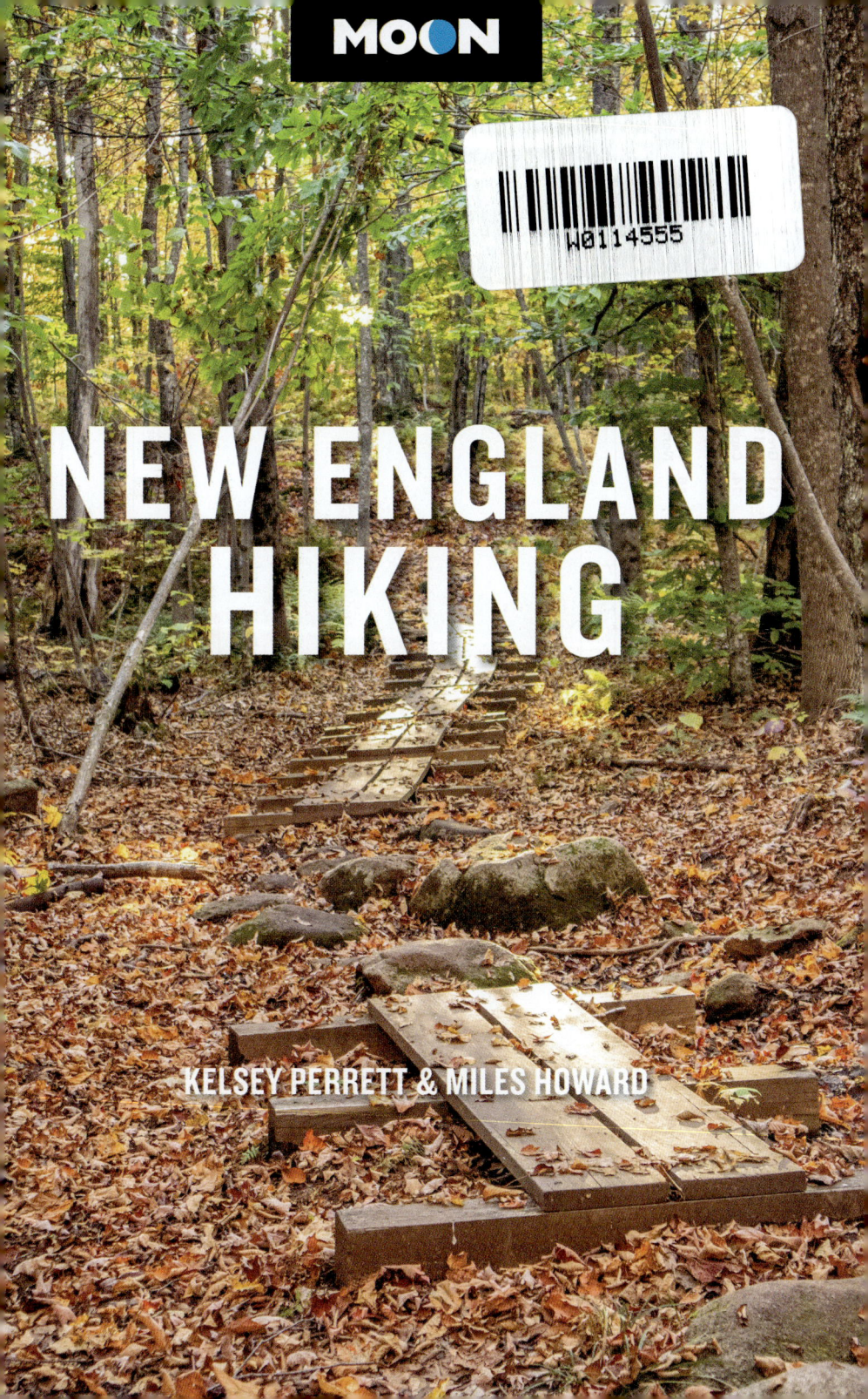

MOON

NEW ENGLAND HIKING

KELSEY PERRETT & MILES HOWARD

NEW ENGLAND HIKING REGIONS

1. Acadia
2. Baxter, the Highlands, and the Carrabassett Valley
3. Midcoast, Casco Bay, and the Maine Beaches
4. The Mahoosucs, Evans Notch, and Rangeley Lakes

5. White Mountain National Forest
6. Great North Woods and Dixville Notch
7. Winnipesaukee and the Lakes District
8. Monadnock, Merrimack Valley, and the Seacoast

9. Northern Green Mountains
10. Southern Green Mountains
11. Champlain Valley and Stowe
12. Northeast Kingdom

13. Greater Boston, North and South Shore
14. Cape Cod and the Islands
15. The Berkshires
16. The Pioneer Valley and North Quabbin

17. Litchfield Hills
18. Metacomet Ridge
19. Rhode Island

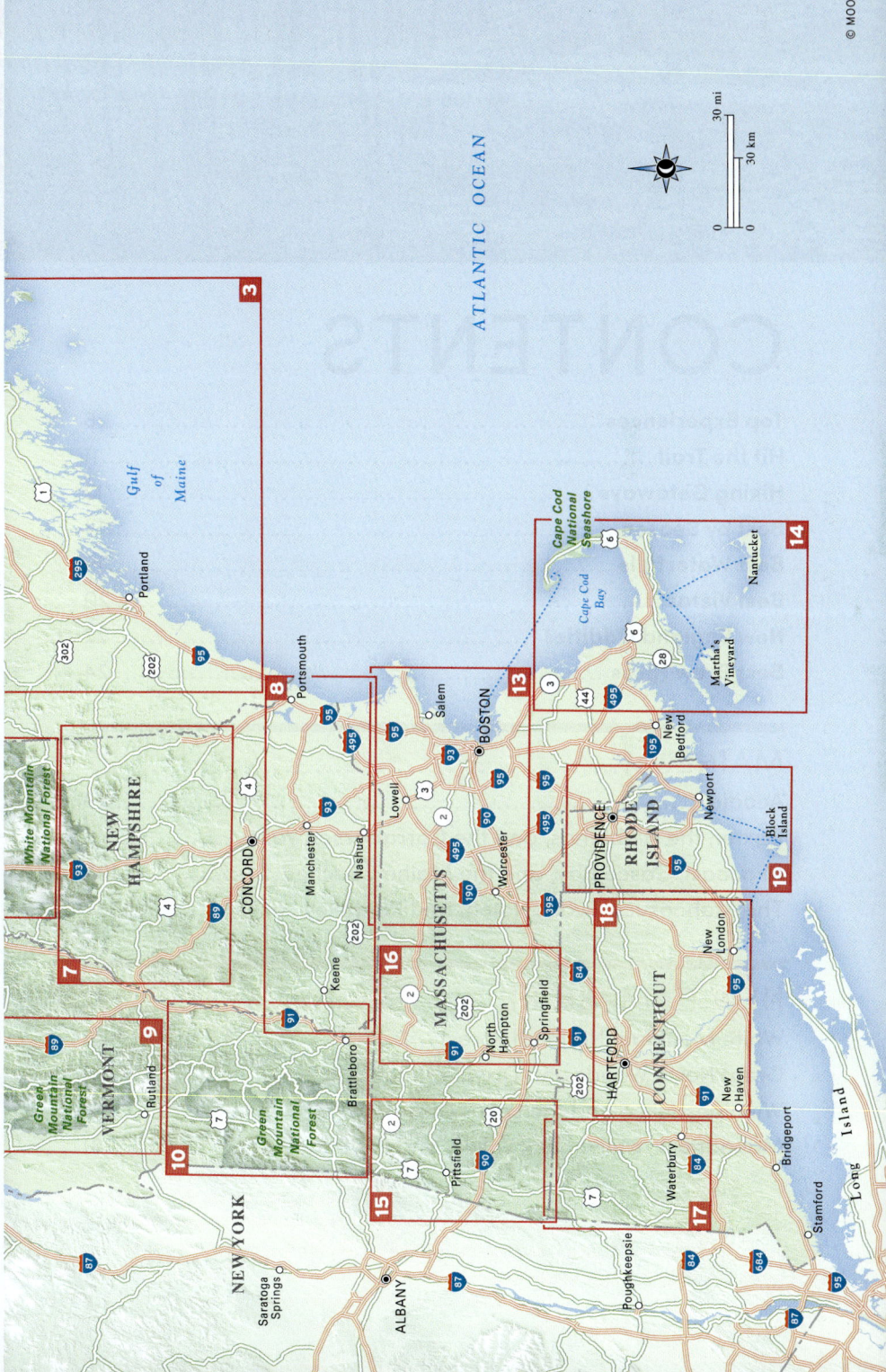

ATLANTIC OCEAN

Gulf of Maine

30 mi
30 km

© MOON.COM

3

14 Cape Cod National Seashore
Nantucket
Cape Cod Bay
Martha's Vineyard

8 Portsmouth
Portland

Salem
13 BOSTON
New Bedford

7 NEW HAMPSHIRE
CONCORD
White Mountain National Forest
Manchester
Nashua
Lowell
Worcester
MASSACHUSETTS
16
Keene
Springfield
North Hampton

18 PROVIDENCE
RHODE ISLAND
Newport
Block Island
19

9 VERMONT
Rutland
Brattleboro
Green Mountain National Forest

HARTFORD
CONNECTICUT
New London
New Haven
Waterbury

10

15 Pittsfield

17

NEW YORK
Saratoga Springs
ALBANY
Poughkeepsie

Long Island
Bridgeport
Stamford

CONTENTS

NEW ENGLAND HIKING
TOP EXPERIENCES

1 Feeling the spray from **majestic waterfalls** like Arethusa Falls (page 198) or Race Brook Falls (page 500).

2 Taking in **classic New England views** at Camel's Hump (page 399), Owls Head Mountain (page 419), or World's End (page 437).

3 Hiking a flat, approachable segment of the **Appalachian Trail** (page 547).

4 Admiring **wildflowers and fall foliage** from the slopes of Caribou Mountain (page 155) and Mount Horrid (page 324).

5 Watching the **sunrise** from the summit of Cadillac Mountain (page 32).

6 Reaching new heights on **high-elevation hikes** from Penobscot Mountain (page 47) to Mount Adams (page 180) to Mount Greylock (page 481).

7 Wandering **secluded paths** at Giant Falls (page 176) or Mount Wachusett (page 446).

8 Rewarding yourself with **tasty local brews** (page 24).

9 Enjoying **ocean breezes** at Mount Megunticook (page 108), Menemsha Hills (page 466), or Sachuest Point (page 625).

10 Catching a glimpse of elusive **wildlife** at Markus Wildlife Sanctuary (page 260) and Thumb Mountain (page 291).

HIT THE TRAIL

Chiaroscuro birch trees. Chuckling streams. Mossy slabs of granite. These are the ancient woodlands that Hawthorne's characters wandered, the waters that the Abenaki Native Americans charted by canoe, and the mountains on which generations of American peak-baggers have left their sweat, blood, and tears.

These regal yet rugged places are the backbone of New England, largely untouched by the breakneck pace of modern life. The forests are thick with curious sounds, lush colors, and inquisitive furry faces. The trails can get steep enough to leave even the most dedicated athletes longing for an ice bath. The alpine zone—where only the toughest flowers and vegetation can grow—is home to some of the most spectacular sunsets, wind gusts, and thunderstorms in the world.

There's something for every adventurer in New England—verdant valleys, roller-coaster ridges, crystal cascades, acres of wildflowers, 17th-century villages—and almost all of it is conveniently located within a day's drive of Boston, the region's largest city and air hub. Every enclave of New England wilderness offers not only natural beauty, but also the opportunity to experience everyday life in such an arresting place. Chase a good day's hike with a bowl of lobster stew, a mug of locally brewed dunkelweizen, or a performance by an outdoor puppet circus famous for its civil rights-era activism. Diverse as these amenities are, all of them are grounded by the serenity and timeless quality of the New England scenery.

Taking a walk in the woods in New England is both exhilarating and humbling. Hiking here has always been an act of discovery, of sublime wonder, and of hell-or-high water, rain-or-shine grit. You will get wet. Your muscles may feel the mileage and, at times, the elevation. But the longer you spend clomping around here and savoring every beguiling sight and sound, the more you'll begin to feel unstuck from time itself.

This is New England. We wouldn't have it any other way.

▼ LITTLE RIVER HISTORY HIKE, VERMONT

Long Strange Coast

Experience the magic of the Maine's seacoast in two nights and three days.

DAY 1

Start your expedition by admiring the ecological diversity of New Hampshire along the **Sweet Trail** (5.6 mi/9 km). From there, head north to Portland, Maine, to explore the city's renowned food and nightlife circuit and spend the night.

DAY 2

In the morning, take a jaunt over to the city forest and hike to **Fore River and Jewell Falls** (3.3 mi/5.3 km). Then jump on US-1, grab a bite to eat at any of the lobster and clam shacks near Wiscasset, and continue north to Rockport for an afternoon climb up **Ragged Mountain** (4.8 mi/7.7 km). Pitch your tent at **Sea Swell Campground Camden Hills** and then motor into nearby Rockland or Belfast for dinner and drinks.

DAY 3

Wake up early the next morning, enjoy a nice local breakfast, and make your way to nearby Camden Hills State Park and climb **Mount Megunticook** (2.8 mi/4.5 km) for a final ocean vista. If you find yourself pining for the beauty of the seacoast as you begin the journey home, stop by **Wells Reserve** (2.8 mi/4.5 km) for a lush, meditative stroll before it's time to hang up your boots.

Alpine Trilogy

Challenge yourself to three mountain summits in three New England states in three days!

DAY 1

Get a good night's sleep and rise at dawn to drive north through the greenery of Vermont to **Camel's Hump** (6.8 mi/10.9 km)—aim to summit before 2pm. Balance the adrenaline rush with a hearty locally sourced dinner and a few craft beers in Montpelier, and spend the night in Vermont's capital.

DAY 2

Get up early the next morning and head east into New Hampshire, where—depending on how tired you

THE EXPOSED FACE OF WELCH
MOUNTAIN, NEW HAMPSHIRE ▶

are after yesterday's formidable ascent—you can work your way up the moderately difficult **Welch and Dickey Mountains** (4.2 mi/6.8 km) or the easier and shorter **Mount Willard** (3 mi/4.8 km). Knock both off if you feel like it! Then drive to either North Conway or Gorham for another round of decadent cooking and craft libations. But don't stay up too late. You'll finish big on day 3.

DAY 3

For on the third and final day, drive north across the Maine border and climb the mighty **Old Speck** (7.6 mi/12.2 km)—one of the most thrilling hikes in this book. At least, that's the ideal finale. If you're feeling beat after two days of summits, you can easily swap Old Speck for **Mount Agamenticus** (2.5 mi/4 km), a shorter route on Maine's southwestern oceanside, a two-hour drive from the White Mountains.

Island Hopper

Hike three of New England's scenic offshore islands on this easygoing tour around the Atlantic seaboard.

DAY 1

Head east through Massachusetts and cross over the bridged canal marking your arrival in idyllic Cape Cod. Park at the Steamship Authority lot in Hyannis and enjoy a leisurely ferry ride to Nantucket. Take a bus or taxi a few minutes outside Nantucket town to explore the varied local terrain on the **Ocean Walk** (5.7 mi/9.2 km) at Sanford Farm, Ram Pasture, and The Woods. Stay and play on the island, or hop back on the ferry to spend the night in Hyannis.

DAY 2

Wake up and drive approximately 25 mi (40 km) southwest to Woods Hole, where you can pick up the Steamship Authority ferry to Martha's Vineyard. From either Vineyard Haven or Oak Bluffs, where the ferries drop off, catch a ride to pastoral Chilmark, about 15 mi (24 km) away, and spend some time admiring the sweeping ocean views from **Prospect Hill and the Great Sand Bank** (3.1 mi/5 km) at Menemsha Hills. Treat yourself to a night on the Vineyard, or return to the Cape for a night among the pitch pines at **Shawme-Crowell State Forest** campground.

DAY 3

Get up early to beat the Cape Cod traffic and get a jump on your two-hour (85-mi/137-km) drive to Rhode Island. From the Cape Cod Canal, make your way west around Buzzards Bay. After a scenic crossing of Narragansett Bay, you'll arrive in Narragansett, where the ferry to Block Island departs. The pleasant ferry cruise will deliver you just a few minutes' drive from Clay Head Preserve and the **Clay Head Nature Trail and the Maze** (2.9 mi/4.7 km), an easy walk around the beach and the imposing clay cliffs of Block Island.

BEST BY SEASON

Fall

MAINE

- **South Bubble and Jordan Pond:** The forests around Jordan Pond are shimmering with gold once October rolls around, and the rocky peak of South Bubble makes for a fine overlook (page 43).

- **Mount Kineo:** Jutting up from an island on Moosehead Lake, this isolated peak features sheer cliffs and a fire tower with stunning views of the autumnal Maine frontier woods (page 84).

- **Caribou Mountain:** The 360-degree vista from the top of Caribou Mountain is already one of the finest in New England, but when you add a palette of fall colors, it's unforgettable (page 155).

NEW HAMPSHIRE

- **Zealand Valley and Thoreau Falls:** A long stroll through Zealand Valley's vast beaver marshes during fall foliage season is pure New England ecstasy (page 191).

- **Mount Lafayette and Franconia Ridge:** Summiting Mount Lafayette is an uncommonly scenic ascent, with spectacular views of Franconia Notch— and the ridge traverse ups the ante (page 204).

- **Table Rock:** The pinnacle of this dizzyingly sheer 700-ft-tall (213-m) rock formation is the perfect crow's nest from which to admire the autumn forests of the remote, quiet Dixville Notch (page 237).

FALL COLORS FROM TABLE ROCK, NEW HAMPSHIRE ▾

VERMONT

- **Long Trail: Brandon Gap to Mount Horrid Great Cliff and Cape Lookout:** Survey a sea of fall color from the Great Cliff of Mount Horrid, an easily reached ledge overlooking a marsh and a series of rolling hills (page 324).

- **Bald Mountain via the Long Pond Trail:** Vermont views do not get any better than those during peak foliage season from this impressive fire tower overlooking Lake Willoughby and the Northeast Kingdom (page 413).

MASSACHUSETTS

- **Mount Greylock via the Money Brook and Appalachian Trails:** Stony Ledge, a secluded vista overlooking the Greylock Range, pops with fall color in mid- to late October (page 481).

- **Hurlburt's Hill and Bartholomew's Cobble:** The expansive view from Hurlburt's Hill looks out on the Berkshires draped in fall color—all for the price of just a short, leisurely hike (page 503).

CONNECTICUT

- **Bear Mountain via the Undermountain Trail:** The highest peak in Connecticut, Bear Mountain is the best place to watch the leaves turn, offering views across three states (page 538).

- **Sleeping Giant via the Blue and Violet Trails:** This commanding mountain in central Connecticut reveals vista after vista as hikers move along its colorful ridgeline (page 582).

Winter

MAINE

- **Mount Agamenticus:** This prominent peak at the southern tip of Maine (complete with ruins of an old ski resort) draws visitors year-round thanks to its views and easy trails (page 130).

- **Androscoggin Riverlands:** When the woods of Androscoggin Riverlands get nice and snowy, winter hikers, cross-country skiers, and even snowmobilers head here to play (page 164).

NEW HAMPSHIRE

- **Mount Willard:** A family favorite for all seasons, Mount Willard offers a gentle ascent, a frozen cascade, and a view of Crawford Notch that would make Robert Redford weep (page 195).

- **Arethusa Falls via Bemis Brook:** New Hampshire's tallest waterfall somehow manages to look even more dramatic when it freezes for the winter—tempting not only hikers, but ice climbers (page 198).

- **Mount Chocorua:** Take the Champney Falls Trail to visit two gorgeous frozen waterfalls, and if you're feeling adventurous, keep climbing to summit the mighty Chocorua itself (page 220).

- **Sweet Trail:** Even when its flora and fauna are buried under snow, the Sweet Trail still makes for a charming woodland stroll to the Great Bay Estuary (page 284).

VERMONT

- **Abbey Pond Trail:** The easy elevation of this short trail makes it ideal for winter hiking, and the peaceful pond is an idyllic place to spot Vermont wildlife (page 315).

- **Stratton Pond Trail:** A long, scenic walk through flat forest culminates in great views of Stratton Pond, a secluded lake at the base of the mountain of the same name (page 363).

MASSACHUSETTS

- **Carriage Paths:** This wind-whipped park, designed by Frederick Law Olmsted, is particularly scenic in the snow, with frosty vistas of the Boston skyline (page 437).

- **Castle Neck Trails:** Take advantage of the quiet off-season months at popular Crane Beach. Not only do frozen dunes make for easier walking, but also chances of spotting majestic snowy owls are at their highest (page 452).

CONNECTICUT

- **Appalachian Trail: Housatonic River Walk:** A flat, gentle section of the Appalachian Trail along the Housatonic River is welcoming even in wintertime (page 547).

RHODE ISLAND

- **Pond, Coney Brook, and Flintlock Loops:** Stroll the banks of quiet Tillinghast Pond along terrain that alternates between quiet forests and snowy fields (page 604).

Spring

MAINE

- **Cadillac Mountain via the Gorge Path:** Beat the summer hordes and take the beautiful Gorge Path up Acadia's highest mountain for one of the most sweeping seacoast vistas anywhere in Maine (page 32).

- **Fore River and Jewell Falls:** For a magical day in Portland, take a walk through the woods of Fore River Sanctuary, where you'll find wildflowers, great blue herons, and a waterfall (page 124).

NEW HAMPSHIRE

- **Giant Falls:** This aptly named yet little-known cascade just north of the White Mountains becomes a rip-roaring 80-ft (24-m) monster during spring snowmelt (page 176).

A LOON IN THE MARSHES OF
MARKUS WILDLIFE SANCTUARY ▶

- **Markus Wildlife Sanctuary:** New Hampshire's iconic loons get restless during the spring season, and you might catch one taking flight around this mossy lakeside sanctuary (page 260).
- **Purgatory Falls:** Spring comes sooner in southern New Hampshire, and the brookside hike to Purgatory Falls is the perfect way to kick off a new season of backcountry exploring (page 301).

VERMONT
- **Lye Brook Falls Trail:** Snowmelt from the peaks of the Green Mountains builds to a rush during spring at this 125-ft (38-m) waterfall, one of the tallest in Vermont (page 360).
- **Hamilton Falls via the West River Trail:** Catch this spectacular waterfall at its finest, when spring rains and snowmelt amp up its flow (page 366).
- **Sterling Pond:** Your boots will get muddy, your quads might quake, but the climb to Vermont's highest-elevation trout pond will leave you feeling serene and rejuvenated (page 381).

MASSACHUSETTS
- **High Ledges via the Sanctuary Road Loop:** Featuring some of the finest displays of wildflowers—including rare orchids—to be found in New England, High Ledges is a must-see in spring (page 515).

CONNECTICUT
- **Appalachian Trail: Prospect Mountain and Rand's View:** Hike to a meadow dotted with wildflowers and emerging greenery on this lovely destination along the Appalachian Trail (page 541).
- **Vista Trail:** A shroud of misty spring rain adds to the mystique of this lore-steeped trail that includes a waterfall, vista, and strange rock formations (page 585).

RHODE ISLAND
- **North South Trail to Stepstone Falls:** This lush path along the Falls River in Arcadia Management Area looks best in the spring colors of fresh greenery and blooming wildflowers (page 607).

Summer

MAINE
- **Mount Katahdin:** The window for summiting New England's toughest mountain is a short one—August and September are your best bets for glorious weather and panoramic views (page 71).
- **Lane's Island Preserve:** This enchanting hike on the island of Vinalhaven—replete with wildflowers and pebble beaches—might make you reconsider your return to the mainland (page 114).
- **Tumbledown Mountain:** Few things are more romantic than catching a golden summer sunset on the banks of Tumbledown Mountain's summit pond or its rolling granite ridge (page 143).

NEW HAMPSHIRE

- **Mount Washington via Tuckerman Ravine:** Scaling the steep and waterfall-festooned bowl of Tuckerman Ravine surpasses the thrill of summiting New England's highest peak (page 184).

- **The Flume:** This 800-ft-deep (244-m) natural gorge is the perfect misty environment in which to cool off during the height of summer, as well as take in some spectacular waterfalls and mossy cliffs (page 208).

VERMONT

- **Falls of Lana and Rattlesnake Cliffs:** Enjoy a vista of lush greenery from the Rattlesnake Cliffs before descending to the Falls of Lana, where you can find multiple swimming holes along the river (page 321).

- **Calm Cove at Niquette Bay:** Take a reprieve from the sun by winding through the woods and wetlands of Niquette Bay State Park to reach an enchanting beach on Lake Champlain (page 378).

- **Mount Pisgah via the North Trail:** Beat the heat after a hike up Mount Pisgah with a swim in the scenic, cliff-bound blue waters of Lake Willoughby (page 416).

MASSACHUSETTS

- **Great Island Trail:** Extraordinary sunsets and swimmable waters make this long beach-and-dune hike on Cape Cod a great destination for summer (page 460).

- **Doane's Falls via the Tully Trail:** Trek from cascade to cascade along the relatively flat Tully Trail, then continue your adventure with a swim or a paddle on sparkling Tully Lake (page 512).

RHODE ISLAND

- **Clay Head Nature Trail and the Maze:** Summer on Block Island is made even more magical with a hike along this scenic clay bluff, which hikers can follow with a dip in the Atlantic Ocean (page 619).

- **Flint Point and Ocean View Loops:** Marvel at the beach rose in bloom on this short hike around the tip of the Rhode Island coast, then spend the rest of the day at one of many nearby beaches (page 625).

BEST WATERFALLS

MAINE
- **Little and Big Niagara Falls:** Hold onto your hat (and camera!) as you stand beside the roaring torrent of these twin cascades in the wilderness of Baxter State Park (page 75).
- **Angel Falls:** Venture into a remote timber forest and discover the misting majesty of this 90-ft (27-m) cascade that spills down sheer cliffs (page 140).

NEW HAMPSHIRE
- **Arethusa Falls via Bemis Brook:** Dipping your head under New Hampshire's tallest year-round waterfall is guaranteed to shock you back to life on a stupefyingly hot day (page 198).
- **Bridal Veil Falls:** Follow the bubbling Coppermine Brook and its namesake trail to the elegant Bridal Veil Falls, where one of the most picturesque swimming holes in the White Mountains awaits (page 201).

VERMONT
- **Falls of Lana and Rattlesnake Cliffs:** After making the climb to Rattlesnake Cliffs, ease into the serene, briskly refreshing pools formed by these impressive falls that tumble down series of rock faces (page 321).
- **Hamilton Falls via the West River Trail:** These dramatic falls are reached via an easy, scenic riverside route (page 366).

MASSACHUSETTS
- **Race Brook Falls and Race Mountain via the Appalachian Trail:** Enjoy views of plunging cascades after a climb along the Appalachian Trail (page 500).
- **Doane's Falls via the Tully Trail:** Treat yourself to an easy stroll with multiple waterfall views (page 512).

CONNECTICUT
- **Pine Knob Loop:** Waterfalls and cascades will accompany you on your quick ascent to the Pine Knob lookout (page 544).
- **Vista Trail:** Covered bridges, cascades, and vista views—this hike in Devil's Hopyard State Park has it all (page 585).

RHODE ISLAND
- **North South Trail to Stepstone Falls:** Take a peaceful hike along the river to admire the falls and spectacular wildflowers (page 607).

◄ BIG NIAGARA FALLS, MAINE

BEST VISTAS

MAINE
- **Mount Katahdin:** The Penobscot Native Americans were right—when it comes to panoramic views of verdant wilderness and crystal-blue lakes, the craggy and titanic Katahdin is truly "the Greatest Mountain" in Maine, and arguably New England (page 71).
- **Caribou Mountain:** The bumpy granite summit of Caribou might sound modest at only 2,850 ft (869 m) above sea level, but hikers who make the climb are amply rewarded with views of the Carter, Mahoosuc, and Presidential ranges and the Cold River valley (page 155).

NEW HAMPSHIRE
- **Mount Washington via Tuckerman Ravine:** On a clear day, you can glimpse the Atlantic Ocean from the notoriously windy pinnacle of New England's tallest mountain—or you might find yourself looking down at a sea of thick white clouds flowing past the summit cone (page 184).
- **South and North Percy Peaks:** The views from these secluded twin mountains that loom above the Nash Stream Forest are worth the scramble up steep and exposed granite slopes, from which you can see the White Mountains, the Connecticut Lakes, and the wilderness of Quebec to the north (page 241).

VERMONT
- **Long Trail: Lincoln Gap to Mount Abraham:** After climbing endless granite slabs to the 4,017-ft (1,224-m) summit of Mount Abraham, hikers are rewarded with 360-degree views from the Champlain Valley to the Adirondack Mountains (page 312).
- **Long Trail: Brandon Gap to Mount Horrid Great Cliff and Cape Lookout:** The Great Cliff is a short hike, and not particularly high, but it overlooks the wide valley of Brandon Gap where the Green Mountains roll out toward Lake Champlain (page 324).
- **White Rocks Cliffs:** This drop-off overlooking glacial ice beds is a unique mountainside vista named for its alabaster-hued Cheshire quartzite (page 343).
- **Mount Mansfield via the Sunset Ridge Trail:** The tip-top of Vermont's tallest mountain offers sterling views of Stowe and the Northeast Kingdom to the east, and the exposed descent down Sunset Ridge is set against the backdrop of Lake Champlain and New York's distant Adirondacks (page 384).
- **Bald Mountain via the Long Pond Trail:** One of the finest fire tower views in New England, this less-traveled trail in Willoughby State Park features an expansive vista of the Northeast Kingdom (page 413).

▲ SUNRISE NEAR THE SUMMIT OF RAGGED MOUNTAIN, CONNECTICUT

MASSACHUSETTS

- **Great Blue Hill via the Skyline Trail:** The iconic Boston skyline is the highlight of the Buck Hill vista in Blue Hills Reservation, but jetliners cruising toward Logan Airport add an air of excitement (page 440).

- **Mount Greylock via the Money Brook and Appalachian Trails:** Stony Ledge is a lesser-known vista on the west slopes of Mount Greylock. This secluded overlook of the Greylock Range and the cavernous Hopper cirque rivals the mountain's summit (page 481).

- **Alander Mountain Trail:** The vistas are nonstop as you wander across the long ridgeline of Alander Mountain, which boasts a strategic vantage point at the corners of Massachusetts, New York, and Connecticut (page 497).

CONNECTICUT

- **Bear Mountain via the Undermountain Trail:** The tallest peak in Connecticut offers iconic views across three states on this last stop before the Appalachian Trail plunges north into Massachusetts (page 538).

- **Appalachian Trail: Prospect Mountain and Rand's View:** Enjoy the spaciousness of an open meadow hemmed by the Berkshire Range on this gem of a hike along the Appalachian Trail (page 541).

- **Ragged Mountain via the Preserve and Metacomet Trails:** Overlook the Hartford skyline and pristine forests surrounding crystal reservoirs from the red traprock outcroppings of the Metacomet Range (page 575).

RHODE ISLAND

- **Long and Ell Pond Trail:** This beloved vista overlooking a glassy pond from a stone bluff was featured in the Wes Anderson hit *Moonrise Kingdom* (page 610).

- **Nelson Pond Trail:** Admire marsh, beach, and the great Atlantic Ocean from the finger-like rock formations of the Nelson Bird Sanctuary (page 622).

NEW ENGLAND ODDITIES

MAINE

- **Perpendicular and Razorback Trails:** This off-the-beaten-path loop hike begins with a steep climb up hundreds of carved stone stairs to the top of Mansell Mountain and concludes with a wild descent down an exposed granite ridge where the natural contours resemble the spiky back of a dinosaur (page 54).

- **Debsconeag Ice Caves:** Nestled deep in a preserve of pristine forests and glacial lakes, these caves retain a foundation of thick ice through the summer months—the entrance resembles a hole in the forest floor, and the ice itself serves as natural air-conditioning when the outside temperatures become punishing (page 81).

NEW HAMPSHIRE

- **Devil's Den Mountain:** This unshakably creepy peak near Merrymeeting Lake looks like the kind of stone pyre on which a human sacrifice might be conducted, and it also contains a hidden slit cave that's rumored to be haunted by a monstrous presence (page 272).

- **Madame Sherri Forest:** These lush woods in southwestern New Hampshire hide the ruins of a castle once owned by a hedonist fashion designer named Madame Antoinette Sherri—who, legend has it, would drive into town wearing nothing but her fur coat (page 294).

VERMONT

- **Long Trail: Lincoln Gap to Mount Abraham:** Follow the Long Trail just past the summit of Mount Abraham to where a small side path leads to the wreckage of a casualty-free 1973 plane crash (page 312).

- **Little River History Hike:** This state park hike burrows through a chirping forest that contains rusting farming equipment and preserved cemeteries of 19th-century homesteading families (page 390).

- **Little Loop and Peacham Bog Trail:** Visit this unique boardwalk to peek inside a pitcher plant and see what insects and other creatures these carnivorous plants have captured to digest with liquid enzymes (page 422).

RUINS AT MADAME SHERRI'S CASTLE, NEW HAMPSHIRE ▶

▲ HERMIT'S CASTLE OVERLOOKING THE MILLERS RIVER, MASSACHUSETTS

MASSACHUSETTS

- **Hurlburt's Hill and Bartholomew's Cobble:** Among the many wonders of the Bartholomew's Cobble trail system is an enormous cottonwood tree, widely believed to be the largest in Massachusetts (page 503).

- **Hermit's Castle via the Metacomet-Monadnock Trail:** This rock formation along the New England Trail was home to the Scottish hermit John Smith for 32 years (page 518).

CONNECTICUT

- **Donkey Trail and Hodge Road Loop:** This unique trail in Mine Hill Preserve takes visitors past relics of the mining industry, including several grated air shafts that have been repurposed as bat hibernacula (page 563).

- **Wolf Den and Indian Chair via the Blue Trail:** Visit the site in Mashamoquet Brook State Park where the last wolf in Connecticut lived and died. The livestock-slaying wolf was shot in 1742 by Israel Putnam, who would later become a major general in the Revolutionary War (page 588).

RHODE ISLAND

- **Walkabout Trail:** This trail has one of the strangest origin stories in New England. It was built by a group of Australian sailors who were stranded in Rhode Island while awaiting the arrival of their new destroyer. In just six weeks the men completed this 8-mi (12.9-km) trail and named it for the Australian tradition of the walkabout (page 598).

- **Foster Cove, Cross Refuge, and Grassy Point Trails:** Before Ninigret National Wildlife Refuge became one of the top bird-watching spots in Rhode Island, it was the Naval Auxiliary Air Station Charlestown, where pilots, including former U.S. president George H. W. Bush, trained for World War II. Runways are still visible today (page 616).

 BEST BREW HIKES

MAINE

- **Cadillac Mountain via the Gorge Path:** The coastal vista from Cadillac's summit seems to stretch on forever, but it's only a short drive to **Atlantic Brewing Company,** which offers not only a mouthwatering roster of seasonal beers but also some of the finest barbecue in northern Maine (page 32).
- **Gulf Hagas:** Once you're done sizing up the waterfalls and slate cliffs in "the Grand Canyon of Maine," drive east through the KI-Jo Mary Forest (past the Katahdin Iron Works ruins) to nearby Milo and reflect with a liberally hopped IPA or jet-black stout at Maine craft beer favorite **Bissell Brothers Three Rivers** (page 87).

NEW HAMPSHIRE

- **Mount Chocorua:** Scrambling up the steep summit cone of Chocorua is a rush, and once you've finished the hike, you'll want to relax—so head straight to nearby **Tuckerman Brewing Company** for a flight of German-style brews and special-batch beers that you won't find in stores (page 220).
- **Odiorne Point State Park:** After a day of ambling through mixed woods and past reptile-rich vernal pools, keep the biodiversity coming by driving over to **Earth Eagle Brewings** for a beer or gruit made with locally foraged ingredients—and then treat yourself to a meal from the inventive brewpub menu (page 287).

VERMONT

- **Falls of Lana and Rattlesnake Cliffs:** A perfect day in Middlebury? Hike and swim at Rattlesnake Cliffs and the Falls of Lana before stopping into **Foley Brothers** for hoppy IPAs and toasty porters (page 321).
- **Killington Peak via the Bucklin Trail:** A trip up the long, tough Bucklin Trail to 4,236-ft (1,291-m) Killington Peak is best followed with a visit to **Long Trail Brewing Company,** where handcrafted beers are paired with a seasonal comfort-food menu (page 327).
- **Mount Ascutney via the Weathersfield Trail:** Climb to the viewing platform of Mount Ascutney for views stretching as far as the White Mountains, and then stop into Windsor's **Harpoon Brewery Taproom and Beer Garden** for a burger and a pint in the beer garden (page 346).
- **Sterling Pond:** Sterling Pond might be one of the most meditative places in Vermont, but there's nothing understated about the deliciously hoppy ales down the road at **The Alchemist,** especially Heady Topper, a double IPA that is one of the most coveted craft beers in America (page 381).

MASSACHUSETTS

- **Ocean Walk:** Fun on Nantucket doesn't get any better than a walk in the fresh ocean air at Sanford Farm followed by music, brews, and food truck offerings in the lively outdoor courtyard at **Cisco Brewers** (page 469).

- **Mount Tom via the Metacomet-Monadnock Trail:** Survey the Pioneer Valley from the peak of Mount Tom, then dip into Easthampton where you can admire views of the mountain with a flight from the tasting room at **Fort Hill Brewery** (page 528).

CONNECTICUT

- **Appalachian Trail: Housatonic River Walk:** After a day on the Appalachian Trail, unwind at **Kent Falls Brewing Company,** a tasting room that holds events and offers tours of its brewery and farm (page 547).
- **Robert Ross and Agnes Bowen Trails:** Follow a hike in People's State Forest with a visit to **Brewery Legitimus,** a craft brewery featuring interesting ales, food trucks, and a variety of live music and other events (page 554).

RHODE ISLAND

- **North South Trail to Stepstone Falls:** Explore this notable section of Rhode Island's North South Trail in the Arcadia Management Area, then head over to **Tilted Barn Brewery,** featuring tours of a historic barn and fresh-off-the-farm brews (page 607).
- **Foster Cove, Cross Refuge, and Grassy Point Trails:** Work up a thirst wandering the trails of the Ninigret National Wildlife Refuge, and then stop in to South Kingstown's **Whalers Brewing Company** for some of Rhode Island's favorite beers (page 616).
- **Flint Point and Ocean View Loops:** Ocean views, shorebirds, and windswept rocks make Sachuest Point National Wildlife Refuge a top hiking destination in the Newport area, and there are plenty of great options nearby for a post-hike drink. **Taproot Brewing** in Middletown is a favorite (page 625).

LONG TRAIL BREWING COMPANY BEER

LONG POND, ACADIA NATIONAL PARK

MAINE

ACADIA

On a little slice of the Maine coast called Mount Desert Island, a secluded universe of exposed peaks, serene beaches, and unrivaled biodiversity welcomes millions each year. Acadia National Park is one of the oldest and most beloved parks in America. One look at a map illustrates why: The waterlocked wonder contains more than 120 mi (195 km) of trails for every taste. You can wander around lagoons and fjords, search the woods for more than 40 species of mammalian wildlife, or scale cliffs steep enough to make you feel like a sponsored athlete. To top it off, the villages of Bar Harbor and Southwest Harbor are your ticket for freshly caught sustenance including lobsters, bluefish, and good old Maine steamers.

▲ VIEW FROM CADILLAC MOUNTAIN

▲ VIEW OF THE BUBBLES FROM JORDAN POND PATH

◄ HADLOCK FALLS AFTER RAINY WEATHER

1 **Cadillac Mountain via the Gorge Path**
DISTANCE: 4.6 mi (7.4 km) round-trip
DURATION: 2.5 hr
EFFORT: Strenuous
PAGE: 32

2 **The Beehive**
DISTANCE: 1.6 mi (2.6 km) round-trip
DURATION: 1 hr
EFFORT: Moderate
PAGE: 36

3 **Ocean Path**
DISTANCE: 3.6 mi (5.8 km) round-trip
DURATION: 1.5 hr
EFFORT: Easy
PAGE: 40

4 **South Bubble and Jordan Pond**
DISTANCE: 3.6 mi (5.8 km) round-trip
DURATION: 3 hr
EFFORT: Moderate
PAGE: 43

5 **Penobscot Mountain via the Jordan Cliffs Trail**
DISTANCE: 3.3 mi (5.3 km) round-trip
DURATION: 2 hr
EFFORT: Strenuous
PAGE: 47

6 **Hadlock Falls**
DISTANCE: 2 mi (3.2 km) round-trip
DURATION: 1 hr
EFFORT: Easy
PAGE: 51

7 **Perpendicular and Razorback Trails**
DISTANCE: 2.6 mi (4.2 km) round-trip
DURATION: 2.5 hr
EFFORT: Moderate
PAGE: 54

8 **Ship Harbor**
DISTANCE: 1.4 mi (2.3 km) round-trip
DURATION: 45 min
EFFORT: Easy
PAGE: 58

ACADIA

US 1 Ellsworth

Hancock

US 1

Sullivan

172

3

Lamoine

Bean Island

Sorrento

Preble Island

3

230

BAR HARBOR AIRPORT

Trenton

HADLEY'S POINT

Mt. Desert Narrows

Frenchman Bay

Salsbury Cove

BAR HARBOR

THOMPSON ISLAND INFORMATION CENTER

3

Alley Island

Mt. Desert Narrows

Town Hill

Hulls Cove

HULLS COVE VISITOR CENTER

Bar Island

Long Porcupine Island

Bar Harbor

102

Mt. Desert

Island

233

ACADIA NATIONAL PARK HEADQUARTERS

1

Eagle Lake

Somesville

Bartlett Island

102

Mount Desert

HTR ACADIA

3

Acadia National Park

Cadillac Mountain

3

SAND BEACH ENTRANCE

2 **3**

Long Pond

Echo Lake

Acadia Mountain

6

Jordan Pond

Thunder Hole

Sand Beach

102

5

4

Otter Creek

Hardwood Island

Acadia National Park

SMUGGLER'S DEN

Seal Harbor

BLACKWOODS

Otter Point

102

7

STANLEY BROOK ENTRANCE

Tinker Island

Northeast Harbor

Sonnes Sound

Seal Harbor

Seal Cove

Southwest Harbor

Sutton Island

102

Little Cranberry Island

Tremont

Islesford

Cranberry Isles

QUIETSIDE CAMPGROUND & CABINS

SEAWALL

Great Cranberry Island

Baker Island

Blue Hill Bay

Bass Harbor

8

BASS HARBOR

Placentia Island

0   2 mi

0   2 km

© MOON.COM

1 Cadillac Mountain via the Gorge Path

ACADIA NATIONAL PARK, BAR HARBOR

This hidden gem of a mountain hike reaches the highest summit in Acadia by negotiating the rocky recesses of an atmospheric gorge complete with waterfalls.

BEST: Spring hikes, brew hikes

DISTANCE: 4.6 mi (7.4 km) round-trip

DURATION: 2.5 hr

ELEVATION GAIN: 1,240 ft (378 m)

EFFORT: Strenuous

TRAIL: Dirt path, rocks, water crossings by rocks, wooden bog bridges

USERS: Hikers

SEASON: June–October

FEES/PASSES: $35 park entrance fee per vehicle, May–October

MAPS: Acadia National Park website

TRAILHEAD: Gorge Path parking lot, Park Loop Rd., Bar Harbor

FACILITIES: None

CONTACT: Acadia National Park; 207/288-3338; www.nps.gov/acad. Hulls Cove Visitor Center is open from April 15 through October 31. Call the park to verify hours.

No trip to Acadia is complete without the superlative climb up Cadillac Mountain, the tallest point on the island at 1,529 ft (466 m) above sea level. Watching the sun come up from the peak is an iconic part of the Acadia National Park experience. In the fall and winter months it's the first place in the United States to see the sunrise. Most visitors take the well-worn North Ridge Trail to the summit, but a better option is to take Gorge Path—a lesser-known, more sublime experience—to the top and then descend via North Ridge.

START THE HIKE

▶ **MILE 0-0.4: Gorge Path Parking Lot to Hemlock Trail Junction**

Begin the hike at the Gorge Path parking lot on the side of Park Loop Road. Walk toward the east side of the stone bridge, where a wooden trail post reads Gorge Path. Descend some stone stairs to the bottom of the bridge, cross the stream, ascend another set of stairs, and then turn left onto the **Gorge Path.** The trail begins as a dirt path that burrows south through a thick and dark hemlock forest. Blue blazes mark the way. After passing into a stretch of white birch forest, the trail crosses creek beds and

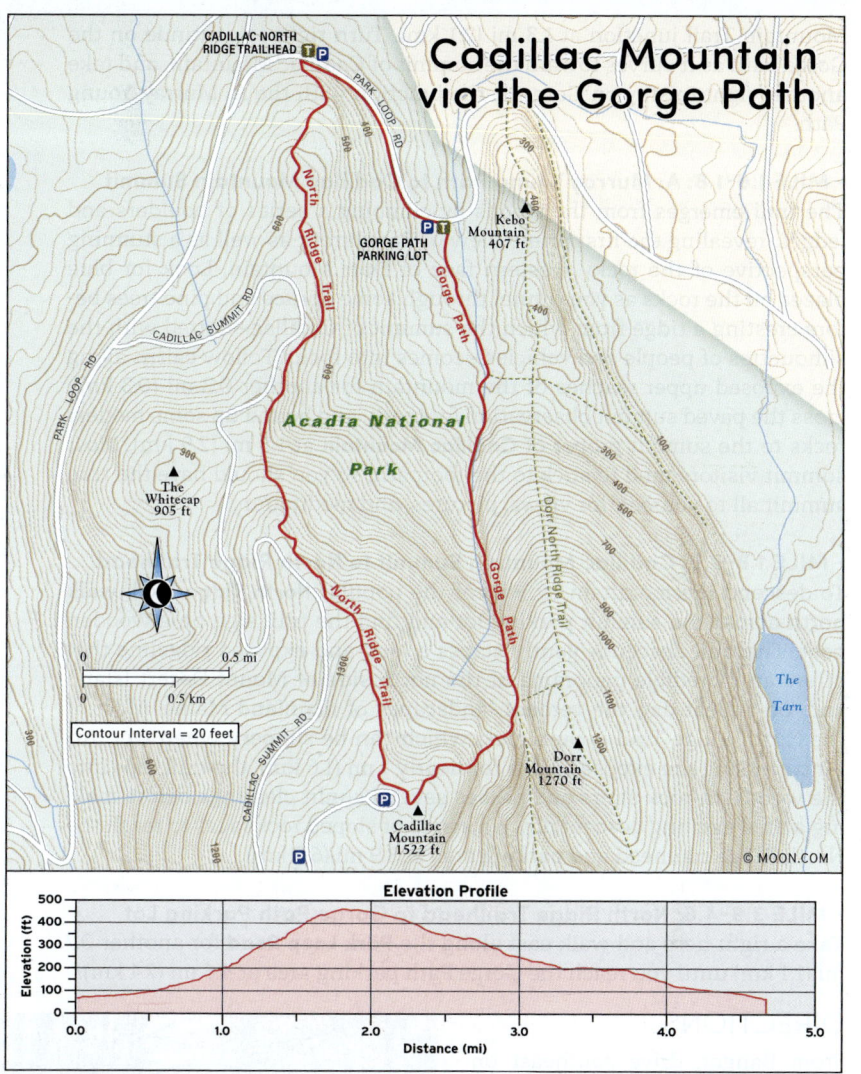

Cadillac Mountain via the Gorge Path

CADILLAC NORTH RIDGE TRAILHEAD

GORGE PATH PARKING LOT

Kebo Mountain 407 ft.

North Ridge Trail

PARK LOOP RD.

CADILLAC SUMMIT RD.

Gorge Path

Acadia National Park

The Whitecap 905 ft

North Ridge Trail

Dorr North Ridge Trail

Dorr Mountain 1270 ft

Cadillac Mountain 1522 ft

The Tarn

0   0.5 mi
0   0.5 km

Contour Interval = 20 feet

© MOON.COM

Elevation Profile

Elevation (ft) | Distance (mi)

wooden bog bridges over muddy areas before reaching the Hemlock Trail junction at 0.4 mi (0.6 km).

▶ MILE 0.4–1.6: Hemlock Trail Junction to A. Murray Young Path

Keep right to stay on Gorge. Cross another pebbly creek bed as the trail becomes a smooth highway of well-placed stones. The grade of the surrounding forest steepens on both sides of the trail. Around 0.6 mi (1 km), the severe rock cliffs of the gorge itself begin to appear, as well as a pretty, silvery cascade. Continue hiking south along the rock pathway past several smaller cascades as the trail gradually steepens. One mi (1.6 km) in, you'll pass a jumble of mossy boulders just before the trail makes a sharp, lung-busting climb out of the gorge with the help of some winding rock staircases. The trail grade becomes gentler as it arrives at the Dorr

Mountain Trail junction at 1.3 mi (2.1 km). Turn right to continue on the Gorge Path as it curves toward the summit of Cadillac Mountain, and take another right to stay on Gorge at the junction with the A. Murray Young Path.

▶ MILE 1.6–1.8: A. Murray Young Path to Cadillac Mountain Summit

The trail emerges from the woods by climbing a series of boulders and ledges, revealing the first primo view of Bar Harbor as well as a stunning perspective of the rocky western face of Dorr Mountain. Look for blue blazes on the rocks as you tunnel through some spruce and pine trees before cresting a ridge from which the summit of Cadillac—dotted with the silhouettes of people and vehicles—comes into focus. Follow cairns along the exposed upper reaches of the mountain for another 0.2 mi (0.3 km), cross the paved summit observation footpath, and bound up some modest rocks to the summit proper of **Cadillac Mountain** at 1.8 mi (2.9 km). Most summit visitors tend to stick to the footpath, so you should have the true summit all to yourself for views, pictures, and meditation.

▶ MILE 1.8–3.9: Cadillac Mountain Summit to North Ridge Trailhead

To descend the mountain by way of the popular **North Ridge Trail,** walk north across the summit parking lot and find the trail sign on a wooden post. The trail descends gently across a long and exposed ridgeline that offers an incredible panorama of the north side of Mount Desert Island and, on a clear day, the verdant landscapes of mainland Maine. Most of the North Ridge Trail is pure rock, which can be slippery when wet. After traversing the exposed ridge for nearly 1 mi (1.6 km), the trail dips into the woods on rock stairs and passes several sunlit clearings before making a final exciting descent down a series of sloped rock faces to reach the North Ridge trailhead and parking area at 3.9 mi (6.3 km).

▶ MILE 3.9–4.6: North Ridge Trailhead to Gorge Path Parking Lot

Take a right here and walk east along the **Park Loop Road** for another 0.7 mi (1.1 km) until you reach the Gorge Path parking area at 4.6 mi (7.4 km).

DIRECTIONS

From Bangor, drive southeast on US-1A E for 25 mi (40 km). After crossing the bridge onto Mount Desert Island, turn left at the fork onto ME-3 E. Continue driving along ME-3 E for about 9 mi (14.5 km) and then turn right onto Paradise Hill Road. Follow this road for 3 mi (4.8 km) as it climbs into the hills near Bar Harbor. As the road ends and merges with Park Loop Road, pull a sharp left and then a right onto Park Loop Road. Drive

THE GORGE PATH TO CADILLAC
MOUNTAIN SUMMIT ▶

▲ SUNRISE FROM CADILLAC MOUNTAIN

north and then southeast along Park Loop Road for roughly 1 mi (1.6 km) until you see the sign for the Gorge Path parking area on your right.

The park's free Island Explorer shuttle bus offers direct service to the North Ridge Trailhead. From Bar Harbor, take the Route 4 or 5 bus to the North Ridge Trailhead and walk 0.7 mi (1.1 km) down Park Loop Road to connect to the trailhead for the Gorge Path.

GPS COORDINATES: 44°22'21.6"N 68°13'19.0"W

BEST NEARBY BITES AND BREWS

Who said the South has a monopoly on barbecue? Cap off your hike with smoky pulled pork, chicken, ribs, and more at **Mainely Meat BBQ on Dreamwood Hill** (369 ME-3, Bar Harbor; 207/288-1100; www.atlanticbrewing.com/mainly-meat-bbq; 11am-8pm daily) and wash it down with a local microbrew from **Atlantic Brewing Company** (15 Knox Rd., Bar Harbor; 207/288-2337; www.atlanticbrewing.com; late-May-mid-October; 11am-7pm daily), which owns and runs the Mainely Meat restaurant.

The hike up Beehive isn't for the faint of heart, but it offers pretty views and a glacial lake to anyone up for the challenge.

DISTANCE: 1.6 mi (2.6 km) round-trip

DURATION: 1 hr

ELEVATION GAIN: 505 ft (154 m)

EFFORT: Moderate

TRAIL: Dirt path, rocks, iron rungs, wooden bog bridges

USERS: Hikers

SEASON: June–October

FEES/PASSES: $35 park entrance fee per vehicle, May–October

MAPS: Acadia National Park website

TRAILHEAD: Sand Beach parking lot, Park Loop Rd., Bar Harbor

FACILITIES: Restrooms

CONTACT: Acadia National Park; 207/288-3338; www.nps.gov/acad. Hulls Cove Visitor Center is open from April 15 through October 31. Call the park to verify hours.

The Beehive might be the most perfectly named peak in Acadia—not only is this handsome little mountain shaped like a hive, but a closer look at its exposed cliffs on a summer day reveals intrepid hikers scaling the mountain like little worker bees. It's another Acadia hike with lots of iron ladder rungs and handrails to aid your perilous journey. If it's wet, or if you have a fear of heights, skip this hike. The ledges and sheer drops make this hike scary for anyone, at any time of year—people have fallen and been injured and killed. Be sure to watch your footing and have both hands free for the duration of the hike.

START THE HIKE

▶ MILE 0-0.2: Sand Beach Parking Lot to Beehive Trail

Begin the hike at the wooden post with signage for Beehive Trail, just north of the entrances to the Sand Beach parking lots. Hike west up a stone path through the woods before reaching a clearing with a signpost for the **Beehive Trail** at 0.2 mi (0.3 km).

▶ MILE 0.2-0.3: Beehive Trail to Split Ledge and Metal Grate

Make a right turn onto the trail, which heads north and immediately begins climbing the Beehive by way of narrow stone stairs. Enjoy the wide ledges and early views here. Follow blue blazes on the trees and cliffs as the trail becomes a series of switchbacks and arrives at a section of split ledge that's bridged with a metal grate at 0.3 mi (0.5 km). Crossing this narrow grate is one of the scarier parts of the hike.

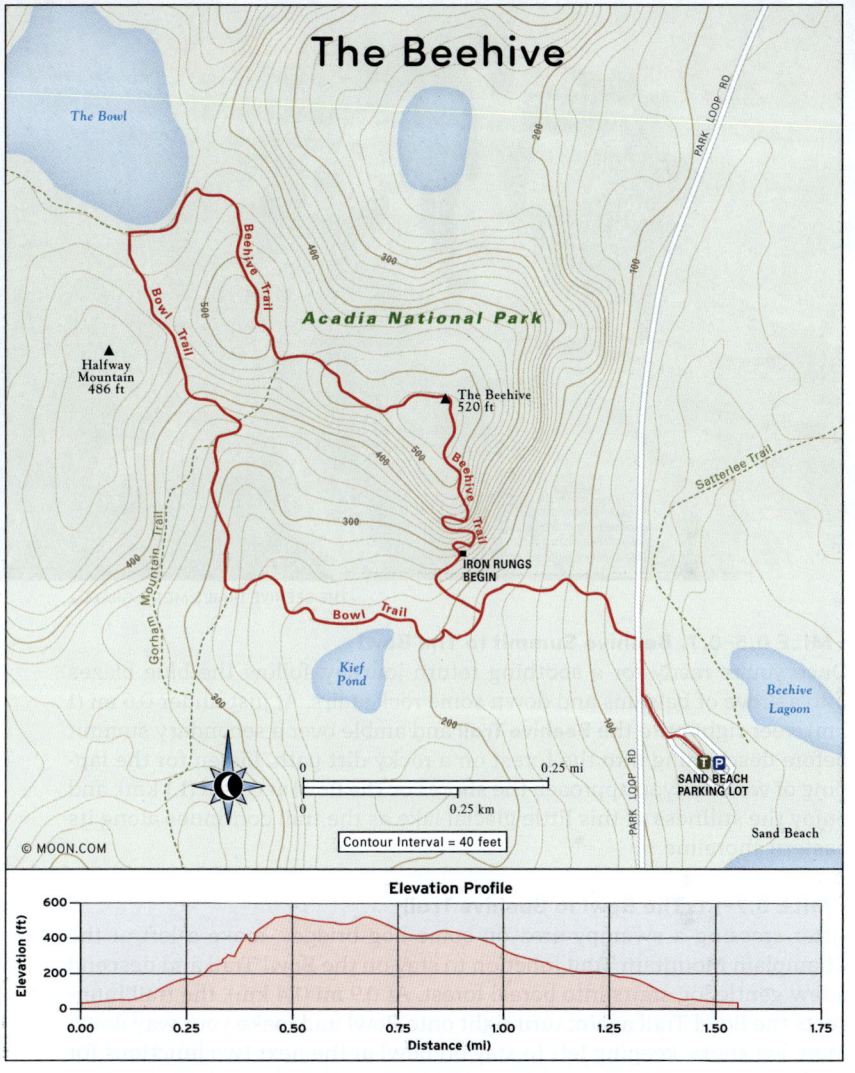

The Beehive

The Bowl

Acadia National Park

Beehive Trail

Bowl Trail

▲ Halfway Mountain 486 ft

▲ The Beehive 520 ft

Satterlee Trail

Gorham Mountain Trail

Beehive Trail

IRON RUNGS BEGIN

Bowl Trail

Kief Pond

Beehive Lagoon

PARK LOOP RD

Contour Interval = 40 feet

0 ——— 0.25 mi
0 ——— 0.25 km

SAND BEACH PARKING LOT

Sand Beach

© MOON.COM

Elevation Profile

Elevation (ft) vs. Distance (mi)

▶ **MILE 0.3-0.5: Split Ledge and Metal Grate to Beehive Summit**
Continue past the grate and carefully make your way up the first round of **iron rungs** and handrails, noting the placement of your feet as you climb. The smooth rungs can sometimes be slippery due to being handled by lots of hikers who've applied sunscreen recently. Squeeze behind some balsam firs and watch your footing as the trail becomes a much higher and narrower ledge that overlooks **Sand Beach.** Take a minute to enjoy the vista and calm your nerves. Beyond this ledge, the trail ascends its most complex series of rungs. Scramble up this final series of ledges, and you'll be standing atop **The Beehive**'s rocky summit at 0.5 mi (0.8 km).

▸ **MILE 0.5–0.7: Beehive Summit to The Bowl**

Once you're ready for a soothing return journey, follow the blue blazes into a grove of balsams and down some rock stairs. At just under 0.6 mi (1 km), veer right onto the **Beehive Trail** and amble over a secondary summit before descending into the forest on a rocky dirt path. Listen for the lapping of water as you approach the shores of **The Bowl** at 0.7 mi (1.1 km), and enjoy the stillness of this little glacial lake as the trail continues along its eastern shoreline.

▸ **MILE 0.7–1.1: The Bowl to Beehive Trail**

After crossing a swampy area on some bog bridges, make a left at the Champlain Mountain Trail junction to stay on the Bowl Trail and descend a few gentle log stairs into boreal forest. At 0.9 mi (1.4 km), the trail intersects the Bowl Trail again; turn right onto Bowl and make your way down more log stairs, keeping left to stay on Bowl at the next two junctions for Gorham Mountain.

▸ **MILE 1.1–1.6: Beehive Trail to Sand Beach Parking Lot**

Enjoy a final view of the Beehive cliffs as the trees open up and the trail returns to the first Beehive Trail cutoff at 1.2 mi (1.9 km). Backtrack down the stone path to Park Loop Road to conclude the hike at 1.6 mi (2.6 km). For a cooldown, cross the road and descend the stairs to the parking lot.

DIRECTIONS

From Bangor, drive southeast on US-1A E for 25 mi (40 km). After crossing the bridge onto Mount Desert Island, turn left at the fork onto ME-3 E. Continue driving along ME-3 E for about 10 mi (16 km) into the town of Bar Harbor, and then drive straight onto Kebo Street. Take Kebo Street south until its terminus and then veer left onto Park Loop Road. Drive along this

▲ THE BEEHIVE'S EXPOSED SOUTH FACE

road to the Sand Beach park entrance station, and then continue south briefly until you see the sign for Sand Beach parking on your left. The entrance to the larger lot comes first and the turnoff for a smaller lot comes immediately after. If both lots are full, roadside parking on the right side of the road is allowed.

GPS COORDINATES: 44°19'53.6"N 68°11'07.1"W

BEST NEARBY BITES

Once you're done savoring flat ground again, head into Bar Harbor for a stacked wood-fired pizza at **Sweet Pea's Café** (854 ME-3, Bar Harbor; 207/801-9099; www.sweetpeascafemaine.com; summer and fall 3pm-8pm Mon. and Thurs., 4pm-8pm Tues.-Wed. and Fri.). If you're in the mood for something more luxurious, enjoy salmon tartine and duck cassoulet from the French-inspired kitchen at **Brasserie Le Brun** (74 Cottage St., Bar Harbor; 207/801-9040; www.lebrunmaine. com; 4pm-midnight daily).

Ocean Path

ACADIA NATIONAL PARK, BAR HARBOR

🐐 ❀ 🐾 🧍 ♿ 🚍

This wildly popular hike along Acadia's eastern shoreline is like walking through a series of postcards that showcase the rugged beauty of coastal Maine.

DISTANCE: 3.6 mi (5.8 km) round-trip
DURATION: 1.5 hr
ELEVATION GAIN: 92 ft (28 m)
EFFORT: Easy
TRAIL: Dirt path, rocks
USERS: Hikers, leashed dogs
SEASON: April–November
FEES/PASSES: $35 park entrance fee per vehicle, May–October
MAPS: Acadia National Park website
TRAILHEAD: Sand Beach Parking Lot, Park Loop Rd., Bar Harbor
FACILITIES: Restrooms
CONTACT: Acadia National Park; 207/288-3338; www.nps.gov/acad. Hulls Cove Visitor Center is open from April 15 through October 31. Call the park to verify hours.

START THE HIKE

▸ **MILE 0-0.7: Sand Beach Parking Lot to Thunder Hole**

Begin the hike in the small parking lot directly above the larger Sand Beach parking area. At the southern end of the lot, find the wooden post labeled **Ocean Path** and pick up the wide gravel trail as it climbs a hillside and then emerges beside Park Loop Road. (Note: The Ocean Path is accessible from Sand Beach to Thunder Hole.) The trail ambles south along the road, passing a series of rocky beaches. At 0.4 mi (0.6 km), you'll enter a corridor of balsam fir and spruce trees. The beaches transition into shelf-like cliffs, and several little spur trails on the left offer vistas of the cliffs and the ocean beyond.

At 0.7 mi (1.1 km), emerge from the woods to reach **Thunder Hole**—a tidal basin through which the incoming waves create a thunder-like booming sound. A metal walkway down to the hole offers a closer look, as well as a chance to get drenched by the waves as they explode against the rock walls of the basin.

▸ **MILE 0.7-1.4: Thunder Hole to Otter Cliffs**

From here, the trail begins to branch away from the road as it passes more shelf cliffs, on which you might see families picnicking or simply enjoying the view. At 1.2 mi (1.9 km), the trail enters a much thicker forest of hemlock-spruce and mossy boulders. The footing gets rootier and rockier

Ocean Path

SAND BEACH
PARKING LOT

Sand
Beach

Great
Head

Newport
Cove

Gorham
Mountain
525 ft

Cadillac Cliffs

Acadia National Park

Old
Soaker

Ocean Path

Gorham Mountain Trail

PARK LOOP RD

THUNDER HOLE
INFORMATION
STATION

Thunder
Hole

Monument
Cove

OTTER CLIFF RD

ATLANTIC

OCEAN

OTTER COVE
OVERLOOK

Otter
Cove

PARK LOOP RD

Boulder
Beach

OTTER CLIFFS
OVERLOOK

Otter
Cliffs

OCEAN VIEW
VISTA

Otter
Point

© MOON.COM

0   0.25 mi

0   0.25 km

Contour Interval = 40 feet

Elevation Profile

Elevation (ft)

One-Way Distance (mi)

henceforth, but the trail remains nearly level, even as it climbs higher above the ocean.

At 1.4 mi (2.3 km), the trees open up once again as the trail reaches **Otter Cliffs**—a destination for rock climbers, who can often be seen scaling the craggy rock faces here.

▶ **MILE 1.4-1.8: Otter Cliffs to Ocean View Vista**
Climb a set of stone stairs to reach an observation walkway that hugs Park Loop Road, walk to the end of the walkway, and descend another staircase to return to the woods. At 1.6 mi (2.6 km), right after descending this staircase, take a moment to look behind you for an incredible view of the Beehive and Champlain Mountain framed by the sea and the sky. Continue as the trail curves southwest through a thick grove of ferns before it delivers you to a final vista that overlooks the ocean at 1.8 mi (2.9 km). Return the way you came.

DIRECTIONS

From Bangor, drive southeast on US-1A E for 25 mi (40 km). After crossing the bridge onto Mount Desert Island, turn left at the fork onto ME-3 E. Continue driving along ME-3 E for about 10 mi (16 km) into the town of Bar Harbor, and then drive straight onto Kebo Street. Take Kebo Street south until its terminus and then veer left onto Park Loop Road. Drive along this road to the Sand Beach entrance station and then continue south to the sign for Sand Beach parking, which will be on your left. The entrance to the larger lot comes first and the turnoff for the small lot (from which the Ocean Path begins) comes immediately after. If both lots are full, roadside parking on the right side is allowed.

The park's free Island Explorer shuttle bus offers direct service to the Sand Beach Parking Lot. From Bar Harbor, take the Route 3 or 4 bus.

GPS COORDINATES: 45°53'11.7"N 68°59'59.1"W

BEST NEARBY BITES

Replicate the serene beauty of your hike with locally sourced and Latin-inspired cuisine such as lobster paella and slow-roasted pork belly at **Havana** (318 Main St., Bar Harbor; 207/288-2822; www.havanamaine.com; 4pm-9pm Wed.-Sun.). Or try any of the wildly creative extra-butterfat ice cream flavors at **Mount Desert Island Ice Cream** (7 Firefly Ln., Bar Harbor; 207/801-4007; www.mdiic.com; summer and fall 11am-10:30pm daily).

This fun hike along Jordan Pond visits the summit of South Bubble, offering vistas, rock climbing, and bog bridges along the way.

BEST: Fall hikes

DISTANCE: 3.6 mi (5.8 km) round-trip

DURATION: 3 hr

ELEVATION GAIN: 498 ft (152 m)

EFFORT: Moderate

TRAIL: Dirt path, rocks, wooden bog bridges, water crossings on stones

USERS: Hikers

SEASON: June–October

FEES/PASSES: $35 park entrance fee per vehicle, May–October

MAPS: Acadia National Park website

TRAILHEAD: Jordan Pond House, Park Loop Rd., Seal Harbor

FACILITIES: Restrooms

CONTACT: Acadia National Park; 207/288-3338; www.nps.gov/acad. Hulls Cove Visitor Center is open from April 15 through October 31. Call the park to verify hours.

START THE HIKE

▶ **MILE 0-0.3: Jordan Pond House to Carriage Road**

Begin the hike at the end of the observation lawn at Jordan Pond House, on the southern shore of the pond. Looking straight out to the pond and the Bubbles, you'll be standing on a groomed gravel path; this is the **Jordan Pond Path.** Head right and stroll through some wildflowers and into the cedar and spruce woods on the pond's eastern shore. Continue north along the shoreline on this gentle section, passing several boat launches and some little rocky beaches. As you circle a larger cove, the forest transitions to hemlocks and passes a cutoff for the Carriage Road at 0.3 mi (0.5 km).

▶ **MILE 0.3-1.3: Carriage Road to Bubbles Trail**

Keep left here and check out the views of the cliffs on neighboring Penobscot Mountain on the western side of the pond. Follow signs for Bubble Rock as the smooth path veers close to the water—close enough to spot trout swimming beneath the surface on a sunny day! One mi (1.6 km) in, you'll cross a wooden footbridge over a creek before approaching the foot of South Bubble. Cross a second bridge to reach a junction for the **Bubbles Trail** at 1.3 mi (2.1 km); pick up the trail and warm up your quads with a moderately graded ascent up rock stairs and through the woods. Blue blazes mark the path.

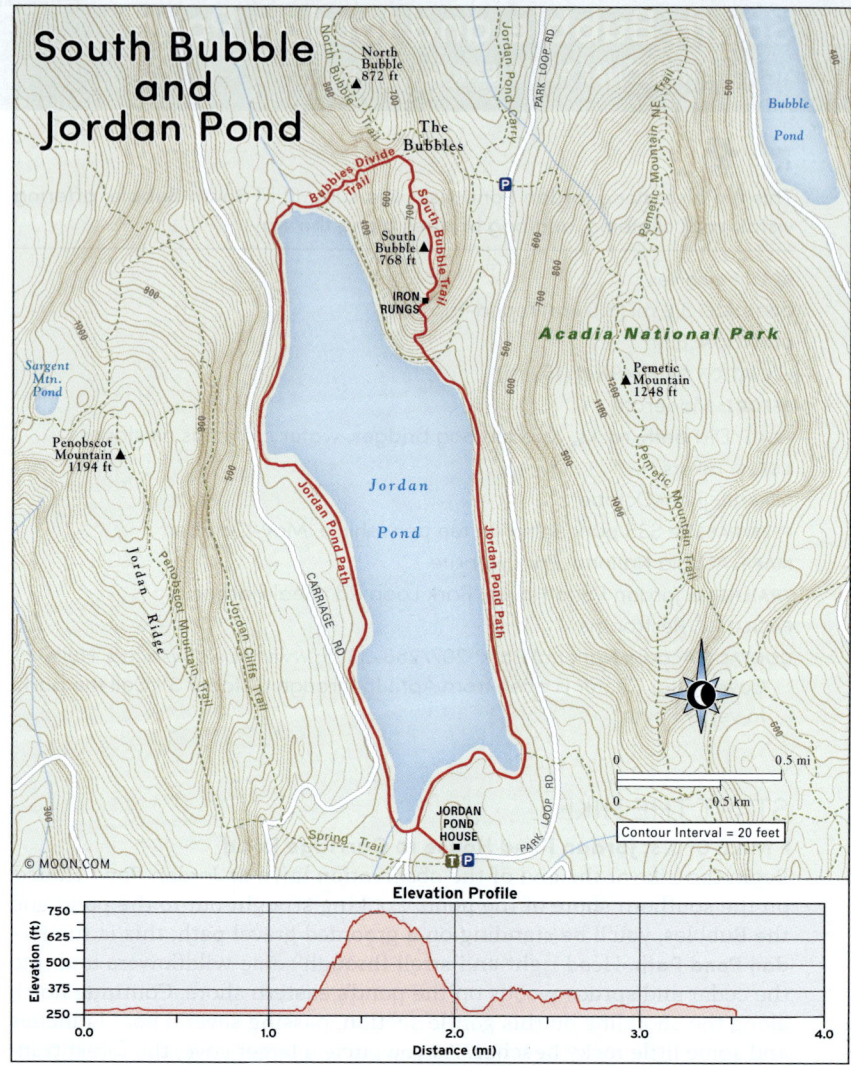

South Bubble and Jordan Pond

Elevation Profile

▶ **MILE 1.3-1.5: Bubbles Trail to South Bubble**

As the stairs become rougher and steeper, the trail emerges from the trees and slabs dramatically up the southern face of the mountain. One trickier section requires passing through a tight crevice of rock. A few iron rungs are placed here and there to help hikers bypass the steeper parts of the climb, which soon levels off and reaches the globular rocky summit of **South Bubble** at 1.5 mi (2.4 km). There are views of Jordan Pond to the south and Pemetic Mountain to the east.

▶ **MILE 1.5-1.6: South Bubble to Summit Rock**

Before continuing onward, scramble down the rock slopes on the eastern edge of the summit to find the mountain's famous glacial erratic—a house-sized rock that's precariously placed on the edge of a cliff!

▲ BRIDGE AT JORDAN POND

▶ MILE 1.6–2.1: **Summit Rock to Bubbles Divide Trail**

Hike north past the summit proper and dip back into the woods and down some log stairs to reach the wooded col (gap) between the two Bubbles. Turn left at the Bubbles Divide junction at 1.8 mi (2.9 km) to take Bubbles Divide Trail and descend a steep and winding rock staircase that becomes more like a boulder field as you approach the waters of Jordan Pond again.

▶ MILE 2.1–2.3: **Bubbles Divide Trail to Jordan Pond Path**

At 2.1 mi (3.4 km), make a right to link back up with the **Jordan Pond Path.** Pass a large pebbly beach and cross a larger wooden footbridge to reach the Deer Brook junction at 2.2 mi (3.5 km). Veer left to stay on Jordan Pond and return along the pond's more densely forested western shores.

▶ MILE 2.3–3.6: **Jordan Pond Path to Jordan Pond House**

The woods on this side of the pond are a lot rockier and darker. The trail stays near the water but makes use of the rougher landscape by rock-hopping across watery sections and weaving between some massive boulders. The grand finale—a long, meandering boardwalk of wooden bog bridges—begins at roughly 2.7 mi (4.3 km). These bridges, many of which are new, traverse a mossy bog-like area of forest. Some of them are a couple of feet above the ground or water, so be sure to watch your balance. After the last bridge, the trail reaches the Carriage Road at 3.6 mi (5.8 km). Merge onto the road and take an immediate left onto the Jordan Pond Path, which delivers you back to the Pond House after just a few yards.

Acadia

MAINE

VIEW OF JORDAN POND FROM SOUTH BUBBLE SUMMIT ▲

DIRECTIONS

From Bangor, drive southeast on US-1A E for 25 mi (40 km). After crossing the bridge onto Mount Desert Island, turn right at the fork and continue south along ME-102 S for about 4 mi (6.4 km) before swinging left onto ME-3 W. Drive southwest for another 5 mi (8 km), make a left turn to stay on ME-3 W, and then take a left at the Stanley Brook entrance for Acadia. Take this road to its terminus, make a slight left onto Park Loop Road, and drive north until you see the Jordan Pond House entrance on your left. If the lot here is full (which it usually is), continue north past the Pond House and turn left to access the overflow parking areas.

GPS COORDINATES: 44°19'22.5"N 68°15'13.4"W

BEST NEARBY BITES

Make a reservation before your visit and enjoy a spread of freshly baked popovers with jam, tea, coffee, and more on the sunny pond-side patio of the legendary **Jordan Pond House Restaurant** (2928 Park Loop Rd., Seal Harbor; 207/813-4342; www.acadiajordanpondhouse.com; 11am–5pm daily).

5 Penobscot Mountain via the Jordan Cliffs Trail

ACADIA NATIONAL PARK, BAR HARBOR

Climb one of Acadia's most popular mountains via a series of dramatic cliff faces for awe-inspiring views of the coast.

DISTANCE: 3.3 mi (5.3 km) round-trip
DURATION: 2 hr
ELEVATION GAIN: 1,027 ft (313 m)
EFFORT: Strenuous
TRAIL: Dirt path, rocks, iron rungs, wooden bog bridges
USERS: Hikers
SEASON: June–October
FEES/PASSES: $35 park entrance fee per vehicle, May–October
MAPS: Acadia National Park website
TRAILHEAD: Jordan Pond House, Park Loop Rd., Seal Harbor
FACILITIES: Restrooms
CONTACT: Acadia National Park; 207/288-3338; www.nps.gov/acad. Hulls Cove Visitor Center is open from April 15 through October 31. Call the park to verify hours.

The most unforgettable way up Penobscot is the Jordan Cliffs Trail—a wildly scenic climb across the rock walls that form the eastern flank of the peak. The trail is not especially steep, but its iron ladders and narrow ledges can make sections of this hike feel like a training run for *American Ninja Warrior*. If the weather is wet, take a different trail to the top. The trail is also occasionally closed if peregrine falcons have been spotted in the area (there is a nesting zone along the trail).

START THE HIKE

▸ **MILE 0-0.3: Jordan Pond House to Jordan Cliffs Trail**
Begin the hike by the restroom entrance outside the Jordan Pond House. Veer left at the wooden trail post to pick up Spring Trail, a gravel path that descends into the forest. Cross the carriage road and continue east over a wooden bridge that crosses a creek. Amble through the woods briefly and then turn right at the junction for **Jordan Cliffs Trail,** which follows blue blazes through a mossier stretch of forest.

The trail swings north and climbs some gentle stone stairs to reach another junction at roughly 0.3 mi (0.5 km). Keep right here as the trail crosses the carriage road once more and continues into the forest on the opposite side.

Acadia

MAINE

Penobscot Mountain
via the Jordan Cliffs Trail

Deer Brook Trail

Sargent Mt Pond

Penobscot East Trail

Penobscot Mountain 1194'

IRON RUNGS
Sheer Cliff Face
BRIDGE

Jordan Cliffs Trail

Penobscot Mountain Trail

Jordan Ridge

Acadia

National

Park

Jordan Pond

Jordan Pond Path

EAGLE-JORDAN CARRIAGE RD

The Amphitheater

Amphitheater Trail

0   0.25 mi

0   0.25 km

Contour Interval = 20 feet

© MOON.COM

Spring Trail

Jordan Stream

JORDAN POND HOUSE

PARK LOOP RD

Elevation Profile

Elevation (ft): 1,200 / 1,000 / 800 / 600 / 400 / 200

Distance (mi): 0.0 0.5 1.0 1.5 2.0 2.5 3.0 3.5

▲ VIEW OF SOMES SOUND FROM PENOBSCOT MOUNTAIN

▶ **MILE 0.3–1.0: Jordan Cliffs Trail to Sheer Cliff Face**

Climbing gradually through airier spruce-and-fir woods, the dirt trail quickly transitions to sloped slabs of rock with a notable peach hue. A few fleeting views of Penobscot's summit appear through the trees on the left. At 0.7 mi (1.1 km), the trail levels out and continues north. Suddenly, the woods on your right will open to reveal the expanse of Jordan Pond several hundred feet below. The footing gets rockier, and the trail climbs higher with the help of steep rock stairs. One mi (1.6 km) in, the trail traverses the first sheer cliff face and becomes much skinnier—watch your step here.

▶ **MILE 1.0–1.6: Sheer Cliff Face to Penobscot East Trail**

After dipping in and out of the woods, the trail arrives at the first obstacle at 1.1 mi (1.8 km): a large boulder that hikers must climb over with the help of a single iron rung and a bar installed in the rock. (Consider this your last chance to turn back.) The trail continues north but becomes much rougher, with lots of exposed tree roots. At 1.3 mi (2.1 km), you'll cross a long balance beam-like wooden bridge with handrails. Descend the stairs at the end of the bridge and prepare to tread carefully—the trail traverses a much longer stretch of exposed cliff here with the help of iron rungs in the rock, including one vertical rung climb of at least 15 ft (4.5 m) that requires the use of handholds in the surrounding rock. Be sure that your boots have a good grip on each rung before stepping onto the next rung.

At the top of this scary stretch, the trail swerves into the woods and climbs a gentler stony path to the junction with the **Penobscot East Trail** at 1.6 mi (2.6 km).

▶ **MILE 1.6–1.9: Penobscot East Trail to Penobscot Mountain Summit**

Swing left onto Penobscot East Trail and hoist your way up some boulders and rock ledges onto the upper heights of Penobscot. The trail meanders across the alpine landscape, following blue-blazed cairns, before climbing to a final height of land and reaching the **Penobscot Mountain** summit signpost at 1.9 mi (3.1 km).

▸ **MILE 1.9–2.8: Penobscot Mountain Summit to Spring Trail**

Enjoy the views while beginning your return journey down the **Penobscot Mountain Trail** from the summit post. The initial descent is a dreamy stroll down the mountain's broad summit, with the south coast of Mount Desert Island serving as an epic backdrop. Continue south for 0.9 mi (1.4 km) as the crops of young spruce trees segue into full-on forest. At 2.8 mi (4.5 km), take a left at the junction onto **Spring Trail.**

▸ **MILE 2.8–3.3: Spring Trail to Jordan Pond House**

The descent becomes very steep after this point, with rock steps, some slabs, and even a wooden boardwalk that hugs a series of sheer cliff faces. It's hair-raising but short-lived. The trail reaches the carriage road again at 3 mi (4.8 km). Cross to the other side and make your way down some rugged rock stairs before reaching the **Jordan Cliffs Trail junction** at 3.1 mi (5 km). Turn right, backtrack to the Jordan Pond House, and complete your hike at a hearty 3.3 mi (5.3 km).

DIRECTIONS

From Bangor, drive southeast on US-1A E for 25 mi (40 km). After crossing the bridge onto Mount Desert Island, turn right at the fork and continue south along ME-102 S for about 4 mi (6.4 km) before swinging left onto ME-3 W. Drive southwest for another 5 mi (8 km), make a left turn to stay on ME-3 W, and then take another left turn at the Stanley Brook entrance for Acadia. Take this road to its terminus, make a slight left onto Park Loop Road, and drive north until you see the Jordan Pond House entrance on your left. If the lot here is full (which it usually is), continue north past the Pond House and turn left to access the overflow parking areas.

The park's free Island Explorer shuttle bus offers direct service to the Jordan Pond House, and catching the bus is a great way to beat the steep parking competition. From Bar Harbor, take the Route 4, 5, or 6 bus.

GPS COORDINATES: 44°19'13.5"N 68°15'15.1"W

6 Hadlock Falls

ACADIA NATIONAL PARK, BAR HARBOR

❀ ♨ 🚶 ♿ 🚌🚉

This quiet and meditative hike to Acadia's prettiest waterfall is a chance to stroll along the famous carriage roads that wind through the island's woods.

DISTANCE: 2 mi (3.2 km) round-trip

DURATION: 1 hr

ELEVATION GAIN: 146 ft (45 m)

EFFORT: Easy

TRAIL: Gravel path, optional rock stairs

USERS: Hikers, cyclists, horseback riders

SEASON: May–October

FEES/PASSES: $35 park entrance fee per vehicle, May–October

MAPS: Acadia National Park website

TRAILHEAD: Parkman Mountain parking lot, Route 3, Mount Desert

FACILITIES: Vault toilet

CONTACT: Acadia National Park; 207/288-3338; www.nps.gov/acad. Hulls Cove Visitor Center is open from April 15 through October 31. Call the park to verify hours.

The modest yet beautiful 40-ft-tall (12-m) Hadlock Falls is among the park's lesser-known attractions (most tourists are focused on the mountains and coastline). If you're on foot, the only way to reach it is to take a walk along Acadia's carriage roads as they meander along the southern flanks of Parkman Mountain and Sargent Mountain. The falls are most impressive during the late spring and early summer, when the flow is more dramatic.

START THE HIKE

▶ MILE 0-0.4: Parkman Mountain Parking Lot to Junction 12

Begin the hike at the north side of the Parkman Mountain parking lot by the large wooden information kiosk for the carriage road. Walk northeast past the sign and make an immediate right turn onto the carriage road. Briefly take the road south through a mixed forest of spruce and birch before turning left at the **13 junction.** (Look for a little sign bearing the number 13 on a tree—all the carriage road junctions are marked numerically like this.)

The road sharply veers northwest and climbs a duet of switchbacks through mossy, boulder-strewn woods. As you pass several cliff faces, note how the baby cedar trees explode out of the rifts in the cliff. As the sound of auto traffic fades away, the road curves northeast and reaches **junction 12** at 0.4 mi (0.6 km).

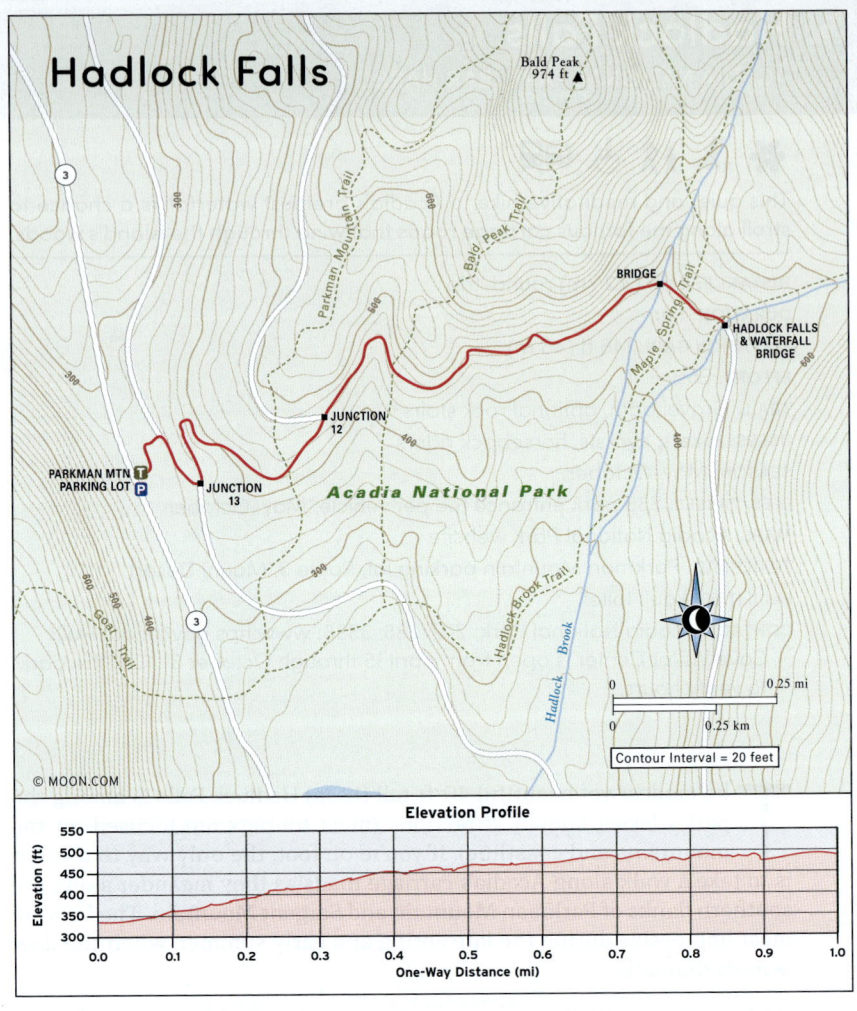

Hadlock Falls

Bald Peak
974 ft ▲

BRIDGE

HADLOCK FALLS
& WATERFALL
BRIDGE

JUNCTION
12

PARKMAN MTN
PARKING LOT

JUNCTION
13

Acadia National Park

Goat Trail

Hadlock Brook Trail

Maple Springs Trail

Parkman Mountain Trail

Bald Peak Trail

Hadlock Brook

© MOON.COM

0   0.25 mi
0   0.25 km
Contour Interval = 20 feet

Elevation Profile

Elevation (ft)

One-Way Distance (mi)

▶ MILE 0.4-0.9: Junction 12 to Arched Stone Bridge

Turn right here and continue hiking along the road as it meanders through a denser corridor of hemlock and balsams. The nearby ripple of a stream offers a teaser of things to come, and the cliffs start to tower over the road in places. Pass by the Bald Mountain Trail cutoff at 0.6 mi (1 km), then enjoy a few glimpses of **Penobscot Mountain** ahead. Suddenly cedar and balsam fir become the dominant trees here. Also take a look along the side of the trail for wildflowers such as asters and goldenrods, especially in late summer or early fall. Continue hiking east for 0.3 mi (0.5 km).

▶ MILE 0.9-1.0: Arched Stone Bridge to Hadlock Falls

At 0.9 mi (1.4 km), the road crosses an arched stone bridge over a creek. Hike past the Maple Springs Trail before arriving at a second arched bridge overlooking **Hadlock Falls.** The bridge is outfitted with a little cleft from which visitors can view the falls, but a set of rock stairs on the left side of the road allows hikers to descend closer to the cascade—which

▲ STONE BRIDGE ALONG ACADIA'S CARRIAGE ROADS

is complemented by a little observation terrace that would be a hell of a place to propose to someone. The rocks at the foot of the falls can get very slick from the moss and water, but as long as you watch your footing, it doesn't take much effort to scramble close enough to feel the cooling mist of Hadlock Falls—the perfect finale to a heavenly hike. Return the way you came.

DIRECTIONS

From Bangor, drive southeast on US-1A E for 25 mi (40 km). After crossing the bridge onto Mount Desert Island, turn right at the fork and continue south along ME-102 S for about 4 mi (6.4 km) before swinging left onto ME-3 W. Drive southwest for another 4 mi (6.4 km) and then take a sharp left at the sign for the Parkman Mountain parking lot.

The park's free Island Explorer shuttle bus offers direct service to the Parkman Mountain parking lot. From Bar Harbor, take the Route 6 bus.

GPS COORDINATES: 44°19'45.5"N 68°17'34.8"W

BEST NEARBY BITES

Just a few minutes north of the Hadlock Falls trailhead, you can dig into a Maine lobster or a heaping bucket of steamers while enjoying a pretty view of Somes Sound at **Abel's Lobster Pound** (13 Abels Ln., Mount Desert; 207-276-8221; www.abelslobstermdi.com; noon–2:30pm and 4:30pm–8pm daily).

Climb hundreds of exquisitely carved stone stairs up the side of Mansell Mountain, then scramble down an exposed rock formation with nice views of Mount Desert Island's southwest woods.

BEST: New England oddities

DISTANCE: 2.6 mi (4.2 km) round-trip

DURATION: 2.5 hr

ELEVATION GAIN: 868 ft (265 m)

EFFORT: Moderate

TRAIL: Dirt path, rocks, iron rungs, wooden bog bridges

USERS: Hikers, leashed dogs

SEASON: June-October

FEES/PASSES: $35 park entrance fee per vehicle, May-October

MAPS: Acadia National Park website

TRAILHEAD: Long Pond parking lot, Long Pond Road, Southwest Harbor

FACILITIES: None

CONTACT: Acadia National Park; 207/288-3338; www.nps.gov/acad. Hulls Cove Visitor Center is open from April 15 through October 31. Call the park to verify hours.

START THE HIKE

▶ **MILE 0-0.2: Long Pond Parking Lot to Perpendicular Trail**

Begin the hike in the parking lot beside the southern end of Long Pond. Walk west toward the pumphouse and look for a wooden post for **Long Pond Trail.** A gravel path along the shore of the pond takes you into the forest. Keep right at the first junction and continue along the pond until you reach the turnoff for **Perpendicular Trail** at 0.2 mi (0.3 km); turn left and start climbing a series of low, gentle rock stairs.

▶ **MILE 0.2-0.3: Perpendicular Trail to Long Pond View**

As you climb through a breezy grove of spruce woods, following blue blazes on the tree trunks, the stairs become switchbacks and then emerge from the trees into an expansive rockslide at around

WINDING SWITCHBACKS OF
PERPENDICULAR TRAIL ▶

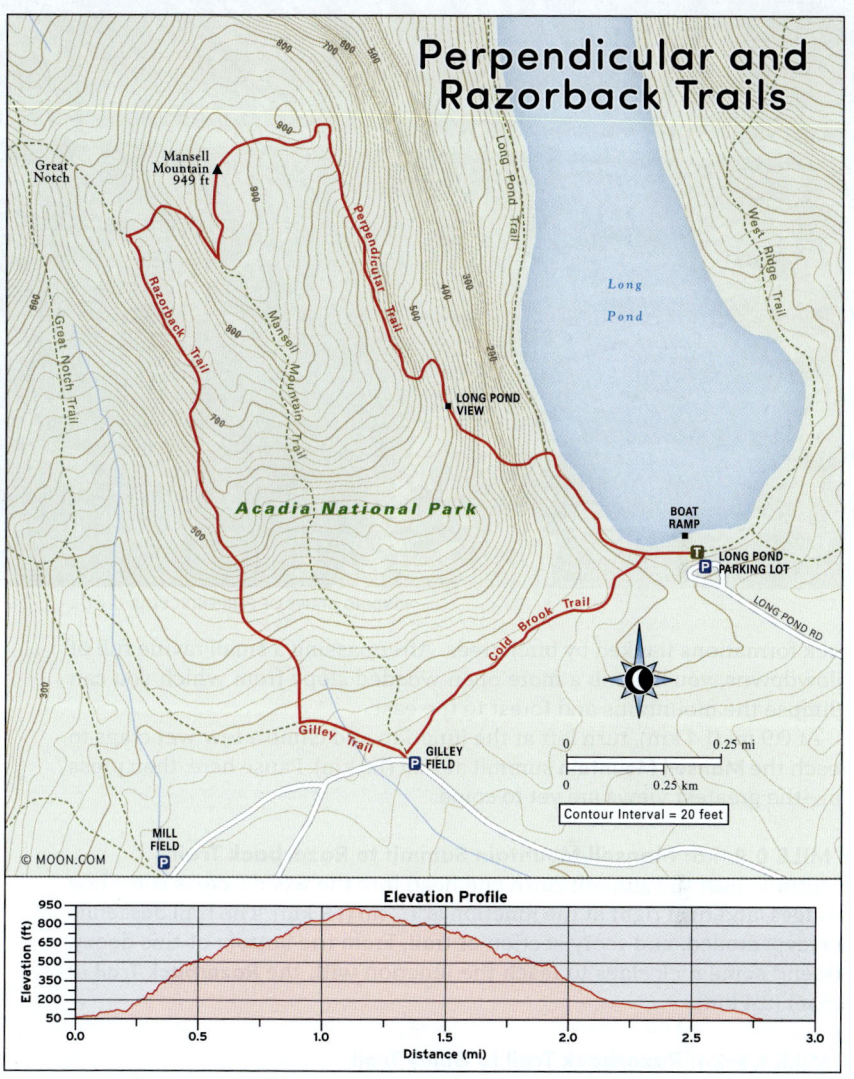

Perpendicular and Razorback Trails

Elevation Profile

0.3 mi (0.5 km). Check out the view of Long Pond below, then continue the ascent. From here, the staircases become steeper, narrower, and more winding.

▶ **MILE 0.3–0.9: Long Pond View to Mansell Mountain Summit**

As the stairs reenter the woods, climb a small set of iron rungs installed into a rock slab that separates two sections of stairs. Cedar trees overtake the spruce as the stairs get rougher and bypass some small boulders. At 0.5 mi (0.8 km), enter a mossier patch of forest and enjoy a brief break from the stairs as the trail hobbles along a sheer cliff face that's often trickling with water runoff. The trail becomes a level wooded ledge for a few hundred yards before transitioning back to stairs. Continue your climb and watch your footing as the trail becomes rougher and ascends several large

Acadia

WINDING STAIRS OF PERPENDICULAR TRAIL ▲

rock formations flanked by birch trees. After passing a small ravine full of blowdowns, you'll climb a more open wooded slope from which you can glimpse the mountains and forest to the east.

At 0.9 mi (1.4 km), turn left at the junction and climb a few wet crags to reach the **Mansell Mountain** summit at 1 mi (1.6 km). Pause here, then press on—the greatest views are yet to come.

▶ MILE 0.9-1.5: Mansell Mountain Summit to Razorback Trail

Continue past the summit cairn and head into the woods, cross some bog bridges, and turn right at the junction at 1.2 mi (1.9 km). The trail descends a steep, eroded, and rooty section of trail. From the bottom of this doozy, ascend some rock slabs to reach the junction with the **Razorback Trail** at 1.5 mi (2.4 km).

▶ MILE 1.5-2.1: Razorback Trail to Gilley Trail

Turn left onto Razorback and hike (or scramble) your way down a series of sawtooth rock faces that can be quite slippery when wet. The outlooks along this section have photo-worthy views of Mount Desert Island's southwest woods.

Keep scrambling along rock faces for another 0.25 mi (0.4 km) before heading back into the woods, where the trail makes a moderately graded descent down a combination of rock stairs and rooty path. At 2 mi (3.2 km), turn left at the **Gilley Trail** junction and follow Gilley to the roundabout at 2.1 mi (3.4 km).

▶ MILE 2.1-2.6: Gilley Trail to Long Pond Parking Lot

Walk straight across the roundabout and pick up the **Cold Brook Trail**, which cruises through the woods past young balsams at a near-level grade. Cross a wooden footbridge over a creek to rejoin the Long Pond

▲ LONG POND

Trail at 2.5 mi (4 km). Turn right and backtrack to the parking lot to complete the loop at 2.6 mi (4.2 km).

DIRECTIONS

From Bangor, drive southeast on US-1A E for 25 mi (40 km). After crossing the bridge onto Mount Desert Island, turn right at the fork onto ME-102 S. Continue south along this road for 10 mi (16 km) and then swing right onto Seal Cove Road. After roughly 0.5 mi (0.8 km), turn right onto Long Pond Road and follow it to its terminus at the southern shore of Long Pond, where you'll see the visitors parking lot. If the lot is full, park alongside the road near the pond.

GPS COORDINATES: 44°18'00.8"N 68°21'01.0"W

BEST NEARBY BITES

Start the day by supporting a good cause and wolfing down some incredible popovers with maple walnut butter at Southwest Harbor's donation-based **Common Good Kitchen Café** (19 Clark Point Rd., Southwest Harbor; 207/266-2733; www.commongoodsoupkitchen. org; 7:30am-11am daily). Cap off your evening with creative Maine-sourced New American fare and an impressive wine list at **Red Sky** (14 Clark Point Rd., Southwest Harbor; 207/244-0476; www. redskyrestaurant.com; 5pm-8pm Wed.-Sat.).

Acadia

MAINE

57

Ship Harbor

ACADIA NATIONAL PARK, SOUTHWEST HARBOR

This secluded ocean hike takes visitors through an otherworldly landscape of pink granite, mixed forests, and that classic Maine fog that regularly envelops the coast.

DISTANCE: 1.4 mi (2.3 km) round-trip
DURATION: 45 min
ELEVATION GAIN: 81 ft (25 m)
EFFORT: Easy
TRAIL: Dirt path, rocks, wooden bog bridges
USERS: Hikers
SEASON: May–October
FEES/PASSES: $35 park entrance fee per vehicle, May–October
MAPS: Acadia National Park website
TRAILHEAD: Ship Harbor parking lot, Seawall Rd., Southwest Harbor
FACILITIES: Vault toilet
CONTACT: Acadia National Park; 207/288-3338; www.nps.gov/acad. Hulls Cove Visitor Center is open from April 15 through October 31. Call the park to verify hours.

START THE HIKE

▶ **MILE 0-0.6: Ship Harbor Parking Lot to Mount Desert Island**

Begin the hike in the **Ship Harbor** parking lot. Pick up the gravel path and briefly descend south into a meadow before veering slightly east and passing a trail information kiosk for Ship Harbor. Continue east through a tunnel of ferns, wildflowers, and mixed trees before the forest widens into a rich green wonderland of massive spruce trees. Keep an eye out for deer, which are active here, and hike east to the fork at roughly 0.1 mi (0.16 km). It's all the same trail, but for the most compelling sequence of sights, take a left here.

As you continue southeast through the woods, the trail passes through verdant blankets of moss. Reach another fork at 0.4 mi (0.6 km), and this time, swing right. Listen for the gentle lapping of the ocean as the trail partially emerges from the woods and meanders along Ship Harbor itself—a shallow, pool-shaped inlet. On your right, you'll notice a few sets of log stairs that offer hikers the chance to descend to a stony beach at the water's edge. The trail becomes rockier and climbs some log stairs to pass into a new forest zone of abundant and very skinny hemlocks. Cross some wooden bog bridges, minding your footing during wet weather, and prepare for another transition as the trail suddenly leaves the woods behind at 0.6 mi (1 km) and arrives at the southern edge of **Mount Desert Island**—a gorgeous landscape of pink granite rocks and gentle waves.

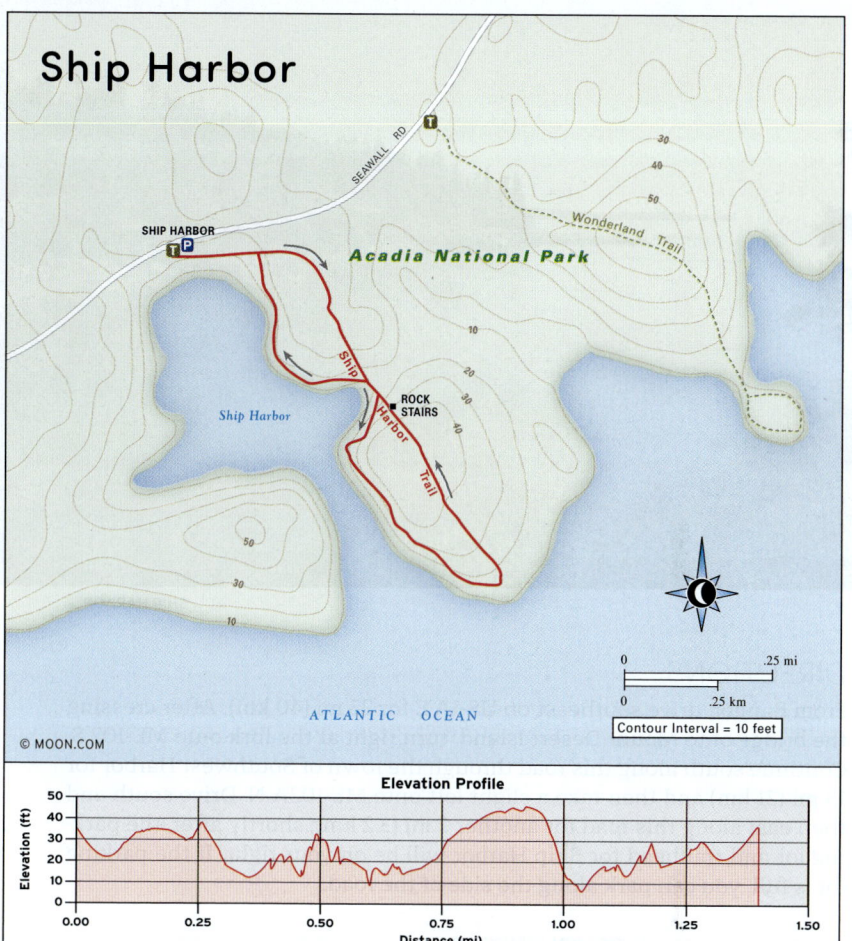

Ship Harbor

Acadia National Park

SHIP HARBOR

Wonderland Trail

SEAWALL RD

Ship Harbor

ROCK STAIRS

Ship Harbor Trail

ATLANTIC OCEAN

0   .25 mi
0   .25 km
Contour Interval = 10 feet

© MOON.COM

Elevation Profile

Elevation (ft)

Distance (mi)

▶ **MILE 0.6–1.0: Mount Desert Island to Rock Stairs**

From here, hikers can choose to scramble around the rocks or stick to the path, which is now flanked by spruce trees small enough to allow for an unobstructed view of the coast. As the trail veers left into some bushes and crosses a few more bog bridges, the pattering of the waves becomes quieter and the trail reenters the forest at 0.7 mi (1.1 km). Continue walking northwest through the forest over more bog bridges and down some spacious **rock stairs** to arrive at a familiar-looking fork at 1 mi (1.6 km). Turn left.

▶ **MILE 1.0–1.4: Rock Stairs to Ship Harbor Parking Lot**

The concluding lap of the hike—which resembles a figure-eight—returns to the inlet, ambling along the water from a higher position. The hemlocks here are even more majestic than the ones in the woods. A final winding descent delivers you to the first fork at 1.3 mi (2.1 km). Take a left turn here and backtrack northwest to the **trailhead** and parking lot to complete the hike at 1.4 mi (2.3 km).

DIRECTIONS

From Bangor, drive southeast on US-1A E for 25 mi (40 km). After crossing the bridge onto Mount Desert Island, turn right at the fork onto ME-102 S. Continue south along this road through the town of Southwest Harbor for 13 mi (21 km) and then take a slight left onto ME-102A N. Drive south and then east along this road for another 2 mi (3.2 km); shortly after, the parking lot and trailhead for Ship Harbor will be on your right. If the parking lot is full, you can park along the side of the road.

GPS COORDINATES: 44°13'56.0"N 68°19'22.4"W

BEST NEARBY BITES

Double down on the maritime theme with a classic oceanside Maine lobster dinner. Head over to Bass Harbor to check out **Thurston's Lobster Pound** (9 Thurston Rd., Bernard; 207/244-7600; www.thurstonforlobster.com; noon-9pm Tues.-Sat.) or drive east to Seawall and visit **Charlotte's Legendary Lobster Pound** (465 Seawall Rd., Southwest Harbor; 207/244-8021; www.charlotteslegendarylobsters.com; 11am-8:30pm daily).

NEARBY CAMPGROUNDS

NAME	LOCATION	FACILITIES	SEASON	FEE
Hadley's Point Campground	33 Hadley Point Rd., Bar Harbor, 44°26'16.1"N 68°18'51.4"W	Tent sites, RV sites, cabins, toilets, showers, potable water, laundry, pool, camp store, Wi-Fi	mid-May through mid-October	$32-110
207/288-4808; www.hadleyspoint.com				
Bar Harbor Campground	409 ME-3, Bar Harbor, 44°25'52.7"N 68°16'15.0"W	Tent sites, RV sites, toilets, showers, potable water, laundry, pool, camp store, Wi-Fi	late May through mid-October	$34-46
207/288-5185; www.thebarharborcampground.com				
Blackwoods Campground	155 Blackwoods Dr., Otter Creek, 44°18'47.0"N 68°12'39.3"W	Tent sites, RV sites, toilets, potable water	May through mid-October	$30-60
207/288-3274; www.recreation.gov				
HTR Acadia Campground	5 Spinnaker Way, Mount Desert, 44°20'15.5"N 68°19'19.5"W	Tent sites, cabin tents, RV sites, cabins, toilets, showers, potable water, pool, Wi-Fi	late May through mid-October	$42-215
207/244-8094; www.htrresorts.com				

NEARBY CAMPGROUNDS (continued)

NAME	LOCATION	FACILITIES	SEASON	FEE
Smuggler's Den Campground	20 Main St., Southwest Harbor, 44°18'03.3"N 68°19'50.0"W	Tent sites, RV sites, RV rentals, cabins, toilets, showers, potable water, laundry, pool, camp store, Wi-Fi	late May through mid-October	$32-260
207/244-9033; www.smugglersdencampground.com				
Bass Harbor Campground	342 Harbor Dr., Bass Harbor, 44°13'50.4"N 68°20'21.6"W	Tent sites, RV sites, cabins, yurts, toilets, showers, potable water, laundry, pool, camp store, Wi-Fi	mid-May through mid-October	$32-114
207/244-5857; www.bassharbor.com				
Seawall Campground	668 Seawall Rd., Southwest Harbor, 44°14'31.8"N 68°18'21.2"W	Tent sites, RV sites, toilets, potable water	late May through mid-October	$22-60
207/244-3600; www.recreation.gov				
Quietside Campground & Cabins	397 Tremont Rd., Bernard, 44°15'03.3"N 68°22'02.8"W	Tent sites, RV sites, cabins, toilets, showers, potable water, laundry, camp store, Wi-Fi	June through mid-October	$28-75
207/244-0566; www.quietsidecampground.com				

BAXTER, THE HIGHLANDS, AND THE CARRABASSETT VALLEY

Northern Maine is a land of superlatives. The tallest mountain, biggest lake, and longest river in the state are all here. The region contains thousands of miles of trails, all of which are surrounded by acre after acre of evergreen frontier. To amble through Maine's northern forests is to experience the Pine Tree State at its most rugged and majestic. For hikers who make the considerable journey here, three wild and wooded wonderlands await: Baxter State Park, the Maine Highlands, and the Carrabassett Valley. Each contains relics of Maine's unique blend of logging and geological history—from old sawmills to older caves, cascades, and remote peaks that seem to poke the sky.

▲ VIEW OF MOUNT KATAHDIN

▲ KINEO RISING FROM MOOSEHEAD LAKE

◄ ORONO BOG BOARDWALK

1 **South Turner Mountain**
DISTANCE: 3.6 mi (5.8 km) round-trip
DURATION: 2.5 hr
EFFORT: Moderate/strenuous
PAGE: 68

2 **Mount Katahdin**
DISTANCE: 9.4 mi (15.1 km) round-trip
DURATION: 8.5 hr
EFFORT: Strenuous
PAGE: 71

3 **Little and Big Niagara Falls**
DISTANCE: 2.4 mi (3.9 km) round-trip
DURATION: 1.5 hr
EFFORT: Easy
PAGE: 75

4 **Blueberry Ledges**
DISTANCE: 3.6 mi (5.8 km) round-trip
DURATION: 1.5 hr
EFFORT: Easy
PAGE: 78

5 **Debsconeag Ice Caves**
DISTANCE: 2 mi (3.2 km) round-trip
DURATION: 1 hr
EFFORT: Easy
PAGE: 81

6 **Mount Kineo**
DISTANCE: 3.5 mi (5.6 km) round-trip
DURATION: 2 hr
EFFORT: Moderate
PAGE: 84

7 **Gulf Hagas**
DISTANCE: 8.2 mi (13.2 km) round-trip
DURATION: 5 hr
EFFORT: Strenuous
PAGE: 87

8 **Mount Bigelow**
DISTANCE: 10 mi (16 km) round-trip
DURATION: 6.5 hr
EFFORT: Strenuous
PAGE: 91

9 **Poplar Stream Falls**
DISTANCE: 4.4 mi (7.1 km) round-trip
DURATION: 2 hr
EFFORT: Easy
PAGE: 95

10 **Orono Bog**
DISTANCE: 1.5 mi (2.4 km) round-trip
DURATION: 45 min
EFFORT: Easy
PAGE: 98

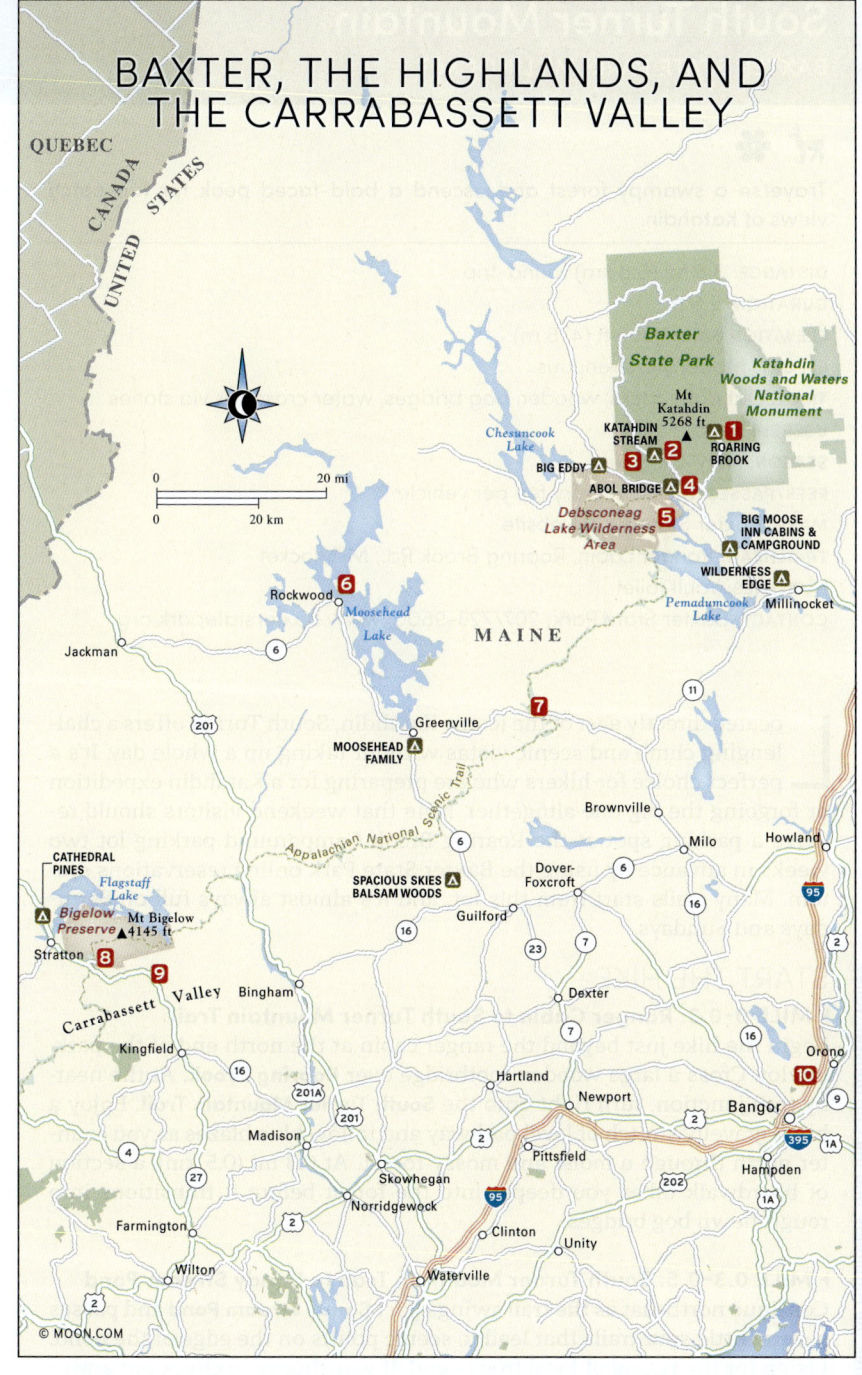

BAXTER, THE HIGHLANDS, AND THE CARRABASSETT VALLEY

QUEBEC

CANADA

UNITED STATES

MAINE

Baxter State Park

Katahdin Woods and Waters National Monument

Chesuncook Lake

Mt Katahdin 5268 ft

KATAHDIN STREAM △ **3** △ **2** △ **1** ROARING BROOK

BIG EDDY △

ABOL BRIDGE △ **4**

Debsconeag Lake Wilderness Area **5**

BIG MOOSE INN CABINS & CAMPGROUND

WILDERNESS EDGE △

Millinocket

Pemadumcook Lake

Rockwood **6**

Moosehead Lake

Jackman

7

Greenville

MOOSEHEAD FAMILY △

Brownville

Howland

Dover-Foxcroft

Milo

CATHEDRAL PINES

Flagstaff Lake

Bigelow Preserve

Mt Bigelow ▲ 4145 ft

Stratton **8** **9**

Carrabassett Valley

Bingham

Kingfield

Appalachian National Scenic Trail

SPACIOUS SKIES BALSAM WOODS △

Guilford

Dexter

Hartland

Newport

Madison

Orono

Bangor

10

Hampden

Farmington

Skowhegan

Norridgewock

Pittsfield

Wilton

Clinton

Unity

Waterville

© MOON.COM

0   20 mi

0   20 km

1 South Turner Mountain

BAXTER STATE PARK, MILLINOCKET

Traverse a swampy forest and ascend a bald-faced peak for top-notch views of Katahdin.

DISTANCE: 3.6 mi (5.8 km) round-trip

DURATION: 2.5 hr

ELEVATION GAIN: 1,558 ft (475 m)

EFFORT: Moderate/strenuous

TRAIL: Dirt path, rocks, wooden bog bridges, water crossings via stones

USERS: Hikers

SEASON: May–October

FEES/PASSES: $16 park entry fee per vehicle

MAPS: Baxter State Park website

TRAILHEAD: Ranger cabin, Roaring Brook Rd., Millinocket

FACILITIES: Vault toilet

CONTACT: Baxter State Park; 207/723-9500; www.baxterstatepark.org

Located directly east of the iconic Katahdin, South Turner offers a challenging climb and scenic vistas without taking up a whole day. It's a perfect choice for hikers who are preparing for a Katahdin expedition or forgoing the big one altogether. Note that weekend visitors should reserve a parking spot at the Roaring Brook Campground parking lot two weeks in advance by using the Baxter State Park online reservations system. Many trails start from this lot, and it's almost always full on Saturdays and Sundays.

START THE HIKE

▶ **MILE 0–0.3: Ranger Cabin to South Turner Mountain Trail**
Begin the hike just beyond the ranger cabin at the north end of the parking lot. Cross a large wooden footbridge over **Roaring Brook.** At the nearby trail junction, turn right onto the **South Turner Mountain Trail.** Enjoy a brief, gravelly stretch of level pathway and follow blue blazes as you saunter north through a moist and mossy forest. At 0.3 mi (0.5 km), a section of boardwalk takes you deeper into the forest before it transitions into rough-hewn bog bridges.

▶ **MILE 0.3–0.5: South Turner Mountain Trail to Sandy Stream Pond**
Continue northeast as the trail swings past **Sandy Stream Pond** and passes several little spur trails that lead to scenic points on the edge of the pond. Listen for the twang of local frogs—and, if you choose to check out any of the scenic cutoffs, watch the shoreline for moose, especially in the late afternoon or evening.

MAINE Baxter, the Highlands, and the Carrabassett Valley

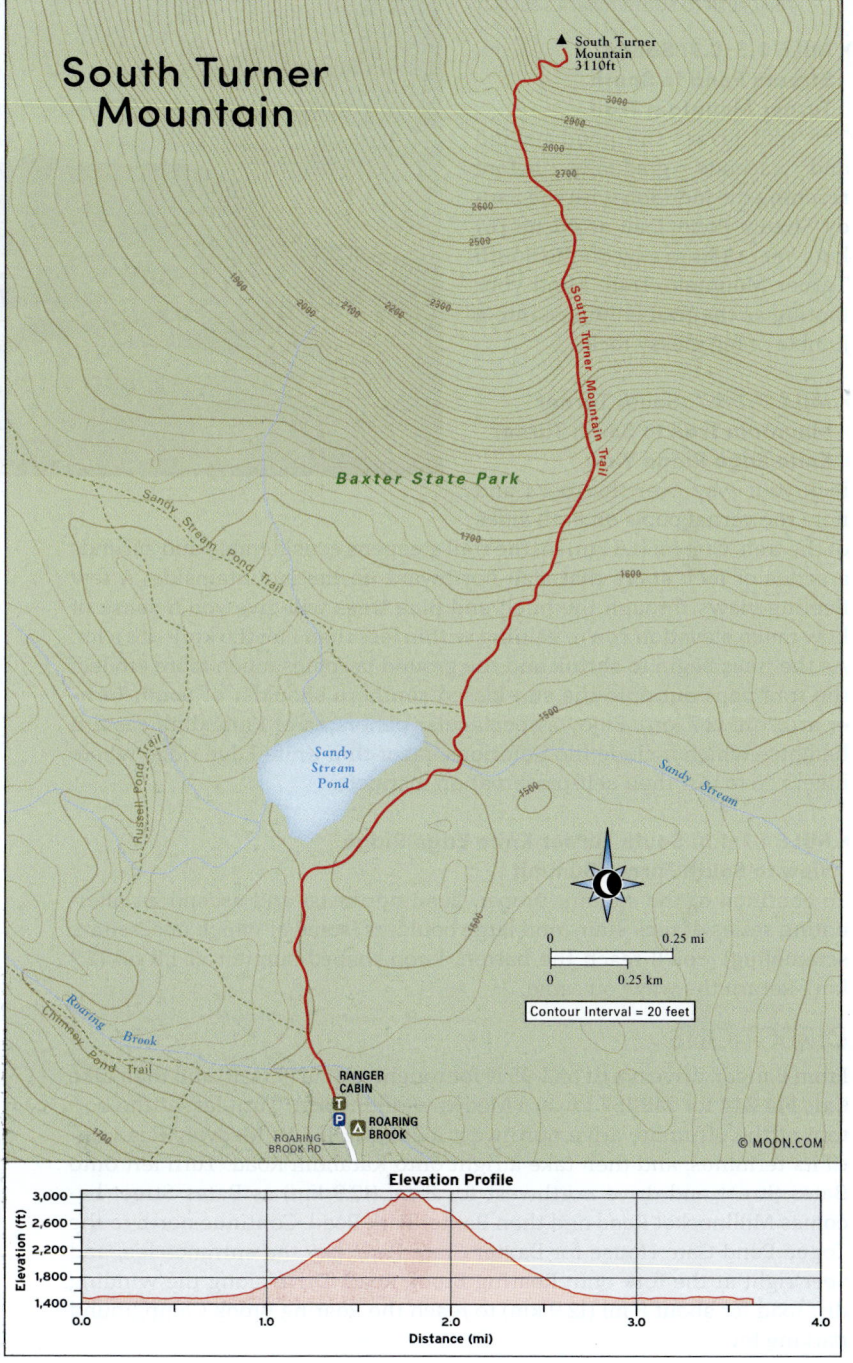

South Turner Mountain

▲ South Turner
Mountain
3110ft

South Turner Mountain Trail

Baxter State Park

Sandy Stream Pond Trail

Sandy Stream Pond

Sandy Stream

Russett Pond Trail

Roaring Brook

Chimney Pond Trail

RANGER
CABIN

ROARING
BROOK

ROARING
BROOK RD

0   0.25 mi

0   0.25 km

Contour Interval = 20 feet

© MOON.COM

Elevation Profile

Elevation (ft)				
3,000				
2,600				
2,200				
1,800				
1,400				
0.0	1.0	2.0	3.0	4.0

Distance (mi)

▶ MILE 0.5–0.7: Sandy Stream Pond to South Turner Mountain Trail

The trail leaves the pond behind and ascends gradually before reaching the junction with the Sandy Stream Pond Trail at 0.7 mi (1.1 km). Veer right to stay on the South Turner Mountain Trail. Mind your footing as the trail crumples into a jumble of big mossy rocks.

▶ MILE 0.7–1.7: South Turner Mountain Trail to South Turner Knife Edge Ridge View

Pick your way over the rocks and note the vernal pools on both sides of the trail. One mi (1.6 km) in, the trail steepens considerably and ascends a series of rock stairs that slab northward up the mountainside. A few fleeting views through the birch and pine trees will give you a sense of how much elevation you're gaining within less than 1 mi (1.6 km)—it's a lot. As the trees begin to shrink and the ground becomes much more eroded, the trail pops out onto the sun-kissed southern shoulder of **South Turner** at 1.7 mi (2.7 km). Enjoy a spectacular panorama of Katahdin's eastern heights—which include the notorious, razor-thin Knife Edge ridge where hikers go to test their self-preservation instincts.

▶ MILE 1.7–1.8: South Turner Knife Edge Ridge View to South Turner Summit

To continue to the summit proper, head northeast and ascend an alternating series of rock stairs and large boulders (some of which necessitate scrambling). You'll reach the barren, knob-shaped summit at 1.8 mi (2.9 km). Return the way you came.

DIRECTIONS

From Bangor, drive north on I-95 N for roughly 58 mi (93 km) and then take Exit 144-244 for ME-157 toward Medway/Millinocket. Turn left at the bottom of the off-ramp, drive northwest along ME-157 W/Medway Road until its terminus, and then take a right onto Katahdin Road. Turn left onto Bates Street and drive northwest for 8 mi (12.9 km) as Bates Street becomes Millinocket Road and then Baxter Park Road. Continue north to the Togue Pond Gate House for Baxter State Park, pay the entrance fee, and veer right at the fork onto Roaring Brook Road. Drive along the winding dirt road for about 8 mi (12.9 km) to reach the Roaring Brook Campground parking lot.

GPS COORDINATES: 45°55'10.8"N 68°51'26.5"W

BAXTER STATE PARK, MILLINOCKET

The tallest mountain in Maine and the northern terminus of the Appalachian Trail is a once-in-a-lifetime climbing experience that will take your breath away.

BEST: Summer hikes, vistas

DISTANCE: 9.4 mi (15.1 km) round-trip

DURATION: 8.5 hr

ELEVATION GAIN: 4,077 ft (1,243 m)

EFFORT: Strenuous

TRAIL: Dirt path, rocks, iron rungs, wooden bridges

USERS: Hikers

SEASON: June–September

FEES/PASSES: $16 park entrance fee, optional $5 parking reservation fee

MAPS: Baxter State Park website

TRAILHEAD: Katahdin Stream Campground parking lot, Park Tote Rd., Millinocket

FACILITIES: Vault toilet

CONTACT: Baxter State Park; 207/723-9500; www.baxterstatepark.org

Various trails lead to the summit, all of which require you to climb hundreds of rock stairs through boreal forests, scale perilous ledges, and scramble through mazes of boulders. Because Katahdin is the northern terminus of the Appalachian Trail, the route below follows the Hunt Trail—the official AT ascent route.

Baxter State Park limits the number of hikers on Katahdin each day. There are three parking lots from which the Katahdin trails depart, and most of the spaces in those lots are reserved by hikers in advance. (A limited number of first-come, first-served spots are handed out when the park opens at 6am each morning, and people will line up to grab them.)

Reservations can be made online or by phone. Maine residents can book summer parking spots in advance starting in April and non-Mainers can reserve their spots two weeks before their hiking date. Weekends are far more competitive, and there is no parking allowed on the sides of the roads in the park.

START THE HIKE

▶ **MILE 0-1.0: Katahdin Stream Campground Parking Lot to The Owl Junction**

Begin the hike in the clearing beside the day-use parking lot. The **Hunt Trail** begins on the north end of the clearing by a post with a white blaze. Follow the Hunt Trail north along a gentle stony path. Veer right at the junction for **The Owl** at 1 mi (1.6 km) and cross Katahdin Stream on a

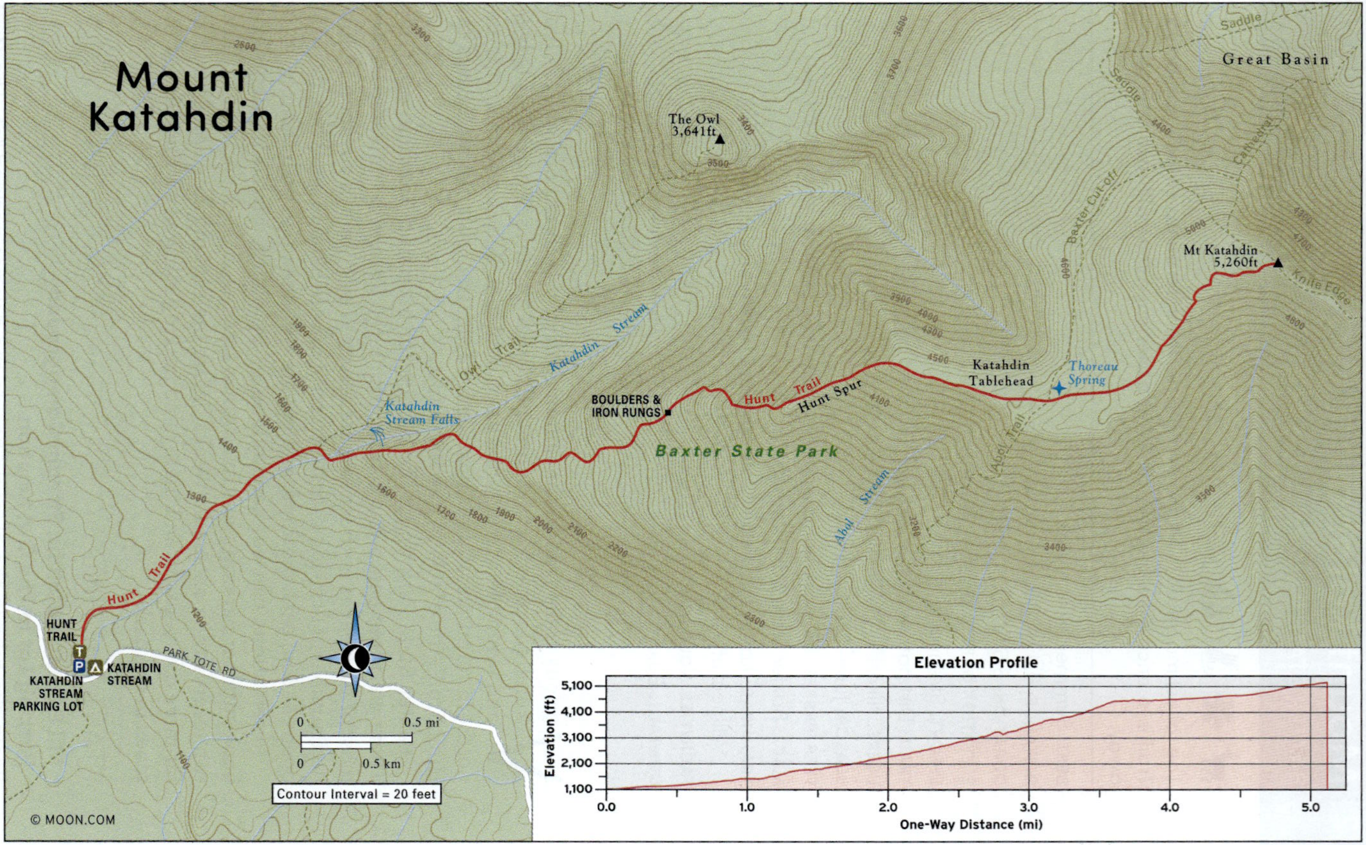

Baxter, the Highlands, and the Carrabassett Valley

Mount Katahdin

Baxter State Park

Mr Katahdin
5,260ft ▲

Great Basin

The Owl
3,641ft ▲

Thoreau Spring

Katahdin Tablehead

Hunt Spur

Hunt Trail

BOULDERS &
IRON RUNGS

Katahdin Stream Falls

HUNT TRAIL

KATAHDIN STREAM PARKING LOT

KATAHDIN STREAM

PARK TOTE RD

Contour Interval = 20 feet

0   0.5 mi

0   0.5 km

© MOON.COM

Elevation Profile

Elevation (ft)

5,100
4,100
3,100
2,100
1,100

0.0   1.0   2.0   3.0   4.0   5.0

One-Way Distance (mi)

rugged wooden bridge. On the other side, be sure to take note of the outhouse beside Katahdin Stream: This is your last chance to relieve yourself in relative comfort.

▶ MILE 1.0-2.5: The Owl Junction to Boulders

From here, the trail ascends a series of sloped rock faces that emerge from the trees and passes the beautiful **Katahdin Stream Falls** at 1.1 mi (1.8 km). Keep following the white blazes as the trail becomes a sequence of rock stairs that grow progressively steeper and rougher for the next 1 mi (1.6 km). Gradually, the stairs transition to dicier rock scrambles, and the trees open up a bit to reveal some killer views of The Owl, a craggy peak that sits to Katahdin's west. Then, quite suddenly, the trail fully emerges from the trees at 2.5 mi (4 km) and arrives at a jumble of house-sized boulders.

▶ MILE 2.5-2.8: Boulders to Hunt Spur

This is where the hike truly becomes a climb, as the Hunt Trail scales the boulders with the assistance of some **iron rungs** and pegs that have been installed along the trail to help hikers pull themselves over the gargantuan rocks. This is a tough and often scary section of trail that requires concentration, caution, and considerable upper-body strength. After bypassing the last of the boulders, the trail levels out and reaches **Hunt Spur** at 2.8 mi (4.5 km). This is one of the most incredible parts of the hike. The upper heights of Katahdin are now in sight, but to get there, you must scale the exposed and dizzyingly steep ridge of Hunt Spur.

▶ MILE 2.8-3.7: Hunt Spur to Katahdin Tableland

For the next 0.3 mi (0.5 km), the trail works its way up the spur, over all manner of crags and cliffs. (Don't stray from the white-blazed climbing route.) Take a break to recover your breath and drink in the beauty of the surrounding landscape: a sea of green trees and blue lakes. After a final stretch of ledges, the trail reaches the tableland of Katahdin at 3.1 mi (5 km) and segues into a gorgeous amble across a windswept plateau of tundra and rocks for the next 0.6 mi (1 km).

▶ MILE 3.7-4.7: Katahdin Tableland to Mount Katahdin Summit

Veer left at the junction with the Abol Trail at 3.7 mi (6 km) to stay on Hunt. Slather on some sunscreen here—it will be at least another hour or two before you're back in the shade of the trees. The trail curves to the northeast and climbs a series of rock steps. Just ahead, you'll likely notice a gaggle of hikers. At 4.7 mi (7.6 km), you will arrive at the summit of **Mount**

Baxter, the Highlands, and the Carrabassett Valley

MAINE

Katahdin, which offers an awe-inspiring panoramic view of Maine's deep green northern wilderness.

▶ **MILE 4.7-9.4: Mount Katahdin Summit to Katahdin Stream Campground Parking Lot**

Take your time at the top and assess your physical condition before making your descent. For hikers uncomfortable with the prospect of venturing down the technical portions of the boulder field, the Abol Trail offers a less technical (but relentlessly steep) alternative descent of 2.9 mi (4.7 km) that finishes at Abol Campground. From here, it's a 2.4 mi (3.9 km) walk along Park Tote Road to reach Katahdin Stream Campground. Otherwise, returning by way of the Hunt Trail is the "easiest" way back down.

DIRECTIONS

From Bangor, drive north on I-95 N for roughly 58 mi (93 km) and then take Exit 144-244 for ME-157 toward Medway/Millinocket. Turn left at the bottom of the off-ramp, drive northwest along ME-157 W/Medway Road until its terminus, and then take a right onto Katahdin Road. Turn left onto Bates Street and drive northwest for 8 mi (12.9 km) as Bates Street becomes Millinocket Road and then Baxter Park Road. Continue north to the Togue Pond Gate House for Baxter State Park, pay the $16 entrance fee, and turn left at the fork onto Park Tote Road. Drive along the winding dirt road for roughly 8 mi (12.9 km) and then turn right at the sign for Katahdin Stream Campground parking.

GPS COORDINATES: 45°53'11.7"N 68°59'59.1"W

BEST NEARBY BITES AND BREWS

Down the road from Togue Pond Gate House, you'll find killer burgers, salads, pastas, and Maine craft beers at the **Loose Moose Bar & Grill** (Big Moose Inn, 5 Fredericka's Way, Millinocket; 207/723-8391; www.bigmoosecabins.com; 5pm-9pm Wed.-Sun.). Head farther into town for a nice selection of bars and home-style eateries such as the **Scootic In Restaurant** (70 Penobscot Ave., Millinocket; 207/723-4566; www.scooticin.com; 3pm-9pm Tues.-Sat.); be sure to make time for a few homemade baked goods and some conversations with thru-hikers at the **Appalachian Trail Café** (210 Penobscot Ave., Millinocket; 207/723-6720; 7am-2pm daily).

Little and Big Niagara Falls

BAXTER STATE PARK, MILLINOCKET

This forest hike visits two explosive waterfalls that spill from the height of Baxter State Park into the valley below.

BEST: Waterfalls
DISTANCE: 2.4 mi (3.9 km) round-trip
DURATION: 1.5 hr
ELEVATION GAIN: 185 ft (56 m)
EFFORT: Easy
TRAIL: Dirt path, rocks, wooden bog bridges
USERS: Hikers
SEASON: June–October
FEES/PASSES: $16 park entrance fee per vehicle
MAPS: Baxter State Park website
TRAILHEAD: Daicey Pond Campground parking lot, Daicey Pond Rd., Millinocket
FACILITIES: Vault toilet
CONTACT: Baxter State Park; 207/723-9500; www.baxterstatepark.org

START THE HIKE

▸ **MILE 0-0.2: Parking Lot to Daicey Pond Nature Trail Junction**
Begin the hike at the southwest corner of the Daicey Pond Campground parking lot by the trails kiosk. Look for the wooden **Appalachian Trail** sign for Little and Big Niagara on a nearby tree; briefly walk east along a dirt path through tall grass, then turn left as the trail veers into a mixed forest of beech and pine. Look for white blazes on trees. The footing quickly becomes rockier and muddier but is made easier by lots of wooden bog bridges. Turn right at the two junctions with the Daicey Pond Nature Trail to continue your hike toward the falls.

▸ **MILE 0.2-0.9: Daicey Pond Nature Trail Junction to Little Niagara Falls**
Listen for the sound of rushing water before the trail reaches **Nesowade-hunk Stream** at 0.3 mi (0.5 km).

As you continue south beside the water, the trail begins to descend through the increasingly mossy and rocky forest at a gentle grade. Big glacial boulders are visible in the surrounding woodland, rich with those classic Maine ferns. The roar of the stream gradually grows louder, and at 0.9 mi (1.4 km) the trail reaches a sign for the cutoff path to **Little Niagara Falls.**

Turn right onto the cutoff and emerge onto an open rock slab that the falls spill around. This cascade resembles a sloped series of rapids, but in times of high water they take on a powerful frothing appearance. The

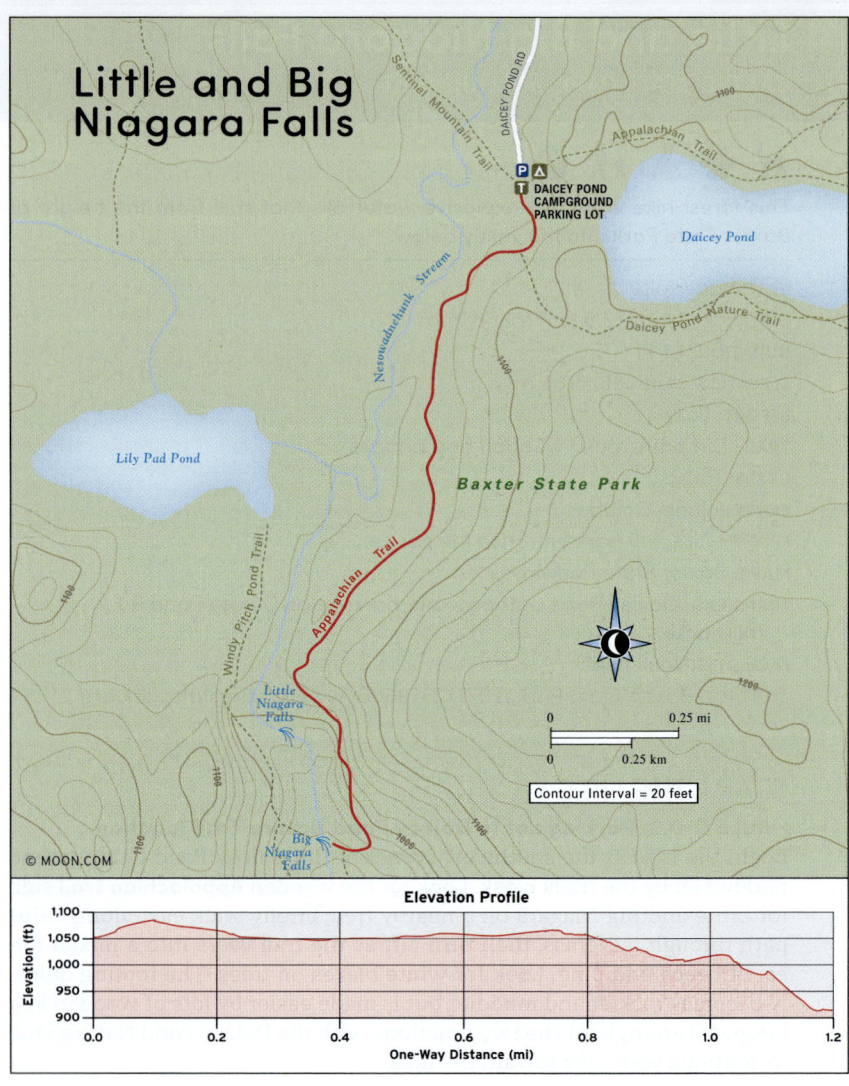

Little and Big Niagara Falls

Elevation Profile

falls' outlook point also offers a killer view of nearby West Peak and Doubletop Mountain to the north.

▶ MILE 0.9–1.2: Little Niagara Falls to Big Niagara Falls

To reach the grand finale, backtrack to the AT and turn right to continue the hike. The trail veers away from the stream and descends at a more moderate grade, with plenty of exposed roots—be careful of these during soggy conditions. As the hemlock woods become more spacious and sunlit, the trail descends several rock stairs to reach the cutoff path for **Big Niagara Falls** at 1.2 mi (1.9 km).

Turn right here and briefly walk through the undergrowth to reach a ledge that overlooks the gargantuan waterfall. Big Niagara Falls lives up to its name, exploding outward in great torrents and spilling down several

▲ LITTLE NIAGARA FALLS

20-ft (6-m) cliffs to form a larger stream below that contains several rock islands on which trees have managed to grow. Chances are you'll be sharing the ledge with some thru-hikers. Return the way you came.

DIRECTIONS

From Bangor, drive north on I-95 N for roughly 58 mi (93 km) and then take Exit 144-244 for ME-157 toward Medway/Millinocket. Turn left at the bottom of the off-ramp, drive northwest along ME-157 W/Medway Road until its terminus, and then take a right onto Katahdin Road. Turn left onto Bates Street and drive northwest for 8 mi (12.9 km) as Bates Street becomes Millinocket Road and then Baxter Park Road. Continue north to the Togue Pond Gate House for Baxter State Park, pay the $16 entrance fee, and turn left at the fork onto Park Tote Road. Drive along the winding dirt road for roughly 10 mi (16 km) and then make a left onto Daicey Pond Road. You'll arrive at the campground parking lot in an exposed grassy area just over 0.5 mi (0.8 km) ahead.

GPS COORDINATES: 45°52'57.5"N 69°01'54.6"W

Baxter, the Highlands, and the Carrabassett Valley

MAINE

BAXTER STATE PARK, MILLINOCKET

Hike through forest to visit one of the most wondrous places in Maine—a massive exposed rock slab decorated with rivulets of rushing water.

DISTANCE: 3.6 mi (5.8 km) round-trip
DURATION: 1.5 hr
ELEVATION GAIN: 263 ft (80 m)
EFFORT: Easy
TRAIL: Dirt path, rocks, wooden bridges
USERS: Hikers
SEASON: May–September
FEES/PASSES: None
MAPS: Baxter State Park website
TRAILHEAD: Day use parking lot, Appalachian Trail, Millinocket
FACILITIES: None
CONTACT: Baxter State Park; 207/723-9500; www.baxterstatepark.org

Blueberry Ledges is a rolling expanse of exposed rock cuts on the southern border of Baxter State Park. What makes this place special are the chutes of water that spill down the rocky ledges—putting the "blue" in blueberry. In spring and early summer, the snowmelt turns the entire mess of slides into a big torrent of rushing water, which funnels into watery chutes that hikers can ride into pools of (very cold) water. This feature makes Blueberry Ledges a popular stop for thru-hikers who've just finished the trail and are craving a celebratory cool-down. And since the main trail to the ledges begins outside the park, you can bypass the usual $16 entrance fee.

START THE HIKE

▶ **MILE 0-0.3: Parking Lot to Baxter State Park**
Begin the hike by the twin woodsheds in the north end of the parking lot. Walk toward the Northern Outdoors sign, pass through the trees, and turn left onto a dirt road. Walk north along the road to an open marsh area and cross a wooden log bridge over a creek. This bridge marks your official entry point into **Baxter State Park.**

▶ **MILE 0.3-0.6: Baxter State Park to Blueberry Ledges Trail**
Enter the forest on the other side of the bridge and continue northwest to the trail information kiosk at 0.4 mi (0.6 km). Make a right turn here onto the **Abol Pond Trail.** The trail climbs a hill before leveling off and reaching a junction for the Blueberry Ledges Trail at 0.6 mi (1 km).

MAINE

Baxter, the Highlands, and the Carrabassett Valley

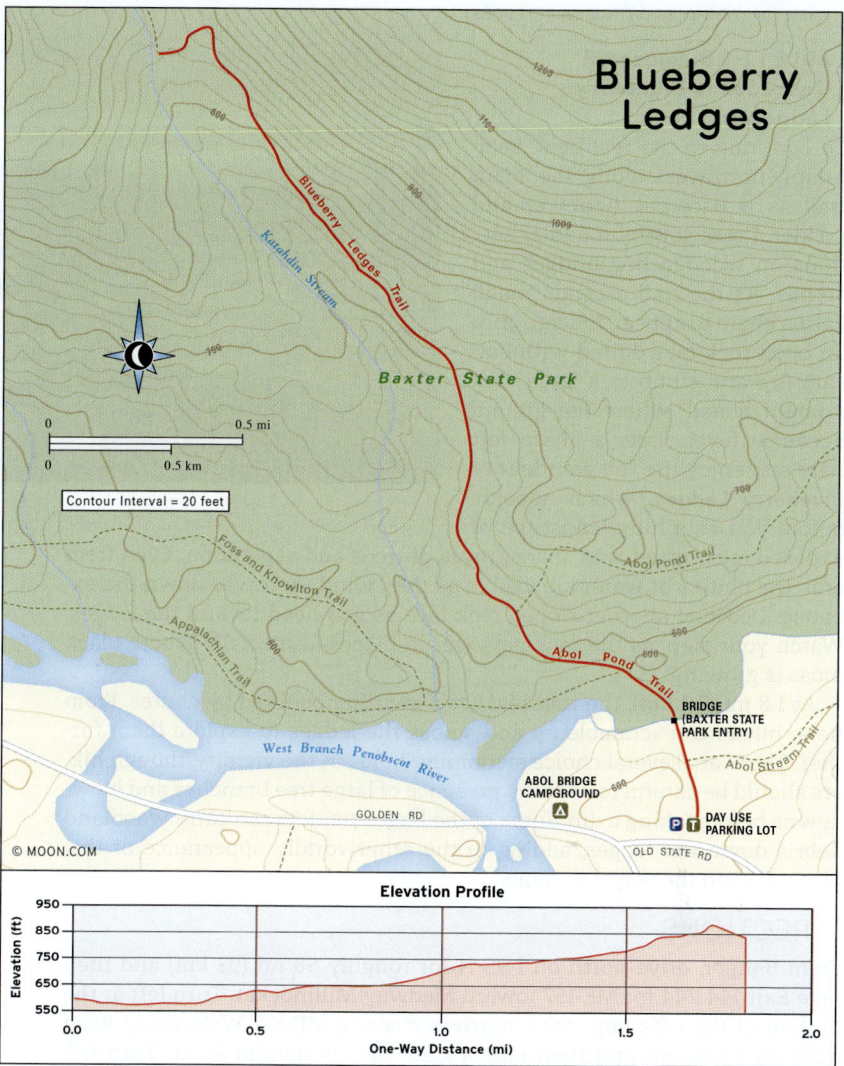

Elevation Profile

▶ MILE 0.6–1.1: Blueberry Ledges Trail to Seasonal Cascades

Turn left onto the Blueberry Ledges Trail and enjoy a meandering stroll through a hall of beautiful white birch trees. The undergrowth is rich with multiple fern species, but the trail remains wide and smooth. As the trail begins to ascend at a gradual grade, the surrounding woods become more diverse, with cedar trees making appearances. At 1.1 mi (1.8 km), keep an eye out for a dirt cutoff path on the left. This little spur leads down to the bottom of a ledge where hikers can admire some seasonal cascades during the wettest months. And this ledge marks the bottom of the more expansive and numerous Blueberry Ledges.

▸ MILE 1.1-1.8: Seasonal Cascades to Blueberry Ledges and Pools

To continue to the real deal, keep hiking northwest along the main trail as it becomes narrower and rockier. Cross several muddier sections on wooden bog bridges and stones. As the trail ascends, small cairns begin to appear. Emerge onto an open rock face dotted with balsam firs and climb to a large rock straight ahead, where the ground becomes level. Take a sharp left here and enjoy the full grandeur of **Blueberry Ledges,** which appears before you as a hilly landscape of exposed rock, water, and spare groves of trees and vegetation. Even from afar, the chutes of water are visible as they wind their way down the expanse. Descend another sloped rock face as you head toward the ledges. Watch your step, as the rock gets wet in places—especially where black moss is growing.

At 1.8 mi (2.9 km), the trail reaches a swirling pool fed by chutes. From here, hikers can scramble up and across the ledges to explore them further. There are several choice swimming holes in the vicinity, though hikers should be careful to note the presence of large tree branches and blowdowns before taking a dip. Some of the larger rivulets can carry woodland debris down the ledges, adding to the otherworldly appearance of this place. Return the way you came.

DIRECTIONS

From Bangor, drive north on I-95 N for roughly 58 mi (93 km) and then take Exit 144-244 for ME-157 toward Medway/Millinocket. Turn left at the bottom of the off-ramp, drive northwest along ME-157 W/Medway Road until its terminus, and then take a right onto Katahdin Road. Turn left onto Bates Street and drive northwest for 8 mi (12.9 km) as Bates Street becomes Millinocket Road and then Baxter Park Road. After passing the Big Moose Inn, take a left and then turn right to merge onto Golden Road. Drive carefully along this pothole-filled logging road for another 10 mi (16 km). As you approach the Abol Bridge Campground store, pull a U-turn-esque right onto an unmarked dirt road (Old State Road), then make another left onto another dirt road (the Appalachian Trail: seriously!). Ahead, on your left, you'll see a gravel parking area with twin woodsheds.

GPS COORDINATES: 45°50'08.5"N 68°57'35.7"W

This gentle wooded path has an awesome surprise at the end—a series of caves that retain their natural ice throughout the year.

BEST: New England oddities
DISTANCE: 2 mi (3.2 km) round-trip
DURATION: 1 hr
ELEVATION GAIN: 158 ft (48 m)
EFFORT: Easy
TRAIL: Dirt path, rocks, wooden bridges, river crossings on stones, metal ladders
USERS: Hikers
SEASON: May-September
FEES/PASSES: None
MAPS: The Nature Conservancy website
TRAILHEAD: Debsconeag Ice Caves trailhead, Water Way, Millinocket
FACILITIES: None
CONTACT: The Nature Conservancy; 207/729-5181; www.nature.org

Hidden deep in the forest of the Debsconeag Wilderness Area, the Debsconeag Ice Caves are chock-full of ice that can last beyond July. Hikers will want to have boots with good tread, and parents with small children might want to skip this one. Traction isn't necessary for exploring the ice caves—boots with good grip, and a healthy dose of caution, will suffice.

START THE HIKE

▸ MILE 0-0.6: Trailhead to Glacial Boulders

From the south end of the parking lot, cross a large wooden bridge, then make a left as the dirt trail veers into the woods. Blue blazes mark the path forward. The trail crosses a few creeks on stones and ambles south through deciduous forest with plenty of young spruce and cedar trees. Look out for bear and moose scat—the woods here have a very active mammal population.

As the trail starts to ascend gradually, the trees on your left will begin to part and offer fleeting views of the Debsconeag Wilderness expanse, including the Penobscot River. Abundant ferns add some color along the trail. Continue hiking south as the trail narrows into a ledge and takes you along the flank of a broad hillside. Note the glacial boulders that begin to appear around 0.6 mi (1 km).

Baxter, the Highlands, and the Carrabassett Valley

MAINE

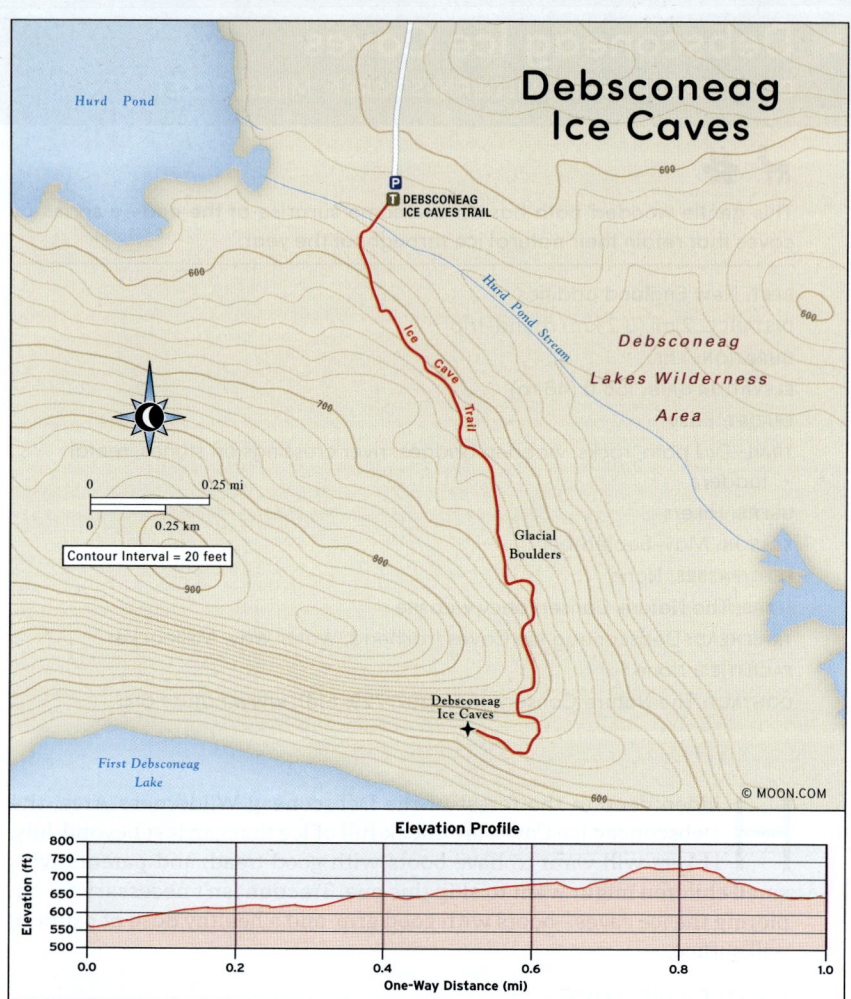

Debsconeag Ice Caves

Hurd Pond

DEBSCONEAG ICE CAVES TRAIL

Hurd Pond Stream

Ice Cave Trail

Debsconeag Lakes Wilderness Area

Glacial Boulders

Contour Interval = 20 feet

Debsconeag Ice Caves

First Debsconeag Lake

© MOON.COM

Elevation Profile

Elevation (ft)

One-Way Distance (mi)

▶ **MILE 0.6-1.0: Glacial Boulders to Debsconeag Ice Caves**

After another 0.2 mi (0.3 km), the trail reaches a junction with a sign for the ice caves. Turn left here, descend through a dreamy, mossy stretch of woods, and then turn right at a second junction (also affixed with a sign for the ice caves). Walk west toward a looming garden of glacial boulders and reach the entrance to the **Debsconeag Ice Caves** at 1 mi (1.6 km).

You can climb down into the caves by using the metal rungs that are installed in the rock walls, but be careful upon reaching the bottom: The floor of the cave is sheer ice and very slippery. A guide rope affixed to the right wall of the cave offers some support. If you feel like venturing deeper into the abyss, you'll want to have a reliable light source. Solo hikers should take extra caution when exploring the cave. When you're done exploring, return the way you came.

▲ DESCENT INTO DEBSCONEAG ICE CAVES

DIRECTIONS

From Bangor, drive north on I-95 N for roughly 58 mi (93 km) and then take Exit 144-244 for ME-157 toward Medway/Millinocket. Turn left at the bottom of the off-ramp, drive northwest along ME-157 W/Medway Road until its terminus, and then take a right onto Katahdin Road. Turn left onto Bates Street and drive northwest for 8 mi (12.9 km) as Bates Street becomes Millinocket Road and then Baxter Park Road. After passing the Big Moose Inn, take a left and then turn right to merge onto Golden Road. Drive carefully along this pothole-filled logging road for another 10 mi (16 km). Immediately after crossing Abol Bridge, turn left onto an unmarked dirt road (Water Way) flanked by a large Nature Conservancy sign. Drive south for about 3 mi (4.8 km). Veer left at the fork and continue for another 1 mi (1.6 km) until you reach the Debsconeag Ice Caves parking lot on the right side.

GPS COORDINATES: 45°47'29.2"N 68°58'41.4"W

BEST NEARBY BITES

Tuck into a nourishing burger or some seafood pasta in the middle of the Millinocket backwoods by making a pit stop at the New England Outdoor Center's lakeside eatery, the **River Drivers Restaurant** (30 Twin Pines Rd., Millinocket; 207/723-8475; www.neoc.com; 11am-9pm Fri.-Mon.).

🦌 ❋

Take a boat ride from the village of Rockwood to an island on Maine's largest lake to climb an arrestingly steep and gorgeous mountain.

BEST: Fall hikes

DISTANCE: 3.5 mi (5.6 km) round-trip

DURATION: 2 hr

ELEVATION GAIN: 724 ft (221 m)

EFFORT: Moderate

TRAIL: Dirt path, rocks, wooden bog bridges

USERS: Hikers

SEASON: May–October

FEES/PASSES: $15 (cash only) per adult round-trip ferry ride from Rockwood to Mount Kineo Golf Course, $3 day-use fee for the trail (honor system)

MAPS: $2 at golf course clubhouse

TRAILHEAD: Ferry dock, Young Rd., Rockwood

FACILITIES: Restroom

CONTACT: Mount Kineo Golf Course, clubhouse 223 Young Rd., Rockwood; 207/534-9012; www.mooseheadlakegolf.com

FERRY HOURS: Every 2 hours on the hour 9am–3pm daily May–June, every hour on the hour 8am–6pm daily July–August, every hour on the hour 9am–4pm daily September–October

START THE HIKE

▶ **MILE 0–1.0: Ferry Dock to Indian Trail**

Pick up the **Carriage Trail** to the left of the ferry dock and stroll northwest along a wide gravel path that meanders along the shore of the island. In the summer, the trail is flanked by wildflowers that sprout from the tall-grass. Notice how the cliffs on your right become taller and more sheer. Within minutes, you'll be heading up there.

Turn right at a signed junction for the **Indian Trail** at 0.6 mi (1 km) and begin the steep, root-festooned climb up Kineo's ledges. Blue blazes and red arrows mark the path, which heads northeast, passing a few ledges that offer spectacular views of the shoreline and the golf course. The trail becomes steeper over the next 0.3 mi (0.5 km), climbing over several rocky steps and narrow ledges that require handholds. Tread slowly and carefully here.

▶ **MILE 1.0–1.9: Indian Trail to Mount Kineo Summit**

About 1 mi (1.6 km) in, the Indian Trail reaches a grassy height of land that offers the best view yet. At 1.1 mi (1.8 km), keep right at the junction for Bridle Trail to stay on Indian Trail, continuing to amble through boreal woods with lots of moss and rocks. A final brief climb delivers you to the proper

Mount Kineo

Elevation Profile

summit of **Mount Kineo** at 1.8 mi (2.9 km). The summit is wooded, but it features a six-story viewing tower that can be climbed for an unbeatable view of Moosehead Lake.

▶ MILE 1.9-2.2: Mount Kineo Summit to Bridle Trail

To return, backtrack down the Indian Trail to the junction for the **Bridle Trail** at 2.2 mi (3.5 km) and turn right onto the Bridle Trail. Descend the western haunch of Kineo at a pleasant grade for just over 0.5 mi (0.8 km) (blue blazes mark this path too). The path is gentler than the Indian Trail, but no less rocky and rooty.

▶ **MILE 2.2–3.5: Bridle Trail to Ferry Dock**

After passing through a grove of hemlock and spruce, the trail crosses some bog bridges and rejoins the **Carriage Trail** at 2.9 mi (4.7 km). Veer left onto the Carriage Road, keep right at the Indian Trail junction just ahead to stay on the Carriage Road, and retrace your steps along the shore until you reach the trailhead at 3.5 mi (5.6 km).

DIRECTIONS

From Portland, drive northeast on I-295 N for 46 mi (74 km) and then merge onto I-95 N to continue heading northeast. Take Exit 150 for Somerset Avenue toward Pittsfield/Hartland. Turn left onto Somerset Avenue at the end of the off-ramp and then take a right onto Spring Road. Follow the road to its terminus and veer left onto ME-152. Drive north on ME-152 until the highway concludes in Cambridge, where you'll make a right turn onto ME-150. Continue along ME-150 to the town of Guilford and turn left onto ME-15 N/ME-6 W. Drive northwest to Greenville, veer left onto Pritham Avenue, and then take a right at the road's end to continue along ME-15 N/ME-6 W. Head northwest along the shores of Moosehead Lake for another 17 mi (27 km), enter the village of Rockwood, and make a final right turn onto Village Road, which descends to the parking lot for the Kineo shuttle ferry.

GPS COORDINATES: 45°40'36.5"N 69°44'18.8"W

Hike through the isolated Maine wilderness into the majestic Gulf Hagas, a breathtaking canyon with an abundance of waterfalls.

BEST: Brew hikes

DISTANCE: 8.2 mi (13.2 km) round-trip

DURATION: 5 hr

ELEVATION GAIN: 1,154 ft (352 m)

EFFORT: Strenuous

TRAIL: Dirt path, rocks, wooden bog bridges, water crossings on stones

USERS: Hikers, leashed dogs

SEASON: June-September

FEES/PASSES: $10 day-use fee per person for nonresidents, $6 for Maine residents

MAPS: North Maine Woods Inc. website

TRAILHEAD: Trail information kiosk at Gulf Hagas lower parking lot, Katahdin Iron Works Rd., Monson

FACILITIES: Vault toilet

CONTACT: North Maine Woods Inc.; 207/435-6213; www.northmainewoods.org

Deep in the Maine wilderness that once housed the Katahdin Iron Works furnaces, you'll find Gulf Hagas, often referred to as "the Grand Canyon of Maine." But this moniker doesn't do the canyon justice—the dark gray slate cliffs are uncharacteristically sheer, the waters of the Pleasant River surge through the canyon with a monotone roar, and the curious glacial rock formations have created an abundance of pretty waterfalls.

START THE HIKE

▶ **MILE 0-0.2: Trail Information Kiosk to Pleasant River**
Start at the trail information kiosk at the north end of the parking area. Pick up the **Appalachian Trail** as it leads into the deciduous forest. At 0.2 mi (0.3 km), you'll ford the Pleasant River, Oregon Trail-style—this crossing is too deep and wide to rock-hop, so either bring water shoes or consider removing your boots for this "initiation" into the realm of Gulf Hagas.

▶ **MILE 0.2-1.5: Pleasant River to Appalachian Trail**
On the other side of the river, veer right and follow white blazes on the trees. The trail curves away from the river and crosses some bog bridges before reaching a T intersection at 0.4 mi (0.6 km). Turn left to stay on the AT and follow the trail for roughly 1 mi (1.6 km) as it gradually climbs west through the woods over rocks and roots.

Baxter, the Highlands, and the Carrabassett Valley

MAINE

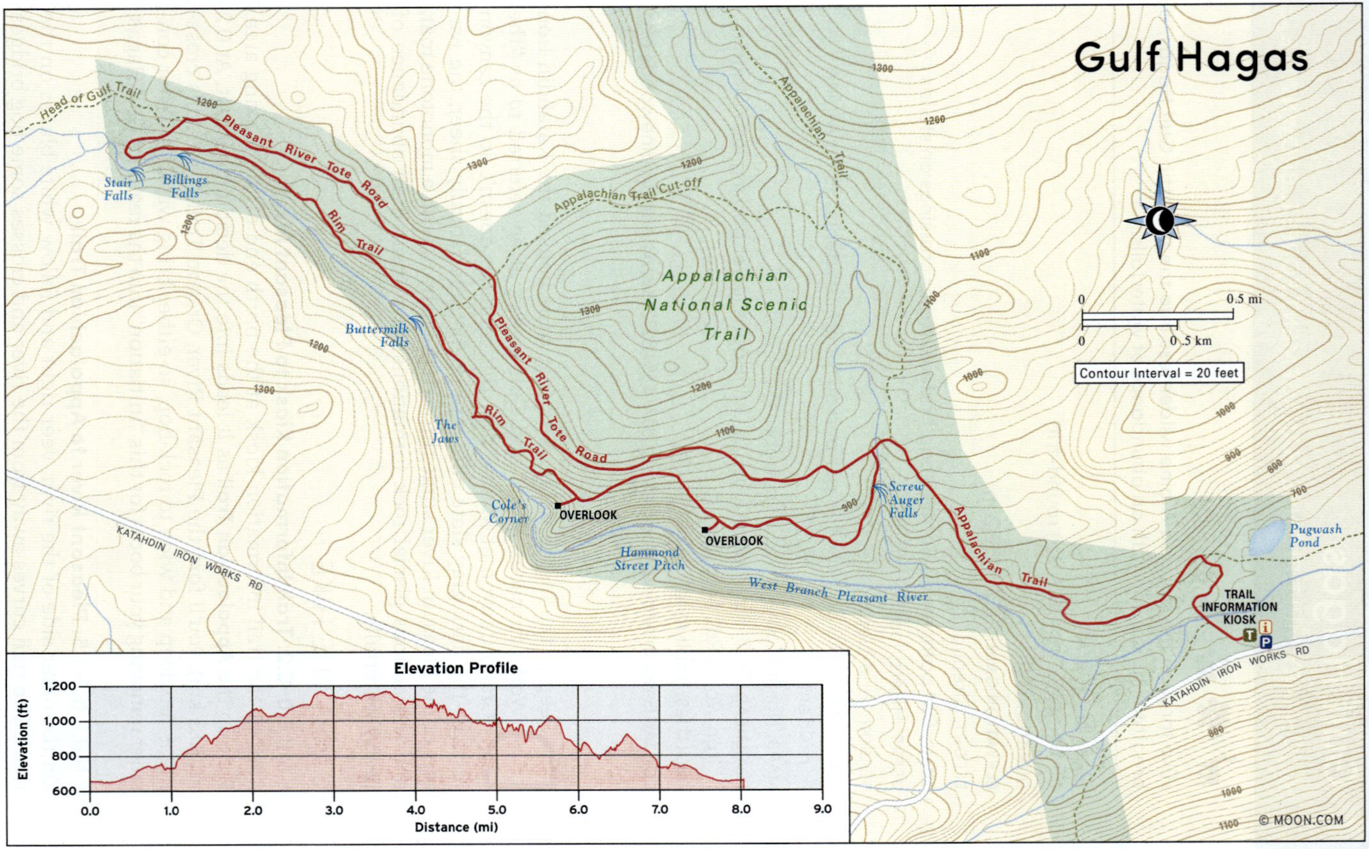

Gulf Hagas

Contour Interval = 20 feet

0.5 mi
0.5 km

© MOON.COM

Puguash Pond

TRAIL INFORMATION KIOSK

Appalachian Trail

Screw Auger Falls

West Branch Pleasant River

Appalachian National Scenic Trail

Appalachian Trail

Appalachian Trail Cut-off

OVERLOOK

Hammond Street Pitch

OVERLOOK

Cole's Corner

Pleasant River Tote Road

Rim Trail

The Jaws

Buttermilk Falls

Rim Trail

Pleasant River Tote Road

Billings Falls

Stair Falls

Head of Gulf Trail

KATAHDIN IRON WORKS RD

KATAHDIN IRON WORKS RD

Elevation Profile

Elevation (ft)

Distance (mi)

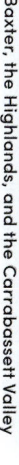

▲ TAKING A REST AT THE HEADWATERS OF GULF HAGAS

▶ MILE 1.5-1.8: **Appalachian Trail to Rim Trail**

At 1.5 mi (2.4 km), cross a stream to reach the junction for the Rim Trail and the Pleasant River Tote Road. Take a left onto the **Rim Trail** and make a rooty descent toward the sound of rushing water to reach your first cascade, **Screw Auger Falls,** at 1.7 mi (2.7 km). A few spur trails on the left lead to overlooks from which you can admire the cascade. (The Rim Trail is replete with such spur paths to canyon vistas, almost all of which are worth checking out.)

▶ MILE 1.8-3.0: **Rim Trail to The Jaws**

Continue gently descending through the woods for another 0.5 mi (0.8 km). As the trail begins to climb the north rim of Gulf Hagas, huff and puff your way up some winding rock staircases for another 0.2 mi (0.3 km). At 2.5 mi (4 km), keep left to stay on Rim Trail at the Tote Road connector junction. Enjoy your first stunning view of the canyon by taking a spur path at 2.6 mi (4.2 km).

Over the next 0.5 mi (0.8 km), the Rim Trail becomes a rocky and root-festooned roller coaster with a few steep sections that require a bit of scrambling. Check out **The Jaws**—a teeth-like rock formation through which the Pleasant River flows—at 3 mi (4.8 km).

▶ MILE 3.0-4.2: **The Jaws to Stair Falls**

As the hemlock forest gets mossier, the trees start to become more spread out and the trail gets sunnier. Pass several exposed ledges that offer killer perspectives of the canyon. At 3.4 mi (5.5 km), you'll reach **Buttermilk Falls,** and the trail climbs steadily onward.

Keep left to stay on Rim at the second junction for the Tote Road. The trail swings in and out of the forest onto more rocky ledges and ambles past overlook points for **Billings Falls** at 4.1 mi (6.6 km) and **Stair Falls** at 4.2 mi (6.8 km).

▸ **MILE 4.2-4.3: Stair Falls to Head of Gulf Hagas**
As the sound of the river dissipates, the Rim Trail dips deeper into the forest before arriving at the **Head of the Gulf** at 4.3 mi (6.9 km). This is the gorgeous delta of waterways that "feed" Gulf Hagas. Here, on a sunny day, you'll find swimmers, fishers, photographers, and maybe even a few thru-hikers taking a scenic detour.

▸ **MILE 4.3-4.5: Head of Gulf Hagas to Pleasant River Tote Road**
The return path seems specifically designed for those tuckered out from the exhausting climb. From the Head, take the **Rim Trail** north to its terminus at the junction with the **Pleasant River Tote Road** at 4.5 mi (7.2 km).

▸ **MILE 4.5-8.2: Pleasant River Tote Road to Trail Information Kiosk**
Turn right onto the Tote Road, which cruises through the woods on a smooth dirt path and over lots of bog bridges at a gradual downhill grade for 2.2 mi (3.5 km). The path effortlessly delivers you back to the beginning of the Rim Trail at 6.7 mi (10.8 km). Turn left onto the **Appalachian Trail,** recross the stream, and backtrack to reach **Katahdin Iron Works Road** at 8.2 mi (13.2 km).

DIRECTIONS

From Bangor, drive north on I-95 N for 13 mi (21 km) and take Exit 199 for ME-16 toward Alton/Lagrange/Milo. At the bottom of the off-ramp, turn left onto ME-16 W and follow it for 15 mi (24 km) before making a slight left onto ME-16 W/ME-6 W as you pass through Lagrange. Drive northwest into Milo and turn right onto Main Street. Take an immediate slight left onto ME-11 N/Park Street and continue for another 12 mi (19 km). As you reach Prairie, veer left onto Ebermee Road, which will soon become Katahdin Iron Works Road. After the road transitions to dirt, you'll reach the KI gatehouse. Stop here to register and pay the fee before continuing west along the road. The Gulf Hagas lower parking lot is clearly marked on your right.

GPS COORDINATES: 45°28'26.4"N 69°17'39.8"W

BEST NEARBY BITES AND BREWS

Those approaching Gulf Hagas from the Greenville (western) side can enjoy a hearty old-school diner breakfast at **Auntie M's** (13 Lily Bay Rd., Greenville; 207/695-2238, 5am-3pm daily); if you're departing Gulf Hagas by heading east to Brownville, reward yourself with a dizzyingly hazy Maine IPA or pale ale at **Bissell Brothers Three Rivers** (157 Elm St., Milo; 207/943-9190; www.bissellbrothers. com; 3pm-8pm Thurs., noon-8pm Fri.-Sat., 10am-4pm Sun.).

Venture deep into the woods to visit a pair of peaks with incredible views of one of Maine's tallest mountains.

DISTANCE: 10 mi (16 km) round-trip
DURATION: 6.5 hr
ELEVATION GAIN: 2,615 ft (797 m)
EFFORT: Strenuous
TRAIL: Dirt path, rocks, wooden bridges, water crossings on stones
USERS: Hikers, leashed dogs
SEASON: June–September
FEES/PASSES: None
MAPS: Maine Department of Agriculture, Conservation, and Forestry website
TRAILHEAD: Fire Warden's Trail parking lot, Stratton Brook Rd., Kingfield
FACILITIES: None
CONTACT: Maine Bureau of Parks and Lands; 207/778-8231; www.maine. gov/bigelowpreserve

Mount Bigelow, one of the highest summits in Maine, is a remote and immense heap of granite that offers multiple peaks. The highest point on Bigelow—West Peak, at 4,145 ft (1,263 m)—is best paired with the nearby Avery Peak for an unforgettable two-for-one climb.

START THE HIKE

▶ **MILE 0-0.7: Fire Warden's Trail Parking Lot to Fire Warden's Trail**
Walk to the trail **information kiosk** at the north end of the parking lot and pick up a rugged logging road, which climbs and then descends a small hill to reach a wooden bridge over Stratton Brook. Cross the bridge and keep right at the junction as the logging road ambles along the brook. Enjoy pretty views of a nearby marshy area and Sugarloaf Mountain in the distance. At 0.7 mi (1.1 km), turn left onto the **Fire Warden's Trail** to leave the brook behind and venture into the Bigelow Preserve.

▶ **MILE 0.7-3.1: Fire Warden's Trail to Moose Falls Campsite**
Climbing steadily at a gentle grade, the trail heads northeast with few deviations over the next 1 mi (1.6 km). After climbing a steep, rocky ridge for 0.3 mi (0.5 km), you'll descend into a boggy stretch of boreal pine and spruce forest at 1.7 mi (2.7 km). Watch your footing on the many bog bridges. Continue ascending into thicker, more deciduous woods where black bears and deer are known to wander. At 2.1 mi (3.4 km), keep right at the Horns Pond Trail junction to stay on the Fire Warden's Trail. Rock-hop across a creek and keep heading northeast, deeper into the woods—the trees are spaced apart just enough to allow you to admire the depth of

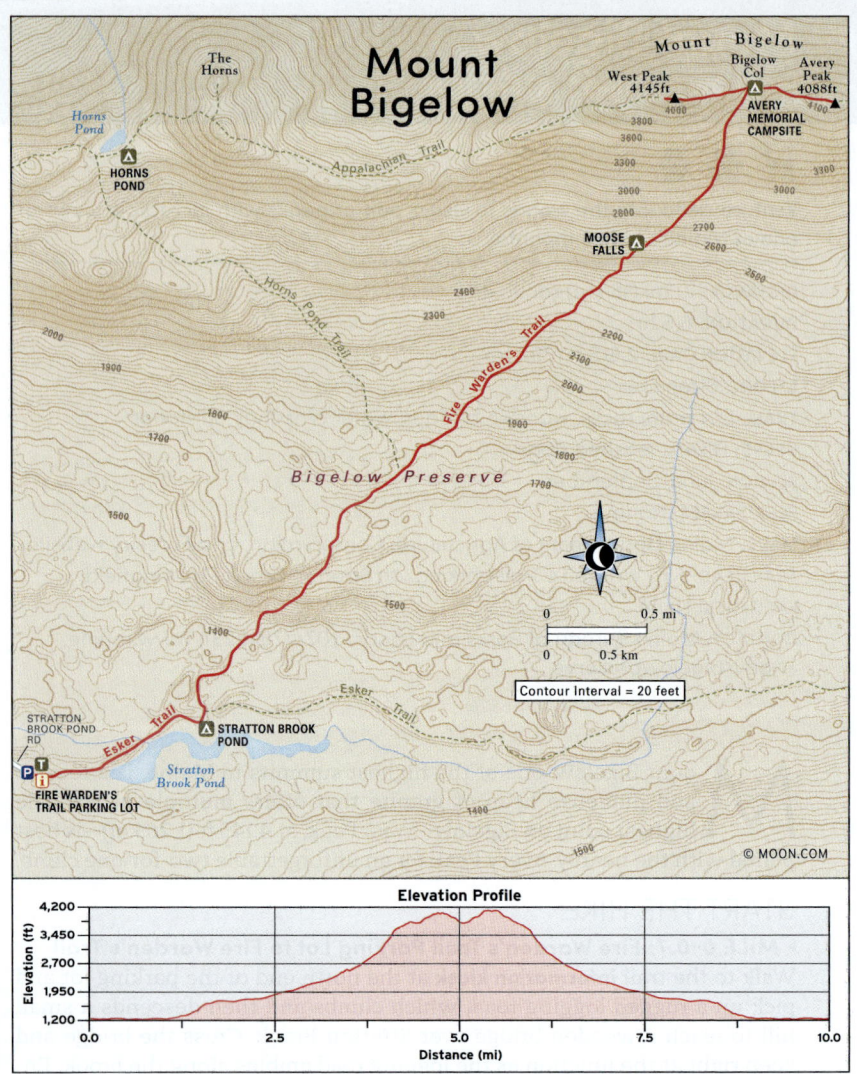

Elevation Profile

color and texture in this forest. The footing slowly becomes rockier and steeper, and the occasional gust of wind through the trees hints at what lies ahead.

At 3.1 mi (5 km), the trail climbs a set of rock stairs to reach **Moose Falls Campsite,** a bare-bones tenting site that is first come, first served and used by hikers doing longer overnight treks in the Bigelow Range.

▶ MILE 3.1–4.2: Moose Falls Campsite to Avery Memorial Campsite

From here, the gradual ascent through the woods comes to an end. The trail crosses a nearby creek and becomes very steep and rocky, ascending a series of winding granite stairs and slabs to break through the foliage. As the boreal trees get thinner and smaller, the green expanse of northern Maine becomes partially visible, making the brutal ascent just a little

▲ MOUNT BIGELOW

more bearable. Keep climbing northeast, keeping left at the junction for **Avery Memorial Campsite** at 4.2 mi (6.8 km) (this is another tenting area for overnight hikers) to stay on Fire Warden's.

▶ **MILE 4.2–5.0: Avery Memorial Campsite to West Peak and Avery Peak Summits**

Enjoy a sudden blast of alpine exposure as you step onto the open ridgeline between **West Peak** and **Avery Peak** at just over 4.2 mi (6.8 km), where the trail finally (mercifully) levels off a bit and concludes at the Appalachian Trail, which visits both summits. From this beautiful juncture, hikers can choose to turn left or right to either peak. The climbs are similar—rocks, boulders, tundra, and abundant views of the Rangeley Lakes, the Carrabassett Valley, and even the Quebec wilderness. Avery Peak also has the stone foundations of an old fire tower. From the AT/Fire Warden's junction, it's about 0.4 mi (0.6 km) round-trip to each summit. Ascend both summits for maximum victory points, then return the way you came.

DIRECTIONS

From Portland, drive northeast on I-295 N for 46 mi (74 km) and then merge onto I-95 N to continue northeast to Exit 113 for ME-3 toward Augusta/Belfast. At the end of the off-ramp, enter the traffic circle and take the third exit to get on ME-3 N. Another traffic circle will appear just ahead. Take the first exit to stay on ME-3 N and drive north for 1 mi (1.6 km) before turning right onto ME-27 N/Civic Center Drive. Follow this road to its terminus and then make a left onto US-2 W. After 1 mi (1.6 km), turn right onto Weeks Mill Road, drive northwest for another 6 mi (9.7 km), and then make a very sharp right onto ME-43 E. At the fork 1 mi (1.6 km) ahead, veer left onto Mosher Hill Road, continue for 3 mi (4.8 km), and swing left onto Ramsdell Road. Follow this road to its end and turn right onto ME-27 N. Drive north for another 33 mi (53 km) and then take a right onto Stratton Brook Road at the sign for Bigelow Preserve. Follow the road to the hiker parking area.

GPS COORDINATES: 45°06'35.6"N 70°20'14.0"W

BEST NEARBY BITES

What good is a mountain hike without a decadent dinner to conclude the day? For locally sourced gourmet international cooking, get thee to the **Coplin Dinner House** (8252 Carrabassett Rd., Stratton; 207/246-0016; www.coplindinnerhouse.com; 4:30pm-9pm Wed.-Thurs., 4:30pm-8:30pm Wed.-Thurs., 4:30pm-9pm Fri.-Sat.). If you're feeling like something heavier, meatier, and saucier, you'll find what you're craving at Sugarloaf ski resort's **The Rack BBQ** (5016 Access Rd., Carrabassett Valley; 207/237-2211; www.racksugarloaf.com; 4pm-9pm Wed.-Sat.).

Poplar Stream Falls
CARRABASSETT VALLEY

Hike through dense and mossy woods to one of northern Maine's more secluded cascades.

DISTANCE: 4.4 mi (7.1 km) round-trip
DURATION: 2 hr
ELEVATION GAIN: 268 ft (82 m)
EFFORT: Easy
TRAIL: Dirt path, wooden bridges, water crossings on stones
USERS: Hikers, leashed dogs
SEASON: June–October
FEES/PASSES: None
MAPS: Maine Huts & Trails website
TRAILHEAD: MHT information kiosk, Gauge Rd., Carrabassett Valley
FACILITIES: None
CONTACT: Maine Huts & Trails; 207/265-2400; www.mainehuts.org

START THE HIKE

▶ **MILE 0-0.1: MHT Information Kiosk to Cutoff Trail**
Begin the hike by the Maine Huts & Trails information kiosk in the parking lot just off Gauge Road. Pick up the grassy **MHT Trail** and follow it north for a brief 0.1 mi (0.16 km) before turning left at the first junction onto the **Cutoff Trail.**

▶ **MILE 0.1-0.5: Cutoff Trail to MHT Trail**
Pick your way over some rocks as the blue-blazed trail climbs a hillside into thick, dark spruce forest. The trail follows **Poplar Stream,** getting steeper in a few places, before merging with the MHT Trail again at a junction at 0.5 mi (0.8 km). Turn left onto the MHT.

▶ **MILE 0.5-1.1: MHT Trail to Larry's Trail**
The MHT Trail continues north, rolling up and down over a brief knoll. The rockier, wider pathway almost feels like a dirt road. At 0.7 mi (1.1 km), turn right at the junction and climb a larger hillside as the trail crosses several small tributaries on wooden bridges. As you pass through a leafier stretch of woods, look for blue diamond markers, bearing the Maine Huts & Trails brand, on the trees, and listen for woodpeckers and other birds. At 1.1 mi (1.8 km), you'll reach a cutoff for Larry's Trail. Turn left to pick up Larry's Trail.

▶ **MILE 1.1-2.0: Larry's Trail to Footbridge**
From here, the trail enters a shadier patch of hemlock forest and becomes much narrower, following the gentle roar of Poplar Stream along a densely

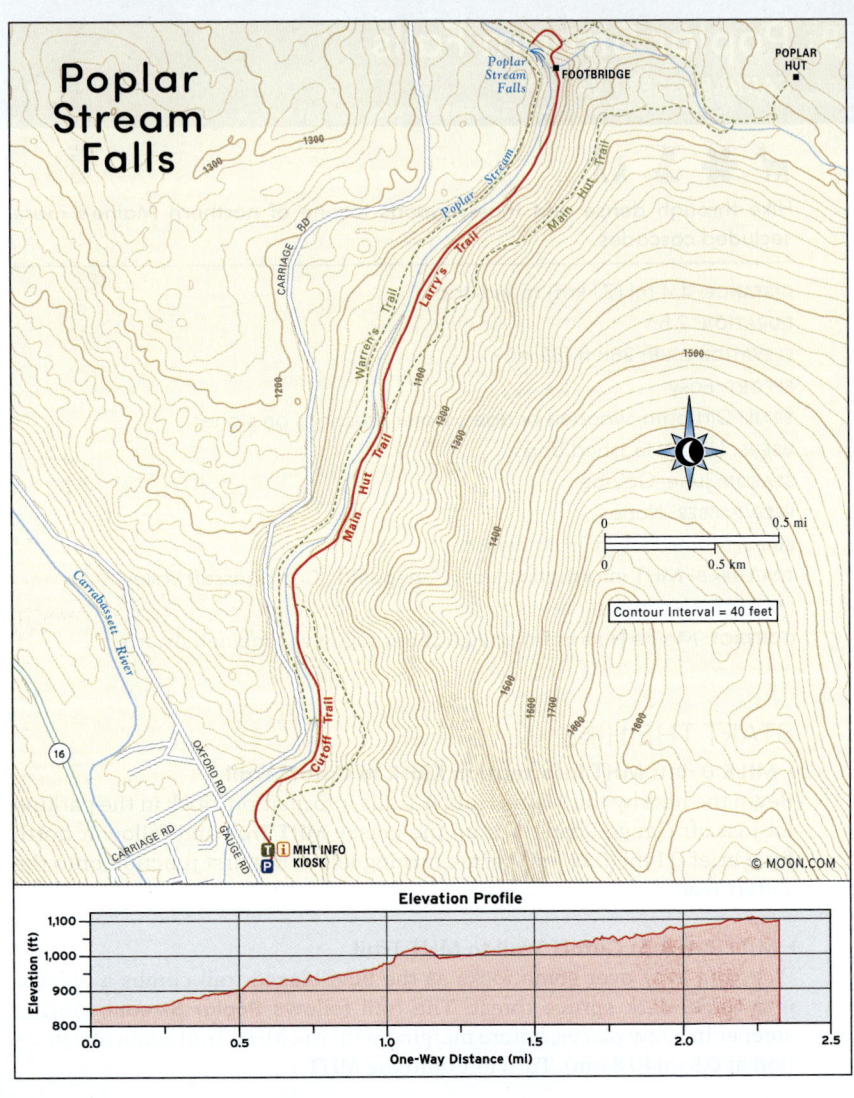

Poplar Stream Falls

POPLAR HUT

FOOTBRIDGE

Poplar Stream Falls

CARRIAGE RD

Poplar Stream

Larry's Trail

Warren's Trail

Main Hut Trail

Main Hut Trail

Cutoff Trail

Carrabassett River

16

OXFORD RD

GAUGE RD

CARRIAGE RD

MHT INFO KIOSK

0.5 mi

0.5 km

Contour Interval = 40 feet

© MOON.COM

Elevation Profile

Elevation (ft)

1,100
1,000
900
800

0.0   0.5   1.0   1.5   2.0   2.5

One-Way Distance (mi)

wooded hillside where the battle cry of the red squirrel is as constant as the sound of the water. Cruise along Larry's Trail through some groves of ferns and make your way over some old bog bridges. Watch your step on exposed tree roots as the trail begins to descend at a moderate grade, arriving at a sturdy **wooden footbridge** over Poplar Stream at 2 mi (3.2 km).

▸ **MILE 2.0-2.2: Footbridge to Poplar Stream Falls**

After crossing the bridge, you'll hear the sound of crashing water echoing through the forest on your right. Continue north along the path until you reach a steep series of stone stairs; turn right here to stay on level ground, skipping the stairs, and continue a few more yards. At 2.2 mi (3.5 km), you'll reach **Poplar Stream Falls,** a roaring chute of water that tumbles 50 ft (15 m) into a stunningly pretty pool. The deep, reflective pool is

▲ POPLAR STREAM FALLS

cold but swimmable in the summer. **Optional add-on:** Hikers interested in checking out nearby Poplar Hut can backtrack to the stone stairs and head up them to the junction for the hut. The hut offers comfy overnight lodging and locally sourced meals by reservation, and day hikers can purchase lunch here from noon to 2pm on Saturday and Sunday during the full-service season (mid-June through September). Otherwise, return the way you came.

DIRECTIONS

From Portland, it's about 2.5 hours to the trailhead. Take I-295 N and I-95 N to ME-3 and ME-27 N until it intersects with US-2 W. Turn left onto US-2 W and continue to West Farmington, where you'll turn right onto ME-27 N once again. Drive north to Carrabassett Valley, turn right onto Carriage Road, and then take the first left to reach the Carrabassett Valley Town Office parking lot. (This is where you'll leave your car.) To reach the trailhead, walk back to Carriage Road, turn left, and continue walking northeast along the road to Gauge Road. Make a right onto Gauge Road, cross a wooden footbridge over Poplar Stream, and take the first left to arrive at the Poplar Stream Falls trailhead.

GPS COORDINATES: 45°04'44.4"N 70°12'27.7"W

BEST NEARBY BITES

Feel like injecting some more fun into your day after a serene waterfall hike? Devour a bacon-laden cheeseburger, sip some suds from an impressive Maine craft beer list, and roll a few games of bowling at **The SugarBowl** (1242 Carrabassett Dr., Carrabassett Valley; 207/235-3300; 4pm-10pm Tues.-Fri., noon-10pm Sat.-Sun.).

Baxter, the Highlands, and the Carrabassett Valley

MAINE

🦌 ✿ 👫 ♿

This boardwalk loop through a beautiful bog is especially nice for bird-watchers, families, and couples on a sunset stroll.

DISTANCE: 1.5 mi (2.4 km) round-trip
DURATION: 45 min
ELEVATION GAIN: 27 ft (8 m)
EFFORT: Easy
TRAIL: Dirt path, boardwalk
USERS: Hikers
SEASON: May–November
FEES/PASSES: None
MAPS: University of Maine Orono Bog Walk website
TRAILHEAD: East Trail trailhead, Tripp Dr., Bangor
FACILITIES: Vault toilet
CONTACT: University of Maine; 207/581-1865; www.umaine.edu/oronobogwalk

Tucked away in Bangor's public forest is Orono Bog—a 616-acre (249-hectare) conservation area that's teeming with wildlife and vivid green peat moss so thick that it actually constitutes a small height of land at the center of the bog. This walk is especially nice during the evening "magic hour" when the lighting is softer.

START THE HIKE

▶ **MILE 0-0.4: East Trail to Orono Bog Boardwalk**
Walk to the northeast end of the parking area to the wooden sign for the **East Trail.** Go 0.3 mi (0.5 km) northeast along this gravel path that meanders through an airy forest of spruce and cedar trees. Upon reaching a clearing with picnic tables and an information kiosk, take a right turn onto the **Orono Bog Boardwalk** entrance.

▶ **MILE 0.4-0.6: Orono Bog Boardwalk to Orono Bog**
Continue northeast along the first section of boardwalk as it takes you through a much thicker, diverse stretch of forest. Some pieces of the boardwalk are actually resting on the bog surface, so don't be worried if they bounce like a floating dock. Colorful signs are placed throughout the boardwalk to give visitors an idea of the many bird, mammal, and reptile species that call the bog home. The boardwalk splits at 0.5 mi (0.8 km); bear right and keep heading northeast through an airier grove of spruce. The landscape suddenly opens up into a panorama of peat moss in countless shades of green. You're officially in **Orono Bog** now.

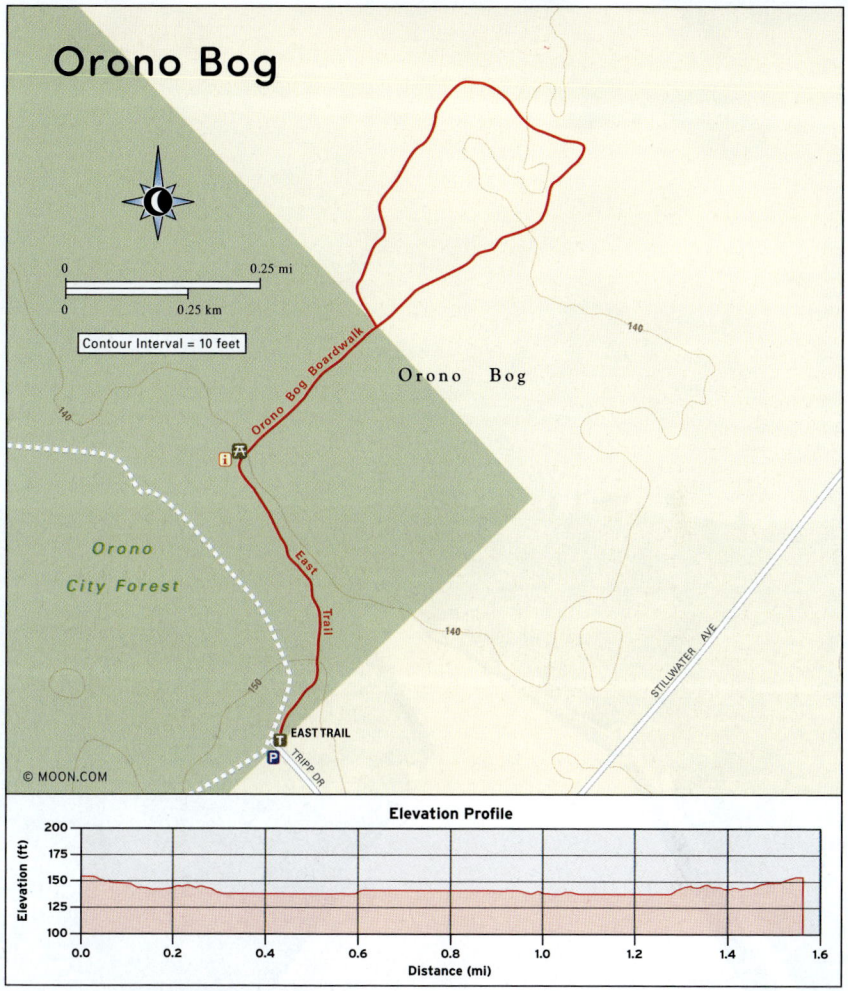

Orono Bog

Orono Bog

Orono Bog Boardwalk

East Trail

EAST TRAIL

Orono
City Forest

STILLWATER AVE

TRIPP DR

Contour Interval = 10 feet

0.25 mi
0.25 km

© MOON.COM

Elevation Profile

Elevation (ft)

Distance (mi)

▶ **MILE 0.6-1.0: Orono Bog**

As the bog boardwalk curves north and then northwest over the next
0.3 mi (0.5 km), watch the sky for northern harriers. Not only do these
medium-size raptors make regular appearances around the bog, but the
trees and shrubs here are less than 10 ft (3 m) tall, offering birders a prime
view. The boardwalk starts to turn west and passes through a stretch of
young spruce. Around here the boardwalk is slightly more raised, but it's
still close enough to the peat for hikers to spot a northern leopard frog
hopping around on the surface.

▶ **MILE 1.0-1.5: Orono Bog to East Trail**

The trail heads southeast for 0.3 mi (0.5 km) as the boardwalk loop draws
toward its close. Be sure to take a good final whiff of the air—some of the
herbs that grow around here are bog variations of laurel and rosemary.
The boardwalk loop enters forest again, reaching its origin point at 1.1 mi

(1.8 km). From here, you can turn left and backtrack to the parking lot or explore more of the Bangor City Forest trails.

DIRECTIONS

From Portland, take I-95 north to the Bangor area. Take Exit 186 for Stillwater Avenue and then turn right onto Stillwater Avenue. Take Stillwater Avenue northeast for 2.6 mi (4.2 km) and then make a left turn onto Tripp Drive. The Bangor City Forest parking lot is at the end of this quiet road.

GPS COORDINATES: 44°51'46.1"N 68°43'42.1"W

BEST NEARBY BITES AND BREWS

The nearby city of Bangor is teeming with restaurants and watering holes, but in Orono, right near the bog, you can get a representative taste of Maine's craft beers and some seriously loaded hot dogs at **The Family Dog** (6 Mill St., Orono; 207/866-2808; www.thefamilydogorono.com; 11am-10pm Mon.-Fri., 9am-10pm Sat., 9am-9pm Sun.).

NEARBY CAMPGROUNDS

NAME	LOCATION	FACILITIES	SEASON	FEE
Roaring Brook Campground	Chimney Pond Trail, Millinocket, 45°55'09.6"N 68°51'24.5"W	Tent sites, lean-tos, bunkhouse, toilets	mid-May through late October	$13-34
207/723-9500; www.baxterstatepark.org				
Katahdin Stream Campground	Appalachian Trail/Katahdin Stream, Millinocket, 45°53'13.2"N 68°59'57.7"W	Tent sites, lean-tos, toilets	mid-May through late October	$34 (plus $16 park entry fee)
207/723-9500; www.baxterstatepark.org				
Big Eddy Campground	Golden Rd., Millinocket, 45°52'32.7"N 69°07'47.9"W	Tent sites, cabins, RV sites, toilets, showers, potable water, Wi-Fi	early May through mid-October	$16-110
207/882-7323; www.bigeddy.chewonki.org				
Abol Bridge Campground	3969 Golden Rd., Mile 19, Millinocket, 45°50'07.1"N 68°57'55.7"W	Tent sites, RV sites, cabins, toilets, showers, camp store, restaurant, Wi-Fi	late May through September	$27-268
207/447-5803; www.webreserv.com/abolbridgecampgroundandstoreme				
Big Moose Inn Cabins & Campground	5 Frederickas Way, Millinocket, 45°43'45.5"N 68°50'16.1"W	Tent sites, lean-tos, RV sites, cabins, hotel rooms, toilets, showers, potable water, camp store, restaurant, Wi-Fi	June-late October	$15-450
207/723-8391; www.bigmoosecabins.com				

NEARBY CAMPGROUNDS (continued)

NAME	LOCATION	FACILITIES	SEASON	FEE
Wilderness Edge Campground	71 Millinocket Lake Rd., Millinocket, 45°40'32.3"N 68°43'24.2"W	Tent sites, rental tents, cabin tents, RV sites, RV rentals, toilets, showers, potable water, laundry, camp store, Wi-Fi	early May through mid-October	$13–325
207/447-8485; www.wildernessedgecampground.com				
Moosehead Family Campground	312 Moosehead Lake Rd., Greenville, 45°26'15.0"N 69°35'24.4"W	Tent sites, RV sites, toilets, showers, potable water, camp store, Wi-Fi	late May through mid-October	$34–56
207/695-2210; www.mooseheadcampground.com				
Spacious Skies Balsam Woods Campground	112 Pond Rd., Abbot, 45°13'00.9"N 69°31'04.9"W	Tent sites, RV sites, cabins, toilets, showers, potable water, laundry, pool, dog park, camp store, Wi-Fi	late May through mid-October	$45–149
207/876-2731; www.spaciousskiescampgrounds.com				
Cathedral Pines Campground	945 The Arnold Trail, Eustis, 45°11'21.4"N 70°27'45.5"W	Tent sites, RV sites, toilets, showers, potable water, laundry, boat rentals, Wi-Fi	mid-May through September	$37–45
207/246-3491; www.gopinescamping.com				

MIDCOAST, CASCO BAY, AND THE MAINE BEACHES

The beauty of the Maine coast is in its seamless pairing of hills and sea. This is the Maine that people dream of—cerulean seas crackling with whitecaps, towering pines rocked by the wind, and the aroma of golden-fried shrimp wafting down the shore. Nowhere else in New England can you scale steeplechase cliffs (flanked with blueberry bushes!) while breathing in that salty sea breeze. The sheer number of islands that speckle the Maine coast—more than 4,500 of them—imbues some local hiking destinations with an expeditionary thrill. And when it's time to refuel, Maine's coastal communities offer an unparalleled smorgasbord of classic maritime and New American culinary delights, plus a booming craft beer scene.

▲ VIEW OF MIRROR LAKE AND ROCKLAND FROM RAGGED MOUNTAIN

▲ WELLS RESERVE

1 **Mount Megunticook**

DISTANCE: 2.8 mi (4.5 km) round-trip
DURATION: 2 hr
EFFORT: Moderate
PAGE: 108

2 **Ragged Mountain**

DISTANCE: 4.8 mi (7.7 km) round-trip
DURATION: 3.5 hr
EFFORT: Moderate/strenuous
PAGE: 111

3 **Lane's Island Preserve**

DISTANCE: 1 mi (1.6 km) round-trip
DURATION: 30 min
EFFORT: Easy
PAGE: 114

4 **Oven's Mouth Preserve**

DISTANCE: 3.1 mi (5 km) round-trip
DURATION: 1.5 hr
EFFORT: Easy
PAGE: 117

5 **Harpswell Cliff Trail**

DISTANCE: 2.2 mi (3.5 km) round-trip
DURATION: 1.5 hr
EFFORT: Easy
PAGE: 121

6 **Fore River and Jewell Falls**

DISTANCE: 3.3 mi (5.3 km) round-trip
DURATION: 1.5 hr
EFFORT: Easy
PAGE: 124

7 **Wells Reserve**

DISTANCE: 2.8 mi (4.5 km) round-trip
DURATION: 1.5 hr
EFFORT: Easy
PAGE: 127

8 **Mount Agamenticus**

DISTANCE: 2.5 mi (4 km) round-trip
DURATION: 2 hr
EFFORT: Easy/moderate
PAGE: 130

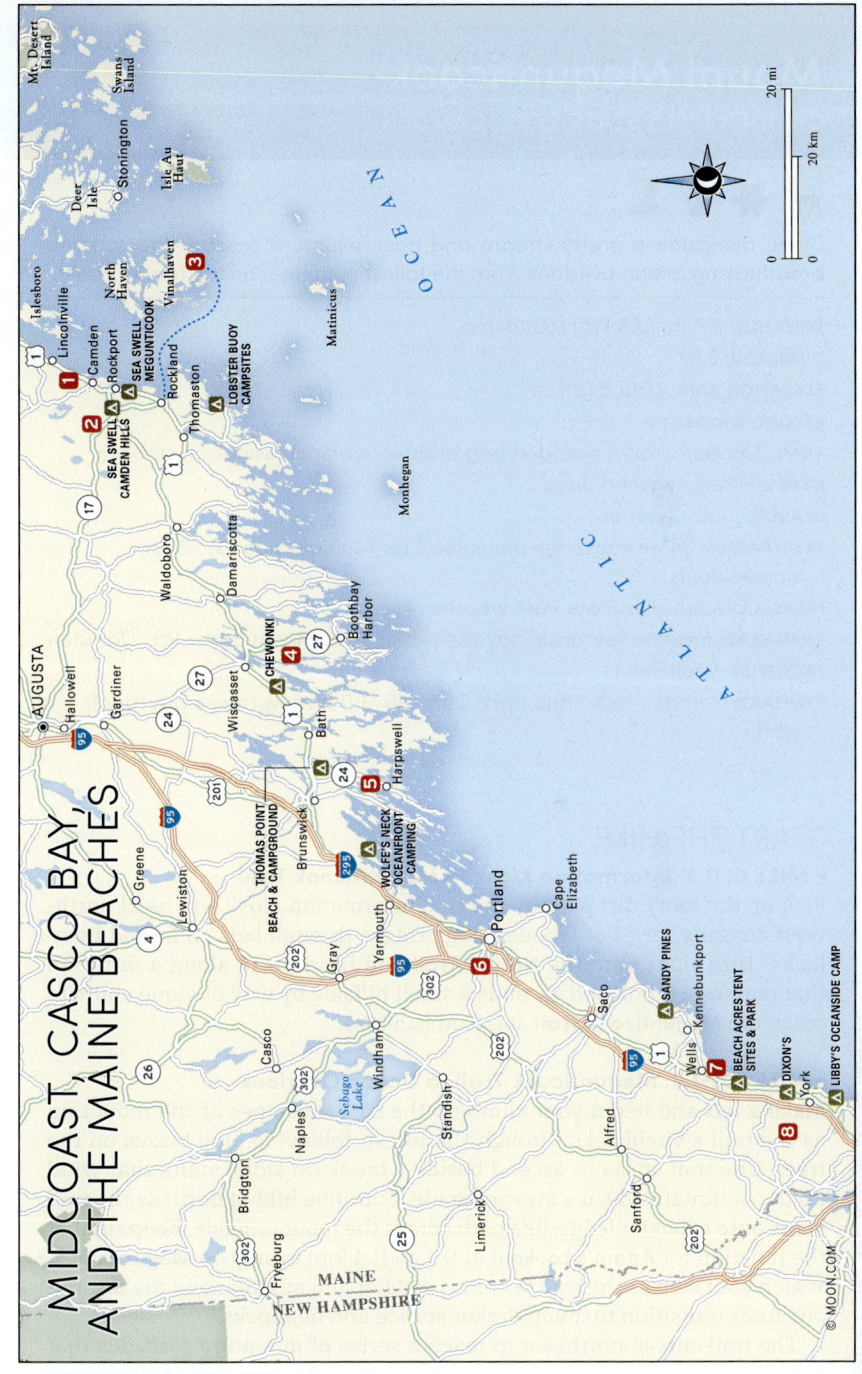

MIDCOAST, CASCO BAY, AND THE MAINE BEACHES

Mt. Desert Island

Swans Island

Stonington

Deer Isle

Isle Au Haut

Islesboro

Lincolnville

Camden

Rockport

SEA SWELL MEGUNTICOOK

Vinalhaven

North Haven

3

Rockland

LOBSTER BUOY CAMPSITES

Thomaston

1

2 **SEA SWELL CAMDEN HILLS**

Waldoboro

Damariscotta

Matinicus

Monhegan

Boothbay Harbor

CHEWONKI **4**

Wiscasset

Bath

Harpswell

Gardiner

Hallowell

● AUGUSTA

THOMAS POINT BEACH & CAMPGROUND

Brunswick

WOLFE'S NECK OCEANFRONT CAMPING **5**

Yarmouth

Portland

Cape Elizabeth

Greene

Lewiston

Gray

6

Saco

SANDY PINES

Kennebunkport

BEACH ACRES TENT SITES & PARK

Casco

Windham

Wells

7

DIXON'S

York

LIBBY'S OCEANSIDE CAMP

8

Naples

Standish

Alfred

Sanford

Bridgton

Fryeburg

Limerick

MAINE

NEW HAMPSHIRE

Sebago Lake

OCEAN

ATLANTIC

20 mi

20 km

© MOON.COM

1 Mount Megunticook

CAMDEN HILLS STATE PARK, CAMDEN

Climb alongside a pretty stream and past miniature cascades to reach a breathtaking ocean overlook from the tallest mountain on the Maine coast.

DISTANCE: 2.8 mi (4.5 km) round-trip

DURATION: 2 hr

ELEVATION GAIN: 1,019 ft (311 m)

EFFORT: Moderate

TRAIL: Dirt path, rocks, wooden bog bridges, water crossings on stones

USERS: Hikers, leashed dogs

SEASON: June-October

FEES/PASSES: $4 entrance fee per vehicle for Maine residents, $6 for nonresidents

MAPS: Camden Hills State Park website

TRAILHEAD: Information kiosk, day use parking lot, Mount Battie Rd., Camden

FACILITIES: Vault toilet

CONTACT: Camden Hills State Park; 207/236-3109; www.maine.gov/dacf/parks

START THE HIKE

▶ **MILE 0-0.3: Information Kiosk to Megunticook Trail**
Pick up the rooty dirt path by the trail information kiosk and head north-west across a series of wooden bog bridges through balsam fir and hemlocks. Turn right onto the **Nature Trail** and head north along a dirt path that crosses a brook and ascends a small hillside by way of stone stairs to reach the **Megunticook Trail** at 0.3 mi (0.5 km).

▶ **MILE 0.3-1.3: Megunticook Trail to Ocean Overlook**
Make a left and begin your climb up the eastern slopes of the mountain as the trail switchbacks through the forest, following blue blazes on the trees. The trail starts to ascend beside a brook on stone stairs that wind up the mountainside at a steeper grade. Continue hiking north as the trail veers onto a rockier ledge-like path across the mountainside. Keep right at the junction for **Adam's Lookout** at 0.9 mi (1.4 km) to stay on Megunticook. Watch your step as the trail becomes soggier and muddier and the deciduous trees transition to much darker spruce and hemlocks.

The trail curves northeast to reach a series of miniature cascades that spill alongside the trail. During rainy weather, the cascades can overflow and transform this stretch of trail into something of a waterway itself. Continue up more stone stairs and some sloped rock slabs that become bigger and steeper as the spruce trees get shorter. The trail levels off at

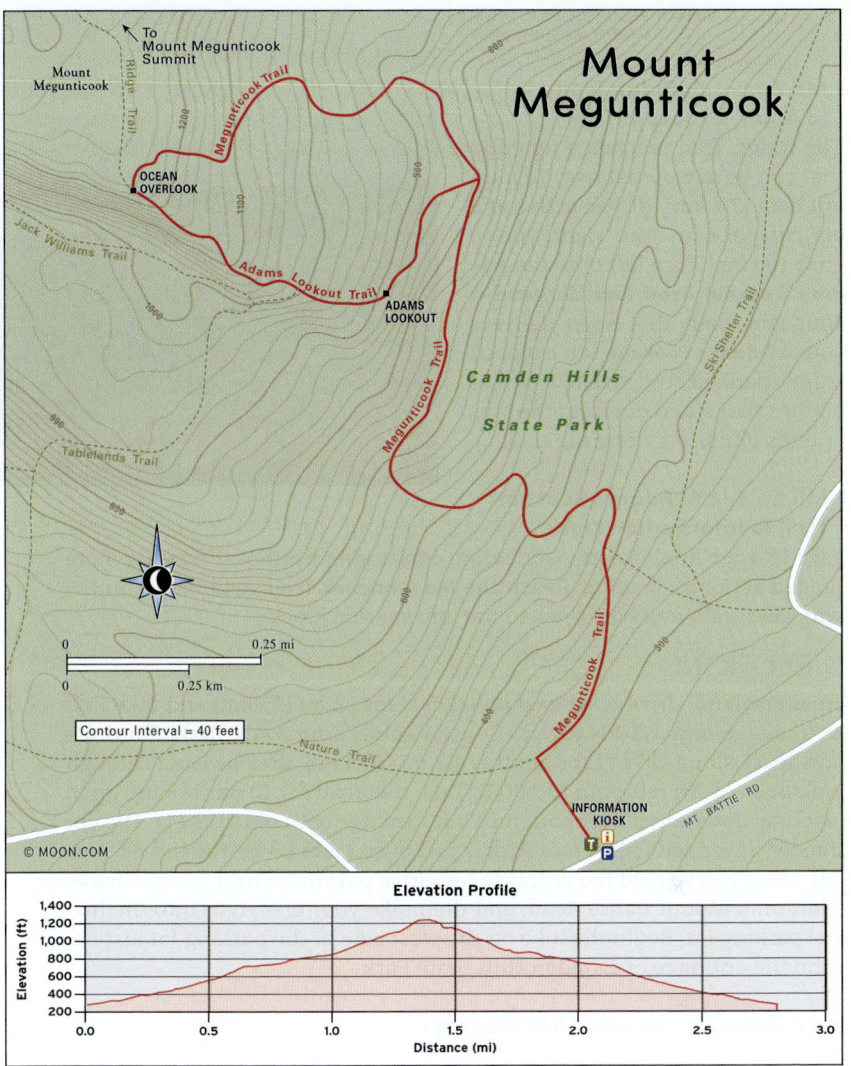

Elevation Profile

a grassy clearing and passes through a grove of trees to arrive at **Ocean Overlook** at 1.3 mi (2.1 km).

▶ MILE 1.3-1.4: Ocean Overlook to Mount Megunticook Summit

Enjoy the ocean vista and the overhead perspective of nearby Mount Battie. Hikers who wish to see the wooded (and mostly view-less) summit proper of **Mount Megunticook** can continue north up the Megunticook Trail.

▶ MILE 1.4-1.5: Ocean Overlook to Ridge Trail

Otherwise, pick up the **Ridge Trail** by following blue blazes that lead southeast down the lichen-crusted rock slabs of Ocean Overlook.

▶ **MILE 1.5–1.8: Ridge Trail to Adam's Lookout Trail**

The Ridge Trail reaches a junction that can be somewhat easy to miss at 1.6 mi (2.6 km). (If you arrive at a big cliff face on your right, you've gone too far.) Turn left onto the **Adam's Lookout Trail** and descend a snug dirt path that soon delivers you to **Adam's Lookout**—an exposed ledge flanked by twisted white birches that stand out from the other trees glimpsed along the trail.

▶ **MILE 1.8–2.8: Adam's Lookout Trail to Information Kiosk**

Take in your final ocean vista before continuing northeast down a more rugged set of rock stairs. Reach the **Megunticook Trail** again at 1.9 mi (3.1 km). Veer right and backtrack to the information kiosk.

DIRECTIONS

From Portland, drive northeast on I-295 N for 22 mi (35 km) and take Exit 28 to merge onto US-1 N toward Coastal Route/Brunswick/Bath. Continue northeast along US-1 N for another 42 mi (68 km); after passing through Waldoboro, turn left onto ME-90 E. Take this road for 10 mi (16 km); upon reaching downtown Rockport, turn left to merge back onto US-1 N. The entrance to Camden Hills State Park is just over 3 mi (4.8 km) ahead on your left. Once you've paid the entrance fee, drive past the ranger station, make a left onto Mount Battie Road, and then take your first right into the hikers' parking lot. Begin the hike on the west side of the parking lot just beyond the entrance of Camden Hills State Park.

GPS COORDINATES: 44°13'48.2"N 69°03'05.4"W

BEST NEARBY BITES

The beauty of Megunticook's Ocean Overlook is best followed by spicy Thai basil-minced chicken and house-made pad seaw noodles at **Long Grain** (20 Washington St., Camden; 207/236-9001; www.longgraincamden.com; 11:30am-2:30pm and 4:30-9pm Tues.-Sat.) or a glass of locally made wine and even a vineyard tour at **Cellardoor Winery** (367 Youngtown Rd., Lincolnville; 207/763-4478; www.mainewine.com; 11am-3pm Sat., noon-5pm Sun.).

2

Ragged Mountain

GEORGES RIVER LAND TRUST, ROCKPORT

🦌 ❀ 🐾

Weave through a boulder-strewn forest and scale a ragged mountainside to enjoy the views from one of coastal Maine's tallest peaks.

DISTANCE: 4.8 mi (7.7 km) round-trip

DURATION: 3.5 hr

ELEVATION GAIN: 1,102 ft (336 m)

EFFORT: Moderate/strenuous

TRAIL: Dirt path, rocks, wooden bridges, water crossings on stones

USERS: Hikers, leashed dogs

SEASON: May–November

FEES/PASSES: None

MAPS: Georges River Land Trust website

TRAILHEAD: Information kiosk, Georges Highland Path parking lot, Rockland Street, Rockport

FACILITIES: None

CONTACT: Georges River Land Trust; 207/594-5166; www.georgesriver.org/ragged-mountain

START THE HIKE

▶ **MILE 0-0.5: Information Kiosk to Georges Highland Path**
Begin the hike at the north end of the parking lot by the trail information kiosk. Descend a small set of wooden stairs into the forest and amble down a stony path to a nearby stream, which you'll cross on a wooden bridge. The **Georges Highland Path** follows blue blazes as it gently rolls through mixed maple and pine woods, cresting a series of knolls with occasional views of Ragged Mountain towering ahead. The sections of ancient stone walls along the path add some historical seasoning.

▶ **MILE 0.5-1.3: Georges Highland Path to Mirror Lake**
After reaching the top of a knoll with a good view of Ragged Mountain's more elongated north face, the trail descends to reach the **Oyster River** (really more of a small brook) at 0.7 mi (1.1 km). Rock-hop across the water and past a big boulder slide as the trail heads southeast beneath the cliffs on Ragged Mountain's west face. As the footing gets rockier and more slippery in places, the trail veers away from the Oyster River briefly but rejoins just before it spills into **Mirror Lake.** Before you reach the shores of the lake, the trail suddenly veers east at 1.3 mi (2.1 km) and climbs at a steeper grade right up the western haunch of Ragged Mountain. From here, you've officially left the foothills behind.

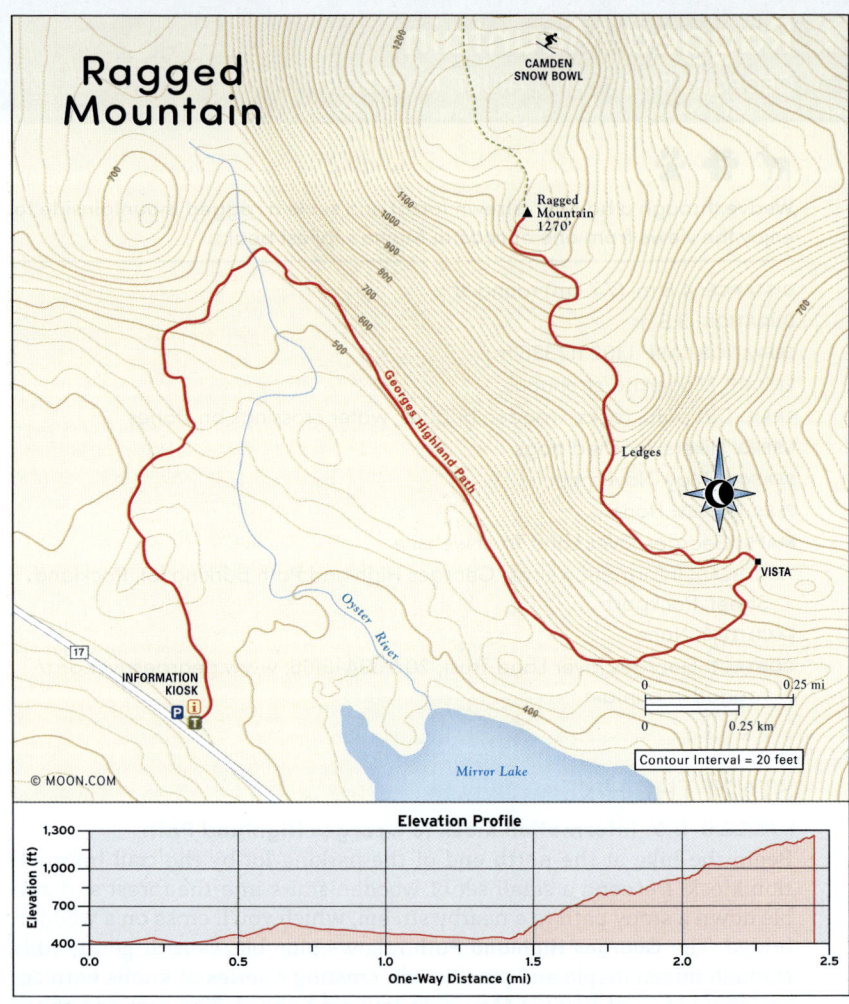

Ragged
Mountain

CAMDEN
SNOW BOWL

Ragged
Mountain
1270'

Georges Highland Path

Ledges

VISTA

Oyster River

17

INFORMATION
KIOSK

0   0.25 mi

0   0.25 km

Contour Interval = 20 feet

Mirror Lake

© MOON.COM

Elevation Profile

Elevation (ft)

1,300
1,000
700
400

0.0   0.5   1.0   1.5   2.0   2.5
One-Way Distance (mi)

▶ **MILE 1.3–1.8: Mirror Lake to Ragged Mountain Ridgeline**

Continue climbing east, enjoying some partial views of Mirror Lake and the nearby coast through the trees on your right. The trail is wider here, but the exposed tree roots can become slippery with rain. As the grade starts to level out a bit, the trail reaches a wooded height of land at 1.6 mi (2.6 km) with a new **vista** perspective—this time, you can gaze out at the Camden Hills and the northern coastline of Downeast Maine. From here, the trail climbs north at a more gradual rate up the ridgeline of Ragged Mountain. A series of exposed, rocky **ledges** at 1.8 mi (2.9 km) offer the best views yet, and a great chance to get a face full of that inimitable Maine sea breeze.

▶ **MILE 1.8–2.4: Ragged Mountain Ridgeline
to Ragged Mountain Summit**

A brief descent into a wooded col (gap) brings you to the final stretch of rocky trail, which is more eroded and rougher on the feet. Ahead, through

the trees, you'll see the summit communications tower. Climb north around a bulbous piece of ridgeline and emerge onto a much more thoroughly exposed granite landscape at 2.1 mi (3.4 km). Little cairns and blue blazes spray-painted on the rock mark the way as you scramble up some slabs and breeze through a few thin stretches of alpine forest to reach the summit "cone." Muscle your way up the concluding lichen-covered rock slabs and step onto the spacious summit of **Ragged Mountain** at 2.4 mi (3.9 km). The summit overlooks Mirror Lake and beyond to the pretty coastal enclaves of Rockport and Rockland. Return the way you came.

DIRECTIONS

From Portland, drive northeast on I-295 N for 22 mi (35 km) and take Exit 28 to merge onto US-1 N toward Coastal Route/Brunswick/Bath. Continue northeast along US-1 N for another 42 mi (68 km); after passing through Waldoboro, turn left onto ME-90 E. Take this road for 8 mi (12.9 km) and make another left turn onto ME-17 W (Rockland Street). The Georges Highland Path parking lot will be on your right just over 2 mi (3.2 km) ahead.

GPS COORDINATES: 44°12'07.1"N 69°09'32.0"W

BEST NEARBY BITES

Ragged Mountain is a stone's throw from Rockland, where no palates are left unsatisfied. Start or conclude the hike with a robust cup of locally roasted espresso and a house-baked pastry at **Atlantic Baking Co.** (351 Main St.; 207/596-2449; www.atlanticbakingco.com; 7am-5pm Mon.-Sat.). When you're ready for something more lavish, take your pick of Rockland's classic seafood and modern American restaurants: The hottest joint in town is chef Melissa Kelly's **Primo** (2 Main St., Rockland; 207/596-0770; www.primorestaurant.com; 5pm-10pm Wed.-Mon. summer, 5pm-9:30pm Wed.-Sat. fall). Primo was featured on Anthony Bourdain's *No Reservations*, but have no illusions: You'll definitely need one!

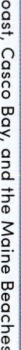

Midcoast, Casco Bay, and the Maine Beaches

MAINE

3

Lane's Island Preserve

LANE'S ISLAND PRESERVE, VINALHAVEN

🦌 ❀ 🐾 🚶

The ferry trip to Vinalhaven is worth it for this dreamy hike that's bursting with wildflowers and gorgeous ocean views.

BEST: Summer hikes

DISTANCE: 1 mi (1.6 km) round-trip

DURATION: 30 min

ELEVATION GAIN: 95 ft (29 m)

EFFORT: Easy

TRAIL: Dirt path, rocks

USERS: Hikers, leashed dogs

SEASON: May–November

FEES/PASSES: Round-trip ferry fares $20, $26 with bike, $49 with vehicle, Rockland terminal day parking $10

MAPS: Vinalhaven Chamber of Commerce website, http://vinalhaven.org/20142015brochure.pdf

TRAILHEAD: Lane's Island Preserve parking lot, Lane's Island Preserve, Vinalhaven

FACILITIES: None

CONTACT: Town of Vinalhaven; 207/863–4471; www.townofvinalhaven.org; Rockland Ferry Services, 517A Main St., Route 1, Rockland, ME; 207/596–5400. Ferry schedule www.maine.gov/mdot/ferry/vinalhaven

START THE HIKE

▶ MILE 0-0.2: Parking Lot to Trail Junction

Pick up the dirt path at the south end of the parking lot and walk south through some tallgrass before emerging into a vast clearing with some picnic tables and views of the ocean. Ahead, to your right, pick up the grassy path to begin your loop around the peninsula. You'll start by walking through a field with a small **cemetery** on your left, where members of the Lane family are buried. Spot Indian paintbrushes and even wild raspberries in the field. Pass under a large apple tree and into a grove of spruce and then veer left at the unmarked trail junction at 0.2 mi (0.3 km).

▶ MILE 0.2-0.4: Trail Junction to Ocean Overlook

The trail becomes rockier here and passes through immense ferns before reaching a viewpoint from which hikers can admire Green's Island to the southwest. This stretch of Lane's Island is also known for its *Rosa rugosa*—bright pink roses that are native to East Asia but are known to pop up in certain parts of coastal Maine. Continue hiking east along the coast past several **pebbly beaches** that can easily be reached. As the trail enters another pocket of woods, turn right at the junction at 0.4 mi (0.6 km).

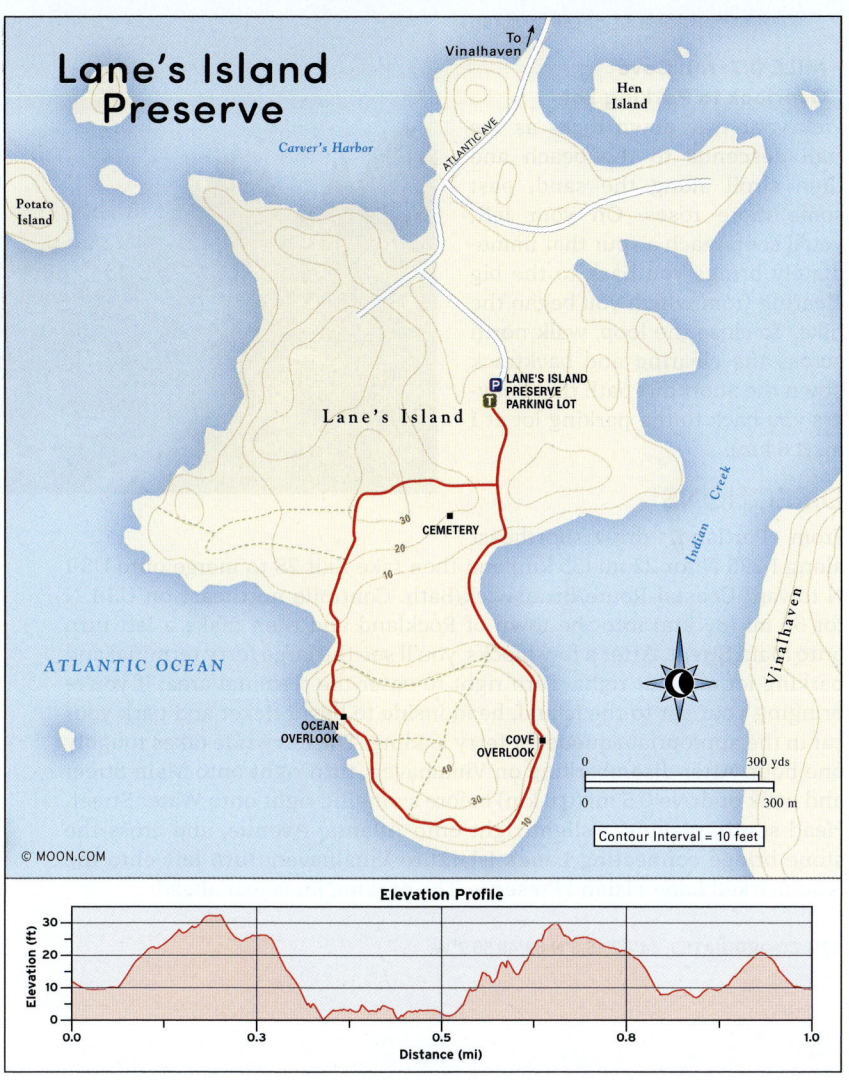

Lane's Island Preserve

Carver's Harbor

Potato Island

Hen Island

To Vinalhaven

ATLANTIC AVE.

LANE'S ISLAND PRESERVE PARKING LOT

Lane's Island

CEMETERY

30

20

10

ATLANTIC OCEAN

OCEAN OVERLOOK

COVE OVERLOOK

40

30

10

Indian Creek

Vinalhaven

300 yds

300 m

Contour Interval = 10 feet

© MOON.COM

Elevation Profile

Elevation (ft)

Distance (mi)

Make a brief climb up a rocky and rooty hill to arrive a grassy height of land with a wooden bench for looking out at the ocean.

▶ MILE 0.4-0.7: Ocean Overlook to Cove Overlook

The trail rolls up and down along some vegetation-rich cliffs and starts to curve northeast. Make another right at a junction at 0.5 mi (0.8 km), pass through some more spruce trees, and ascend a small ledge to a sunny ridge. From here, the trail dips in and out of pockets of trees, with constant ocean views to the east. Finally, at 0.7 mi (1.1 km), the trail reaches a slabby open **cliff top** that overlooks a cove with its own beach.

▶ **MILE 0.7-1.0: Cove Overlook to Parking Lot**

Pick your way down rocks as the trail descends to the beach and then stroll along the sand, past some more roses. On your left, you'll soon reach a spur that immediately brings you back to the big clearing from which you began the hike. To close the loop, walk north across the clearing and backtrack down the short dirt path that delivers you back to the parking lot at 1 mi (1.6 km).

DIRECTIONS

From Portland, drive northeast along I-295 N for 22 mi (35 km) and then take Exit 28 to merge onto US-1 N toward Coastal Route/Brunswick/Bath. Continue northeast on US-1 N for 55 mi (89 km) into the town of Rockland and then make a left turn onto Main Street. After a few blocks, you'll see the large ferry terminal and parking lot on your right. Turn right to enter the terminal area. If you're bringing your car to the island, head inside to buy a ticket and park your car in the appropriate queue for ferry loading. The ferry ride takes roughly one hour. After disembarking on Vinalhaven, turn right onto Main Street and walk or drive 0.5 mi (0.8 km) before swinging right onto Water Street. Head south, making a slight right onto Atlantic Avenue, and cross the stone bridge connecting Lane's Island to Vinalhaven; turn left onto the road marked Lane's Island Preserve. The parking lot is just ahead.

GPS COORDINATES: 44°02'15.5"N 68°49'56.7"W

4

Oven's Mouth Preserve

BOOTHBAY REGION LAND TRUST, BOOTHBAY

This coastal forest hike follows a saltwater channel to reach a beautiful tidal basin where revolution-era warships used to hide.

DISTANCE: 3.1 mi (5 km) round-trip
DURATION: 1.5 hr
ELEVATION GAIN: 248 ft (76 m)
EFFORT: Easy
TRAIL: Dirt path, rocks, wooden bridges
USERS: Hikers, leashed dogs
SEASON: May-October
FEES/PASSES: None
MAPS: Boothbay Region Land Trust website
TRAILHEAD: Oven's Mouth Preserve parking lot, Dover Rd., Boothbay
FACILITIES: None
CONTACT: Boothbay Region Land Trust; 207/633-4818; www.bbrlt.org

START THE HIKE

▶ **MILE 0-0.2: Parking Lot to Back River**

Begin the hike on the west side of the parking area. Pick up the **White Trail** and enter a lush pine forest on a rooty dirt path. Veer right at the fork and follow white blazes north. At 0.2 mi (0.3 km), the trail emerges from the thicker greenery onto a wooded yet sunny hillside on the shores of the **Back River.**

▶ **MILE 0.2-0.9: Back River to Oven's Mouth Bridge**

This "river" is actually one of the coves that formerly sheltered warships during the American Revolutionary War. Continue north along the Back River as the trail rolls up and down the hillside, occasionally descending close enough to the water for hikers to veer off-trail and immerse their feet. The trail curves west around the tip of the east peninsula, following a narrower channel with lots of rushing water.

Pass through a grove of spruce trees to reach a wooden bench at 0.6 mi (1 km) with a view of **Oven's Mouth.** The trail curves south and hugs the shoreline before arriving at a handsome wooden **bridge** at 0.9 mi (1.4 km).

▶ **MILE 0.9-1.1: Oven's Mouth Bridge to White Trail**

Cross over to the west peninsula, and then turn right again to enter the rockier and more densely wooded part of the preserve. The trail climbs steeply to a ridge that curves to the west, offering a pretty overhead perspective of the channel. At 1.1 mi (1.8 km), keep right at the **Blue Trail junction** to stay on White Trail and descend toward the water.

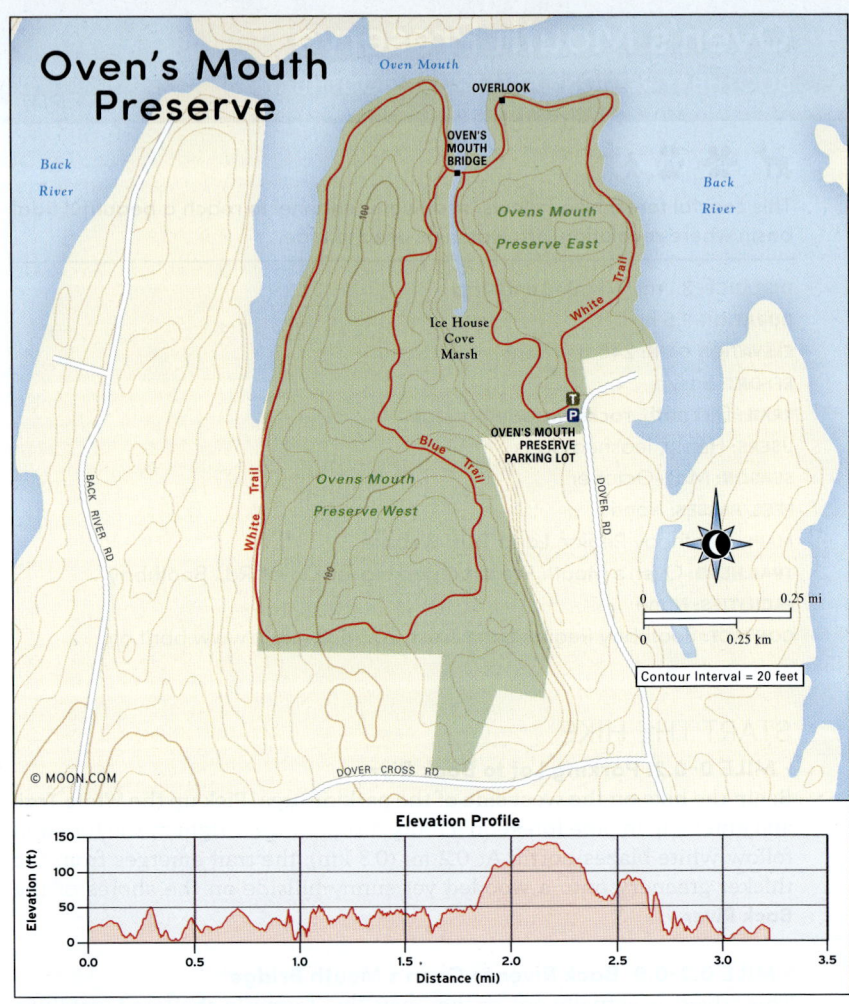

Oven's Mouth Preserve

Oven Mouth

OVERLOOK

OVEN'S MOUTH BRIDGE

Back River

Back River

Ovens Mouth Preserve East

White Trail

Ice House Cove Marsh

OVEN'S MOUTH PRESERVE PARKING LOT

Blue Trail

BACK RIVER RD

Ovens Mouth Preserve West

White Trail

DOVER RD

0   0.25 mi
0   0.25 km

Contour Interval = 20 feet

© MOON.COM

DOVER CROSS RD

Elevation Profile

Elevation (ft)

Distance (mi)

▶ MILE 1.1–2.2: White Trail to Blue Trail

Hike south for 0.5 mi (0.8 km) along a smaller cove on the far edge of the west peninsula. The footing becomes much softer—a classic Maine foundation of pine needles and soil. At 1.6 mi (2.6 km), a series of steeper and much rockier climbs and dips begins. The spruce woods around here are darker and thicker (and the red squirrels are especially feisty). As the cove narrows into something resembling a creek, the trail slabs up a larger hillside and climbs gradually to a height of land that's covered in ferns, spruce, and beech trees. At 2.2 mi (3.5 km), turn left onto the **Blue Trail,** following blue blazes on a level walk across a broader wooded ridge.

▶ MILE 2.2–2.8: Blue Trail to Oven's Mouth Bridge

Descend an especially fertile slope of ferns and wildflowers to reach a set of closely interspersed junctions at 2.4 mi (3.9 km). Turn right at the first split and follow combined blue and yellow blazes to the second junction at 2.6 mi (4.2 km); turn left onto this cutoff trail, which heads north and

quickly merges with the **White Trail** again, making a steep and rocky descent to return to the Oven's Mouth bridge at 2.8 mi (4.5 km).

▶ **MILE 2.8–3.1: Oven's Mouth Bridge to Parking Lot**

Cross the bridge, turn right this time, and enjoy a final victory lap through **Ice House Cove**—a sprawling marsh where eagles and herons are sometimes spotted. As you hike south along the marsh, a series of bog bridges will deliver you back to the fork at the beginning of your hike. Turn right to reach the parking lot at 3.1 mi (5 km).

DIRECTIONS

From Portland, drive northeast on I-295 N for 22 mi (35 km) and take Exit 28 to merge onto US-1 N toward Coastal Route/Brunswick/Bath. Continue northeast along US-1 N for another 21 mi (34 km) and then, after crossing a large bridge in Wiscasset, make a right turn onto ME-27 S. Drive south along this road for 7 mi (11.3 km), turn right onto Adams Pond Road, and then take a right onto Dover Road. Continue north and keep right at the fork to stay on Dover Road. The Oven's Mouth parking lot will be on your left less than 0.5 mi (0.8 km) ahead.

GPS COORDINATES: 43°55'45.9"N 69°38'24.4"W

BEST NEARBY BITES

If you want the pinnacle of classic no–frills Maine seafood, head into Wiscasset, brave the long takeout line, and enjoy the biggest, most meaty and buttery lobster roll of your life at **Red's Eats** (41 Water St., Wiscasset; 207/882-6128; www.redseatsmaine.com; 11:30am–5pm Tues.-Sun.). If you'd rather savor something finer and more potent, head slightly north of Oven's Mouth and try the organic rum, vodka, and whiskey at **Split Rock Distilling** (16 Osprey Point Rd., Newcastle; 207/563-2669; www.splitrockdistilling.com; noon–5pm Wed.–Sat.).

5

Harpswell Cliff Trail

HARPSWELL HERITAGE LAND TRUST, HARPSWELL

🦌 ❀ 🐾 ⛲ 🚶‍♂️

Wander through a magical woodland full of handmade fairy houses to reach some of the most dramatic coastal cliff faces in the region.

DISTANCE: 2.2 mi (3.5 km) round-trip
DURATION: 1.5 hr
ELEVATION GAIN: 329 ft (100 m)
EFFORT: Easy
TRAIL: Dirt path, rocks, wooden bridges
USERS: Hikers, leashed dogs
SEASON: May-November
FEES/PASSES: None
MAPS: Harpswell Heritage Land Trust website
TRAILHEAD: Harpswell Town Office parking lot, Mountain Rd., Harpswell
FACILITIES: Restroom
CONTACT: Harpswell Heritage Land Trust; 207/721-1121; www.hhltmaine.org

START THE HIKE

▶ **MILE 0-0.4: Harpswell Town Office Parking Lot to Old Town Road Intersection**

Begin the hike in the northwest corner of the parking lot. Pick up the dirt trail and cross a wooden footbridge into the forest, where you'll quickly arrive at a sign for the **Cliff Trail.** Follow white blazes north as the paved path snakes through hemlock and spruce trees, occasionally skirting the edge of the woods for some sightings of **Strawberry Creek.** As the creek becomes marshier, the trail itself gets softer under your feet. Continue north as the trail veers away from Strawberry Creek and crosses a gulch on another footbridge. Keep straight at the three-way intersection with Old Town Road at 0.4 mi (0.6 km) and cross another bridge to reach a series of seasonal **cascades.**

▶ **MILE 0.4-0.9: Old Town Road Intersection to Harpswell Cliffs**

Around this point, you may start seeing **fairy houses** along the trail. (Fairy houses are pretty little model dwellings made of twigs, stones, shells, moss, and other natural materials found in the woods. Stop and build one of your own, if inspired!) Continue strolling north through the woods as chipmunks and red squirrels rustle through the branches overhead. At 0.6 mi (1 km), make a right turn at the **Henry Creek Lookout junction**. The trail crosses some bog bridges and ascends a mossy hillside. (In the evening, this part of the trail is alive with the sound of peepers.) A brief descent down the opposite side of the hill delivers you to the first of the cliffs at 0.9 mi (1.4 km).

Harpswell Cliff Trail

HENRY CREEK LOOKOUT JUNCTION

Cliff Trail

Cascades

Cut-Off Trail

Strawberry Creek

HARPSWELL TOWN OFFICE PARKING LOT

TOWN OFFICES

Cliff Trail

COMMUNITY DRIVE

MOUNTAIN RD

Cliff Trail

Harpswell Cliffs

Long Reach

ORR'S ISLAND OVERLOOK

© MOON.COM

0   0.25 mi

0   0.25 km

Contour Interval = 40 feet

Elevation Profile

Elevation (ft) / Distance (mi)

▶ **MILE 0.9–1.4: Harpswell Cliffs to Orr's Island Overlook**
The trail transforms into a wooded ledge and heads south along the cliffs, rolling up and down. The views of the ocean are stunning, and the trail itself never feels perilous or vertigo-inducing. A rockier and slightly steeper ascent leads to the ultimate cliff overlook at 1.4 mi (2.3 km), where hikers can gaze out at nearby Orr's Island. Savor this concluding vista before returning south back into the forest.

▶ **MILE 1.4–2.0: Orr's Island Overlook to Community Drive**
Pass through another fairy house building zone and descend gradually down the slopes of a large hillside known as Long Reach Mountain. The trail soon flattens and meanders through a shrubbier patch of woods before emerging onto the shoulder of Community Drive at 2 mi (3.2 km).

▶ **MILE 2.0-2.2: Community Drive to Harpswell Town Office Parking Lot**

Turn right onto the road and make an immediate left into the parking lot for the Harpswell Transfer Station. Walk northwest across the lot and down a grassy embankment to a grove of trees; walk through the grove to the Harpswell Town Office parking lot to complete the loop at 2.2 mi (3.5 km).

DIRECTIONS

From Portland, drive northeast on I-295 N for 17 mi (27 km) and take Exit 24 for US-1 toward Freeport. Make a left onto US-1 N at the end of the off-ramp and continue northeast for roughly 3 mi (4.8 km) before swinging right onto Highland Road. At the four-way intersection, turn left onto Pleasant Hill Road and take it east to its terminus at Maine Street. Make a right onto Maine Street and then make a slight right to stay on Maine Street, which becomes Mere Point Road. Shortly ahead, veer slightly left onto Middle Bay Road and then turn right onto ME-123 S. Drive south along this road for 3.5 mi (5.6 km) and then swing left onto Mountain Road. The Harpswell Town Offices parking lot will be on your left just over 1 mi (1.6 km) ahead.

GPS COORDINATES: 43°48'51.6"N 69°56'34.7"W

BEST NEARBY BITES

Gaze out over Casco Bay while tucking into parmesan-crusted haddock or seafood lasagna at **The Dolphin** (515 Basin Point Rd., Harpswell; 207/833-6000; www.thedolphin.me; 11am–8pm daily) or enjoy classic New England chowder, steamed soft shell lobsters, clams, and an epic view of the Cribstone Bridge at **Cook's Lobster & Ale House** (68 Garrison Cove Rd., Bailey Island; 207/833-2818; www.cookslobster.com; 11:30am–8pm Wed.–Sat., 11:30am–4pm Sun.).

Midcoast, Casco Bay, and the Maine Beaches

MAINE

6

Fore River and Jewell Falls

FORE RIVER SANCTUARY, PORTLAND

🦌 🍀 🐾 ⚔ 🏃 🚌

Hike through bird-filled salt marsh and mixed woods to a beautiful waterfall—all within the city limits of Portland.

BEST: Spring hikes

DISTANCE: 3.3 mi (5.3 km) round-trip

DURATION: 1.5 hr

ELEVATION GAIN: 147 ft (45 m)

EFFORT: Easy

TRAIL: Dirt path, wooden bridges

USERS: Hikers, leashed dogs

SEASON: May–November

FEES/PASSES: None

MAPS: Portland Trails website

TRAILHEAD: Southern Maine Pediatric Dentistry parking lot, Frost Street, Portland

FACILITIES: None

CONTACT: Portland Trails; 207/775-2411; www.trails.org

START THE HIKE

▶ **MILE 0-0.2: Parking Lot to Fore River Estuary**

Begin the hike in the north end of the parking lot. Pick up the trail, which begins as a few sections of wooden boardwalk that run parallel to the parking lot before dipping into a grove of trees. Follow white blazes down a hillside to reach the mouth of the Fore River. Cross a long wooden bridge at 0.2 mi (0.3 km), take a good whiff of salty air, and enter the Fore River estuary.

▶ **MILE 0.2-1.0: Fore River Estuary to Fore River Bridge**

The trail heads northwest along the river on sandy footing, which is helpful for minimizing your audible impact and thereby improving your chance of spotting a heron traipsing through the tall grass.

Curving west into a more wooded region, the trail crosses a few small wooden bridges before taking a sharp right and crossing a much larger bridge at 0.8 mi (1.3 km). A brief climb up a sandy hillside takes you into the cool, verdant depths of a spruce and pine forest. Keep right at the trail junction at the top of the hill. One mi (1.6 km) in, you'll reach another junction where a rickety wooden bridge crosses the Fore River.

▶ **MILE 1.0-1.5: Fore River Bridge to Jewell Falls Junction**

Turn left here (skipping the bridge) and continue deeper into the woods, following blue blazes. The trail meanders through a boggier stretch of

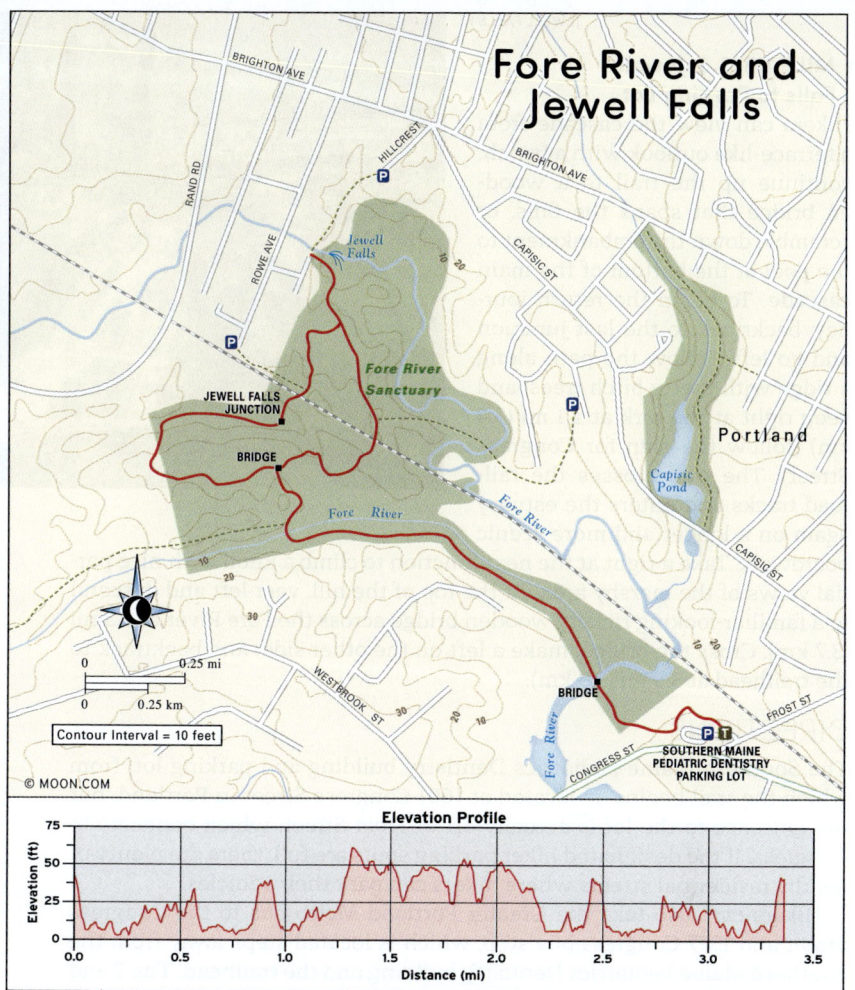

Fore River and Jewell Falls

Fore River Sanctuary

Portland

JEWELL FALLS JUNCTION

BRIDGE

BRIDGE

SOUTHERN MAINE PEDIATRIC DENTISTRY PARKING LOT

Jewell Falls

Capisic Pond

Fore River

0   0.25 mi
0   0.25 km
Contour Interval = 10 feet

© MOON.COM

Elevation Profile

forest and crosses some mudflats on bog bridges—the distant rumble of city traffic pairs surprisingly well with the croaking of frogs.

At 1.2 mi (1.9 km), veer right at the trail split to climb a larger hill. (The blazes become red at this point.) Cross into a sun-splashed zone of woods, where the trail levels off and passes some industrial buildings on the edge of the forest. At 1.5 mi (2.4 km), turn left at a signed junction to Jewell Falls; follow blue blazes down some wooden stairs to a railroad crossing.

▶ MILE 1.5-1.8: Jewell Falls Junction to Jewell Falls

The trail descends from the tracks into a wooded ravine and reaches a final junction at 1.7 mi (2.7 km). Make a left at this split, follow white blazes once again, and gently descend a hillside before the trail transitions to a charming stretch of wooden boardwalk. Schlep your way up to a small, eroded height of land and arrive at the resplendent 30-ft-tall (9-m) **Jewell Falls** at 1.8 mi (2.9 km).

▶ **MILE 1.8–3.3: Jewell Falls to Parking Lot**

Hikers can view the cascade from a terrace-like outlook with a bench, continue up the trail to a wooden bridge that spans the falls, or scramble down the embankment to the pool at the bottom of the main cascade. To begin the return journey, backtrack to the last junction and go left. Follow the path along a ridge with pretty birch trees, and keep right at the fork at 2.1 mi (3.4 km) (follow the sign for Congress Street). The trail crosses the railroad tracks and enters the estuary again on a longer and more scenic boardwalk. Take a right at the next junction to climb a knoll with nice partial views of the marshy area. At the top of the hill, veer left and descend to a familiar-looking rickety wooden bridge across the Fore River at 2.3 mi (3.7 km). Cross the bridge, make a left on the other side, and backtrack to the trailhead at 3.3 mi (5.3 km).

DIRECTIONS

The Southern Maine Pediatrics Dentistry building and parking lot, from which the trail begins, is located at 1601 Congress Street in Portland, but the entrance to the lot is actually off of Frost Street, which connects to Congress. If the designated hiker parking spots are full, there are plenty of nearby residential streets where hikers can park their vehicles.

Hikers can also take the Greater Portland Metro bus to the Congress Street and 1577 Congress bus stop, which is located steps away from the Southern Maine Pediatrics Dentistry building and the trailhead. The 2 and 5 buses drop off and pick up here.

GPS COORDINATES: 43°39′37.6″N 70°18′24.7″W

BEST NEARBY BREWS

Portland was named one of *Bon Appetit's* top restaurant cities in 2018, which gives you an idea of the plethora of dining and drinking options you'll find in neighborhoods like Old Port, Back Cove, and Munjoy Hill. But if you want to keep your forays extra local, take a 20-minute stroll east from the Fore River Sanctuary trailhead on the relatively new Fore River Trail and pay a visit to what many consider the best microbrewery in Maine—the seriously hopped-up **Bissell Brothers Portland** (38 Resurgam Pl., Portland; 207/808-8258; www.bissellbrothers.com; 11am–8pm Mon.–Thurs., 11am–11pm Sat.–Sun.).

7

Wells Reserve
WELLS RESERVE AT LAUDHOLM, WELLS

🦌 🍀 🚶

Explore one of the most biodiverse coastal environments in Maine, with mixed woods, estuaries, and a windswept beach.

DISTANCE: 2.8 mi (4.5 km) round-trip

DURATION: 1.5 hr

ELEVATION GAIN: 63 ft (19 m)

EFFORT: Easy

TRAIL: Dirt path, wooden bridges

USERS: Hikers

SEASON: May–October

FEES/PASSES: $5 adult, $1 ages 7-16, free ages 6 and under

MAPS: Wells Reserve website

TRAILHEAD: Wells Reserve Visitor Center, Skinner Mill Rd., Wells

FACILITIES: Restroom

CONTACT: Wells Reserve; 207-646-1555; www.wellsreserve.org. The visitor center is open 10am-4pm daily from Memorial Day weekend through mid-October, and then 10am-4pm daily in late October, November, April, and May.

The Maine coast is a melting pot of flora and fauna. The mixed woods here are alive with the cries of gulls and red squirrels. The spiny spruce trees give way to salty estuaries where tallgrass blows in the wind. This biodiversity is best experienced by taking a jaunt through Wells Reserve—a 2,250-acre estuarine research area with a vast network of trails that meander through fields, forests, beaches, boardwalk, and tidal marshes.

START THE HIKE

▶ **MILE 0-0.4: Wells Reserve Visitor Center to Muskie Trail Boardwalk**
Begin the hike on the north side of the visitor center. Walk west down the grassy hill to the right of the visitor center and pick up the **Muskie Trail,** which cuts through a sunny meadow speckled with flowers and buzzing with insects. (Be sure to do a tick check after the hike.) Shortly after the trail begins, you'll cross an access road and walk along a stretch of boardwalk that tunnels through a forest of pine and sugar maple before popping back out into a larger meadow.

▶ **MILE 0.4-0.8: Muskie Trail Boardwalk to Webhannet Estuary**
Continue hiking west as the trail segues from boardwalk to a flat grassy path at 0.5 mi (0.8 km). The trail curves north through a red oak and spruce corridor and concludes at a cutoff trail for **Webhannet Estuary** at 0.8 mi

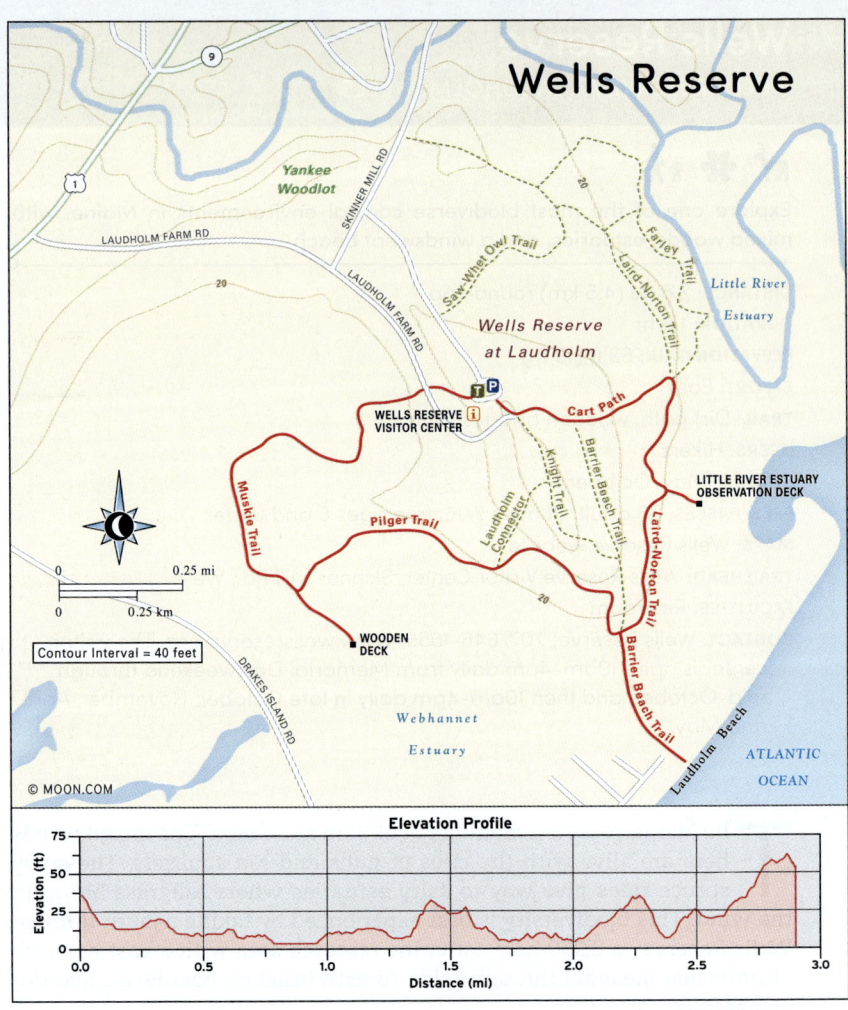

Wells Reserve

Yankee Woodlot

LAUDHOLM FARM RD

SKINNER MILL RD

Saw-Whet Owl Trail

LAUDHOLM FARM RD

Wells Reserve at Laudholm

Farley Trail

Laird-Norton Trail

Little River Estuary

Cart Path

WELLS RESERVE VISITOR CENTER

Knight Trail

Barrier Beach Trail

LITTLE RIVER ESTUARY OBSERVATION DECK

Muskie Trail

Pilger Trail

Laudholm Connector

Laird-Norton Trail

Barrier Beach Trail

0   0.25 mi
0   0.25 km

Contour Interval = 40 feet

WOODEN DECK

DRAKES ISLAND RD

Webhannet Estuary

Laudholm Beach

ATLANTIC OCEAN

© MOON.COM

Elevation Profile

Elevation (ft): 75, 50, 25, 0

Distance (mi): 0.0, 0.5, 1.0, 1.5, 2.0, 2.5, 3.0

(1.3 km). To visit the estuary lookout, keep right and take a brief southward stroll to reach a **wooden deck** that overlooks the briny marsh.

▶ **MILE 0.8-1.6: Webhannet Estuary to Barrier Beach Connector**
To continue deeper into the reserve, turn right at the junction to pick up the **Pilger Trail,** which heads east into a shrubbier stretch of woods with lots of sunlight and fruit trees bearing black cherries and apples. At 1.3 mi (2.1 km), turn right at the junction with Laudholm Connector and make a brief descent through groves of slender trembling aspen trees. At 1.6 mi (2.6 km), reach a four-way intersection and turn right onto the **Barrier Beach Connector,** a spacious dirt road that emerges from the woods to bisect two estuaries.

▶ **MILE 1.6-2.0: Barrier Beach Connector to Laird-Norton Trail**
Continue south through a stone gate and pass some houses. A boardwalk takes you down to the dune-like sprawl of **Laudholm Beach** at 1.8 mi

(2.9 km). This beach is much quieter and more pristine than the heavily trafficked ones closer to Wells. Once you've had your fill of surf and sand, backtrack north along the Barrier Beach Connector; at the junction, swing right onto the **Laird-Norton Trail**.

▶ **MILE 2.0-2.8: Laird-Norton Trail to the Wells Reserve Visitor Center**
Head northeast for another 0.3 mi (0.5 km) as the Laird-Norton Trail transitions from dirt to a gorgeous highway of boardwalk that weaves through towering maples and yellow birches; there are plenty of wooden benches along the boardwalk for taking in the scenery. At 2.3 mi (3.7 km), the trail passes a cutoff for the Little River Estuary observation deck and continues southwest through vividly green ferns and sphagnum moss. At 2.5 mi (4 km), turn left onto the **Cart Path** and walk west along a gravel trail that takes you out of the hemlocks and up a gentle exposed hillside to return to the visitor center at 2.8 mi (4.5 km).

DIRECTIONS

From Portland, take I-295 S to merge onto I-95 S and then drive south for 23 mi (37 km). Take Exit 25 toward ME-35/Kennebunk/Kennebunkport. Swing left onto Alewife Road and then make a right turn onto ME-35 S/Fletcher Street. Continue to the traffic circle, take the first exit onto Storer Street, and follow it to the four-way intersection with US-1 S/York Street and Water Street. Turn right onto US-1 S/York Street, drive south for another 3 mi (4.8 km), and make a left onto Laudholm Farm Road. Shortly ahead, veer left onto Skinner Mill Road and take the first turnoff on your right to reach the parking lot for Wells Reserve.

GPS COORDINATES: 45°53'11.7"N 68°59'59.1"W

Midcoast, Casco Bay, and the Maine Beaches

MAINE

BEST NEARBY BITES AND BREWS

If you're in town for a morning ramble, pick up some king-sized crullers and sprinkled confections at **Congdon's Doughnuts** (1090 Post Rd., Wells; 207/646-4219; www.congdons.com; 6am-2pm Thurs.-Sun.). And for midafternoon nourishment, wet your whistle with house-made ales and pizza at **Battery Steele Kitchen + Bar** (60 Mile Rd., Wells; 207/360-0333; www.batterysteele.com; noon-7pm Mon., 3pm-9pm Thurs.-Fri., noon-9pm Sat., noon-8pm Sun.).

Mount Agamenticus

MOUNT AGAMENTICUS CONSERVATION REGION, YORK

This family-friendly mountain hike offers an unbeatable 360-degree view of northeastern New England at a bargain cardiovascular price.

BEST: Winter hikes

DISTANCE: 2.5 mi (4 km) round-trip

DURATION: 2 hr

ELEVATION GAIN: 492 ft (150 m)

EFFORT: Easy/moderate

TRAIL: Dirt path, paved path, rocks, wooden bridges

USERS: Hikers, leashed dogs

SEASON: April-October

FEES/PASSES: None

MAPS: Mount Agamenticus Conservation Region website

TRAILHEAD: Cedar Trail parking lot, Mountain Rd., York

FACILITIES: None

CONTACT: Mount Agamenticus Conservation Region; 207/361-1102; www.agamenticus.org

Mount Agamenticus rises a mere 692 ft (211 m) above sea level, but there's nothing modest about its panoramic vistas and wildlife-rich forests. Located near the coastal town of York, Agamenticus was once home to a ski resort. Now it features a network of volunteer-maintained trails that have become wildly popular with hikers of all ages.

START THE HIKE

▶ **MILE 0-0.4: Cedar Trail Parking Lot to Goosefoot Trail**

Begin your hike from the parking lot on the **Cedar Trail,** a wide dirt road. At 0.2 mi (0.3 km), turn left at the sign for **Beaver Loop.** This brief detour will take you past a marsh where you can admire beaver lodges and their industrious makers. The Beaver Loop rejoins the Cedar Trail at 0.3 mi (0.5 km). Turn left back onto the Cedar Trail and

A STRETCH OF AGAMENTICUS'S WHEELCHAIR-ACCESSIBLE SUMMIT PATHWAY ▶

MAINE

Midcoast, Casco Bay, and the Maine Beaches

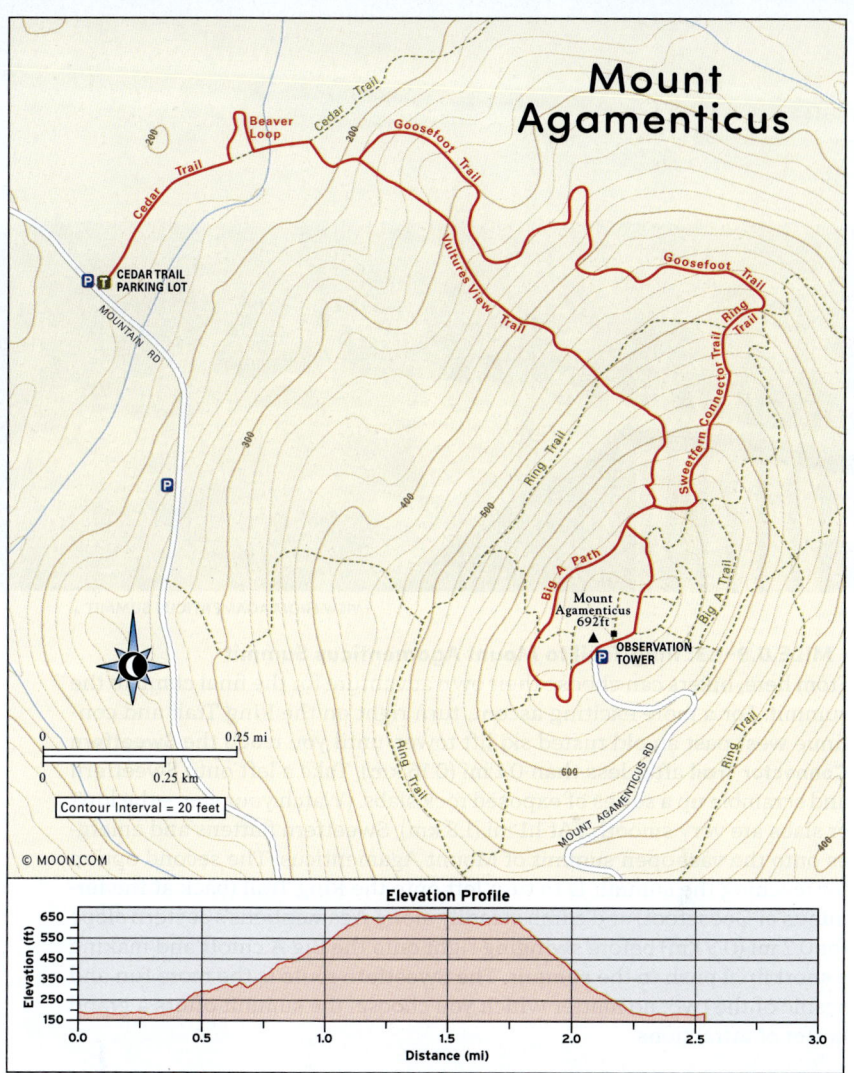

Mount Agamenticus

CEDAR TRAIL PARKING LOT

Beaver Loop

Cedar Trail

Goosefoot Trail

Vultures View Trail

Goosefoot Trail

Ring Trail

Sweetten Connector Trail

Ring Trail

Big A Path

Mount Agamenticus 692ft

OBSERVATION TOWER

Big A Trail

MOUNTAIN RD

MOUNT AGAMENTICUS RD

Ring Trail

0   0.25 mi
0   0.25 km
Contour Interval = 20 feet

© MOON.COM

Elevation Profile

continue for just under 0.1 mi (0.16 km) before arriving at the junction with the **Goosefoot Trail.**

▶ MILE 0.4-0.9: Goosefoot Trail to Ring Trail

Veer left onto the Goosefoot Trail. Climbing the northern flank of Agamenticus at a gentle grade, the Goosefoot Trail is wide but rocky enough to necessitate careful footing at times. Keep an eye out for grouse, which often wander the woods around Agamenticus and give hikers the amusing impression that they're being followed. (The grouse are actually warding hikers away from their nests!) The trail zigzags southeast through a corridor of spruce, ascending steadily for 0.5 mi (0.8 km) until it reaches the **Ring Trail** at 0.9 mi (1.4 km).

VIEW FROM AGAMENTICUS SUMMIT ▲

▶ **MILE 0.9–1.3: Ring Trail to Mount Agamenticus Summit**

From here, hikers can choose their own adventure for the final climb to the summit. For a more exciting ascent, turn right on the Ring Trail and continue west past an old rusted ski lift tower, until you reach the **Sweetfern Connector Trail** after less than 0.1 mi (0.16 km). Take a left onto Sweetfern and scramble up a series of exposed rock slabs. (Watch your step—the lower slabs are very smooth.) At 1.1 mi (1.8 km), Sweetfern flattens and emerges onto the vast open summit of Mount Agamenticus. The second option for reaching the summit is to turn left onto the Ring Trail (back at the terminus of Goosefoot) and climb steadily along Agamenticus's eastern slope for 0.2 mi (0.3 km) before swinging right onto the Big A cutoff and making a short final push to the summit. The Sweetfern route is the more fun and scenic of the two; no matter which you choose, the summit offers a grand buffet of attractions.

▶ **MILE 1.3–1.6: Mount Agamenticus Summit to
Big A Path and Observation Tower**

Continue on Sweetfern for 0.1 mi (0.16 km) until you reach the wheelchair-accessible Big A summit path (also accessible via the Agamenticus auto road). Take a right onto the **Big A Path,** cross a wooden bridge, and enjoy the north-facing views of New Hampshire and Maine as you amble along the path in a southwesterly direction. On clear days, Mount Washington is visible from here. Big A soon curves north and passes a rocky overlook point called Blueberry Bluff before delivering you to the summit proper and its nearby **observation tower** at 1.6 mi (2.6 km). From the tower, you can gaze out to the Atlantic Ocean and spot the Isles of Shoals.

▶ **MILE 1.6–2.5: Observation Tower to Cedar Trail Parking Lot (via Big A Path)**

For a more interesting return journey, pick up the Vultures View Trail from the Big A Path—back by the wooden summit bridge—and descend some sunny stone stairs into the woods. Vultures View intersects with Goosefoot at 2.2 mi (3.5 km). Keep left at this final junction and retrace your steps to the parking lot.

DIRECTIONS

From Boston, drive north on Route 1 for 15 mi (24 km) and then merge onto I-95 N. Continue for 47 mi (76 km) through New Hampshire and into Maine until you reach Exit 7 toward ME-91. Turn left at the top of the exit ramp, then take an immediate right onto Chases Pond Road. Drive north on Chases Pond Road for 6 mi (10 km) as it curves northwest and becomes Mountain Road. Continue past the Mount Agamenticus auto road for one last mile. The paved road becomes a dirt road and the Cedar Trail parking lot is ahead on the right. If the Cedar Trail lot is full, there's also a hiker parking lot back by the auto road entrance.

GPS COORDINATES: 43°13'39.3"N 70°42'06.0"W

BEST NEARBY BITES AND BREWS

If you have a soft spot for craft beer, prepare to go weak in the knees when you try the oyster stout and farmhouse saisons at **Tributary Brewing Company** (10 Shapleigh Rd., Kittery; 207/703-0093; www.tributarybrewingcompany.com; noon-7pm Wed.-Sat., 1pm-6pm Sun.). And just up the road from here, you'll find baskets of crispy clams and other maritime morsels at **Bob's Clam Hut** (315 Route 1, Kittery; 207/439-4233; www.bobsclamhut.com; 11am-7pm daily).

NEARBY CAMPGROUNDS

NAME	LOCATION	FACILITIES	SEASON	FEE
Sea Swell Campground Camden Hills	30 Applewood Rd., Rockport, 44°10'55.8"N 69°07'05.9"W	Tent sites, RV sites, toilets, showers, potable water, laundry, pool, camp store, Wi-Fi	mid-May through mid-October	$35-58
207/236-2498; www.seaswellcampgrounds.com				
Sea Swell Campground Megunticook	620 Commercial St., Rockport, 44°09'35.9"N 69°05'05.5"W	Tent sites, RV sites, cabins, toilets, showers, potable water, laundry, pool, camp store, Wi-Fi	mid-May through mid-October	$40-67
207/594-2428; www.seaswellcampgrounds.com				
Lobster Buoy Campsites	280 Waterman Beach Rd., South Thomaston, 44°01'32.9"N 69°07'21.2"W	Tent sites, RV sites, toilets, showers, potable water, camp store	mid-May through mid-October	$32-75
207/594-7546; www.lobsterbuoycampsites.wixsite.com				
Chewonki Campground	235 Chewonki Neck Rd., Wiscasset, 43°57'24.2"N 69°43'08.8"W	Tent sites, RV sites, toilets, showers, potable water, pool, camp store, Wi-Fi	mid-June through mid-October	$65-98
207/882-7426; www.chewonkicampground.com				
Thomas Point Beach & Campground	29 Meadow Rd., Brunswick, 43°53'47.3"N 69°53'39.0"W	Tent sites, RV sites, toilets, showers, potable water, laundry, camp store, Wi-Fi	May through October	$35-60
207/725-6009; www.thomaspointbeach.com				

NAME	LOCATION	FACILITIES	SEASON	FEE
Wolfe's Neck Oceanfront Camping	134 Burnett Rd., Freeport, 43°49'50.1"N 70°04'06.1"W	Tent sites, RV sites, cabin tents, cabins, toilets, showers, potable water, laundry, camp store, restaurant, Wi-Fi	May through October	$36-350
207/865-9307; www.freeportcamping.com				
Sandy Pines Campground	277 Mills Rd., Kennebunkport, 43°24'03.8"N 70°25'55.7"W	Tent sites, rental tents, RV sites, cabin tents, cabins, toilets, showers, potable water, laundry, pool, camp store, Wi-Fi	mid-May through mid-October	$61-259
207/967-2483; www.sandypinescamping.com				
Beach Acres Tent Sites & Park	76 Eldridge Rd., Wells, 43°17'27.1"N 70°35'14.1"W	Tent sites, RV sites, toilets, showers, potable water, laundry, pool, Wi-Fi	mid-May through September	$50-64
207/646-5612; www.beachacres.com				
Dixon's Campgrounds	1740 US-1, Cape Neddick, 43°13'11.1"N 70°36'39.3"W	Tent sites, RV sites, yurts, toilets, showers, potable water, pool, camp store, Wi-Fi	mid-May through mid-September	$44-650
207/363-3626; www.dixonscampground.com				
Libby's Oceanside Camp	725 York St., York, 43°08'49.7"N 70°37'34.4"W	Pop-up tent sites, RV sites, toilets, showers, potable water, laundry, Wi-Fi	mid-May through mid-October	$70-130
207/363-4171; www.libbysoceancamping.com				

THE MAHOOSUCS, EVANS NOTCH, AND RANGELEY LAKES

If New Hampshire's White Mountains had wilder, quieter, more artsy cousins, the mountains and forests of western Maine would fit the bill. Everything about this part of the state feels starker. The trees here come in darker shades of green. The rocks are more jagged and the boulders more unwieldy. The lonesome peaks that tower above the valleys here are too remote to be spoiled by the cacophony of summer and fall tourism. And western Maine's lakes and rivers are the stuff of legend for canoeing enthusiasts. In other words, western Maine is what hikers and outdoor adventurers live for—pure, isolated wilderness, far from the madding crowds and bountiful for those who make the pilgrimage.

▲ VIEW FROM THE SUMMIT OF TUMBLEDOWN MOUNTAIN

▲ ANGEL FALLS

◄ VIEW OF GRAFTON NOTCH

1 Angel Falls
DISTANCE: 1.4 mi (2.3 km) round-trip
DURATION: 1 hr
EFFORT: Easy
PAGE: 140

2 Tumbledown Mountain
DISTANCE: 5.8 mi (9.3 km) round-trip
DURATION: 4 hr
EFFORT: Strenuous
PAGE: 143

3 Dunn Falls
DISTANCE: 2.6 mi (4.2 km) round-trip
DURATION: 1.5 hr
EFFORT: Moderate
PAGE: 147

4 Old Speck
DISTANCE: 7.6 mi (12.2 km) round-trip
DURATION: 4.5 hr
EFFORT: Strenuous
PAGE: 151

5 Caribou Mountain
DISTANCE: 6.7 mi (10.8 km) round-trip
DURATION: 4.5 hr
EFFORT: Strenuous
PAGE: 155

6 Bickford Slides
DISTANCE: 2.3 mi (3.7 km) round-trip
DURATION: 1 hr
EFFORT: Easy/moderate
PAGE: 158

7 Lord Hill
DISTANCE: 4.3 mi (6.9 km) round-trip
DURATION: 2 hr
EFFORT: Easy
PAGE: 161

8 Androscoggin Riverlands
DISTANCE: 7.2 mi (11.6 km) round-trip
DURATION: 3.5 hr
EFFORT: Moderate
PAGE: 164

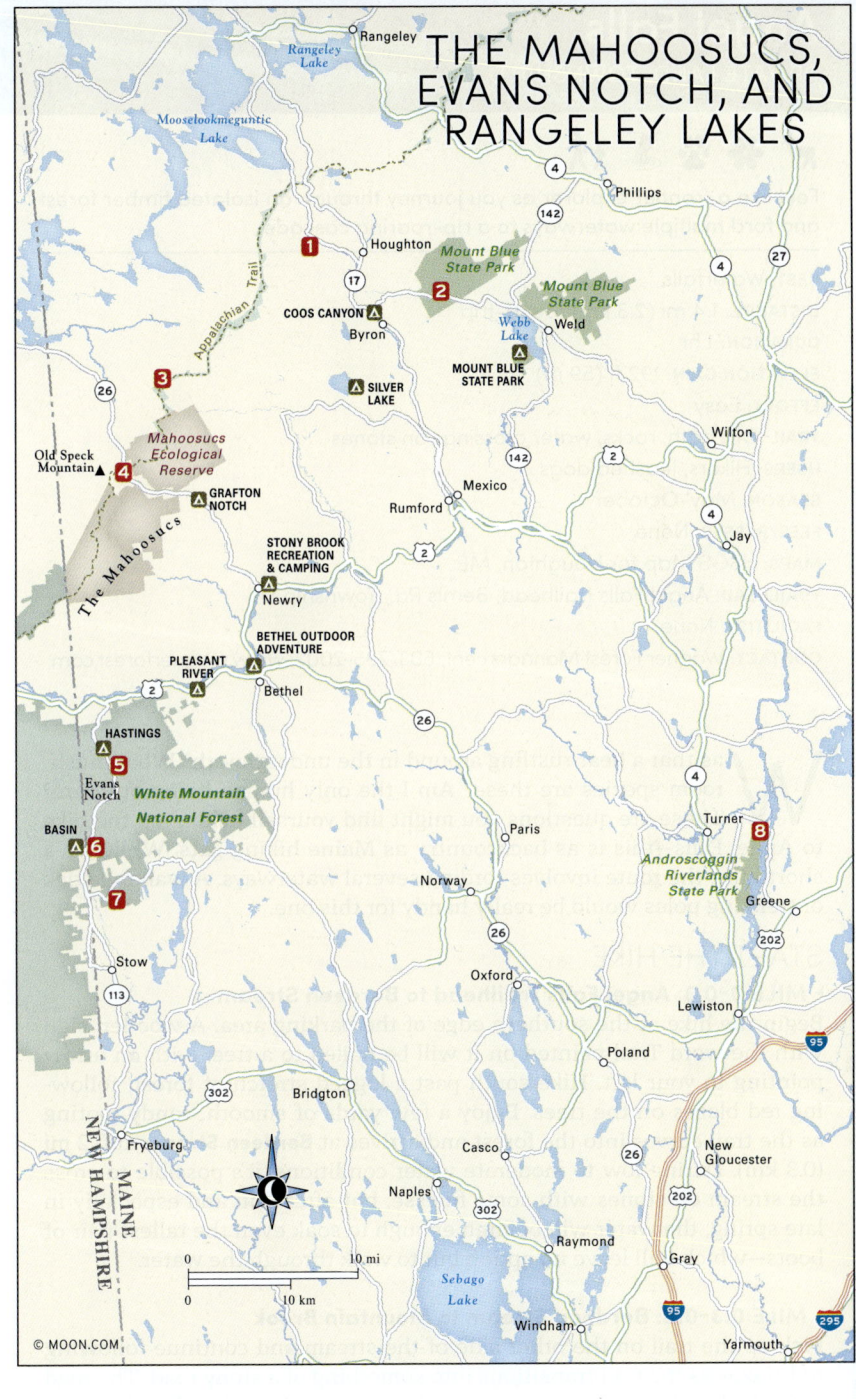

THE MAHOOSUCS, EVANS NOTCH, AND RANGELEY LAKES

Rangeley

Rangeley Lake

Mooselookmeguntic Lake

1

Houghton

Phillips

2

Mount Blue State Park

COOS CANYON

Byron

Mount Blue State Park

Webb Lake

Weld

SILVER LAKE

MOUNT BLUE STATE PARK

Wilton

3

Mahoosucs Ecological Reserve

Old Speck Mountain

4

GRAFTON NOTCH

Mexico

Rumford

The Mahoosucs

STONY BROOK RECREATION & CAMPING

Newry

Jay

BETHEL OUTDOOR ADVENTURE

PLEASANT RIVER

Bethel

HASTINGS

5

Evans Notch

White Mountain National Forest

Paris

Turner

8

Androscoggin Riverlands State Park

BASIN

6

Norway

Greene

7

Stow

Oxford

Lewiston

Bridgton

Poland

Fryeburg

Casco

New Gloucester

Naples

Raymond

Gray

Sebago Lake

Windham

Yarmouth

NEW HAMPSHIRE

MAINE

0   10 mi

0   10 km

© MOON.COM

Angel Falls

PRIVATE LAND, TOWNSHIP D

Feel like a frontier explorer as you journey through an isolated timber forest and ford multiple waterways to a rip-roaring cascade.

BEST: Waterfalls
DISTANCE: 1.4 mi (2.3 km) round-trip
DURATION: 1 hr
ELEVATION GAIN: 192 ft (59 m)
EFFORT: Easy
TRAIL: Dirt path, rocks, water crossings on stones
USERS: Hikers, leashed dogs
SEASON: May–October
FEES/PASSES: None
MAPS: USGS Map for Houghton, ME
TRAILHEAD: Angel Falls trailhead, Bemis Rd., Township D
FACILITIES: None
CONTACT: Wagner Forest Management; 603/795-2002; www.wagnerforest.com

Was that a bear rustling around in the undergrowth? What mushroom species are these? Am I the only human being out here? These are questions you might find yourself asking on the hike to Angel Falls—this is as backcountry as Maine hiking gets. While it's a short hike, the route involves fording several waterways. A walking stick or trekking poles would be really handy for this one.

START THE HIKE

▸ **MILE 0-0.3: Angel Falls Trailhead to Berdeen Stream**
Begin the hike at the southern edge of the parking area. A wooden sign with the word Trail painted on it will be nailed to a tree, with an arrow pointing to your left. Hike south past a logged stretch of forest, following red blazes on the trees. Enjoy a few yards of smooth, sandy footing as the trail curves into the forest and arrives at **Berdeen Stream** at 0.2 mi (0.3 km). During low to moderate water conditions, it's possible to cross the stream on stones with some finesse, but after rain and especially in late spring, the water will be high enough to soak even the tallest pair of boots—which will leave no option but to walk through the water.

▸ **MILE 0.3-0.5: Berdeen Stream to Mountain Brook**
Pick up the trail on the other side of the stream and continue following red blazes as the trail transitions into something of a stony road. The road is flanked with wildflowers and a variety of trees including beech, white birch, and spruce. After passing an open grassy area, the trail veers southwest into a much darker and thicker section of spruce woods and climbs

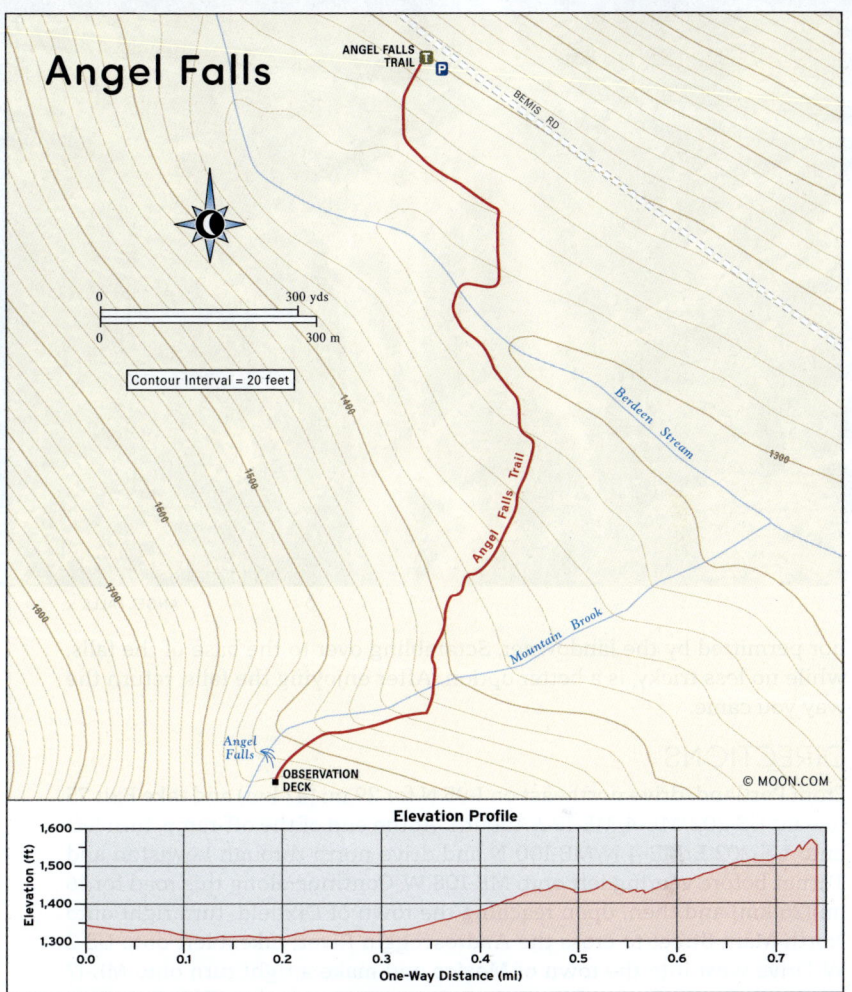

Angel Falls

ANGEL FALLS
TRAIL

BEMIS RD.

0 ——— 300 yds
0 ——— 300 m

Contour Interval = 20 feet

Angel Falls Trail

Berdeen Stream

Mountain Brook

1300

1400

1500

1600

1700

1800

Angel Falls

OBSERVATION DECK

© MOON.COM

Elevation Profile

Elevation (ft) — 1,600 / 1,500 / 1,400 / 1,300

One-Way Distance (mi) — 0.0 0.1 0.2 0.3 0.4 0.5 0.6 0.7

gradually. The footing becomes twisted with roots and quite rocky in places. After popping out onto an exposed and slippery ledge, the trail arrives at **Mountain Brook** at 0.5 mi (0.8 km). The water level isn't quite as high here, but the "stepping" stones are rough and ragged.

▶ MILE 0.5-0.7: Mountain Brook to Angel Falls Observation Deck
Hike west alongside Mountain Brook and watch your footing as the trail crosses the brook two more times, with comparably treacherous footing in places. After the third crossing, the trail climbs the bank of the brook at a steeper grade and bypasses some boulders. A dull roar from up ahead grows louder. Navigate a final pitch of rock slabs and you'll find yourself at a rough-hewn observation "deck" at 0.7 mi (1.1 km). Here you can admire and even feel the misty majesty of **Angel Falls,** a 90-ft-tall (27-m) cascade that crashes down a sheer cliff. Daredevil hikers might be tempted to scramble farther up the rocky embankment toward the top of the falls, but this is essentially bushwhacking and is neither recommended

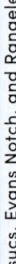

ANGEL FALLS ▲

nor permitted by the landowner. Scrambling over to the base of the falls, while no less tricky, is a better option. After enjoying the falls, return the way you came.

DIRECTIONS

From Portland, drive northeast on I-95 N for 29 mi (47 km) and take Exit 75 toward US-202/ME-4/ME-100/Auburn. At the end of the off-ramp, turn left onto US-202 E/ME-4 N/ME-100 N and drive north through Lewiston and Turner before veering left onto ME-108 W. Continue along this road for 16 mi (26 km) and then, upon reaching the town of Dixfield, turn right onto North Main Street to cross the Androscoggin River; take a left onto US-2 W. Drive west into the town of Mexico and make a right turn onto ME-17 W. Continue northwest for another 17 mi (27 km), make a left turn onto Houghton Road, and then turn right onto Bemis Road. The route becomes a dirt logging road. Drive northwest for 2 mi (3.2 km) or so until you reach a Y junction where you'll see a crude sign for the falls nailed to a tree. Turn left at this junction and arrive at the parking area.

GPS COORDINATES: 44°47'18.4"N 70°42'29.6"W

BEST NEARBY BITES

If you see hiking as more of a prelude to a raspberry sundae or a stacked chocolate waffle cone, motor down the road to Andover and enjoy some post–trail ice cream at **Kate's Kones** (52 S. Main St.; variable hours).

2

Tumbledown Mountain

TUMBLEDOWN PUBLIC LANDS, WELD

Make an exciting ascent—complete with cave spelunking—to an otherworldly summit with amazing views and an alpine pond.

BEST: Summer hikes

DISTANCE: 5.8 mi (9.3 km) round-trip

DURATION: 4 hr

ELEVATION GAIN: 1,899 ft (579 m)

EFFORT: Strenuous

TRAIL: Dirt path, rock scrambling, ladder climb, water crossings via stones and bog bridges

USERS: Hikers

SEASON: June–October

FEES/PASSES: None

MAPS: Maine Bureau of Parks and Lands website

TRAILHEAD: Loop trailhead, Byron Rd., Weld

FACILITIES: None

CONTACT: Maine Bureau of Parks and Lands; 207/778-8231; www.maine. gov/dacf/parks

Standing tall and defiant in the modest hills of Franklin County, Tumbledown Mountain, at 3,054 ft (931 m), is a dramatic sight. Hikers can reach this enchanting summit by two routes: the short, easier Brook Trail, or the more exciting Loop Trail, which is recommended for those who aren't afraid of heights, rock scrambling, or mild spelunking. Note that the Loop Trail should not be hiked during wet weather.

START THE HIKE

▶ **MILE 0-0.7: Loop Trailhead to Tumbledown Boulder**
Starting from the Loop trailhead, follow blue blazes as the rock-strewn trail snakes north through the woods for 0.2 mi (0.3 km). After crossing a creek, the trail starts to climb at a moderate grade before reaching the absurdly massive **Tumbledown Boulder** at 0.7 mi (1.1 km).

▶ **MILE 0.7-1.2: Tumbledown Boulder to Fat Man's Misery Cave**
From here, the real workout begins as the trail immediately climbs steeply up the lower haunch of Tumbledown Mountain through a jumble of boulders and roots. Catch your breath at a clearing at 1 mi (1.6 km) that offers a primo view of Tumbledown's sheer south face. Briefly descend into a patch of boreal forest before climbing straight up a rift in the south face at an even steeper grade than before. The trail here is somewhat eroded and bypasses rock slabs, some of which require handholds. At 1.2 mi (1.9 km), you'll come upon the infamous **Fat Man's Misery cave,** a narrow and damp

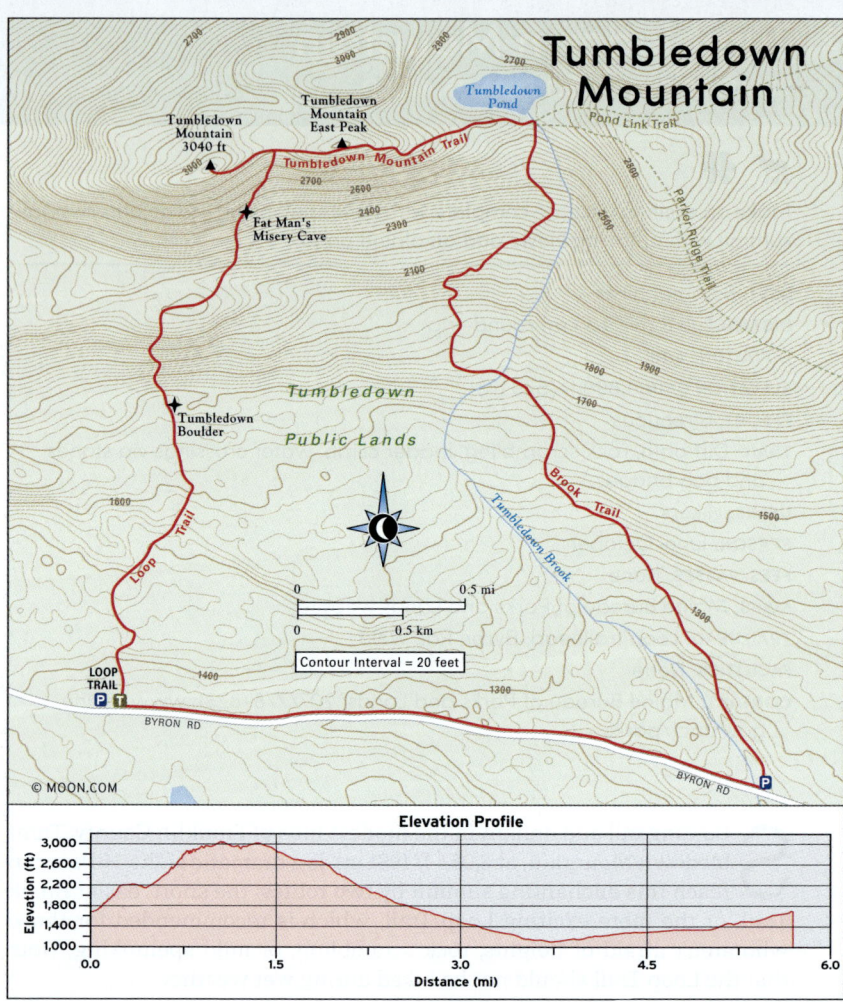

Tumbledown
Mountain

Elevation Profile

chimney cave through which hikers must hoist themselves with the help of three iron rungs that are attached to the interior walls. This doesn't require much upper-body strength but it's a tricky maneuver, so take your time.

▶ **MILE 1.2–1.8: Fat Man's Misery Cave to Tumbledown Mountain Summit**

After exiting the cave, the worst is over. Continue briefly up some rocks and at 1.6 mi (2.6 km), turn left onto **Tumbledown Mountain Trail** and hike west up a series of sloped slabs. You'll reach the summit of **Tumbledown Mountain** at 1.8 mi (2.9 km).

▶ **MILE 1.8–2.3: Tumbledown Mountain Summit to Tumbledown Mountain Trail**

After gazing across the lush panorama of western Maine, backtrack east to the junction of the Loop Trail and the Tumbledown Mountain Trail and

The Mahoosucs, Evans Notch, and Rangeley Lakes

▲ VIEW OF TUMBLEDOWN POND

veer left to continue along the Tumbledown Mountain Trail, which meanders across a windswept ridgeline for 0.5 mi (0.8 km). (Notice how the metamorphic rock contains visible flows of sediment!)

▶ **MILE 2.3–2.4: Tumbledown Mountain Trail to Tumbledown Pond**
A pleasant descent delivers you to the shores of **Tumbledown Pond**—a heavenly body of cerulean water with its own lightly forested island.

▶ **MILE 2.4–4.4: Tumbledown Pond to Brook Trail**
At 2.4 mi (3.9 km), pick up the **Brook Trail** beside the pond. Hike southeast down a mess of rocks strewn throughout the woods for about 0.6 mi (1 km), before the trail softens and widens into an old streambed at 3 mi (4.8 km). Continue along the path through corridors of white birches, rock-hopping your way across a series of streams, over the next 1.4 mi (2.3 km). Mind your step: Tiny eastern American toads are active here.

▶ **MILE 4.4–5.8: Brook Trail to Byron Road and Loop Trailhead**
The Brook Trail reaches **Byron Road** at 4.4 mi (7.1 km). Turn right and walk west along the sunlit road for an easy 1.4 mi (2.3 km) back to the Loop Trail parking area, completing the hike at 5.8 mi (9.3 km).

DIRECTIONS

From Boston or Portland, drive north on I-95 toward Lewiston/Augusta. Take Exit 75 and turn left onto ME-100 N/ME-4 N/US-202 E. Drive into Lewiston and continue straight onto ME-4 N. Take this road north for 20 mi (32 km) and then turn left onto ME 108-W. Drive northwest for another 16 mi (26 km) to Dixfield and then take a right onto Main Street over the bridge; then make another right onto US-2 E. Head east briefly before taking a left onto ME-142 N and continuing north into Carthage. Turn left

SHORE OF TUMBLEDOWN POND ▲

onto West Road and continue north past Webb Lake until you reach Byron Road. Take a final left onto Byron Road and follow the dirt road west past the Brook Trail parking lot to the nearby Loop Trail parking area. Begin your hike in the parking area along Byron Road. Cross the road to the trailhead sign for the Loop Trail and enter a thick deciduous forest.

GPS COORDINATES: 44°43'52.8"N 70°33'17.4"W

BEST NEARBY BITES AND BREWS

After gazing out at Webb Lake from the top of Tumbledown, take in the lake from a different perspective at **Kawanhee Inn** (12 Anne's Way, Weld; 207/585-2000; www.kawanheeinn.com), where you'll find hearty comfort food and Maine beers at the **in-house pub** (5pm-9pm Tues.-Sun. summer). Call the inn to inquire about limited dining hours during the fall.

Visit two towering and thunderous cascades along one of the most remote segments of the Appalachian Trail.

DISTANCE: 2.6 mi (4.2 km) round-trip

DURATION: 1.5 hr

ELEVATION GAIN: 492 ft (150 m)

EFFORT: Moderate

TRAIL: Dirt path, water crossings on rocks, wooden bog bridges

USERS: Hikers, leashed dogs

SEASON: June–early October

FEES/PASSES: None

MAPS: USGS map for B Pond, ME

TRAILHEAD: Appalachian Trail parking lot, East B Hill Rd., North Andover Surplus

FACILITIES: None

CONTACT: Town of Andover; 207/392-3302; www.andovermaine.org

Thru-hikers often cite western Maine as one of the most brutal sections of the Appalachian Trail because of how relentlessly rocky and isolated the trail can get. Dunn Falls, a duo of crashing cascades folded into the forest on the north edge of the Mahoosucs, offers an ethereal respite from the long slog. And as a day trip, the loop hike to Dunn Falls offers just enough climbing, scrambling, and rock-hopping to make you feel like you're earning your AT wings. If you've got waterproof boots, you'll want them for this hike.

START THE HIKE

▶ **MILE 0–0.7: Appalachian Trail Parking Lot to Ellis River**

Begin the hike in the parking lot for the Appalachian Trail. Walk south down East B Hill Road for about 100 yards, until you see a white blazed trail disappearing into the woods on both sides of the road. Turn right and pick up the **Appalachian Trail** as it descends stone stairs toward the rippling of a brook. Almost immediately, the trail reaches a signed junction. Turn left onto the **Cascade Trail** and follow yellow blazes alongside the brook, as the rocky, rooty trail descends at a moderate grade and passes several small waterfalls. Consider these a foreshadowing of sights to come. After making the first of several water crossings at 0.6 mi (1 km), the trail climbs and descends a wooded ridge at a steeper grade, delivering you to the West Branch of the **Ellis River.** Rock-hop across the wider, faster Ellis River and follow it through fern-festooned woods, listening for a deep roar up ahead.

The Mahoosucs, Evans Notch, and Rangeley Lakes | MAINE

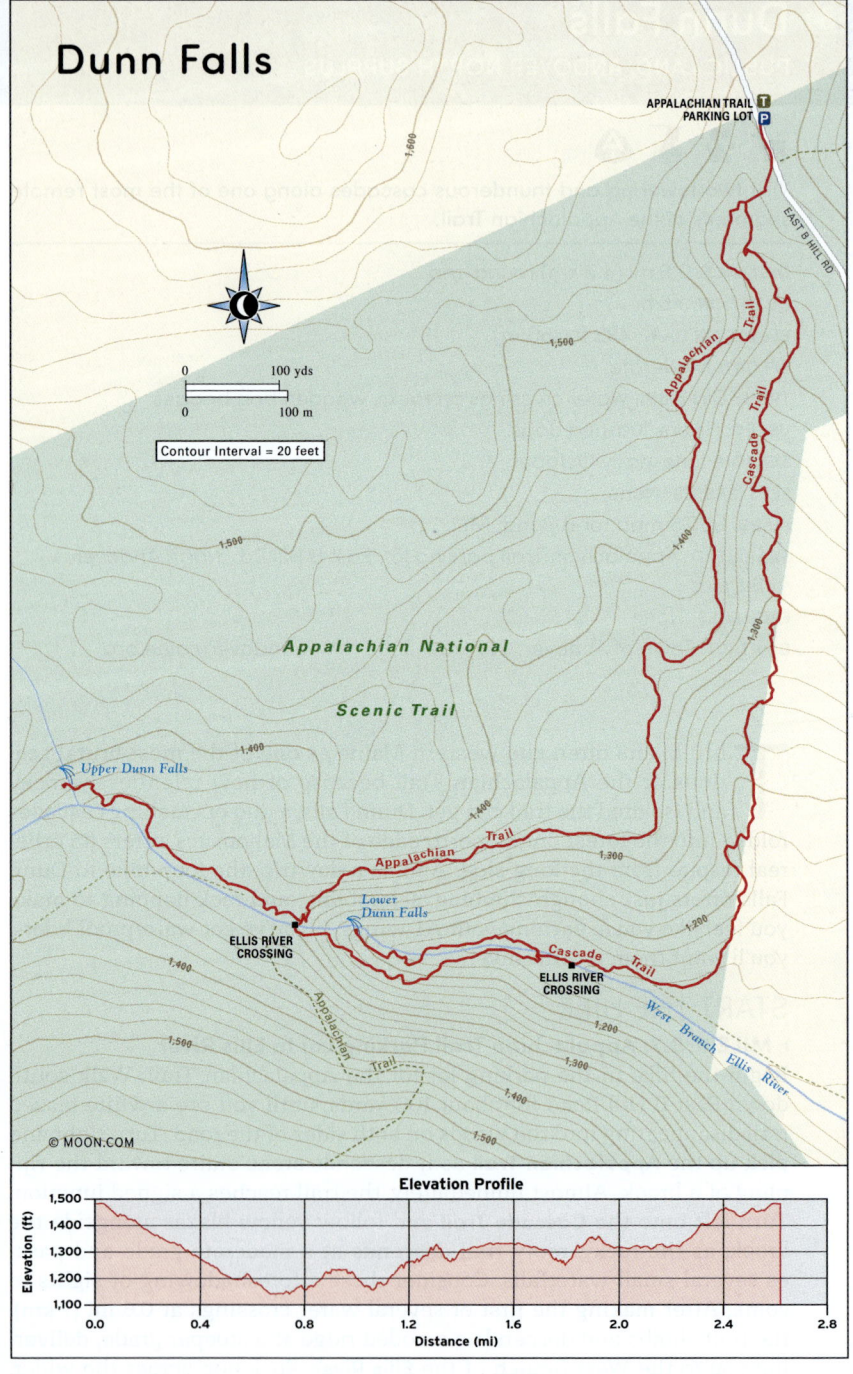

Dunn Falls

APPALACHIAN TRAIL
PARKING LOT

EAST B HILL RD

Appalachian Trail

Cascade Trail

1,600

1,500

0   100 yds
0   100 m

Contour Interval = 20 feet

1,500

1,500

Appalachian National

Scenic Trail

1,400

Upper Dunn Falls

1,400

1,400

Appalachian   Trail

1,300

Lower
Dunn Falls

1,200

ELLIS RIVER
CROSSING

Cascade   Trail

1,400

ELLIS RIVER
CROSSING

West Branch Ellis River

Appalachian

Trail

1,200

1,500

1,300

1,400

1,500

© MOON.COM

Elevation Profile

Elevation (ft)

1,500
1,400
1,300
1,200
1,100

0.0   0.4   0.8   1.2   1.6   2.0   2.4   2.8

Distance (mi)

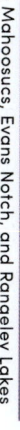

▲ LOWER DUNN FALLS

▶ **MILE 0.7-1.2: Ellis River to Top of Lower Dunn Falls**

At 0.7 mi (1.1 km), the trail forks. Turn right to begin your approach to Lower Dunn Falls on the blue-blazed cutoff path. As you enter the depths of a narrow, dank ravine, watch your footing as the trail becomes little more than a thin ledge of slippery stone surfaces. The 80-ft (24-m) plume of **Lower Dunn Falls** appears suddenly at 0.9 mi (1.4 km), like a torrent of white lightning. To reach the base of the falls, you can scramble your way through some boulders amassed below the cascade. Or you can admire it from a safer distance.

To continue, backtrack to the fork and turn right to pick up the Cascade Trail again, as it climbs the shoulder of the ravine at a moderately steep grade. Upon leveling out at 1.2 mi (1.9 km), the trail ends at the top of **Lower Dunn Falls,** where the Appalachian Trail crosses the Ellis River.

▶ **MILE 1.2-1.5: Top of Lower Dunn Falls to Upper Dunn Falls**

Cross the river once again and pull yourself up the eroded embankment with exposed tree roots. Then make a left turn onto a blue-blazed path that branches off the AT and continues uphill alongside the river. You'll pass several inviting pools and likely a few campfire rings from thru-hikers drawn to the placid river. At 1.5 mi (2.4 km), the full 70-ft (21-m) heft of the fan cascade of **Upper Dunn Falls** comes into view. It's a sublime sight that many hikers miss in their haste to visit the better-known lower falls.

▶ **MILE 1.5–2.6: Upper Dunn Falls to Appalachian Trail Parking Lot**

Retrace your steps to the junction and make a left onto the Appalachian Trail. The return journey to the parking lot involves a surprising amount of roller-coastering terrain, as the trail negotiates several forested hills. At 1.8 mi (2.9 km), look through the trees on your right for a partial view of the woodlands you traversed to reach the falls. After several tributary crossings, at 2.4 mi (3.9 km) the trail finally arrives back at the brook from where you began your hike on the Cascade Trail. Keep left this time and follow the Appalachian Trail up to East B Hill Road and the parking lot.

DIRECTIONS

From Portland, drive northeast on I-295 N for 1 mi (1.6 km) and take Exit 8 for ME-26/Washington Avenue. Continue north on ME-26 for 4 mi (6.4 km), and then make a right onto the toll road that connects ME-26 to I-95. Make a right to merge onto I-95 N and drive north for 10 mi (16 km). Take Exit 63 for US-202/ME-115/ME-4 toward ME-26/Gray/New Gloucester. At the bottom of the off-ramp, turn left onto US-202 W and then make an immediate right onto ME-26A N. Continue north along this road as it becomes ME-26 N and take it all the way to the town of Woodstock, where you'll turn right onto ME-232 N. Drive to its terminus in Hanover, turn left onto US-2 W, and then make a right onto ME-5 N. Follow this local highway to the town of Andover and turn left onto Upton Road. The road ascends into the woods and becomes East B Hill Road. After 8 mi (12.9 km), look for the Appalachian Trail parking lot on your right.

GPS COORDINATES: 44°40'05.9"N 70°53'35.4"W

BEST NEARBY BREWS

For a sudsy post-hike reward, sidle up to the bar and order a local lager at **The Knotty Moose** (1359 Roxbury Notch Rd., Roxbury; 207/670-8778; 11am–8pm Thurs.–Sun.).

4 Old Speck

GRAFTON NOTCH STATE PARK, NEWRY

Maine's third-tallest mountain has it all—alpine flowers, cascades, and gorgeous vistas.

DISTANCE: 7.6 mi (12.2 km) round-trip

DURATION: 4.5 hr

ELEVATION GAIN: 2,913 ft (889 m)

EFFORT: Strenuous

TRAIL: Dirt path, rocks, iron rungs, wooden bog bridges, water crossings on stones

USERS: Hikers

SEASON: June–October

FEES/PASSES: $3 day-use fee for Maine residents, $4 for nonresidents

MAPS: Grafton Notch State Park website

TRAILHEAD: Information kiosk, Old Speck parking lot, Route 26, Newry

FACILITIES: Vault toilet

CONTACT: Grafton Notch State Park; 207/824-2912; www.maine.gov/graftonnotch

The third-tallest mountain in Maine at 4,170 ft (1,271 m), which rises high above the craggy Grafton Notch, can be seen from many miles away on a clear day. The hike to the top is challenging, with some rock climbing up and across the exposed cliffs on the lower eastern face of the mountain, but the reward at the top is worth it. Just be sure to save Old Speck for a clear day—it gets slippery during rainy weather.

START THE HIKE

▶ **MILE 0-0.9: Information Kiosk to Grafton Notch Overlook**

Begin the hike in the parking lot by the trail information kiosk. Pick up the **Appalachian Trail** and walk along a stony path into birch and beech woods. Turn right onto the **Eyebrow Trail** at 0.1 mi (0.16 km). Follow orange blazes as the trail crosses several bog bridges before climbing some steep and winding rock stairs. Ascend into a denser and greener stretch of spruce woods before reaching an obstacle of sorts at 0.5 mi (0.8 km). The trail climbs an extremely steep series of **rock slabs** with the aid of steel cables anchored into the rock on posts. Use the cables as handholds as you ascend the slabs to arrive at a sloped and exposed cliff face. Carefully cross the cliff face with the aid of metal rungs affixed to the rock and reach a small ladder on the other side that takes you back into the woods. Climb a final set of iron rungs up the steep and mossy wooded hillside to reach surer footing.

Continue ascending steeply along the rocky trail as it ascends the eastern face of the mountain. Partial views of Grafton Notch through the trees

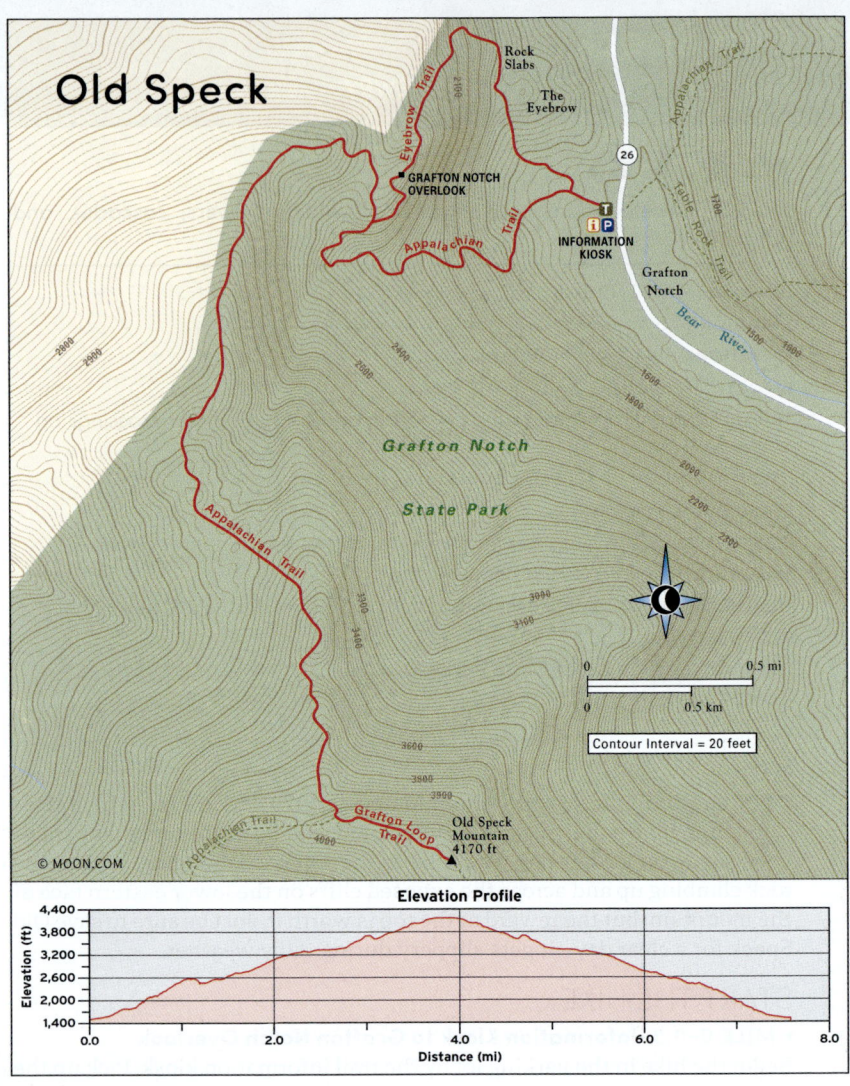

Old Speck

Elevation Profile

will try to fool you into thinking you're almost there—you're not, but a beautiful reward lies ahead at 0.9 mi (1.4 km), where the trail reaches a height of land with a stunning and picturesque **Grafton Notch overlook.** The dome-like summit of Old Speck looms ahead to the south.

▶ **MILE 0.9–3.6: Grafton Notch Overlook to Grafton Loop Trail and Old Speck Summit**

The trail ambles up and down a wooded ridge with lots of boreal spruce trees. At 1.2 mi (1.9 km), turn right onto the **Appalachian Trail.**

After briefly heading north, the AT shifts south to begin the long and steady 2.4-mi (3.9-km) climb up Old Speck's elongated northern slopes. The rock up here glitters with traces of mica and feldspar, which is noticeable even on gray, foggy days. Follow white blazes and cairns up rock stairs

▲ THE LOOMING PINNACLE OF OLD SPECK

and slabs as the trail dips in and out of the trees. Check out the views to the east to see Maine's Table Rock and to the west to see the boglands of northern New Hampshire. Here the exposure and alpine tundra become constant. At 3.5 mi (5.6 km), turn left onto **Grafton Loop Trail** and stroll up the gently graded summit spur to arrive at the **Old Speck summit** at 3.6 mi (5.8 km). The 360-degree view from the mossy and exposed peak is one for the ages, with sweeping views into northern New Hampshire, Maine, and Canada. Brave hikers can climb the ladder up the 40-ft-tall (12-m) summit fire tower for an even wilder view. (This rickety, steep climb is not for the faint of heart.)

▶ **MILE 3.6–7.6: Old Speck Summit to Appalachian Trail and Information Kiosk**

To begin the return journey, backtrack along the Grafton Loop Trail, turn right onto the AT again, and retrace your steps down the north ridge to the junction with **Eyebrow Trail** at 6.1 mi (9.8 km). This time turn right to stay on the AT, which descends rock stairs beside a series of chuckling cascades that spill and swirl beside the trail. As the grade and the ground conditions soften, the trail crosses a creek on rocks, then segues to a rooty dirt path that meets the Eyebrow Trail again at 7.5 mi (12.1 km). Keep right on the AT and continue to the parking lot to conclude the loop at 7.6 mi (12.2 km).

DIRECTIONS

From Portland, drive southwest on I-295 S and take Exit 1 for I-95 N. Merge onto I-95 N and drive north for 17 mi (27 km). Take Exit 63 for US-202/ME-115/ME-4 toward ME-26/Gray/New Gloucester. At the bottom of the off-ramp, turn left onto US-202 W and then make an immediate right onto ME-26A N. Continue north along this road as it becomes ME-26 N and take

it all the way to the town of Bethel, where you'll turn right onto US-2 E. Drive north to Newry and then make a left turn onto ME-26 N. Continue northwest for 12 mi (19 km) as the road enters Grafton Notch State Park and watch for the Old Speck parking lot on your left.

GPS COORDINATES: 44°35'23.4"N 70°56'49.9"W

BEST NEARBY BITES AND BREWS

Believe it or not, some of the best pork-pulling and brisket smoking in the north country is happening in a humble food truck parked near Grafton Notch; if you're looking for a celebratory feast after coming down Old Speck, drive south to **Smokin' Good BBQ** (212 Mayville Rd., Bethel; 207/824-4744; www.smokingoodbarbecue.com; 11:30am-7:30pm Fri.-Sun.). If you prefer your victory dance in liquid form, try the Pine Hill Porter or the Whitecap Blueberry wheat ale over at **Steam Mill Brewing** (96 Sunday River Rd., Bethel; 207/824-1149; www.steammillbrew.com; 2pm-8pm Mon.-Tues., 2pm-9pm Thurs., noon-9pm Fri.-Sat., noon-7pm Sun.).

5 Caribou Mountain

EVANS NOTCH, SOUTH OXFORD

Climb this modest peak for one of the most beautiful panoramic views in the Northeast.

BEST: Fall hikes, vistas

DISTANCE: 6.7 mi (10.8 km) round-trip

DURATION: 4.5 hr

ELEVATION GAIN: 1,898 ft (579 m)

EFFORT: Strenuous

TRAIL: Dirt path, rocks, wooden bog bridges, water crossings on stones

USERS: Hikers, leashed dogs

SEASON: June–October

FEES/PASSES: None

MAPS: White Mountain National Forest website

TRAILHEAD: Mud Brook trailhead, Route 113, South Oxford

FACILITIES: Vault toilet

CONTACT: White Mountain National Forest; 603/536-6100; www.fs.usda.gov/detail/whitemountain

START THE HIKE

▶ **MILE 0-1.6: Mud Brook Trailhead to Mud Brook Crossing**
From the east end of the parking lot, walk south toward the sign for the **Mud Brook Trail.** Step into the forest on a spacious dirt path that weaves through mixed woods. Follow yellow blazes, listening for water echoing from ahead. Reach **Mud Brook** at 0.3 mi (0.5 km) and hike east along the brook as the trail narrows into a shelf-like path. Climb along the hillside, ascending at an easy grade while the path becomes rockier and rootier. The grade is surprisingly gentle for the next 1 mi (1.6 km), with only a few notable dips and rises. After crossing some tributaries, descend **rock stairs** at 1.6 mi (2.6 km) and cross the brook.

▶ **MILE 1.6-3.0: Mud Brook Crossing to Caribou Mountain Summit**
Continue the gradual ascent to another brook crossing at 1.9 mi (3.1 km). From here, the real climb begins as the trail steepens considerably and by-passes several rock staircases. Through the trees, glimpses of nearby mountains offer a sense of how much elevation you've gained. The trail slowly becomes a thin, wooded ledge along a very steep stretch of mountainside. Note that the trail is rather eroded in places. Scramble up some rock slabs into darker boreal spruce trees. At 2.8 mi (4.5 km), the trail reaches a scenic **overlook** atop some cliffs. A brief descent takes you back into the woods before your final steeper schlep. Climb rock stairs and slabs through the

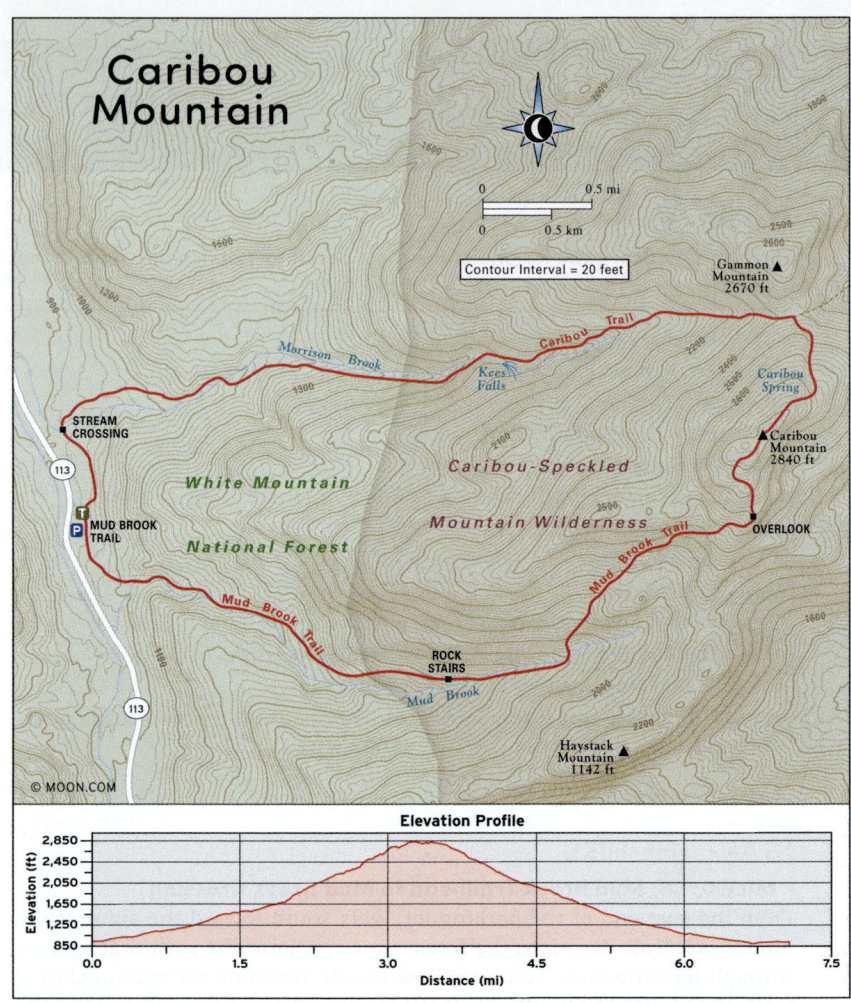

Caribou
Mountain

Gammon
Mountain
2670 ft

Caribou Trail

Morrison Brook

Kees
Falls

Caribou
Spring

STREAM
CROSSING

Caribou
Mountain
2840 ft

113

Caribou-Speckled

White Mountain

Mountain Wilderness

OVERLOOK

MUD BROOK
TRAIL

National Forest

Mud Brook Trail

Mud Brook Trail

ROCK
STAIRS

113

Mud Brook

Haystack
Mountain
1142 ft

© MOON.COM

Contour Interval = 20 feet

0   0.5 mi

0   0.5 km

Elevation Profile

increasingly mossy forest for 0.2 mi (0.3 km) before emerging onto a granite
summit at 3 mi (4.8 km). This marks the official summit of **Caribou Mountain.** The vista from the top of Caribou Mountain is truly incredible. On a
semi-clear day, you can gaze out to the Whites, the Great North Woods, the
Mahoosucs, the Rangeley Lakes, and the hills of southwestern Maine.

▶ **MILE 3.0–4.0: Caribou Mountain Summit to Caribou Trail**
To continue the loop, follow little cairns on the summit and look for yellow blazes on the rocks. The path alternates between exposed rock and a
ribbon-like trail through the boreal forest and tundra, skirting northeast
along the broad upper slopes of the mountain. After descending a longer
stretch of granite, the trail dips back into the forest and descends some
steep slabs and slippery rock stairs to reach the Caribou Trail junction
at 3.7 mi (6 km). Turn left onto the **Caribou Trail** and descend through a
strange section of forest with lots of blowdowns and unusually high sun
exposure before entering a more deciduous ravine.

▶ **MILE 4.0-6.7: Caribou Trail to Mud Brook Trailhead**

At 4 mi (6.4 km), a stream presents the first of many crossings on the way down. As the trail grade becomes more gradual, passing several cascades along the stream, the forest transitions to tall spruce and hemlocks. Mind your footing on the rockier sections of the descent. At 5.3 mi (8.5 km), the trail levels, becoming a cruise through the woods. At 5.7 mi (9.2 km), make another stream crossing, after which the trail becomes wider and smoother before reaching the final and largest of the **stream crossings** at 6.4 mi (10.3 km); some ruins of an old wooden bridge remain here. (The water level at this crossing can become high enough to saturate boots.) On the other side, climb a few sets of stone stairs, pick your way over some exposed roots, and then descend to the trailhead parking lot at 6.7 mi (10.8 km).

DIRECTIONS

From Portsmouth, New Hampshire, drive north on NH-16 N to the town of Conway. Keep right at the junction for NH-16 N and NH-113 E to continue driving east on NH-113 E. After 2 mi (3.2 km), turn left onto US-302 W and then make a right onto East Conway Road. Drive northeast for 6 mi (9.7 km) and then swing a right onto West Fryeburg Road. Here you'll briefly cross into Maine as you continue north along West Fryeburg Road, which eventually becomes Stow Road. At the junction with ME-113B, veer slightly right to stay on Stow Road and follow it north for another 11 mi (18 km). As you approach Evans Notch, the road becomes ME-113. After passing Bull Brook Campground on the left, look for a hiker sign on the right and turn onto the cutoff road here to reach the parking lot for Caribou Mountain. Begin the hike on the east end of the parking lot.

GPS COORDINATES: 44°20'09.0"N 70°58'31.8"W

BEST NEARBY BITES

Coming down from a view as splendorous as Caribou's can be hard, so make the transition easier with a sumptuous dinner of braised lamb shank, wild mushroom gnocchi, or one of many other indulgent options at **The Elizabeth** (32 Main St., Bethel; 207/824-1089; www.theelizabethmaine.com; 4pm–9pm Wed.–Sun.).

The Mahoosucs, Evans Notch, and Rangeley Lakes

MAINE

Visit a pretty series of cascades that tumble through a dark and densely forested ravine.

DISTANCE: 2.3 mi (3.7 km) round-trip

DURATION: 1 hr

ELEVATION GAIN: 609 ft (186 m)

EFFORT: Easy/moderate

TRAIL: Dirt path, water crossings on stones

USERS: Hikers, leashed dogs

SEASON: June–October

FEES/PASSES: $5 day-use fee (per vehicle)

MAPS: White Mountain National Forest website

TRAILHEAD: Brickett Place parking lot, Route 113, Stow

FACILITIES: Vault toilet

CONTACT: White Mountain National Forest; 603/536-6100; www.fs.usda.gov/detail/whitemountain

Some of the best-kept secrets of the White Mountains are housed in ravines—those wooded, rocky clefts sandwiched between the more heavily trafficked mountains. On the southern end of Evans Notch, a splendid series of waterfalls known as the Bickford Slides await hikers curious enough to venture into the narrow space between Sugarloaf Mountain and Blueberry Mountain.

START THE HIKE

▶ **MILE 0-0.6: Brickett Place Parking Lot to Blueberry Ridge Trail**
Find the wooden sign for the **Bickford Brook Trail** at the east side of the parking lot. Pick up the dirt trail as it enters an airy birch forest. The trail, rooty and rocky at first, climbs a hillside at a moderate grade heading northeast before leveling out briefly and then resuming the climb at a gentler angle. Continue your ascent, stepping over some rock water bars.

The trail gets smoother and more spacious as the mixed trees transition into much taller hemlocks. Listen for the promising sound of rippling water as the trail climbs into the ravine between Sugarloaf and Blueberry along a wooded hillside. Down the slope to your right, you can see and hear **Bickford Brook**. At 0.6 mi (1 km), turn right onto **Blueberry Ridge Trail**.

▶ **MILE 0.6-0.9: Blueberry Ridge Trail to Bickford Slides Trail**
A brief descent to Bickford Brook delivers you to another junction with the Bickford Slides Trail. The positioning of the sign here is slightly confusing—to continue in the right direction, make a slight left toward the smaller sign that reads Trail (attached to a tree just beyond the Bickford Slides

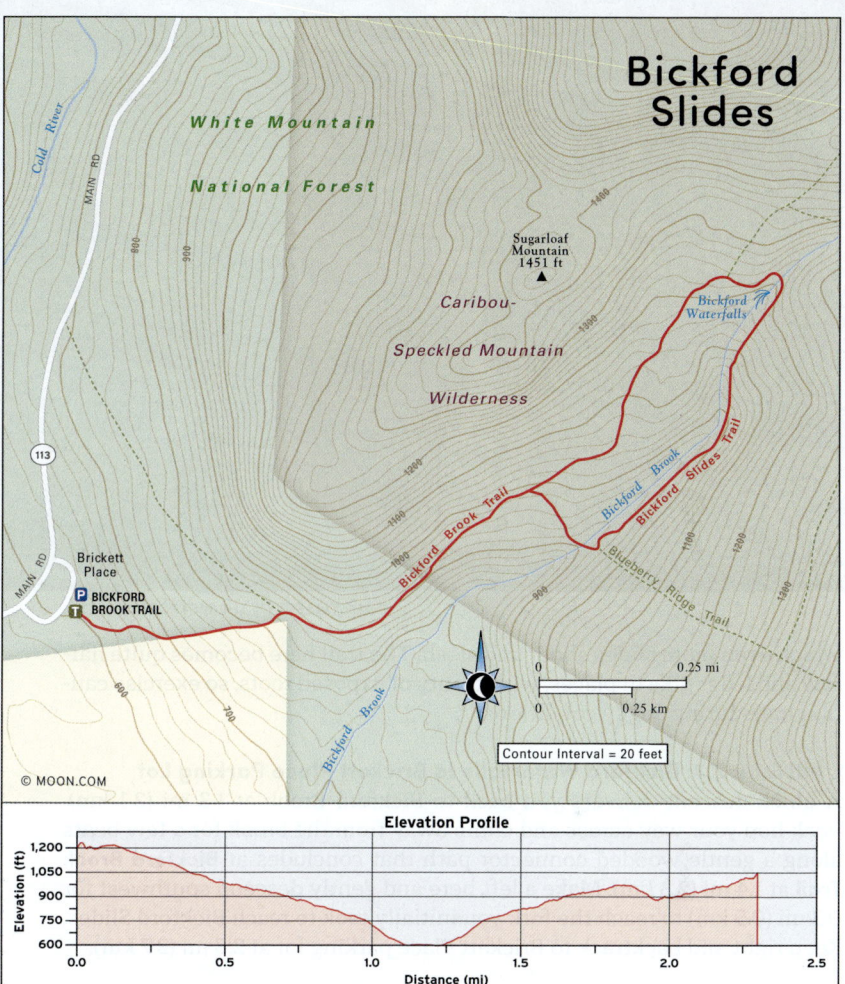

Bickford Slides

White Mountain
National Forest

Sugarloaf
Mountain
1451 ft

Caribou-
Speckled Mountain

Wilderness

Bickford
Waterfalls

Bickford Brook Trail

Bickford Brook

Bickford Slides Trail

Blueberry Ridge Trail

Brickett
Place

BICKFORD
BROOK TRAIL

Bickford Brook

Cold River

MAIN RD

113

MAIN RD

0   0.25 mi

0   0.25 km

Contour Interval = 20 feet

© MOON.COM

Elevation Profile

Elevation (ft): 1,200 / 1,050 / 900 / 750 / 600

Distance (mi): 0.0 / 0.5 / 1.0 / 1.5 / 2.0 / 2.5

sign), and cross Bickford Brook on rocks. On the other side of the brook, veer left to take the **Bickford Slides Trail.** Amble along the brook on a much skinnier dirt path that bypasses several little tributaries and a few muddier zones. Continue hiking northeast along the increasingly lively brook as the woods get mossier, denser, and darker.

▶ **MILE 0.9–1.1: Bickford Slides Trail to Bickford Waterfalls**

A set of miniature cascades at 0.9 mi (1.4 km) marks the beginning of the slides. Make a steeper ascent along a more eroded stretch of trail, catching glimpses of more silvery slides before reaching a reflecting pool into which a big, beautiful 40-ft-tall (12-m) **waterfall** spills. The trail passes above the pool, but you can scramble down the embankment to your left to reach the water for a better view. The trail climbs alongside the falls at a steep grade; watch your footing as you make this ascent. A small wooden arrow confirms that you're on the right track. Once you reach the top of the big slide, enjoy a gentler stroll along the rim of a little "canyon" through

which even more slides shoot and slosh. The trail here becomes quite narrow and ledge-like in places, with plenty of exposed roots, so exercise caution here during soggy conditions.

▶ **MILE 1.1–2.3: Bickford Waterfalls to Brickett Place Parking Lot**
A quick descent delivers you back to Bickford Brook at 1.3 mi (2.1 km). Rock-hop your way across and climb away from the brook for a few beats along a gentle wooded connector path that concludes at **Bickford Brook Trail** at 1.4 mi (2.3 km). Make a left here and gently descend southwest for 0.3 mi (0.5 km) to reach the fork you initially took to reach Bickford Slides. Keep right and backtrack to Brickett Place parking lot at 2.3 mi (3.7 km).

DIRECTIONS

From Portsmouth, New Hampshire, drive north on NH-16 N to the town of Conway. Keep right at the junction for NH-16 N and NH-113 E to continue driving east on NH-113 E. After 2 mi (3.2 km), turn left onto US-302 W and then make a right onto East Conway Road. Drive northeast for 6 mi (9.7 km) and then swing right onto West Fryeburg Road. You'll briefly cross into Maine as you continue north along West Fryeburg Road, which eventually becomes Stow Road. At the junction with ME-113B, veer slightly right to stay on Stow Road and follow it north for another 7 mi (11.3 km) as you cross back into New Hampshire. The road will become ME-113 as you enter Evans Notch. After passing a large sign for The Basin on your left, a sign for Brickett Place will appear on your right almost immediately. Turn right onto the cutoff road here and park in the lot beside the preserved farmhouse.

GPS COORDINATES: 44°16'01.5"N 71°00'14.5"W

🦌 ❀ 🐾 🚶

Hike past ruins and through two distinct forest areas to a pretty pond vista.

DISTANCE: 4.3 mi (6.9 km) round-trip

DURATION: 2 hr

ELEVATION GAIN: 811 ft (247 m)

EFFORT: Easy

TRAIL: Dirt path, rocks, wooden bridges, river crossings on stones, metal ladders

USERS: Hikers, leashed dogs

SEASON: May–October

FEES/PASSES: None

MAPS: White Mountain National Forest website

TRAILHEAD: Conant trailhead, Deer Hill Rd., Stow

FACILITIES: None

CONTACT: White Mountain National Forest; 603/536-6100; www.fs.usda.gov/detail/whitemountain

A stroll up Lord Hill offers a unique and enchanting walk from a traditional New Hampshire forest zone to a traditional Maine one. Along the way, you'll encounter backcountry relics such as crumbling stone walls, a graveyard, and even an abandoned mining site that awaits hikers near the top of the 1,257-ft-tall (383-m) "hill."

START THE HIKE

▶ **MILE 0-1.2: Conant Trail to Mine Loop Junction**
Turn left onto the **Conant Trail,** which is really a rocky, eroded road. The road ambles east through an open stretch of marshland before tunneling into a deciduous forest of beech trees. Climb gently through the woods as the road passes an A-frame house and some cottages. Veer right at the sign for **Lord Hill** at 0.4 mi (0.6 km) and walk on. The trail continues east and swings by a small graveyard before arriving at an **unmarked junction** at 0.6 mi (1 km). Take a left here to stay on the Conant Trail and ascend a steeper hillside.

As the road curves left, continue straight as the Conant Trail becomes narrower and rockier and enters a darker stretch of forest. The trail follows an old creek bed as it begins a steady, occasionally steep climb through spruce and birch trees (look for yellow blazes henceforth). Turn left at the Mine Loop junction at 1.2 mi (1.9 km) to stay on the Conant Trail.

▶ **MILE 1.2-2.3: Mine Loop Junction to Lord Hill Summit**
Continue a gentle ascent, meandering past some old stone walls that have been reclaimed by the forest. After rolling up and down mildly for a bit,

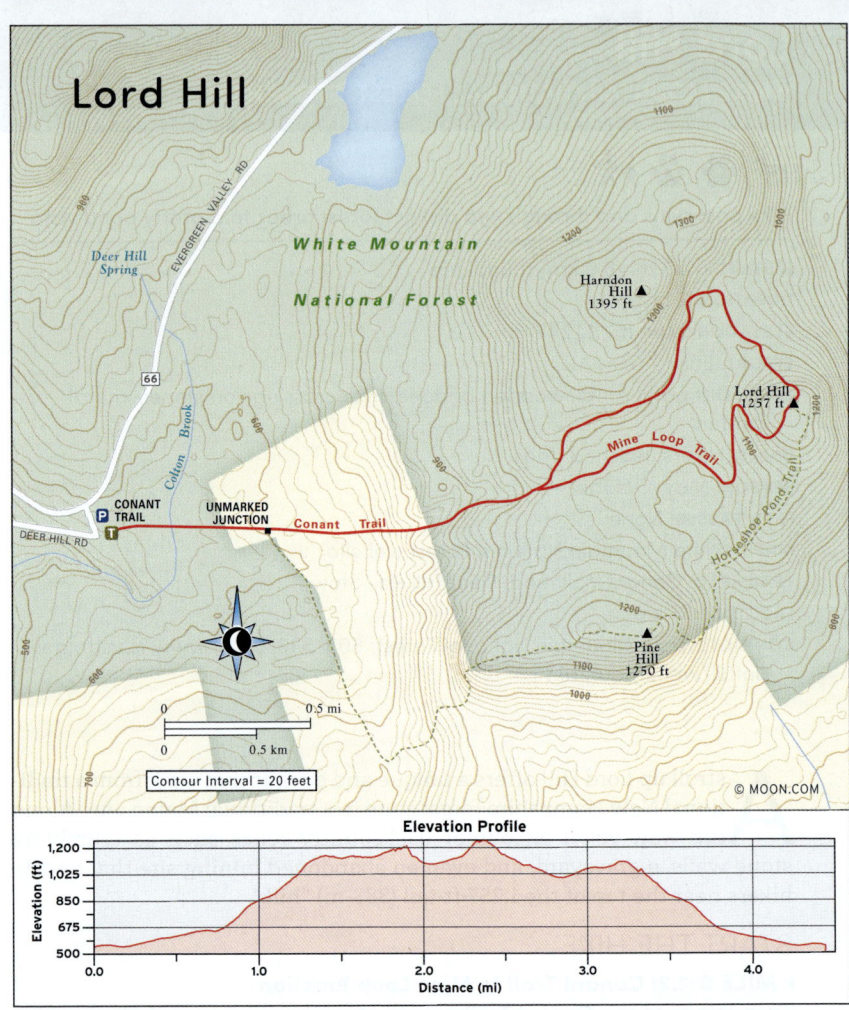

Lord Hill

Elevation Profile

the trail suddenly enters an airier stretch of pine and spruce forest around 1.8 mi (2.9 km). The greenery of the trees and the abundant moss is dizzying, and the breeze foreshadows what's just ahead.

At 2.1 mi (3.4 km), turn right at the Horseshoe Pond Trail junction to stay on the Conant Trail. Climb a steeper pitch, arriving at the top of **Lord Hill** at 2.3 mi (3.7 km). On a clear day, the summit offers a primo view of **Horseshoe Pond,** which is shaped exactly like you'd expect.

▶ MILE 2.3-2.7: Lord Hill Summit to Mine Loop Trail

Once you've had your fill, pick up the **Mine Loop Trail** at the sign on the summit and hike west along the top of the hill. Check out the abandoned mining site just a couple of steps beyond the summit; this dugout of rocks is rich with glittering feldspar specimens. The Mine Loop Trail veers south and makes a moderate rocky descent into the woods before arriving at a grassy clearing with a junction at 2.7 mi (4.3 km).

▶ **MILE 2.7–4.3: Mine Loop Trail to Conant Trail**

Turn right to stay on the Mine Loop Trail and stroll through an emerald corridor of ferns, tallgrass, and white birch trees. You'll make several creek crossings on stones before the trail enters darker spruce woods once again. Make a brief, steep descent to reach the **Conant Trail** again at 3.2 mi (5.1 km). Turn left onto Conant here and retrace your steps for a little over 1 mi (1.6 km) back to the parking area to finish the loop at 4.3 mi (6.9 km).

DIRECTIONS

From Portland, take ME-22 W to its junction with ME-14 N. Turn right onto ME-14 N and then, at the traffic circle, take the second exit onto ME-112 S. Continue straight through the next traffic circle to stay on ME-112 S; at the subsequent circle, take the second exit onto ME-25 W/Ossipee Trail E. Drive northwest for around 8 mi (12.9 km), veer right onto ME-113 N, and follow the road northwest to its terminus in Fryeburg. Turn right onto ME-5 N/Main Street and drive north for 4 mi (6.4 km) before taking a left onto Fish Street. Follow Fish Street to its end, turn right onto North Fryeburg Road, and drive north for 2.5 mi (4 km), as North Fryeburg Road becomes Stow Road. Take a slight right to stay on Stow Road and continue north for about 5 mi (8 km) to reach the turnoff for Deer Hill Road. Turn right onto Deer Hill Road and rumble along a dirt road with some potholes. Swing left at the first fork and then take a right at the next junction. Drive southeast and look for a sign on the right pointing to the Conant Trail. Take this final right turn onto a cutoff road. The parking area and trailhead will be just ahead on your left.

GPS COORDINATES: 44°13′12.0″N 70°59′08.3″W

Androscoggin Riverlands

ANDROSCOGGIN RIVERLANDS STATE PARK, TURNER AND LEEDS

🦌 ❀ 🐾 🚶 🧗

Explore the lush and wildlife-rich woodlands along the Androscoggin River while bypassing the ruins of old farms and settlements that once existed here.

BEST: Winter hikes

DISTANCE: 7.2 mi (11.6 km) round-trip

DURATION: 3.5 hr

ELEVATION GAIN: 662 ft (202 m)

EFFORT: Moderate

TRAIL: Dirt path, rocks, wooden bridges

USERS: Hikers, leashed dogs, cyclists, ATV riders

SEASON: June–October

FEES/PASSES: None

MAPS: Maine Bureau of Parks and Lands website

TRAILHEAD: Information kiosk, Androscoggin Riverlands State Park parking lot, Center Bridge Rd., Turner

FACILITIES: Vault toilet

CONTACT: Range Pond State Park; 207/998-4104; www.maine.gov/dacf/parks

The Androscoggin Riverlands, one of the Maine's newer state parks, is a mixed-use recreational forest on the western banks of the big, blue Androscoggin River. It's home to hundreds of bird and mammal species, as well as ruins of the farms and outposts that once operated here. The park's abundant trails are popular with long-distance runners (the Riverlands 100—Maine's first 100-mile endurance race—is held here), mountain bikers, and ATV riders.

START THE HIKE

▶ MILE 0-0.5: Information Kiosk to Homestead Trail

Find the wooden trail information kiosk in the day parking area, pick up **Old River Road Trail** (a dirt ATV trail), and walk south through the orange gate and up a small hill. Immediately after, you'll see a wooden sign for the Homestead Trail on your left. Veer left onto the **Homestead Trail** and leave the road behind as you enter a vast, resplendent forest of pine, spruce, and beech.

▶ MILE 0.5-1.2: Homestead Trail to Androscoggin River

Follow blue blazes as the trail rolls up and down over the hills, and keep your ears open for the songs of hermit thrushes and pine warblers. You'll reach the mossy foundations of an ancient house at 0.6 mi (1 km).

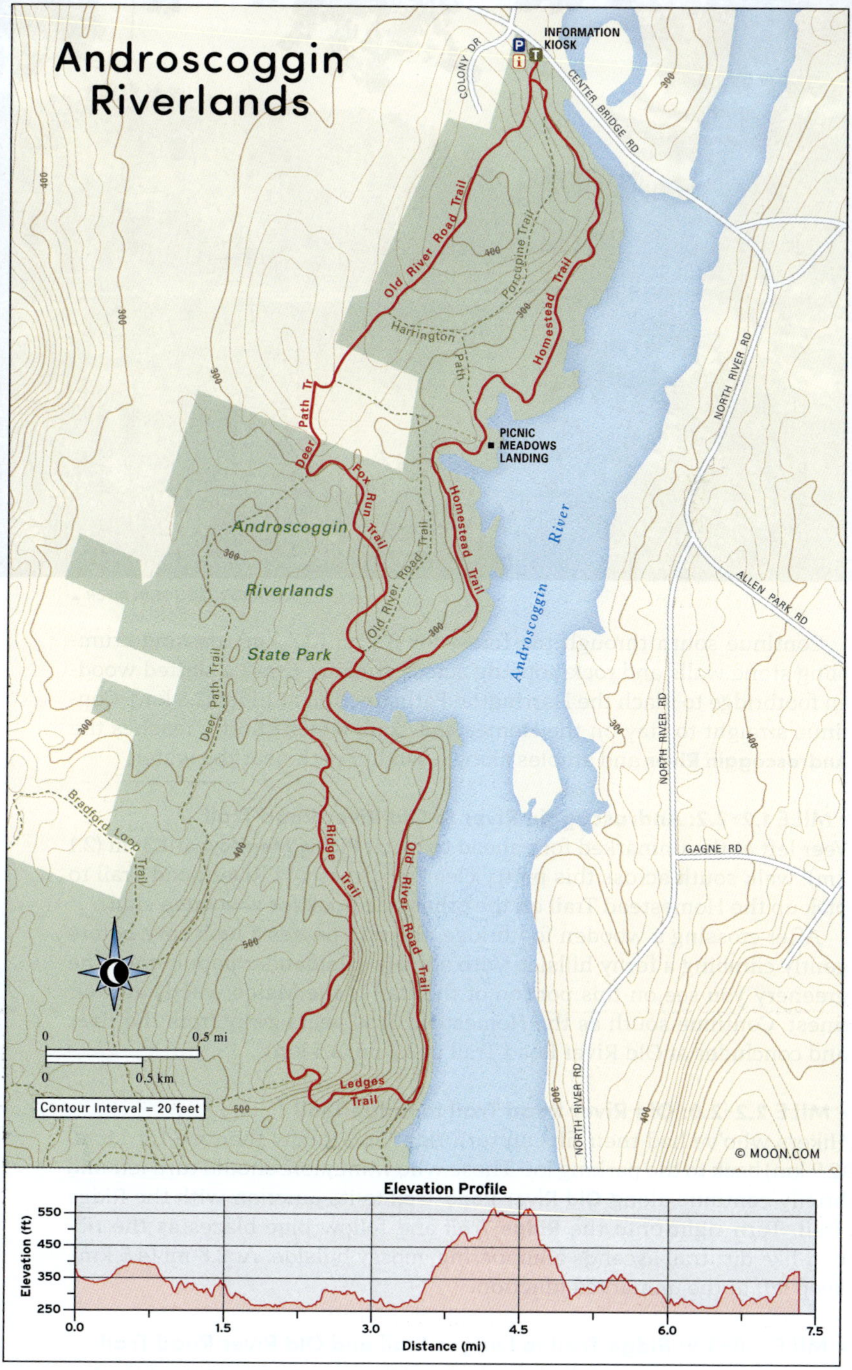

Androscoggin Riverlands

INFORMATION KIOSK

COLONY DR

CENTER BRIDGE RD

Old River Road Trail

Porcupine Trail

Homestead Trail

Harrington

Path

Deer Path Tr

PICNIC MEADOWS LANDING

Fox Run Trail

Androscoggin

Riverlands

State Park

Homestead Trail

Old River Road Trail

Deer Path Trail

Bradford Loop Trail

Androscoggin River

NORTH RIVER RD

ALLEN PARK RD

NORTH RIVER RD

GAGNE RD

Ridge Trail

Old River Road Trail

Ledges Trail

NORTH RIVER RD

0   0.5 mi
0   0.5 km

Contour Interval = 20 feet

© MOON.COM

Elevation Profile

Elevation (ft)

550
450
350
250

0.0   1.5   3.0   4.5   6.0   7.5

Distance (mi)

THE ANDROSCOGGIN RIVER ▲

Continue south through the forest for 0.5 mi (0.8 km), passing crumbling stone walls and rock-hopping across streams. Cross a slatted wooden footbridge to reach the Harrington Path junction at 1.1 mi (1.8 km). Continue straight to stay on the Homestead Trail, which shortly reaches the **Androscoggin River** and ambles along a sandier path near the water.

▶ MILE 1.2–2.2: Androscoggin River to Old River Road Trail
Veer left at the unmarked fork ahead to reach **Picnic Meadow** at 1.3 mi (2.1 km); walk south across this pretty clearing. Cross Old River Road Trail to pick up the Homestead Trail on the other side (look for a wooden sign).

After crossing a wooden footbridge, the trail passes a lush cove before gently climbing a ferny hillside with a lively salamander population. The greenery you see on this portion of the trail is the Maine woods at their finest. Continue south as the Homestead Trail veers away from the river and concludes at Old River Road Trail at 2.2 mi (3.5 km).

▶ MILE 2.2–2.8: Old River Road Trail to Ridge Trail
Hikers who've had their fill can turn right and follow the road for 1.8 mi (2.9 km) back to the parking lot. Those who want more should turn left and briefly continue along **Old River Road Trail** to its junction with the Ridge Trail. Turn right onto the **Ridge Trail** and follow blue blazes as the ribbon-like dirt trail ascends a lumbering, mossy hillside. At 2.8 mi (4.5 km), keep left at the unmarked junction.

▶ MILE 2.8–3.9: Ridge Trail to Ledges Trail and Old River Road Trail
Continue your ascent of the hill, enjoying the breeze and views of the river. Amble across the gentler, rocky hilltop until you reach the Ledges Trail junction at 3.5 mi (5.6 km). Turn left onto the **Ledges Trail** and watch your step as you descend a thrillingly steep switchback of rock stairs. Continue

through the woods and down a final staircase to rejoin Old River Road Trail at 3.9 mi (6.3 km).

▶ MILE 3.9–5.3: Old River Road Trail to Fox Run Trail

Turn left onto the road and walk for just over 1 mi (1.6 km), past the Ridge Trail sign and a marshy area, until you reach the Fox Run Trail at 5.2 mi (8.4 km). Turn left onto **Fox Run Trail** and head back into dense forest, ambling past some meadows where deer sightings are a regular occurrence.

▶ MILE 5.3–5.9: Fox Run Trail to Deer Path Trail

Cross a rickety wooden bridge to reach the junction with the appropriately named Deer Path Trail at 5.9 mi (9.5 km), where you'll turn right.

▶ MILE 5.9–7.2: Deer Path Trail to the Information Kiosk

Ascend a small rocky hillside on a sandier path. Turn right at an unmarked junction and pass a jumble of boulders before arriving at an ATV trail roundabout at 6.2 mi (10 km). Walk north across the roundabout to pick up **Old River Road Trail** one last time. Continue northeast along the road for about 1 mi (1.6 km) as it climbs a series of knolls before descending back to the trailhead sign at 7.2 mi (11.6 km).

DIRECTIONS

From Portland, drive south on I-295 S for roughly 4 mi (6.4 km) and take Exit 1 to merge onto I-95 N. Drive north on I-95 toward Lewiston/Augusta and take Exit 75. At the end of the off-ramp, turn left onto ME-100 N/ME-4 N/US-202 E. Drive north through Lewiston for 12 mi (19 km) and then take a right onto Upper Street. Follow this hillside road to its terminus at Center Bridge Road and make a left onto Center Bridge Road. The turnoff for the Androscoggin Riverlands State Park parking area will be on your right just over 1.5 mi (2.4 km) ahead. Look for an easily missed dark brown wooden sign by the side of the road.

GPS COORDINATES: 44°15'40.7"N 70°11'18.4"W

BEST NEARBY BITES AND BREWS

If you're driving through Lewiston, take a few minutes to sample an indelible Maine IPA and many other admirable brews at **Baxter Brewing Co.** (130 Mill St., Lewiston; 207/333-6769; www.baxterbrewing.com; 11:30am-9pm Sun.-Thurs., 11:30am-11pm Fri.-Sat.). Make your foodie friends jealous and experience a farm-to-table breakfast or lunch on an actual Maine farm by visiting **Nezinscot Farm** (284 Turner Center Rd., Turner; 207/225-3231; www.nezinscotfarm.com; 7am-5pm Thurs.-Sun.).

NEARBY CAMPGROUNDS

NAME	LOCATION	FACILITIES	SEASON	FEE
Coos Canyon Campground	445 Swift River Rd., Byron, 44°43'09.3"N 70°37'50.8"W	Tent sites, lean-tos, RV sites, cabins, toilets, showers, potable water, laundry, camp store, Wi-Fi	May through October	$32-175
207/364-3880; www.cooscanyoncamping.com				
Mount Blue State Park Campground	187 Webb Beach Rd., Weld, 44°40'47.7"N 70°27'22.9"W	Tent sites, lean-tos, toilets, showers, potable water	mid-May through September	$30-40
207/585-2261; www.maine.gov/dacf/parks				
Silver Lake Campground	261 Main St., Roxbury, 44°39'23.6"N 70°39'30.6"W	Tent sites, RV sites, cabins, toilets, showers, potable water, laundry, Wi-Fi	mid-May through September	$28-48
207/545-0416; www.silverlakecampground.com				
Grafton Notch Campground	1472 Bear River Rd., Route 26, Newry, 44°33'52.7"N 70°51'21.9"W	Tent sites, RV sites, toilets, showers, potable water	mid-May to mid-October	$30
207/824-2292; www.campgrafton.com				
Stony Brook Recreation & Camping	3036 Main St., Hanover, 44°29'19.6"N 70°46'30.4"W	Tent sites, lean-tos, RV sites, toilets, showers, potable water, laundry, pool, boat rentals, camp store, Wi-Fi	year-round	$39-49
207/824-2836; www.stonybrookrec.com				

NEARBY CAMPGROUNDS (continued)

NAME	LOCATION	FACILITIES	SEASON	FEE
Bethel Outdoor Adventure	121 Mayville Rd., Bethel, 44°25'06.5"N 70°47'50.6"W	Tent sites, RV sites, toilets, showers, potable water, laundry, boat rentals, camp store, Wi-Fi	mid-May to mid-October	$28–48
207/824-4224; www.betheloutdooradventure.com				
Pleasant River Campground	800 W. Bethel Rd., Bethel, 44°24'02.0"N 70°52'02.3"W	Tent sites, RV sites, cabins, toilets, showers, potable water, pool, camp store, Wi-Fi	May through October	$36–56
207/836-2000; www.pleasantrivercampground.com				
Hastings Campground	State Rte 113, Bethel, 44°21'07.8"N 70°59'01.6"W	Tent sites, toilets, potable water	late May through mid-October	$22
www.recreation.gov				
Basin Campground	ME/NH border, Basin Rd., Chatham, NH, 44°16'04.2"N 71°01'19.7"W	Tent sites, toilets, potable water	late May through mid-October	$22
603/447-5448; www.recreation.gov				

NEW HAMPSHIRE

WHITE MOUNTAIN NATIONAL FOREST

New Hampshire's White Mountains dominate the Northeast like the Beatles once ruled pop music. These craggy peaks— including Mount Washington, the tallest in New England—are wildly popular, scenically diverse, and, sometimes, a bit dangerous. The abundance of mountains over 4,000 ft (1,220 m) here is unparalleled by anything in New England, and there's something for everyone. Whether you fancy a gentle stroll to some hidden waterfalls or following cairns up a bumpy ridge, you'll find it. The trails here range from meditatively gentle to relentlessly steep. You'll share the woods with deer, pine martens, beavers, and bears. And come sundown, you can pair your hike with award-winning cuisine and artisanal libations.

▲ CAIRNS AT THE SUMMIT OF MOUNT MOOSILAUKE

▲ MOUNT WILLARD IN WINTER

1 **Giant Falls**
DISTANCE: 3 mi (4.8 km) round-trip
DURATION: 1.5 hr
EFFORT: Easy
PAGE: 176

2 **Mount Adams**
DISTANCE: 8.6 mi (13.8 km) round-trip
DURATION: 7 hr
EFFORT: Strenuous
PAGE: 180

3 **Mount Washington via Tuckerman Ravine**
DISTANCE: 8.2 mi (13.2 km) round-trip
DURATION: 8 hr
EFFORT: Strenuous
PAGE: 184

4 **Basin Rim**
DISTANCE: 4.4 mi (7.1 km) round-trip
DURATION: 3 hr
EFFORT: Moderate
PAGE: 188

5 **Zealand Valley and Thoreau Falls**
DISTANCE: 9.4 mi (15.1 km) round-trip
DURATION: 4.5 hr
EFFORT: Moderate
PAGE: 191

6 **Mount Willard**
DISTANCE: 3 mi (4.8 km) round-trip
DURATION: 1.5 hr
EFFORT: Easy
PAGE: 195

7 **Arethusa Falls via Bemis Brook**
DISTANCE: 2.8 mi (4.5 km) round-trip
DURATION: 2 hr
EFFORT: Easy/moderate
PAGE: 198

8 **Bridal Veil Falls**
DISTANCE: 4.4 mi (7.1 km) round-trip
DURATION: 2.5 hr
EFFORT: Easy/moderate
PAGE: 201

9 **Mount Lafayette and Franconia Ridge**
DISTANCE: 8.4 mi (13.5 km) round-trip
DURATION: 5.5 hr
EFFORT: Strenuous
PAGE: 204

10 **The Flume**
DISTANCE: 2 mi (3.2 km) round-trip
DURATION: 1 hr
EFFORT: Easy
PAGE: 208

11 **Mount Carrigain**
DISTANCE: 10.4 mi (16.7 km) round-trip
DURATION: 6 hr
EFFORT: Strenuous
PAGE: 211

12 **Mount Moosilauke**
DISTANCE: 7.6 mi (12.2 km) round-trip
DURATION: 5 hr
EFFORT: Strenuous
PAGE: 214

13 **Greeley Ponds**
DISTANCE: 4.2 mi (6.8 km) round-trip
DURATION: 2.5 hr
EFFORT: Easy/moderate
PAGE: 217

14 **Mount Chocorua**
DISTANCE: 7.4 mi (11.9 km) round-trip
DURATION: 4.5 hr
EFFORT: Moderate/strenuous
PAGE: 220

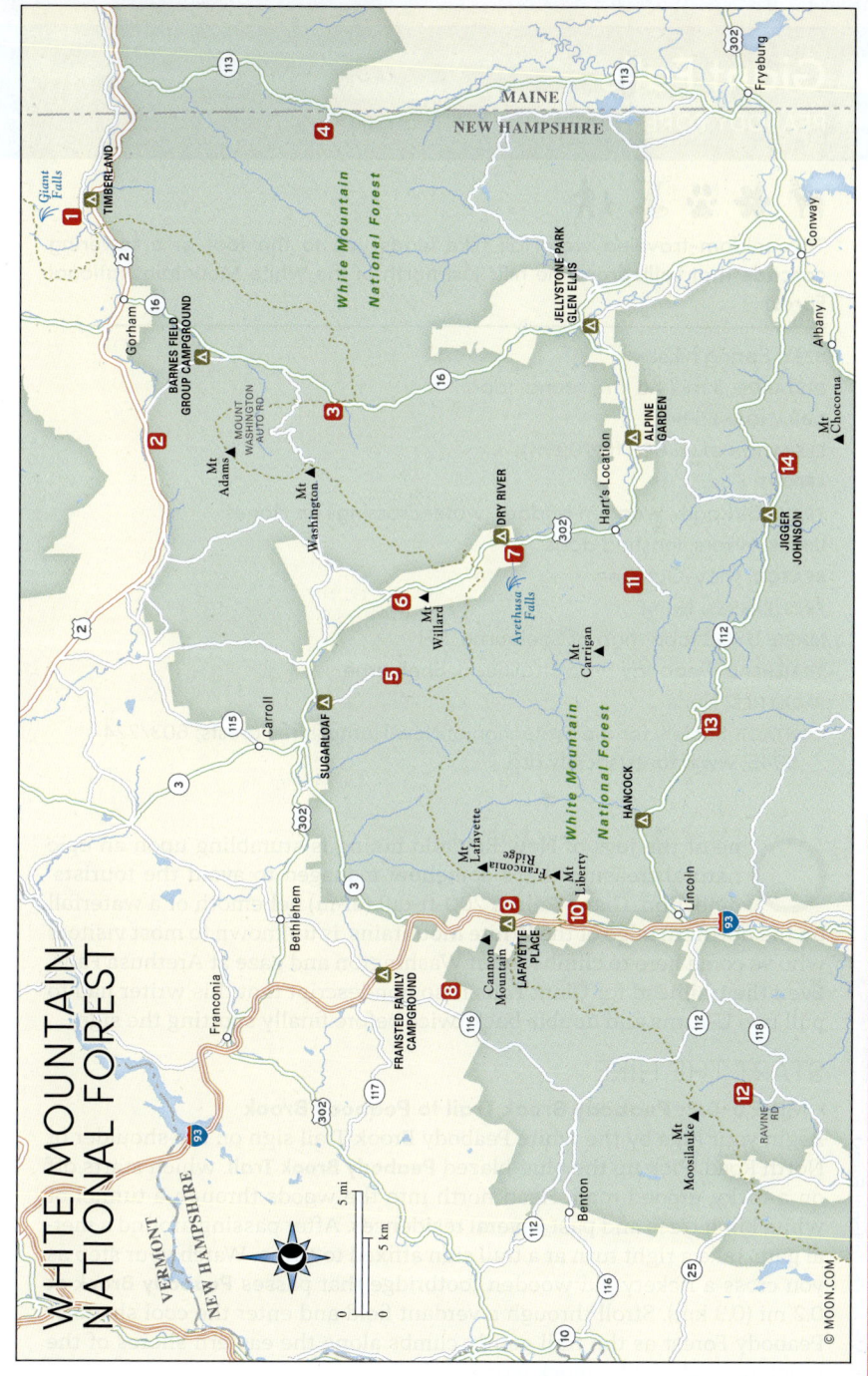

WHITE MOUNTAIN NATIONAL FOREST

VERMONT

NEW HAMPSHIRE

MAINE

NEW HAMPSHIRE

White Mountain National Forest

Giant Falls

TIMBERLAND

Gorham

BARNES FIELD GROUP CAMPGROUND

MOUNT WASHINGTON AUTO RD

Mt Adams

Mt Washington

DRY RIVER

Arethusa Falls

Mt Willard

JELLYSTONE PARK
GLEN ELLIS

ALPINE GARDEN

Hart's Location

Conway

Albany

Mt Chocorua

JIGGER JOHNSON

Mt Carrigan

SUGARLOAF

Carroll

Bethlehem

Franconia

Mt Lafayette

Franconia Ridge

Mt Liberty

HANCOCK

Lincoln

Cannon Mountain

LAFAYETTE PLACE

FRANSTED FAMILY CAMPGROUND

Benton

Mt Moosilauke

RAVINE RD

White Mountain National Forest

5 mi

5 km

© MOON.COM

1 Giant Falls

PEABODY FOREST, SHELBURNE

This seldom-traveled waterfall hike leads you to the foot of a towering cascade that spills from the hills just north of the White Mountain National Forest.

BEST: Spring hikes

DISTANCE: 3 mi (4.8 km) round-trip

DURATION: 1.5 hr

ELEVATION GAIN: 685 ft (209 m)

EFFORT: Easy

TRAIL: Dirt path, wooden bridges, water crossings on stones

USERS: Hikers, leashed dogs

SEASON: May–October

FEES/PASSES: None

MAPS: USGS topo map of Shelburne, NH

TRAILHEAD: Peabody Brook trailhead, Shelburne

FACILITIES: None

CONTACT: Society for the Protection of New Hampshire Forests; 603/224-9945; www.forestsociety.org

One of the joys of New England hiking is stumbling upon an epic natural treasure that's somehow managed to avoid the tourists' detection. Giant Falls, a 200-ft-tall (61-m) behemoth of a waterfall on the northern edge of the White Mountains, is unknown to most visitors who've come here to climb Mount Washington and gaze at Arethusa Falls. Even the trailhead for Giant Falls is so nondescript that this writer had to pull two U-turns and double back twice before finally spotting the sign.

START THE HIKE

▶ MILE 0-0.2: Peabody Brook Trail to Peabody Brook

Begin your hike by the white Peabody Brook Trail sign on the shoulder of North Road. Pick up the blue-blazed **Peabody Brook Trail**, which starts off on a rocky, eroded road. Head north into the woods through a tunnel of white birch trees and past several residences. After passing around a metal gate, take a right turn at a trail sign affixed to a tree. Watch your step as you cross a rickety old wooden footbridge that passes **Peabody Brook** at 0.2 mi (0.3 km). Stroll through a verdant field and enter the cool shade of Peabody Forest as the trail gently climbs along the eastern shores of the brook through the hemlock woods.

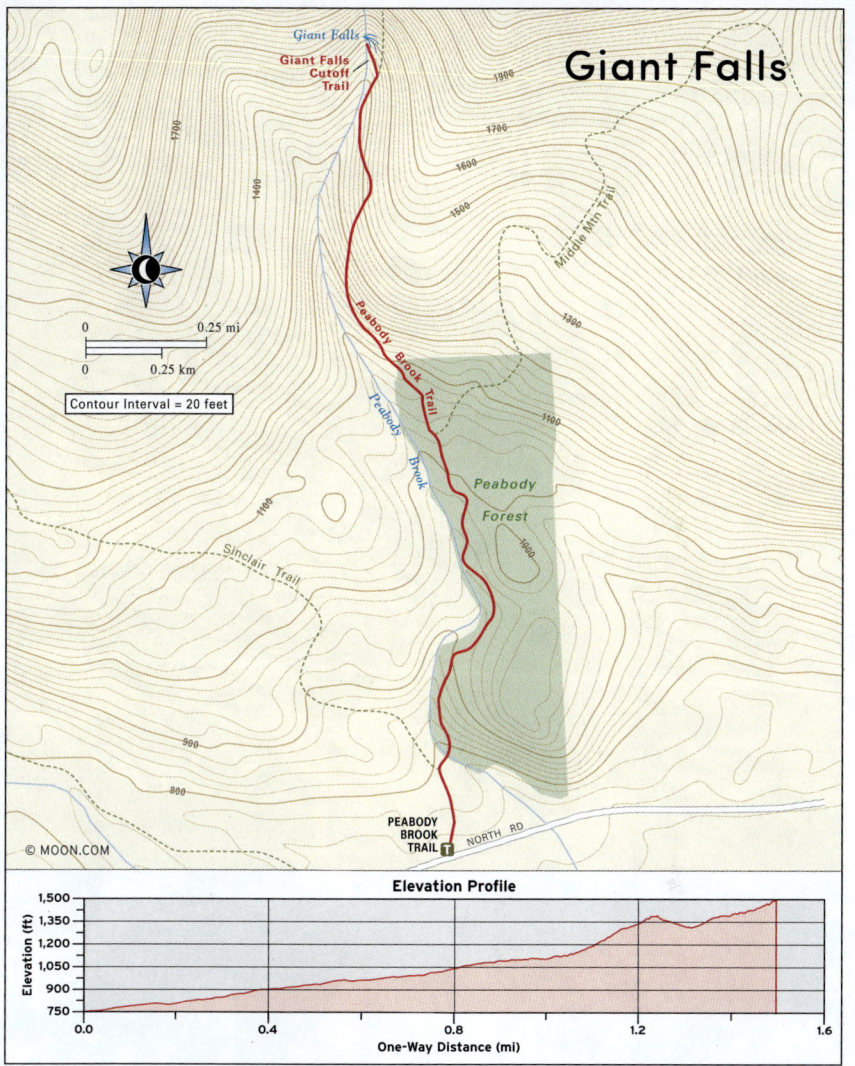

Elevation Profile

▸ MILE 0.2–1.2: Peabody Brook to Giant Falls Cutoff Trail

The trail here alternates between a smooth dirt path lined with ferns and wider stretches that are bursting with tallgrass. (Be sure to do a tick check after completing the hike.) You may also notice the abundance of colorful wild mushrooms that grow along the path. At 0.8 mi (1.3 km), take a left turn at the Peabody Brook Trail sign and continue your ascent as the trail becomes rockier and steeper with each step. Climb higher above Peabody Brook and work your way up stone staircases past a series of glacial boulders and some sheer cliff faces. The trail grade eventually softens and reaches a signed cutoff trail for **Giant Falls** at 1.2 mi (1.9 km).

GIANT FALLS DURING SPRING MELT ▲

▶ **MILE 1.2–1.5: Giant Falls Cutoff Trail to Giant Falls**

Turn left at the sign, descending a rooty dirt path to Peabody Brook at a moderate grade. The cutoff reaches the brook at 1.4 mi (2.3 km) and climbs north alongside some small cascades. A dull roar beckons from just ahead. After scrambling up a final steeper pitch, the trail arrives at a rocky perch at 1.5 mi (2.4 km) that offers a pristine view of **Giant Falls.** Nimble hikers can carefully make their way down from the perch and reach the base of the falls, but the rocks here can be quite slippery, especially during the spring when snowmelt turns the falls into a rip-roaring monster that's as beautiful as it is dangerous. Return the way you came.

DIRECTIONS

From Concord, drive north on I-93 N to the White Mountain National Forest. After passing through Franconia Notch, take Exit 35 and merge onto US-3 N to Lancaster/Twin Mountain. Continue north on US-3 N for 12 mi (19 km) before turning right onto NH-115 N. Take this road northeast to its terminus and then take a right onto US-2 E. Drive east into Gorham and turn right onto US-2 E/Main Street. Continue for roughly 7 mi (11.3 km) and then take a left onto Meadow Road. Cross a bridge over the Androscoggin River and take your final right turn onto North Road. The Peabody Brook trailhead will be on your left, just past 267 North Road.

GPS COORDINATES: 44°24'47.7"N 71°06'15.5"W

2 Mount Adams

WHITE MOUNTAIN NATIONAL FOREST, RANDOLPH

This mountain hike ascends a beautiful and narrow rocky ridgeline to reach the summit of New Hampshire's second-tallest peak and returns by way of a lush forest trail with waterfalls.

DISTANCE: 8.6 mi (13.8 km) round-trip

DURATION: 7 hr

ELEVATION GAIN: 4,465 ft (1,361 m)

EFFORT: Strenuous

TRAIL: Dirt path, rocks

USERS: Hikers

SEASON: June–September

FEES/PASSES: None

MAPS: White Mountain National Forest website

TRAILHEAD: Appalachia parking lot, US-2, Randolph

FACILITIES: None

CONTACT: White Mountain National Forest; 603/536-6100; www.fs.usda.gov/recarea/whitemountain

Mount Adams is arguably the most thrilling summit in the White Mountains—a barren and dizzyingly high tower of rocks that seems to poke the cosmos. At 5,794 ft (1,766 m) above sea level, it's the second-highest mountain in the Granite State. It's everything that Mount Washington (a more developed and lumbering peak) would seem to be, given its moniker as the tallest peak. Adams is a beauty and a beast of a climb, no matter which route you take.

START THE HIKE

▶ MILE 0-1.0: Appalachia Parking Lot to Randolph Path

Begin the hike on the south side of the Appalachia parking lot by the trail information kiosk. Follow a dirt path into a meadow through which power lines run, then turn right at the junction to pick up the blue-blazed **Airline Trail** as it heads south into a dense deciduous forest full of mossy boulders and twittering birds. The footing is rooty and rocky as the Airline crosses a stream on rocks and then ascends through ferns at a steady grade. Keep straight to stay on Airline as Sylvan Way bisects the trail, turn right at the nearby junction with Beechwood Way, and then make a left at the Short Line Trail fork.

After reaching the **Randolph Path** crossing at roughly 1 mi (1.6 km), keep straight as the Airline steepens considerably and transitions from dirt to large and unwieldy stone stairs. It soon becomes a ledge-like path that climbs sharply up the north spur of Mount Adams.

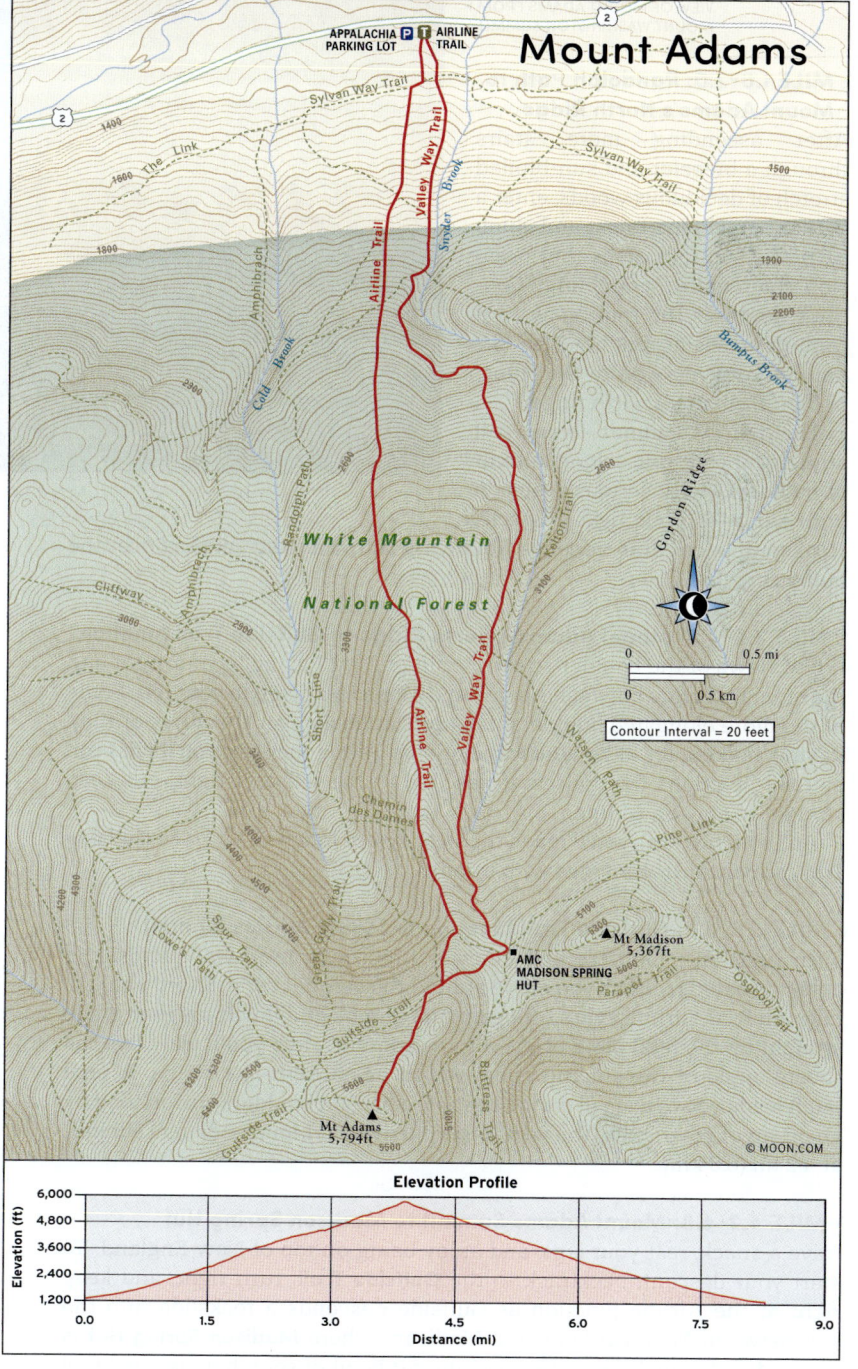

Mount Adams

APPALACHIA PARKING LOT
AIRLINE TRAIL

Sylvan Way Trail
Valley Way Trail
Snyder Brook
Airline Trail
The Link
Amphibrach
Cold Brook
Randolph Path
Amphibrach
Cliffway
Short Line
Spur Trail
Lowe's Path
Great Gully Trail
Chapin des Dames
Gulfside Trail
Gulfside Trail

Sylvan Way Trail
Bumpus Brook
Gordon Ridge
Kelton Trail
Watson Path
Pine Link
Buttress Trail
Parapet Trail
Osgood Trail

White Mountain
National Forest

▲ Mt Madison
5,367ft

AMC
MADISON SPRING
HUT

▲ Mt Adams
5,794ft

0   0.5 mi
0   0.5 km

Contour Interval = 20 feet

© MOON.COM

Elevation Profile

Elevation (ft): 6,000 / 4,800 / 3,600 / 2,400 / 1,200

Distance (mi): 0.0 1.5 3.0 4.5 6.0 7.5 9.0

▶ MILE 1.0-2.0: Randolph Path to Mount Adams's North Ridge

After ascending more stairs through a breezier and sun-broiled stretch of deciduous woods, enter a darker boreal pine forest and climb several steep rock slabs that occasionally require scrambling. Continue south as the trail breaks out from the trees at roughly 2 mi (3.2 km) and delivers you to the "foot" of Mount Adams's north ridge.

The pointy summit looms tall straight ahead, but a long tumult of boulders—with serious drops on both sides—is your next obstacle. Hike south along this ridgeline, following cairns and scrambling over the bulbous rocks.

▶ MILE 2.0-3.6: Mount Adams's North Ridge to Gulfside Trail Junction

Enjoy views of the boulder-strewn basin of King Ravine to your right and the emerald ravine between Adams and Mount Madison to your left. Some of the more elongated boulders hang precariously over the abyss of King Ravine, making for killer landscape photos. Along the way, you'll pass numerous junctions for trails that descend to the left and right, but keep straight to stay on Airline.

At 3.6 mi (5.8 km), you'll reach the windswept junction with the **Gulfside Trail,** which Airline merges with briefly.

▶ MILE 3.6-4.2: Gulfside Trail Junction to Mount Adams Summit

Turn right onto Gulfside and enjoy a brief, more level walk across big lichen-crusted rocks as you curve around the summit cone. Shortly ahead, take a left as Airline splits off again and climbs at a much tougher grade straight up the final pitch of the Adams summit. Here you'll truly feel the severe angle of the summit cone, which has a horn-like shape. A final pitch leads you to a small crow's nest of rocks and boulders surrounded by an ocean of green hills. You've officially arrived at Mount Adams's summit at 4.2 mi (6.8 km).

▶ MILE 4.2-4.8: Mount Adams Summit to Madison Spring Hut

Have a snack, rest your legs, and enjoy being on top of New England. To start your descent, backtrack to the **Gulfside Trail,** turn right, and keep right at the Airline junction as Gulfside descends a rockslide into the gap between Mount Adams and Madison, where **Madison Spring Hut** is reached at 4.8 mi (7.7 km). (A post-summit bowl of soup here is ideal fuel for the return journey ahead.)

▶ MILE 4.8-5.9: Madison Spring Hut to Valley Way Trail

From the hut, pick up the **Valley Way Trail,** marked by blue blazes, and hike north as it makes a very rocky and steep descent into boreal forest before segueing to a more manageable dirt path at 5.5 mi (8.9 km) with plenty of knee-creaking rock stairs. Continue north and keep straight as you pass several marked cutoffs that branch off to the left and right of the Valley Way trail. The trail is flanked with plenty of moss tuffets in places, which can make for a nice place to rest your legs and enjoy a partial view of the valley below.

▶ MILE 5.9-7.9: Valley Way Trail to Snyder Brook

A final series of stone staircases into deciduous woods leads to the junction with Brookside Trail at 7.7 mi (12.4 km). Turn left here, then right at the Beechwood Way fork, continuing on Valley Way at both junctions. Enjoy a gentler dirt path that ambles along several chuckling cascades on **Snyder Brook**—a great place to take a shockingly rejuvenating dip.

▶ MILE 7.9-8.6: Snyder Brook to Appalachia Parking Lot

The trail soon levels and leaves the brook behind to pass through a grove of ferns and hemlocks. Keep straight as Valley Way bisects Sylvan Way and emerge into the meadow with the Airline junction at 8.5 mi (13.7 km). Stroll (or drag your tired carcass) to the parking lot ahead to complete the hike at 8.6 mi (13.8 km)!

DIRECTIONS

From Concord, drive north on I-93 N. After passing through Franconia Notch, take Exit 35 and merge onto US-3 N to Lancaster/Twin Mountain. Continue north on US-3 N for 12 mi (19 km) before turning right onto NH-115 N. Take this road northeast to its terminus and then take a right onto US-2 E. Drive east for another 7 mi (11.3 km). The Appalachia parking lot will be on your left. If it's a busy summer day, you may have to park off the shoulder of the road before or after the parking lot.

GPS COORDINATES: 44°22'16.5"N 71°17'20.7"W

BEST NEARBY BITES

Prepare for your climb by stopping in Gorham for a breakfast sandwich, hot coffee, or a smoothie at the **White Mountain Café & Bookstore** (212 Main St, Gorham; 603/466-2511; www.whitemountaincafe.com; 7am-4pm Thurs.-Tues.). When the sun goes down and you're (hopefully) off the mountain, circle back for a hearty dinner of haddock puttanesca, chicken marsala, or many other Italian delicacies at **Nonna's Kitchen** (19 Exchange St., Gorham; 603/915-9203; www.nonnasgorham.com; 4pm-8:30pm Wed.-Sat.).

Mount Washington via Tuckerman Ravine

WHITE MOUNTAIN NATIONAL FOREST, GORHAM

Hike through a gigantic bowl-like ravine filled with waterfalls, wildflowers, and glacial boulders to reach the highest summit in New England.

BEST: Summer hikes, vistas

DISTANCE: 8.2 mi (13.2 km) round-trip

DURATION: 8 hr

ELEVATION GAIN: 4,265 ft (1,300 m)

EFFORT: Strenuous

TRAIL: Dirt path, rocks, wooden bridges

USERS: Hikers

SEASON: June–September

FEES/PASSES: None

MAPS: White Mountain National Forest website

TRAILHEAD: Tuckerman Ravine Trail, NH-16, Gorham

FACILITIES: Restrooms

CONTACT: Appalachian Mountain Club Pinkham Notch Visitor Center; 603/466-2727; www.outdoors.org. Summer and fall visitor center hours are 6:30am-9pm daily.

You haven't really hiked in New England until you've pulled yourself over the lip of Mount Washington's peak only to find yourself surrounded by tourists in flip-flops clutching chili dogs and struggling to stay upright against the wind. The highest summit in all of New England is definitely an attraction—it has its own weather observatory, a museum, and a cafeteria where you can buy fast food. It's reachable by foot, car, and even train.

The most epic route to the top of Mount Washington is the Tuckerman Ravine Trail, which scrambles straight up the sloped walls of Tuckerman Ravine. In the summer, the ravine blooms into a paradise of cascades and alpine flora, and it's arguably better than the peak itself.

START THE HIKE

▶ **MILE 0-0.4: Tuckerman Ravine Trail to Crystal Cascade**

Walk toward the large wooden sign for the **Tuckerman Ravine Trail** just to the left of the visitor center and turn right to pick up the stony trail as it ventures into the woods behind the visitor center. Cross the **Ellis River** on a wooden footbridge. As the trail begins to climb a hillside at a moderate grade, you'll pass a rock staircase that leads to a lookout spot at 0.4 mi (0.6 km), from which you can view the **Crystal Cascade**—a shimmering 100-ft-tall (30-m) waterfall that's a promising sign of things to come.

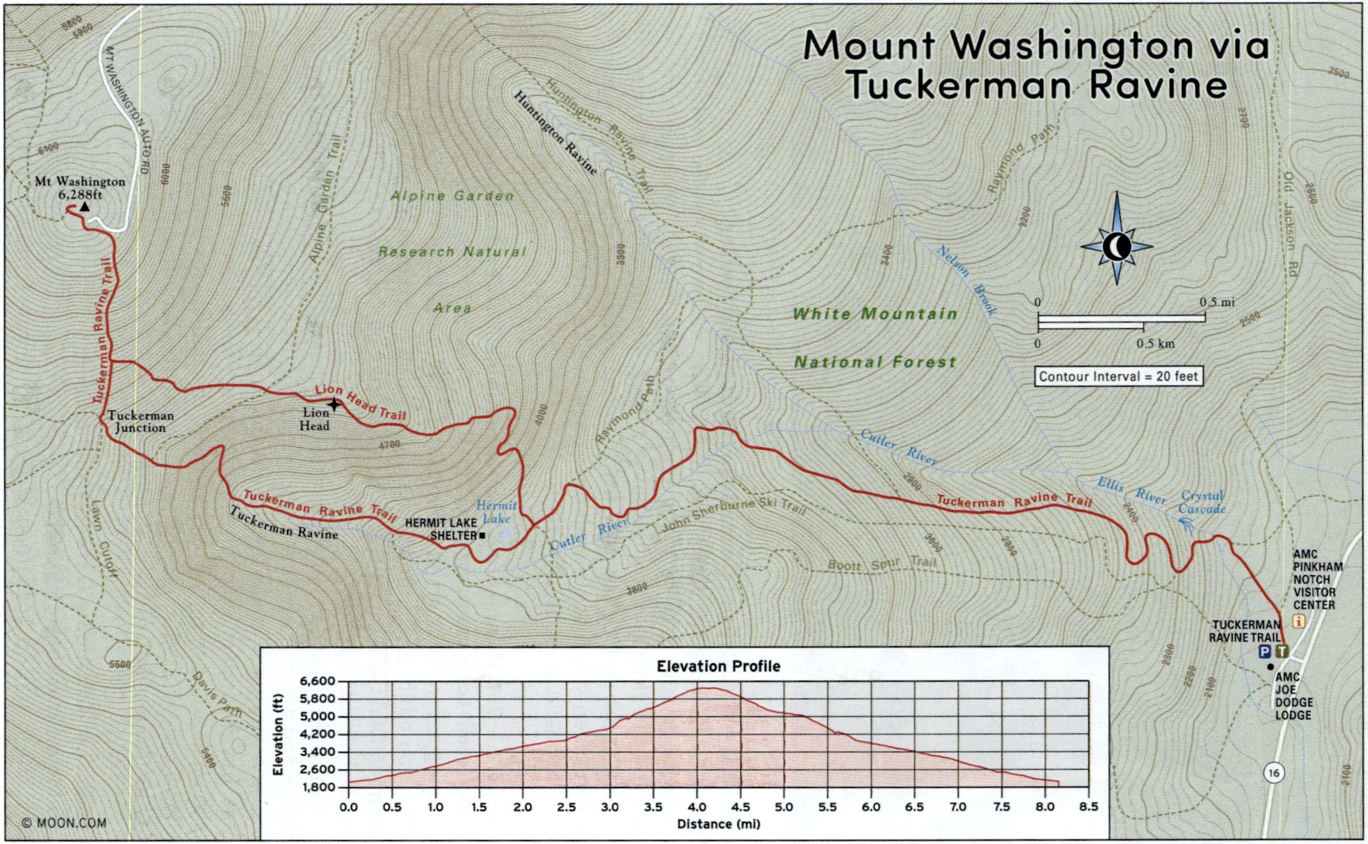

Mount Washington via Tuckerman Ravine

Old Jackson Rd

AMC PINKHAM NOTCH VISITOR CENTER

AMC JOE DODGE LODGE

16

TUCKERMAN RAVINE TRAIL

Crystal Cascade

Ellis River

White Mountain National Forest

Nelson Brook

Raymond Ravine Trail

Cutler River

Tuckerman Ravine Trail

Boott Spur Trail

John Sherburne (Ski) Trail

Huntington Ravine

Huntington Ravine Trail

Alpine Garden Research Natural Area

Lion Head Trail

Lion Head

Cutler River

Hermit Lake

HERMIT LAKE SHELTER

Tuckerman Ravine Trail

Tuckerman Ravine

Alpine Garden Trail

Tuckerman Junction

Tuckerman Ravine Trail

Davis Path

Lawn Cutoff

MT WASHINGTON AUTO RD

Mt Washington 6,288ft

0   0.5 mi

0   0.5 km

Contour Interval = 20 feet

Elevation Profile

Elevation (ft): 1,800 / 2,600 / 3,400 / 4,200 / 5,000 / 5,800 / 6,600

Distance (mi): 0.0, 0.5, 1.0, 1.5, 2.0, 2.5, 3.0, 3.5, 4.0, 4.5, 5.0, 5.5, 6.0, 6.5, 7.0, 7.5, 8.0, 8.5

© MOON.COM

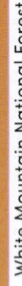

THE CLIMB UP TUCKERMAN RAVINE'S HEADWALL ▲

▶ **MILE 0.4–2.4: Crystal Cascade to Hermit Lake Shelter**
Climb west along the rocky trail, navigating moderately steep switchbacks for roughly 2 mi (3.2 km). With each turn, the trail becomes sunnier and the skyline offers flashes of Mount Washington's distant upper slopes. At 2.4 mi (3.9 km), take a water break and slather on some sunscreen when you reach **Hermit Lake Shelter.** The bowl of the ravine lies straight ahead in all its glory.

▶ **MILE 2.4–3.4: Hermit Lake Shelter to Alpine Garden Trail Junction**
From **Hermit Lake,** continue for 0.7 mi (1.1 km) as the trail becomes steeper, climbing several rock stairs to reach the floor of the bowl at 3.1 mi (5 km). Here, you might encounter a looming ice arch that can last well into the summer. Don't walk near the arch, as chunks of ice the size of boulders regularly break off.

Continue past several misting waterfalls that spill down the bowl of the ravine, and get your quads ready. The trail begins to scramble up the headwall at a very steep grade; there are surprisingly few ledges with drop-offs here, but the trail is rough and maintaining your balance is crucial. After skirting around the rim of the headwall, the trail climbs a modest jumble of rocks, breaking through the tree line and reaching the junction for the Alpine Garden Trail at 3.4 mi (5.5 km).

▶ **MILE 3.4–4.2: Alpine Garden Trail Junction
to Mount Washington Summit**
Turn left to stay on Tuckerman Ravine and be sure to take a look behind you—the view of the Carter-Wildcat Range from here is incredible.

Continue up a mess of rocks and make a right at the second junction at 3.6 mi (5.8 km) to stay on the Tuckerman Ravine Trail. With the cone of Washington towering ahead, the trail steepens and navigates its way across larger lichen-crusted boulders and rock slabs. Well-placed cairns keep hikers on the correct trajectory. At 3.7 mi (6 km), veer left at the Lion Head Trail junction to stay on Tuckerman and carefully schlep your way up the final rocks until you step onto the Mount Washington Auto Road at 4 mi (6.4 km). Turn left, walk up the road to the parking lot, and climb two wooden staircases to reach the summit of Washington at 4.2 mi (6.8 km).

▶ **MILE 4.2–5.9: Mount Washington Summit to Lion Head Trail**
Hikers can choose to come back the way they came, but a less brutal option is to backtrack to the Lion Head Trail junction at 4.7 mi (7.6 km) and then turn left to take **Lion Head Trail** down the northern flank of the ravine. The trail is steep with plenty of rock stairs and slabs, but it's not as dizzying as the headwall itself. (An added bonus: The upper stretches of Lion Head are rich with alpine wildflowers in the summer.)

▶ **MILE 5.9–8.2: Lion Head Trail to Tuckerman Ravine Trail**
Arrive back at Hermit Lake Shelter at 5.9 mi (9.5 km) and hop back on the **Tuckerman Ravine Trail** to return to Pinkham Notch Visitor Center, completing the loop at 8.2 mi (13.2 km).

DIRECTIONS

From Concord, drive north on I-93 N for 74 mi (119 km) and take Exit 35 for US-3 N toward Lancaster/Twin Mountain. Merge onto US-3 N and take it for 11 mi (18 km) before veering right onto NH-115 N. Drive along this local highway until its terminus at US-2. Make a right onto US-2 E and drive northeast into the town of Gorham. As you pass the town common, turn right onto NH-16 S and continue south into Pinkham Notch for a final 10 mi (16 km). After you pass the Wildcat Mountain ski lift, look for the entrance to Pinkham Notch Visitor Center on your right and make a final right turn into the facility parking lot.

GPS COORDINATES: 44°15'26.2"N 71°15'11.6"W

BEST NEARBY BITES AND BREWS

Once you've completed the hike, drive to North Conway and reward yourself with a frothy mug of Czech-style pilsner and a flatbread pizza or pile of barbecue at **Moat Mountain Smokehouse & Brewing Co.** (3378 White Mountain Hwy., North Conway; 603/356-6381; www.moatmountain.com; 11:30am-8pm Sun.-Tues., 11:30am-9pm Fri.-Sat.).

Basin Rim

EVANS NOTCH, CHATHAM

This forest hike bypasses a spellbinding glacial lake and a waterfall before climbing to exposed cliffs with excellent views into western Maine.

DISTANCE: 4.4 mi (7.1 km) round-trip

DURATION: 3 hr

ELEVATION GAIN: 1,251 ft (381 m)

EFFORT: Moderate

TRAIL: Dirt path, rocks, wooden bridges, water crossings on stones

USERS: Hikers, leashed dogs

SEASON: June–October

FEES/PASSES: None

MAPS: White Mountain National Forest website

TRAILHEAD: Basin boat launch, Basin Rd., Chatham

FACILITIES: Restroom

CONTACT: White Mountain National Forest; 603/536-6100; www.fs.usda.gov/recarea/whitemountain

Straddling eastern New Hampshire and western Maine, Evans Notch is a mysterious and under-visited place where multiple mountain ranges converge. One of the most memorable oddities found here is The Basin—a glacial cirque, a feature that hikers normally encounter at much higher elevations in places like the Rockies.

START THE HIKE

▶ **MILE 0-0.7: Basin Boat Launch to Basin Brook**

Start at the wooden Basin Trail sign. Step into a deciduous forest on the rooty dirt path of the **Basin Trail,** marked by yellow blazes. Warm up with some gentle ups and downs along the southern shore of the lake as the trail chugs west. The trail descends some rock stairs and emerges from the woods at 0.7 mi (1.1 km) by the edge of **Basin Brook,** which you'll have to cross on stones. The water here can get high enough to fully saturate a boot, so consider removing your hiking shoes for the crossing.

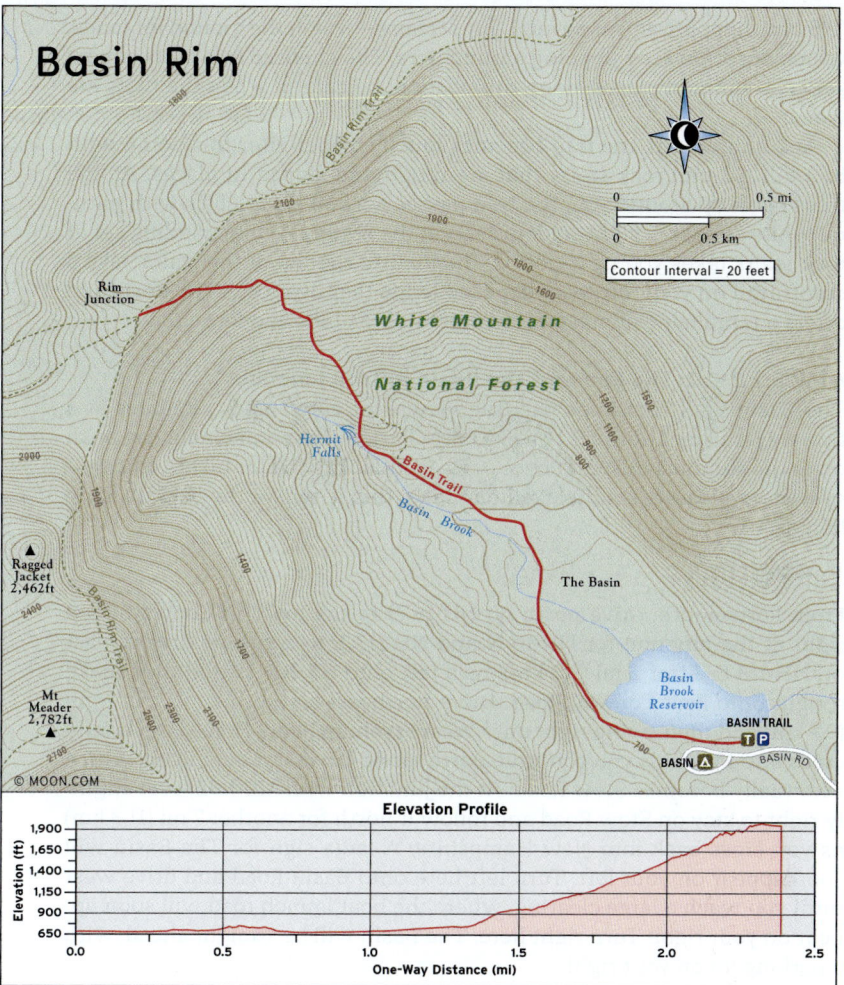

Basin Rim

White Mountain
National Forest

Rim
Junction

Hermit
Falls

Basin Trail

Basin Brook

Ragged
Jacket
2,462 ft

The Basin

Basin
Brook
Reservoir

BASIN TRAIL

BASIN

BASIN RD

Mt
Meader
2,782 ft

© MOON.COM

Contour Interval = 20 feet

0   0.5 mi
0   0.5 km

Elevation Profile

Elevation (ft): 1,900 / 1,650 / 1,400 / 1,150 / 900 / 650

One-Way Distance (mi): 0.0 / 0.5 / 1.0 / 1.5 / 2.0 / 2.5

▶ **MILE 0.7–1.4: Basin Brook to Hermit Falls**
Pick up the trail on the other side of Basin Brook and hike northwest along an old streambed. Cross another tributary on a wooden footbridge and then venture deeper into a vast forest replete with glacial boulders. The grade here is almost flat, with fewer roots and rocks. At 1.3 mi (2.1 km), you'll reach a junction for Hermit Falls; turn left and follow a creek along a narrower stony path as a rush of water echoes from ahead. The trail steepens considerably before reaching **Hermit Falls** at 1.4 mi (2.3 km). This spattering cascade tumbles 30 ft (10 m) along a series of cliffs, and the trail climbs alongside the falls by way of rock slabs and exposed roots.

▶ **MILE 1.4–2.0: Hermit Falls to The Rim and The Basin**
Continue climbing the steep hillside beyond the falls. At 1.5 mi (2.4 km), take a left at the junction to remerge with the **Basin Trail.**
  Now the hike becomes a more labored, rocky ascent up the southwestern haunch of West Royce Mountain. Climb through the woods for 0.5 mi

(0.8 km), hopping across several tiny streams—watch the ground for toads, which are often seen hopping around here. The exposed tree roots almost serve as stairs in places along this section; be careful when the roots are wet.

At 2 mi (3.2 km), the trail becomes much steeper after this point, with foot-tall (30-cm) rock stairs that are rough and sloped in places. As the trees open up around you, the trail passes several sheer cliffs with natural white streaks, a sight seldom seen in the region. A final winding set of rock stairs takes you up a cleft in **The Rim.** At the top of the stairs, take a cutoff trail on your left to an exposed ledge that overlooks **The Basin** and offers a tantalizing glimpse of western Maine's hills and farmlands.

▶ **MILE 2.0-2.2: The Rim and The Basin to Trail Junction**
The Basin Trail continues past the viewpoint cutoff and concludes at a five-way trail junction at 2.1 mi (3.4 km). Gluttons for punishment can push on to the summits of West Royce or Ragged Jacket, but for hikers who fancy a more pleasant and relaxed day hike, this is where the backtracking begins.

DIRECTIONS

From Portsmouth, drive north on NH-16 N to the town of Conway. Keep right at the junction for NH-16 N and NH-113 E to continue driving east on NH-113 E. After 2 mi (3.2 km), turn left onto US-302 W and then make a right onto East Conway Road. Drive northeast along this road for 6 mi (9.7 km) and then swing right onto West Fryeburg Road. Here you'll briefly cross into Maine as you continue north along West Fryeburg Road, which eventually becomes Stow Road. At the junction with ME-113B, veer slightly right to stay on Stow Road and follow it north for another 7 mi (11.3 km) as you cross back into New Hampshire. A large sign for The Basin will soon appear on your left. Turn left here onto Basin Road and drive west until you reach a large clearing, where the boat launch road will soon appear on your right. Turn right here. The Basin will be straight ahead, with a parking lot on your right.

GPS COORDINATES: 44°16'09.0"N 71°01'12.1"W

BEST NEARBY BITES AND BREWS

Make the most of your afternoon in this quiet corner of the White Mountains by swinging down to Fryeburg, Maine, for some seriously hopped-up ales like the Murder Hornets Nest imperial IPA at **Saco River Brewing** (10 Jockey Cap Ln., Fryeburg; 207/256-3028; www. sacoriverbrewing.com; 1pm-8pm Mon.-Thurs., 1pm-9pm Fri., noon-9pm Sat., noon-6pm Sun.). If you're feeling extra indulgent, dig into a mountain of ribs and pulled pork with southern fixins at **302 West Smokehouse & Tavern** (636 Main St., Fryeburg; 207/935-3021; www.302west.com; 11:30am-9pm Thurs.-Mon.).

This long yet gentle waterfall hike winds through a beaver bog and traverses a breathtaking white rockslide before concluding with one of the prettiest waterfalls in New Hampshire.

BEST: Fall hikes
DISTANCE: 9.4 mi (15.1 km) round-trip
DURATION: 4.5 hr
ELEVATION GAIN: 425 ft (130 m)
EFFORT: Moderate
TRAIL: Dirt path, rocks, wooden bog bridges, water crossings via stones
USERS: Hikers, leashed dogs
SEASON: June-October
FEES/PASSES: $5 day-use fee per vehicle
MAPS: White Mountain National Forest website
TRAILHEAD: Zealand Trail parking lot, Zealand Rd., Bethlehem
FACILITIES: Vault toilet
CONTACT: White Mountain National Forest; 603/536-6100; www.fs.usda.gov/recarea/whitemountain

It's no secret that Henry David Thoreau had a hankering for beautiful and isolated places, so it's fitting that he got his very own cascade right in the thick of New Hampshire's Pemigewasset Wilderness. Thoreau Falls, which spills 80 ft (24 m) down a series of ledges that overlook the verdant "Pemi" woods, is a classic.

START THE HIKE

▶ **MILE 0-2.3: Zealand Trail to A-Z Trail Junction**
Pick up the **Zealand Trail** as it heads south through a tight corridor of birch and pine trees before entering a more spacious deciduous forest. After gentle ups and downs over a rocky hillside, the smooth dirt trail crosses a wooden footbridge at 0.3 mi (0.5 km) and follows an old railroad bed through the forest. The trail ambles along the **Zealand River** for a bit before veering deeper into the woods and crossing several streams on wooden bridges and rocks.

Curving southwest, the trail suddenly emerges into a vast bogland at 1.7 mi (2.7 km) and crosses a long stretch of boardwalk that marks your entrance into the Zealand Valley. Continue through the bogland as the trail alternates between forest and tallgrass. (Look out for the resident beavers and moose here.) The trail traverses two more streams on rocks and reaches the A-Z Trail junction at 2.3 mi (3.7 km).

White Mountain National Forest

NEW HAMPSHIRE

Zealand Valley and Thoreau Falls

ZEALAND TRAIL

ZEALAND RD

Zealand River

Zealand Trail

Mt Field Brook

Mt Tom ▲ 4,051ft

A-Z Trail

AMC ZEALAND FALLS HUT

Zealand Pond

Zealand Falls

White Mountain

National Forest

Twinway

Ethan Pond Trail

Whitewall Brook

Zeacliff Outlook

Zeacliff Trail

Whitewall Mountain 3,045ft

0   0.5 mi

0   0.5 km

Contour Interval = 40 feet

Thoreau Falls

North Fork

Ethan Pond Trail

Shoal Pond Trail

© MOON.COM

Elevation Profile

Elevation (ft)

2,500
2,400
2,300
2,200
2,100
2,000

0.0   1.0   2.0   3.0   4.0   5.0

One-Way Distance (mi)

▲ THE PATH ALONG WHITEWALL ROCK SLIDE MARKS YOUR EXIT FROM ZEALAND VALLEY.

▶ **MILE 2.3–2.5: A–Z Trail Junction to Zealand Falls**
Keep right to stay on the Zealand Trail and enjoy the view of Zealand Mountain from a wooden footbridge just ahead. Listen for the roar of a nearby waterfall as you reenter the forest and pass **Zealand Pond** on your right. At 2.5 mi (4 km), a huge glacial boulder marks the junction with the Ethan Pond Trail and the Twinway Trail. If you feel like a bowl of soup and a scenic vista, turn right onto the Twinway and scramble up a steep rock staircase to **Zealand Falls Hut,** one of the Appalachian Mountain Club's mountain huts, which offers fresh food and a front-row seat to **Zealand Falls,** which literally rumbles down the mountainside just beyond the hut's doorstep.

▶ **MILE 2.5–3.7: Zealand Falls to Whitewall**
To continue to Thoreau Falls, pick up the **Ethan Pond Trail** at the junction (part of the Appalachian Trail and marked by white blazes) and hike south through a thicker, tighter deciduous forest. Continue along the paved, flat path, which gradually becomes rockier with some twists and turns, for 1.2 mi (1.9 km). At 3.7 mi (6 km), you'll emerge onto an open ledge that cuts right across a massive slide of white rocks known as **Whitewall.** Take a moment to admire the immensity of the slide as well as the stunning views of Zealand Valley behind you and the Pemigewasset territory that lies ahead.

▶ **MILE 3.7–4.7: Whitewall to Thoreau Falls**
After crossing Whitewall, the trail dips back into the trees and crosses several bog bridges as the surrounding woodlands become marshier, with lots of tributaries running through the terrain. Continue south for just under 1 mi (1.6 km) until you reach one last junction at 4.6 mi (7.4 km); turn right onto the **Thoreau Falls Trail.** Descend down a rooty path as a dull rush of water becomes louder, and arrive at the upper ledges of **Thoreau Falls**

at 4.7 mi (7.6 km). The upper ledge offers photo opportunities, swimming holes, and plenty of space for picnicking. Curious hikers can continue down the Thoreau Trail for a different perspective of the cascade before beginning the return journey back through the valley.

DIRECTIONS

From Concord, drive north on I-93 N for 73 mi (117 km). After passing through Franconia Notch, take Exit 35 for US-3 N toward Lancaster/Twin Mountain. Merge onto US-3 N and continue northwest for roughly 10 mi (16 km) before taking a right turn onto US-302 E. Drive east along US-302 E for another 2 mi (3.2 km) and then make a final right onto Zealand Road. Cross the bridge over the Ammonoosuc River; watch your speed, as the road becomes a dirt road that weaves through the woods for about 3 mi (4.8 km) before crossing a final wooden bridge and arriving at the Zealand Trail parking lot. Overflow parking is available just before the final bridge; the day-use fee is payable by cash or check at the self-serve kiosk by the trailhead sign at the south end of the parking lot.

GPS COORDINATES: 44°13'29.7"N 71°28'41.9"W

BEST NEARBY BREWS

Cool off with a nitro stout or a hoppy red ale at **Rek-Lis Brewing** (2085 Main St., Bethlehem; 603/991-2357; www.reklisbrewing.com; 4pm–9pm Mon.–Tues. and Thurs., noon–9pm Fri.–Sun.). The brewery also offers a mean fried chicken sandwich among other gastropub noshes, which is best enjoyed in the open-air beer garden with a view of the Presidential Range to the east.

NEW HAMPSHIRE

White Mountain National Forest

Mount Willard
CRAWFORD NOTCH STATE PARK, CARROLL

🦌 ❄️ 🐾 🏞️ 🚶 🚌

A rite of passage for New Englanders, this classic family-friendly mountain hike ascends to an exposed lookout ledge that offers the most awe-inspiring view of Crawford Notch.

BEST: Winter hikes
DISTANCE: 3 mi (4.8 km) round-trip
DURATION: 1.5 hr
ELEVATION GAIN: 874 ft (266 m)
EFFORT: Easy
TRAIL: Dirt path, rocks, water crossings on stones
USERS: Hikers, leashed dogs
SEASON: June–October
FEES/PASSES: None
MAPS: Crawford Notch State Park website
TRAILHEAD: Crawford Notch Depot, US–302, Carroll
FACILITIES: Restrooms
CONTACT: Crawford Notch State Park; 603/374-2272; www.nhstateparks.org

For those who are just getting started with hiking, the little tuft-like Mount Willard is the equivalent of a bicycle with training wheels. The ascent itself is a gentle and pleasant walk in the woods, offering a lively waterfall along the way to Willard's upper slopes. But the summit of Mount Willard is a legend—a windy, exposed ledge with sheer drops and an amazing panoramic view of Crawford Notch that's too vast and epic to be contained within most camera frames.

START THE HIKE

▶ **MILE 0-0.2: Crawford Notch Depot to Mount Willard Trail**
Begin the hike by the boarding area at Crawford Notch Depot. Cross the railroad tracks and pick up the dirt trail on the other side. Walk west through a small field into the woods and turn left onto the yellow-blazed **Mount Willard Trail.** Head south through the rich birch and spruce forest, snaking through the forest at a level grade and crossing a series of streams on rocks.

▶ **MILE 0.2-0.5: Mount Willard Trail to Centennial Pool**
The trail begins to curve southwest, ascending the northern haunch of Mount Willard up stone stairs at a relaxed grade. Up ahead, the hulking profile of nearby Mount Avalon looms through the boreal spruce trees as the trail continues climbing gradually, meeting up with a stream that spills beside the trail.

White Mountain National Forest

NEW HAMPSHIRE

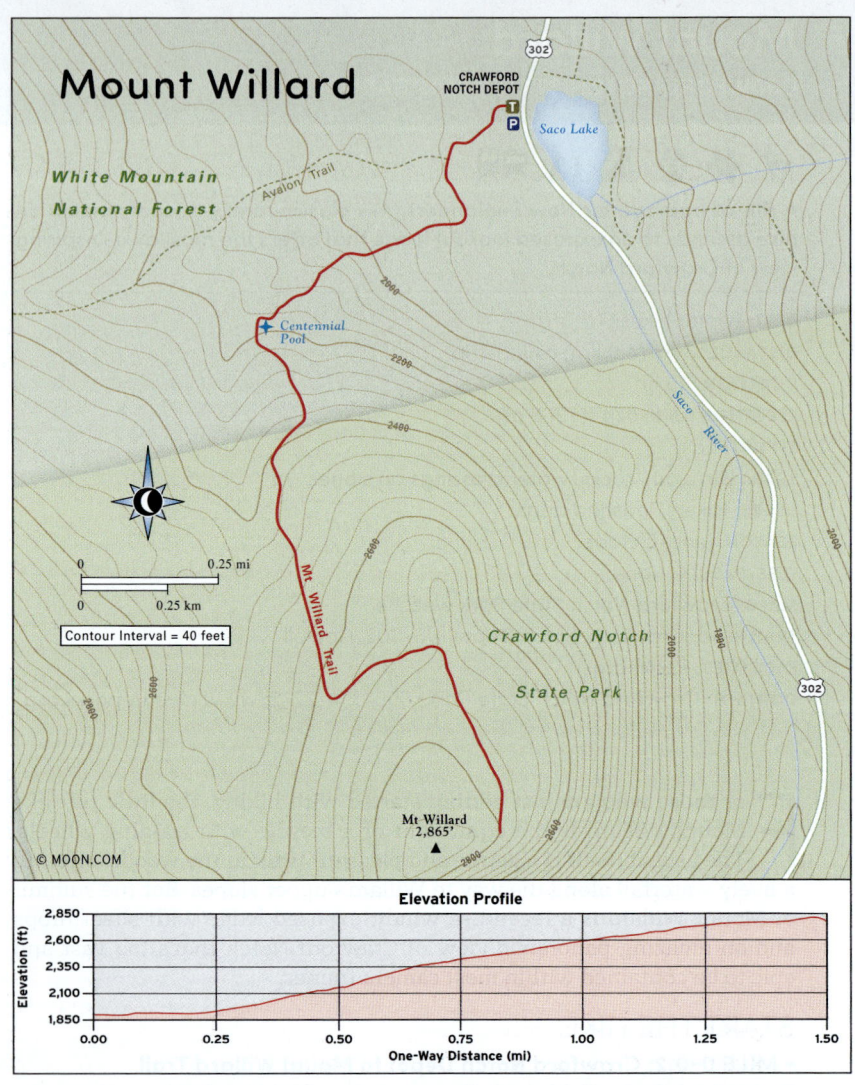

Mount Willard

CRAWFORD NOTCH DEPOT

Saco Lake

White Mountain National Forest

Avalon Trail

Centennial Pool

Saco River

0   0.25 mi

0   0.25 km

Contour Interval = 40 feet

Mt Willard Trail

Crawford Notch State Park

302

Mt Willard 2,865'

© MOON.COM

Elevation Profile

Elevation (ft): 2,850 / 2,600 / 2,350 / 2,100 / 1,850

One-Way Distance (mi): 0.00 — 0.25 — 0.50 — 0.75 — 1.00 — 1.25 — 1.50

Continue west along the stream until you reach **Centennial Pool** at 0.5 mi (0.8 km). This little cascade is worth a look—the water spatters down a beautifully carved cliff into a reflective basin that you can scramble down to.

▶ **MILE 0.5-1.5: Centennial Pool to Ledges of Mount Willard**

The Mount Willard Trail climbs south from here and ascends some taller rock stairs before transitioning into a wider and rockier path that's often bisected by ancient concrete water pipes. The strong pine aroma here foreshadows the forests of the upper slopes. At 1.1 mi (1.8 km), you'll reach the slopes, as the trail flattens and swerves east into dark, mossy woods.

A brief series of moist, sloped rock slabs through the boreal pine woods delivers you to a long corridor of trees where the path becomes a much

▲ VIEW FROM MOUNT WILLARD

smoother dirt highway across the mountaintop. Far ahead, a distant orb of daylight shines like the metaphorical "light at the end of the tunnel." Head south again toward the light and step out onto the famous ledges of **Mount Willard** at 1.5 mi (2.4 km). Watch your step around the rim of the ledge, especially on a gusty day, and enjoy one of the most disarmingly beautiful vistas in New Hampshire. The notch—a vast glacial gorge filled with woodlands—is framed by Mount Webster on the left and Mount Willey on the right. Beyond, well-known peaks such as Carrigain and Chocorua tickle the clouds. Return the way you came—if you can bring yourself to leave.

DIRECTIONS

From Concord, drive north on I-93 N for 73 mi (117 km). After passing through Franconia Notch, take Exit 35 for US-3 N toward Lancaster/Twin Mountain. Merge onto US-3 N and continue northwest for roughly 10 mi (16 km) before taking a right turn onto US-302 E. Drive east along US-302 E for another 8 mi (12.9 km). You'll then see the Appalachian Mountain Club's Highland Center lodge on your right. Turn right into the Highland Center parking lot, where hikers can park their vehicles. The Crawford Notch Depot train station is next to the Highland Center and accessible by a short dirt path that cuts across a field.

GPS COORDINATES: 44°13'04.1"N 71°24'40.8"W

7 Arethusa Falls via Bemis Brook

CRAWFORD NOTCH STATE PARK, HART'S LOCATION

This popular hike to New Hampshire's tallest waterfall takes a rugged detour to visit a series of hidden cascades along Bemis Brook.

BEST: Winter hikes, waterfalls
DISTANCE: 2.8 mi (4.5 km) round-trip
DURATION: 2 hr
ELEVATION GAIN: 928 ft (283 m)
EFFORT: Easy/moderate
TRAIL: Dirt path, rocks, wooden bridges, water crossings on stones
USERS: Hikers, leashed dogs
SEASON: May–October
FEES/PASSES: None
MAPS: Crawford Notch State Park website
TRAILHEAD: Arethusa Falls trailhead parking lot, US–302, Hart's Location
FACILITIES: None
CONTACT: Crawford Notch State Park; 603/374–2272; www.nhstateparks.org

A trip to the Whites wouldn't be complete without gawking at the towering wonder that is Arethusa Falls. At nearly 200 ft (61 m) tall, this silvery cascade tumbles down a sheer cliff face right in the heart of Crawford Notch State Park. The direct-access route, the Arethusa Falls Trail, is popular during all seasons—even winter, when ice climbers tempt fate by scaling the frozen falls. But the coolest way to reach Arethusa Falls is taking the lesser-known Bemis Brook Trail cutoff, which features a gorgeous pair of smaller waterfalls that spill through the forest in which Arethusa Falls is tucked away.

START THE HIKE

▶ MILE 0-0.1: Arethusa Falls Trailhead Parking Lot to Bemis Brook Trail Junction

Begin your hike in the Arethusa Falls parking lot, directly off Route 302. Walk up the concrete road to the railroad tracks and look for the Arethusa Falls trailhead to your left. Cross the tracks and pick up the trail as it gently climbs west into a forest of birches and pine. Follow the blue-blazed trail up a root-festooned path for a few minutes before quickly reaching the **Bemis Brook Trail** junction.

▶ MILE 0.1-0.3: Bemis Brook Trail to Coliseum Falls

Turn left here and pick up the Bemis Brook Trail as it efficiently descends to Bemis Brook itself. After reaching the stream, the yellow-blazed trail follows the boulder-strewn brook while ascending at a modest grade.

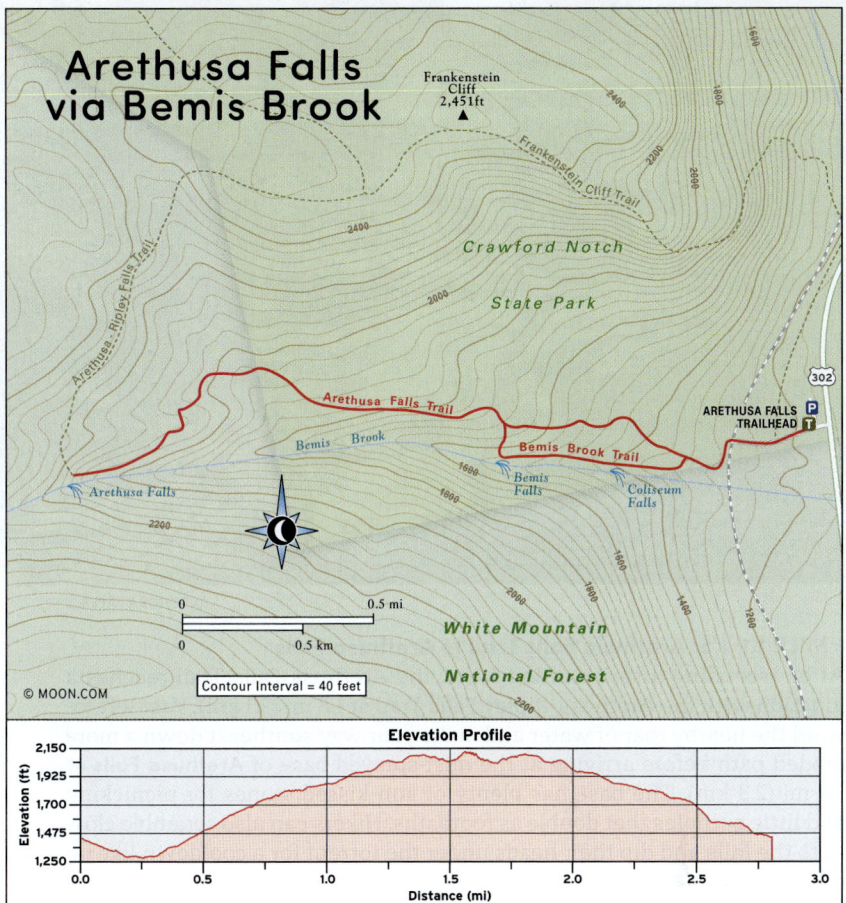

Arethusa Falls
via Bemis Brook

Elevation Profile

The dynamic rush of water announces your arrival at **Coliseum Falls** at roughly 0.3 mi (0.5 km). The lower portion of this lively 25-ft-tall (8-m) cascade spatters down a series of natural rock steps that resemble a miniature amphitheater.

▶ **MILE 0.3–0.5: Coliseum Falls to Bemis Falls**
Continue along the brook for another 0.2 mi (0.3 km) before reaching **Bemis Falls,** a larger trifecta of falling waters with a wonderful outlook ledge.

▶ **MILE 0.5–1.1: Bemis Falls to Arethusa Falls Trail**
From here, the trail takes a sharp right and makes a steep, rocky climb back up to the main trail. Upon reaching the junction at 0.6 mi (1 km), continue left on the Arethusa Falls Trail, which weaves west through the woods at an agreeable grade for 0.5 mi (0.8 km) and widens into a smoother, gravelly path with occasional stone stairs. Cross two wooden footbridges at 1.1 mi (1.8 km) and keep an eye out for lady's slippers, which bloom here during the spring and early summer.

▶ **MILE 1.1-1.5: Arethusa Falls Trail to Arethusa Falls**
After ascending a series of log steps, the Arethusa Falls Trail reaches a junction with the Arethusa-Ripley Falls Trail at 1.3 mi (2.1 km). Veer left toward the nearby roar of water and make your way southeast down a more eroded path before arriving at the mist-sprayed base of **Arethusa Falls** at 1.4 mi (2.3 km). The base has plenty of sun-kissed stones for picnicking and little potholes that double as footbaths. Hikers can also scramble closer to the falls and dip their heads under the torrent for a cooldown like no other.

▶ **MILE 1.5-2.8: Arethusa Falls to Arethusa Falls Trailhead Parking Lot**
Once you feel optimally serene, backtrack east along the Arethusa Falls Trail. This time, when you reach the Bemis Brook Trail junction, take a left to stay on the main trail, which descends at a moderate grade through the woods for roughly 0.5 mi (0.8 km) over exposed roots and small rocks before delivering you back to the Arethusa Falls trailhead at 2.8 mi (4.5 km).

DIRECTIONS

From Boston, drive north on I-93 N for 139 mi (224 km) across the New Hampshire border and into the White Mountains. Take Exit 35 for US-3 N toward Lancaster/Twin Mountain and continue until you reach the junction with US-302 E. Turn right onto US-302 E and drive southeast for roughly 15 mi (24 km) as you pass the sign for Crawford Notch State Park and descend into the notch itself. A sign on your right clearly marks the turnoff for the Arethusa Falls parking area.

GPS COORDINATES: 44°08'53.3"N 71°21'59.1"W

8

Bridal Veil Falls

WHITE MOUNTAIN NATIONAL FOREST, FRANCONIA

This forest hike features one of New Hampshire's most elegant cascades, a sumptuous swimming hole, and a haunting memento of Hollywood history.

BEST: Waterfalls
DISTANCE: 4.4 mi (7.1 km) round-trip
DURATION: 2.5 hr
ELEVATION GAIN: 966 ft (294 m)
EFFORT: Easy/moderate
TRAIL: Dirt path, rocks, wooden bridge, water crossings via rocks
USERS: Hikers, leashed dogs
SEASON: May-October
FEES/PASSES: None
MAPS: White Mountain National Forest website
TRAILHEAD: Coppermine Trail parking lot, Coppermine Rd., Franconia
FACILITIES: None
CONTACT: White Mountain National Forest; 603/536-6100; www.fs.usda.gov/recarea/whitemountain

One of New Hampshire's most elegant and aptly named cascades, Bridal Veil Falls spills from a pitcher-like cleft of rock in a ravine on Cannon Mountain's western haunch. The top of this 80-ft-tall (24-m) cascade resembles the silky veil of a bride, and the access route to the falls—the Coppermine Trail—makes for a breezy day hike with enough climbing to get the blood pumping. The trail is rustling with deciduous vegetation and critters, and it also contains a legend that has intrigued visitors for decades.

START THE HIKE

▶ **MILE 0-1.0: Coppermine Trail Parking Lot to Coppermine Brook**
Begin your hike in the parking area on Coppermine Road. Turn left and walk east on Coppermine Road. Keep right at the fork with Beechwood Lane and at 0.2 mi (0.3 km), look for a metal hiker sign on a tree on your left. Turn left onto the dirt path by the sign. This is the start of the **Coppermine Trail.** As you step into a thick forest of pine trees, the trail curves southeast (following yellow blazes) and ambles upward at a gentle grade. The footing gets rockier and rootier, but the generous trail width makes the going pleasant. Around 0.6 mi (1 km), you'll start to hear the promising sound of rushing water.

Passing through some white birch trees, the trail reaches **Coppermine Brook** at 1 mi (1.6 km). Before you continue southeast along the water, take a minute to pick your way down to the brook from the trail: One of the boulders here contains a bronze plaque memorializing Arthur Farnsworth, a

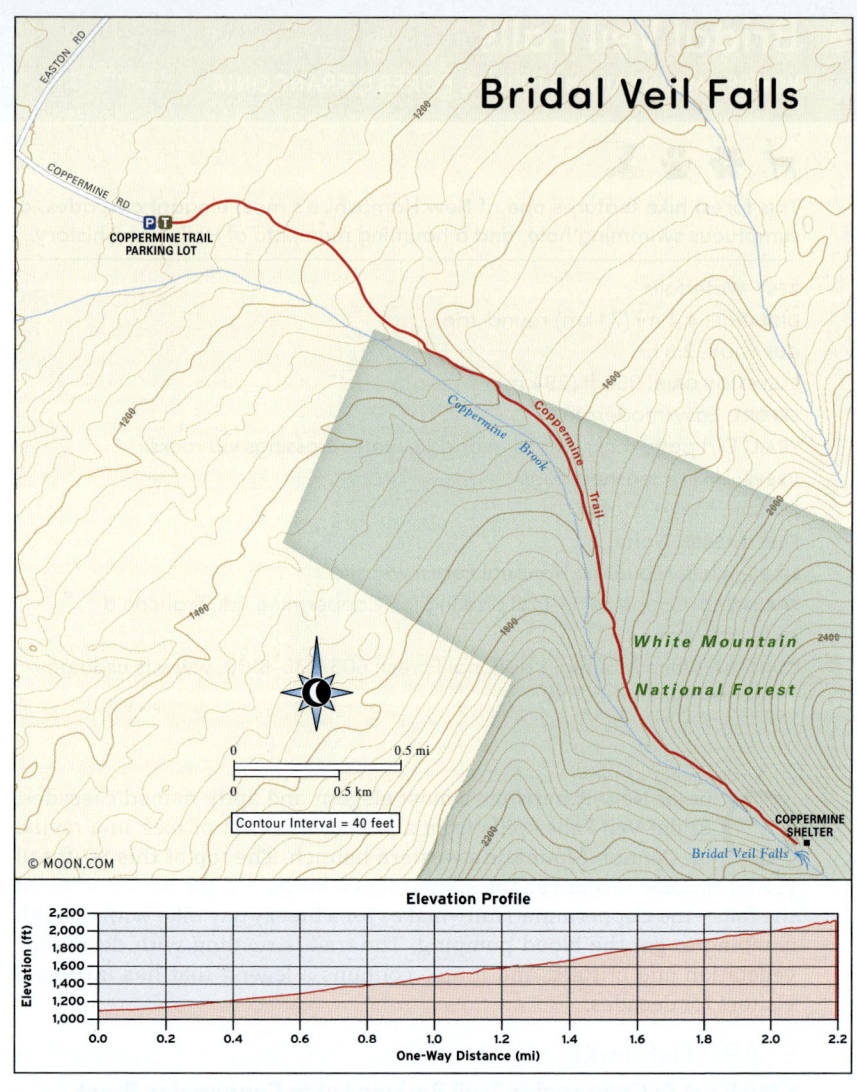

Bridal Veil Falls

Elevation Profile

local innkeeper who became the second husband of Hollywood icon Bette Davis. Local legend has it that Davis herself had the plaque placed there—though it's not 100 percent confirmed. (The plaque, which refers to Farnsworth as "The Keeper of Stray Ladies," cites Davis as "A Grateful One.")

▶ MILE 1.0–2.1: Coppermine Brook to Coppermine Shelter

Once you've either found the plaque or given up, continue along the brook and savor this final stretch of laid-back terrain, for the Coppermine Trail steepens at 1.4 mi (2.3 km) and begins to veer away from the brook. After climbing the western flank of Cannon Mountain for roughly 0.5 mi (0.8 km)—passing into a mixture of deciduous and boreal forest—the trail rejoins Coppermine

NEW HAMPSHIRE
White Mountain National Forest

Brook and crosses it on a wooden bridge at 1.9 mi (3.1 km). Shortly after, at 2.1 mi (3.4 km), you'll arrive at **Coppermine Shelter**—a grungy lean-to for overnight hikers.

► **MILE 2.1-2.2: Coppermine Shelter to Bridal Veil Falls**
The Coppermine Trail continues past the shelter and crosses the brook on stones one final time. Listen for the sound of crashing water; at 2.2 mi (3.5 km), emerge from the forest at the foot of Bridal Veil Falls' bottom half—a water slide that tumbles down an open slope of granite. The pool at the base of the slide is ideal for a brisk swim before scrambling up the rocks and roots along the left side of the lower falls (the trail concludes at the pool) and reaching the upper half of **Bridal Veil Falls**—the veil-like part for which it's named. There are plenty of nearby rocks for sitting and admiring the view. Return the way you came.

DIRECTIONS

From Boston, drive north on I-93. Once you've crossed the New Hampshire border, continue north and take Exit 34C. Turn left onto NH 8 N. Veer left at the junction with Profile Road, after which NH 8 becomes Wells Road. Continue to the end of Wells Road and turn right on NH 116. Coppermine Road is 0.5 mi (0.8 km) ahead. Turn left on Coppermine Road and park in the hiker parking area that you'll see on your immediate left.

GPS COORDINATES: 44°10'49.0"N 71°45'13.9"W

BEST NEARBY BITES AND BREWS

Start the day with a stack of maple syrup-coated flapjacks at **Polly's Pancake Parlor** (672 NH-117, Sugar Hill; 603/823-5575; www.pollyspancakeparlor.com; 7am-2pm Thurs.-Mon.). After your hike, hop over to Littleton and reflect with a malty doppelbock or any of the other European-inspired artisanal brews at **Schilling Beer Co.** (18 Mill St., Littleton; 603/444-4800; www.schillingbeer.com; noon-8pm Sun.-Thurs., noon-9pm Fri.-Sat.).

White Mountain National Forest

NEW HAMPSHIRE

9

Mount Lafayette and Franconia Ridge

FRANCONIA NOTCH STATE PARK, LINCOLN

Summit the tallest mountain on the Franconia Ridge, along with two others, and make a thrillingly steep descent of several large waterfalls.

BEST: Fall hikes

DISTANCE: 8.4 mi (13.5 km) round-trip

DURATION: 5.5 hr

ELEVATION GAIN: 3,812 ft (1,162 m)

EFFORT: Strenuous

TRAIL: Dirt path, rocks, wooden bog bridges

USERS: Hikers

SEASON: June–October

FEES/PASSES: None

MAPS: Franconia Notch State Park website

TRAILHEAD: Old Bridle Path, Lafayette Place parking lot, I-93, Lincoln

FACILITIES: Vault toilet

CONTACT: Franconia Notch State Park; 603/823-8800; www.nhstateparks.org

Mount Lafayette greets visitors to the White Mountains as they approach from the south on I-93. It's the tallest point along the breathtaking Franconia Ridge, which also contains comparably mighty mountaintops such as Mount Lincoln and Little Haystack. Ascending to Lafayette by way of the Old Bridle Path is one of the most generously scenic ridge climbs in New Hampshire. But the fun doesn't stop there—as any peak-bagger worth their salt would say, why summit just one mountain when you could experience a trilogy? That's exactly what this loop offers—an opportunity to climb Lafayette, Lincoln, and Haystack in one fell swoop.

START THE HIKE

▶ **MILE 0-2.1: Old Bridle Path to The Three Agonies**
Pick up the **Old Bridle Path** by the trail sign and step into the forest on a rocky path that ambles over to **Walker Brook.** Veer left at the junction for Falling Waters Trail at 0.2 mi (0.3 km) to stay on Old Bridle Path and hike northwest as the trail meanders up the foothills of **Lafayette** at a pleasant grade. As the footing becomes rockier and steeper, the trail ascends a series of slabby switchbacks. At 1.5 mi (2.4 km), you'll reach the first of many exposed ledges on Lafayette's curvy southern ridgeline. Lafayette and the Franconia ridgeline beckon beyond this lookout point.

From here, the Old Bridle Path roller-coasters up and down the Lafayette ridgeline. The views of **Franconia Ridge** and the deep deciduous valley below are constant, with only a few forays into the trees. At just over

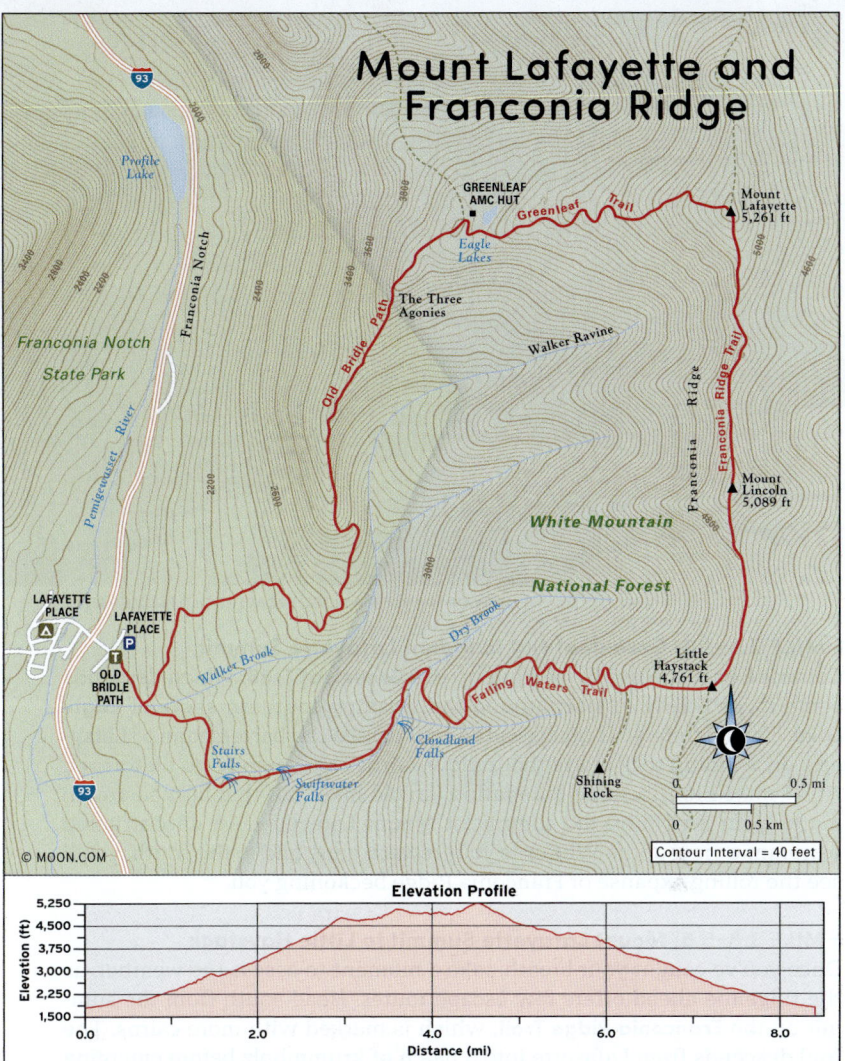

Mount Lafayette and Franconia Ridge

Elevation Profile

2 mi (3.2 km), you'll reach **"The Three Agonies"**—a trio of very steep and rocky ledge climbs. (The first Agony consists of smooth red rock that can become super slippery when wet.)

▶ **MILE 2.1-2.8: The Three Agonies to Greenleaf Hut**

After this trifecta of obstacles, the trail levels off and emerges from boreal forest into the alpine zone. Here, at 2.8 mi (4.5 km), you'll reach **Greenleaf Hut,** where you can buy soup, tea, or—if so desired—a bunk bed and a five-course dinner. (Reservations are recommended and can be made at www. outdoors.org.)

VIEW OF FRANCONIA RIDGE FROM THE OLD BRIDLE PATH ▲

▶ **MILE 2.8-3.8: Greenleaf Hut to Mount Lafayette Summit**
Continue past the hut by picking up the **Greenleaf Trail,** which descends
some rocks briefly to skirt around the swampy southern shore of **Eagle
Lake.** Then, ignite your quads as the trail climbs the barren cone of Lafayette on winding rock stairs that follow cairns that seem to go on forever.
At 3.8 mi (6.1 km), a stone foundation (an old hiker hut that burned down)
marks your arrival on the summit of Mount Lafayette. An unobstructed
panoramic view of the Whites is your reward here, and to the south, you'll
see the rolling expanse of Franconia Ridge beckoning you.

▶ **MILE 3.8-5.5: Mount Lafayette Summit to Little Haystack**
Once you've caught your breath, take a moment to assess the weather, as
the ridgeline ahead offers few escape routes. Head south from the summit on the **Franconia Ridge Trail,** which is marked with more cairns. The
trail descends from Lafayette into a patch of krummholz before emerging
again and traveling up and down along the verdant, exposed, and often
very narrow ridgeline to visit **Mount Lincoln** at 4.7 mi (7.6 km) and **Little
Haystack** at 5.5 mi (8.9 km).

▶ **MILE 5.5-6.8: Little Haystack to Dry Brook**
The path is alternately rocky and smooth, weaving along and over the
bumpy ridgeline like a dirt ribbon. Complemented by the rich green moss
and krummholz, it's one of the most beautiful and dreamy trails in New
England—with no trees to obstruct the view.

Your return journey begins from the top of Little Haystack. From the
summit, turn right onto the **Falling Waters Trail,** which is clearly marked
with a sign on the summit. Follow blue blazes and descend west back
into the boreal spruce forest at a steep grade down rock slabs and some
very rough stairs before entering more deciduous woods. The churning of

NEW HAMPSHIRE

White Mountain National Forest

water precedes your first crossing of the ironically named **Dry Brook** at 6.8 mi (10.9 km).

▶ **MILE 6.8-8.2: Dry Brook to Walker Brook**
Rock-hop across the brook a few more times to arrive at **Cloudland Falls**—an 80-ft-tall (24-m) behemoth of a waterfall that the trail descends alongside at a steep grade. The trail stays close to the brook and passes two more cascades before leveling out, making a final crossing, and heading north to a bridge across the familiar Walker Brook at 8.2 mi (13.2 km).

▶ **MILE 8.2-8.4: Walker Brook to Old Bridle Path**
Turn left onto **Old Bridle Path** after the bridge and backtrack to the trailhead to complete the hike at 8.4 mi (13.5 km).

DIRECTIONS

From Concord, drive north on I-93 N for 69 mi (111 km) into Franconia Notch. Take the Trailhead Parking exit for Lafayette Place. If the lot is full, continue north on I-93, take Exit 34B, turn left at the bottom of the off-ramp, drive under the highway, and then pull an immediate left to merge back onto I-93, heading south this time. Backtrack to Lafayette Place and take the Trailhead Parking exit off I-93 S. The two lots are connected by a pedestrian tunnel underneath the highway. The outhouses are up a short concrete path that ascends east from the lot. Begin the hike on the I-93 N side of the Lafayette Place parking lot.

GPS COORDINATES: 44°08'30.6"N 71°40'51.4"W

White Mountain National Forest

NEW HAMPSHIRE

10

The Flume

FRANCONIA NOTCH STATE PARK, LINCOLN

This waterfall hike takes visitors through a misty gorge with plenty of cascades, boardwalks, covered bridges, and views of the Franconia ridgeline.

BEST: Summer hikes

DISTANCE: 2 mi (3.2 km) round-trip

DURATION: 1 hr

ELEVATION GAIN: 527 ft (160 m)

EFFORT: Easy

TRAIL: Dirt path, wooden bridges and staircases

USERS: Hikers

SEASON: June–October

FEES/PASSES: $21 adult, $19 child ages 6–12, free ages 5 and under

MAPS: New Hampshire State Parks website

TRAILHEAD: Flume Gorge Visitor Center, US-3, Lincoln

FACILITIES: Restrooms

CONTACT: Franconia Notch State Park; 603/823-8800; www.nhstateparks. org; visitor center 8am–5pm daily mid–May to late October (these are the hours when the trail is "open" to hikers)

D iscovered in 1808 by a 93-year-old woman who was looking for a good place to fish, The Flume is one of New Hampshire's most popular natural wonders. This 800-ft-deep (244-m) gorge sits at the base of Mount Liberty and contains an eye-popping series of waterfalls that hikers can glimpse up close thanks to the ingeniously constructed boardwalk system that runs through The Flume and links up with a path that traverses a forest of wildflowers, moss, and glacial boulders above the gorge itself.

START THE HIKE

▶ **MILE 0–0.2: Flume Gorge Visitor Center to Flume Trail**
Start the hike at the back end of the visitor center. Walk up the road into the woods, following signs for the Flume hiking trails. This will deliver you to the **Great Boulder.** Turn right to pick up the **Flume Trail,** which begins as a wide gravel path that descends a broad hillside to a handsome covered bridge over the **Pemigewasset River.**

▶ **MILE 0.2–0.4: Flume Trail to Table Rock Falls**
From the bridge, the trail climbs gradually through a beech forest and reaches **Flume Brook** at 0.3 mi (0.5 km). Continue climbing east alongside the brook past several miniature cascades before ascending a rockier and slightly steeper pitch to arrive at **Table Rock Falls.** This waterfall spills down a vast sloped rock face and marks your arrival to the gorge at 0.4 mi (0.6 km).

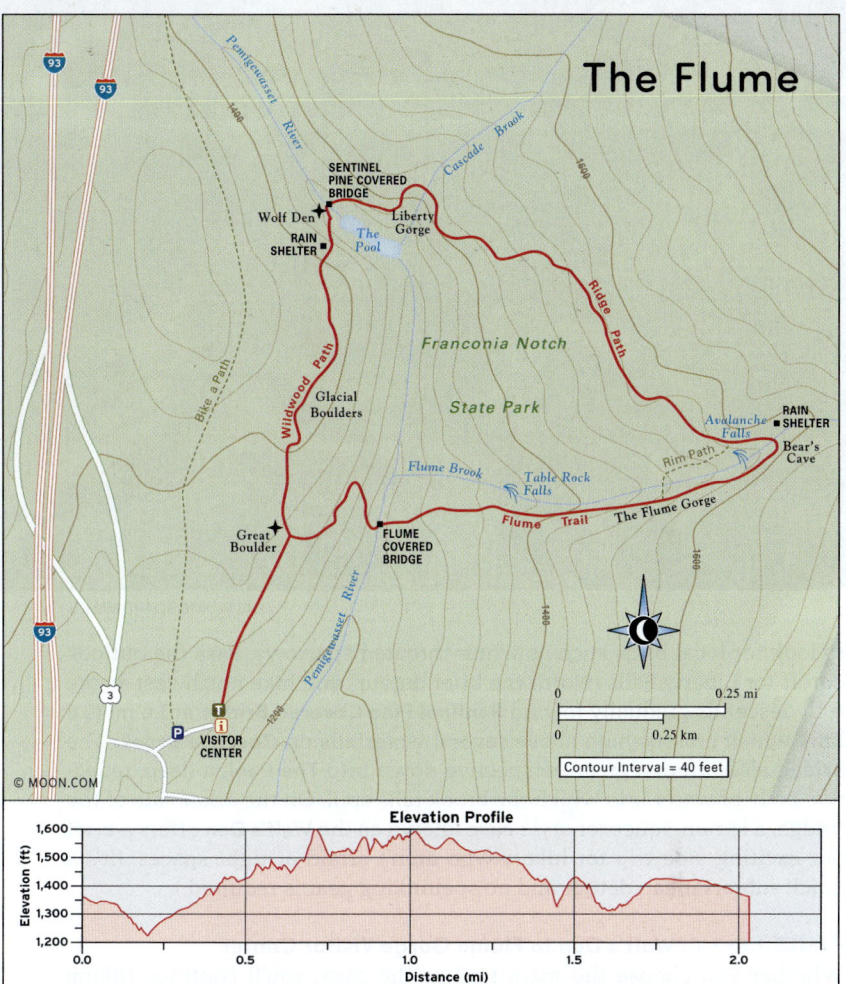

The Flume

Elevation Profile

▶ **MILE 0.4–0.9: Table Rock Falls to Avalanche Falls**

Staying eastward, the trail enters **The Flume** and transitions to boardwalk at 0.5 mi (0.8 km), just as the damp walls of the gorge are becoming more pronounced. Stroll along the boardwalk and up flights of precariously tilted wooden stairs, beneath which Flume Brook crashes and spills down several miniature cascades. You'll notice that the air in The Flume is remarkably moist and cool—this contributes to the many species of moss you'll observe growing on the walls. A final round of stairs delivers you to **Avalanche Falls** at 0.9 mi (1.4 km).

Take a moment to admire this thundering 45-ft-tall (14-m) torrent of water before stepping off the last stretch of the boardwalk and onto a level gravel path. You'll leave the gorge and head into the rim forest.

▶ **MILE 0.9–1.6: Avalanche Falls to Wolf's Den**

The trail ambles through the trees for a few beats. This is a good place for hikers to take in partial views of the Kinsman mountains to the west and

THE FLUME BOARDWALK ▲

to look for local birds such as white-throated sparrows. Pass the outlook cutoff for Liberty Falls (worth the brief detour) and hike northwest as the trail descends gradually toward **Sentinel Pine Covered Bridge** at 1.6 mi (2.6 km), which crosses high above several waterfalls on **Cascade Brook.** The bridge also offers a great perspective down into **The Pool,** a deep, reflective body of water into which the brook falls spill. On the other side of the bridge, a lemon-squeezer-style cave known as the **Wolf's Den** offers a brief but exciting side trip for hikers who aren't afraid of tight spaces. (It's a quick subterranean detour and no spelunking gear is required.)

▸ **MILE 1.6–2.0: Wolf's Den to Flume Gorge Visitor Center**
Whether you choose the main trail or the cave, you'll continue hiking south and eventually pass into a much rockier stretch of forest that's chock-full of glacial erratics at 1.7 mi (2.7 km). This final portion of the hike feels like a stroll through a sculpture park. Enjoy a bit of light climbing and descending through these knolly woods and reemerge at Great Boulder and then the visitor center.

DIRECTIONS

From Concord, drive north on I-93 N for 66 mi (106 km) and take Exit 34A to merge onto US-3 N toward the Flume Gorge. Turn right at the first sign for the Flume Gorge Visitor Center and park in the visitor lots ahead. Enter the center to buy your ticket and pass through the admission gate to the back end of the center.

GPS COORDINATES: 44°05'53.2"N 71°40'45.5"W

11

Mount Carrigain

WHITE MOUNTAIN NATIONAL FOREST, HART'S LOCATION

Venture deep into the isolated Pemigewasset Wilderness to ascend the long, scenic ridgeline of this cone-shaped peak, which has a lookout tower offering the finest vista in New Hampshire.

DISTANCE: 10.4 mi (16.7 km) round-trip

DURATION: 6 hr

ELEVATION GAIN: 3,474 ft (1,059 m)

EFFORT: Strenuous

TRAIL: Dirt path, rocks, wooden bog bridges, water crossings on stones

USERS: Hikers, leashed dogs

SEASON: June–October

FEES/PASSES: None

MAPS: White Mountain National Forest website

TRAILHEAD: Signal Ridge trailhead, Sawyer River Rd., Hart's Location

FACILITIES: None

CONTACT: White Mountain National Forest; 603/536-6100; www.fs.usda.gov/recarea/whitemountain

START THE HIKE

▶ **MILE 0–0.5: Signal Ridge Trailhead to Whiteface Brook**

Cross Sawyer River Road and head for the wooden trailhead sign to pick up the yellow-blazed **Signal Ridge Trail.** Head northwest, warming up your quads as the trail gently ascends a hemlock-spruce forest. Watch your step on the abundant roots and rocks. To your right, the constant rippling of **Whiteface Brook** provides a soothing soundtrack. The trail heads directly northwest alongside the brook, crossing the occasional log bridge and passing some little sputtering cascades at 0.5 mi (0.8 km).

▶ **MILE 0.5–1.7: Whiteface Brook to Carrigain Brook**

As the woods become sunnier and breezier, a moderately graded stone staircase takes you away from the brook to a higher stretch of beechwood forest. Continue northwest as the trail transitions into a smoother expressway of rock and stone that cruises through the woods. Up ahead, the titanic mass of Carrigain looms through the trees. At 1.5 mi (2.4 km), the trail passes a fork with an unmarked side path. Veer right here to stay on Signal Ridge Trail—note that the yellow blazes become less frequent henceforth. At 1.7 mi (2.7 km), the trail arrives on the stony banks of **Carrigain Brook**. Shortly ahead, the trail crosses the brook on rocks. The water level here can easily get high enough to cover the stepping-stones and saturate a boot, so be prepared to ford barefoot if you don't want to squelch your way to the top of Carrigain.

White Mountain National Forest

NEW HAMPSHIRE

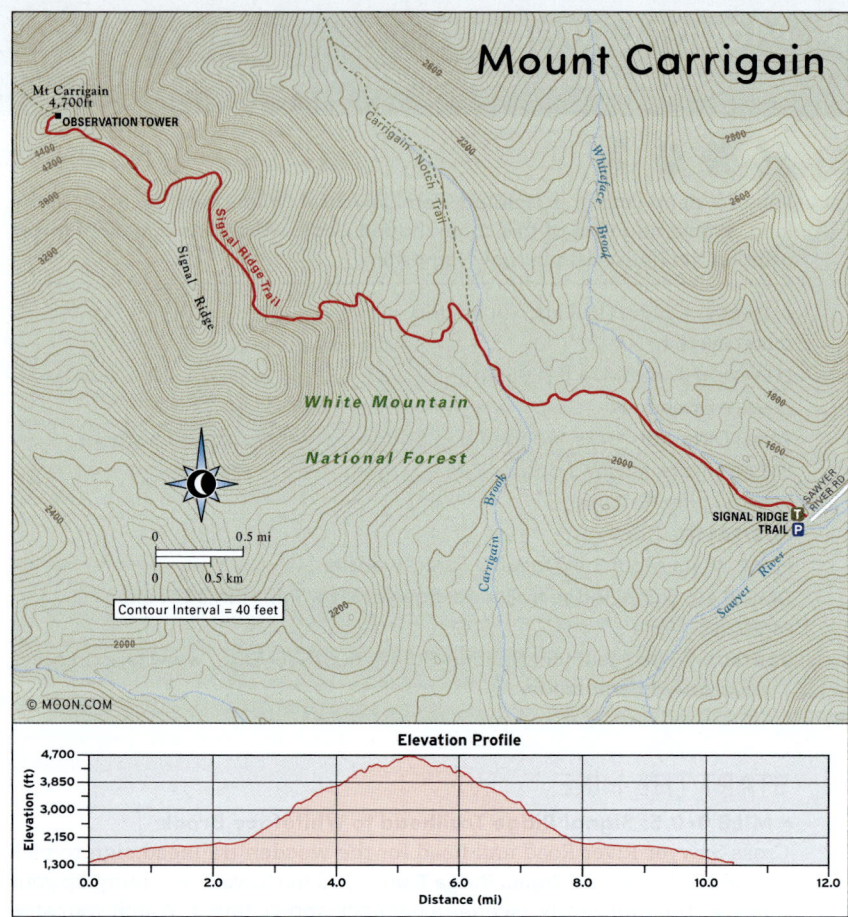

Mount Carrigain

Mt Carrigain
4,700ft
OBSERVATION TOWER

Carrigain Notch Trail

Whiteface Brook

Signal Ridge Trail

Signal Ridge

White Mountain

National Forest

Carrigain Brook

SIGNAL RIDGE TRAIL

SAWYER RIVER RD

Sawyer River

0   0.5 mi
0   0.5 km

Contour Interval = 40 feet

© MOON.COM

Elevation Profile

Elevation (ft)

4,700
3,850
3,000
2,150
1,300

0.0   2.0   4.0   6.0   8.0   10.0   12.0

Distance (mi)

▶ **MILE 1.7–3.2: Carrigain Brook to Signal Ridge**

Shortly after the brook crossing, the trail passes through a beaver marsh before reaching the junction with Carrigain Notch Trail at 2.2 mi (3.5 km). Make a left here to stay on Signal Ridge Trail as it approaches the mountain base. Then, quite suddenly, the terrain changes from level ambling to steep rock stairs and slabs through mossier boreal woods. Consider this the "toll booth" to reach the more exposed and scenic ridgeline. Be sure to pause and enjoy the partial views of nearby peaks such as **Mount Lowell,** especially as the forest thins out and the trees start to shrink. The trail climbs steadily and steeply, heading northeast before reaching the gustier and sunnier southern end of **Signal Ridge** at roughly 3.2 mi (5.1 km).

▶ **MILE 3.2–5.2: Signal Ridge to Mount Carrigain Observation Tower**

Over the next 1 mi (1.6 km), the climb is a much more gradual and enjoyable saunter across the wooded ridgeline. The evergreen trees up here are small enough to offer near-constant views of the vast Pemi wilderness, as well as the Presidentials and the Sandwich Range. The footing is a mixture of dirt and rocks as the trail closes in on the summit. A brief dip into

the trees at 4.7 mi (7.6 km) takes you to the final ascent—a steeper and rockier pitch that slabs up to the top of the summit cone before fully emerging from the alpine woods and reaching the famous summit **observation tower** at 5.2 mi (8.4 km). Unlike the other, more terrifying lookout towers in the Whites, this one is short enough for almost anyone to scramble up and enjoy. On a clear day, you can gaze out at Mount Washington and Co. to the north and the craggy Sandwich Range to the south. Return the way you came.

DIRECTIONS

From Concord, drive north on I-93 N for 73 mi (117 km). After passing through Franconia Notch, take Exit 35 for US-3 N toward Lancaster/Twin Mountain. Merge onto US-3 N and continue northwest for roughly 10 mi (16 km) before taking a right turn onto US-302 E. Drive east along US-302 E for another 19 mi (31 km) and then make a right turn onto Sawyer River Road. Follow this dirt road up into the woods for roughly 1 mi (1.6 km). The parking lot for the Signal Ridge Trail will be on your left immediately after crossing a bridge over Whiteface Brook. Hikers should check the White Mountain National Forest website to ensure that Sawyer River Road is open. If the road is closed, hikers should park alongside the road at the access gate and walk up the road to the Signal Ridge trailhead. This will add about 4 mi (6.4 km) to the already taxing round-trip distance.

GPS COORDINATES: 44°04'11.8"N 71°23'01.4"W

BEST NEARBY BREWS

Enjoy some of the finest internationally inspired gourmet cooking in the north country, along with several varieties of craft cider, at the **White Mountain Cider Co.** (207 US-302, Glen; 603/383-9061; www.ciderconh.com; 5pm–9pm Wed., 8am–9pm Thurs.–Sun.).

White Mountain National Forest

12

Mount Moosilauke

WHITE MOUNTAIN NATIONAL FOREST, BENTON

🦌 🍀 🐾 ⚠️

This mountain hike climbs alongside a series of peaceful waterways to reach a peak that serves as the gateway to the White Mountains along the Appalachian Trail.

DISTANCE: 7.6 mi (12.2 km) round-trip
DURATION: 5 hr
ELEVATION GAIN: 2,438 ft (743 m)
EFFORT: Strenuous
TRAIL: Dirt path, rocks, wooden bridges, water crossings on stones
USERS: Hikers, leashed dogs
SEASON: June–October
FEES/PASSES: None
MAPS: Moosilauke Ravine Lodge website
TRAILHEAD: Moosilauke Ravine Lodge, Ravine Rd., Warren
FACILITIES: Restrooms
CONTACT: Dartmouth Outdoors; 603/646-2428; www.outdoors.dartmouth.edu

START THE HIKE

▶ **MILE 0-0.4: Moosilauke Ravine Lodge to Gorge Brook**
A small cutoff trail on the west side of the lodge's guest parking lot takes you down a hill to a big wooden footbridge that crosses the **Baker River.** Turn left onto the **Hurricane Trail** on the other side of the bridge and walk along the river briefly before veering right into the woods. Shortly ahead, turn right at the signed junction to pick up the **Gorge Brook Trail.** The trail climbs north through the woods at a patient grade up rocks and some stone stairs.

You'll reach **Gorge Brook** at 0.4 mi (0.6 km) and climb alongside the waterway on rockier footing.

▶ **MILE 0.4-0.8: Gorge Brook to Gorge Brook Trail**
At 0.5 mi (0.8 km), veer right at the junction with Snapper Trail to stay on Gorge Brook, and then cross an ominously creaky footbridge over the brook. From the end of the bridge, the trail passes a discontinued section of the Gorge Brook Trail that's been barred with rocks and tree limbs. Keep left here as the trail climbs away from the brook and up more stone stairs to a connector path at 0.8 mi (1.3 km). Turn right onto the connector and enter a boreal forest of pine and spruce.

▶ **MILE 0.8-3.7: Gorge Brook Trail to Moosilauke Summit**
The trail becomes a gulch-like ribbon that weaves through the woods, merging with the original Gorge Brook Trail again.

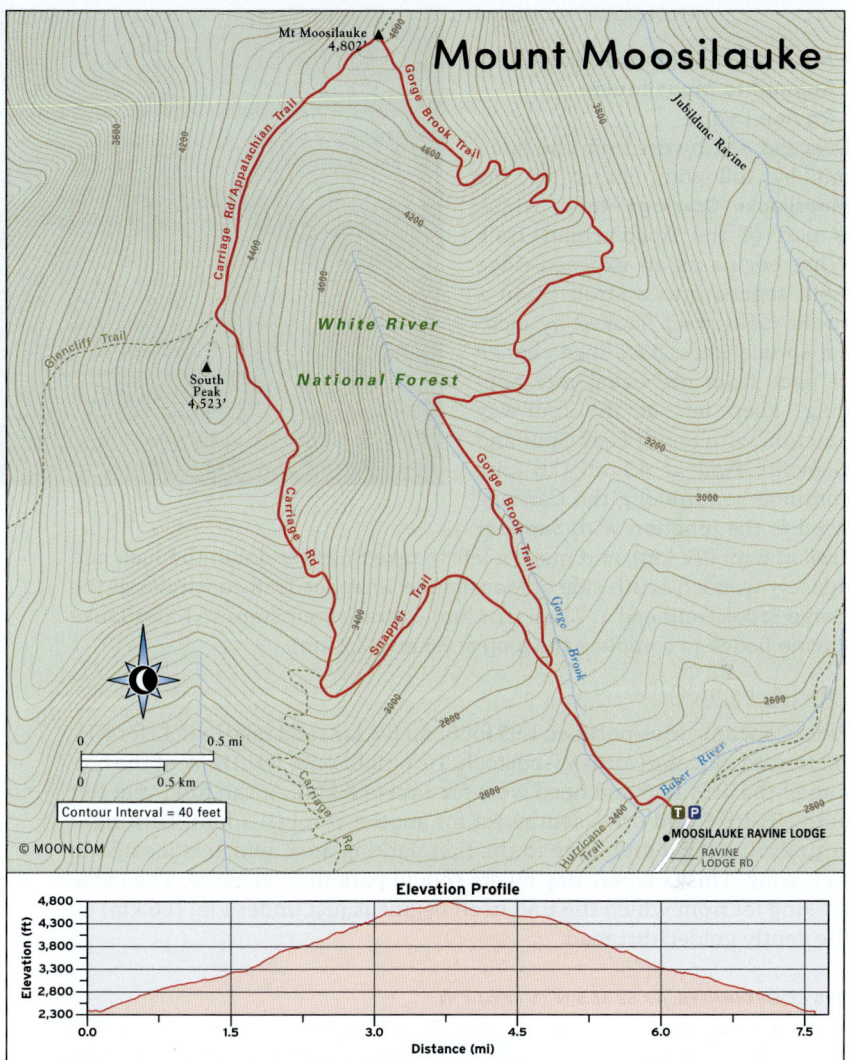

Mount Moosilauke

Elevation Profile

At 1.3 mi (2.1 km), you'll reach the brook again, where another bridge crossing awaits. Hop across some tributaries that feed the brook and climb north at a steeper grade alongside the brook. This rugged ascent continues for roughly 1 mi (1.6 km) up the eastern shoulder of Moosilauke.

At 3 mi (4.8 km), the trail transforms into a rocky road across the upper slopes of the mountain, with plenty of krummholz and tundra. (Moosilauke is one of the broader and gentler summits in the Whites.) A final ascent up some rock stairs delivers you to the pinnacle of the mountain at 3.7 mi (6 km), where hikers can size up the Presidentials to the east and the Green Mountains to the west.

▶ **MILE 3.7–7.6: Moosilauke Summit to Moosilauke Ravine Lodge**

Descend southwest from the summit by following signs for the **Moosilauke Carriage Road,** which is part of the Appalachian Trail. What begins as an exposed ridge walk segues into a stroll down a sunlit rocky road flanked by modest spruce trees. It's a nice change of pace from the usual rock-hopping. Keep left at the four-way junction with South Peak Spur and Glencliff Trail at 4.7 mi (7.6 km), continue south along the Carriage Road to the junction with **Snapper Trail** at 6 mi (9.7 km), and make a left to take Snapper down the lush and densely wooded south side of Moosilauke. Snapper Trail concludes at the Gorge Brook trailhead at 7.1 mi (11.4 km). Retrace your steps to Moosilauke Ravine Lodge to complete the loop at 7.6 mi (12.2 km).

DIRECTIONS

From Concord, drive north on I-93 for 61 mi (98 km) and take Exit 32 for NH-112 toward Lincoln/North Woodstock. Turn right onto NH-112 W at the bottom of the off-ramp and head west for 3 mi (4.8 km). At the fork, veer left onto NH-118 S and drive southwest for another 7 mi (11.3 km). Turn right onto Ravine Road and drive to the first parking area, which is located in a clearing. This is where day hikers should park their vehicles. The lodge parking lot from which the trail itself begins is just under 1 mi (1.6 km) up the gently graded dirt road.

GPS COORDINATES: 43°59'37.5"N 71°48'53.7"W

BEST NEARBY BREWS

Replenish your spent calories post-hike by heading to North Woodstock and tucking into a multicourse comfort food dinner and a flight of seasonal craft beers at the **Woodstock Inn Station & Brewery** (135 Main St., North Woodstock; 603/745-3951; www.woodstockinnbrewery.com; 11:30am–11pm Sun.–Wed., 4pm–11pm Thurs., 11:30am–midnight Fri.–Sat.).

13

Greeley Ponds

WHITE MOUNTAIN NATIONAL FOREST, WOODSTOCK

🦌 ❄️ 🐾 🚶

This forest hike passes through the southern reaches of the Pemigewasset Wilderness and into Mad River Notch to visit two of the most beautiful bodies of water in New Hampshire.

DISTANCE: 4.2 mi (6.8 km) round-trip

DURATION: 2.5 hr

ELEVATION GAIN: 378 ft (115 m)

EFFORT: Easy/moderate

TRAIL: Dirt path, roots, rocks, wooden bog bridges, water crossings on stones

USERS: Hikers, leashed dogs

SEASON: June-October

FEES/PASSES: None

MAPS: White Mountain National Forest website

TRAILHEAD: Greeley Ponds Trail parking lot, Kancamagus Highway, Lincoln

FACILITIES: None

CONTACT: White Mountain National Forest; 603/536-6100; www.fs.usda.gov/recarea/whitemountain

I n a state as compact yet bustling with hiker activity as New Hampshire, certain outdoor experiences can be trickier to achieve—say, standing beside a quietly rippling boreal pond as the setting sun fills the sky with shades of violet. But Greeley Ponds offers that sumptuous mix of beauty and isolation, and that's why these twin bodies of water are a New England hiking classic for folks who regularly visit the Whites. Nestled in Mad River Notch—which serves as kind of a border zone between the Pemi and the Sandwich Range—the ponds are ideal for picnicking, birding, and meditating. The upper pond is deep enough for swimming (though you may have to contend with muck and possibly some leeches) and both ponds are stocked with trout, which are fair game for anyone willing to bring a rod and tackle box into the backcountry.

START THE HIKE

▶ **MILE 0-1.2: Greeley Ponds Trailhead to Mount Osceola Trail Junction**
Begin the hike at the wooden trail sign at the south end of the Greeley Ponds Trail parking lot. Climb south up a small rocky hillside festooned with exposed tree roots—you'll be walking on a lot of these—and enter a thickly vegetated pine forest. Follow yellow blazes on the trees as the trail crosses a series of trickling creeks before entering a stretch of evergreen woods with more "breathing room" and better opportunities for bird sightings. (Woodpeckers often add to the natural soundtrack around here.) The footing is consistently rooty but mostly dirt otherwise, and the trail ascends at a very patient grade through the forest.

White Mountain National Forest

NEW HAMPSHIRE

217

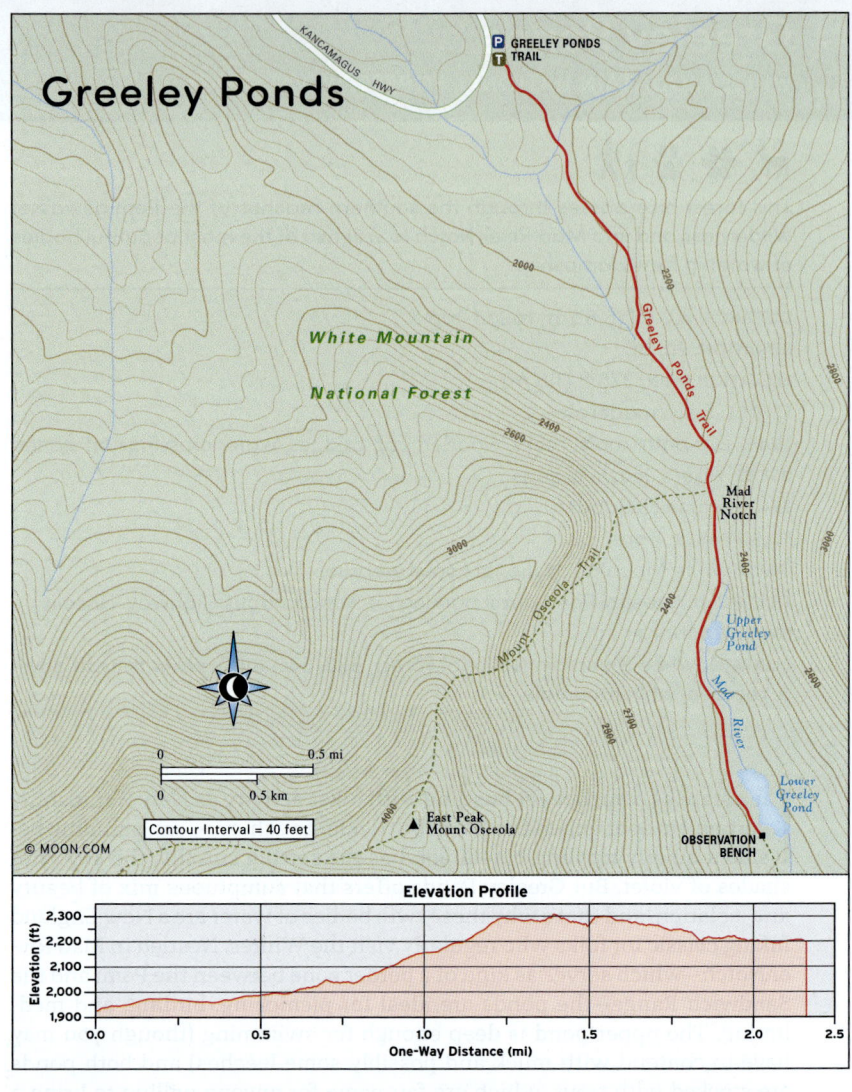

Greeley Ponds

GREELEY PONDS TRAIL

White Mountain

National Forest

Mad River Notch

Upper Greeley Pond

Lower Greeley Pond

Mount Osceola Trail

East Peak Mount Osceola

OBSERVATION BENCH

Greeley Ponds Trail

Mad River

KANCAMAGUS HWY

0   0.5 mi
0   0.5 km
Contour Interval = 40 feet
© MOON.COM

Elevation Profile

Elevation (ft): 2,300 / 2,200 / 2,100 / 2,000 / 1,900

One-Way Distance (mi): 0.0 / 0.5 / 1.0 / 1.5 / 2.0 / 2.5

The sound of rushing water precedes your arrival at a stream crossing at 0.3 mi (0.5 km). Pick your way over the water on rocks and step onto the first of many wooden bog bridges that take you over some muddier patches of the trail. After passing some mossy boulders, the trail climbs a hillside at a slightly steeper grade to arrive at the junction with the Mount Osceola Trail at 1.2 mi (1.9 km).

▶ **MILE 1.2–1.6: Mount Osceola Trail Junction to Mount Osceola Lookout**
Take a left turn to stay on the Greeley Ponds Trail and enjoy some softer, sandier footing—a hint of what lies ahead. Pass an enormous fortress-like rock the size of a garage and reach a second junction at 1.4 mi (2.3 km), where you can go right to stay on Greeley Ponds Trail or take a left to follow a brief ski path to a pebbly beach on **Upper Greeley Pond.**

(The ski path-to-beach approach is much more scenic and gets you closer to the water.) Upper Greeley Pond is deeper and less boggy than Lower Greeley, which makes it the better pond for aquatic activities. To hike along the pond from the pebbly beach, walk to the right across the beach and up a small hill to link back up with the Greeley Ponds Trail. Amble along the pond's western shore, which is replete with young spruce trees. As you approach the southern edge of the pond, keep an eye out for a dirt cutoff on your left, which leads to a scenic lookout from which you can see the cliff faces of nearby Mount Osceola.

▶ **MILE 1.6–1.9: Mount Osceola Lookout to Lower Greeley Pond**
The main trail continues south and descends through the forest by way of a rocky former streambed before reaching some more bog bridges. Emerging from the woods, the trail arrives at Lower Greeley Pond at 1.9 mi (3.1 km) and ambles through a rich landscape of ferns and maple trees along the western shore.

▶ **MILE 1.9–2.1: Lower Greeley Pond to Observation Bench**
Look for a spur cutoff on your right at 2.1 mi (3.4 km). This will take you to a beautiful little beach surrounded by hemlocks and complete with an observation bench made from logs. It also marks the conclusion of your hike! Return the way you came.

DIRECTIONS

From Concord, drive north on I-93 N for 60 mi (97 km) and then take Exit 32 for NH-112 toward Lincoln/North Woodstock. Turn left onto NH-112 E at the bottom of the off-ramp. Drive east along the Kancamagus Highway for roughly 9 mi (14.5 km). The Greeley Ponds trailhead parking lot will be on your right.

GPS COORDINATES: 44°01'53.0"N 71°31'00.5"W

White Mountain National Forest

NEW HAMPSHIRE

14

Mount Chocorua

WHITE MOUNTAIN NATIONAL FOREST, ALBANY

This hike to one of New Hampshire's sharpest and most recognizable peaks features some of the prettiest waterfalls in the state—and a thrilling finale of steep climbing.

BEST: Winter hikes, brew hikes
DISTANCE: 7.4 mi (11.9 km) round-trip
DURATION: 4.5 hr
ELEVATION GAIN: 2,125 ft (648 m)
EFFORT: Moderate/strenuous
TRAIL: Dirt path, rocks, wooden bog bridges
USERS: Hikers, leashed dogs
SEASON: June-October
FEES/PASSES: $5 day-use fee per vehicle
MAPS: White Mountain National Forest website
TRAILHEAD: Champney Brook Trail parking lot, Kancamagus Highway, Albany
FACILITIES: Vault toilet
CONTACT: White Mountain National Forest; 603/536-6100; www.fs.usda.gov/recarea/whitemountain

When you look at the Sandwich Range of the White Mountains from afar, one sharp horn-like peak stands out from the rest. Mount Chocorua's distinctive peak has a relatively modest height of 3,478 ft (1,060 m) compared to the 4,000-footers, but it's still a formidable climb, and the Champney Brook Trail makes it a fun one. With lush forest, crashing waterfalls, gorgeous vistas, and some seriously steep rock scrambling near the top, this is one of the most enjoyable hikes in the state.

START THE HIKE

▶ **MILE 0-0.5: Champney Brook Trail Parking Lot to Champney Brook**
Follow yellow blazes as the trail enters deciduous forest, crosses a brook on stones, and turns southeast. Hike through the trees along a wide dirt path with plenty of exposed roots, and listen for the sound of rushing water echoing through the undergrowth. At 0.5 mi (0.8 km), the trail reaches **Champney Brook.**

▶ **MILE 0.5-1.4: Champney Brook to Champney Falls Loop Trail**
Continue along the brook as the trail begins to ascend the northwestern flank of Mount Chocorua at a patient grade. After climbing higher above Champney Brook for about 1 mi (1.6 km), you'll reach a wooden sign for the **Champney Falls Loop Trail** at 1.4 mi (2.3 km).

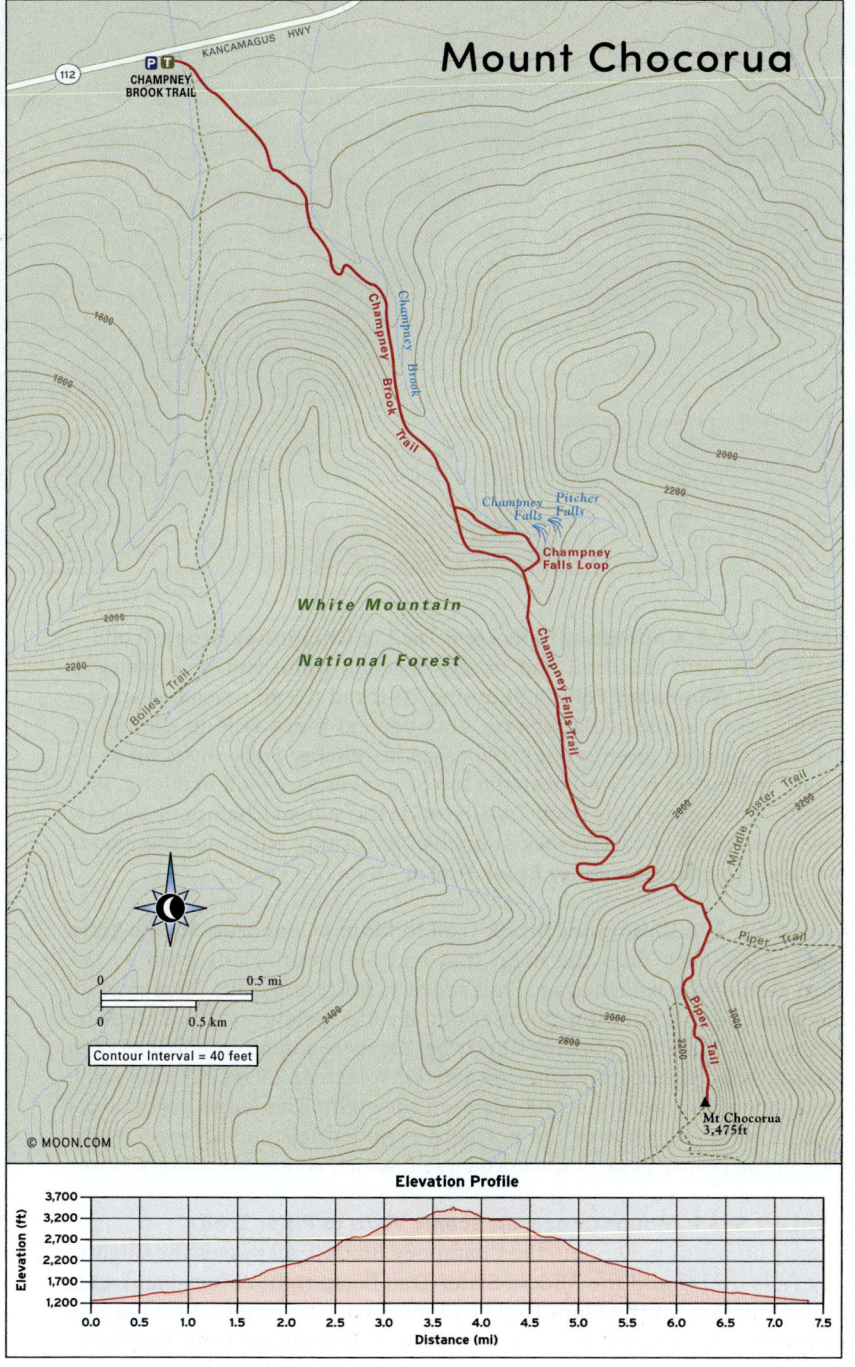

Mount Chocorua

KANCAMAGUS HWY

112

CHAMPNEY
BROOK TRAIL

Champney Brook

Champney Brook Trail

Champney Falls

Pitcher Falls

Champney Falls Loop

White Mountain

National Forest

Boles Trail

Champney Falls Trail

Middle Sister Trail

Piper Trail

Piper Trail

N

0   0.5 mi

0   0.5 km

Contour Interval = 40 feet

Mt Chocorua
3,475ft

© MOON.COM

Elevation Profile

Elevation (ft)

3,700
3,200
2,700
2,200
1,700
1,200

0.0 0.5 1.0 1.5 2.0 2.5 3.0 3.5 4.0 4.5 5.0 5.5 6.0 6.5 7.0 7.5

Distance (mi)

▶ **MILE 1.4–1.8: Champney Falls Loop Trail to Champney Brook Trail**
Take a left onto this trail and briefly descend some wet rock stairs to the foot of **Champney Falls**, a stunning 70-ft-tall (21-m) cascade that can become quite explosive after rain. Just beyond these falls to the left of the trail, an even more remarkable cascade—**Pitcher Falls**—lives up to its name, spilling 50 ft (15 m) from the top of a sheer rock wall in a long, thin stream. Champney Falls Loop Trail ascends the side of Champney Falls by way of exquisitely carved rock stairs before turning back into the woods and rejoining the **Champney Brook Trail** at 1.8 mi (2.9 km).

▶ **MILE 1.8–2.9: Champney Brook Trail to Mount Chocorua Scenic Vista**
Make a left back onto the main trail and feel your quads burn as the once-gentle path becomes a rockier series of stairs and slabs. Yard by yard, the trees open up, offering glimpses of the valley below and the Three Sisters mountains to the north of Chocorua. Traverse some switchbacks with exposed rock faces before entering a boreal forest. At 2.9 mi (4.7 km), you'll come upon a sign for a scenic **vista** on the right. The ledge beyond this sign offers a fine view of the northern Presidentials and an even better look at the pointy peak of Chocorua itself, which is now startlingly close.

▶ **MILE 2.9–3.1: Mount Chocorua Scenic Vista to Piper Trail**
Shortly after this viewpoint, the Champney Brook Trail passes the Champney Falls Cutoff and the Middle Sister Trail (keep right at both) and ends at the junction for the **Piper Trail** at 3.1 mi (5 km). Turn right onto the Piper Trail and make a left at the nearby West Side Trail junction. Keep looking for yellow blazes as the trail tunnels through more boreal forest before popping out onto the rocky upper reaches of Chocorua.

▸ MILE 3.1-3.8: Piper Trail to Chocorua Summit

From this point, the trail becomes an exciting climb up very steep rock slabs and ledges. You truly "feel" the sharpness of the peak here. Some sections may require the use of handholds for balance, but the rock also has plenty of natural steps to make the ascent easier. Turn left at the junction with the Brook Trail at 3.7 mi (6 km) to stay on Piper Trail, scramble up a final pitch of rock faces, and plant your boots on the Chocorua summit at 3.8 mi (6.1 km). (It's a very small and raised summit, so keep low to the rock if it's especially windy.)

▸ MILE 3.8-5.8: Chocorua Summit to Champney Brook Trail

The return journey is a simple backtrack along the Piper Trail to Champney Brook Trail. That said, at the Champney Falls Loop Trail junction at 5.8 mi (9.3 km)—remember, this is the cutoff loop path that you took to view the falls—hikers can go left and stick to the Champney Brook Trail on the way down for a shorter, less rocky descent.

▸ MILE 5.8-7.4: Champney Brook Trail to Champney Brook Trail Parking Lot

The Champney Brook Trail passes the start of the falls observation loop at 6 mi (9.7 km), and the remainder of the return is an easy amble through the deciduous woods, finishing at the parking lot at 7.4 mi (11.9 km).

DIRECTIONS

From Concord, drive north on I-93 N for 60 mi (97 km) and take Exit 32 for NH-112 toward Lincoln/North Woodstock. Turn left onto NH-112 E at the bottom of the off-ramp and then drive along the famous Kancamagus Highway for about 24 mi (39 km). The Champney Brook trailhead will be on your right by the outhouses.

GPS COORDINATES: 43°59'24.4"N 71°17'57.5"W

BEST NEARBY BREWS

Kick back like a local and pair your hike with an afternoon or evening glass of dark brown altbier and a veggie-laden brick-oven pizza at **Tuckerman Brewing Company** (66 Hobbs St., Conway; 603/447-5400; www.tuckermanbrewing.com; 2pm-7pm Mon.-Thurs., noon-8pm Fri.-Sat., noon-7pm Sun.).

NEARBY CAMPGROUNDS

NAME	LOCATION	FACILITIES	SEASON	FEE
Timberland Campground	809 US-2, Shelburne, 44°24'29.3"N 71°05'19.6"W	Tent sites, RV sites, RV rentals, cabins, toilets, showers, potable water, laundry, pool, camp store, Wi-Fi	mid-May through early October	$30-135
603/466-3872; www.timberlandcampgroundnh.com				
Barnes Field Group Campground	Dolly Copp Rd., Gorham, 44°20'20.7"N 71°13'05.1"W	Tent sites, toilets, potable water	mid-May through mid-October	$45-85
603/466-2713; www.fs.usda.gov				
Sugarloaf Campground	Campground Rd. and Zealand Rd., Jefferson, 44°15'37.3"N 71°30'10.8"W	Tent sites, toilets, potable water	mid-May–mid-October	$22
603/536-6100; www.fs.usda.gov				
Fransted Family Campground	974 Profile Rd., Franconia, 44°13'02.0"N 71°43'49.2"W	Tent sites, RV sites, toilets, showers, potable water, laundry, camp store, Wi-Fi	mid-May through early October	$48-62
603/823-5675; www.franstedcampground.com				
Lafayette Place Campground	2 Franconia Notch State Park, Franconia, 44°08'35.6"N 71°40'59.1"W	Tent sites, toilets, showers, potable water, camp store	year-round (no services in winter)	$25
603/823-9513; www.nhstateparks.org				

NAME	LOCATION	FACILITIES	SEASON	FEE
Dry River Campground	2057 US-302, Bartlett, 44°09'19.0"N 71°21'48.1"W	Tent sites, lean-tos, toilets, showers, potable water	mid-May through mid-October	$25
603/374-2272; www.nhstateparks.org				
Jellystone Park Glen Ellis	83 Glen Ellis Campground Rd., Glen, 44°06'18.9"N 71°10'56.3"W	Tent sites, RV sites, cabins, toilets, showers, potable water, laundry, camp store, private beach, pool, mini-golf, Wi-Fi	late-May through mid-October	$44-292
603/383-4567; www.glenellisjellystone.com				
Alpine Garden	1255 US-302, Bartlett, 44°04'41.0"N 71°16'28.4"W	Tent sites, RV sites, cabins, toilets, showers, potable water, winery, pool, camp store, Wi-Fi	May through October	$75-300
603/374-5154; www.alpinegardenglamping.com				
Hancock Campground	133 Hancock Campground, Lincoln, 44°03'52.2"N 71°35'37.7"W	Tent sites, toilets, potable water	year-round (no services in winter)	$27
603/536-6100; www.fs.usda.gov				
Jigger Johnson Campground	Kancamagus Hwy., Albany, 43°59'41.5"N 71°20'07.6"W	Tent sites, toilets, potable water	mid-May through mid-October	$27
www.fs.usda.gov				

GREAT NORTH WOODS AND DIXVILLE NOTCH

Beyond the hubbub of the Whites lies a remote and pristine territory where even the most active New England hikers rarely venture. The Great North Woods, Dixville Notch, and Nash Stream Forest are New Hampshire at its most rugged and eerily beautiful. Getting here is a hike itself, but the trails are worth the pilgrimage. You'll step back in time on quiet paths that take you deep into New Hampshire's logging capital to otherworldly sights such as the origin of the Connecticut River or the scariest precipice in the Granite State. Plus, the lack of human activity will magnify your chances of having an unforgettable encounter with some of New England's rarest (and endangered) creatures—such as the golden eagle or the Canada lynx.

▲ MOOSE NEAR FOURTH CONNECTICUT LAKE

▲ NEW HAMPSHIRE FUNGI IN THE DEVIL'S HOPYARD

◄ VIEW OF TABLE ROCK THROUGH DIXVILLE NOTCH

1 Fourth Connecticut Lake

DISTANCE: 2.1 mi (3.4 km) round-trip
DURATION: 2 hr
EFFORT: Moderate
PAGE: 230

2 Little Hellgate Falls

DISTANCE: 1.5 mi (2.4 km) round-trip
DURATION: 1 hr
EFFORT: Easy
PAGE: 233

3 Table Rock

DISTANCE: 1.6 mi (2.6 km) round-trip
DURATION: 1 hr
EFFORT: Moderate/strenuous
PAGE: 237

4 South and North Percy Peaks

DISTANCE: 4.6 mi (7.4 km) round-trip
DURATION: 4 hr
EFFORT: Strenuous
PAGE: 241

5 The Devil's Hopyard

DISTANCE: 2 mi (3.2 km) round-trip
DURATION: 1 hr
EFFORT: Easy
PAGE: 245

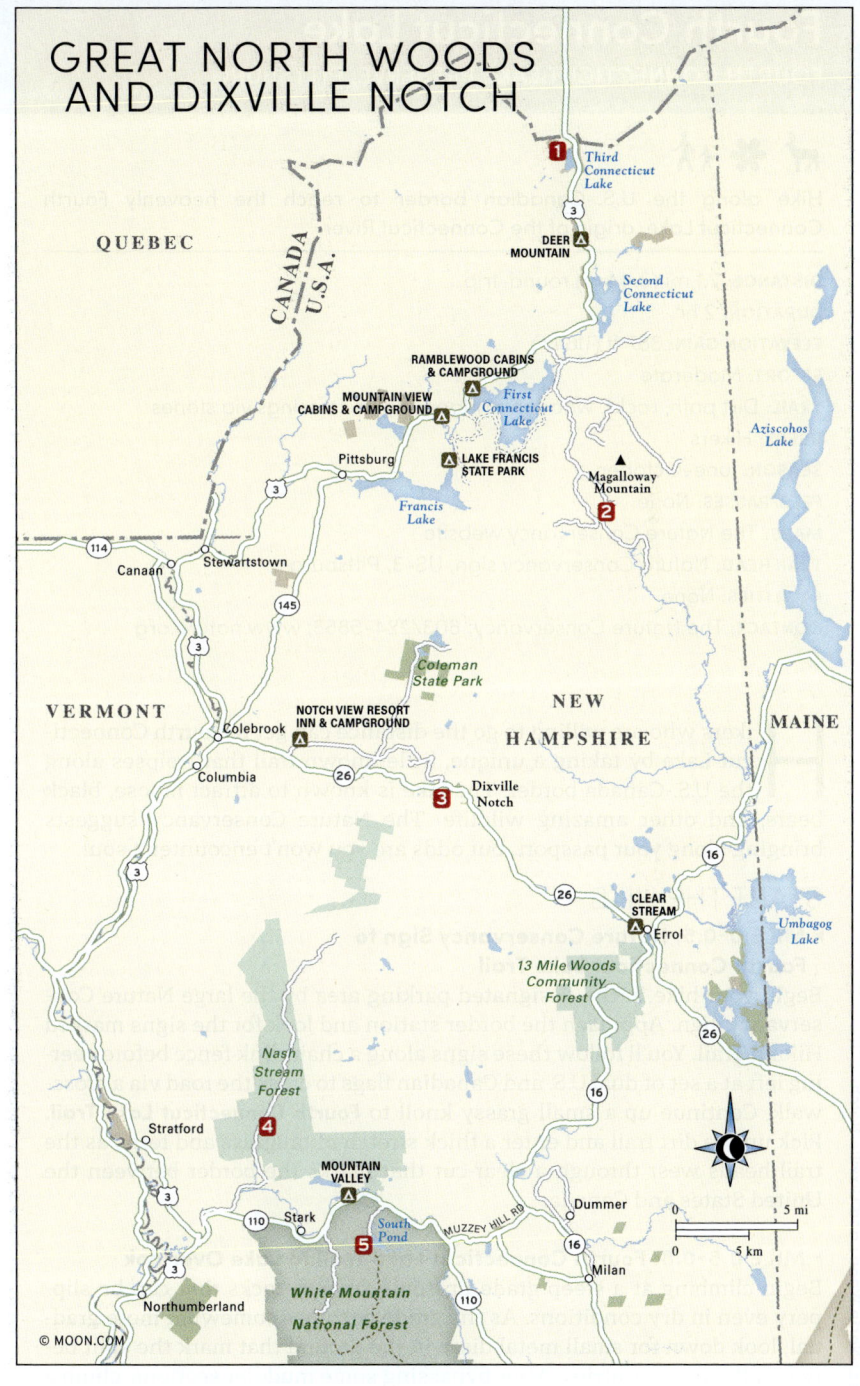

GREAT NORTH WOODS
AND DIXVILLE NOTCH

QUEBEC

CANADA
U.S.A.

Third
Connecticut
Lake

1

**DEER
MOUNTAIN**

Second
Connecticut
Lake

Aziscohos
Lake

**RAMBLEWOOD CABINS
& CAMPGROUND**

First
Connecticut
Lake

**MOUNTAIN VIEW
CABINS & CAMPGROUND**

Pittsburg

**LAKE FRANCIS
STATE PARK**

Magalloway
Mountain

2

114

Canaan

Stewartstown

Francis
Lake

145

3

Coleman
State Park

3

**NEW
HAMPSHIRE**

MAINE

VERMONT

Colebrook

**NOTCH VIEW RESORT
INN & CAMPGROUND**

Columbia

26

Dixville
Notch

3

16

Umbagog
Lake

3

26

**CLEAR
STREAM**

Errol

**13 Mile Woods
Community
Forest**

Nash
Stream
Forest

16

Stratford

4

**MOUNTAIN
VALLEY**

3

110

Stark

South
Pond

MUZZEY HILL RD

Dummer

16

Milan

0   5 mi

0   5 km

3

5

110

Northumberland

**White Mountain
National Forest**

© MOON.COM

Hike along the U.S.-Canadian border to reach the heavenly Fourth Connecticut Lake, origin of the Connecticut River.

DISTANCE: 2.1 mi (3.4 km) round-trip

DURATION: 2 hr

ELEVATION GAIN: 387 ft (118 m)

EFFORT: Moderate

TRAIL: Dirt path, rocks, wooden bridges, water crossings via stones

USERS: Hikers

SEASON: June–October

FEES/PASSES: None

MAPS: The Nature Conservancy website

TRAILHEAD: Nature Conservancy sign, US-3, Pittsburg

FACILITIES: None

CONTACT: The Nature Conservancy; 603/224-5853; www.nature.org

Hikers who are willing to go the distance can get to Fourth Connecticut Lake by taking a unique, little-known trail that traipses along the U.S.-Canada border. The lake is known to attract moose, black bears, and other amazing wildlife. The Nature Conservancy suggests bringing along your passport, but odds are you won't encounter a soul.

START THE HIKE

▶ **MILE 0-0.5: Nature Conservancy Sign to Fourth Connecticut Lake Trail**

Begin your hike in the designated parking area by the large Nature Conservancy sign. Approach the border station and look for the signs marked Hiking Trail. You'll follow these signs along a chain-link fence before veering left at a set of dual U.S. and Canadian flags to cross the road via a crosswalk. Continue up a small grassy knoll to **Fourth Connecticut Lake Trail.** Pick up the dirt trail and enter a thick stretch of tallgrass and ferns as the trail heads west through a clear-cut that marks the border between the United States and Canada.

▶ **MILE 0.5-0.8: Fourth Connecticut Lake Trail to Lake Overlook**

Begin climbing at a steep grade up some smooth rocks that can be slippery even in dry conditions. As the grade becomes somewhat more gradual, look down for small metal discs in the ground that mark the split between the two countries. After bypassing some muddier sections, climb a final steep pitch before reaching a height of land at 0.6 mi (1 km), where the trail transitions from dirt to pure granite. At 0.7 mi (1.1 km), you'll reach a wooden sign for **Fourth Connecticut Lake;** veer left into the thick spruce

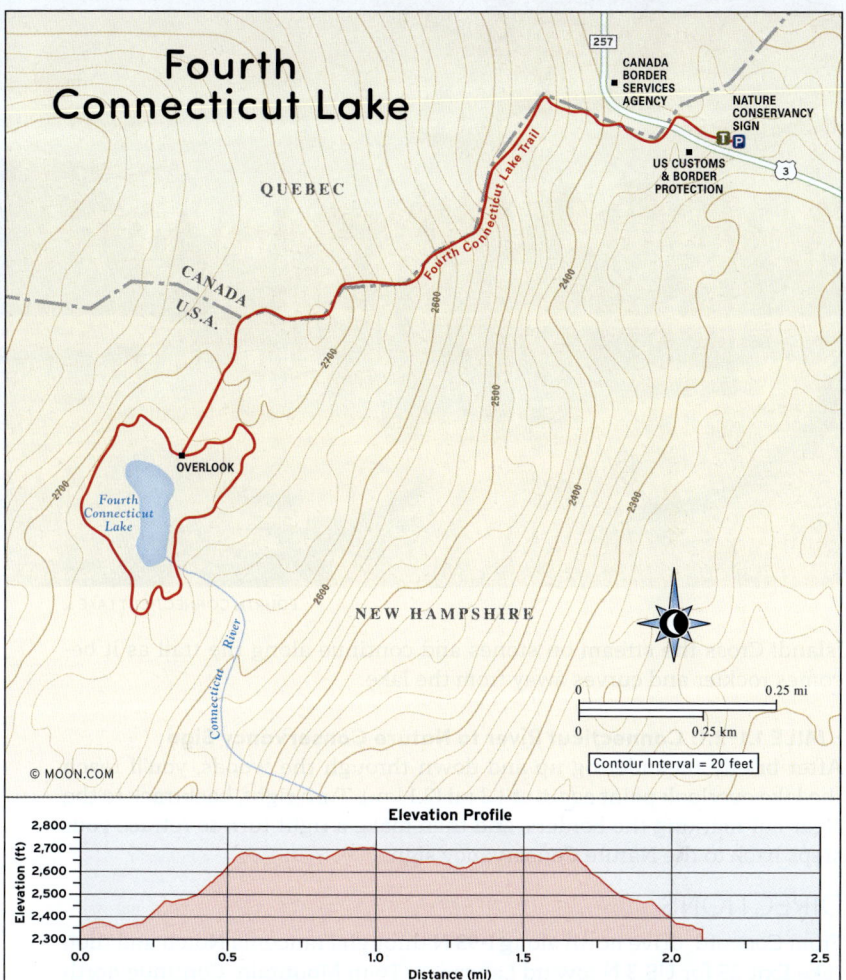

Fourth Connecticut Lake

Elevation Profile

and white birch forest and cross a few wooden bog bridges as the trail gently descends into the preserve area. Look for green diamond-shaped signs bearing yellow arrows on the trees.

At 0.8 mi (1.3 km), you'll arrive at a scenic **overlook** on the northern banks of Fourth Connecticut Lake. From the overlook, the trail loops around the lake.

▶ MILE 0.8-1.1: Lake Overlook to Connecticut River

Turn right at the overlook and notice how the trail begins to resemble a dirt ribbon weaving in and out of the mossy forest, never straying too far from the water. After crossing several aging bog bridges at 1 mi (1.6 km), enjoy the finest lake views yet on your left. Watch your footing beyond here as the trail becomes bumpier and more grown-in.

At 1.1 mi (1.8 km), arrive at a stream that flows from the lake down into the nearby woods. This little trickle of water is nothing less than the start of the Connecticut River, which flows 400 mi (645 km) south to Long

Island! Cross the stream on stones and continue along the trail as it becomes rockier and curves away from the lake.

▶ **MILE 1.1–2.1: Connecticut River to Nature Conservancy Sign**

After briefly meandering up and down through the woods, you'll reach the lake overlook point again at 1.3 mi (2.1 km). Turn right, backtrack to the clear-cut marking the borders, and then make a right turn to retrace your steps back to the Nature Conservancy sign.

DIRECTIONS

From Concord, drive north along I-93 N through Franconia Notch and then take Exit 35 for US-3 N toward Lancaster/Twin Mountain. Continue north along US-3 N to the town of Colebrook and then turn right onto NH-145 N. Drive north for 13 mi (21 km) to the road's terminus and then turn right onto US-3 N again. Take this road through the town of Pittsburg, past the larger Connecticut Lakes, and into the northern foothills of the area until the road finishes at the U.S.-Canada border station. Park by the big Nature Conservancy sign.

GPS COORDINATES: 45°15'10.0"N 71°12'17.4"W

2 Little Hellgate Falls

CLARKSVILLE

Traverse a remote and very underexplored forest to reach a towering cascade with a dark and tragic history.

DISTANCE: 1.5 mi (2.4 km) round-trip
DURATION: 1 hr
ELEVATION GAIN: 322 ft (98 m)
EFFORT: Easy
TRAIL: Dirt path, rocks, log stairs
USERS: Hikers, leashed dogs
SEASON: June–September
FEES/PASSES: None
MAPS: USGS topo map for Magalloway Mountain, New Hampshire
TRAILHEAD: Information kiosk, Cedar Stream Rd., Clarksville
FACILITIES: None
CONTACT: NH Division of Forests and Lands; 603/788-4157; www.nh.gov/nhdfl

Not too long ago, thousands of loggers spent the peaks of their lives cutting timber in the Great North Woods. Quite often, this occupation caused their demise. Little Hellgate Falls is a particularly infamous place in local logging history. This crashing 40-ft-tall (12-m) cascade is fed by a mighty brook that served as a natural "flume" for logs. But the narrow opening at the top of the falls caused frequent logjams, and more than a few loggers died while trying to restart the flow of timbers—hence the name "Hellgate." The hike to this pretty and mostly unknown waterfall might feel like a dreamy jaunt through evergreen woods, but even the local wood itself is an ode to what happened here.

START THE HIKE

▶ MILE 0-0.1: Information Kiosk to Falls Trail

Begin the hike by the wooden trail information kiosk on the shoulder of Cedar Stream Road. A few yards south of the kiosk, you'll see a snowmobile junction for trails 20 and 137. Take a left turn here onto the unnamed dirt road that branches off from Cedar Stream Road. Walk around the orange access gate ahead and cross a wooden bridge over Rowell Brook. Continue east along the road past a clear-cut (logging still happens in the Great North Woods). A small wooden sign that says **Falls Trail** will soon appear on your left just beyond the clear-cut. Turn left here to leave the road behind and begin your true foray to Little Hellgate Falls.

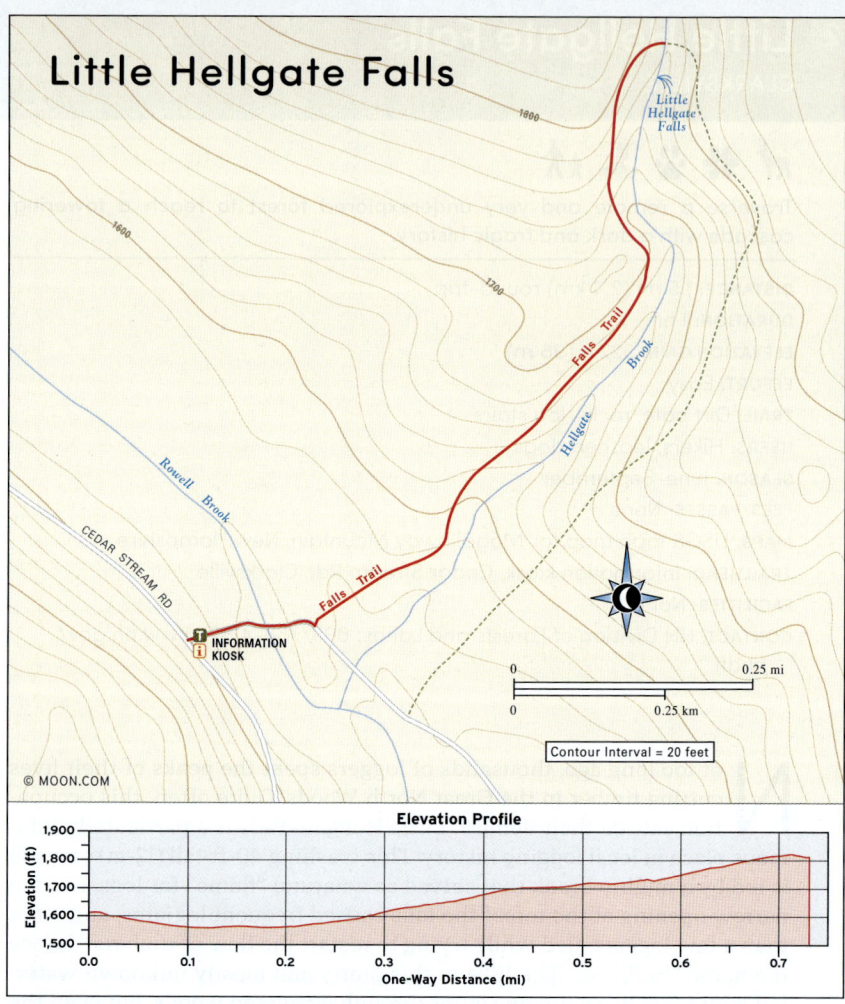

Little Hellgate Falls

Little
Hellgate
Falls

Falls Trail

Hellgate Brook

Rowell Brook

CEDAR STREAM RD

Falls Trail

INFORMATION
KIOSK

Contour Interval = 20 feet

0   0.25 mi

0   0.25 km

© MOON.COM

Elevation Profile

Elevation (ft)

One-Way Distance (mi)

▶ **MILE 0.1–0.6: Falls Trail to Little Hellgate Falls**

Follow the winding dirt path northeast through a rich forest of spruce and pine trees—a testament to nature's ability to make a comeback after decades of ravaging. As the trail climbs a sun-splashed hillside on notched and beautifully carved log stairs, you'll reach the edge of the rejuvenated forest and pass by a much larger logging zone at 0.3 mi (0.5 km). After skirting this border between the two forest zones briefly, the trail descends more log stairs into a wooded ravine. The rush of water that you hear echoing from below is **Hellgate Brook.** Continue northeast through the ravine, following the sound of the brook, and make another brief climb past mossy boulders and tuffets into a hemlock forest. Once again, the trail emerges from the woods to make a quick foray through the logging zone before returning to the greenery of the trees and moss—the latter of which is truly abundant here, lending the forest a distinctly Scandinavian feel.

▲ LITTLE HELLGATE FALLS

Turn right onto the spur path at 0.6 mi (1 km); quite suddenly, you'll find yourself standing on a dirt ledge that overlooks **Little Hellgate Falls.** A little log picnic table nearby offers a great place to have a snack, while hikers who don't mind a bit of bushwhacking can carefully descend the steep overlook slopes to the falls' base. To reach the top of the falls, pick up the main trail again and continue hiking northeast as it climbs above the cascade at a moderate grade before reaching a height of land.

▶ MILE 0.6-0.75: Little Hellgate Falls to Hellgate Brook

Make a final descent down some more log stairs to reach a sunny little beach beside Hellgate Brook at 0.75 mi (1.2 km). To your right, a few yards down the brook, you'll see the narrowing rock walls that caused all those deadly logjams not so long ago. This spot marks the finish of your hike. Dip your feet in the water and reflect before returning the way you came.

DIRECTIONS

From Concord, drive north along I-93 N through Franconia Notch and then take Exit 35 for US-3 N toward Lancaster/Twin Mountain. Continue north along US-3 N to the town of Colebrook and then turn right onto NH-145 N. Drive north for 13 mi (21 km) to the road's terminus and then turn right onto US-3 N again. Take this road through the town of Pittsburg for another 11 mi (18 km) and then make a right onto Magalloway Road, a well-maintained dirt road with numerical mile marker signs. Drive southeast along this unmarked road for 3 mi (4.8 km) and make the first right onto Buckhorn Road. Follow Buckhorn Road for a few miles to a juncture where another unmarked road intersects; stay straight to continue onto Cedar Stream Road. Drive along this road for a final 2-3 mi (3.2-4.8 km), past two cabins, and you'll see the trail kiosk on your left. Park on the side of the road.

GPS COORDINATES: 45°01'27.8"N 71°10'47.2"W

Table Rock
DIXVILLE NOTCH STATE PARK, DIXVILLE TOWNSHIP

Hike to the top of one of New England's most beautiful (and scary) natural attractions.

BEST: Fall hikes

DISTANCE: 1.6 mi (2.6 km) round-trip

DURATION: 1 hr

ELEVATION GAIN: 754 ft (230 m)

EFFORT: Moderate/strenuous

TRAIL: Dirt path, rocks, river crossings on stones

USERS: Hikers, leashed dogs

SEASON: May-October

FEES/PASSES: None

MAPS: USGS topo map of Coos County, New Hampshire

TRAILHEAD: Climbing Trail trailhead on the shoulder of NH-26, Colebrook

FACILITIES: None

CONTACT: New Hampshire Division of Parks and Recreation; 603/271-3556; www.nhstateparks.org

North of the White Mountains in the isolated wild of Dixville Notch, Table Rock awaits the bold traveler. This spire of crumbling granite looms 700 ft (213 m) above the road through Dixville Notch, erupting from the forest like a wizard's tower in *Lord of the Rings.* And luckily for hikers, there are two different ways to reach the top of Table Rock. The first trail—the Climbing Trail, which is the more popular of the two routes—is a near-vertical scramble through the woods on the east side of Table Rock. You'll gain a dizzying 754 ft (230 m) in less than 0.5 mi (0.8 km)! The second, less severe route, the Table Rock Trail, takes a more gradual and civilized approach to the payoff. Both trails are located on NH-26, roughly 20 minutes apart by foot, and they can be combined for a longer hike.

Note that this hike should not be attempted in wet weather.

START THE HIKE

▶ **MILE 0-0.3: Climbing Trail Trailhead to Table Rock**
Begin the hike on the shoulder of NH-26 S directly behind the Welcome to Dixville Notch State Park sign. The **Climbing Trail** up to Table Rock is marked with a wooden sign on a tree. Warm up your leg muscles by ascending a series of stone stairs that wind through a mossy, boulder-strewn forest. The trail grade steepens considerably with each little twist and turn, and you might have to pick your way up and over blowdowns here and there.

As the trail climbs above the floor of Dixville Notch—with fleeting views through the trees to measure your progress—the footing becomes

Great North Woods and Dixville Notch

NEW HAMPSHIRE

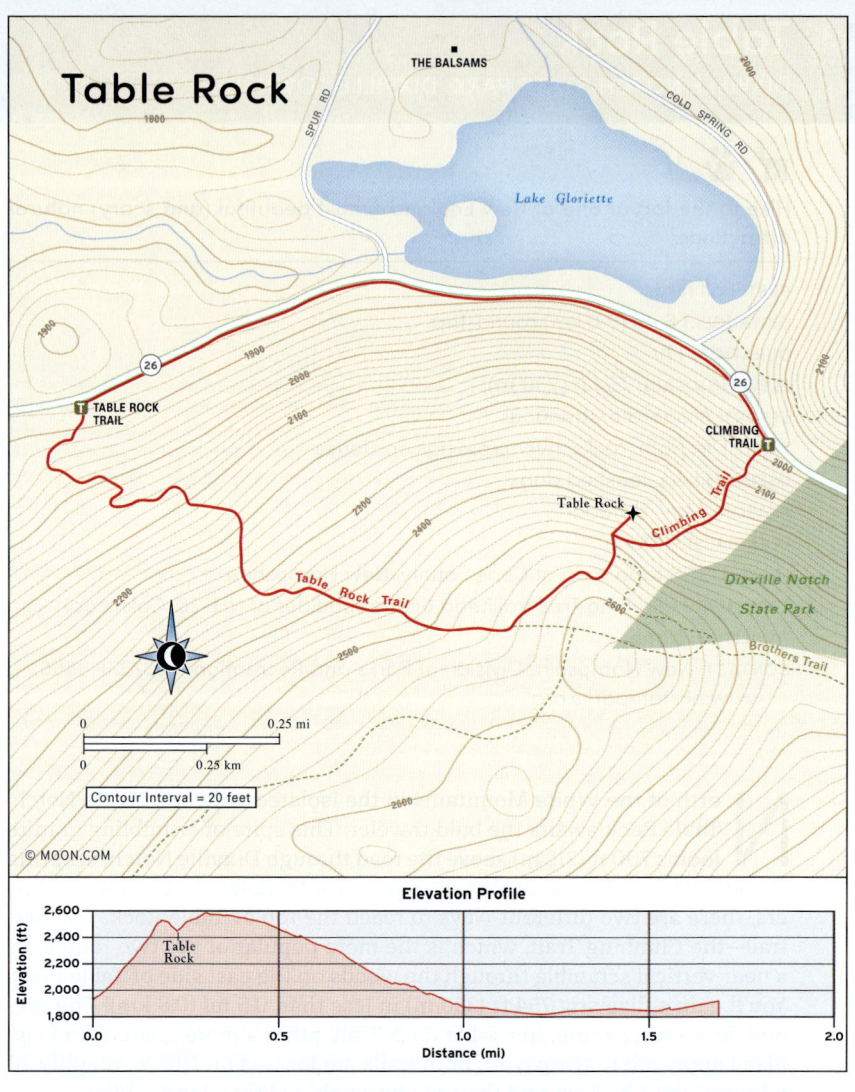

Table Rock

THE BALSAMS

Lake Gloriette

26

TABLE ROCK
TRAIL

CLIMBING
TRAIL

Table Rock

Climbing Trail

26

Dixville Notch
State Park

Table Rock Trail

Brothers Trail

0   0.25 mi

0   0.25 km

Contour Interval = 20 feet

© MOON.COM

Elevation Profile

Table
Rock

Elevation (ft)

2,600
2,400
2,200
2,000
1,800

0.0   0.5   1.0   1.5   2.0

Distance (mi)

more eroded in places, with lots of exposed tree roots. In some places, you may even find yourself using the roots themselves as handholds. The pine and spruce trees start to shrink and the trail becomes more sunlit. A few glimpses of Table Rock's sheer pinnacle offer hope as the Climbing Trail approaches its terminus.

After reaching a rocky height of land at 0.25 mi (0.4 km), the Climbing Trail arrives at an unmarked trail junction. Take a right turn and tread carefully as the trail emerges onto the tip-top of Table Rock. Hikers can decide how far out they wish to venture onto the "summit," which is barely 7 ft (2 m) wide at its farthest point—with a 700-ft (213-m) vertical drop on three sides! The views of Dixville Notch are unbeatable, and the vertigo is similarly unique.

▲ THE SPIRE OF TABLE ROCK

▶ **MILE 0.3–1.6: Table Rock to Climbing Trail Trailhead**

Return by descending the much less steep **Table Rock Trail.** When you reach the parking lot at 1.1 mi (km), turn right and walk along the shoulder of NH-26 for roughly 0.5 mi (km) to reach your car again and complete the loop hike.

Note that the extremely steep Climbing Trail should only be done as the ascent portion the hike, with the Table Rock Trail serving as the descent.

You can also opt to skip the Climbing Trail and instead follow the Table Rock Trail as an out-and-back hike: Begin your hike in the **parking area** for the **Table Rock Trail**—a small dugout on the shoulder of NH-26 S, immediately west of the now-closed **Balsams** resort. Enter a deciduous forest of beech and white birches and climb gradually up a series of switchbacks. The trail then crosses a trickling creek and begins to ascend southeast at a moderate grade. Watch for loose rocks in some of the more eroded sections, especially during rain or soggy conditions. The trail steepens considerably at 0.4 mi (0.6 km) for several yards before merging with and then crossing another creek.

As you continue your climb, notice the shards of dark gray stone that litter the trail—these slick, sometimes glittering rocks are native to the far north of New Hampshire. The ferns that line the trail thicken as the forest transitions into a boreal mixture of pine, spruce, and birch. The trail grade starts to soften at 0.6 mi (1 km) and curves southeast through the upper woods before reaching an unmarked four-way junction at 0.7 mi (1.1 km). Turn left and descend a sunny knoll to arrive at the junction with the Climbing Trail. Veer left here to reach the top of Table Rock at 0.8 mi (1.3 km). Return the way you came.

DIRECTIONS

From Concord, drive north on I-93 N. After passing through Franconia Notch, take Exit 35 for US 3-N toward Lancaster/Twin Mountain. Merge onto US-3 N and continue north to the town of Colebrook. Take a right turn onto NH-26 E and drive east for roughly 10 miles. The Table Rock Trail parking area will be on your right just before you reach the Balsams resort property (now closed). To reach the Climbing Trail, continue east along NH-26E past the resort and pull into one of the dugouts on the right shoulder of the road. Park here and walk east along the road to the nearby Welcome to Dixville Notch sign.

GPS COORDINATES: Climbing Trail 44°51'53.5"N 71°18'03.3"W

BEST NEARBY BITES AND BREWS

Beer is a big deal in far northern New England, and you'll find suitably piney ales *and* melt-in-your mouth artisan pizza at **Coös Brewing Company** (30 Bill Bromage Dr., Colebrook; 603/460-4069; www.coosbeer.com; 3pm-8pm Thurs.-Fri., 1pm-8pm Sat.). Morning visitors will find extra-large muffins in flavors beyond the wildest imaginations at the unambiguously named **Mostly Muffins** (51 Parson St., Colebrook; 603/237-4582; www.facebook.com/mostlymuffins.colebrook; 6am-noon Mon.-Fri., 7am-11am Sat.).

This hike to New Hampshire's most visually stunning peaks north of the White Mountains offers sweeping views of the Nash Stream Forest, as well as a profound feeling of isolation.

BEST: Vistas
DISTANCE: 4.6 mi (7.4 km) round-trip
DURATION: 4 hr
ELEVATION GAIN: 2,785 ft (849 m)
EFFORT: Strenuous
TRAIL: Dirt path, rocks, wooden bridges, water crossings on stones
USERS: Hikers
SEASON: June–September
FEES/PASSES: None
MAPS: USGS topo map of Percy Peaks, New Hampshire
TRAILHEAD: North Percy Trail parking lot, Nash Stream Rd., Stratford
FACILITIES: None
CONTACT: NH Division of Forests and Lands; 603/788-4157; www.nh.gov/nhdfl

South and North Percy Peaks are gargantuan outliers in a region of modest mountains, lakes, and woods. They tower above the Nash Stream Forest and the nearby villages of Stratford and Stark like twin volcanic cones. And hikers who are willing to follow the rugged, overlooked path to the evergreen-rich saddle between the Percy Peaks are rewarded with one of the most scenic and exciting hikes north of the White Mountains. Abundant tuffets of moss and dramatic slides of exposed granite pave the way to the top, and the act of summiting each peak requires some good old New England rock scrambling. The slabby slopes of North Percy Peak, in particular, are steep and exposed enough to get the adrenaline pumping (and they shouldn't be traversed when the ground is wet!). Summiting the Percy Peaks also includes briefly linking up with the Cohos Trail, a 170-mi (274-km) trail from the heart of the White Mountains to the U.S.-Canada border, built by volunteers and finished in 2011. Altogether, the climb to South and North Percy Peaks is a big, bold showcase of northern New Hampshire's most wondrous hiking attractions.

START THE HIKE

▶ **MILE 0-1.5: North Percy Trail Parking Lot to Cohos Trail**
Begin the hike on the shoulder of Nash Stream Road, where a small pull-out offers parking for Percy Peaks hikers. Walk north up the road, over a bridge, and turn right onto the orange-blazed **Percy Peaks Trail.** Follow the meditative ripple of nearby Slide Brook as the trail climbs at a patient grade through a mix of maple and beech trees. The occasional mossy rocks

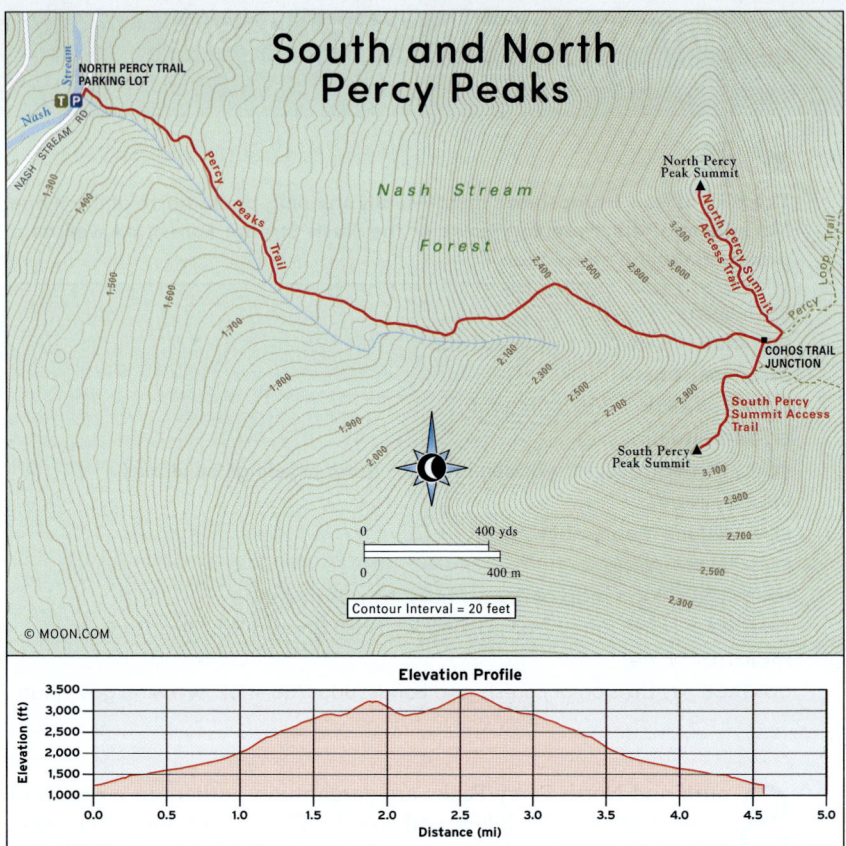

South and North Percy Peaks

NORTH PERCY TRAIL PARKING LOT

Nash Stream

NASH STREAM RD

Percy Peaks Trail

Nash Stream Forest

North Percy Peak Summit

North Percy Summit Access Trail

Percy Loop Trail

COHOS TRAIL JUNCTION

South Percy Summit Access Trail

South Percy Peak Summit

400 yds

400 m

Contour Interval = 20 feet

© MOON.COM

Elevation Profile

Elevation (ft) / Distance (mi)

and ferns that appear alongside the rooty trail hint at what awaits farther along the trail.

At 1 mi (1.6 km), the trail arrives at a bungalow-sized boulder perched above the brook and makes a hard left turn. Now the climbing truly begins. Continue east as the Percy Peaks Trail ascends the col between the two peaks via stone stairs and somewhat eroded dirt sections, at a much steeper grade. At 1.2 mi (1.9 km), you'll reach the first of several exposed granite slabs, where landslides of yesteryear sheared off the local vegetation. Enjoy partial views of the Stratford area, and continue up more stone steps as the trail gradually starts to level out. The sudden presence of wind sweeping through the trees indicates the end of your climb to the saddle between the peaks—as does the verdant explosion of ferns. Follow the trail through boreal trees to a junction for the Cohos Trail at 1.5 mi (2.4 km).

▶ **MILE 1.5-1.8: Cohos Trail to South Percy Peak**

Make a right turn onto the Cohos Trail and follow yellow blazes as the trail makes a brief descent to the foot of South Percy's summit cone. Keep right here, as the Cohos Trail branches off to the left, and continue on the **South Percy summit access trail.** Use your hands and legs to pull or push yourself

▲ VIEW OF NORTH PERCY'S EXPOSED SLOPE FROM SOUTH PERCY PEAK

up through a jumble of roots and mossy boulders as the trail becomes much more ragged and steep. And take a moment to admire the seemingly boundless carpet of moss that covers the rocky forest floor up here. As the trail breaks through wispy boreal spruce, look over your shoulder for a stunning view of North Percy Peak, whose immense granite slabs you'll soon be monkeying up and down. At 1.8 mi (2.9 km), the summit access trail reaches **the South Percy Peak summit.**

▶ **MILE 1.8–2.4: South Percy Peak to North Percy Peak**
Once you've had your fill of South Percy, carefully make your way back down the mess of stones and roots. Turn left onto the Cohos Trail and backtrack to the junction for the Percy Peaks Trail at 2.1 mi (3.4 km). This time veer right to continue through the saddle on the Cohos Trail. After a brief steep scramble up perpetually damp stones, the trail reaches a junction for the **North Percy summit access trail,** where a trail registration kiosk is affixed to a tree. Turn left to begin ascending North Percy.

Climb through the mossy forest at an increasingly steep grade and prepare to be wowed as the trail emerges from the overstory onto the barren granite slopes of North Percy's cone. Carefully scramble up the exposed mountainside: The slabs are quite steep in places, but in dry weather, the granite should still offer plenty of grip for shoes and boots. Once you get into the swing of things, keep an eye out for the blueberries that grow in the shrubs of North Percy, and keep climbing until you arrive at a surprisingly flat height of land. You've arrived at the **North Percy summit,** the taller mountain at 3,430 ft (1,045 m) above sea level.

▶ **MILE 2.4–4.6: North Percy Peak to North Percy Trail Parking Lot**
The return journey will involve retracing your steps. But do take extra time and caution when descending North Percy's slabs. (When in doubt,

sit down and crab-walk.) Upon reaching the Cohos Trail again, turn right, backtrack to the Percy Peaks Trail, and follow it to Nash Stream Road again, where you'll conclude your hike at 4.6 mi (7.4 km).

DIRECTIONS

From Concord, drive north along I-93 N through Franconia Notch and then take Exit 35 for US-3 N toward Lancaster/Twin Mountain. Continue north along US-3 N to the town of Northumberland and then turn right onto NH-110 E. Drive northeast for 2 mi (3.2 km) and make a left onto Emerson Road, which eventually becomes Northside Road. Follow the road to its terminus and turn left onto Nash Stream Road. The pavement transitions to dirt, and the hiker parking lot for the Percy Peaks Trail is located 2.7 mi (4.3 km) up the road, on the right shoulder.

GPS COORDINATES: 44°39'55.7"N 71°27'27.8"W

BEST NEARBY BITES

Step into the inviting, old-school digs of a roadside diner and fuel up for your climb with comfort food essentials like corned beef hash or eggs Benedict at **Claudette & Dean's Place** (1858 US-3, North Stratford; 603/922-3299; www.claudetteanddeansplace.weebly.com; 6am-2pm Mon.-Wed., 6am-8pm Thurs.-Sun.). The recurring pot roast dinner special also makes for a savory and succulent reward for finishing the Percy Peaks ascent.

Burrow through the forest into the depths of an eerie gorge and scramble over a jumble of mossy rocks that conceal an active stream.

DISTANCE: 2 mi (3.2 km) round-trip
DURATION: 1 hr
ELEVATION GAIN: 145 ft (44 m)
EFFORT: Easy
TRAIL: Dirt path, rocks, wooden bridges, river crossings on stones
USERS: Hikers
SEASON: June-October
FEES/PASSES: $7 day-use fee per vehicle
MAPS: White Mountain National Forest website
TRAILHEAD: South Pond Recreation Area, South Pond Rd., Stark
FACILITIES: Vault toilet
CONTACT: White Mountain National Forest; 603/536-6100; www.fs.usda.gov/recarea/whitemountain

The Devil's Hopyard is a dark, vegetation-rich gorge that lies deep in the quiet woods north of the White Mountains. Exploring the Hopyard requires scrambling up and down a mess of rocks beneath which a river runs, filling the gorge with strikingly cool moisture that can take hikers by surprise. Because the access route for the Devil's Hopyard departs from the idyllic summer camp-esque beaches of South Pond, the dramatic change of scenery along the hike can feel like, well, taking a journey into the underworld.

START THE HIKE

▶ **MILE 0-0.5: South Pond Recreation Area to Kilkenny Ridge Trail**
Begin the hike in the trees by the beach at South Pond Recreation Area. Find the sign for the **Kilkenny Ridge Trail,** which starts as a narrow dirt path along the water. (During early summer, this area is often blooming with tiny wildflowers.) Yellow blazes mark the way through a corridor of spruce and white birch trees. As the mostly level trail becomes rockier, it starts to veer south away from the pond. Hike into a thicker and darker stretch of deciduous forest and rock-hop across a few small tributaries that feed a larger stream.

▶ **MILE 0.5-0.8: Kilkenny Ridge Trail to Devil's Hopyard**
After crossing the stream by way of an aging log bridge, the trail reaches the junction for the **Devil's Hopyard Trail** at 0.6 mi (1 km).
Make a right turn onto Devil's Hopyard at the junction and follow the stream deeper into the forest. The trail crosses the water once again on

245

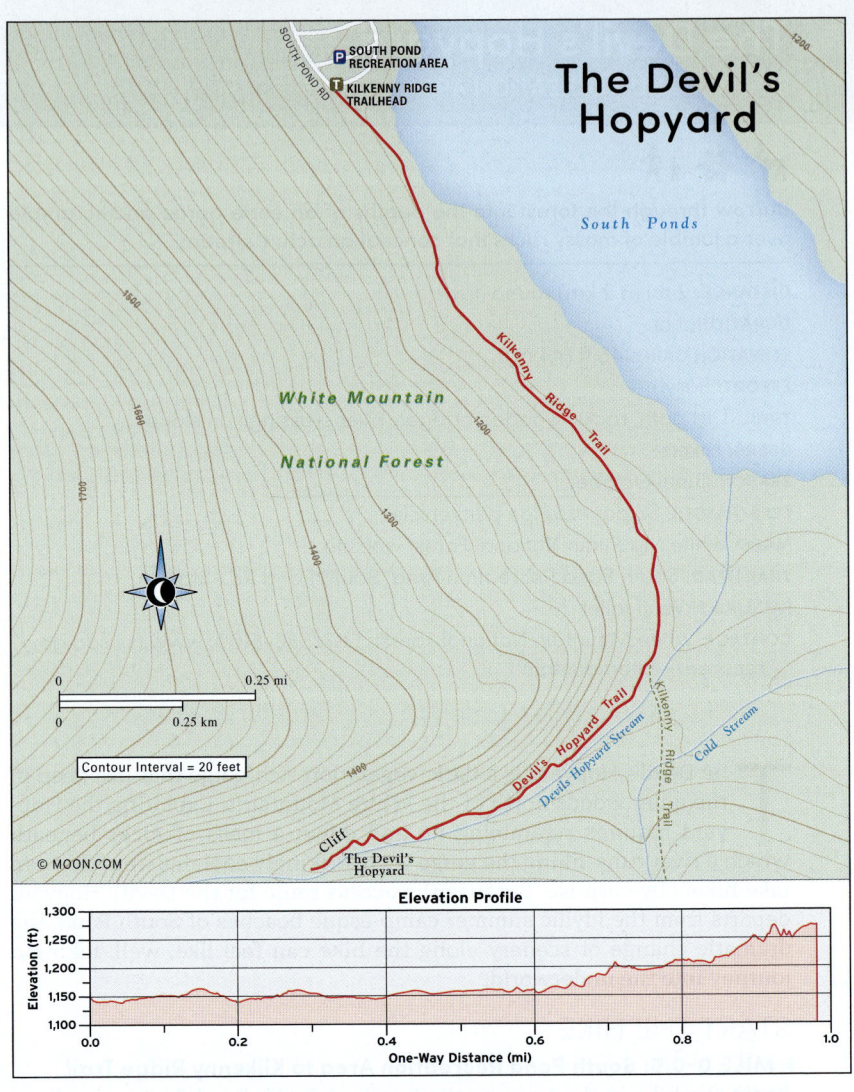

The Devil's Hopyard

SOUTH POND
RECREATION AREA
KILKENNY RIDGE
TRAILHEAD

South Ponds

Kilkenny Ridge Trail

White Mountain

National Forest

0   0.25 mi
0   0.25 km

Contour Interval = 20 feet

Devil's Hopyard Trail

Devils Hopyard Stream

Kilkenny Ridge Trail

Cold Stream

Cliff

The Devil's
Hopyard

© MOON.COM

Elevation Profile

Elevation (ft)

1,300
1,250
1,200
1,150
1,100

0.0   0.2   0.4   0.6   0.8   1.0

One-Way Distance (mi)

a second log bridge, and the surrounding vegetation gradually becomes lush with emerald ferns. As you walk along the trail here, you'll notice that the air is becoming colder, indicating that the Hopyard is close. As the trail climbs uphill at a subtle grade, the footing gets considerably rougher, with lots of loose rocks that can become quite slick during rainy weather due to the growth of moss and algae. Then, quite suddenly, the crumbling walls of the gorge appear at 0.8 mi (1.3 km), marking your entry into the Hopyard.

▶ MILE 0.8-1.0: **Devil's Hopyard to Cliff**

From here, you'll scramble up a jumble of rocks and boulders through the recesses of the gorge. As you carefully make your way through the gorge, streams of chilly and moist air will blast upward through the gaps between

the rocks. And, if you listen closely, you can hear the rushing of water beneath the rocks; that's the sound of the stream that you've followed to this point. The gorge walls get taller, darker, and more dramatic as the trail climbs the rockfall. Finally, the trail reaches its terminus at a looming vertical **cliff** at roughly 1 mi (1.6 km). Return the way you came.

DIRECTIONS

From Concord, drive north along I-93 N through Franconia Notch and then take Exit 35 for US-3 N toward Lancaster/Twin Mountain. Continue north along US-3 N to the town of Northumberland and then turn right onto NH-110 E. Drive along this road for 10 mi (16 km) and then swing a right onto South Pond Road. Keep right at the forks for Short Road and Normand Road, and then take a sharper right to stay on South Pond Road. Follow the road past a gate to its end at the South Pond Recreation Area. The gate is usually opened for the season in mid-June and closes in mid-October, but off-season visitors can park on the shoulder just before the closed gate and walk down the final stretch of road to the South Pond Recreation area.

GPS COORDINATES: 45°'3'11"7"N 68°59'59.1"W

BEST NEARBY BITES AND BREWS

The Devil's Hopyard might not be the toughest hike in the book, but that's no reason to turn down an Irish red ale or any of the other microbrews you'll find at **Copper Pig Brewery** (1 Middle St., Lancaster; 603/631-2273; www.copperpigbrewery.com; 11:30am-8:30pm Thurs.-Sat., 8am-noon Sun.). Hearty stick-to-your-ribs breakfast and lunch classics are offered in generous portions at **The Granite Grind** (70 Main St.; 603/788-8211; www.facebook.com/granitegrind; 7am-2pm Tues.-Fri., 8am-2pm Sat.).

Great North Woods and Dixville Notch

NEW HAMPSHIRE

NEARBY CAMPGROUNDS

NAME	LOCATION	FACILITIES	SEASON	FEE
Deer Mountain Campground	5309 N. Main St., Pittsburg, 45°11′28.0″N 71°11′30.1″W	Tent sites, toilets, potable water	late May–early October	$23
603/538–6965; www.nhstateparks.org				
Ramblewood Cabins & Campground	3256 N. Main St., Pittsburg, 45°06′08.3″N 71°16′58.8″W	Tent sites, lean-tos, RV sites, cabins, toilets, showers, potable water, laundry, camp store, Wi-Fi	year-round	$30–275
603/538–6948; www.ramblewoodcabins.com				
Mountain View Cabins & Campground	2787 N. Main St., Pittsburg, 45°05′09.3″N 71°18′32.6″W	Tent sites, RV sites, cabins, toilets, showers, potable water, laundry, camp store, restaurant, Wi-Fi	year-round	$30–175
603/538–6305; www.mountainviewcabinsandcampground.com				
Lake Francis State Park	439 River Rd., Pittsburg, 45°03′35.4″N 71°18′09.8″W	Tent sites, RV sites, toilets, showers, potable water, camp store	late May–early October	$25–35
603/538–6965; www.nhstateparks.org				

NEARBY CAMPGROUNDS (continued)

NAME	LOCATION	FACILITIES	SEASON	FEE
Notch View Resort Inn & Campground	54 Forbes Hill Rd., Colebrook, 44°53'37.4"N 71°25'37.1"W	Tent sites, RV sites, RV rentals, hotel rooms, toilets, showers, potable water, laundry, swimming pool, camp store, Wi-Fi	May-October	$50
603/237-4237; www.notchviewresort.com				
Clear Stream Campground	33 Chabot Rd., Errol, 44°46'56.6"N 71°08'37.1"W	Tent sites, RV sites, toilets, showers, potable water	late May-mid-September	$45-55
603/482-3888; www.clearstreamcampground.com				
Mountain Valley Campground	63 Meacham Rd., Stark, 44°37'22.4"N 71°23'06.5"W	Tent sites, RV sites, hotel rooms, toilets, showers, potable water, private beach	late May-mid-October	$30-60
603/856-3101; www.mountainvalleycarp.com				

WINNIPESAUKEE AND THE LAKES DISTRICT

Most of us have heard illustrious tales of summers on Lake Winnipesaukee, but in New Hampshire, the famed lake is just the start. The Lakes District is home to many such bodies of water, all of which provide the type of aquatic bliss that's worth traveling for. Just as essential are the local trails that can make a swim more refreshing. In the Lakes District, you can climb a mountain without completely wearing out your calves, glimpse wild animals and birds without disappearing into wild territory, and enjoy old-school cooking and shopping in towns such as Tamworth and Sandwich. And if your heart desires, you can even rent a boat and do your best *Miami Vice* impression on New Hampshire waters.

▲ VISTA FROM WEST RATTLESNAKE MOUNTAIN

▲ THE EXPOSED FACE OF WELCH MOUNTAIN

◄ VIEW OF THE WHITE MOUNTAINS FROM THE WELCH-DICKEY LOOP TRAIL

NEW HAMPSHIRE

Winnipesaukee and the Lakes District

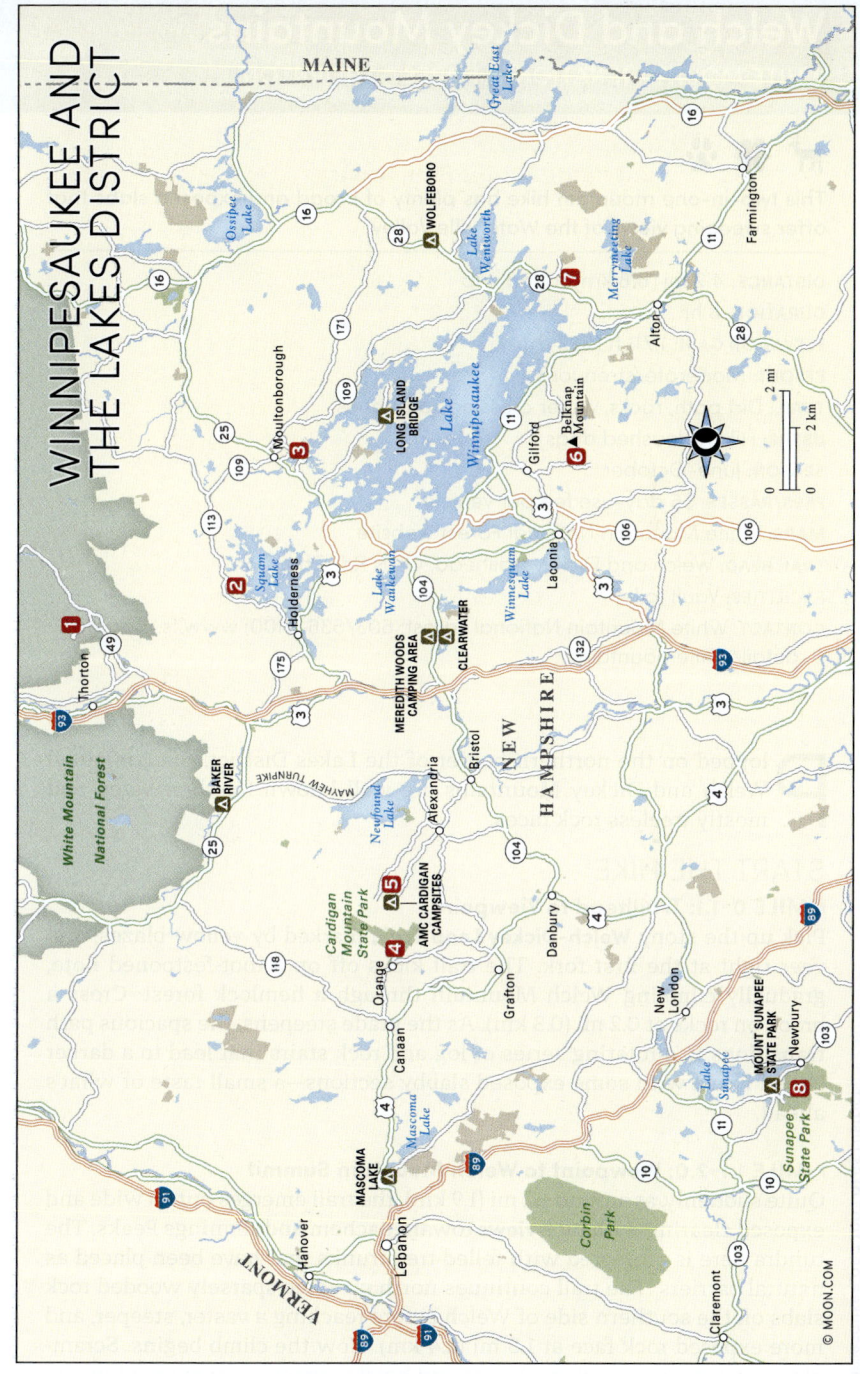

WINNIPESAUKEE AND THE LAKES DISTRICT

MAINE

Great East Lake

MOON.COM

1

Welch and Dickey Mountains

WHITE MOUNTAIN NATIONAL FOREST, THORNTON

This two-in-one mountain hike has plenty of broad and exposed slabs that offer sweeping views of the Waterville Valley.

DISTANCE: 4.2 mi (6.8 km) round-trip

DURATION: 3 hr

ELEVATION GAIN: 1,711 ft (522 m)

EFFORT: Moderate/strenuous

TRAIL: Dirt path, rocks, water crossings on stones

USERS: Hikers, leashed dogs

SEASON: June–October

FEES/PASSES: $5 day-use fee per vehicle

MAPS: White Mountain National Forest website

TRAILHEAD: Welch and Dickey trailhead, Orris Rd., Thornton

FACILITIES: Vault toilet

CONTACT: White Mountain National Forest; 603/536-6100; www.fs.usda.gov/detail/whitemountain

Plopped on the northern border of the Lakes District, the conjoined Welch and Dickey Mountains are well known for their steep and mostly treeless rock faces.

START THE HIKE

▶ MILE 0-1.1: Trailhead to Viewpoint

Pick up the stony **Welch-Dickey Loop Trail,** marked by yellow blazes, and veer right at the first fork. The trail kicks off on a root-festooned note, gradually climbing Welch Mountain through a hemlock forest. Cross a brook on rocks at 0.2 mi (0.3 km). As the grade steepens, the spacious path transitions to a rotating series of log and rock stairs that lead to a darker boreal forest with some exposed slabby sections—a small taste of what's ahead.

▶ MILE 1.1-2.0: Viewpoint to Welch Mountain Summit

Quite suddenly, at around 1.2 mi (1.9 km), the trail emerges onto a wide and exposed clearing with nice **views** toward Sachem and Jennings Peaks. The tundra here is protected with felled tree trunks that have been placed as natural barriers. The trail continues north up some sparsely wooded rock slabs on the southern side of Welch before reaching a vaster, steeper, and more exposed rock face at 1.5 mi (2.4 km). Now the climb begins. Scramble your way up the epic rock face and hoist yourself up some boulders to reach the summit of **Welch Mountain** at 2 mi (3.2 km). Look out to see the pinnacle of the larger Dickey Mountain directly ahead.

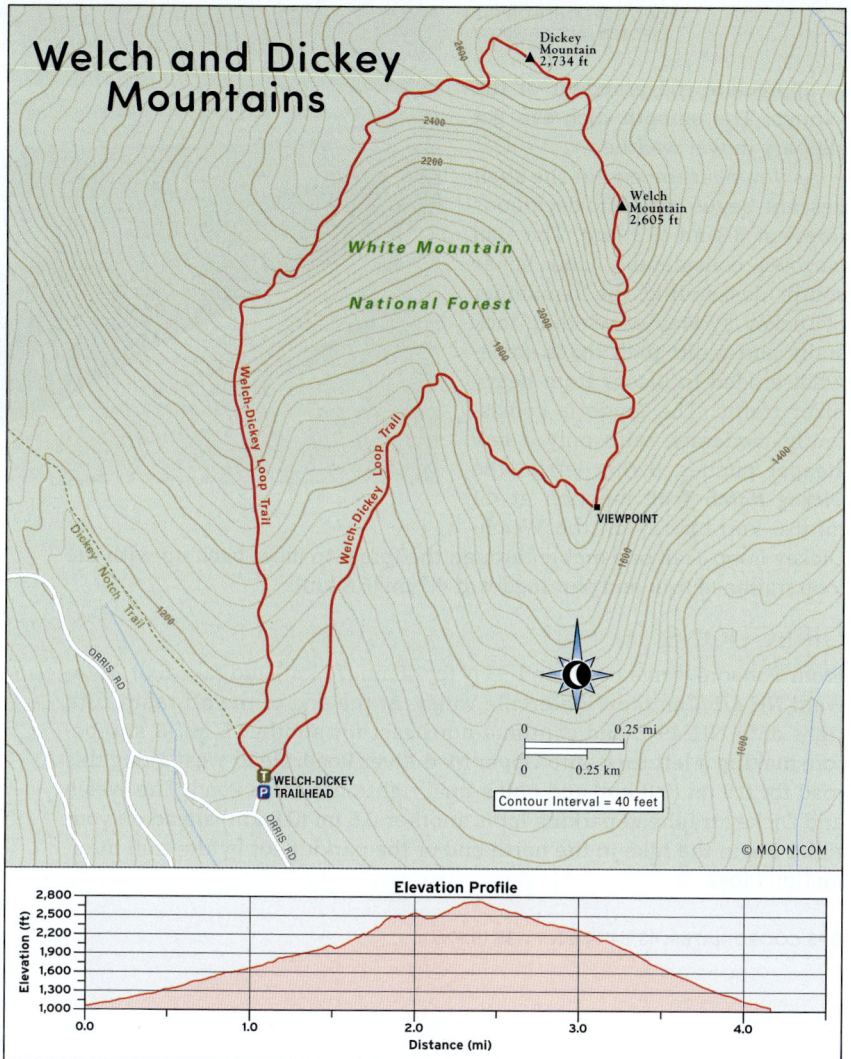

Welch and Dickey Mountains

Dickey Mountain
2,734 ft

Welch Mountain
2,605 ft

White Mountain

National Forest

Welch-Dickey Loop Trail

Welch-Dickey Loop Trail

Dickey Notch Trail

ORRIS RD

VIEWPOINT

0   0.25 mi

0   0.25 km

Contour Interval = 40 feet

WELCH-DICKEY
TRAILHEAD

ORRIS RD

© MOON.COM

Elevation Profile

Elevation (ft)

2,800
2,500
2,200
1,900
1,600
1,300
1,000

0.0   1.0   2.0   3.0   4.0

Distance (mi)

▶ **MILE 2.0-2.4: Welch Mountain Summit to Dickey Mountain Summit**
Continue on the trail to descend into the col (gap) between the two mountains. At the bottom of the col, pass by an enormous cairn at 2.1 mi (3.4 km) and make a brief foray back into boreal woods before scaling an even steeper and more exposed section of slabby rock faces. At 2.4 mi (3.9 km), step onto the summit of **Dickey Mountain,** where you can savor a view of the deep green Pemigewasset Wilderness to the north.

▶ **MILE 2.4-4.2: Dickey Mountain Summit to Trailhead**
As you begin your descent of the mountain's southern haunch, get ready for the best part yet—a long walk down a barren rock shelf with a sheer drop on one side, and killer views of Welch. This shelf is a great place

to appreciate the grandeur of the Whites. The smooth rock can get slippery in wet weather.

As you near the end of the shelf descent, segue back into deciduous forest at 3.3 mi (5.3 km). The trail narrows considerably and heads south, descending the remainder of Dickey by way of winding rock stairs and a dirt path that's somewhat eroded in places from heavy hiker traffic. The grade is consistently moderate, with only a few steeper pitches. Swing left at the **Dickey Notch Trail** junction at 4.1 mi (6.6 km) to stay on the Welch-Dickey Loop Trail and amble through the forest to meet back up with the loop trailhead fork and parking lot at 4.2 mi (6.8 km).

DIRECTIONS

From Concord, drive north on I-93 N for 48 mi (77 km) and take Exit 28 toward NH-175/Campton/Waterville Valley. At the end of the off-ramp, turn right onto NH-49 E and continue northeast for another 5 mi (8 km) before making a left turn onto Upper Mad River Road. Head west along this road for 0.5 mi (0.8 km) and pull a final right onto Orris Road. The Welch and Dickey trailhead parking lot is another 0.5 mi (0.8 km) ahead on your right. Begin the hike in the north end of the parking lot by the trail information kiosk.

GPS COORDINATES: 43°54'14.8"N 71°35'19.9"W

BEST NEARBY BITES

The Mad River region offers several solid options for a pre-summit breakfast. For a damn fine cup of locally roasted coffee and a decadent egg sandwich, head to **Mad River Coffee** (18 Six Flags Rd., Campton; 603/726-7793; www.madrivercoffeeroasters.com; 6am-6pm daily). If you're craving something more rustic and old-fashioned—say, a tower of blueberry pancakes—check out **Benton's Sugar Shack** (2010 NH-175, Thornton; 603/726-3867; www.bentonssugarshack.com; 7am-noon Thurs.-Fri., 7am-2pm Sat.-Sun.).

2

West and East Rattlesnake Mountains

ARMSTRONG NATURAL AREA, SANDWICH

This family-friendly mountain hike visits two neighboring peaks with views of Squam Lake that would make Ansel Adams weep.

DISTANCE: 3.8 mi (6.1 km) round-trip

DURATION: 2 hr

ELEVATION GAIN: 609 ft (186 m)

EFFORT: Easy/moderate

TRAIL: Dirt path, rocks

USERS: Hikers, leashed dogs

SEASON: June–October

FEES/PASSES: None

MAPS: New Hampshire Division of Forests and Lands website

TRAILHEAD: Old Bridal Path trailhead, NH-113, Sandwich

FACILITIES: None

CONTACT: New Hampshire Division of Forests and Lands; 603/271-2214; www.nh.gov/nhdfl

Rising from the northern shores of Squam Lake, the modest West and East Rattlesnake Mountains form a popular destination for families with small children and couples making proposals. A gentle ascent up West Rattlesnake leads to a vast, heavily visited lookout ledge with one of the most awe-inducing panoramic lake views anywhere in New England. The neighboring East Rattlesnake is more quiet and rugged, but it features a comparably beautiful vista with a more romantic ambience.

START THE HIKE

▶ MILE 0-0.4: Trailhead to Old Bridle Path

Begin the hike in the south end of the parking lot, where you'll see a wooden trail information kiosk. Pick up the **Old Bridle Path** by the kiosk and head southeast up log stairs into the forest. The trail is wide and mostly dirt, with a few odd rocks scattered about. Follow yellow diamond markers on the trees as the trail flows through oaks and beech, gradually curving south and ascending some gently sloped rock slabs near the entrance to a University of New Hampshire revegetation area at 0.4 mi (0.6 km) (UNH manages portions of the land here).

▶ MILE 0.4-0.9: Old Bridle Path to West Rattlesnake Lookout

Climbing steadily up the western flank of West Rattlesnake, the trail passes into an airy stretch of red pines, where the terrain alternates between flat stony floor and rock stairs. Glimpses of blue through the trees hint at the nearby lookout. At 0.8 mi (1.3 km), turn left at the junction with the

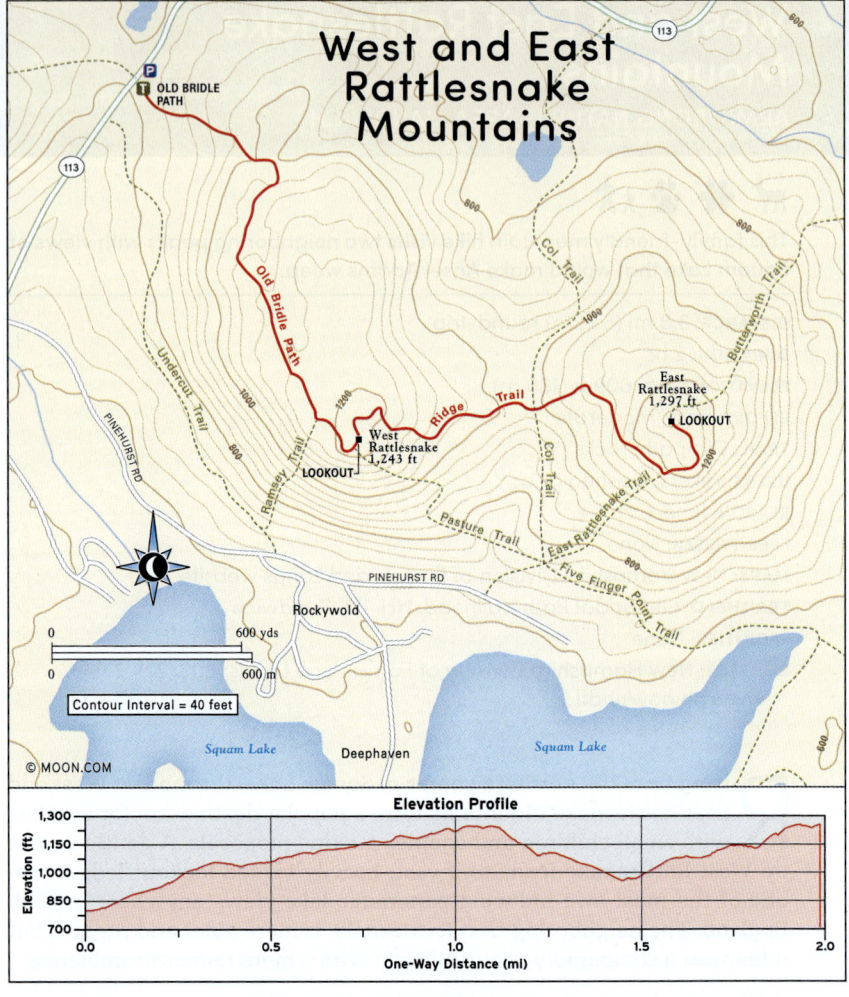

West and East Rattlesnake Mountains

Elevation Profile

Map labels:
OLD BRIDLE PATH
113
Old Bridle Path
Col Trail
Butterworth Trail
East Rattlesnake 1,297 ft
LOOKOUT
Ridge Trail
West Rattlesnake 1,243 ft
LOOKOUT
PINEHURST RD
Undercut Trail
Ramsey Trail
Col Trail
Pasture Trail
East Rattlesnake Trail
Five Finger Point Trail
PINEHURST RD
Rockywold
0   600 yds
0   600 m
Contour Interval = 40 feet
© MOON.COM
Squam Lake
Deephaven
Squam Lake

Elevation profile axis: Elevation (ft) — 1,300 / 1,150 / 1,000 / 850 / 700; One-Way Distance (mi) — 0.0 / 0.5 / 1.0 / 1.5 / 2.0

Ramsey Trail to stay on Old Bridle. Ascend a series of exposed and sloping rock faces to reach another set of log stairs that delivers you to the scenic **West Rattlesnake lookout** at 0.9 mi (1.4 km). The rock here has a deep glowing tan that's reminiscent of landscapes in the American Southwest, and the view is spectacular. The lookout ledge is generally a bit crowded.

▶ **MILE 0.9-1.5: West Rattlesnake Lookout to Ridge Trail**

To continue onward to more peaceful surroundings, pick up the **Ridge Trail** by the junction sign on the ledge and head northeast back into the woods, where you'll quickly reach the wooded summit of West Rattlesnake at 1 mi (1.6 km). The narrower dirt trail, marked by green diamond markers, plows through a breezy ridge forest before making a steeper descent into a much darker forest in the col (gap) between the two mountains. A rugged climb out of the col brings you to the junction with the aptly named **Col Trail** at 1.4 mi (2.3 km). Turn left here, and then take an immediate right at a second junction ahead to stay on the Ridge Trail.

▶ **MILE 1.5–1.7: Ridge Trail to East Rattlesnake Trail**

Climb northeast along the sunnier southern slopes of East Rattlesnake for another 0.2 mi (0.3 km). Watch your step on the countless exposed roots along this stretch of trail, which can become quite eroded during drier summer conditions. At 1.7 mi (2.7 km), you'll reach the junction for **East Rattlesnake Trail;** veer left to take East Rattlesnake and continue along a narrow ledge-like path.

▶ **MILE 1.7–1.9: East Rattlesnake Trail to East Rattlesnake Summit**

Climb steadily up the mountain before reaching the gorgeous **East Rattlesnake lookout** at 1.8 mi (2.9 km). The lookout ledge is perfectly framed by trees that have bent to form a circular opening in the woods. (The intimate scale of this ledge, paired with the beauty of Squam Lake, would make this a fine place to propose.) The wooded summit of East Rattlesnake is 0.1 mi (0.16 km) farther up the trail, which continues north from the ledge into the woods. Top off the summit and then return the way you came.

DIRECTIONS

From Concord, drive north on I-93 N for 36 mi (58 km) and take Exit 24 for US-3/NH-25 toward Ashland/Holderness. At the bottom of the off-ramp, turn right onto NH-25 E/US-3 S and continue along this road for 4 mi (6.4 km). As you enter downtown Holderness, pull a left onto NH-113 and drive northeast and then north for another 5 mi (8 km). The West Rattlesnake parking lot will be on your right at the top of a hill.

GPS COORDINATES: 43°47'19.8"N 71°32'54.3"W

BEST NEARBY BITES

Fresh Maine scallops, ahi tuna salad, and crispy maple pork belly are just a few of the gourmet line items you'll find in the lakeside dining room at **Walter's Basin** (859 US-3, Holderness; 603/968-4412; www.waltersbasin.com; 3pm-9pm Mon.-Thurs., 11:30am-9pm Fri.-Sat., 11:30am-8pm Sun.).

Winnipesaukee and the Lakes District

NEW HAMPSHIRE

3 Markus Wildlife Sanctuary

MARKUS WILDLIFE SANCTUARY, MOULTONBOROUGH

This wildlife-rich trail takes hikers through a lush forest, wetlands, and along the shores of Lake Winnipesaukee to visit an active loon nest.

BEST: Spring hikes
DISTANCE: 2 mi (3.2 km) round-trip
DURATION: 1 hr
ELEVATION GAIN: 75 ft (23 m)
EFFORT: Easy
TRAIL: Dirt path, rocks, wooden bridges
USERS: Hikers
SEASON: May-October
FEES/PASSES: None
MAPS: Loon Preservation Committee website
TRAILHEAD: The Loon Center parking lot, Lee's Mill Rd., Moultonborough
FACILITIES: Restroom
CONTACT: Loon Preservation Committee; 603/476-5666; www.loon.org

Countless mammal, bird, and reptile species reside along the waterfront woodlands in the Lakes District. The Markus Wildlife Sanctuary is a lush preserve that offers hiking trails through the conjoined ecosystems of Lake Winnipesaukee. The crown jewel of the sanctuary is the loon nest, a special place that draws native loons each year. Midsummer is the best season to hear their distinct cry.

START THE HIKE

▶ **MILE 0-0.2: The Loon Center to Forest Trail**
Begin your hike in the parking lot by the Loon Center building. Find the Trails sign and walk east, toward a large wooden bridge that spans a brook. Cross the bridge into the woods, pick up the Loon Nest Trail for a few yards, and then take an immediate left onto the **Forest Trail** loop. Stroll through a corridor of pine trees marked with red blazes and keep an ear open for birdsong.

▶ **MILE 0.2-0.5: Forest Trail to Loon Nest Trail**
Upon reaching the end of the Forest Trail loop, turn left back onto **Loon Nest Trail,** following yellow blazes along a smooth dirt path that weaves through the woods along the brook. At 0.3 mi (0.5 km), cross a second wooden footbridge as the trail curves away from the brook. Continue along some sections of wooden boardwalk through a wetter area of the forest and enjoy a few glimpses of Lake Winnipesaukee between the trees. The

Markus Wildlife Sanctuary

LEE'S MILL RD

THE LOON CENTER

Forest Loop Trail

Halfway Brook

Markus

Wildlife

Sanctuary

Loon Nest Trail

LEE'S MILL BOAT RAMP

Lake Winnipesaukee

Rock Formation

LOOKOUT POINT

0   0.25 mi
0   0.25 km

Contour Interval = 20 feet

© MOON.COM

Elevation Profile

Elevation (ft) — 550, 540, 530, 520, 510, 500

Distance (mi) — 0.0, 0.5, 1.0, 1.5, 2.0

trail passes through a patch of bogland, becoming rockier with each yard, before entering a darker forest of pine.

▶ **MILE 0.5-1.2: Loon Nest Trail to Lookout Point**

After crossing a stream on rocks, you'll reach a trail junction at 0.7 mi (1.1 km); the Loon Nest Trail diverges in two directions to form a loop. Make a left and note how intensely green the forest becomes. The abundance of moss here feels more like the Pacific Northwest. As the path rolls up and down mildly through the woods, you'll really hear the melodies of native bird species. At 1.1 mi (1.8 km), emerge from the forest by a marsh and hike northwest along the banks of the lake until you reach a bench at 1.2 mi (1.9 km). This is the lookout point for the loon nest.

▶ **MILE 1.2-2.0: Lookout Point to the Loon Center**

Take a seat, watch the reeds of the marsh for rustling, and listen for that unmistakable cry that the White Mountains are famous for. From the

lookout, the trail turns back into the woods, passing some muddier terrain before arriving at a massive glacial **rock formation** that hikers must squeeze their way through. The trees around here are often speckled with wild discus-shaped mushrooms that grow on the bark and can become quite large. Continue along the rocky, rooty path for another 0.2 mi (0.3 km) before reaching the end of the Loon Nest Trail loop at 1.4 mi (2.3 km). Turn left and backtrack over the boardwalk and along the brook to return to the trailhead and end your hike at 2 mi (3.2 km).

DIRECTIONS

From Concord, drive north on I-93 N for 30 mi (48 km) and take Exit 23 for NH-104/NH-132 toward Meredith/New Hampton. Turn right onto NH-104 E/NH-132 N at the bottom of the off-ramp and drive east for 8 mi (12.9 km). Veer right onto US-3 N and then make another right onto NH-25 E/Winnipesaukee Street. Take this road northeast for another 9 mi (14.5 km) before turning right onto Blake Road. Follow the road to its terminus and then turn right onto Lee's Mill Road. The Loon Center visitors building and parking area will be on your left shortly after this turn.

GPS COORDINATES: 43°44'15.2"N 71°23'27.1"W

4 Mount Cardigan

CARDIGAN MOUNTAIN STATE PARK, ORANGE

This tough but short mountain hike is a rock scrambler's paradise—and the beautiful views into Vermont aren't bad either.

DISTANCE: 3.4 mi (5.5 km) round-trip

DURATION: 3 hr

ELEVATION GAIN: 1,191 ft (363 m)

EFFORT: Moderate/strenuous

TRAIL: Dirt path, rocks, wooden bridges, water crossings on stones

USERS: Hikers, leashed dogs

SEASON: June–October

FEES/PASSES: None

MAPS: Cardigan Mountain State Park website

TRAILHEAD: West Ridge trailhead, Cardigan Mountain State Park parking lot, Cardigan Mountain Rd., Orange

FACILITIES: Vault toilet

CONTACT: Cardigan Mountain State Park; 603/227-8745; www.nhstateparks.org

I n the 1950s, a devastating forest fire left some mountains stripped of vegetation at their highest points, including Mount Cardigan. This makes for an exhilarating climb to the top, with panoramic vistas of the surrounding wilderness and plenty of smooth rock slabs to be scaled.

START THE HIKE

▶ **MILE 0-0.4: West Ridge Trailhead to West Ridge Trail**
Starting from the east side of the parking lot, climb a set of log stairs into the woods and head northwest up **West Ridge Trail,** marked by orange blazes. Step carefully on the abundant tree roots that squiggle across the trail, and look out for some prized plant species such as lady's slippers. Cross a winding stream on rocks before reaching a junction with South Ridge Trail at 0.4 mi (0.6 km); keep left to stay on West Ridge Trail.

▶ **MILE 0.4-1.4: West Ridge Trail to Cardigan Mountain Summit Dome**
The trail becomes rockier and steeper as the surrounding woods transition into a more boreal collection of trees. A brief and more level reprieve from the climb leads to a wooden bridge at 0.8 mi (1.3 km).

From here, the ascent resumes at a steep grade almost immediately and ascends sloped slabs and rock stairs to the Skyland Trail junction at 1 mi (1.6 km). Make a left turn to stay on West Ridge and keep left again at the Ranger Cabin Trail junction shortly ahead. Emerge from the woods at 1.4 mi (2.3 km) onto the massive and exposed summit dome of Cardigan Mountain.

Winnipesaukee and the Lakes District

NEW HAMPSHIRE

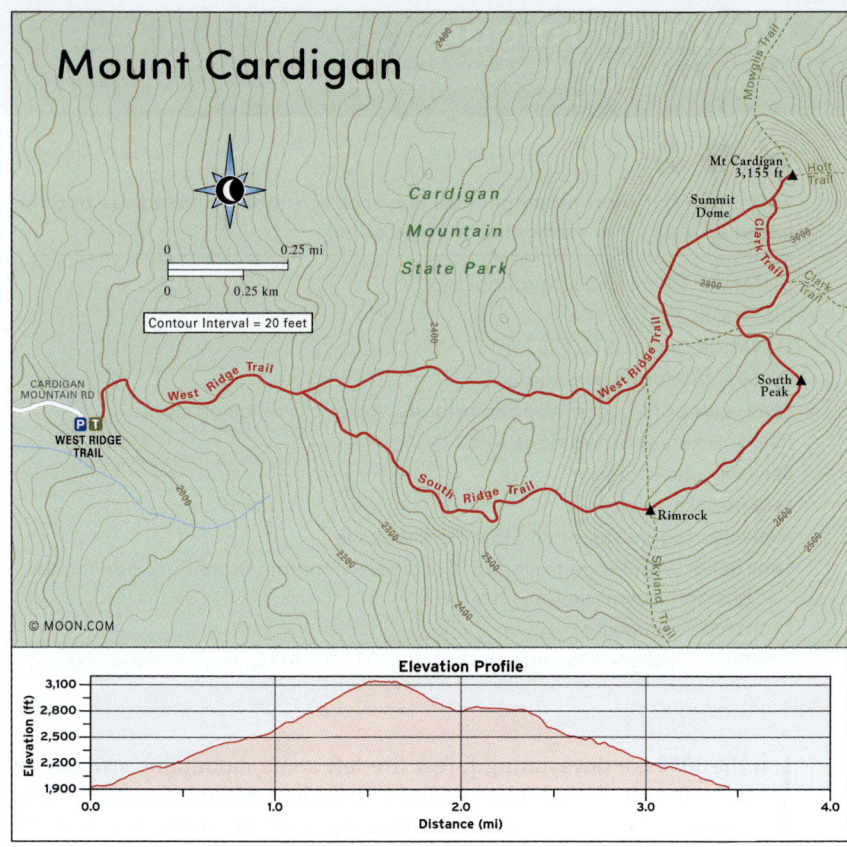

Mount Cardigan

Cardigan Mountain State Park

Contour Interval = 20 feet

Mt Cardigan 3,155 ft

Summit Dome

South Peak

Rimrock

West Ridge Trail

South Ridge Trail

Clark Trail

Mowglis Trail

Holt Trail

Skyland Trail

CARDIGAN MOUNTAIN RD

WEST RIDGE TRAIL

© MOON.COM

Elevation Profile

▶ **MILE 1.4-1.6: Cardigan Mountain Summit Dome to Cardigan Mountain Summit**

The home stretch of the West Ridge Trail is a thrilling climb straight up the barren granite slopes of Cardigan's summit. Follow the cairns and watch out for algae on the rocks during wet weather. Be sure to take a look behind you and gaze out toward White River Junction, Mount Killington, and Camel's Hump in nearby Vermont. Climb a final and less sheer pitch of stone before reaching the victory point at 1.6 mi (2.6 km)—the summit of **Cardigan Mountain.** Scale the **fire tower** and look to the east to see the mighty Presidentials looming like a gathering of green giants. Just northeast of Cardigan's summit lies **The Firescrew**—a partially wooded ridge where a fire that ravaged Cardigan in the 1800s left a spiral-shaped section of exposed rock amid the trees.

▶ **MILE 1.6-2.3: Cardigan Mountain Summit to South Ridge Trail**

Pick up the **Clark Trail** by following cairns that head south from the summit to the junction with South Ridge Trail at 1.7 mi (2.7 km). Turn right here to pick up the **South Ridge Trail** and descend an even steeper side of the exposed dome. (Scrambling on your hands and knees may prove necessary.) Keep left at the fork for the old Cardigan ranger cabin and make another right at the Hurricane Gap Trail junction at 1.9 mi (3.1 km) to stay

▲ VALLEY VIEW FROM CARDIGAN'S SUMMIT

on South Ridge. Hike across a wooded ridge to the South Cardigan summit and then down to the nearby **Rimrock** peak at 2.3 mi (3.7 km). Stay straight on South Ridge and continue down into the boreal forest.

▶ **MILE 2.3–3.4: South Ridge Trail to West Ridge Trailhead**
The descent continues through the mossy woods on Cardigan's south face at an increasingly gradual grade. Hike for another 0.5 mi (0.8 km), crossing some streams on rocks and passing through wildflowers and berry bushes. At 3 mi (4.8 km), link back up with the **West Ridge Trail.** Make a left and backtrack to the trailhead.

DIRECTIONS

From Concord, drive north on I-93 N for 5 mi (8 km) and take Exit 17 for US-4 toward US-3/NH-132/Boscawen/Penacook. Merge onto US-4/Hoit Road and drive to the traffic circle, where you'll take the first exit, US-4 W. At the fork ahead, make a slight left to stay on US-4 W and continue for 15 mi (24 km). Make a right turn onto US-4 and drive north for another 11 mi (18 km). Pull a right onto Turnpike Road and then a second right onto Millbrook Road. Follow this road to its terminus and then turn left onto Burnt Hill Road. Drive north for 2 mi (3.2 km) more and make a final right turn onto Cardigan Mountain Road, which leads to the hiker parking lot and trailhead.

GPS COORDINATES: 43°38'38.9"N 71°56'06.4"W

BEST NEARBY BITES
The town of Hanover—less than 30 minutes west of Cardigan—is an edible mecca of dining options. But if you'd rather stay local, you can't go wrong with the old-school diner comforts and made-to-order breakfast counter classics at **Chappy's in Canaan** (1182 US-4, Canaan; 603/523-9255; 6am-2pm Tues.-Sun.).

Winnipesaukee and the Lakes District

NEW HAMPSHIRE

Welton Falls

WELTON FALLS STATE FOREST, ALEXANDRIA

Follow a pretty brook through the forest to a cascade that spills from a rift in the cliffs.

DISTANCE: 2.6 mi (4.2 km) round-trip

DURATION: 2 hr

ELEVATION GAIN: 472 ft (144 m)

EFFORT: Easy

TRAIL: Dirt path, water crossings via stones

USERS: Hikers, leashed dogs

SEASON: May–October

FEES/PASSES: None

MAPS: Appalachian Mountain Club, "Southern New Hampshire Trail Map"

TRAILHEAD: Lower Manning trailhead, shoulder of Shem Valley Rd., Alexandria

FACILITIES: Restroom at Cardigan Lodge

CONTACT: Appalachian Mountain Club Cardigan Lodge; 603/466-2727; www.outdoors.org

START THE HIKE

▶ **MILE 0-1.0: Lower Manning Trailhead to Clark Brook Crossing**
Begin the hike from the shoulder of Shem Valley Road; look for the wooden sign for **Lower Manning Trail** and walk east into a hemlock forest past several tent sites and a pair of outhouses. Yellow blazes mark the way as the path crosses a ski trail and descends a series of log stairs into the forest. Rock-hop your way across a chuckling stream and listen for the roar of **Clark Brook** as the air suddenly becomes much cooler and moist.

At 0.3 mi (0.5 km), the trail reaches the first viewpoint of the brook and then turns sharply to the north. Make your way down a few more sets of log and stone stairs and enjoy a more agreeable grade as you follow Clark Brook, which flows north alongside the trail. Watch your footing on several more stream crossings—some of them quite muddy—and take a moment to admire the brook from a few more outlook points. After a

CABLE GUARDRAILS ON A PATH
NEAR WELTON FALLS ▶

Winnipesaukee and the Lakes District

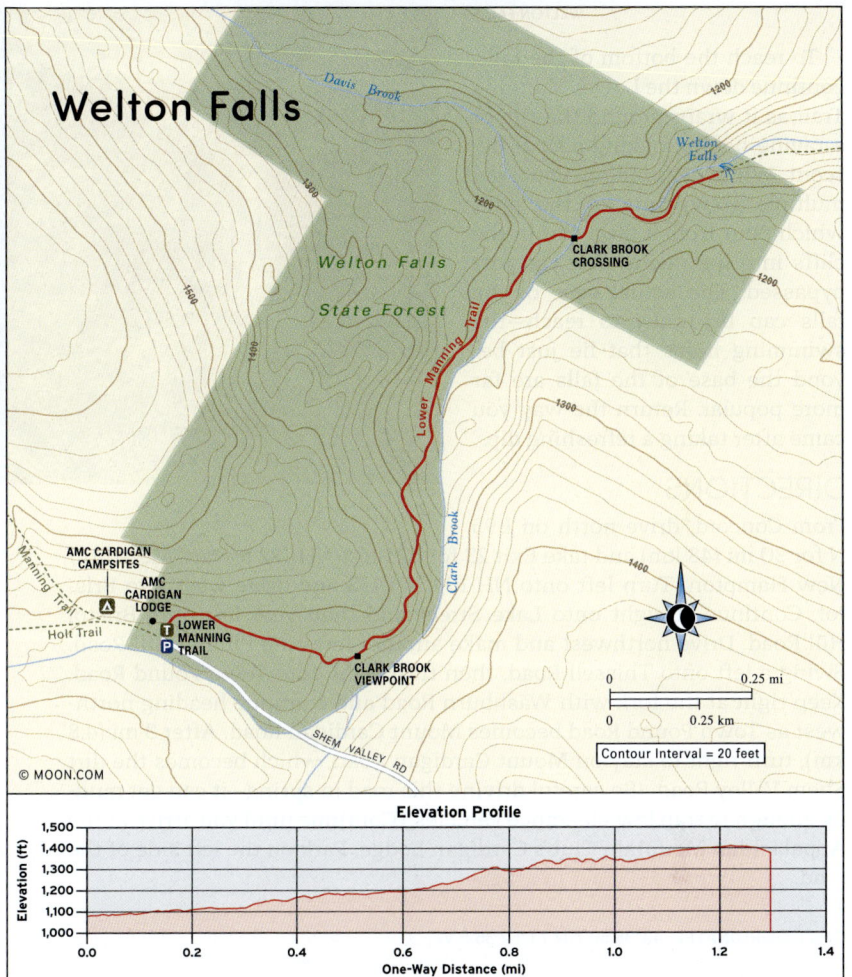

Welton Falls

Davis Brook

Welton Falls

CLARK BROOK
CROSSING

Welton Falls
State Forest

Lower Manning Trail

Manning Trail

AMC CARDIGAN
CAMPSITES

AMC CARDIGAN
LODGE

Holt Trail

LOWER
MANNING
TRAIL

Clark Brook

CLARK BROOK
VIEWPOINT

SHEM VALLEY RD

0   0.25 mi

0   0.25 km

Contour Interval = 20 feet

© MOON.COM

Elevation Profile

brief, higher climb above the brook, the trail descends to the rocky **Clark Brook crossing** at 1 mi (1.6 km). Be sure to exercise caution crossing here, especially during the late spring when snowmelt can cause the water level to rise. Look for a double yellow blaze on a tree on the opposite side of the brook to stay along the trail.

▶ **MILE 1.0–1.3: Clark Brook Crossing to Welton Falls**

Continue hiking northeast as the trail veers deeper into the woods and starts to scramble up a steeper series of knolls with lots of exposed tree roots. Crest a height of land and mind your footing as the trail suddenly makes a steep, winding descent and arrives at the top of **Welton Falls** at 1.3 mi (2.1 km). For a unique perspective of the 30-ft-tall (9-m) cascade, take the marked viewpoint path onto a ledge that wraps around a large cliff to an **overlook** where you can view the falls from above. An old cable fence offers some measure of protection from the drop, but it's best not to test its limits.

To reach the bottom of the falls, continue down the Lower Manning Trail as it wraps around the rim of a ravine before making a final descent. While descending, you'll get multiple viewpoints of the falls, which pour from a little slot in the cliffs into the ravine that you just bypassed. The actual base of the falls can be tricky to reach—the swimming holes that lie just beyond the base of the falls are far more popular. Return the way you came after taking a refreshing dip.

DIRECTIONS

From Concord, drive north on I-93 N for 30 mi (48 km) and take Exit 23 for NH-104/NH-132 toward Meredith/New Hampton. Turn left onto NH-104/NH-132 and drive west into Bristol. Continue straight onto Lake Street and then veer left onto Bristol Hill Road. Drive northwest and make another left onto Plumer Hill Road. Swing a left onto Thissell Road, then turn right onto Town Pound Road. Keep right at the fork with Washburn Road and continue heading northwest as Town Pound Road becomes Mount Cardigan Road. After 3 mi (4.8 km), turn right to stay on Mount Cardigan Road, which becomes the dirt Shem Valley Road. (Be careful driving this road in spring—it can get muddy enough to trap low-clearance vehicles.) Continue until you arrive at the Appalachian Mountain Club's Cardigan Lodge. Park on the left side of the road.

GPS COORDINATES: 43°38'56.7"N 71°52'35.5"W

Escape the tourist hordes of Lake Winnipesaukee on this hike, which passes the ruins of a crashed plane and ends at a fire tower with supreme views of the lakes.

DISTANCE: 2.5 mi (4 km) round-trip

DURATION: 1.5 hr

ELEVATION GAIN: 726 ft (221 m)

EFFORT: Moderate

TRAIL: Dirt path, rock scrambling, water crossings via stones and wooden bridges

USERS: Hikers, leashed dogs

SEASON: May–October

FEES/PASSES: None

MAPS: Belknap Range Trails website

TRAILHEAD: Belknap Mountain parking lot, Carriage Rd., Gilford

FACILITIES: None

CONTACT: Belknap Range Trails; www.belknaprangetrails.org

Pristine Belknap Mountain, the tallest peak in the area at a modest 2,382 ft (726 m), features what might be the finest view of Winnipesaukee.

START THE HIKE

▶ **MILE 0-0.2: Belknap Mountain Parking Lot to Blue Trail**

Walk toward the trailhead sign at the north end of the parking lot and climb a set of stone stairs (known as **"Wayne's Way"** and marked with a sign) to reach a small clearing that overlooks the eastern flank of Belknap. Turn right into the woods, walk toward a wooden utility shed, and veer left at the shed to pick up the **Blue Trail** at a tree marked with double blue blazes.

▶ **MILE 0.2-0.8: Blue Trail to Plane Crash Wreckage**

Descend north on a well-trod dirt path lined with arranged rocks. Hop over a few streams before beginning the climb at 0.3 mi (0.5 km). The trail becomes rockier and ascends the west side of the mountain at a gradual grade. Stone and log staircases offer stable footing as the trail becomes muddy in places.

At 0.6 mi (1 km), the trail starts to level out before reaching a junction with the Saddle Trail. Keep right to stay on the Blue Trail. Climb a steeper set of stone stairs and emerge into a sloped, sunny meadow with tiny white starflowers. Around 0.8 mi (1.3 km), look for a piece of colored tape

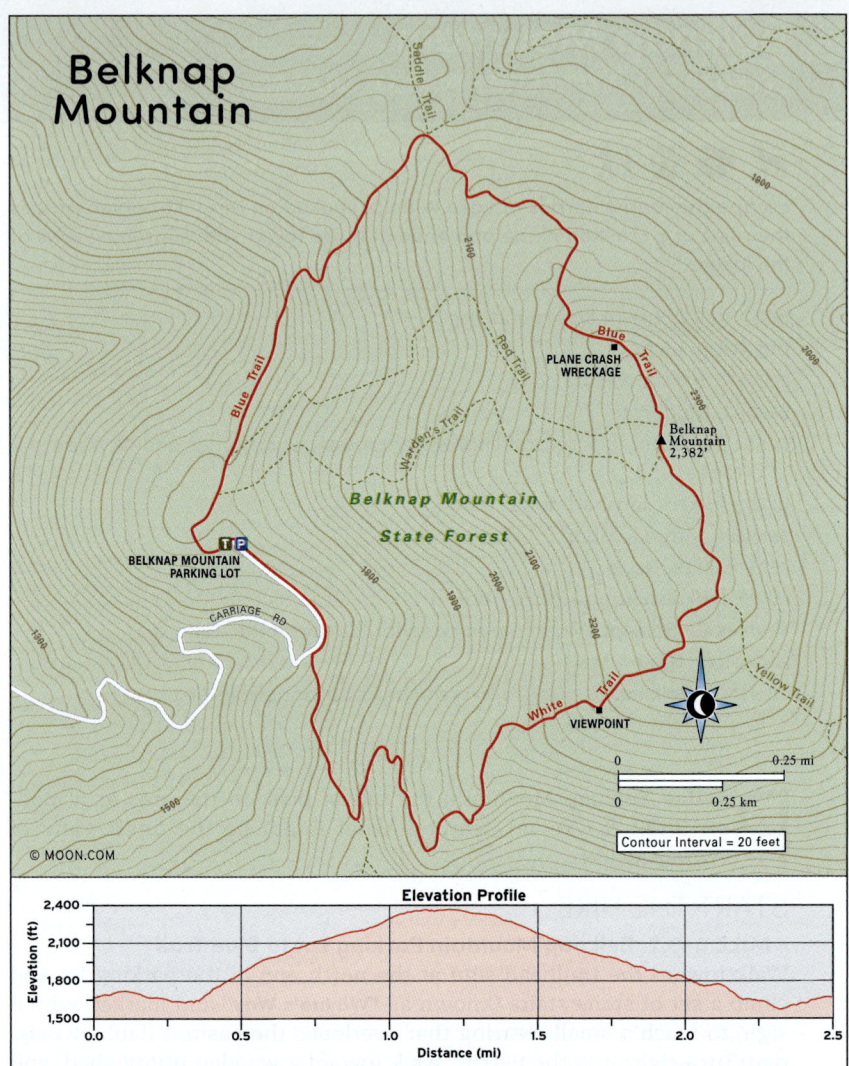

Belknap Mountain

PLANE CRASH WRECKAGE

Blue Trail

Red Trail

Warden's Trail

Seddie Trail

Belknap Mountain 2,382'

Belknap Mountain State Forest

BELKNAP MOUNTAIN PARKING LOT

CARRIAGE RD

White Trail

VIEWPOINT

Yellow Trail

Blue Trail

0   0.25 mi
0   0.25 km

Contour Interval = 20 feet

© MOON.COM

Elevation Profile

Elevation (ft)

2,400
2,100
1,800
1,500

0.0   0.5   1.0   1.5   2.0   2.5

Distance (mi)

tied to a tree branch on the left. You can find the plane crash **wreckage** just off the trail from this point—if you don't mind a little bushwhacking.

▶ **MILE 0.8–1.1: Plane Crash Wreckage to Belknap Mountain Summit**
Continue southeast for 0.3 mi (0.5 km) into an airier boreal forest before arriving at the summit of **Belknap Mountain** at 1.1 mi (1.8 km).

A fire tower looms at the summit, and while it's safe to climb—and the glorious view of the Lakes District from the top is worth it—be aware that the staircases are quite steep and the railings are low. Exercise caution on the up-and-down.

▶ **MILE 1.1-1.3: Belknap Mountain Summit to Yellow/White Trail**

Pick up the **Yellow/White Trail** (marked with yellow and white blazes, naturally) on the east side of the tower and walk along the power lines that run across the ridge of Belknap before descending into a mossier swath of forest.

▶ **MILE 1.3-2.0: Yellow/White Trail to White Trail**

At 1.3 mi (2.1 km), reach a rocky clearing and turn right onto the **White Trail** as it heads south across an exposed ridge with cairns. Mind your footing on the numerous slippery rock slabs.

Descend a ramp-like stone ledge at around 1.6 mi (2.6 km) with a killer **view** of Winnipesaukee, then continue south down a larger rock face.

▶ **MILE 2.0-2.5: White Trail to Belknap Mountain Parking Lot**

At 2 mi (3.2 km), you'll reach a three-way junction; take a right and enjoy the final stretch of the trail as it winds through deciduous beech and delivers you back to Carriage Road at 2.3 mi (3.7 km). Turn right and walk up the road to the parking lot.

DIRECTIONS

From Concord, drive north on NH-106 N for 20 mi (32 km). Merge right onto the ramp for NH-11 E/US-3 N/Laconia-Gilford Bypass and then take the NH-11A exit toward Gilford/Laconia. Turn right onto NH-11A and continue northwest for just over 1 mi (1.6 km) before making a right onto Hoyt Road. Drive south for another 2 mi (3.2 km) as Hoyt Road merges with Belknap Mountain Road. Make a final left onto Carriage Road and watch your speed as the road transitions to dirt, enters the forest, and climbs the eastern slope of Belknap. The road is narrow, winding, and steep, with several bridge crossings. As you reach the end of Carriage Road, the trail parking lot will be on your left.

GPS COORDINATES: 43°30'55.8"N 71°22'36.9"W

BEST NEARBY BITES

Dine on pepper-crusted filet mignon inside a regal 19th-century barn at **Ellacoya Barn & Grille** (2667 Lake Shore Rd., Gilford; 603/293-8700; www.ellacoyabandg.com; 11:30am-8pm Sun.-Thurs., 11:30am-9pm Fri.-Sat.).

Winnipesaukee and the Lakes District

NEW HAMPSHIRE

This spooky, little-known hike visits a desolate mountaintop with a cave that's rumored to be haunted by a monstrous presence.

BEST: New England oddities
DISTANCE: 5.4 mi (8.7 km) round-trip
DURATION: 2.5 hr
ELEVATION GAIN: 478 ft (146 m)
EFFORT: Easy/moderate
TRAIL: Dirt path, rocks
USERS: Hikers
SEASON: May–October
FEES/PASSES: None
MAPS: USGS topo map of Strafford County, NH
TRAILHEAD: Dirt access road off Hayes Rd., Alton
FACILITIES: None
CONTACT: LandVest Inc.; 603/228-2020; www.landvest.com

Hidden in a relatively quiet corner of the Lakes District and rising 1,050 ft (320 m) above sea level, the craggy Devil's Den Mountain offers a killer view of Lake Winnipesaukee—but its moody atmosphere is what makes it unique. The trail to the mountaintop, while easy to follow, is mostly unmarked, and the mountain's most infamous feature—a slit cave from which locals have reported hearing ferocious hissing sounds—requires a bit of hunting around the summit area.

START THE HIKE

▶ **MILE 0-1.3: Dirt Access Road to T Intersection**
Begin your hike by picking up the dirt access road just beyond the gate and heading southeast into the forest. This road will be your trail for most of the hike. Walk along the road as it cuts southeast through a forest of pine, birches, and stone walls. At 0.3 mi (0.5 km), take a left at the fork and continue onward as the road ascends at a very gentle grade. The pine trees here are green and numerous enough to make you feel like you've stepped into an episode of *Twin Peaks*.

As the road becomes sandier, you can often glimpse fresh animal tracks cutting across the ground. At 0.7 mi (1.1 km), keep straight at the split and hike past a clearing full of young trees. Look out for a partial glimpse of the Devil's Den Mountain summit just ahead, around 0.9 mi (1.4 km). Continue hiking southeast for another 0.4 mi (0.6 km) before reaching a T intersection at 1.3 mi (2.1 km); take a left and start to climb the east haunch of Devil's Den Mountain. Look to your right and you'll glimpse a series of granite

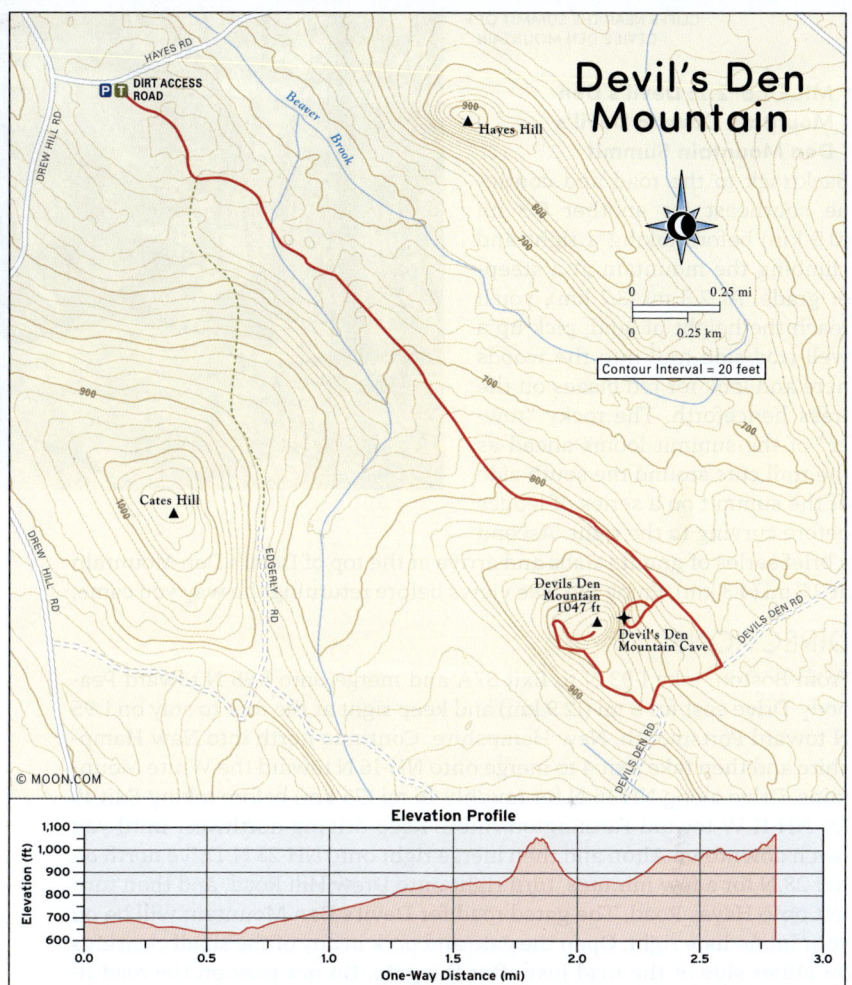

Devil's Den Mountain

HAYES RD

DIRT ACCESS ROAD

DREW HILL RD

Beaver Brook

Hayes Hill

900

800

700

Cates Hill

1000

DREW HILL RD

EDGERLY RD

700

800

900

700

Devils Den Mountain 1047 ft

Devil's Den Mountain Cave

DEVILS DEN RD

DEVILS DEN RD

900

© MOON.COM

0   0.25 mi

0   0.25 km

Contour Interval = 20 feet

Elevation Profile

Elevation (ft)

1,100
1,000
900
800
700
600

0.0   0.5   1.0   1.5   2.0   2.5   3.0

One-Way Distance (mi)

cliffs and boulders in the woods. This is where the infamous haunted cave is located.

▶ MILE 1.3–1.8: T Intersection to Devil's Den Mountain Cave

To find the **cave,** keep an eye peeled for a rough-hewn and slightly over-grown side path that appears on your right at roughly 1.7 mi (2.7 km); it's marked with felled tree trunks. Continue for roughly 0.1 mi (0.16 km) to reach the cliffs, then look for a red arrow spray-painted on a jumble of boulders. Scramble up the jumble and you'll find the opening to the cave on a ledge that overlooks the forest. The interior of the cave is damp and tight—and then there are the accounts of hissing and a large shadow moving on the walls. So, proceed at your own risk.

▶ MILE 1.8–2.7: Devil's Den Mountain Cave to Devil's Den Mountain Summit

Backtrack to the road and continue southeast for another 0.3 mi (0.5 km) before taking a right and climbing the mountain at a steeper grade. At 2.3 mi (3.7 km), you'll reach the height of land; pick up a well-trod side trail into the woods here and look for red blazes on the trees henceforth. The rocky "tower" of the summit looms ahead as the trail cuts around the south side of the summit on a series of ledges before curving to the right. Ascend a brief series of granite slabs and arrive at the top of Devil's Den Mountain at 2.7 mi (4.3 km). Enjoy the lake views before returning the way you came.

DIRECTIONS

From Boston, take I-93 N to Exit 37A and merge onto I-95 N toward Peabody. Drive east for 8 mi (12.9 km) and keep right at the fork to stay on I-95 N toward Portsmouth, New Hampshire. Continue north into New Hampshire and then take Exit 4 to merge onto NH-16 N toward the White Mountains. Drive along NH-16 N for roughly 16 mi (26 km) before taking Exit 15 for NH-11 W toward Farmington/Alton. Keep driving northwest until you reach downtown Alton and then merge right onto NH-28 N. Drive north on NH-28 N for a few minutes, turn right onto Drew Hill Road, and then turn left onto Hayes Road. The gated road for Devil's Den Mountain will be on your immediate right. Open the gate and park in any of the small clearings on either side of the road just after the gate. Do not park on the road itself—it must remain clear for emergency vehicles.

GPS COORDINATES: 43°31'45.9"N 71°11'38.8"W

BEST NEARBY BREWS

Try a key lime saison or a liberally dry-hopped red ale at **Burnt Timber Brewing & Tavern** (96 Lehner St., Wolfeboro; 603/515-1079; www.burnttimbertavern.com; 4pm-9pm Wed.-Fri., noon-9pm Sat., 11am-3pm Sun.). And consider soaking up the suds with onsite offerings like kimchi and brisket tacos or the sweet potato quinoa veggie burger.

NEW HAMPSHIRE

Winnipesaukee and the Lakes District

MOUNT SUNAPEE STATE PARK, NEWBURY

Hike through the secluded woods on the north slopes of Mount Sunapee to a beautiful lake that lies just below the summit.

DISTANCE: 4.2 mi (6.8 km) round-trip
DURATION: 2 hr
ELEVATION GAIN: 948 ft (289 m)
EFFORT: Easy/moderate
TRAIL: Dirt path, rocks, wooden bog bridges
USERS: Hikers, leashed dogs
SEASON: June–October
FEES/PASSES: $5 day-use fee per adult
MAPS: Mount Sunapee Resort website
TRAILHEAD: End of Park Rd., Newbury
FACILITIES: Restrooms at Mount Sunapee State Park Campground
CONTACT: Mount Sunapee State Park; 603/763-5561; www.nhstateparks.org

START THE HIKE

▶ **MILE 0-0.7: Park Road to Rim Trail**

Begin the hike at the end of Park Road in a clearing festooned with pieces of old ski lift machinery. Pick up the **Rim Trail** at the trail sign on the edge of the forest and follow yellow blazes into the woods heading southeast. Rock-hop across **Johnson Brook** and climb a series of gently graded stone steps through the beech trees. The stone stairs are older and some of them might be a bit loose. Listen to the chattering of red squirrels and gray jays in the branches overhead.

▶ **MILE 0.7-1.0: Rim Trail to Newbury Trail**

The trail levels off a bit before reaching a junction with Newbury Trail at 0.8 mi (1.3 km); make a right onto **Newbury Trail** (marked by orange blazes) and climb south up a steep and eroded stretch that quickly delivers you to an exposed rocky ledge called **Eagle's Nest Outlook,** which has a stunning view out to Lake Sunapee. From here, the trail ascends the north side of Sunapee for a little while before flattening at roughly 1 mi (1.6 km) and peacefully weaving through an unusually lush ridge forest that's bursting with ferns and wildflowers.

▶ **MILE 1.0-1.8: Newbury Trail to Jack and June Junction**

The footing gets rockier and rootier as the trail goes up and down some knolls before reaching the four-way Jack and June Junction at 1.8 mi (2.9 km). Here, you can choose between a water-side view of the lake or an overhead vista.

Winnipesaukee and the Lakes District

NEW HAMPSHIRE

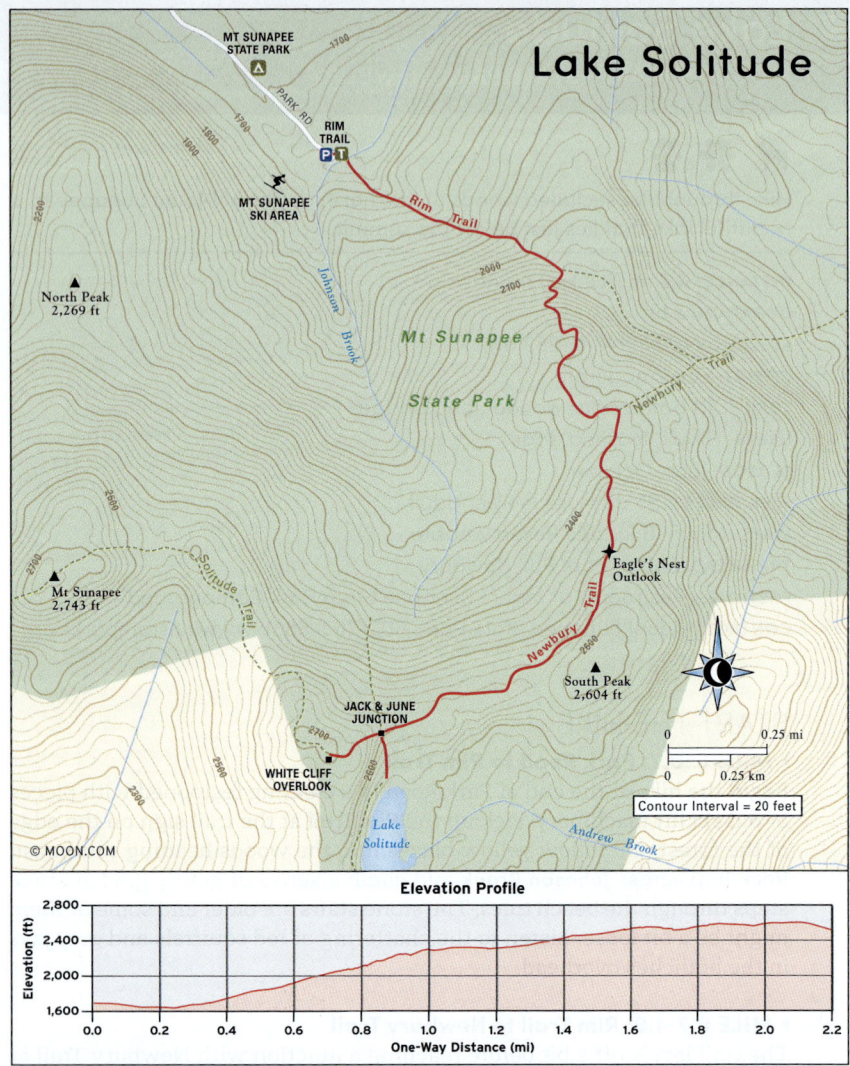

Lake Solitude

Elevation Profile

▶ **MILE 1.8–1.9: Jack and June Junction to Lake Solitude**

For the former, turn left onto the Mount Sunapee Greenway South and descend a rocky trail for 0.1 mi (0.16 km) that cuts through deciduous woods before arriving quite suddenly on the northern banks of **Lake Solitude.** Stop here or continue south on the trail for a little while as it follows the western shore of the lake.

▶ **MILE 1.9–2.2: Lake Solitude to White Cliff Overlook**

To reach the overhead vista, backtrack to Jack and June Junction and take the Mount Sunapee Greenway North/Solitude Trail up a comparably rocky trail for 0.2 mi (0.3 km) to reach **White Cliff Overlook**—a shelf-like ledge perched just above the lake. If you still have some gas in the tank, you can continue up the Mount Sunapee Greenway North/Solitude Trail to the

▲ LAKE SOLITUDE BENEATH THE SUMMIT OF MOUNT SUNAPEE

summit of Mount Sunapee itself, roughly 0.8 mi (1.3 km) up the trail. Otherwise, return the way you came.

DIRECTIONS

From Concord, take I-93 S briefly and merge onto I-89 N toward Lebanon/White River Junction (VT). Drive northeast for 20 mi (32 km) and then take Exit 9 for NH-103 toward Warner/Bradford. Follow this local highway for another 16 mi (26 km) to reach the entrance to Mount Sunapee Resort. Upon reaching the entrance, turn left onto NH-103B S and continue straight onto Sunapee Road to enter the resort itself. Shortly ahead, make a left turn onto Park Road, a rugged dirt road that climbs the north slopes of the mountain. Follow the road for about 1 mi (1.6 km) and you'll reach the entrance to Mount Sunapee State Park Campground on your left. Park on the right side of the road, across from the campground entrance. Continue on foot beyond the gate to the end of Park Road.

GPS COORDINATES: 43°19'27.4"N 72°03'53.2"W

BEST NEARBY BITES

Treat yourself to a scenic Lake Sunapee dinner cruise by stepping aboard the **MV Sunapee Lake Queen** (1 Lake Ave., Sunapee; 603/938-6465; www.sunapeecruises.com; 6:30pm daily Memorial Day-Labor Day, 5:30pm daily after Labor Day), or stick to the land and indulge in some smoked bratwurst and baby back ribs at **Wildwood Smokehouse** (45 Main St., Sunapee; 603/763-1178; www.wildwoodsmokehousesunapee.com; 4pm-8pm Tues.-Sat.).

NEARBY CAMPGROUNDS

NAME	LOCATION	FACILITIES	SEASON	FEE
Baker River Campground	56 Campground Rd., Rumney, 43°47'13.7"N 71°46'37.9"W	Tent sites, RV sites, toilets, showers, potable water, camp store	mid-May through mid-October	$40-63
603/786-9707; www.bakerrivercampground.com				
Mascoma Lake Campground	92 NH-4A, Lebanon, 43°38'35.9"N 72°10'37.2"W	Tent sites, RV sites, cabins, cottages, tiny houses, toilets, showers, potable water, laundry, camp store, Wi-Fi	early May through mid-October	$33-98
603/448-5076; www.mascomalake.com				
AMC Cardigan Campsites	774 Shem Valley Rd., Alexandria, 43°38'58.2"N 71°52'39.5"W	Tent sites, toilets, potable water	year-round	$35
603/466-2727; www.outdoors.org				
Clearwater Campground	556 NH-104, Meredith, 43°37'08.1"N 71°35'09.5"W	Tent sites, RV sites, toilets, showers, potable water, laundry, camp store, Wi-Fi	mid-May through early October	$37-66
603/279-7761; www.clearwatercampground.com				

NEARBY CAMPGROUNDS (continued)

NAME	LOCATION	FACILITIES	SEASON	FEE
Meredith Woods Camping Area	551 NH-104, Meredith, 43°37'16.1"N 71°34'46.6"W	Tent sites, RV sites, toilets, showers, potable water, laundry, pool, camp store, Wi-Fi	late May through mid-October	$44-65
603/279-5449; www.meredithwoods.com				
Long Island Bridge Campground	29 Long Island Rd., Moultonborough, 43°40'00.5"N 71°20'49.4"W	Tent sites, RV sites, toilets, showers, potable water, laundry, Wi-Fi	mid-May through mid-October	$42-75
603/253-6053; www.longislandbridgecampgroundnh.com				
Wolfeboro Campground	61 Haines Hill Rd., Wolfeboro, 43°38'04.9"N 71°09'14.4"W	Tent sites, RV sites, toilets, showers, potable water, camp store, Wi-Fi	late May through early October	$35-40
603/569-9881; www.wolfeborocampground.com				
Mount Sunapee State Park	Park Rd., Newbury, 43°19'35.1"N 72°04'03.5"W	Tent sites, lean-tos, toilets, potable water	late May through mid-October	$23-29
603/763-5561; www.nhstateparks.org				

MONADNOCK, MERRIMACK VALLEY, AND THE SEACOAST

Southern New Hampshire is the delta for northern New England's famous mountains, forests, and seacoast. Far from being just a place between Boston and popular summer destinations like the White Mountains and Acadia, the southern reaches of New Hampshire are a taster's menu of adventures for first-time hikers and experienced backcountry trekkers. The numerous suburbs and small cities of the region are surrounded by mile after mile of sunny forests, angular hills, and coastal marshes and beaches that are often singing with visiting birds and native wildlife. In southern New Hampshire, you can saunter past a farm, over hills, and through swamps before arriving at a secluded beach. It's just that easy.

▲ DUSK AT LOWER PURGATORY FALLS

▲ CASTLE RUINS IN MADAME SHERRI FOREST

1 Sweet Trail
DISTANCE: 5.6 mi (9 km) round-trip
DURATION: 2.5 hr
EFFORT: Easy
PAGE: 284

2 Odiorne Point State Park
DISTANCE: 3.3 mi (5.3 km) round-trip
DURATION: 2 hr
EFFORT: Easy
PAGE: 287

3 Skatutakee Mountain and Thumb Mountain
DISTANCE: 5 mi (8 km) round-trip
DURATION: 4 hr
EFFORT: Moderate
PAGE: 291

4 Madame Sherri Forest
DISTANCE: 4 mi (6.4 km) round-trip
DURATION: 3 hr
EFFORT: Easy/moderate
PAGE: 294

5 Monte Rosa and Mount Monadnock
DISTANCE: 4.6 mi (7.4 km) round-trip
DURATION: 3.5 hr
EFFORT: Strenuous
PAGE: 297

6 Purgatory Falls
DISTANCE: 5 mi (8 km) round-trip
DURATION: 2.5 hr
EFFORT: Easy/moderate
PAGE: 301

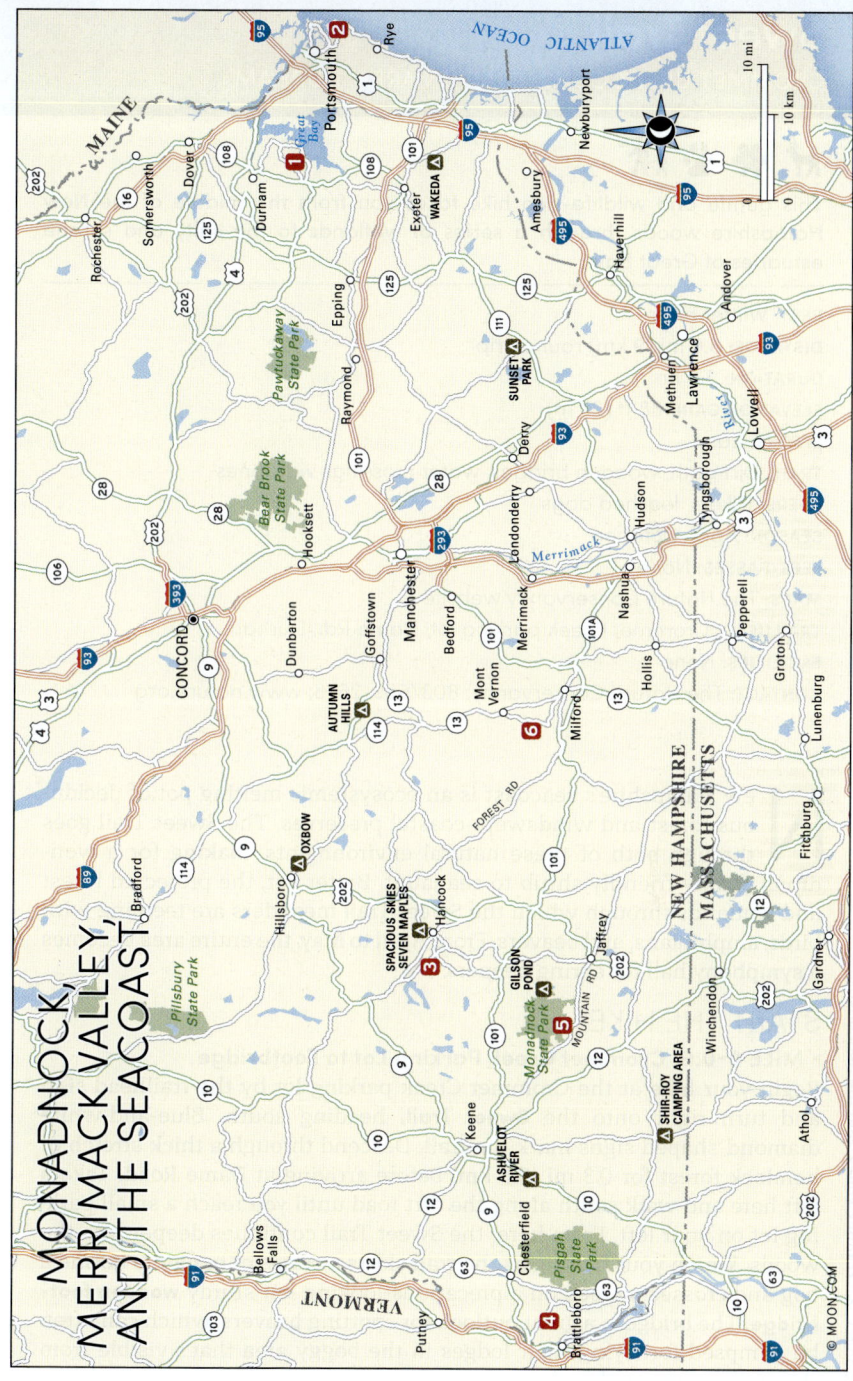

MONADNOCK, MERRIMACK VALLEY, AND THE SEACOAST

ATLANTIC OCEAN

MAINE

VERMONT

NEW HAMPSHIRE

MASSACHUSETTS

Rye
Portsmouth
Newburyport
Somersworth
Dover
Durham
Rochester
Amesbury
Haverhill
Andover
Exeter
WAKEDA
Methuen
Lawrence
Lowell
Epping
Raymond
Tyngsborough
Pawtuckaway State Park
SUNSET PARK
Derry
Londonderry
Hudson
Nashua
Pepperell
Bear Brook State Park
Hooksett
Manchester
Merrimack
Hollis
Groton
Lunenburg
Concord
Dunbarton
Goffstown
Bedford
Mont Vernon
Milford
Fitchburg
AUTUMN HILLS
Bradford
OXBOW
Hillsboro
SPACIOUS SKIES SEVEN MAPLES
Hancock
Jaffrey
Winchendon
Gardner
Pillsbury State Park
GILSON POND
Monadnock State Park
SHIR-ROY CAMPING AREA
Athol
Bellows Falls
Keene
ASHUELOT RIVER
Pisgah State Park
Putney
Chesterfield
Brattleboro

© MOON.COM

NEW HAMPSHIRE

283

Sweet Trail

CROMMET CREEK CONSERVATION AREA, DURHAM

This gentle and wildlife-rich hike takes you from the middle of the New Hampshire woods through a series of wetlands to the salty and serene estuaries of Great Bay.

BEST: Winter hikes

DISTANCE: 5.6 mi (9 km) round-trip

DURATION: 2.5 hr

ELEVATION GAIN: 88 ft (27 m)

EFFORT: Easy

TRAIL: Dirt path, wooden bridges, water crossings via stones

USERS: Hikers, leashed dogs

SEASON: April–October

FEES/PASSES: None

MAPS: The Nature Conservancy website

TRAILHEAD: Crommet Creek parking lot, Dame Rd., Durham

FACILITIES: None

CONTACT: The Nature Conservancy; 603/659–2678; www.nature.org

New Hampshire's seacoast is an ecosystemic melting pot of deciduous forest and windswept coastal preserves. The Sweet Trail goes through both of these natural environments, making for a wondrous, family-friendly shrub-to-sea jaunt. Better yet, the protected forest and wetlands through which the Sweet Trail meanders are teeming with birds, amphibians, and beavers. From April to May, the entire area becomes a symphony hall for spring peepers.

START THE HIKE

▶ **MILE 0-0.6: Crommet Creek Parking Lot to Footbridge**

Begin your hike at the Crommet Creek parking lot by the trailhead sign and turn right onto the **Sweet Trail,** heading south. Blue-and-white diamond-shaped signs mark the trail. Descend through a thick stretch of hemlock forest for 0.3 mi (0.5 km) before arriving at Dame Road. Take a left here and walk south along the dirt road until you reach a small parking lot on your left. From here, the Sweet Trail continues deeper into the woods. Watch your footing as the trail skirts a series of boulders beside a bog and crosses a creek on a precarious-looking but sturdy **wooden footbridge.** The bridge is a great outlook for spotting beavers, which can often be glimpsed fortifying their lodges in the boggy area that's visible from this point of the trail.

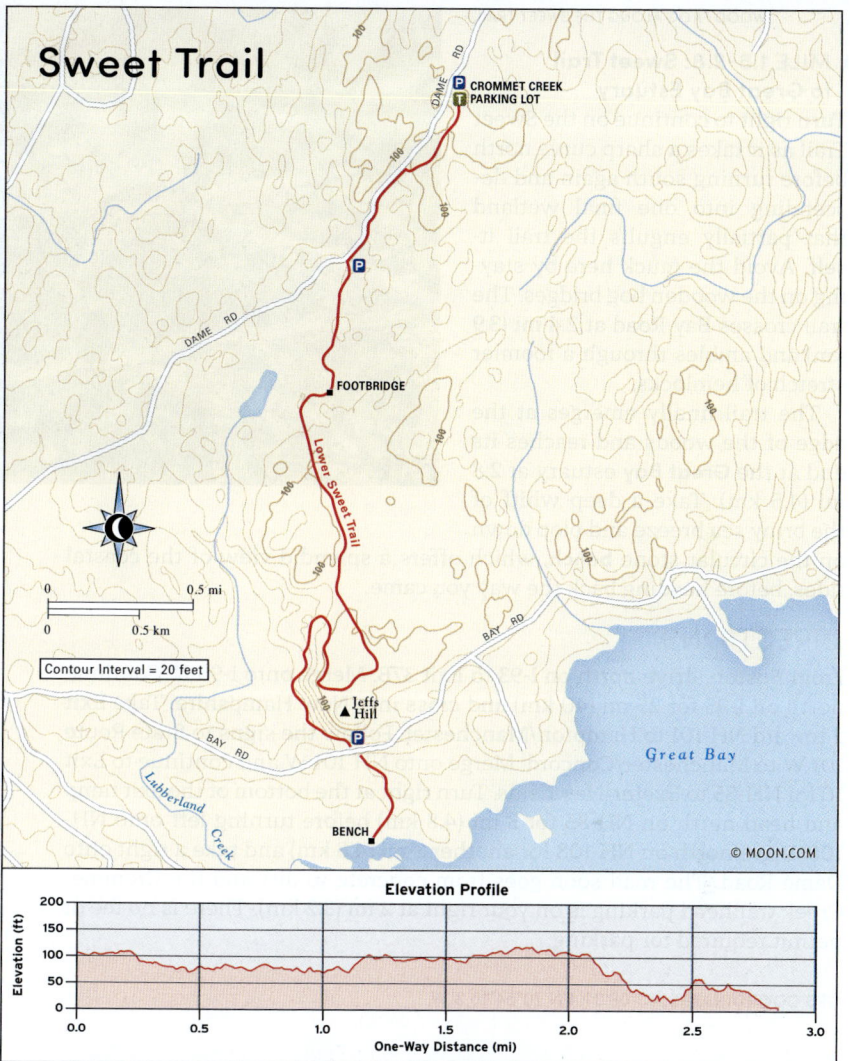

Sweet Trail

CROMMET CREEK
PARKING LOT

DAME RD

FOOTBRIDGE

Lower Sweet Trail

BAY RD

Jeffs
Hill

Great Bay

BAY RD

Lubberland
Creek

BENCH

© MOON.COM

0   0.5 mi

0   0.5 km

Contour Interval = 20 feet

Elevation Profile

Elevation (ft)

200
150
100
50
0

0.0   0.5   1.0   1.5   2.0   2.5   3.0

One-Way Distance (mi)

▶ **MILE 0.6–1.8: Footbridge to Sweet Trail**

Leaving the bog and creek behind, the trail continues south and crosses a smaller stream on rocks at 0.9 mi (1.4 km) before curving to the southeast and widening into a smoother dirt path. The trail ambles through a hall of hemlocks and birches before skirting a second, larger series of wetlands. Tread lightly and quietly here: Not only do spotted salamanders and wood frogs regularly cross the forest floor, but the dead white pine snags of the nearby wetlands are the nesting grounds for a small group of great blue herons who occasionally make appearances. Keep an ear open for their deep-throated croak as you pass through here.

At 1.8 mi (2.9 km), the Sweet Trail reaches the upper flank of **Jeff's Hill.** At this junction, hikers can choose to continue over the hill or stick with the Sweet Trail.

▶ **MILE 1.8–2.8: Sweet Trail to Great Bay Estuary**

Turn right to continue on the Sweet Trail as it takes a sharp curve north before turning south again and descending into one final wetland that partially engulfs the trail itself. Avoid the muck here by staying on the wooden bog bridges. The trail crosses Bay Road at 2.4 mi (3.9 km) and ambles through a roomier stretch of hemlocks.

The trail finally emerges at the edge of the woods and reaches its end at the **Great Bay** estuary at 2.8 mi (4.5 km). Take a deep whiff of the briny sea breeze and plop down on the circular stone **bench,** which offers a splendid view of the coastal tides, before heading back the way you came.

DIRECTIONS

From Boston, drive north on I-93 to Exit 37B. Merge onto I-95 N. Continue north on I-95 for 25 mi (40 km) and cross into New Hampshire. Take Exit 2 toward NH-101 to Hampton/Manchester. Follow the signs to State Route 101 W to Manchester/Concord. Merge onto NH-101 W and continue to Exit 10 for NH-85 to Exeter/Newfields. Turn right at the bottom of the exit ramp and head north on NH-85 for 3 mi (4.8 km) before turning left onto NH-108. Drive north on NH-108 for another 3 mi (4.8 km) and take a right onto Dame Road. The road soon goes from concrete to dirt and the Crommet Creek trailhead parking is on your right at 2 mi (3.2 km). There is no fee or permit required for parking.

GPS COORDINATES: 43°06'01.4"N 70°54'16.3"W

BEST NEARBY BREWS

The nearby towns of Durham and Dover have plenty of dining options, from savory burgers to Southeast Asian cuisine, but before you make your decision, stop for a hazy wheat IPA or a tart Berliner weisse at **Deciduous Brewing Company** (12 Weaver St., Newmarket; 603/292-5809; www.deciduousbrewing.com; 4pm-8pm Wed.-Thurs., 2pm-8pm Fri., noon-8pm Sat., noon-6pm Sun.).

NEW HAMPSHIRE

Monadnock, Merrimack Valley, and the Seacoast

This seaside stroll across one of New Hampshire's finest coastal conservation areas bypasses sandy and rocky beaches, tidepools, spooky World War II–era bunkers, and a drowned forest.

BEST: Brew hikes

DISTANCE: 3.3 mi (5.3 km) round-trip

DURATION: 2 hr

ELEVATION GAIN: 74 ft (23 m)

EFFORT: Easy

TRAIL: Dirt path, sandy beaches, rocks, wooden bridges

USERS: Hikers

SEASON: Year-round

FEES/PASSES: $4 adult, $2 child ages 6–11 (late May through October)

MAPS: Odiorne Point State Park website

TRAILHEAD: Odiorne Point State Park boat launch parking lot, NH-1A, Rye

FACILITIES: None

CONTACT: Odiorne Point State Park; 603/436-7406; www.nhstateparks.org

Roughly 30 minutes north of the casinos and clam shacks that occupy Hampton Beach lies one of the Granite State's premier coastal preserves. Odiorne Point State Park—named for the family who settled the land in the mid-17th century—offers a colorful palette of natural environments that includes white pine and hemlock woods, beaches, and the ruins of an ancient forest that has since been swallowed by the sea. The park also contains a marine science center and some abandoned bunkers and artillery batteries that were built to defend the New England coast during World War II.

The trails around the park—while numerous, very short, and interconnected—are not always marked or even named, so it's best to print a map of the park before your visit.

START THE HIKE

▶ MILE 0-0.2: Odiorne Point Boat Launch to Heritage Trail

Begin your hike in the Odiorne Point boat launch parking lot at the northwest end of the park. Cross the wooden bridge by the Trails sign and then immediately take a right onto a dirt path that passes through a thicket of briars before reaching the **Heritage Trail.** Turn right onto the Heritage Trail and hike through the forest at an even grade.

▶ MILE 0.2-0.6: Heritage Trail to Memorial Point

The Heritage Trail ends at Frost Point Road at 0.3 mi (0.5 km). Turn left onto the road and then make an immediate right onto the **Sugar Maple**

Odiorne Point State Park

Frost Point Breakwater

Frost Point

FROST POINT OUTLOOK

Frost Point Loop

Piscataqua River

Sagamore Trail

WWII STRUCTURE

Heritage Trail

Frost Point Rd.

Odiorne Point State Park

ATLANTIC OCEAN

ODIORNE POINT BOAT LAUNCH

P T

OCEAN BLVD

Bike Path

Sugar Maple Trail

MEMORIAL POINT

Monument Way

1A

Columbus Rd.

SEACOAST SCIENCE CENTER

Rabbit Run

P

Bike Path

0   0.25 mi

0   0.25 km

Contour Interval = 20 feet

Odiornes Point

Periwinkle Cove

1A

© MOON.COM

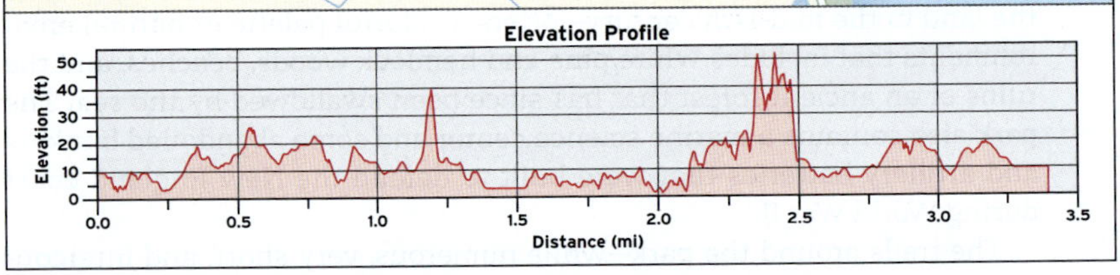

Elevation Profile

Elevation (ft) — Distance (mi)

Trail at 0.3 mi (0.5 km); the first bunker will appear on your right. Continue southeast on the Sugar Maple Trail through a sun-splashed corridor of hemlocks until you reach **Memorial Point** at 0.6 mi (1 km). This grassy clearing has grade A ocean views, stone walls, and a monument to New Hampshire's earliest settlers.

▶ **MILE 0.6–1.3: Memorial Point to Periwinkle Cove**

Head south along Monument Way for 0.2 mi (0.3 km). Upon reaching the **Odiorne Point Seacoast Science Center** parking lot, you'll see a hill in front of you with wooden stairs. Climb these stairs to reach another bunker and descend the hill toward the science center. From here, walk south across the parking lot and turn right on the spur trail at its end. This trail will immediately deliver you to the Odiorne Point bike path. Take a left onto the

▲ THE ROCKY SHORES NEAR ODIORNE POINT ARE FULL OF TIDEPOOLS.

bike path; just a few moments later, you'll reach the beach known as **Per-iwinkle Cove** at 1.2 mi (1.9 km).

Veer left to enter the beach. At low tide, you can observe the ancient decaying stumps of trees that once stood tall here—Odiorne Point's "drowned forest."

▶ MILE 1.3–2.7: Periwinkle Cove to Frost Point Outlook

Head northwest along the pebble-strewn beach, cutting back up to the grassier upper shore when the going gets too rocky; maintain your northerly shoreline hike with the ocean on your right. The beach becomes sandier at 1.7 mi (2.7 km) and passes several tidepools and a large meadow where white-tailed deer make regular appearances.

When you reach a **beached dock wreck** at 2.2 mi (3.5 km), take a sharp left and pick up a narrow sandy path at the top of the beach. Hike west back into the forest briefly before reaching a massive gun battery built into a hillside at 2.5 mi (4 km). A small path to the right will take you up the hill to the final bunker. From here, turn right and descend the hill on an eroded, wooded path that delivers you to the grassy, gusty **Frost Point** outlook at 2.7 mi (4.3 km). A stone jetty extends far into the Atlantic for the intrepid to explore, and the picnic tables at Frost Point make for an ideal lunch spot.

▶ MILE 2.7–3.3: Frost Point Outlook to Odiorne Point Boat Launch

Once you've had your fill of the maritime vista, finish your hike by picking up the **Sagamore Trail** from Frost Point. Head southwest through the white pines along the shoreline for just under 0.5 mi (0.8 km) before reaching a salt marsh and arriving back at the bridge and parking lot from which you began your adventure.

ODIORNE POINT'S COASTLINE ▲

DIRECTIONS

From Boston, head north on I-93 N and continue 9 mi (14.5 km) to Exit 37A for I-95 N. Merge onto I-95 N toward Peabody. Keep right at the fork to stay on I-95 N toward Portsmouth, New Hampshire, and continue for another 32 mi (51 km). After crossing the New Hampshire border, take Exit 3 for NH-33. Turn right at the bottom of the exit ramp and briefly drive east on NH-33 E/Greenland Road before taking a right onto Peverly Hill Road. Keep driving east to the traffic circle and continue straight onto NH-1A. After a just over 1 mi (1.6 km), you'll see the Odiorne Point State Park boat launch parking lot on your left.

GPS COORDINATES: 43°02'55.1"N 70°43'37.9"W

BEST NEARBY BITES AND BREWS

Local oysters, littleneck clams, and salmon tartare are just a few of the raw-bar treats you'll find at **The Carriage House** (2263 Ocean Blvd., Rye; 603/964-8251; www.carriagehouserye.com; 4:30pm-9:30pm Tues.-Wed., 4:30pm-10pm Thurs.-Sat.). Nearby in Portsmouth, you can sample gruit ales with locally foraged herbs and have a hearty lunch or dinner at the prolific **Earth Eagle Brewings** (175 High St., Portsmouth; 603/502-2244; www.eartheaglebrewings.com; noon-9pm Tues.-Thurs., noon-10pm Fri.-Sat., noon-6pm Sun.).

3 Skatutakee Mountain and Thumb Mountain

HARRIS CENTER FOR CONSERVATION EDUCATION, HANCOCK

This family-friendly hike traverses a forest with an active bobcat population and visits two neighboring peaks that offer views of the Monadnocks and the Wapack Range.

DISTANCE: 5 mi (8 km) round-trip
DURATION: 4 hr
ELEVATION GAIN: 892 ft (272 m)
EFFORT: Moderate
TRAIL: Dirt path, rocks, water crossings by stones
USERS: Hikers, leashed dogs
SEASON: May-October
FEES/PASSES: None
MAPS: Harris Center website
TRAILHEAD: Harris Center parking lot, Kings Hwy., Hancock
FACILITIES: Restrooms
CONTACT: Harris Center for Conservation Education; 603/525-3394; www.harriscenter.org

START THE HIKE

▶ **MILE 0-0.2: Harris Center to Harriskat Trail**

Begin your hike in the parking lot for the Harris Center by the Trails sign. Follow a dirt path down to the adjacent road (Kings Highway) and cross the road to pick up the **Harriskat Trail,** marked with white rectangles on trees. The trail begins with a pleasant meander through mossy, boulder-strewn woods with plenty of vernal pools and a few creeks to hopscotch across. Some of the hemlocks here are riddled with woodpecker holes.

▶ **MILE 0.2-1.7: Harriskat Trail to Skatutakee Summit**

Continue along this stretch for 0.6 mi (1 km) before reaching the intersection of Harriskat and the Thumbs Down Trail. Turn left to continue on Harriskat. The trail segues into a series of switchbacks that ascend the northeastern haunch of **Skatutakee Mountain** at a surprisingly laid-back grade. As the trees start to thin out and the trail becomes rockier, it reaches the summit of Skatutakee at 1.7 mi (2.7 km), which is marked with a massive cairn. The summit resembles a high-altitude meadow with panoramic views of Keene, the Monadnocks, and the Wapack Range just across the state border in Massachusetts.

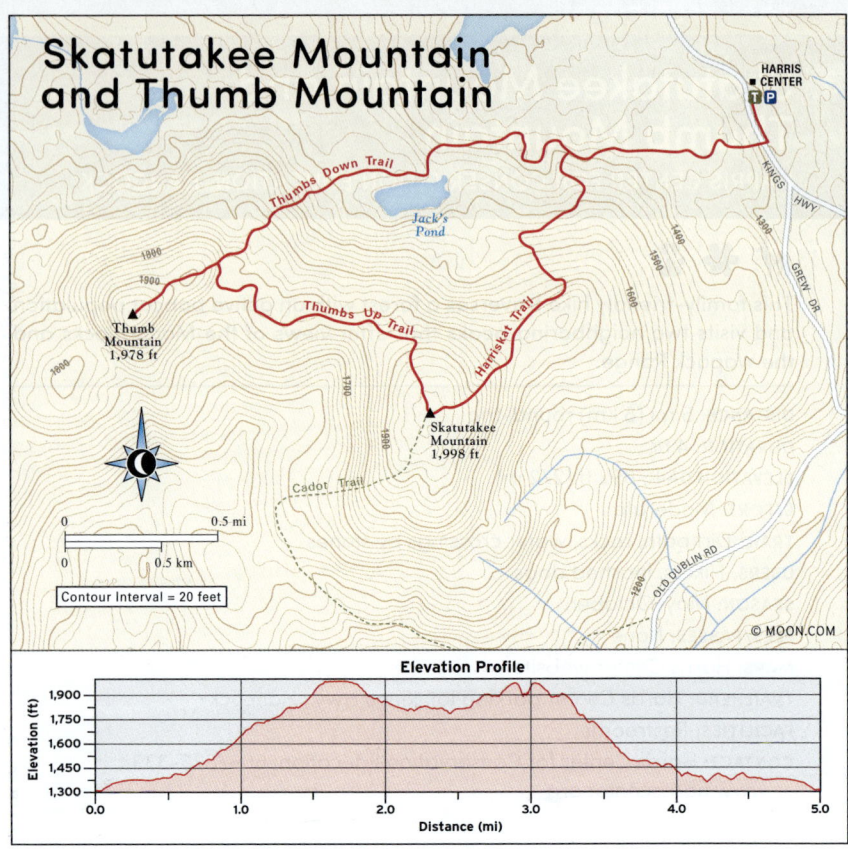

Skatutakee Mountain
and Thumb Mountain

HARRIS CENTER

Thumb Mountain 1,978 ft

Skatutakee Mountain 1,998 ft

Jack's Pond

Thumbs Down Trail

Thumbs Up Trail

Harriskat Trail

Cadot Trail

KINGS HWY

GREW. DR

OLD DUBLIN RD

0   0.5 mi
0   0.5 km

Contour Interval = 20 feet

© MOON.COM

Elevation Profile

Elevation (ft): 1,900 / 1,750 / 1,600 / 1,450 / 1,300

Distance (mi): 0.0 / 1.0 / 2.0 / 3.0 / 4.0 / 5.0

▶ **MILE 1.7–2.3: Skatutakee Summit to Thumbs Up Trail**

To continue the loop, turn right onto the **Thumbs Up Trail** at the summit junction with the Harriskat and Cadot Trails. (Look for white triangles on this section.) After a brief and relaxing descent from the top of Skatutakee, the trail veers west and begins its ascent to **Thumb Mountain** at 2.3 mi (3.7 km). The grade is somewhat gentler, but with more rocks and exposed roots.

▶ **MILE 2.3–2.9: Thumbs Up Trail to Thumb Mountain Summit**

Climb until you reach a junction with the Thumbs Down Trail at 2.6 mi (4.2 km). Turn left to stay on Thumbs Up and continue at a steeper angle for 0.3 mi (0.5 km) before arriving at the summit proper at 2.9 mi (4.7 km). The top of Thumb is more grown-in with foliage than Skatutakee, but a clearing—complete with a stone victory bench—offers a direct and superior view of **Mount Monadnock.**

▶ **MILE 2.9–3.3: Thumb Mountain Summit to Thumbs Down Trail**

Begin the return journey by backtracking down the Thumbs Up Trail to the junction and turning left onto the **Thumbs Down Trail,** which is marked with yellow rectangles. The descent grade is moderate, but the trail here is more rugged and less traveled. Keep an eye peeled for any of the local

▲ VIEW FROM THUMB MOUNTAIN

forest's resident bobcats, which occasionally make brief but unforgettable appearances in the presence of lucky hikers.

▶ **MILE 3.3–5.0: Thumbs Down Trail to Harris Center**
Continue the descent for roughly 0.5 mi (0.8 km). The grade smoothens once the trail passes **Jack's Pond** at 3.9 mi (6.3 km), and the remaining 0.5 mi (0.8 km) is nearly level. At 4.4 mi (7.1 km), the Thumbs Down Trail concludes at the **Harriskat Trail.** Turn left onto Harriskat to return to the parking lot.

DIRECTIONS

From Boston, pick up I-93 N and drive north for 73 mi (117 km) into New Hampshire. Shortly after passing through the toll booth, take Exit 5 to merge onto I-89 N. Drive north for 9 mi (14.5 km) and use the left lane to take Exit 5 onto US-202 W/NH-9 toward Henniker/Keene. Continue heading west and then southwest along NH-9 for 27 mi (43 km) before taking a left onto NH-123. Turn right onto Hunts Pond Road and take it to its end, where you'll turn left onto Kings Highway. The road transitions from concrete to dirt and the Harris Center parking lot will be on your left.

GPS COORDINATES: 42°58'41.9"N 72°01'13.8"W

BEST NEARBY BITES
Reward yourself for a solid double mountain hike by trucking up to nearby Harrisville and enjoying a few house-made doughnuts or a piping-hot bowl of seasonal vegetable soup at the historic **Harrisville General Store** (29 Church St., Harrisville; 603/827-3138; www.historiccharrisville.org; 8am-6pm Mon.-Sat., 8am-2pm Sun.).

Madame Sherri Forest

MADAME SHERRI FOREST, CHESTERFIELD

Hike through lush forest and past the ruins of an old castle to a romantic vista overlooking the hills of Massachusetts.

BEST: New England oddities
DISTANCE: 4 mi (6.4 km) round-trip
DURATION: 3 hr
ELEVATION GAIN: 531 ft (162 m)
EFFORT: Easy/moderate
TRAIL: Dirt path, rocks, wooden bridges
USERS: Hikers, leashed dogs
SEASON: May–October
FEES/PASSES: None
MAPS: Society for the Protection of New Hampshire Forests website
TRAILHEAD: Madame Sherri Forest parking lot, Gulf Rd., Chesterfield
FACILITIES: None
CONTACT: Society for the Protection of New Hampshire Forests; 603/224-9945; www.forestsociety.org

Back in the Gilded Age, a New York costume designer named Antoinette Sherri laid claim to this thick pocket of woods in the southwest tip of New Hampshire. Today, the ruins of her old forest castle form one of the region's most evocative sights. Beyond the castle is vivid emerald foliage, amphibian-rich wetlands, and the wooded knoll known as Daniels Mountain. The park is a paradise for hikers who appreciate grown-in trails and the ambience of undeveloped (and undervisited) woodlands.

START THE HIKE

▶ **MILE 0-0.7: Madame Sherri Forest Parking Lot to Anne Stokes Loop**
Begin your hike in the Madame Sherri Forest parking lot by crossing a wooden bridge and picking up the **Anne Stokes Loop.** Immediately, you'll encounter a sign for the castle ruins. Veer right up a small hill to take a good gander at the ruins before merging back onto the Anne Stokes Loop, which is marked with brown diamonds bearing the name of the loop. Hike southeast past a marsh into a denser section of northern hardwood conifers. Turn left at the loop junction sign at 0.2 mi (0.3 km) and continue 0.5 mi (0.8 km) as the trail becomes rockier and rootier. Watch your step—frogs and garter snakes make regular crossings along this stretch of the trail.

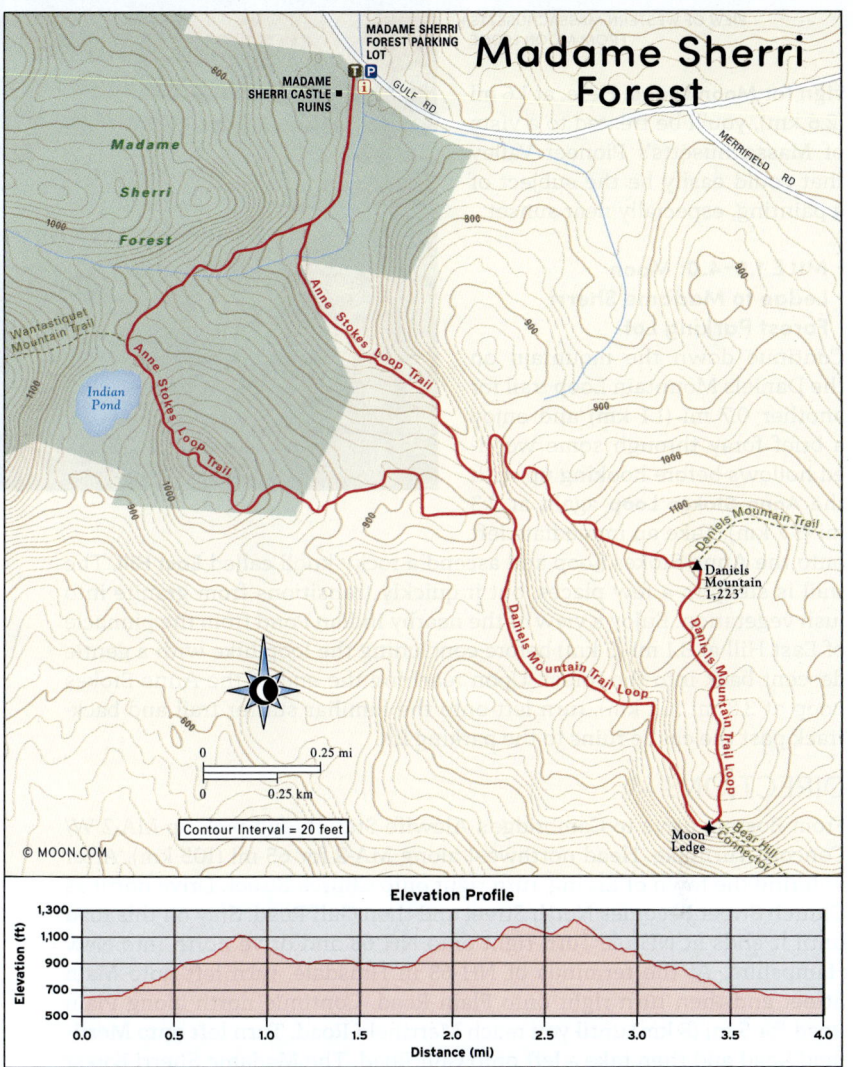

Elevation Profile

▶ MILE 0.7–1.2: Anne Stokes Loop to Daniels Mountain Summit

As the trail begins to ascend, turn left at the junction with the **Daniels Mountain Loop** at 0.7 mi (1.1 km). Head north briefly before the trail takes a sharp right and slabs up the northern flank of Daniels Mountain at a moderate grade. The path contains many exposed roots, so be mindful of your footing during wet weather. An exposed ledge offers a stunning view of the forest at 0.8 mi (1.3 km). Continue for another 0.4 mi (0.6 km) on the final ascent to the top of Daniels Mountain.

▶ MILE 1.2–1.6: Daniels Mountain Summit to Moon Ledge

At 1.2 mi (1.9 km), you'll be at the summit. Ironically, though, the best view is just below the summit. Turn right at the summit junction to continue along the loop trail and descend for 0.4 mi (0.6 km) until you reach the

sign for **Moon Ledge.** Here, at 1.6 mi (2.6 km), you'll be treated to a vista of Massachusetts's Pioneer Valley that could easily be the subject of a painting, especially near sunset.

▶ **MILE 1.6-4.0: Moon Ledge to Madame Sherri Forest Parking Lot**

Continue down the mountain on the Daniels Mountain Loop trail for another 0.7 mi (1.1 km) and enjoy a brief foray through some wooded hollows before hooking up with the **Anne Stokes Loop** again at 2.3 mi (3.7 km). Take an immediate left onto the Anne Stokes Loop and ascend a rocky knoll called **East Hill.** The trail is steep in a few places, but it quickly transitions from granite into lush vegetation. Enjoy a view of the nearby Indian Pond from the pinnacle of East Hill at 3.1 mi (5 km) before concluding the loop hike with a gentle descent back into the forest. Upon reaching the end of the Anne Stokes Loop at 3.8 mi (6.1 km), turn left onto the familiar starter trail and backtrack past the castle ruins to the parking lot.

DIRECTIONS

From Boston, drive to Cambridge's Alewife Station and pick up MA-2 W/ Concord Turnpike. Head northwest along MA-2 for 65 mi (105 km). After entering the town of Erving, turn right onto Church Street. Drive north as Church Street becomes North Street and then Gulf Road. Stay on this road until it ends at NH-63. Turn right onto NH-63 and drive north into New Hampshire. At the terminus of NH-63 in Hinsdale, turn left onto Main Street and then turn right onto Plain Road. Continue north along Plain Road for 5 mi (8 km) until you reach Merrifield Road. Turn left onto Merrifield Road and then take a left onto Gulf Road. The Madame Sherri Forest trailhead and parking lot will be on your left, and a spillover parking area is located directly across the road on the right side.

GPS COORDINATES: 42°51′53.0″N 72°31′05.2″W

BEST NEARBY BREWS

Traipse over the nearby New Hampshire-Vermont border to enjoy the restaurant scene in Brattleboro, and be sure not to miss the phenomenal New American sour ales at **Hermit Thrush Brewing** (29 High St. #101C, Brattleboro; 802/257-2337; www.hermitthrushbrewery.com; 11am-7pm Mon. and Thurs.-Sat., 11am-6pm Sun.).

This thrilling and under-the-radar route up America's most climbed mountain features two summits, plenty of rock scaling, and an unbeatable view of southern New England.

DISTANCE: 4.6 mi (7.4 km) round-trip

DURATION: 3.5 hr

ELEVATION GAIN: 1,509 ft (460 m)

EFFORT: Strenuous

TRAIL: Dirt path, rock scrambling

USERS: Hikers

SEASON: May-October

FEES/PASSES: $5 parking fee per vehicle (cash only)

MAPS: New Hampshire State Parks website

TRAILHEAD: Monadnock State Park Ranger Booth, Mountain Rd., Jaffrey

FACILITIES: Vault toilet

CONTACT: Monadnock State Park; 603/532-8862; www.nhstateparks.org

Mount Monadnock attracts more visitors per year than any other mountain in the continental United States. This leads to over-crowding and erosion on some of the most popular trails, but luckily, Monadnock features almost as many ascent routes as it does humans. And the Monte Rosa loop on the west side is the prettiest and most physically invigorating.

START THE HIKE

▶ **MILE 0-1.2: Monadnock State Park Ranger Booth to Cart Path**

Begin your hike just beyond the ranger station, to the left of the toll road itself, where you'll see a sign for the **Old Halfway House Trail.** Turn left onto the trail and ascend north through a forest of white pine and northern hardwoods. The footing is deceptively soft and gentle. Amble through the woods for 1.2 mi (1.9 km) before reaching a junction with the Cart Path.

▶ **MILE 1.2-1.3: Cart Path to Old Halfway House Site**

Turn right on the Cart Path, emerge onto the toll road, and make a left to continue up the road for another 0.1 mi (0.16 km) to the old Halfway House site. This grassy clearing once featured a hotel for hikers, but today it offers an alluring view of Monadnock's upper flanks and summit.

▶ **MILE 1.3-1.6: Old Halfway House Site to Monte Rosa Trail**

From the Halfway House site, pick up the White Arrow Trail and head north briefly before turning left onto the **Monte Rosa Trail** at 1.4 mi (2.3 km). The

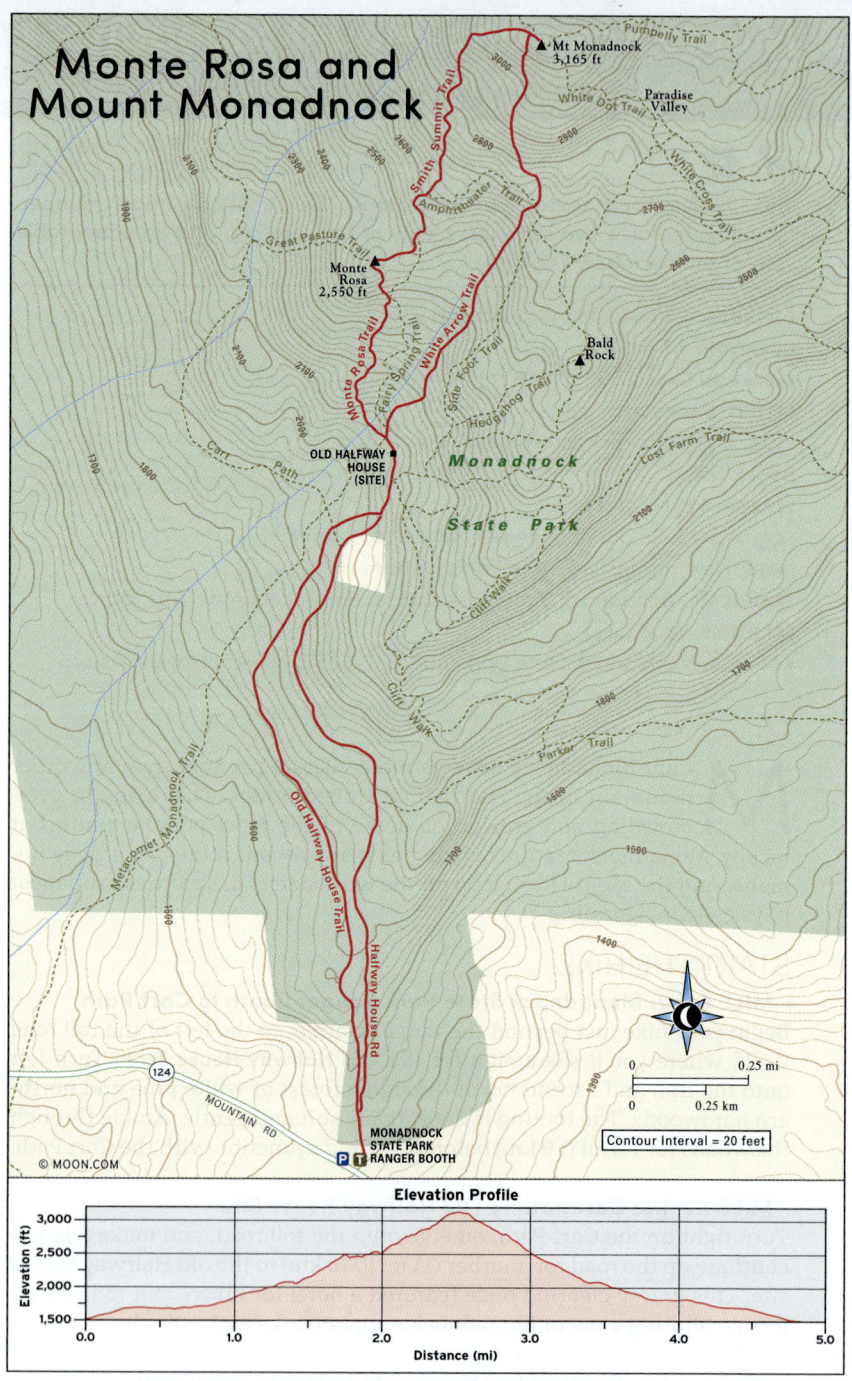

Monte Rosa and Mount Monadnock

Mt Monadnock
3,165 ft

Pumpelly Trail

Paradise Valley

White Dot Trail

White Cross Trail

Smith Summit Trail

Amphitheater Trail

Great Pasture Trail

Monte Rosa
2,550 ft

Monte Rosa Trail

Fairy Spring Trail

White Arrow Trail

Side Foot Trail

Hedgehog Trail

Bald Rock

OLD HALFWAY HOUSE (SITE)

Monadnock

Lost Farm Trail

State Park

Cart Path

Metacomet Monadnock Trail

Cliff Walk

Parker Trail

Old Halfway House Trail

Halfway House Rd

124

MOUNTAIN RD

MONADNOCK STATE PARK RANGER BOOTH

0   0.25 mi
0   0.25 km

Contour Interval = 20 feet

© MOON.COM

Elevation Profile

▲ THE MONTE ROSA WEATHERVANE

trail steepens dramatically here, climbing straight up a torrent of roots, rocks, and loose soil.

▶ MILE 1.6–1.8: Monte Rosa Trail to Monte Rosa Summit
Keep climbing for 0.2 mi (0.3 km) past the Fairy Spring Cutoff until you reach a rocky height of land at 1.8 mi (2.9 km) where the trees recede to shrub-like krummholz. This is the summit of Monte Rosa, marked by a weathervane on a steel post.

▶ MILE 1.8–2.4: Monte Rosa Summit to Mount Monadnock Summit
Pick up the **Great Pasture Trail,** make a left turn onto the **Smith Summit Trail** just a few yards ahead, and climb northeast up the west face of Monadnock. (Look for white S's spray-painted on the rock.) Watch your footing on the well-worn rock slabs as you scramble upward for 0.6 mi (1 km) before arriving at the summit of Mount Monadnock at 2.4 mi (3.9 km). Odds are you'll have to wait in line to stand at the highest point, but the 360-degree views of Massachusetts, the Green Mountains, and New Hampshire's Lakes District should be more than enough to satisfy.

▶ MILE 2.4–4.6: Mount Monadnock Summit to Monadnock State Park Ranger Booth
Briefly backtrack down the Smith Summit Trail and turn left onto the **White Arrow Trail.** For the next 0.4 mi (0.6 km), you'll lower yourself down steep, craggy rock faces marked with white arrows before transitioning back into the woods and enjoying easier, less sheer footing. Continue through the forest as you pass the Monte Rosa Trail entrance (keep left here) and arrive back at the Old Halfway House site at 3.3 mi (5.3 km). Take the Old Halfway House Trail again or descend the final 1.3 mi (2.1 km) by staying on the smoother old toll road itself.

DIRECTIONS

From Boston, drive to Cambridge's Alewife Station and pick up MA-2 W/ Concord Turnpike. Head northwest along MA-2 for 39 mi (63 km) and then merge onto MA-140 N in Westminster. Keep heading northwest as MA-140 merges with MA-12 N near Winchendon. Take a sharp right onto US-202 and continue north into New Hampshire. Once you reach the town of Jaffrey, turn left onto NH-124 W (Mountain Road) and drive west for 5 mi (8 km). The Monadnock Ranger Booth and the parking lot will be on your right.

GPS COORDINATES: 42°50'07.7"N 72°06'53.8"W

BEST NEARBY BREWS

Enjoy a round of liquid replenishment with a Velvety Antlers brown ale or passion fruit sour ale at **Granite Roots Brewing** (244 N. Main St., Troy; 603/242-3435; www.graniterootsbrewing.com; 4pm-7pm Thurs.-Fri., noon-7pm Sat., noon-6pm Sun.). Consider leveling up and ordering one of the wood-fired pizzas that the brewery dishes up each Saturday.

Purgatory Falls
PURGATORY BROOK WATERSHED, MONT VERNON

This relaxing and refreshing hike visits two gorgeous waterfalls by way of a brook that weaves and tumbles through the western woods of the Merrimack River valley.

BEST: Spring hikes
DISTANCE: 5 mi (8 km) round-trip
DURATION: 2.5 hr
ELEVATION GAIN: 317 ft (97 m)
EFFORT: Easy/moderate
TRAIL: Dirt and gravel paths, wooden bridges, water crossings via stones and logs
USERS: Hikers, leashed dogs
SEASON: April–October
FEES/PASSES: None
MAPS: Town of Mont Vernon website
TRAILHEAD: Purgatory Brook trailhead, Purgatory Rd., Mont Vernon
FACILITIES: None
CONTACT: Town of Mont Vernon; 603/673-6080; www.montvernonnh.us/conservation-commission

Tucked away in the hills north of Nashua, the Purgatory Brook Trail is an under-the-radar gem compared to the heavily trafficked trails of the nearby Monadnocks. While this makes for serene hiking, it also means that the trail can be overgrown. For a confusion-free trip, bring a printout of the trail map found on the Mont Vernon Conservation Commission website and watch the tree trunks for the yellow plastic strips that mark the path. If you're hiking in late May or June, throw some bug spray in your day pack too: Those 4-5 weeks are blackfly season in New Hampshire, and blackflies love running water.

START THE HIKE

▶ **MILE 0-0.3: Purgatory Brook Trailhead to Lower Purgatory Falls**
Begin on the **Purgatory Brook Trail** heading west. Bear left at a Y junction to stay on the main dirt path, which ambles through hemlocks at an even grade. After passing several reptile-rich vernal pools, the trail curves northwest and makes a quick descent to **Lower Purgatory Falls** at 0.3 mi (0.5 km). The shoreline that circles the pool of the explosive 25-ft-tall (8-m) cascade is ideal for picnickers and landscape photographers, making this a popular place.

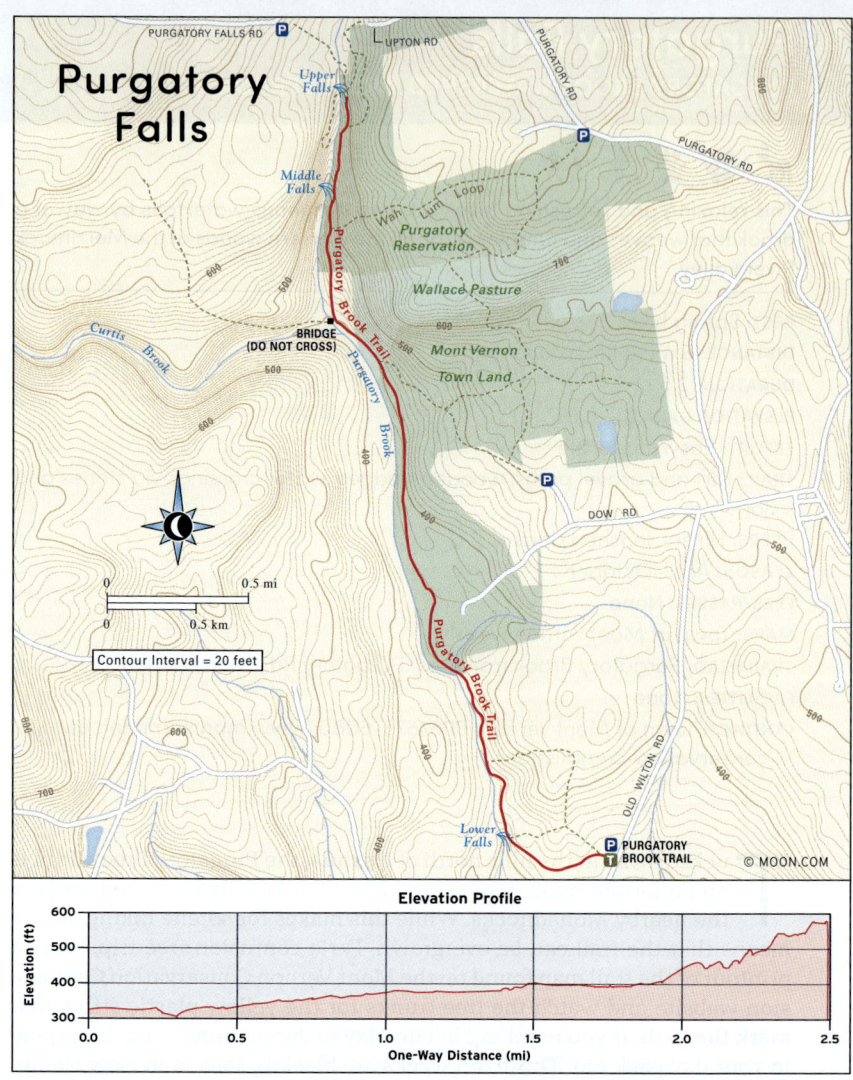

Purgatory Falls

Elevation Profile

Elevation (ft)

One-Way Distance (mi)

© MOON.COM

▶ **MILE 0.3–1.7: Lower Purgatory Falls to Purgatory Brook**

Leaving the crowds behind, the trail climbs the right side of the lower falls and flattens into a narrow, rockier path through mossy woods. Hugging the shore of **Purgatory Brook,** continue north and cross several mud patches on wooden plank bridges and logs. At 0.8 mi (1.3 km), turn right to avoid a bridge over Purgatory Brook. Continue for 0.9 mi (1.4 km) as the forest expands into a great hall of deciduous hardwoods. Occasionally the trees part wide enough to offer pleasant views of Purgatory Brook, which are often complemented by rock slabs and boulders large enough to host a small group of picnickers.

▸ **MILE 1.7-2.5: Purgatory Brook to Upper Purgatory Falls**

The trail briefly merges with a gravel access road at 1.75 mi (2.8 km) before veering sharply to the right to avoid another wooden bridge. Note that the markings on this right turn are a little tough to see if you're not looking for them, especially since the intuitive thing to do when hikers encounter a bridge is to cross it. Bottom line: Don't cross the **bridge.** Turn right instead.

Now it's time for the final climb. The trail ascends a wooded ravine at a moderate grade for 0.7 mi (1.1 km). Be mindful of slippery exposed roots and loose rocks. Keep an ear open for the rumble of Upper Purgatory Falls and look for a small wooden sign; the falls can be viewed from an outlook just beyond this sign at 2.5 mi (4 km). The crashing 50-ft-tall (15-m) falls are surrounded by sheer walls of granite. Extra-curious hikers can get a closer look by carefully scrambling down a steep gully to the pool. Return the way you came.

DIRECTIONS

From Boston, drive north on I-93 to Exit 37B. Merge onto I-95 S and drive 5.5 mi (8.9 km) before turning right onto US-3 N. Continue north on US-3 N for 27.6 mi (44.4 km) into New Hampshire. Take Exit 8 toward Somerset Parkway and turn right onto NH-101A W. Drive 7 mi (11.3 km) and turn left onto NH-101 W at the junction. Continue as the road heads north and becomes Purgatory Road. Look for the Lower Purgatory Falls parking lot on the left. If the parking lot is full, park on the shoulder of Purgatory Road. The trailhead can be found in the parking lot.

GPS COORDINATES: 42°51'31.6"N 71°41'40.1"W

BEST NEARBY BITES

Take a walk on the chic side of southern New Hampshire with wine tastings, a vineyard tour, and farm-to-table bistro fare at **LaBelle Winery** (345 NH-101, Amherst; 603/672-9898; www.labellewinery. com; noon-9pm Wed.-Sat., 11am-5pm Sun.).

Monadnock, Merrimack Valley, and the Seacoast

NEW HAMPSHIRE

NEARBY CAMPGROUNDS

NAME	LOCATION	FACILITIES	SEASON	FEE
Wakeda Campground	294 Exeter Rd., Hampton Falls, 42°56'58.6"N 70°54'47.6"W	Tent sites, RV sites, cabins, toilets, showers, potable water, laundry, camp store, restaurant, Wi-Fi	mid-May-September	$48-97
603/772-5274; www.wakedacampground.com				
Sunset Park Campground	104 Emerson Ave., Hampstead, 42°52'36.9"N 71°10'19.2"W	Tent sites, RV sites, yurts, toilets, showers, potable water, Wi-Fi	late May-early October	$42-90
603/329-6941; www.sunsetparknh.com				
Oxbow Campground	8 Oxbow Rd., Deering, 43°06'25.6"N 71°53'09.4"W	Tent sites, RV sites, cabins, toilets, showers, potable water, laundry, camp store, Wi-Fi	mid-May-mid-October	$55-75
603/464-5952; www.oxbowcampground.net				
Autumn Hills Campground	285 S. Stark Hwy., Weare, 43°02'23.2"N 71°40'13.0"W	Tent sites, RV sites, rental RVs, toilets, showers, potable water, laundry, camp store, Wi-Fi	May-mid-October	$55-150
603/529-2425; www.autumnhillscampground.com				

NAME	LOCATION	FACILITIES	SEASON	FEE
Spacious Skies Seven Maples Campground	24 Longview Rd., Hancock, 42°59'03.0"N 71°58'41.8"W	Tent sites, RV sites, cabins, toilets, showers, potable water, laundry, pool, camp store, Wi-Fi	mid-May-mid-October	$42-112
603/525-3321; www.spaciousskiescampgrounds.com				
Ashuelot River Campground	152 Pine St., Swanzey, 42°52'45.6"N 72°19'33.7"W	Tent sites, RV sites, cabins, toilets, showers, potable water, laundry, camp store, Wi-Fi	May-October	$49-59
603/357-5777; www.ashuelotrivercampground.com				
Gilson Pond Campground	116 Poole Rd., Jaffrey, 42°51'37.9"N 72°03'47.1"W	Tent sites, toilets, showers, potable water	May-October	$18-25
603/532-8862; www.nhstateparks.org				
Shir-Roy Camping Area	136 Athol Rd., Richmond, 42°44'40.7"N 72°16'08.9"W	Tent sites, RV sites, toilets, showers, potable water, laundry, camp store, Wi-Fi	late May-early October	$40-55
603/239-4768; www.shir-roy.com				

▲ VIEW FROM THE GREAT CLIFF OF MOUNT HORRID

VERMONT

NORTHERN GREEN MOUNTAINS

The northern region of the 399,151-acre (161,531-hectare) Green Mountain National Forest and its surrounding parks contain some of the most prized wildlands in the Northeast. Here, the Long Trail traverses the bald granite "backbone" of Vermont, where views of rolling hills unfold and plunge into swaths of rich farmland. Additional paths lead to sparkling ponds and cascading falls, many secluded within pristine wilderness areas. Hikes range from challenging all-day climbs to easygoing jaunts that can be completed in a few hours. Many of these routes are an easy drive from the Middlebury area, which is a great jumping-off point for adventures of all types.

▲ ABBEY POND

▲ BRIDGE ACROSS BREWER'S BROOK TO KILLINGTON PEAK

◄ LONG TRAIL ON MOUNT HORRID

1 **Long Trail: Lincoln Gap to Mount Abraham**
DISTANCE: 4.8–5 mi (7.7–8 km) round-trip
DURATION: 3.25 hr
EFFORT: Strenuous
PAGE: 312

2 **Abbey Pond Trail**
DISTANCE: 4.4 mi (7.1 km) round-trip
DURATION: 2 hr
EFFORT: Easy/moderate
PAGE: 315

3 **Skylight Pond Trail and Long Trail to Breadloaf Mountain**
DISTANCE: 6.9 mi (11.1 km) round-trip
DURATION: 4 hr
EFFORT: Moderate
PAGE: 318

4 **Falls of Lana and Rattlesnake Cliffs**
DISTANCE: 4.9 mi (7.9 km) round-trip
DURATION: 2.5 hr
EFFORT: Moderate
PAGE: 321

5 **Long Trail: Brandon Gap to Mount Horrid Great Cliff and Cape Lookout**
DISTANCE: 3.6 mi (5.8 km) round-trip (with a shorter option)
DURATION: 2.5 hr
EFFORT: Moderate/strenuous
PAGE: 324

6 **Killington Peak via the Bucklin Trail**
DISTANCE: 7.4 mi (11.9 km) round-trip
DURATION: 4 hr
EFFORT: Strenuous
PAGE: 327

7 **Mount Tom via Mountain Road**
DISTANCE: 3.6 mi (5.8 km) round-trip
DURATION: 1.75 hr
EFFORT: Moderate
PAGE: 330

VERMONT | Northern Green Mountains

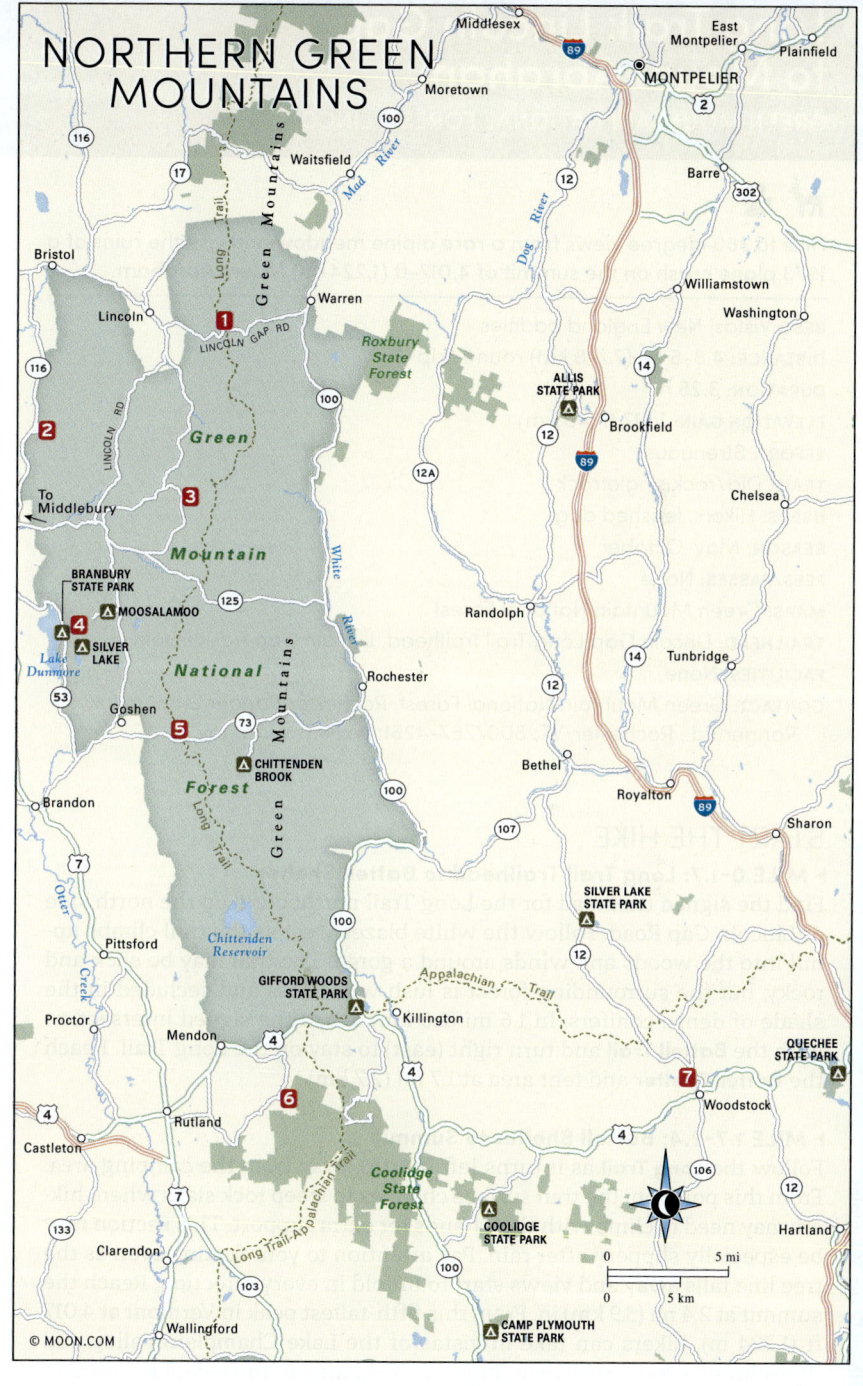

NORTHERN GREEN MOUNTAINS

© MOON.COM

1

Long Trail: Lincoln Gap to Mount Abraham

GREEN MOUNTAIN NATIONAL FOREST, LINCOLN

Hike to 360-degree views from a rare alpine meadow and visit the ruins of a 1973 plane crash on the summit of 4,017-ft (1,224-m) Mount Abraham.

BEST: Vistas, New England oddities
DISTANCE: 4.8–5 mi (7.7–8 km) round-trip
DURATION: 3.25 hr
ELEVATION GAIN: 1,617 ft (493 m)
EFFORT: Strenuous
TRAIL: Dirt/rock singletrack
USERS: Hikers, leashed dogs
SEASON: May–October
FEES/PASSES: None
MAPS: Green Mountain National Forest
TRAILHEAD: Lincoln Gap Long Trail trailhead, Lincoln Gap Rd., Lincoln
FACILITIES: None
CONTACT: Green Mountain National Forest, Rochester Ranger Station, 99 Ranger Rd., Rochester, VT; 800/767-4261; www.fs.usda.gov

START THE HIKE

▶ **MILE 0-1.7: Long Trail Trailhead to Battell Shelter**

Find the signed trailhead for the Long Trail northbound on the north side of Lincoln Gap Road. Follow the white blazes west as the trail climbs uphill into the woods and winds around a gorge. The trail may be slick and rocky, but the surrounding forest is lush with moss and secluded in the shade of dense conifers. In 1.6 mi (2.6 km), reach the signed intersection with the **Battell Trail** and turn right (east) to stay on the Long Trail. Reach the **Battell Shelter** and tent area at 1.7 mi (2.7 km).

▶ **MILE 1.7-2.4: Battell Shelter to Summit**

Follow the **Long Trail** as it turns left (north) away from the camping area. From this point on, the trail surface changes to steep rock slabs where hikers may need to climb with their hands for extra support. This section may be especially slippery after rain. Pay attention to your footing even as the tree line falls away and views start to unfold in every direction. Reach the summit at 2.4 mi (3.9 km) in. From this fifth-tallest peak in Vermont at 4,017 ft (1,224 m), hikers can take in vistas of the Lake Champlain valley and the Adirondacks to the west, Sugarbush ski area to the east, Lincoln Gap to the south, and the rolling green peaks of Mount Ellen and the Monroe Skyline to the north. Enjoy the 360-degree views from the trail only—the roped-off area protects a delicate alpine meadow that can be damaged by

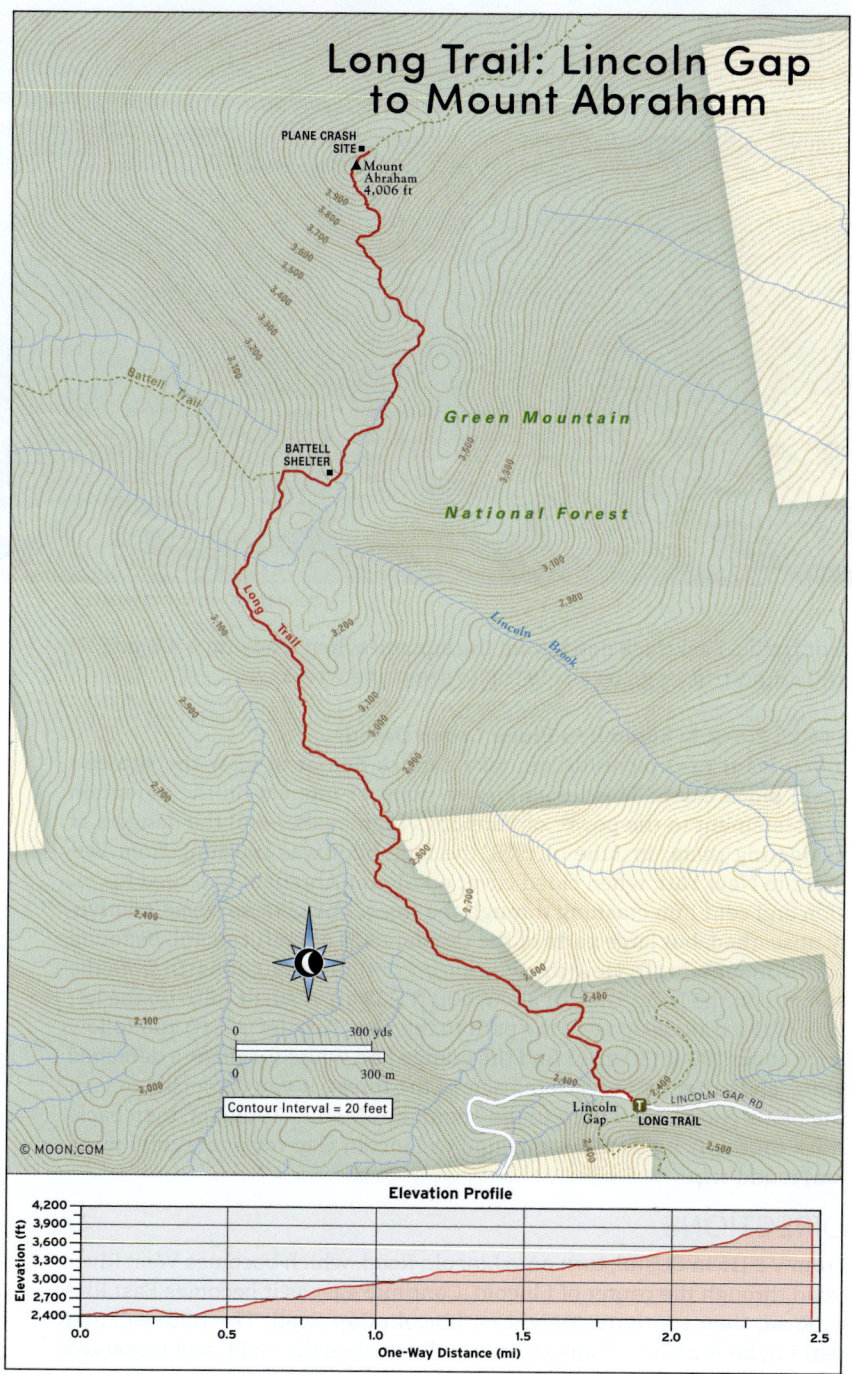

Long Trail: Lincoln Gap to Mount Abraham

PLANE CRASH SITE

Mount Abraham 4,006 ft

Green Mountain

National Forest

BATTELL SHELTER

Battell Trail

Long Trail

Lincoln Brook

Contour Interval = 20 feet

Lincoln Gap

LONG TRAIL

LINCOLN GAP RD

© MOON.COM

Elevation Profile

Elevation (ft)

One-Way Distance (mi)

SUMMIT OF MOUNT ABRAHAM ▲

foot traffic. Backtrack down from the summit when ready for a 4.8-mi (7.7-km) round-trip, or go on a side trip to see plane wreckage.

▶ MILE 2.4–2.5: Summit to Plane Crash Detour

If you want to explore further, take a quick detour to view the site of a small **plane crash.** This lesser-known point of interest on the mountain is a testament to the power of Vermont's high peaks—and the dangers of navigating them. In June of 1973, the lone pilot was traveling from Vermont to New York when cloud cover on Mount Abraham obscured his vision and sent him crashing through the trees. The pilot survived relatively unscathed, but large parts of the Cessna 182N aircraft can still be found on the mountain. To view the wreckage, continue straight north from the summit on the Long Trail for about 400 ft (122 m). A small cairn on the left side of the trail designates the path to the site. Turn left (east) and follow it for about 100 ft (30 m) to find the orange and white fuselage, a detached wing, and other parts scattered across the forest. If you do decide to visit the plane crash site, return to the summit of Mount Abraham, then backtrack on the Long Trail southbound to Lincoln Gap for a total of 5 mi (8 km) round-trip.

DIRECTIONS

From VT-116 in Bristol, turn onto Lincoln Road, which becomes West River Road through the center of Lincoln. Continue east as it becomes East River Road, then continue straight on Lincoln Gap Road. The trailhead and parking lot is about 3.5 mi (5.6 km) up the road on the right, and is marked by signs for the Long Trail.

GPS COORDINATES: 44°05'41.7"N 72°55'44.5"W

2

Abbey Pond Trail

GREEN MOUNTAIN NATIONAL FOREST, MIDDLEBURY

This easygoing trail leads past cascades and slightly uphill to tranquil Abbey Pond, a great spot for wildlife viewing.

BEST: Winter hikes

DISTANCE: 4.4 mi (7.1 km) round-trip

DURATION: 2 hr

ELEVATION GAIN: 1,173 ft (358 m)

EFFORT: Easy/moderate

TRAIL: Dirt/rock singletrack

USERS: Hikers, leashed dogs

SEASON: May–October

FEES/PASSES: None

MAPS: Green Mountain National Forest

TRAILHEAD: Abbey Pond trailhead, Abbey Pond Rd., Ripton

FACILITIES: None

CONTACT: Green Mountain National Forest, Rochester Ranger Station, 99 Ranger Rd., Rochester; 802/767-4261; www.fs.usda.gov

START THE HIKE

▶ **MILE 0-0.3: Abbey Pond Trailhead to Abbey Cascades**

Hike east from the parking lot on a wide gravel path that slopes gradually uphill. Follow the blue blazes around some large rock formations and pass a gravel **quarry** on your left (west). There is also a quarry to the right, which may be heard but not seen from the trail. The fern-lined trail, shaded by a mixed hardwood forest, reaches a bridge crossing over the upper

and lower **Abbey Cascades** at 0.3 mi (0.5 km). The upper falls plunge through a tumble of high granite boulders to the right (east), pass under the bridge to the left (west), and fall across a slide of mossy rocks before the stream rushes around the corner to the north. In warm weather, the lower falls are a fine place to dunk your feet, while in winter the upper falls freeze into dramatic icicles.

◀ ABBEY CASCADES

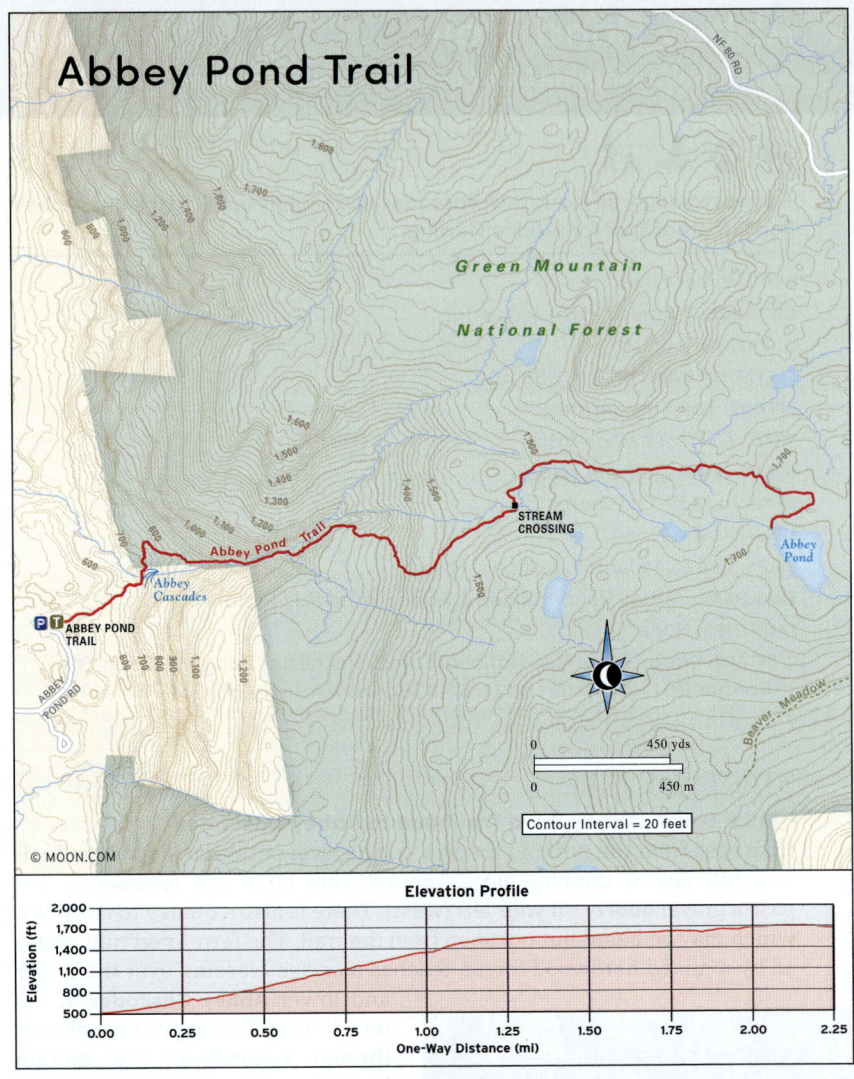

Abbey Pond Trail

Green Mountain

National Forest

STREAM CROSSING

Abbey Pond Trail

Abbey Cascades

Abbey Pond

ABBEY POND TRAIL

ABBEY POND RD

Beaver Meadow

NF 80 RD

0   450 yds

0   450 m

Contour Interval = 20 feet

© MOON.COM

Elevation Profile

Elevation (ft)	

One-Way Distance (mi)

▶ MILE 0.3-1.0: Abbey Cascades to Stream Crossing

From the falls, the rocky path steepens and continues east upstream to the music of rushing water. In another 0.3 mi (0.5 km), the trail crosses the stream at a narrow junction where hikers can hop across. There are some more steep sections and rolling hills as the trail climbs upward, but the terrain evens out after about 0.4 mi (0.6 km).

▶ MILE 1.0-2.2: Stream Crossing to Abbey Pond

After it flattens, the trail meanders through a deciduous forest along the stream then crosses the stream again on a line of large flat stepping stones in 0.3 mi (0.5 km). Use caution during or after wet weather as the rocks may be slick. Arrive on the quiet banks of **Abbey Pond** after another 0.9 mi (1.4 km). The trail ends on the rocky shore of the pond, which is

▲ ABBEY POND

surrounded by reeds and marsh grasses that serve as the nesting area for great blue herons. Part of the trail may be closed during nesting season. The rocky perch is a great spot to sit quietly and scope out wildlife across the pond, especially at the prime feeding hours of dawn and dusk. Enjoy the view from the rocks where the trail ends, then backtrack the same route to return to the start.

DIRECTIONS

From Middlebury, travel south on US-7 for 4 mi (6.4 km) until it intersects with VT-125. Travel east on VT-125 for approximately 0.5 mi (0.8 km) to the intersection with VT-116. Turn left onto VT-116 and continue 4.5 mi (7.2 km) until the sign for the Abbey Pond Trail on the right. Turn onto the gravel road and follow it to the parking area at the end.

GPS COORDINATES: 44°01'51.5"N 73°05'17.3"W

Northern Green Mountains

VERMONT

3

Skylight Pond Trail and Long Trail to Breadloaf Mountain

GREEN MOUNTAIN NATIONAL FOREST, MIDDLEBURY

This climb to a secluded pond and vista is the jewel of the Green Mountains' pristine Breadloaf Wilderness.

DISTANCE: 6.9 mi (11.1 km) round-trip

DURATION: 4 hr

ELEVATION GAIN: 1,902 ft (580 m)

EFFORT: Moderate

TRAIL: Dirt/rock singletrack

USERS: Hikers, leashed dogs

SEASON: May–October

FEES/PASSES: None

MAPS: Green Mountain National Forest

TRAILHEAD: Skylight Pond trailhead, Steam Mill Rd., Ripton

FACILITIES: None

CONTACT: Green Mountain National Forest, Rochester Ranger Station, 99 Ranger Rd., Rochester; 802/767-4261; www.fs.usda.gov

START THE HIKE

▶ **MILE 0-0.4: Skylight Pond Trailhead to Middlebury River Footbridge**
Go east from the parking lot to reach the trailhead and pass a sign marking the entrance to the **Breadloaf Wilderness.** The tree-lined dirt track heads straight east, briefly paralleling a stream, and reaches a crossing at 0.2 mi (0.3 km). When water is low, hikers should be able to hop right over this crossing, but the stream widens after rain, so waterproof boots are a good idea. After the stream crossing, the wide doubletrack trail is marked with blue blazes. Continue straight (southeast) for another 0.2 mi (0.3 km) and cross the Middle Branch of the Middlebury River on a wooden footbridge.

▶ **MILE 0.4-2.2: Middlebury River Footbridge to Skylight Pond**
The path narrows into a single track through a thick forest and over several rolling hills as it makes its way east toward the slopes of

SKYLIGHT LODGE ▶

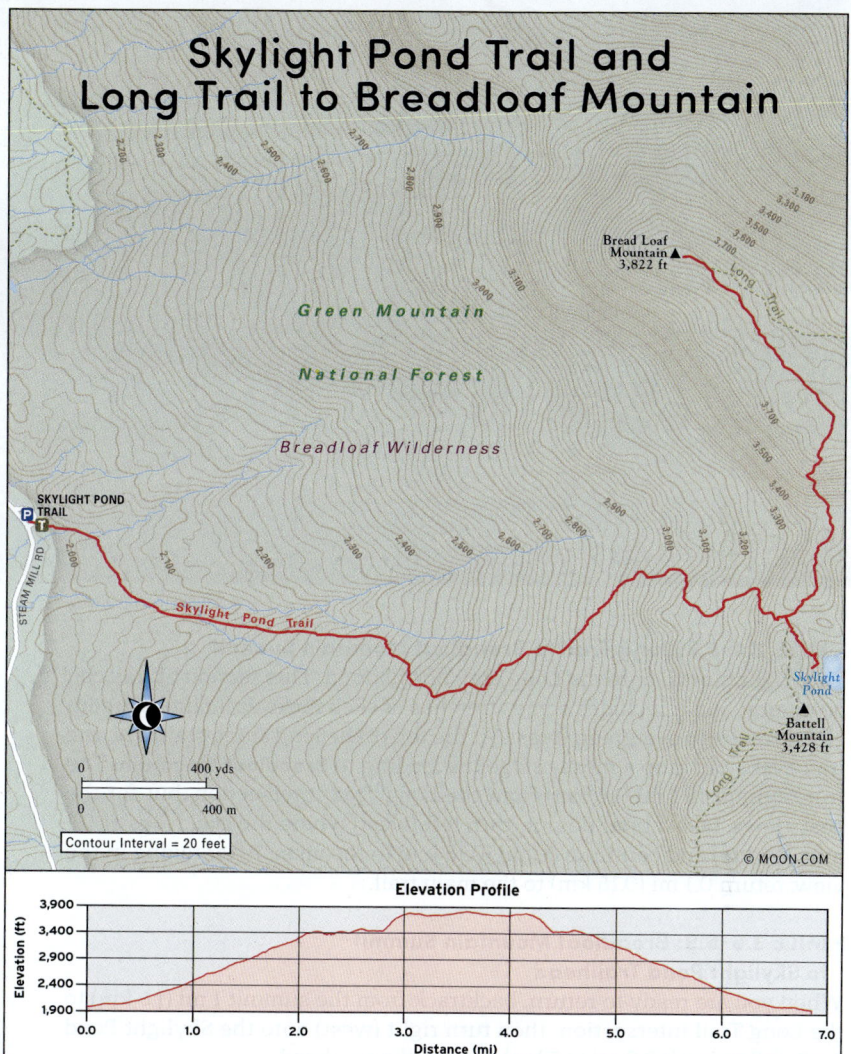

Skylight Pond Trail and Long Trail to Breadloaf Mountain

Green Mountain

National Forest

Breadloaf Wilderness

SKYLIGHT POND TRAIL

STEAM MILL RD

Skylight Pond Trail

Bread Loaf
Mountain ▲
3,822 ft

Long Trail

Skylight
Pond

Battell
Mountain
3,428 ft

Long Trail

0   400 yds
0   400 m

Contour Interval = 20 feet

© MOON.COM

Elevation Profile

Battell Mountain. The trail steepens after 1 mi (1.6 km), then climbs northeast for 1.1 mi (1.8 km) to a hemlock-bound ridgeline. Follow the trail southeast along the ridge to reach the signed four-way intersection with the **Long Trail** at 2.2 mi (3.5 km). Continue straight (east) through the intersection and downhill to **Skylight Pond.**

▶ **MILE 2.2–2.4: Skylight Pond to Long Trail**
The pond sits below the **Skylight Lodge** cabin/shelter at 2.3 mi (3.7 km). Hikers can explore this peaceful, boggy oasis with views of distant ridgelines before backtracking 0.1 mi (0.16 km) to the **Long Trail** intersection.

SKYLIGHT POND ▲

▶ **MILE 2.4–3.6: Long Trail to Breadloaf Mountain Summit**

Turn right (north) onto the Long Trail northbound. This section of trail can be muddy, and it includes some stretches of slick rocks as it climbs gradually through an evergreen forest. At the top of the long stone staircase, the trail evens out atop a mossy ridgeline leading to **Breadloaf Mountain.** The true summit is 1 mi (1.6 km) from the Long Trail intersection, but for the best views, take a brief detour; turn left (west) where the trail forks at 0.9 mile (1.4 km) and continue 0.1 mi (0.16 km) to the vista. After taking in the view, return 0.1 mi (0.16 km) to the main trail.

▶ **MILE 3.6–6.9: Breadloaf Mountain Summit
to Skylight Pond Trailhead**

When you are ready to return, backtrack from the summit 1 mi (1.6 km) to the Long Trail intersection, then turn right (west) onto the Skylight Pond Trail, following it 2.2 mi (3.5 km) back to the trailhead.

DIRECTIONS

From Middlebury, travel south on US-7 for 4 mi (6.4 km) until it intersects with VT-125. Travel east on VT-125 for approximately 6.5 mi (10.5 km), then turn left onto Forest Road 59 (Steam Mill Road). The free parking area for Skylight Pond is marked with a small sign on the right after 6.6 mi (10.6 km).

GPS COORDINATES: 43°59'23.2"N 72°57'56.6"W

Falls of Lana and Rattlesnake Cliffs

GREEN MOUNTAIN NATIONAL FOREST, SALISBURY

This forest hike visits a dramatic multilevel waterfall before ascending to an exposed cliff that offers stellar views of nearby Lake Dunmore and all the way into upstate New York.

BEST: Summer hikes, waterfalls, brew hikes

DISTANCE: 4.9 mi (7.9 km) round-trip

DURATION: 2.5 hr

ELEVATION GAIN: 1,627 ft (496 m)

EFFORT: Moderate

TRAIL: Dirt path, rocks, wooden bridges, water crossings on stones

USERS: Hikers, leashed dogs

SEASON: June–October

FEES/PASSES: None

MAPS: Green Mountain and Finger Lakes National Forests website

TRAILHEAD: Information kiosk, Silver Lake parking lot, Lake Dunmore Rd., Salisbury

FACILITIES: None

CONTACT: Green Mountain and Finger Lakes National Forests; 802/747-6700; www.fs.usda.gov/main/gmfl/home

START THE HIKE

▶ MILE 0-0.5: Information Kiosk to Falls of Lana

Begin by the trail information kiosk on the east side of the parking lot for Silver Lake. Climb a set of stone stairs into a boulder-strewn forest of spruce and maple trees and follow a brief dirt path to a dirt road. Turn right onto the road and ascend a series of switchbacks before arriving at a clearing. A big, black water supply pipe passes through here on stilt-like supports. As you pass underneath the line, you'll hear the churning of water inside the pipe and the brighter crashing of water ahead. The trail dips back into the forest and pops around a curve.

At 0.5 mi (0.8 km), you'll reach a rocky overlook on your left that allows you to gaze down into the frothing torrent and reflective pools of **Falls of Lana.**

▶ MILE 0.5-0.7: Falls of Lana to Rattlesnake Cliffs Trail

From the falls you can reach additional pools and cascades by backtracking to the water supply pipe, following the pipe downhill, and then bushwhacking right into the woods. Be careful around the overlook during wet weather—it gets quite slippery.

From the falls, the trail ascends north at a gentle grade along **Sucker Brook,** which feeds the cascades. At 0.6 mi (1 km), you'll reach a junction with the Silver Lake Trail; keep left here and continue to a wooden bridge that crosses the brook. Turn right onto the **Rattlesnake Cliffs Trail,** marked by blue blazes.

Falls of Lana and Rattlesnake Cliffs

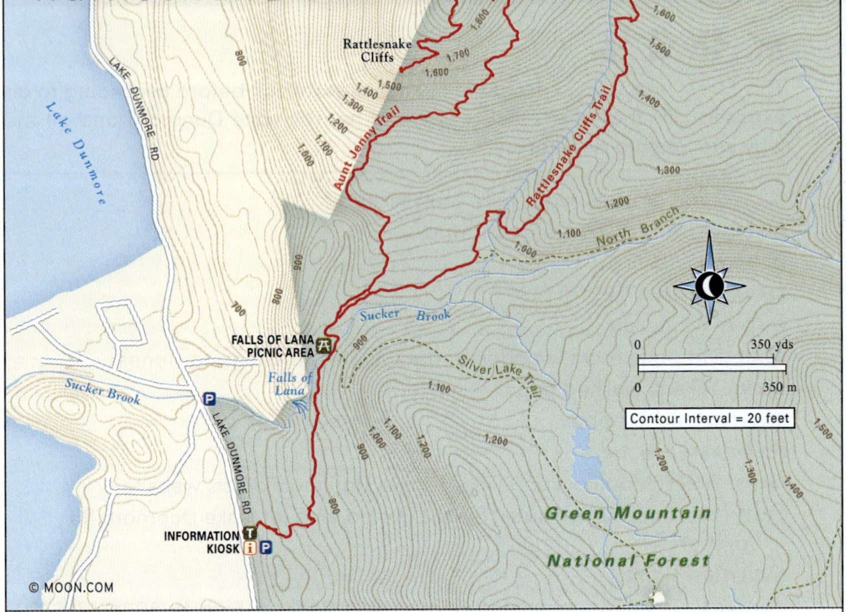

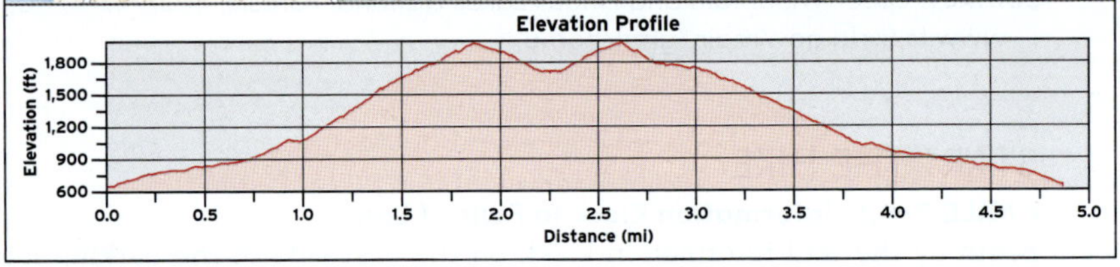

Rattlesnake Cliffs

FALLS OF LANA PICNIC AREA

Falls of Lana

INFORMATION KIOSK

Green Mountain
National Forest

© MOON.COM

Lake Dunmore

Sucker Brook

Aunt Jenny Trail

Rattlesnake Cliffs Trail

North Branch

Silver Lake Trail

LAKE DUNMORE RD.

Contour Interval = 20 feet

0 — 350 yds
0 — 350 m

Elevation Profile

Elevation (ft): 1,800 / 1,500 / 1,200 / 900 / 600

Distance (mi): 0.0 — 5.0

▶ MILE 0.7–1.7: Rattlesnake Cliffs Trail to Aunt Jenny Trail

At 0.7 mi (1.1 km), turn left to pick up the **Aunt Jenny Trail,** which ascends steadily through the forest on a wide path that's swimming with tree roots. A slight curve to the northwest takes you across a ledge-like section of trail that bypasses a very steep and wooded hillside. The hemlocks here are spaced enough to offer some partial views of **Lake Dunmore.**

At 1 mi (1.6 km), the trail swings north again and begins climbing at a steeper grade. As the trail becomes narrower and steeper,

ONE OF SEVERAL "STORIES" OF ROARING CASCADES YOU'LL FIND AT FALLS OF LANA ▶

winding rock stairs become a recurring feature. Continue north, climbing higher into the forest as the trees start to open up and the the trail scrambles up some darker slabs of rock.

▶ MILE 1.7–2.3: Aunt Jenny Trail to Rattlesnake Cliffs

At 1.7 mi (2.7 km), you'll reach another junction for the **Rattlesnake Cliffs Trail.** Turn left onto the Rattlesnake Cliffs Trail, which switchbacks up a series of steeper rocky ledges before heading west through a thinner forest that's rich with birdsong (peregrine falcons are known to nest here). You'll pass a junction with Oak Ridge Trail in 0.2 mi (0.3 km); keep left to stay on Rattlesnake Cliffs Trail. After another 0.1 mi (0.16 km), you'll step onto the exposed, rocky majesty of Rattlesnake Cliffs.

▶ MILE 2.3–4.0: Rattlesnake Cliffs to North Branch Trail Junction

Return by backtracking down Rattlesnake Cliffs Trail to the Aunt Jenny Trail junction. Turn left to stay on Rattlesnake Cliffs Trail and descend a gently graded dirt path. After crossing several little streams on rocks, the trail begins to descend a steeper dirt path that becomes rockier as the surrounding forest again transitions from deciduous trees to hemlocks.

At 3.5 mi (5.6 km), you'll pass a pyre-like rock formation and hear the nearby rippling of Sucker Brook again, which the trail crosses on rocks at 3.8 mi (6.1 km). Continue to hike southwest along the brook into a meadow for 0.2 mi (0.3 km) until you reach a junction with the North Branch Trail. Keep right to continue on **Rattlesnake Cliffs Trail,** which heads back into the forest.

▶ MILE 4.0–4.9: North Branch Trail Junction to Information Kiosk

After the North Branch Trail junction, at 4.2 mi (6.8 km) you'll arrive at the **Aunt Jenny Trail junction** again. Turn left to stay on Rattlesnake Cliffs Trail and backtrack over the bridge and past the Falls of Lana to the parking lot to complete your loop hike.

DIRECTIONS

From Burlington, drive south on US-7 S for 25 mi (40 km); upon reaching downtown Middlebury, turn left onto Court Square and then right onto US-7 S/Court Street. Continue south for another 7 mi (11.3 km) before swinging left onto VT-53, which eventually becomes Lake Dunmore Road. Drive for roughly 4 mi (6.4 km) past Lake Dunmore and you'll soon see the hiker parking lot for Falls of Lana and the Silver Lake Trail on your left.

GPS COORDINATES: 43°54'04.2"N 73°03'51.4"W

BEST NEARBY BREWS

Middlebury and Vergennes—not far north from the trailhead—are your best bets for dining. But if you appreciate the science of beer, head south and sample some of the locally beloved suds (especially the IPAs) at **Foley Brothers** (79 Stone Dam Mill Rd., Brandon; 802/465-8413; www.foleybrothersbrewing.com; 11am–5pm Tue.–Sat.).

5 Long Trail: Brandon Gap to Mount Horrid Great Cliff and Cape Lookout

GREEN MOUNTAIN NATIONAL FOREST, GOSHEN

This short hike to one of the Green Mountains' most prized vistas can be extended with a trek through lush forests to Cape Lookout Mountain.

BEST: Fall hikes, vistas

DISTANCE: 3.6 mi (5.8 km) round-trip (with a shorter option)

DURATION: 2.5 hr

ELEVATION GAIN: 1,195 ft (364 m)

EFFORT: Moderate/strenuous

TRAIL: Dirt/rock singletrack

USERS: Hikers, leashed dogs

SEASON: May–October. This trail may be closed between March and August to protect nesting peregrine falcons. Please heed posted signs.

FEES/PASSES: None

MAPS: Green Mountain National Forest

TRAILHEAD: Brandon Gap Long Trail parking lot, Brandon Mountain Rd., Goshen

FACILITIES: None

CONTACT: Green Mountain National Forest, Rochester Ranger Station, 99 Ranger Rd., Rochester; 800/767-4261; www.fs.usda.gov

START THE HIKE

▶ **MILE 0-0.1: Long Trail Parking Lot to Joseph Battell Wilderness**

From the parking lot, cross to the north side of Brandon Mountain Road (VT-73) and find the narrow path and sign for the **Long Trail** northbound. Reach a larger trailhead sign in about 0.1 mi (0.16 km), then turn left (north) through a tangle of raspberry and blackberry bushes and into the woods, where you'll enter the **Joseph Battell Wilderness.**

▶ **MILE 0.1-0.8: Joseph Battell Wilderness to Great Cliff**

The trail quickly steepens, ascending switchbacks and stone

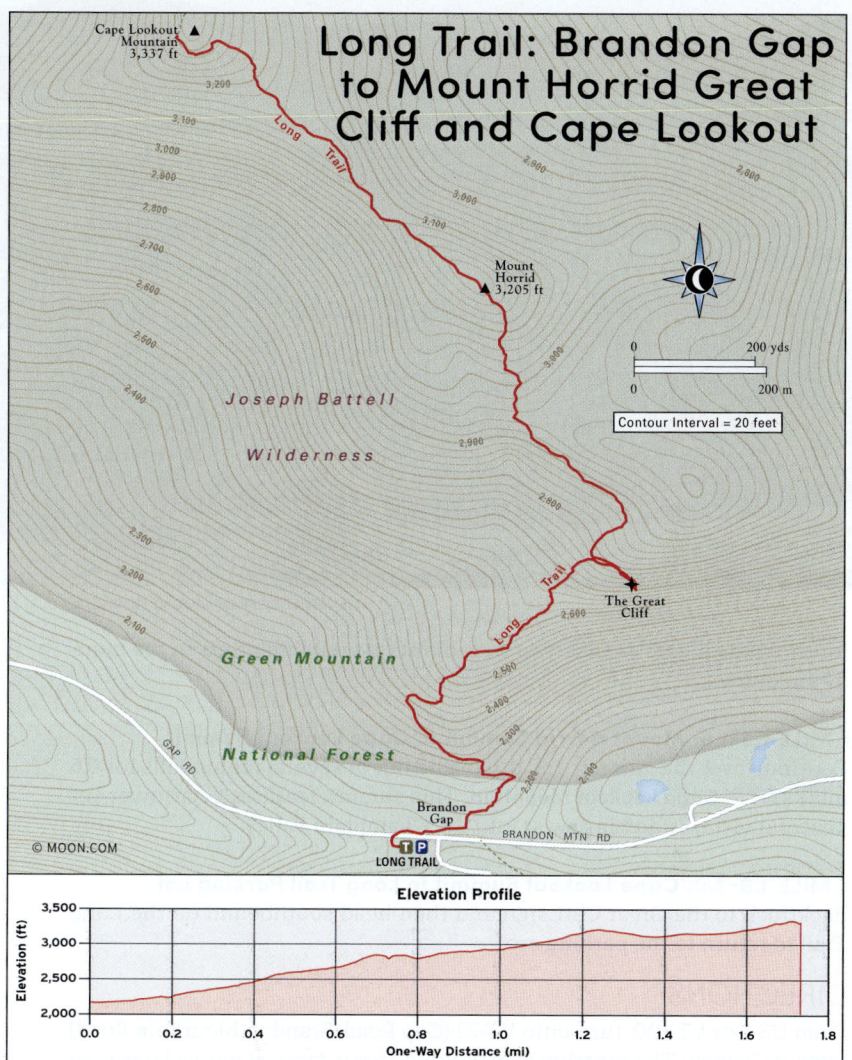

Long Trail: Brandon Gap to Mount Horrid Great Cliff and Cape Lookout

Contour Interval = 20 feet

Elevation Profile

staircases through a birch forest. Reach a sign for the **Great Cliff** at 0.6 mi (1 km) and stay straight (east). The cliff is another 0.1 mi (0.16 km) down the trail. This steep granite face perched above Brandon Gap has great views of the deep valley, stretching east to west. Glimpses of the Champlain Valley peer out from the west, while wildlife can often be spotted in the marsh directly below the cliff. Many hikers, fulfilled by this impressive vista, will turn around here for a total hike of 1.6 mi (2.6 km).

▶ **MILE 0.8-1.3: Great Cliff to Mount Horrid Summit**
For a longer hike, backtrack 0.1 mi (0.16 km) to the sign for the Great Cliff and continue right (north) for 0.4 mi (0.6 km) toward the summit of **Mount Horrid.** The summit is enclosed by trees, so there are not any vistas here, but this lightly traveled section of trail snakes through a dense, shady

forest where hikers are likely to stumble across wildlife prints in the muddy singletrack.

▶ **MILE 1.3–1.9: Mount Horrid Summit to Cape Lookout Summit**
Continue over the summit and dip in and out of several rolling hills for 0.6 mi (1 km) to **Cape Lookout Mountain.** This summit features a narrower yet peaceful vista, stretching west into the Champlain Valley.

▶ **MILE 1.9–3.6: Cape Lookout Summit to Long Trail Parking Lot**
Backtrack to the Great Cliff sign and then head southbound on the Long Trail to return to the parking area.

DIRECTIONS

From US-7 or VT-100, turn onto VT-73 (Gap Road/Brandon Mountain Road) toward Goshen. The Brandon Gap parking area is marked with a large sign on the south side of the road.

GPS COORDINATES: 43°50'22.9"N 72°58'03.3"W

A steep traverse up the west side of Killington, the quiet, water-lined Bucklin Trail has great views from the Green Mountains' second-highest peak.

BEST: Brew hikes
DISTANCE: 7.4 mi (11.9 km) round-trip
DURATION: 4 hr
ELEVATION GAIN: 2,305 ft (703 m)
EFFORT: Strenuous
TRAIL: Dirt/rock singletrack
USERS: Hikers, leashed dogs
SEASON: May–October
FEES/PASSES: None
MAPS: Green Mountain Club, "Killington Area Trail Map"
TRAILHEAD: Brewer's Corner parking area, Wheelerville Rd., Mendon
FACILITIES: None
CONTACT: Coolidge State Forest, 855 Coolidge State Park Rd., Plymouth; 802/672-3612; www.vtstateparks.com/coolidge

START THE HIKE

▸ **MILE 0-0.2: Brewer's Corner Parking Area to Brewer's Brook Bridge**
Starting from the Bucklin trailhead at Brewer's Corner, hike east following the blue blazes on a flat and easygoing trail. Cross over the four-way intersection with the signed Cross Country Ski Trail and continue straight (east) toward the sound of the rushing Brewer's Brook. Reach another trailhead sign at the bridge at 0.2 mi (0.3 km).

▸ **MILE 0.2-3.3: Brewer's Brook Bridge to Long Trail (Appalachian Trail)**
Cross the **bridge** and continue straight (east). The path bends north near the brook at 0.5 mi (0.8 km), then crosses over a series of timber steps and bog bridges lined with lush ferns, grasses, and hobblebush. Follow the trail straight over Brewer's Brook on another large **bridge** at 1.3 mi (2.1 km), and continue over a narrow, rocky doubletrack that climbs above the stream. At 1.9 mi (3.1 km), the trail

◂ BRIDGE OVER BREWER'S BROOK

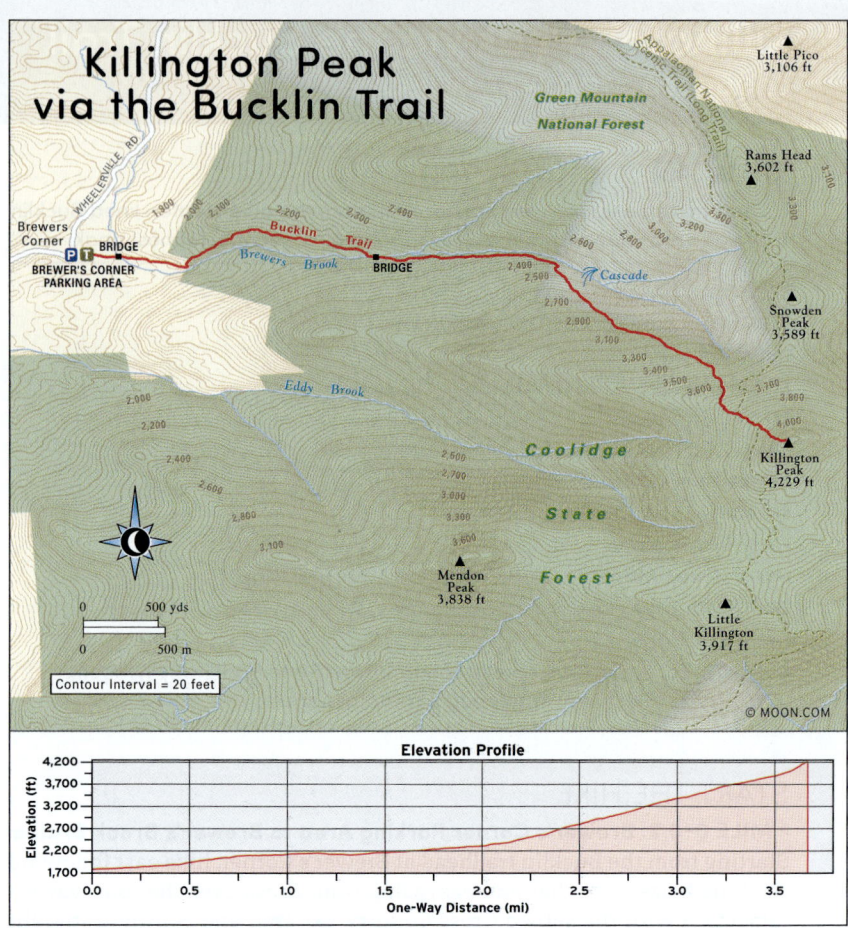

Killington Peak via the Bucklin Trail

Little Pico
3,106 ft

Green Mountain
National Forest

Rams Head
3,602 ft

Brewers
Corner
BRIDGE
BREWER'S CORNER
PARKING AREA

Bucklin   Trail

Brewers   Brook

BRIDGE

Cascade

Snowden
Peak
3,589 ft

Eddy   Brook

Coolidge

State

Forest

Killington
Peak
4,229 ft

Mendon
Peak
3,838 ft

Little
Killington
3,917 ft

0   500 yds

0   500 m

Contour Interval = 20 feet

© MOON.COM

Elevation Profile

Elevation (ft)

One-Way Distance (mi)

overlooks a small **cascade** plunging to meet Brewer's Brook to the left. Shortly after, the trail steepens dramatically, climbing southeast away from the brook for 1.4 mi (2.3 km). Here, it reaches a signed intersection with the **Long Trail (AT).**

▶ **MILE 3.3–3.5: Long Trail (Appalachian Trail) to Killington Spur**
Continue straight (east) at the intersection, on the Long Trail (AT) southbound, following the white blazes. Reach the **Cooper Lodge/tent area** and a sign for the **Killington Spur** trail at 3.5 mi (5.6 km).

▶ **MILE 3.5–3.7: Killington Spur to Killington Summit**
Follow the blue-blazed spur trail straight southeast on a steep, rocky climb toward the summit. Hikers may be required to use their hands on this challenging stretch of rocks, especially if they are slick with rain. Reach the summit, marked with a communication tower, at 3.7 mi (6 km). There are 360-degree views of sprawling mountains from the bald granite rocks atop this second-highest peak in Vermont (4,229 ft/1,289 m). Return to the parking area via the same route.

▲ BUCKLIN TRAIL TO KILLINGTON PEAK

DIRECTIONS

From Rutland, drive east on US-4/Woodstock Avenue. In 5 mi (8 km), turn right onto Wheelerville Road. The trailhead and a large parking area are marked with a sign about 4 mi (6.4 km) down this dirt road.

GPS COORDINATES: 43°37'09.2"N 72°52'36.8"W

BEST NEARBY BREWS

No hiker should travel through Vermont without visiting **Long Trail Brewing Company** (550 US-4, Bridgewater Corners; 802/672-5011; https://longtrail.com; noon-6pm Sun.-Thurs., noon-8pm Fri.-Sat., hours vary seasonally) for a riverfront beer-tasting and seasonal pub grub. It's 21 mi (34 km) from the trailhead.

Experience Vermont's only national park on mountain roads winding through pond, meadow, and forest on the way to Mount Tom's South Peak.

DISTANCE: 3.6 mi (5.8 km) round-trip

DURATION: 1.75 hr

ELEVATION GAIN: 615 ft (187 m)

EFFORT: Moderate

TRAIL: Gravel road, dirt singletrack

USERS: Hikers, leashed dogs, horseback riders

SEASON: May–October

FEES/PASSES: None

MAPS: Town of Woodstock, "Walk Woodstock Map"

TRAILHEAD: Billings Farm and Museum parking lot, Old River Rd., Woodstock

FACILITIES: Restrooms and water available in the Billings Farm and Museum or the Carriage Barn Visitor Center when open

CONTACT: Marsh–Billings–Rockefeller National Historical Park

START THE HIKE

▶ **MILE 0-1.5: Billings Farm and Museum to Four-Way Intersection**

From the **Billings Farm and Museum,** a dairy farm and agricultural history museum (April-November daily 10am-5pm; $16 per person per day), follow the walkway alongside the building, straight west across VT-12 and into the park. Turn left (south) up the hill, passing the **Carriage Barn Visitor Center** on your right.

Continue on, passing beautiful gardens and the mansion on your left. Once you reach the Belvedere (the white building on the left 0.2 mi/0.3 km from the parking area), bear right (northwest) up the hill onto a carriage road lined with huge pine trees. Continue along the road, stay straight past the horse barn on the right, and bend right (north) to keep the trail on your right. Climb the trail as it gradually moves uphill to the left (west). When you reach an intersection (marked by a stone birdbath) at 1.2 mi (1.9 km), continue straight (west)

MEADOW VIEWS ALONG MOUNT TOM ROAD ▶

VERMONT

Northern Green Mountains

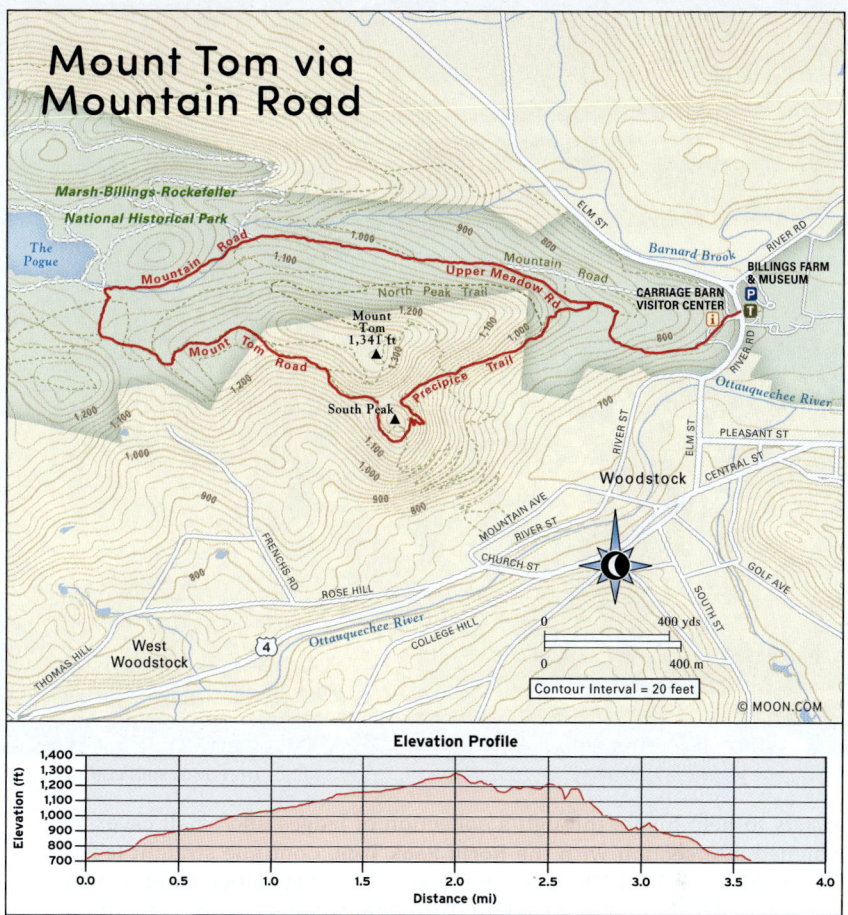

Mount Tom via Mountain Road

Elevation Profile

onto Mountain Road. You'll catch glimpses of a pasture to your right and views of another field on the left where the trail flattens. Come to a signed **four-way intersection** at 1.5 mi (2.4 km). Optional: Continue straight (west) for 200 ft (61 m) to view The Pogue, a beautiful pond lined with wildflowers and featuring reflective mountain views.

▶ **MILE 1.5-2.5: Four-Way Intersection to South Peak**
Turn left (south) on **Mount Tom Road,** following signs for South Peak. The Mount Tom carriage road skirts the edge of a field, then bends east through a forest. Shortly after emerging from the forest, the path slopes downhill under a series of ledges for about 1 mi (1.6 km) in order to reach the **South Peak.** This summit is encircled by a loop trail with multiple vistas. The first vista features a scenic west-facing bench.

▶ **MILE 2.5-3.6: South Peak to Billings Farm and Museum**
Continue around the loop for more views of Woodstock village below, then turn right (east) onto the **Precipice Trail** at 2.6 mi (4.2 km). This adventurous 0.5-mi (0.8-km) descent features steep switchbacks with handrail

assists to help hikers through a collection of ledges and small caves to a signed intersection with the **North Peak Trail.** Continue straight (east) on the Precipice Trail. Then bear left (east) toward **Mountain Road,** which you will reach after 0.1 mi (0.16 km). Turn right (southeast) onto Mountain Road and retrace your steps 0.4 mi (0.6 km) back to the farm and museum.

DIRECTIONS

From US-4/Woodstock center, go east and then turn left onto Elm Street. In 0.3 mi (0.5 km), turn right onto VT-12 N. After 0.2 mi (0.3 km), turn right onto Old River Road, then turn right into the large paved parking area for the Billings Farm and Museum. The entrance to the historical park is across VT-12.

GPS COORDINATES: 43°37'58.3"N 72°31'00.3"W

BEST NEARBY BITES AND BREWS

Downtown areas in the Northern Green Mountains are few and far between, and you can often travel for miles without coming across so much as an old-timey general store. Luckily for hikers, most of our trails are centered on the fun college hub of **Middlebury.** The town's hip downtown area has a wealth of great coffee, craft beer, and local foods, so options for post-hike refreshments are numerous. Here are some of our favorites.

- Sink your teeth into massive and reasonably priced sandwiches on delicious freshly baked breads at **Noonie's Deli** (137 Maple St., Middlebury; 802/388-0014; www.nooniesdeli.com; 10am-2:30pm Mon.-Fri.). Salads, quiches, baked goods, and other specials are available daily.

- The **Mad Taco** (3 Mill St., Middlebury; 802/382-9070; www.themadtaco.com; noon-8pm daily) is a local Vermont chain specializing in slow-roasted carnitas tacos and burly burritos. The Middlebury location has excellent outdoor seating overlooking Otter Creek.

- **Drop-In Brewing Co.** (610 Route 7 South, Middlebury; 802/989-7414; https://dropinbrewing.com; noon-5pm Mon.-Thurs., noon-6pm Fri.-Sat.), a low-key, uncrowded taproom, invites you to "drop in" for a glass or tasting. Visitors are welcome to bring a sandwich or a salad from the Grapevine Grille next door.

- Described as a "return to bread's roots," the wood-fired pizzas at **American Flatbread** (137 Maple St., Middlebury; 802/388-3300; https://americanflatbread.com; 5pm-9pm Wed.-Sat., 11am-3pm Sun.) are crafted with local ingredients and served with creative cocktails or beers and ciders on tap.

- The tandoor oven at **Taste of India** (1 Bakery Ln., Middlebury; 802/388-4856; www.tasteofindiavt.com; 11:30am-2pm and 4:30pm-8:30pm Tues.-Sun.) is the secret behind the flavorful marinated meats and freshly baked Indian breads. The menu includes lunch specials and Sunday brunch.

▼ MIDDLEBURY'S OTTER CREEK

NEARBY CAMPGROUNDS

Dispersed primitive camping and shelters are available within Green Mountain National Forest.

NAME	LOCATION	FACILITIES	SEASON	FEE
Allis State Park	284 Allis State Park Rd., Randolph, 44°03′04.8″N 72°37′38.9″W	18 tent sites, 8 lean-to sites; restrooms	late May–early September	$20–38
802/276-3175; www.vtstateparks.com/allis.html				
Moosalamoo Campground	Forest Road 24, Salisbury, 43°55′09.3″N 73°01′41.7″W	19 RV/tent sites; vault toilets; no water	late May–mid-October	$15
802/767-4261; www.fs.usda.gov				
Branbury State Park	3570 Lake Dunmore Rd., Brandon, 43°54′20.3″N 73°03′58.1″W	36 tent sites, 7 lean-to sites; restrooms	mid-May–mid-October	$20–38
802/247-5925; www.vtstateparks.com/branbury.html				
Silver Lake Campground	Silver Lake Rd., Salisbury, 43°53′52.6″N 73°02′59.2″W	15 tent sites; vault toilets; no water	late May–mid-October	$10
Hike-in access only; 802/767-4261; www.fs.usda.gov				
Chittenden Brook Campground	Forest Road 45, Chittenden, 43°49′32.1″N 72°54′35.2″W	17 RV/tent sites; vault toilets; no water	late May–mid-October	$15
802/767-4261; www.fs.usda.gov				

NEARBY CAMPGROUNDS (continued)

NAME	LOCATION	FACILITIES	SEASON	FEE
Silver Lake State Park	20 State Park Beach Rd., Barnard, 43°43'52.9"N 72°37'00.1"W	39 RV/ tent sites, 7 lean-to sites; restrooms	late May- early September	$20-38
802/234-9451; www.vtstateparks.com/silver.html				
Gifford Woods State Park	34 Gifford Woods Acc., Killington, 43°40'34.5"N 72°48'39.4"W	21 RV/tent sites, 19 lean-to sites, 4 cabins; restrooms	mid-May- mid-October	$20-68
802/775-5354; www.vtstateparks.com/Gifford.html				
Quechee State Park	5800 Woodstock Rd., Hartford, 43°38'13.6"N 72°24'03.1"W	45 RV/tent sites, 7 lean-to sites, 6 cabins; restrooms	mid-May- mid-October	$20-68
802/295-2990; www.vtstateparks.com/quechee.html				
Coolidge State Park	855 Coolidge State Park Rd., Plymouth, 43°33'05.2"N 72°41'48.5"W	26 RV/tent sites, 36 lean-to sites; restrooms	late May- early October	$20-38
802/672-3612; www.vtstateparks.com/Coolidge.html				
Camp Plymouth State Park	2008 Scout Camp Rd., Ludlow, 43°28'34.0"N 72°41'43.2"W	6 lean- to sites, 4 cottages, horse camping area; restrooms	late May- early October	$27-97
802/228-2025; www.vtstateparks.com/Plymouth.html				

SOUTHERN GREEN MOUNTAINS

Nestled among the quaint villages and productive farms of southern Vermont, the lower section of the Green Mountain National Forest sprawls over a terrain of granite peaks, peaceful lakes, and some of the most impressive gushing waterfalls in the state. Just outside the national forest, a number of state, town, and independently run parks protect a diversity of geological features, from historic quarries to explorable, stalactite-decorated caves. Whether you peak-bag on the Long Trail or wander the green shires of the state's southwest corner, southern Vermont's trails never fail to delight.

▲ CAIRNS ON THE TRAIL TO WHITE ROCKS CLIFFS

▲ FARMLAND VIEWS AT MERCK FOREST

VERMONT
Southern Green Mountains

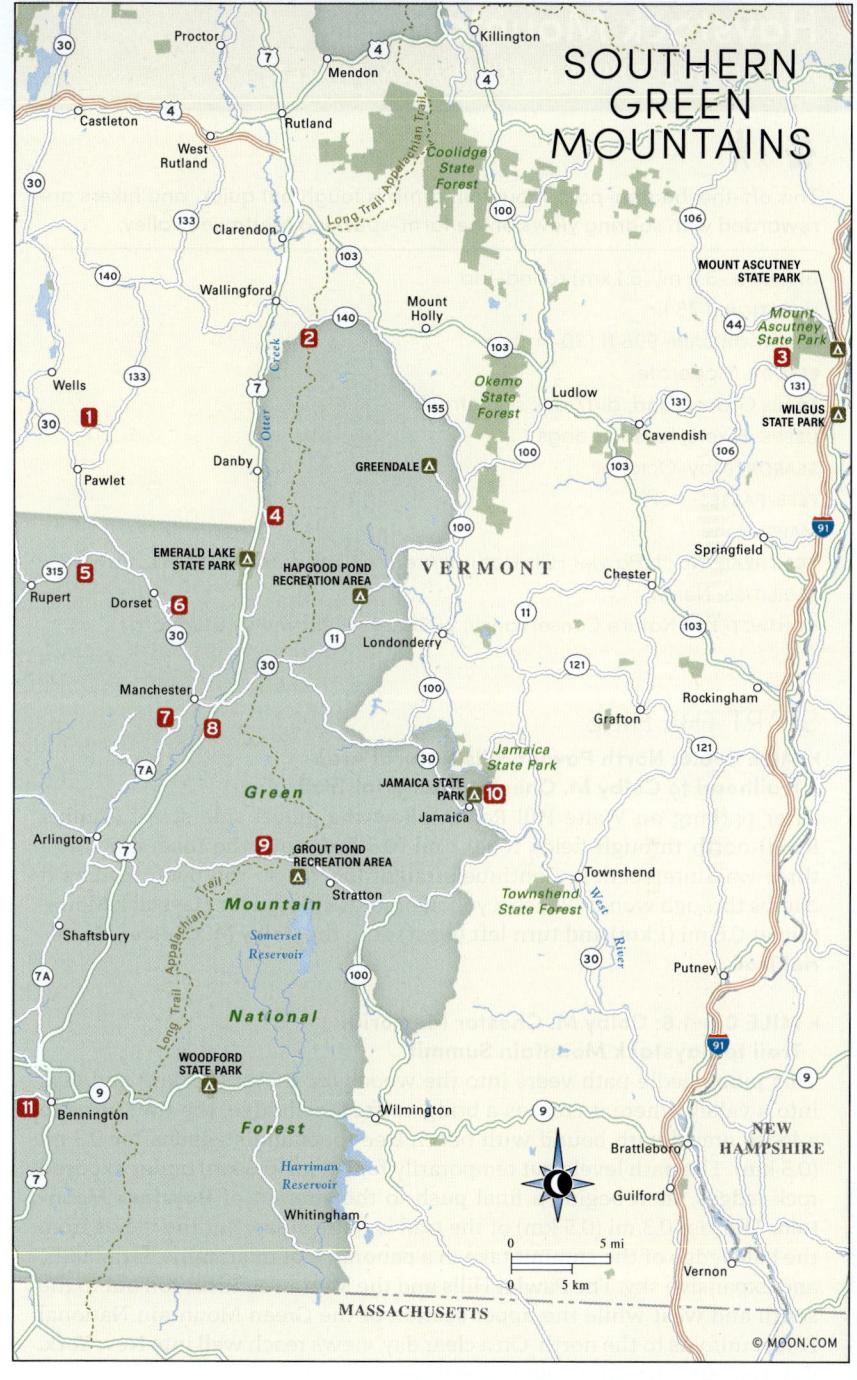

SOUTHERN GREEN MOUNTAINS

Killington

Proctor

30

Mendon

7

4

4

Castleton

West Rutland

4

Rutland

Coolidge State Forest

100

106

30

133

Clarendon

Long Trail-Appalachian Trail

103

MOUNT ASCUTNEY STATE PARK

140

Wallingford

140

Mount Holly

Mount Ascutney State Park

44

Wells

133

103

Okemo State Forest

Ludlow

131

131

WILGUS STATE PARK

1

30

155

Cavendish

106

Pawlet

Danby

7

GREENDALE ⛺

103

91

4

100

315

5

EMERALD LAKE STATE PARK ⛺

VERMONT

Springfield

Rupert

Dorset

6

HAPGOOD POND RECREATION AREA ⛺

Chester

30

11

103

Manchester

30

11

Londonderry

121

7

8

100

Rockingham

7A

30

Grafton

121

Green

Jamaica State Park

JAMAICA STATE PARK ⛺ 10

Arlington

7

9

GROUT POND RECREATION AREA ⛺

Jamaica

Townshend

Shaftsbury

Mountain

Stratton

Townshend State Forest

West River

7A

Somerset Reservoir

National

100

30

Putney

WOODFORD STATE PARK ⛺

91

11

9

Bennington

Wilmington

9

NEW HAMPSHIRE

7

Forest

Harriman Reservoir

Brattleboro

Whitingham

Guilford

0   5 mi

0   5 km

Vernon

MASSACHUSETTS

© MOON.COM

Haystack Mountain

NORTH PAWLET HILLS NATURAL AREA, PAWLET

This off-the-beaten-path mountain climb is tough but quick, and hikers are rewarded with soaring views of the farm-speckled Mettawee Valley.

DISTANCE: 3.2 mi (5.1 km) round-trip
DURATION: 1.75 hr
ELEVATION GAIN: 998 ft (304 m)
EFFORT: Moderate
TRAIL: Gravel road, dirt/rock singletrack
USERS: Hikers, leashed dogs
SEASON: May-October
FEES/PASSES: None
MAPS: None
TRAILHEAD: North Pawlet Hills Natural Area trailhead, Waite Hill Rd., Pawlet
FACILITIES: None
CONTACT: The Nature Conservancy; 802/229-4425; www.nature.org

START THE HIKE

▶ **MILE 0-0.6: North Pawlet Hills Natural Area Trailhead to Colby M. Chester Memorial Trail**

After parking on Waite Hill Road, follow the gravel side street (Tunket Road) north through fields for 0.2 mi (0.3 km) until the road splits at a three-way intersection. Continue straight (north) on the main road as it climbs through woods. Reach a yellow-and-green sign for Haystack Mountain at 0.6 mi (1 km) and turn left (west) onto the **Colby M. Chester Memorial Trail.**

▶ **MILE 0.6-1.6: Colby M. Chester Memorial Trail to Haystack Mountain Summit**

This pine needle path veers into the woods for 0.2 mi (0.3 km) and dips into a valley where it crosses a bridge. After the bridge, the trail turns to a loose gravel path bound with beech tree roots and steepens for 0.3 mi (0.5 km). The path levels out temporarily for 0.2 mi (0.3 km) under exposed rock ledges, then begins a final push to the summit of **Haystack Mountain.** The last 0.3 mi (0.5 km) of the trail is quite steep, but the views from the bald ledge of the summit take in a panorama of mountains, farmlands, and expansive sky. The Pawlet Hills and the Mettawee River roll out to the south and west while the upper section of the Green Mountain National Forest unfolds to the north. On a clear day, views reach well into New York. Carefully use the same route to return.

▲ HAYSTACK MOUNTAIN SUMMIT

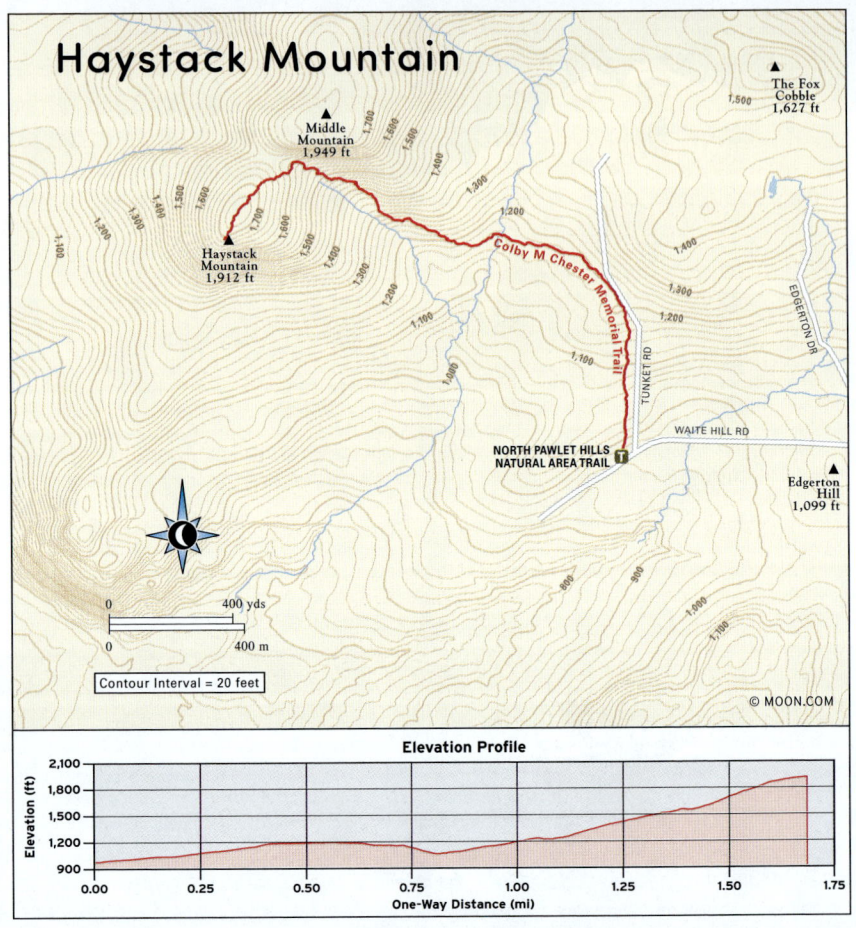

DIRECTIONS

Follow VT-30 north through the center of Pawlet and continue for 1.7 mi (2.7 km). Turn right onto Waite Hill Road and drive east for about 0.4 mi (0.6 km) to the intersection with Tunket Road. A small green-and-yellow sign on the left side designates the start of the trail. Park along the left side of Waite Hill Road.

GPS COORDINATES: 43°22'38.2"N 73°09'53.8"W

2

White Rocks Cliffs

WHITE ROCKS NATIONAL RECREATION AREA, WALLINGFORD

Climb to a sheer face of exposed white quartzite on this beautifully forested section of trail.

BEST: Vistas

DISTANCE: 3.6 mi (5.8 km) round-trip

DURATION: 2.5 hr

ELEVATION GAIN: 1,186 ft (361 m)

EFFORT: Moderate/strenuous

TRAIL: Dirt/rock singletrack

USERS: Hikers, leashed dogs

SEASON: May–October

FEES/PASSES: None

MAPS: Green Mountain National Forest

TRAILHEAD: Keewaydin trailhead, White Rocks Picnic Area, Wallingford

FACILITIES: Vault toilet, picnic tables, trail map

CONTACT: Green Mountain National Forest, Manchester Ranger District; 802/362-2307; www.fs.usda.gov

START THE HIKE

▶ **MILE 0–1.1: Keewaydin Trail to Long Trail (Appalachian Trail)**
Find the **Keewaydin Trail** on the east end of the parking area and hike south for 0.2 mi (0.3 km). Bear right along the stream and climb uphill for 0.3 mi (0.5 km) on a wide dirt path as it travels above a waterfall. The path gets narrow and rocky as it reaches the signed intersection with the **Long Trail (Appalachian Trail).** Bear right (east) to follow the white blazes southbound toward White Rocks Mountain. Continue steadily uphill to another signed junction at 1.1 mi (1.8 km).

▶ **MILE 1.1–1.8: Long Trail (Appalachian Trail) to White Rocks Cliff Trail and Overlook**
Turn right (west) to stay on the Long Trail (AT) southbound for 0.5 mi (0.8 km) as it edges west around the mountain, crossing several bubbling creeks and mossy slabs of rock amid the shade of tall conifers. Wind through a forest of spruce saplings and reach a sign surrounded by white rock cairns. Turn right (west) to follow the blue blazes of **White Rocks Cliff Trail** toward the **White Rocks Cliff overlook.** After a slight downhill through a pine grove, the trail dead-ends at the sheer, white cliff face, 0.2 mi (0.3 km) from the start of the blue blazes. The vista overlooks the white quartzite tumble of an ice bed exposed by glaciers, as wells as the sprawling Taconic and Adirondack Ranges in the distance. Backtrack to the parking area via the same route.

Southern Green Mountains

VERMONT

343

THE QUARTZITE FACE OF THE WHITE ROCKS CLIFFS ▲

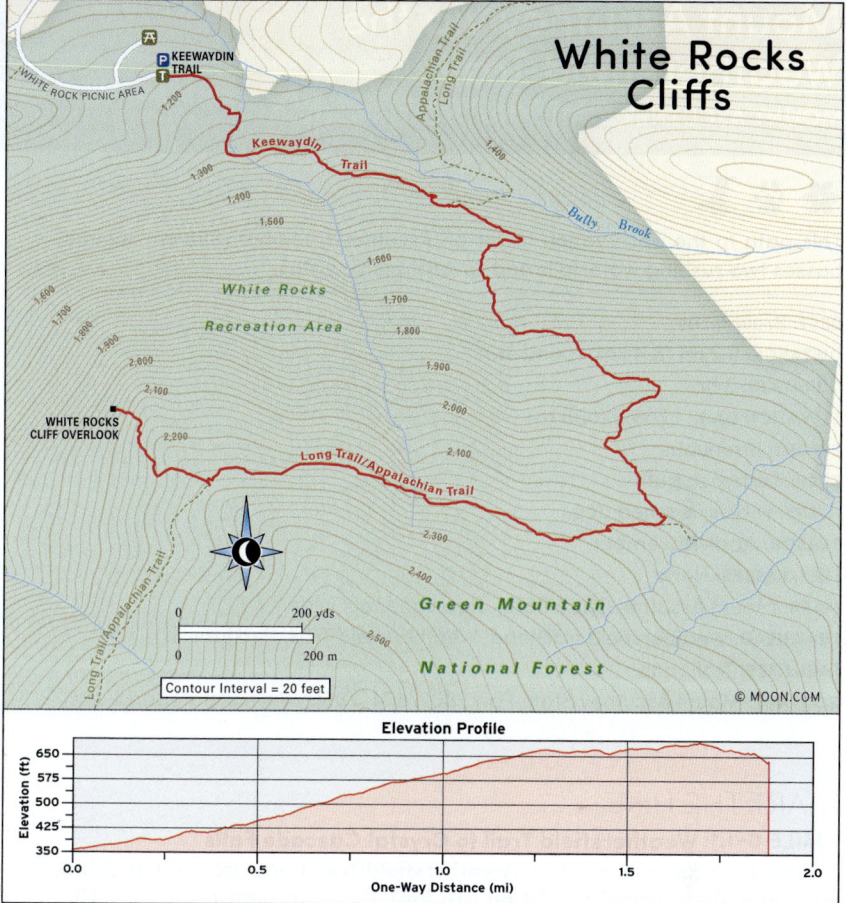

DIRECTIONS

Follow US-7 N to the center of Wallingford and then turn right onto VT-140 E. In 2 mi (3.2 km), bear slightly right onto Russell Road (Sugar Hill Road) and then turn right into the White Rock Picnic Area. There is a large parking lot.

GPS COORDINATES: 43°27'03.4"N 72°56'36.3"W

BEST NEARBY BITES

The Rustic Rooster Restaurant Bar and Grill (5446 Route 103, Cuttingsville; 802/492-3433; www.vtrusticrooster.com; 5pm-9pm Wed.-Fri., noon-9pm Sat., 10am-9pm Sun.) is a local favorite for lunch, dinner, or Sunday brunch. It is 7 mi (11.3 km) from the trailhead.

Southern Green Mountains

VERMONT

3

Mount Ascutney via the Weathersfield Trail

MOUNT ASCUTNEY STATE PARK, WEATHERSFIELD

✹ 🐾 🌊

This path to the observation tower on Ascutney's 3,144-ft (958-m) summit passes two rushing waterfalls and several scenic vistas.

BEST: Brew hikes
DISTANCE: 5.2 mi (8.4 km) round-trip
DURATION: 3 hr
ELEVATION GAIN: 1,766 ft (538 m)
EFFORT: Strenuous
TRAIL: Dirt/rock path
USERS: Hikers, leashed dogs
SEASON: April–November
FEES/PASSES: None
MAPS: Mount Ascutney State Park, "Recreational Guide"
TRAILHEAD: Weathersfield trailhead, Weathersfield Trail, Perkinsville
FACILITIES: Trail map
CONTACT: Mount Ascutney State Park; 802/674-2060; www.vtstateparks.com

START THE HIKE

▶ **MILE 0-1.1: Weathersfield Trail to Crystal Cascade Falls**
Follow the white blazes of the **Weathersfield Trail** north from the parking area on a slight uphill for 0.4 mi (0.6 km). Cross straight (east) over **Little Cascade Falls** and commence climbing the hill. At the top of the hill, at 0.5 mi (0.8 km), hop over the small stream. Pass under a huge ledge and then climb the ladder to a small rocky vista. Edge along the west side of the hill to reach a signed intersection at 1 mi (1.6 km). Continue straight (west) on the Weathersfield Trail toward **Crystal Cascade Falls.** Reach the falls and vista at 1.1 mi (1.8 km).

▶ **MILE 1.1-2.1: Crystal Cascade Falls to Gus's Lookout**
This sliding cascade drops steeply to the left (west), revealing views of Little Ascutney Mountain along the horizon. Use caution at the top of the falls; the rocks can be very

THE LADDER ON WEATHERSFIELD TRAIL ▶

VERMONT

Southern Green Mountains

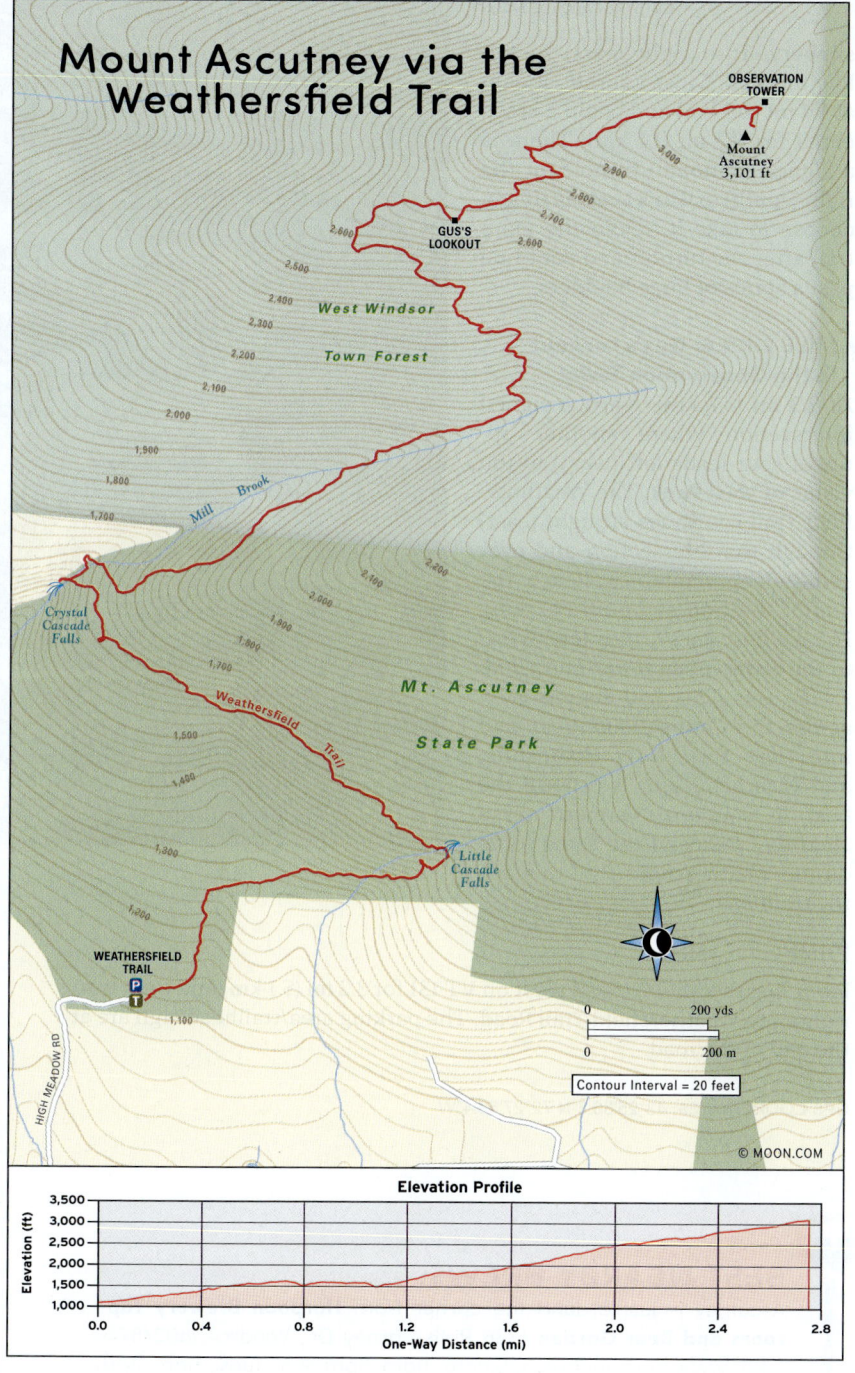

Mount Ascutney via the Weathersfield Trail

OBSERVATION TOWER

Mount Ascutney 3,101 ft

GUS'S LOOKOUT

3,000

2,900

2,800

2,700

2,600

2,800

2,500

West Windsor

2,400

2,300

Town Forest

2,200

2,100

2,000

1,900

1,800

1,700

Mill Brook

2,200

2,100

Crystal Cascade Falls

2,000

1,900

1,800

Weathersfield

1,700

Mt. Ascutney

Trail

State Park

1,500

1,400

Little Cascade Falls

1,300

1,200

WEATHERSFIELD TRAIL

1,100

HIGH MEADOW RD

0   200 yds.

0   200 m

Contour Interval = 20 feet

© MOON.COM

Elevation Profile

Elevation (ft)

3,500
3,000
2,500
2,000
1,500
1,000

0.0   0.4   0.8   1.2   1.6   2.0   2.4   2.8

One-Way Distance (mi)

slippery. Turn right (east) to follow the trail. Cross another stream at 1.4 mi (2.3 km) and begin a steep climb for 0.7 mi (1.1 km). There is a signed (optional) turnoff on the right (south) to **Gus's Lookout.** If you choose to take it, rejoin the main trail after the turnoff and continue past a series of huge boulders.

▶ **MILE 2.1–2.6: Gus's Lookout to the Observation Tower**

At 2.3 mi (3.7 km), reach a signed intersection where another optional spur leads left (west) to the vistas of **West Peak.** The Weathersfield Trail continues straight (east) through the intersection and over some steep scrambles. Reach the end of the trail at 2.6 mi (4.2 km). For the best views, turn left (west) to the **observation tower** and climb to the top. This 360-degree view across the Connecticut River and into New York, New Hampshire, and Massachusetts is among the best in southern Vermont on a clear day. Descend the same route on the Weathersfield Trail to reach the trailhead.

DIRECTIONS

From Weathersfield, travel west on VT-131 for 3.2 mi (5.1 km) and then turn right onto Weathersfield Trail Road. The parking area/trailhead sign are at the end of the road.

GPS COORDINATES: 43°25'36.7"N 72°27'59.4"W

BEST NEARBY BREWS

Ascutney is just around the corner from **Harpoon Brewery Taproom and Beer Garden** (336 Ruth Carney Dr., Windsor; 802/674-5491; www.harpoonbrewery.com; 11am–6pm Sun.-Tues., 11am–8pm Wed.-Sat.). Take a tour and then enjoy a fresh draft and some root beer barbecue wings in the taproom. The taproom is 13 mi (21 km) from the trailhead.

The wet and wild Big Branch Wilderness is the star of this loop that features a mountain peak, a lake, and a cascading river.

DISTANCE: 8.4 mi (13.5 km) round-trip
DURATION: 4.5 hr
ELEVATION GAIN: 2,045 ft (623 m)
EFFORT: Strenuous
TRAIL: Dirt/rock singletrack
USERS: Hikers, leashed dogs
SEASON: May-October
FEES/PASSES: None
MAPS: Green Mountain National Forest
TRAILHEAD: Lake Trail trailhead, South End Rd., Mount Tabor
FACILITIES: Trail map
CONTACT: Green Mountain National Forest, Manchester Ranger District; 802/362-2307; www.fs.usda.gov

START THE HIKE

▶ **MILE 0-0.9: Lake Trail Trailhead to Big Branch Wilderness**
Hike straight south from the trailhead and climb gently uphill on the pine needle-covered **Lake Trail.** The trail winds over a gorge with a stream running through it and crosses the water on stepping-stones at 0.3 mi (0.5 km); the water may be several inches high after rains. At approximately 0.9 mi (1.4 km), you will enter the **Big Branch Wilderness** at a sign, and the trail begins to switchback up a steep hillside bound by tall pines and mossy ledges.

▶ **MILE 0.9-3.0: Big Branch Wilderness to Baker Peak**
Cross a bridge under a rocky ledge at 1.5 mi (2.4 km), and follow the trail right (east) past a series of **waterfalls.** There is another **stream crossing** at 1.9 mi (3.1 km). Cross straight (east) over the stream and reach a signed intersection. Turn left (north) and follow the blue blazes toward Baker Peak. The narrow trail cuts across a white birch hill and reaches the signed intersection with the **Long Trail**

◀ VIEWS FROM THE SUMMIT OF BAKER PEAK

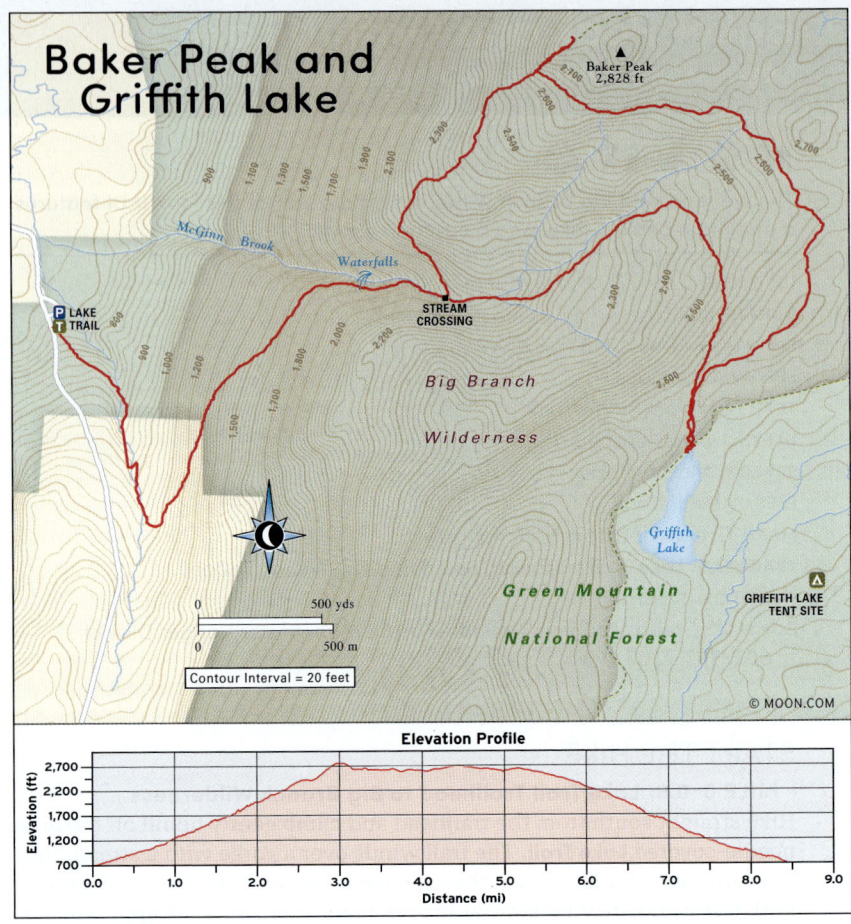

Baker Peak and Griffith Lake

Baker Peak
2,828 ft

McGinn Brook

Waterfalls

STREAM
CROSSING

P LAKE
T TRAIL

Big Branch

Wilderness

Griffith
Lake

Green Mountain

GRIFFITH LAKE
TENT SITE

National Forest

0   500 yds

0   500 m

Contour Interval = 20 feet

© MOON.COM

Elevation Profile

Elevation (ft)

2,700
2,200
1,700
1,200
700

0.0   1.0   2.0   3.0   4.0   5.0   6.0   7.0   8.0   9.0

Distance (mi)

(Appalachian Trail) at 2.8 mi (4.5 km). To view the summit of **Baker Peak,** turn left (north) and follow the white blazes up to a ridge of bare granite. The best views are at about 3 mi (4.8 km).

▶ MILE 3.0–5.0: **Baker Peak to Griffith Lake**

Before the trail enters the woods, turn around and backtrack 0.2 mi (0.3 km) to the signed intersection with the Long Trail. Turn left (east) onto the **Long Trail,** following signs southbound toward **Griffith Lake.** The white-blazed trail descends through a lush forest, arriving at the signed intersection with the **Lake Trail** at 4.8 mi (7.7 km). Turn left (south) to see the lake, which you will reach at 5 mi (8 km).

▶ MILE 5.0–8.4: **Griffith Lake to Lake Trail Trailhead**

After enjoying the secluded mountain lake—a great spot to see wildlife—backtrack 0.2 mi (0.3 km) to the intersection with the Lake Trail and bear left (northeast) onto the Lake Trail. This narrow, sometimes muddy path crosses several bubbling streams and arrives at the intersection with the trail to Baker Peak at 6.5 mi (10.5 km). Cross the stream and continue

▲ GRIFFITH LAKE

straight (west) down the Lake Trail, which will return to the parking lot in 1.9 mi (3.1 km).

DIRECTIONS

From US-7, turn east onto South End Road (Forest Road 259). The trailhead and parking lot are about 0.5 mi (0.8 km) down the road on the left, marked with a Forest Service sign.

GPS COORDINATES: 43°18'45.5"N 72°59'12.9"W

BEST NEARBY BITES

Mach's Market (18 School St., Pawlet; 802/325-3405; https://machsmarket.com; 6am-8pm daily) in downtown Pawlet carries everything from gourmet gifts to grocery staples. They also cook up specialty wood-fired pizzas and deli sandwiches featuring Vermont cheeses and their own sourdough. It's 3 mi (5 km) from the trailhead.

Southern Green Mountains

VERMONT

Antone Mountain via Old Town Road

MERCK FOREST AND FARMLAND CENTER, RUPERT

Pick raspberries as you walk through a pastoral working farm and catch views from its highest peak.

DISTANCE: 5.2 mi (8.4 km) round-trip
DURATION: 2.75 hr
ELEVATION GAIN: 828 ft (252 m)
EFFORT: Moderate
TRAIL: Gravel/grass doubletrack
USERS: Hikers, leashed dogs, horseback riders, cross-country skiers
SEASON: Year-round
FEES/PASSES: None
MAPS: Merck Forest and Farmland Center
TRAILHEAD: Merck Forest and Farmland Center, VT-315, Rupert
FACILITIES: Vault toilet
CONTACT: Merck Forest and Farmland Center; 802/394-7836; www.merckforest.org

START THE HIKE

▶ **MILE 0-0.3: Merck Forest and Farmland Center to Old Town Road Vista**

From the Merck Forest and Farmland Center, head southeast on **Old Town Road,** a wide gravel path that travels through the main section of **farm.** At 0.3 mi (0.5 km), bear right (southwest) to stay on Old Town Road. This vista, sometimes bustling with livestock, looks out over the farm to the **Rupert Valley** in the west.

▶ **MILE 0.3-1.5: Old Town Road Vista to Clark's Clearing Cabin**

Heading southwest from the farm, the road enters a mixed hardwood forest and steadily ascends for 0.6 mi (1 km). Reach a signed intersection and continue straight (south) on **Antone Road** toward **Antone Mountain.** The grassy doubletrack works its way along a ridgeline for 0.6 mi (1 km) and into a field where hikers can pick raspberries in the late summer/early fall. At the **Clark's Clearing Cabin,** follow the sign straight (south) to stay on Antone Road.

▶ **MILE 1.5-2.4: Clark's Clearing Cabin to End of Antone Road**

The path narrows and climbs steeply for 0.5 mi (0.8 km). Here, it dips into a flat saddle and reaches another signed intersection. Go straight (west) past the Lookout Trail junction and follow Antone Road to its end at 2.4 mi (3.9 km).

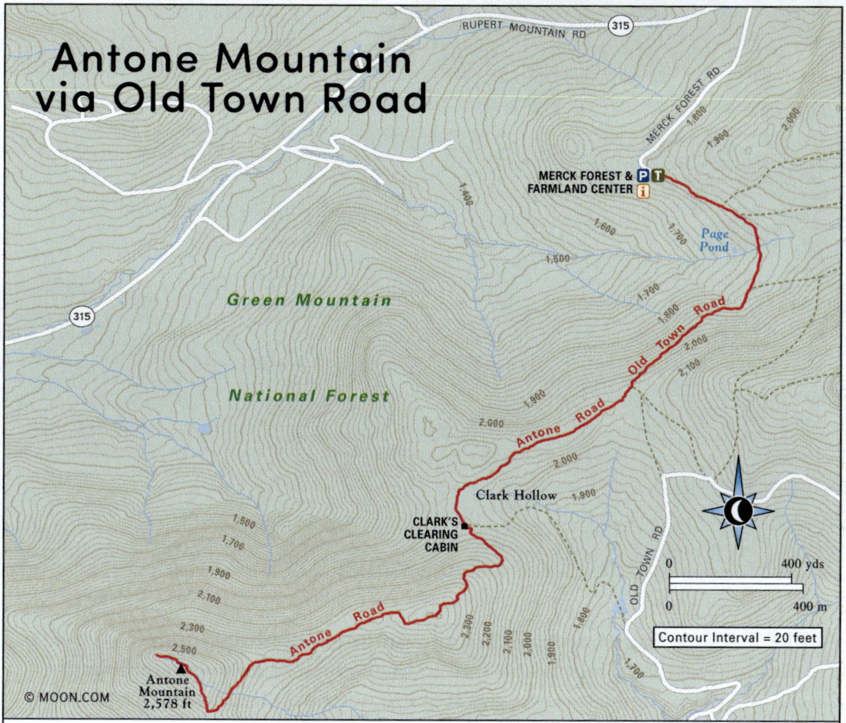

Antone Mountain
via Old Town Road

RUPERT MOUNTAIN RD   315

MERCK FOREST & FARMLAND CENTER   P T i

Page Pond

MERCK FOREST RD

Old Town Road

Green Mountain

315

National Forest

Antone Road

Clark Hollow

OLD TOWN RD

CLARK'S CLEARING CABIN

Antone Road

0   400 yds
0   400 m

Contour Interval = 20 feet

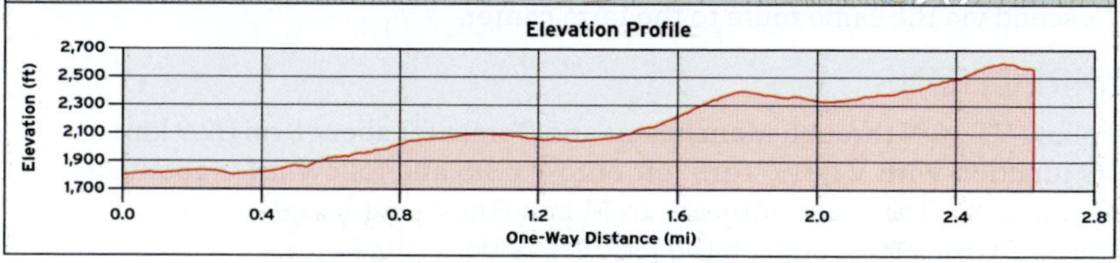

Antone Mountain 2,578 ft

© MOON.COM

Elevation Profile

Elevation (ft)		
2,700		
2,500		
2,300		
2,100		
1,900		
1,700		

0.0   0.4   0.8   1.2   1.6   2.0   2.4   2.8

One-Way Distance (mi)

◀ LAMB AT MERCK FOREST AND FARMLAND CENTER

ANTONE MOUNTAIN ▲

▶ **MILE 2.4–2.6: End of Antone Road to Antone Mountain Summit**
Turn right (west) and follow the trail to the **summit of Antone Mountain** at
2.6 mi (4.2 km). The best views are looking northeast back over the farm.
Descend via the same route to the farm center.

DIRECTIONS

Follow VT-30 N through Manchester and Dorset for about 8 mi (12.9 km) to
its junction with VT-315. Turn left onto VT-315 and follow it for about 2.6
mi (4.2 km). The main entrance to Merck Forest and Farmland Center is
marked with a large sign on the left-hand side.

GPS COORDINATES: 43°16'51.8"N 73°10'08.5"W

BEST NEARBY BITES

Dorset Bakery (3239 Route 30, Dorset; 802/867-7021; www.
dorsetbakeryvt.com; 7:30am–3pm daily), a cozy eatery with outdoor
seating, offers sandwiches, soups, and salads, plus amazing coffee
drinks and baked goods. It's 5 mi (8 km) from the trailhead.

6

Gettysburg Quarry and Gilbert Lookout

OWLS HEAD TOWN FOREST, DORSET

Visit the quarry that supplied headstones for casualties of the Battle of Gettysburg and continue to a peaceful vista of the Taconic Range.

DISTANCE: 3.4 mi (5.5 km) round-trip

DURATION: 1.5 hr

ELEVATION GAIN: 936 ft (285 m)

EFFORT: Moderate/strenuous

TRAIL: Gravel path, dirt/rock singletrack

USERS: Hikers, leashed dogs

SEASON: April–October

FEES/PASSES: None

MAPS: Owls Head Town Forest

TRAILHEAD: Blue Trail trailhead, Ken's Camp Rd., Dorset

FACILITIES: Trail map

CONTACT: Town of Dorset; 802/362-4571; http://dorsetvt.org

START THE HIKE

▶ **MILE 0-0.4: Blue Trail to Gettysburg Quarry**

Follow the blue blazes of the **Blue Trail** north for 0.4 mi (0.6 km) from the parking lot to Gettysburg Quarry. The wide dirt path, lined with a variety of wildflowers, carries straight uphill past an old root cellar and the turnoff for Klondike Quarry. Reach **Gettysburg Quarry,** an enormous former marble quarry, at 0.4 mi (0.6 km). The croak of frogs and sound of water droplets echo in the pools that have formed under the excavated sections of these rock cliffs. To the left (west) hikers can take in views of the Dorset hills and quarries from the knoll of the Art's Bench overlook.

▶ **MILE 0.4-1.7: Gettysburg Quarry to Gilbert Lookout**

When you're done here, follow the trail to the right (south) where it continues toward **Owls Head** and the Gilbert Lookout. Walk along the staircases to a small vista of the quarries at 1.1 mi (1.8 km). From

◀ GETTYSBURG QUARRY

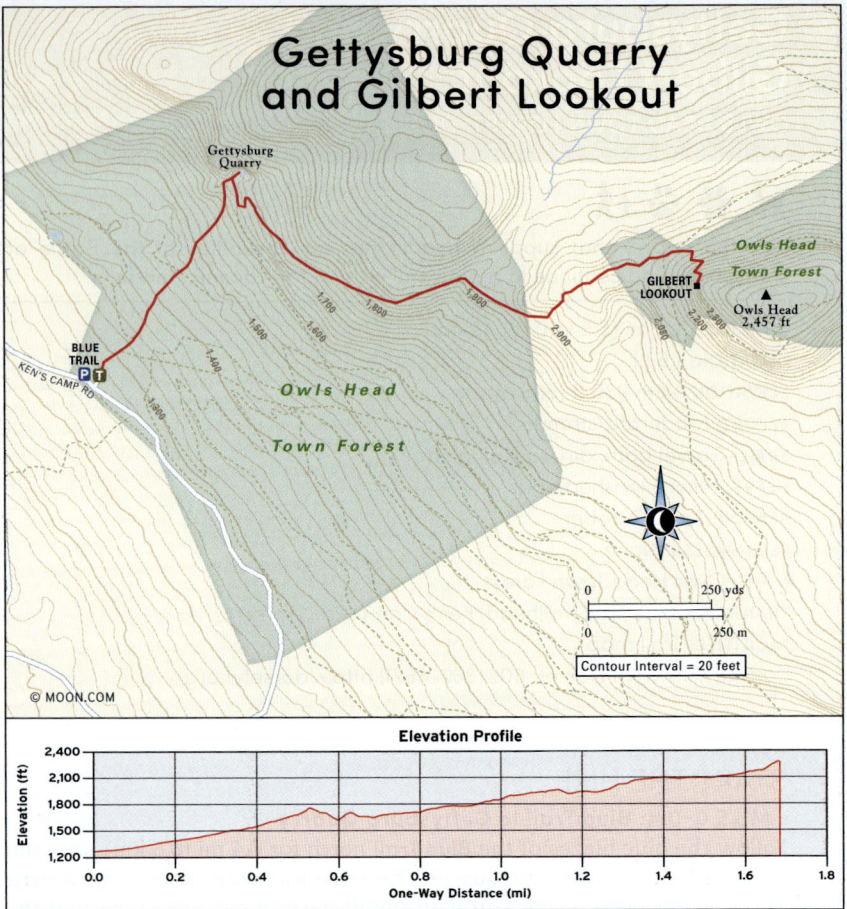

Gettysburg Quarry and Gilbert Lookout

Elevation Profile

here, continue along the trail for 0.3 mi (0.5 km) to the shoulder of Owls Head. Flagging and signs mark the trail as it climbs 0.3 mi (0.5 km) of switchbacks up a steep, ledgy hill to the **Gilbert Lookout.** This rocky, blueberry-lined perch boasts great views west across the Taconic Range; the hill drops steeply into the green valley below. Follow the same route back to the parking lot. Cool off with a dip in **Norcross-West (Dorset) Quarry** at the end of Black Rock Lane.

DIRECTIONS

Take VT-30 to just south of Dorset center and then turn onto Black Rock Lane. At the fork, bear right to stay on Black Rock Lane and then turn right onto Ken Camp Road. The trailhead is marked with a sign at the end of Ken Camp Road.

GPS COORDINATES: 43°14'44.8"N 73°04'50.7"W

While you can drive to the top of this tallest Taconic peak, hiking to its 360-degree views on the long, steep summit trail is much more rewarding.

DISTANCE: 5.4 mi (8.7 km) round-trip

DURATION: 3.25 hr

ELEVATION GAIN: 2,772 ft (845 m)

EFFORT: Strenuous

TRAIL: Gravel road, dirt/rock singletrack

USERS: Hikers, leashed dogs

SEASON: May–October

FEES/PASSES: None

MAPS: Equinox Preservation Trust, "Trail Map and Guide"

TRAILHEAD: Trailhead gate, W. Union St., Manchester

FACILITIES: None

CONTACT: Equinox Preservation Trust; 802/366-1400; www.equinoxpreservationtrust.org

START THE HIKE

▸ **MILE 0-1.6: Trailhead Gate to Blue Trail (and Bench)**
Hike north through the gate and past the trailhead sign on the main dirt road surrounded by oaks. At the signed intersection at 0.4 mi (0.6 km), bear right (west) for the blue summit trail. Follow the blue blazes west along the road, which inclines to another signed intersection at 0.7 mi (1.1 km). Keep straight (west) to stay on the blue trail. The trail climbs through a quiet wood. Reach a bench with a sign at 1.6 mi (2.6 km).

▸ **MILE 1.6-2.7: Blue Trail (and Bench) to Visitor Center**
Turn right (west) at the bench to follow the blue trail uphill on a steep and rocky trajectory with intermittent mountain views. Reach an intersection at 2.5 mi (4 km) and go straight (west) at the intersection, following signs for the summit/visitor center. The trail curls north around a communications tower, then turns left (south) to reach the summit and visitor center at 2.7 mi (4.3 km).

▸ **MILE 2.7-5.4: Visitor Center to Lookout Rock and Trailhead Gate**
The **visitor center's lookouts** and marble benches allow hikers to survey views of the Taconic Range and beyond. Inside the visitor center are restrooms and information. Backtrack 2.7 mi (4.3 km) to the start on the blue-blazed trail, or (optional) follow the **Lookout Rock Spur** trail straight north from the visitor center for 0.5 mi (0.8 km) to **Lookout Rock** for a vista of Manchester below.

Southern Green Mountains

VERMONT

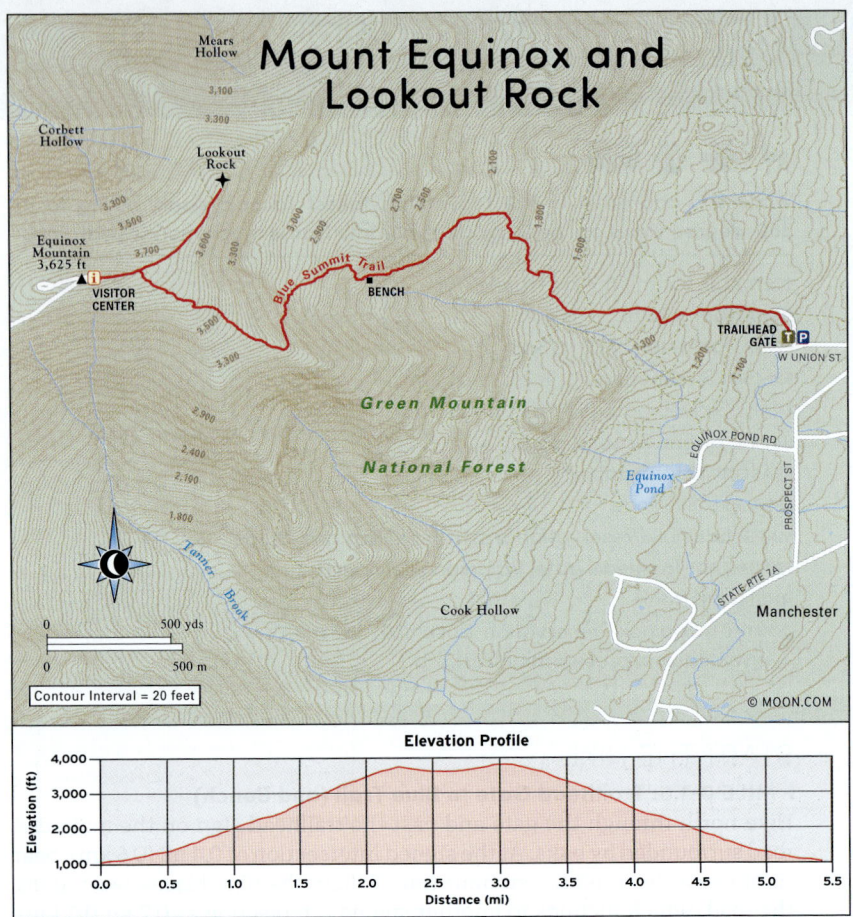

DIRECTIONS

From Main Street in Manchester, go south on VT-7A for about 1.5 mi (2.4 km), then turn right onto Seminary Avenue. Continue onto Prospect Street, then turn right onto West Union Street. The large parking area is marked with a sign on the right side of the road.

GPS COORDINATES: 43°09'48.3"N 73°04'57.7"W

BEST NEARBY BITES

Manchester is full of swanky restaurants, but for an affordable yet totally tasty option, try **Thai Basil** (4950 Main St., Manchester; 802/768-8433; https://thaibasilvt.com; 11:30am-3pm and 5pm-9pm Mon., Tues., Thurs., and Sun., 11:30am-3pm Wed., 11:30am-3pm and 5pm-10pm Fri.-Sat.), renowned for its noodle entrées. It is 2 mi (3.2 km) from the trailhead.

▲ BIRCHES ALONG THE BLUE SUMMIT TRAIL

This out-and-back hike to a stunning 160-ft (49-m) falls follows a relatively easy route over old logging roads.

BEST: Spring hikes

DISTANCE: 4.4 mi (7.1 km) round-trip

DURATION: 2.25 hr

ELEVATION GAIN: 936 ft (285 m)

EFFORT: Moderate

TRAIL: Dirt singletrack

USERS: Hikers, leashed dogs

SEASON: Year-round

FEES/PASSES: None

MAPS: Green Mountain National Forest

TRAILHEAD: Lye Brook Falls trailhead, Glen Rd., Manchester

FACILITIES: None

CONTACT: Green Mountain National Forest, Manchester Ranger District; 802/362-2307; www.fs.usda.gov

START THE HIKE

▶ **MILE 0-0.4: Lye Brook Falls Trail to Lye Brook Wilderness**
Head east on the **Lye Brook Falls Trail,** following the blue blazes for 0.4 mi (0.6 km). The trail wraps south toward the brook on a nice, flat track to a sign marking the entrance to the **Lye Brook Wilderness.** Hop over two narrow streams that flow across the trail and head downhill into the Lye Brook Wilderness.

▶ **MILE 0.4-1.8: Lye Brook Wilderness to Trail Fork**
The trail begins a mild elevation gain 0.6 mi (1 km) from the Lye Brook Wilderness sign. As you make your way up the loose, gravelly trail, listen for the ethereal call of wood thrushes in the canopy of tall, thin hemlocks. Reach a signed fork at approximately 1.8 mi (2.9 km) and bear right (west) toward the falls.

▶ **MILE 1.8-2.2: Trail Fork to Lye Brook Falls**
This section of trail is narrow as it snakes along the edge of a densely vegetated hillside and across a slide of large rocks. The path ends at a rocky cliff near the falls at 2.2 mi (3.5 km). The best views of **Lye Brook Falls** are to the left (east), slightly uphill. You can also view the lower falls from the brook downhill to the right (west). Backtrack along the same route to return to the parking lot.

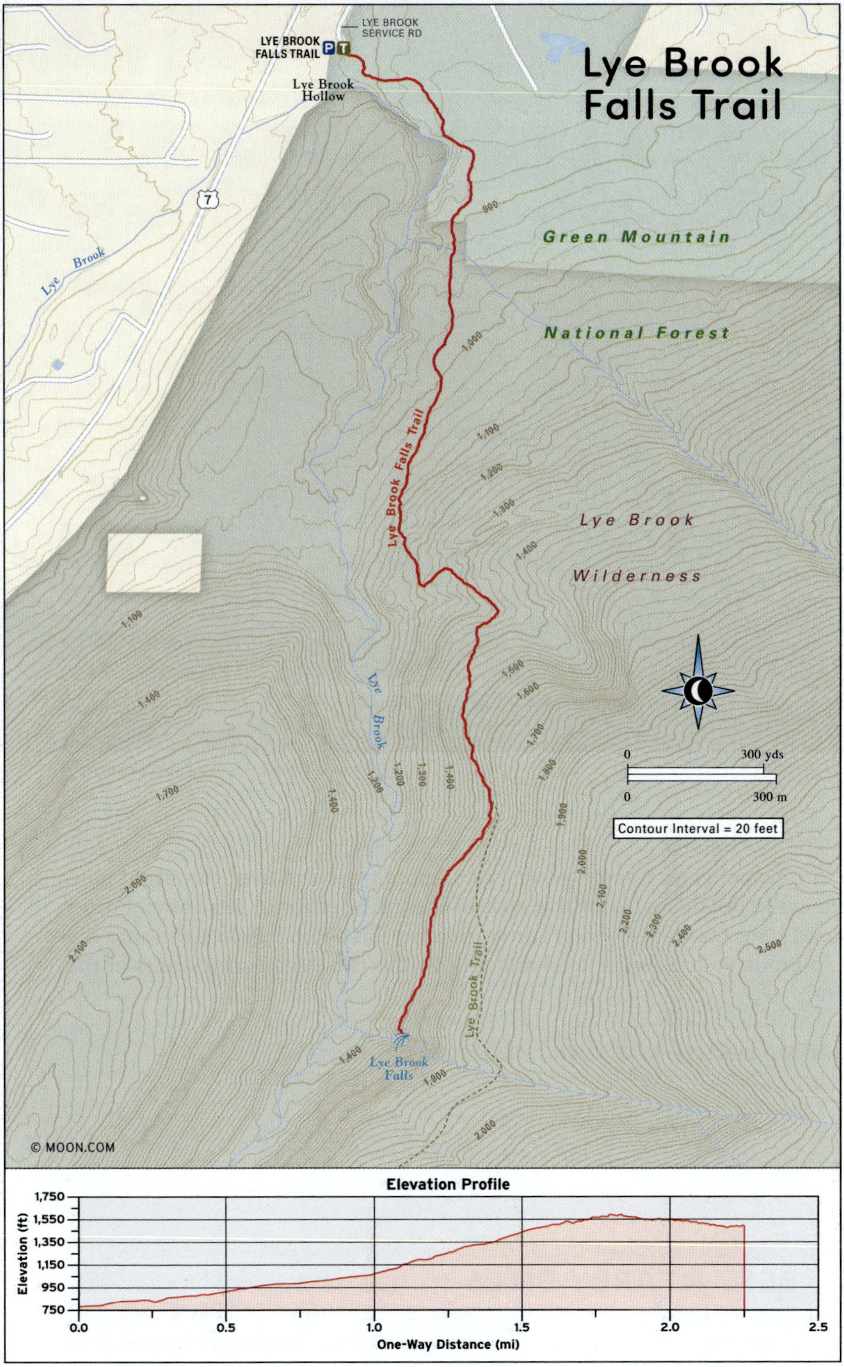

Lye Brook
Falls Trail

LYE BROOK
SERVICE RD

LYE BROOK
FALLS TRAIL

Lye Brook
Hollow

Green Mountain

National Forest

900

7

Lye Brook

1,000

1,100

Lye Brook Falls Trail

1,200

1,300

Lye Brook

Wilderness

1,400

1,100

1,400

Lye Brook

1,500

1,700

1,200

1,600

1,400

1,700

2,000

1,300

1,400

1,800

1,900

2,100

Lye Brook Trail

2,000

2,200

2,300

2,400

2,500

0   300 yds

0   300 m

Contour Interval = 20 feet

1,400

Lye Brook
Falls

1,800

2,000

© MOON.COM

Elevation Profile

1,750					
1,550					
1,350					
1,150					
950					
750					

Elevation (ft)

0.0   0.5   1.0   1.5   2.0   2.5

One-Way Distance (mi)

LYE BROOK FALLS ▲

DIRECTIONS

From Manchester Center, go east on Depot Street and then turn right onto Richville Road. Just past the post office, turn left onto East Manchester Road. Cross under US-7 and turn right onto Glen Road. Bear right onto the Lye Brook Falls Service Road and follow it to the large parking area at the end.

GPS COORDINATES: 43°09'32.9"N 73°02'29.4"W

BEST NEARBY BITES

Choose between the two outposts of local favorite **Zoey's** (www. zoeys.com): Enjoy a lunch or dinner of creative American entrées at **Zoey's Double Hex Restaurant** (1568 Depot St., Manchester; 802/362-4600; 11am-9pm Wed.-Sun.), or grab a quick bite at its sister sandwich shop, **Zoey's Deli** (539 Depot St., Manchester; 802/362-0006; 8:30am-3pm Wed.-Mon.).

This peaceful pond at the base of Stratton Mountain is the largest body of water along the Long Trail.

BEST: Winter hikes
DISTANCE: 7.4 mi (11.9 km) round-trip
DURATION: 3.75 hr
ELEVATION GAIN: 677 ft (206 m)
EFFORT: Easy/moderate
TRAIL: Dirt singletrack
USERS: Hikers, leashed dogs
SEASON: April-October
FEES/PASSES: None
MAPS: Green Mountain National Forest
TRAILHEAD: Stratton Pond Trail parking, Stratton Arlington Rd., Peru
FACILITIES: None
CONTACT: Green Mountain National Forest, Manchester Ranger District; 802-362-2307; www.fs.usda.gov

START THE HIKE

▶ **MILE 0-3.5: Stratton Pond Trail to Long Trail (Appalachian Trail)**
The **Stratton Pond Trail** starts from the sign on the road in front of the parking area. Follow the blue blazes northeast for 2 mi (3.2 km) on the thin, muddy path as it carries through a dense mixed forest. A series of bog bridges add bounce to the path while protecting the trail from erosion. The trail crosses straight (east) over the Catamount XC Ski Trail, following the blue blazes. The scenery is dotted with paper birch, a dense fern ground cover, and large, moss-coated boulders. Reach another signed intersection at 3.5 mi (5.6 km) and turn left (north), following signs for Stratton Pond. Almost immediately after the signed intersection, the trail meets the **Long Trail (Appalachian Trail).**

▶ **MILE 3.5-3.7: Long Trail (Appalachian Trail) to Stratton Pond**
Turn left (west) onto the Long Trail and follow the white blazes. The

◀ STRATTON POND

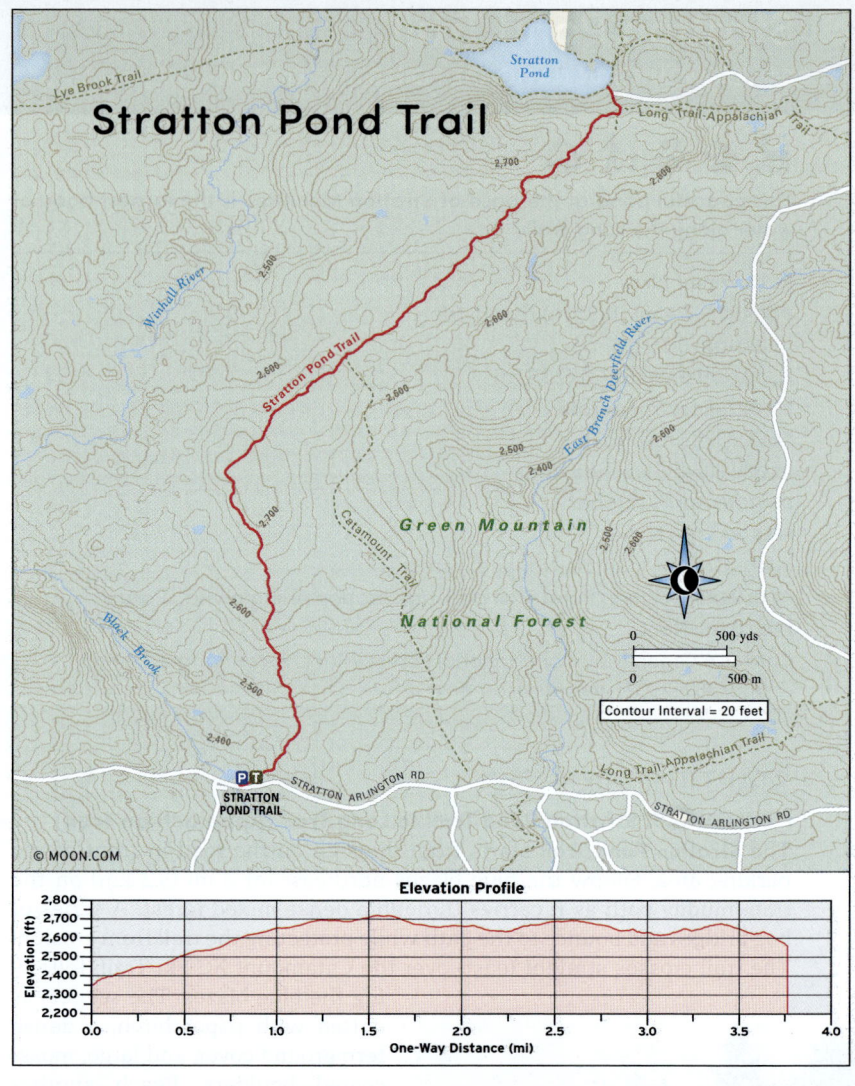

Stratton Pond Trail

Elevation Profile

trail meets **Stratton Pond** at 3.7 mi (6 km). This expansive body of water is hemmed in by large trees and a ring of trails along the banks. You can explore the banks via the Long Trail northbound or the Lye Brook Trail to the west. Both include lovely water views and plenty of chances to glimpse wildlife, especially on a quiet morning or evening. Stay on designated trails; this heavily trafficked trail is at high risk for erosion. Return on the Stratton Pond Trail via the same route.

▲ BOG BRIDGE ON THE STRATTON POND TRAIL

DIRECTIONS

From VT-100, turn west onto Stratton Arlington Road toward Stratton Village. Continue for 7.7 mi (12.4 km) to the Stratton Pond Trailhead sign on the right. Just after the sign is a dirt parking area.

GPS COORDINATES: 43°03'41.7"N 72°59'12.8"W

BEST NEARBY BREWS

Head south to Dover and relax with pub fare creations, beer, live music, and arcade games at **The Last Chair Bar & Grill** (267 Route 100, Dover; 802/464-1143; www.lastchairvt.com; 1pm-9:30pm Tues.-Sat., 4pm-8pm Sun.). It's 13 mi (21 km) from the trailhead.

Hamilton Falls via the West River Trail

JAMAICA STATE PARK, JAMAICA

Hamilton Falls is one of the most dramatic falls in Vermont, accessed via a scenic route along the West River.

BEST: Spring hikes, waterfalls

DISTANCE: 4.3 mi (6.9 km) round-trip

DURATION: 2.5 hr

ELEVATION GAIN: 948 ft (289 m)

EFFORT: Easy/moderate

TRAIL: Gravel multiuse path, dirt singletrack

USERS: Hikers, cyclists, leashed dogs

SEASON: May–October

FEES/PASSES: None

MAPS: Jamaica State Park, "Recreational Trails Guide"

TRAILHEAD: West River trailhead at Ball Mountain Dam, Ball Mountain Ln., Jamaica

FACILITIES: None

CONTACT: U.S. Army Corps of Engineers, New England District; 978/318-8238; www.nae.usace.army.mil and Jamaica State Park; 802/874-4600; www.vtstateparks.com

START THE HIKE

▶ **MILE 0-0.4: West River Trailhead to Ball Mountain Dam**

Follow the paved West River Trail downhill (northeast) from the parking lot. At 0.2 mi (0.3 km), the trail turns to gravel as you pass under the access road to reach the **Ball Mountain Dam.** Turn left (north) to climb to the top of the dam. Looking west toward Ball Mountain Lake, you'll catch fantastic views of Stratton Mountain. Reach the top of the dam in 0.2 mi (0.3 km).

▶ **MILE 0.4-1.2: Ball Mountain Dam to Switch Road Trail**

At the top of the dam, turn right (east) and follow a series of steep switchbacks down to the base. In

SIGNS ALONG THE HAMILTON FALLS TRAIL WARN AGAINST SWIMMING. ▶

VERMONT

Southern Green Mountains

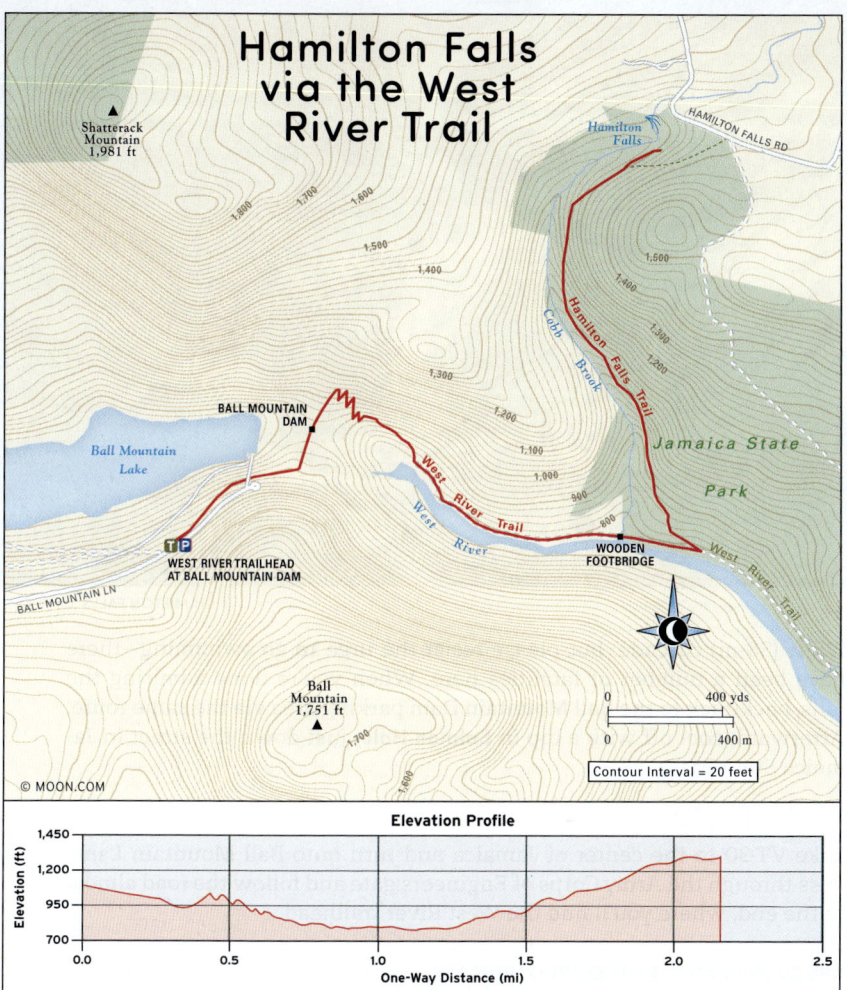

Hamilton Falls via the West River Trail

Shatterack Mountain 1,981 ft

Hamilton Falls

HAMILTON FALLS RD

BALL MOUNTAIN DAM

Ball Mountain Lake

West River Trail

Cobb Brook

Hamilton Falls Trail

Jamaica State Park

West River

WOODEN FOOTBRIDGE

West River Trail

WEST RIVER TRAILHEAD AT BALL MOUNTAIN DAM

BALL MOUNTAIN LN

Ball Mountain 1,751 ft

© MOON.COM

0   400 yds
0   400 m

Contour Interval = 20 feet

Elevation Profile

Elevation (ft)

1,450
1,200
950
700

0.0   0.5   1.0   1.5   2.0   2.5

One-Way Distance (mi)

0.2 mi (0.3 km) the trail flattens and enters the woods. At the fork where the trail meets the bank of the West River in 0.1 mi (0.16 km), turn left. The trail winds through a low canopy of birch trees with rock formations to the north and the river to the south. In 0.4 mi (0.6 km), cross over a wooden footbridge and continue straight on the wide, crushed stone path. At the sign for Hamilton Falls in in 0.1 mi (0.16 km), turn left (north) onto the Switch Road Trail.

▶ **MILE 1.2–2.1: Switch Road Trail to Hamilton Falls**
Continue uphill on the rocky, blue-blazed path, which climbs high over the Cobb River gorge with small cascades flowing below. The trail, originally an old wagon road, evens out and softens to a smooth dirt surface atop a wooded ridgeline. Reach a sign pointing left (north) to Hamilton Falls in 0.8 mi (1.2 km). Turn left (north) past the sign and descend the wooden stairs. Then, travel right (east) on the sloping dirt path along the hillside to reach the falls in 0.1 mi (0.16 km). Enjoy marveling at this impressive

HAMILTON FALLS ▲

125-ft (38-m) cascade, but please resist the urge to go swimming—there have been a number of fatalities here. When you're done admiring the falls, backtrack to the Ball Mountain Dam parking area via the same route. Afterward, cool off with a dip in **Salmon Hole,** just down the street in Jamaica State Park.

DIRECTIONS

Take VT-30 to the center of Jamaica and turn onto Ball Mountain Lane. Pass through the Army Corps of Engineers gate and follow the road almost to the end, where you'll find the West River trailhead.

GPS COORDINATES: 43°07'32.3"N 72°46'37.1"W

BEST NEARBY BITES

Just up the road in Winhall, **The Workhorse Café** (59 Route 30, Winhall; 802/856-7190; 9am-5pm Mon.-Thurs., 9am-7pm Fri., 7am-7pm Sat., 7am-3pm Sun.) serves generously portioned hot sandwiches, fries, lunch bowls, and more that make for perfect post-hike fare. Enjoy your grub at a picnic table along the Winhall River. It's 7 mi (11.3 km) from the trailhead.

VERMONT   Southern Green Mountains

Hike these quiet trails on the Southern Vermont College campus to Everett Cave, a marble solution cave with high chambers to explore.

DISTANCE: 2.7 mi (4.3 km) round-trip

DURATION: 1.5 hr

ELEVATION GAIN: 252 ft (77 m)

EFFORT: Easy

TRAIL: Gravel road, dirt singletrack

USERS: Hikers, leashed dogs, mountain bikers

SEASON: April–November

FEES/PASSES: None

MAPS: Bennington Area Trail System, "Trail Map"

TRAILHEAD: Everett Path trailhead, Mansion Dr., Bennington

FACILITIES: None

CONTACT: Bennington Area Trail System; https://batsvt.org

START THE HIKE

▶ **MILE 0-0.3: Everett Path Trailhead to Halloween Tree Trail**
Depart west from the trailhead and then turn right (north) onto **Everett Path,** a wide gravel road with red blazes. Continue past the water tank and the run-down stonework and statues above the **Everett Mansion.** At 0.3 mi (0.5 km), bear left (west) to follow the red blazes onto the **Halloween Tree Trail.**

▶ **MILE 0.3-1.8: Halloween Tree Trail to Cave Trail**
The path winds through a shady forest on the edge of the Southern Vermont College fields for 0.2 mi (0.3 km), with great views of the Green Mountains across campus. At the intersection with Ursa Way, continue straight (north) for 0.2 mi (0.3 km). Then, reach another intersection with the Lower Beacon Trail. Turn right (northeast) to stay on the Halloween Tree Trail, which winds through a hilly birch forest for 0.2 mi (0.3 km). After climbing a series of rolling switchbacks for another 0.2 mi (0.3 km), the trail meets an unmarked fork at 1.1 mi (1.8 km). Turn left (north) to stay on the Halloween Tree Trail. The path crosses under the power lines and reaches the **"Halloween Tree"** at 1.2 mi (1.9 km). This spooky sugar maple is a sight to behold, with its massive gnarled trunk and weighty branches. From the tree, the trail switchbacks far to the west for 0.3 mi (0.5 km), then doubles back east to meet the yellow-blazed **Cave Trail** at 1.8 mi (2.9 km).

▶ **MILE 1.8-2.2: Cave Trail to Everett Cave**
Go straight (south) onto the Cave Trail for approximately 0.4 mi (0.6 km), where it meets an intersection with the spur trail to Everett Cave. Turn

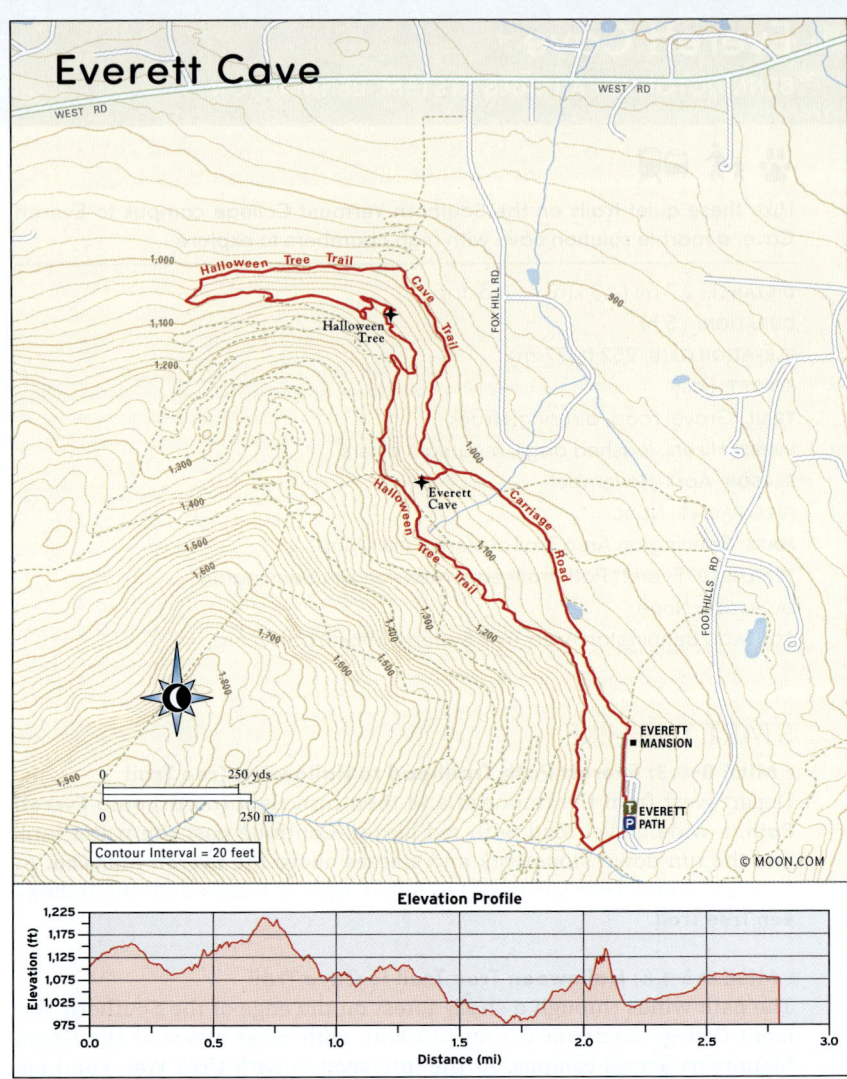

Everett Cave

Elevation Profile

right (west) onto the spur trail and climb the slope for 210 ft (64 m) to the mouth of the cave. This mossy, rocky formation may not look like much from the outside, but bring a flashlight and travel west through the narrow opening to arrive in a cool and spacious chamber composed of marble drip formations.

▶ **MILE 2.2–2.7: Everett Cave to Everett Path Trailhead**
After exploring the cave, backtrack to the intersection with the **Cave Trail** and continue right (south) on the yellow-blazed **carriage road.** This historic cobblestone road leads back to the elegant stone **Everett Mansion** at 2.7 mi (4.3 km). Walk through or around the mansion to arrive back at the parking lot. (Note: The mansion sometimes hosts weddings and other events, so be sure not to crash one in your hiking clothes!)

▲ CARRIAGE ROAD VISTA

DIRECTIONS

From Main Street in the center of Bennington, go west for 1 mi (1.6 km) and then turn left onto West Road. At the first intersection, turn right onto Monument Avenue and continue for 0.5 mi (0.8 km). Then, turn right onto Regwood Road. At the fork, bear left onto Mansion Drive and follow it to the parking lot at the end. Parking for trails is marked with signs at the southwest corner of the lot.

GPS COORDINATES: 42°51'56.9"N 73°13'07.2"W

BEST NEARBY BITES AND BREWS

Bennington is a little-known foodie gem. Check out local favorite **Madison Brewing Company Pub and Restaurant** (428 Main St., Bennington; 802/442-7397; www.madisonbrewingco.com; 11:30am-9pm Mon.-Sat., 11:30am-4:30pm Sun.), 2 mi (3.2 km) from the trailhead, for hot pub grub and house-made brews and sodas.

NEARBY CAMPGROUNDS

Dispersed primitive camping and shelters are available within Green Mountain National Forest.

NAME	LOCATION	FACILITIES	SEASON	FEE
Mount Ascutney State Park	1826 Back Mountain Rd., Windsor, 43°26'16.4"N 72°24'20.5"W	38 tent/ RV sites, 10 lean-to sites, 5 cabins; restrooms	late May– mid-October	$20–68
802/674-2060; www.vtstateparks.com/ascutney.html				
Wilgus State Park	3985 Route 5, Weathersfield, 43°23'23.3"N 72°24'25.7"W	15 RV/tent sites, 9 lean-to sites, 4 cabins; restrooms	early May– early October	$20–68
802/674-5422; www.vtstateparks.com/wilgus.html				
Greendale Campground	698 Greendale Rd., Weston, 43°21'02.8"N 72°49'14.6"W	11 RV/tent sites; vault toilets; no water	late May– mid-October	$10
802/362-2307; www.fs.usda.gov				
Emerald Lake State Park	65 Emerald Lake Ln., East Dorset, 43°16'53.1"N 73°00'17.6"W	66 RV/tent sites, 37 lean-to sites; restrooms	late May– mid-October	$20–38
802/362-1655; www.vtstateparks.com/emerald.html				

NEARBY CAMPGROUNDS (continued)

NAME	LOCATION	FACILITIES	SEASON	FEE
Hapgood Pond Recreation Area	1615 Hapgood Pond Rd., Peru, 43°15'09.3"N 72°53'27.4"W	28 tent sites; restrooms, water	late May–mid-October	$20
802/888-1349; www.fs.usda.gov				
Jamaica State Park	48 Salmon Hole Ln., West Townshend, 43°06'20.1"N 72°46'24.2"W	41 RV/tent sites, 18 lean-to sites; restrooms	early May–early October	$20–38
802/874-4600; www.vtstateparks.com/Jamaica.html				
Grout Pond Recreation Area	Forest Road 263, Stratton, 43°02'44.4"N 72°57'14.0"W	6 RV sites, 11 walk-in tent sites; vault toilets, pump water	year-round	$16
802/362-2307; www.fs.usda.gov				
Woodford State Park	142 State Park Rd., Bennington, 42°53'27.0"N 73°02'14.4"W	76 RV/tent sites, 20 lean-to sites, 4 cabins; restrooms	May–mid-October	$20–68
802/447-7169; www.vtstateparks.com/woodford.html				

CHAMPLAIN VALLEY AND STOWE

Sweeping green hills. Red farmhouses with cow pastures. Great lumbering mountains that seem to cast shadows over the lush landscape. This is Vermont as many imagine it. The landscape around the Champlain Valley and Stowe is an unlikely mix of soft farmlands and titanic peaks that contain some of the toughest trails in Vermont—many of which offer indelible views of Lake Champlain's deep-blue waters. And thanks to the proximity of growing towns like Burlington, a day in the backcountry here can be complemented by a glass of imperial IPA and a dinner of oyster ssäm with local kimchi, followed by a maple creemee. It's almost excessively Vermont! But a little decadence never hurt anyone—especially after a tough hike.

▲ MEADOWS ON STOWE PINNACLE

▲ VIEW FROM MOUNT MANSFIELD SUMMIT

◄ PROFILE OF CAMEL'S HUMP

CHAMPLAIN VALLEY AND STOWE

Franklin

Lake Carmi

105

105

Enosburg Falls

Bakersfield

Montgomery

Missisquoi River

108

Isle La Motte

36

Saint Albans

105

89

Fairfield

36

7

Long Trail State Forest

109

108

Lake Champlain

Grand Isle

2

South Hero

104

Fairfax

Lamoille River

Jeffersonville

Johnson

Westford

Milton

BREWSTER RIVER

15

Long Trail

Niquette Bay State Park

89

7

128

15

Mount Mansfield

2

MALLETTS BAY

Colchester

Underhill

UNDERHILL STATE PARK

108

NORTH BEACH

Winooski

Jericho

100

Essex Junction

Mount Mansfield State Forest

Stowe

Burlington

Williston

GOLD BROOK

4

C.C. Putnam State Forest

116

SHELBURNE CAMPING AREA

Richmond

LITTLE RIVER STATE PARK

5

6

Shelburne

7

89

Waterbury Reservoir

Shelburne Pond

Hinesburg

Camels Hump State Park

Waterbury

Charlotte

Lewis Creek

Huntington River

Duxbury

2

Middlesex

89

8

MOUNT PHILO STATE PARK

7

116

Long Trail

Moretown

Ferrisburg

Starksboro

© MOON.COM

Vergennes

17

Waitsfield

MAPLE HILL CAMPSITES

NEW YORK

VERMONT

Black Creek

MOUNT PHILO RD

0   5 mi

0   5 km

Calm Cove at Niquette Bay

NIQUETTE BAY STATE PARK, COLCHESTER

This rare Vermont "coastal" hike meanders through immersive forests, wetlands, and hidden coves on the eastern shores of Lake Champlain.

BEST: Summer hikes

DISTANCE: 3.7 mi (6 km) round-trip

DURATION: 2–3 hr

ELEVATION GAIN: 581 ft (177 m)

EFFORT: Easy/moderate

TRAIL: Dirt path, rocks, wooden bog bridges, wooden stairs

USERS: Hikers

SEASON: May–October

FEES/PASSES: Day-use fee $5/adult

MAPS: Niquette Bay State Park website

TRAILHEAD: Niquette Bay State Park parking lot, Raymond Rd., Colchester

FACILITIES: Vault toilet

CONTACT: Niquette Bay State Park; 802/893-5210; www.vtstateparks.com/niquette.html

Lake Champlain's crown jewel might just be Calm Cove, a secluded bay where a sun-baked rock slab at the water's edge functions as a beach, inviting hikers and off-leash dogs alike to take a brisk swim.

START THE HIKE

▶ **MILE 0-0.9: Niquette Bay State Park Parking Lot to Beach Bypass Trail**

Begin the hike by the trail kiosk in the parking lot as you walk south into the forest on a wide groomed path. Turn left onto the **Ledges Trail,** a more rugged pathway with blue blazes that climbs through mossy stones to a height of land with eastern white pine trees and sugar maples. At 0.6 mi (1 km), the trail descends a flight of wooden **stairs** to the edge of a beautiful arbor-speckled wetland.

Cross through the wetland on wooden bog bridges and continue along a wooded ridge on the lake's edge. You'll reach a three-way junction for the **Beach Bypass Trail** and the Allen Trail at 0.9 mi (1.4 km). An opening in the trees here reveals a **sandy beach.** Dogs should remain on-leash here, but humans are welcome to roam more freely.

▶ **MILE 0.9-1.6: Beach Bypass Trail to Calm Cove**

Veer left to pick up the Beach Bypass Trail, which immediately climbs a larger set of stairs before ambling along another ridgeline. Occasional blue blazes guide the way, and additional stairs take you even higher to some of the finest water views along the hike. Through the trees you'll see

VERMONT | Champlain Valley and Stowe

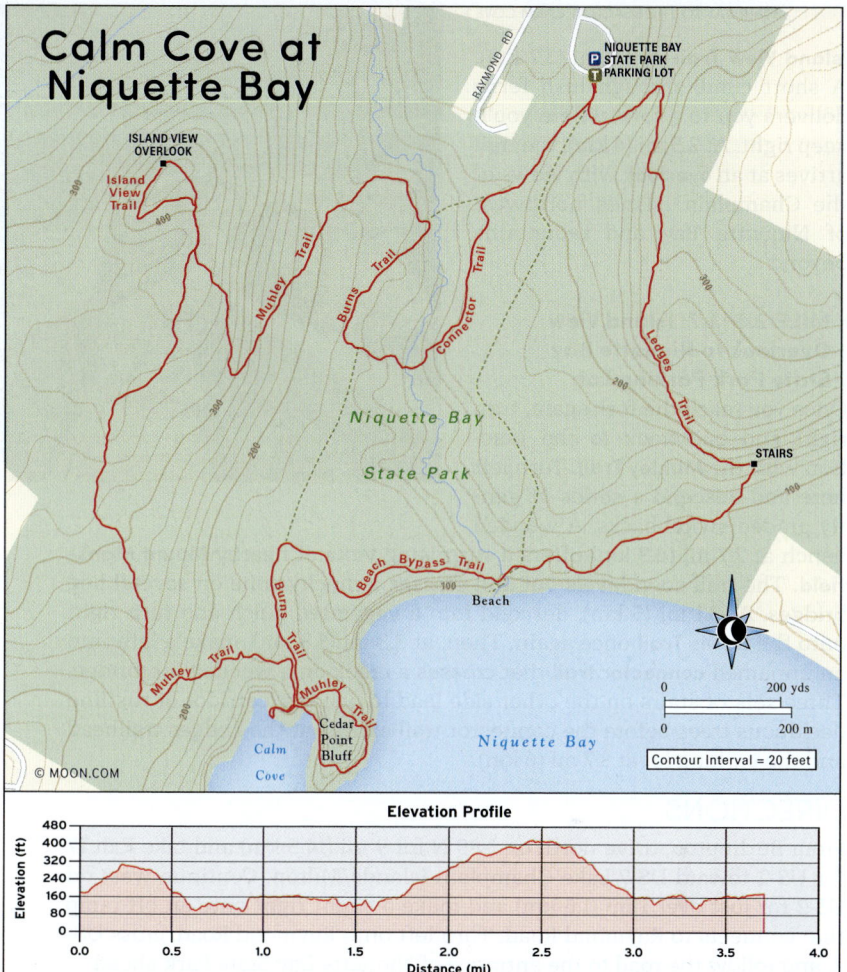

Calm Cove at Niquette Bay

ISLAND VIEW OVERLOOK

Island View Trail

RAXMOND RD

NIQUETTE BAY STATE PARK PARKING LOT

Muhley Trail

Burns Trail

Connector Trail

Ledges Trail

STAIRS

Niquette Bay

State Park

Beach Bypass Trail

Burns Trail

Beach

Muhley Trail

Muhley Trail

Cedar Point Bluff

Calm Cove

Niquette Bay

© MOON.COM

0   200 yds

0   200 m

Contour Interval = 20 feet

Elevation Profile

Elevation (ft)

480
400
320
240
160
80
0

0.0   0.5   1.0   1.5   2.0   2.5   3.0   3.5   4.0

Distance (mi)

Cedar Point Bluff, a knob-like peninsula that resembles a green porcupine, thanks to its evergreen conifers. At 1.1 mi (1.8 km), turn left onto the **Burns Trail** to approach the bluff, watching your footing among the tree roots running across the trail. Upon reaching another junction at 1.3 mi (2.1 km), keep left to stay on the Burns Trail. Almost immediately, you'll hit a *third* junction, where you'll turn left to begin a circumferential traverse of Cedar Point Bluff. The trail roller-coasters up and down the bluff slopes with the help of stone stairs. Once you've closed the loop and returned to the junction at 1.6 mi (2.6 km), turn left (a sign here reads Pet Swim Area) and descend several wooden staircases to the stone slab beach at **Calm Cove.**

▶ **MILE 1.6–2.5: Calm Cove to Island View Overlook**

Backtrack up the stairs and turn left onto the Burns Trail again. Then, at the next junction, veer left to pick up the **Muhley Trail.** Ascend back into the forest at a patient grade, following blue blazes once again and passing the remnants of stone walls from ancient farmsteads. Turn left onto the

Island View Trail at 2.3 mi (3.7 km). A short climb through lush ferns delivers you to a fork, where you'll keep right. At 2.5 mi (4 km), the trail arrives at an **overlook** with views of the Champlain Islands northwest of Niquette Bay and mountains beyond.

▶ **MILE 2.5-3.7: Island View Overlook to Niquette Bay State Park Parking Lot**

Once you reach the fork again, turn right and backtrack to the junction with the **Muhley Trail.** Turn left here and descend a series of gently graded switchbacks. A wooden bench at 2.7 mi (4.3 km) offers a surprising vista of nearby **Mount Mansfield.** The trail soon levels out and crosses a mucky zone on several bog bridges. At 3.1 mi (5 km), descend into a vegetated gulch and turn right onto the **Burns Trail** once again. Then, at 3.3 mi (5.3 km), make a left onto an unnamed **connector trail** that crosses a creek on a wooden footbridge. Three sets of stairs on the other side lead to one last corridor of rustling deciduous trees before the connector trail arrives at the Ledges trailhead and the parking lot at 3.7 mi (6 km).

DIRECTIONS

From Burlington, drive north on I-89 N for 9 mi (14.5 km) and take Exit 17 for US-2 toward US-7/Lake Champlain Islands/Milton. Continue west on US-2 for just over 1 mi (1.6 km) and make a slight right onto an off-ramp that connects to Raymond Road. Turn left onto Raymond Road, cross US-2, and follow the road to the entrance of Niquette Bay State Park ahead.

GPS COORDINATES: 44°35'19.6"N 73°11'31.3"W

BEST NEARBY BITES AND BREWS

If you're heading back to Burlington, take a detour through Essex Junction and try a freshly brewed glass of smoked porter or mango IPA at **1st Republic Brewing Company** (39 River Rd. #6, Essex Junction; 802/857-5318; www.1strepublicbrewingco.com; 3pm-9pm Mon.-Fri., noon-9pm Sat., 1pm-6pm Sun.). Enjoy a nice big bowl of savory pho at **Viet Thai** (118 Pearl St., Essex; 802/288-1688; www.vietthaiessex. com; 11:15am-2:15pm and 4:30pm-8:30pm Mon.-Tues. and Thurs., 4:30pm-8:30pm Wed., 11am-9pm Fri., noon-9pm Sat.).

🦌 ❀ 🐾

This mountain hike gives your calves a solid workout before delivering you to Vermont's highest-elevation trout pond.

BEST: Spring hikes, brew hikes

DISTANCE: 2.6 mi (4.2 km) round-trip

DURATION: 3 hr

ELEVATION GAIN: 1,040 ft (317 m)

EFFORT: Moderate

TRAIL: Dirt path, rock and wood stairs, wooden bog bridges, water crossings on stones

USERS: Hikers, leashed dogs

SEASON: May–October

FEES/PASSES: None

MAPS: Smugglers' Notch State Park website

TRAILHEAD: Smugglers' Notch visitor center, VT-108, Stowe

FACILITIES: Restrooms

CONTACT: Smugglers' Notch State Park; 802/253-4014; www.vtstateparks.com/smugglers.html

Sitting pretty in the northeastern heights of Smugglers' Notch—a wooded cleft between Mount Mansfield and Spruce Peak through which Prohibition-era bootleggers trafficked shipments of hooch—Sterling Pond is one of Vermont's most elegant and tranquil bodies of water. It's also stocked with trout, which makes it a popular hangout for adventurous fly-fishers. The most direct access route is the Sterling Pond Trail, which climbs from the notch floor and merges with Vermont's famous Long Trail (the oldest long-distance backpacking trail in America) to reach the pond.

START THE HIKE

▶ **MILE 0–0.2: Smugglers' Notch Visitor Center to Sterling Pond Trail**
Begin the hike in the Smugglers' Notch visitor center parking lot on Mountain Road. Walk east across the road and pick up the **Sterling Pond Trail** by the trailhead sign. Blue blazes mark the way forward. Heading east through a forest of birch and maple trees, the trail kicks off with a steep and winding staircase of rocks and thick tree roots. The widely spaced trees offer nice views of the road below. You may be surprised by how efficiently the trail gains elevation. The footing here tends to be slippery due to streams that spill alongside the trail and create mud, so be extra mindful when stepping over those tree roots.

Champlain Valley and Stowe

VERMONT

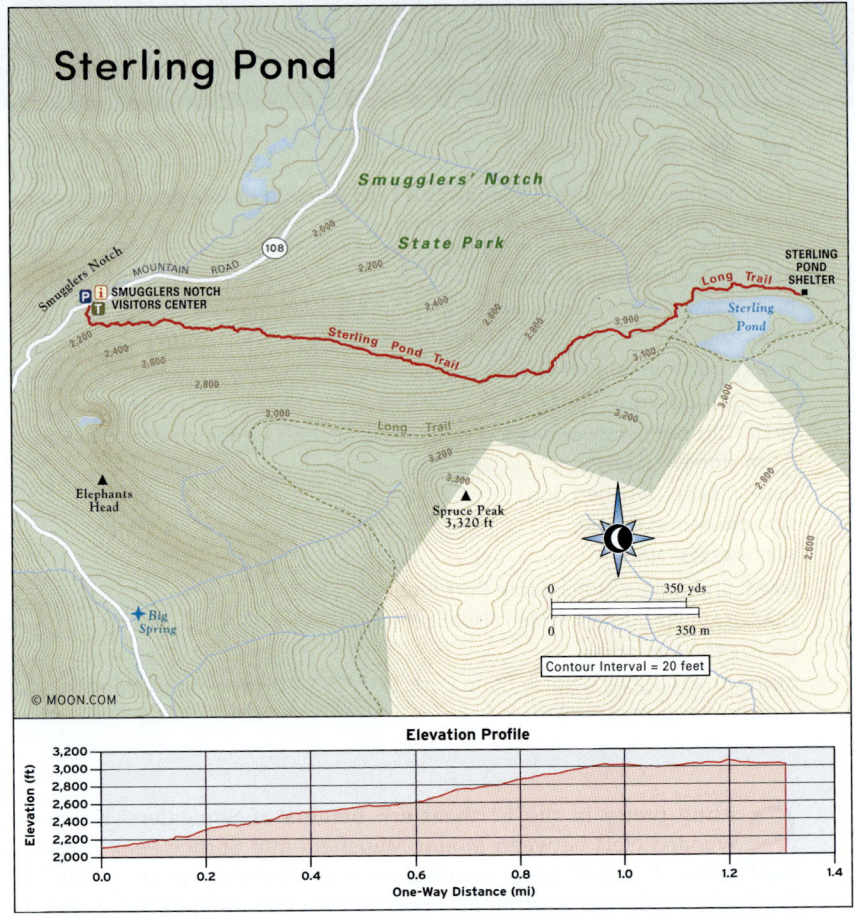

Sterling Pond

Smugglers' Notch State Park

STERLING POND SHELTER

Long Trail

Sterling Pond

MOUNTAIN ROAD 108

Smugglers Notch

SMUGGLERS NOTCH VISITORS CENTER

Sterling Pond Trail

Long Trail

Elephants Head

Spruce Peak 3,320 ft

Big Spring

© MOON.COM

0   350 yds
0   350 m

Contour Interval = 20 feet

Elevation Profile

Elevation (ft): 3,200 / 3,000 / 2,800 / 2,600 / 2,400 / 2,200 / 2,000

One-Way Distance (mi): 0.0   0.2   0.4   0.6   0.8   1.0   1.2   1.4

▶ **MILE 0.2-1.0: Sterling Pond Trail to Long Trail**

The trail climbs steadily up the western slopes of Spruce Peak. As the leafy deciduous trees transition into thinner boreal arbors, partial views of Smugglers' Notch and the northward hills of Jeffersonville become a fixture. As the trail gradually curves northeast—bypassing some smooth yet perpetually soggy slabs of rock—the grade starts to soften a bit, allowing your calves a reprieve. Weave through the woods over rock and root on a wider stretch of path for the final 0.2 mi (0.3 km) of the climb before emerging from the woods on the ridge of Spruce Peak and reaching the **Long Trail** at 1 mi (1.6 km).

▶ **MILE 1.0-1.1: Long Trail to Sterling Pond**

Turn left to head east down a sun-splashed and rockier path toward the sound of lapping water. After another 0.1 mi (0.16 km), the Long Trail arrives at the boggy western shore of **Sterling Pond.** Hikers can dip their feet in the cool water and sun themselves on several large nearby rocks before continuing to the climactic pond overlook point.

▶ **MILE 1.1–1.2: Sterling Pond
to Sterling Pond Trail**

Hop back onto the Sterling Pond Trail and head east as the trail enters the pond-side woods and climbs a steep wooden staircase. As you amble through the forest on the pond's northern shore, keep an eye peeled for falcons, who occasionally dive-bomb the pond for fish.

At 1.2 mi (1.9 km), the trail pops out of the woods again and crosses beneath the towers of Sterling Chairlift—part of the skiing infrastructure at the nearby Smugglers' Notch Resort.

▶ **MILE 1.2–1.3: Sterling Pond Trail to Sterling Pond Shelter**

Reenter the forest and ascend a final stretch of rocky ground before reaching the **Sterling Pond Shelter** at 1.3 mi (2.1 km). Here you'll find a scenic pond overlook complete with a cute little log bench for hikers. It's the perfect note on which to conclude the hike. Return the way you came.

DIRECTIONS

From Boston, drive north on I-93 through New Hampshire and into northeastern Vermont. Exit onto I-91 N to St. Johnsbury and then take Exit 21 to merge onto US-2 W. Continue driving west and turn right at the junction for VT-15 W. Drive northwest on VT-15 W until you reach the traffic circle with the exit for VT-108. Take the VT-108 exit and drive south toward Smugglers' Notch. (Watch your speed as the road narrows and twists around several large trees and boulders.) The Smugglers' Notch visitor center parking lot will be on your left.

GPS COORDINATES: 44°33'23.8"N 72°47'40.1"W

BEST NEARBY BITES AND BREWS

It's impossible to talk about Vermont craft beer without describing the pine-scented double IPA known as Heady Topper, which can be procured in glasses and cans at **The Alchemist** (100 Cottage Club Rd., Stowe; 802/253-6708; www.alchemistbeer.com; 11am-6pm daily). Down the road in Stowe, you can kick back with more Vermont brews and an impressive menu of farm-raised comfort food at **Doc Ponds** (294 Mountain Rd., Stowe; 802/760-6066; www.docponds.com; 4pm-9pm Tues.-Thurs., noon-9pm Fri.-Sun.).

Champlain Valley and Stowe

VERMONT

3

Mount Mansfield via the Sunset Ridge Trail

UNDERHILL STATE PARK, UNDERHILL

Scale Vermont's tallest peak—at sunset, ideally—to get an unbeatable panorama of the Champlain Valley.

BEST: Vistas

DISTANCE: 5.2 mi (8.4 km) round-trip

DURATION: 4.5 hr

ELEVATION GAIN: 2,429 ft (740 m)

EFFORT: Strenuous

TRAIL: Dirt path, rocks, wooden bridges

USERS: Hikers, leashed dogs

SEASON: May–October

FEES/PASSES: Day-use fee $5/adult

MAPS: Underhill State Park website

TRAILHEAD: Eagle Cut trail parking lot, Mountain Rd., Underhill

FACILITIES: Restrooms

CONTACT: Underhill State Park; 802/636-7220; www.vtstateparks.com/underhill.html

START THE HIKE

▸ **MILE 0-0.7: Eagle Cut Trail Parking Lot to Sunset Ridge Trail**

Begin your hike in the Eagle Cut Trail parking lot and walk uphill to the east end of the lot. Pick up the **Eagle Cut connector trail,** which ascends gently through the deciduous woods for 0.4 mi (0.6 km) before ending at a gravel access road. Turn left onto the road and walk northeast for 0.3 mi (0.5 km) until you reach the register for the Sunset Ridge Trail. Write your name in the register before beginning the **Sunset Ridge Trail,** marked with blue blazes.

▸ **MILE 0.7-1.4: Sunset Ridge Trail to Cantilever Rock Junction**

The Sunset Ridge Trail crosses a series of streams on wooden bridges and snakes northward through a sun-splashed forest of birch and beech. Upon reaching the junction for the Laura Cowles Trail at 0.8 mi

DESCENT DOWN SUNSET RIDGE ▸

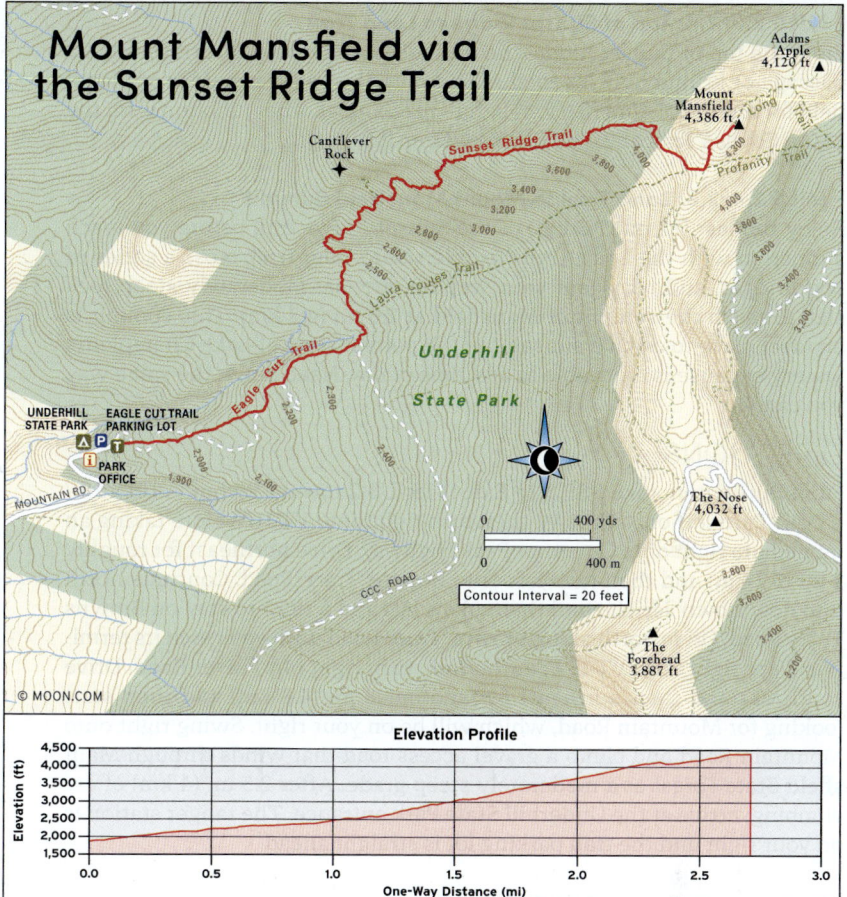

Mount Mansfield via the Sunset Ridge Trail

Adams Apple 4,120 ft ▲

Mount Mansfield 4,386 ft ▲

Cantilever Rock +

Sunset Ridge Trail

Profanity Trail

Laura Coules Trail

Long

Underhill

State Park

UNDERHILL STATE PARK

EAGLE CUT TRAIL PARKING LOT

Eagle Cut Trail

PARK OFFICE

MOUNTAIN RD

The Nose 4,032 ft ▲

0   400 yds

0   400 m

Contour Interval = 20 feet

CCC ROAD

The Forehead 3,887 ft ▲

© MOON.COM

Elevation Profile

Elevation (ft) axis: 4,500 / 4,000 / 3,500 / 3,000 / 2,500 / 2,000 / 1,500

One-Way Distance (mi): 0.0   0.5   1.0   1.5   2.0   2.5   3.0

(1.3 km), keep left to stay on Sunset Ridge Trail and climb gradually up a series of wooden staircases and rock steps. After passing some open ledges around 1.4 mi (2.3 km), the trail arrives at the spur cutoff for **Cantilever Rock**—a long, wafer-shaped rock that's precariously balanced atop a heap of boulders. (It's well worth the 0.2-mi/0.3-km detour.)

▶ **MILE 1.4–2.0: Cantilever Rock Junction to Top of Sunset Ridge**

From this junction, veer right and keep climbing to stay on the Sunset Ridge Trail. Feel the adrenaline kick in as the trail ascends some very steep, exposed rock ledges that require hand and foot scrambling. Enjoy the breeze as you emerge onto the base of **Sunset Ridge** around 1.5 mi (2.4 km). As you ascend the ridge for roughly 0.5 mi (0.8 km), keep an eye out above for hawks—and below for wet rocks. The smooth and lichen-covered rock slabs up here can be slippery, even in dry conditions. After roughly 0.5 mi (0.8 km) of exposed climbing, the trail reaches a height of land that marks the top of Sunset Ridge at 2 mi (3.2 km).

▶ **MILE 2.0-2.4: Top of Sunset Ridge to Long Trail**
From the top of Sunset Ridge, the trail takes a sharp right turn through a passage of krummholz. Keep climbing onto the south shoulder of Mansfield for another 0.4 mi (0.6 km) before reaching another junction with the Laura Cowles Trail at 2.4 mi (3.9 km). Keep left.

▶ **MILE 2.4-2.6: Long Trail to Mount Mansfield Summit**
Enjoy the last 0.2 mi (0.3 km) of the Sunset Ridge Trail before you reach a junction with the Long Trail. Turn left onto **Long Trail,** cross a series of bog bridges, and billy-goat your way up one last moderately steep rock slab to reach the summit of Mansfield at 2.6 mi (4.2 km). This summit is an ideal place to catch a sunset, but the perfect view of Lake Champlain's watery expanse is enjoyable at any time of day. Head down the same way you came.

DIRECTIONS

From Burlington, take I-89 S to Exit 11 for US-2 toward Richmond/Bolton/VT-117. Turn left onto US-2 W, then turn right onto VT-117 before taking an immediate right onto Governor Peck Highway. Drive northeast for roughly 2 mi (3.2 km) and then turn left onto Browns Trace Road. Continue north into downtown Jericho and then take a left and a right to stay on Browns Trace Road. Drive north along Browns Trace Road until you reach its terminus. Veer right onto VT-15 E; at the fork, turn right onto River Road. Drive southeast and then northeast for another 3 mi (4.8 km) and then start looking for Mountain Road, which will be on your right. Swing right onto Mountain Road and climb a gravel access road that winds through Mansfield State Forest at a moderately steep grade. After 2.5 mi (4 km) of car climbing, arrive at the Underhill State Park entrance. The ranger station is on your right and the trail parking lot is straight ahead.

GPS COORDINATES: 44°13'12.0"N 70°59'08.3"W

BEST NEARBY BITES
For a meal with a view, hike south along Mansfield's ridgeline on the Long Trail, turn left onto the Cliff Trail, and then take one more left turn to reach the beautiful **Cliff House Restaurant** (5781 Mountain Rd., Stowe; 802/253-3665; www.gostowe.com; June-Oct., call for hours). If you're famished upon returning to your car, swing by Underhill and purchase a small-batch fruit or cream pie from the self-service shed at the popular **Poorhouse Pies** (419 VT-15, Underhill; 802/858-9129; www.poorhousepies.com; 7am-4pm Tues.-Sun.).

4

Stowe Pinnacle

C. C. PUTNAM STATE FOREST, STOWE

This beloved mountain hike has everything—pretty wildflowers, fun rock scrambles, and breathtaking views.

DISTANCE: 3.4 mi (5.5 km) round-trip

DURATION: 2.5 hr

ELEVATION GAIN: 1,449 ft (442 m)

EFFORT: Moderate

TRAIL: Dirt path, rocks, wooden bog bridges

USERS: Hikers, leashed dogs

SEASON: May–October

FEES/PASSES: None

MAPS: Green Mountain Club, "Mount Mansfield and the Worcester Range"

TRAILHEAD: Stowe Pinnacle trailhead parking lot, Upper Hollow Rd., Stowe

FACILITIES: None

CONTACT: Green Mountain Club; 802/244-7037; www.greenmountainclub.org

The Stowe Valley is best known as a ritzy skiing destination for the well-heeled, but when the snow melts, locals and visitors of all walks flock to Stowe Pinnacle—a mountain that might sound modest at only 2,682 ft (817 m), but in fact offers a breathtaking view of the regional landscape. And the wildlife is perhaps the trail's best feature; be on the lookout for white-tailed deer, grouse, and even the occasional moose, especially in the rolling meadows toward the end of the hike.

START THE HIKE

▶ **MILE 0-0.5: Stowe Pinnacle Trailhead Parking Lot to Log Tepee**
Begin your hike in the trailhead parking lot. Walk toward the sign for the **Stowe Pinnacle Trail** at the east end of the parking lot and set off through a meadow that's chock-full of daffodils before entering the forest. Cross several bog bridges and look for blue blazes on the trees as the dirt trail gradually ascends southeast through a shady stretch of birch trees. Pass an enormous tepee made of logs at 0.5 mi (0.8 km).

▶ **MILE 0.5-1.1: Log Tepee to Pinnacle Meadow Trail Junction**
After the tepee the trail crosses a creek on stones and begins to steepen with each turn. Around 0.7 mi (1.1 km), stone cairns begin to appear on the trail to help guide you to the summit. Ascend a set of rock steps and arrive at the junction for the trail to Pinnacle Meadow at 1.1 mi (1.8 km).

Champlain Valley and Stowe

VERMONT

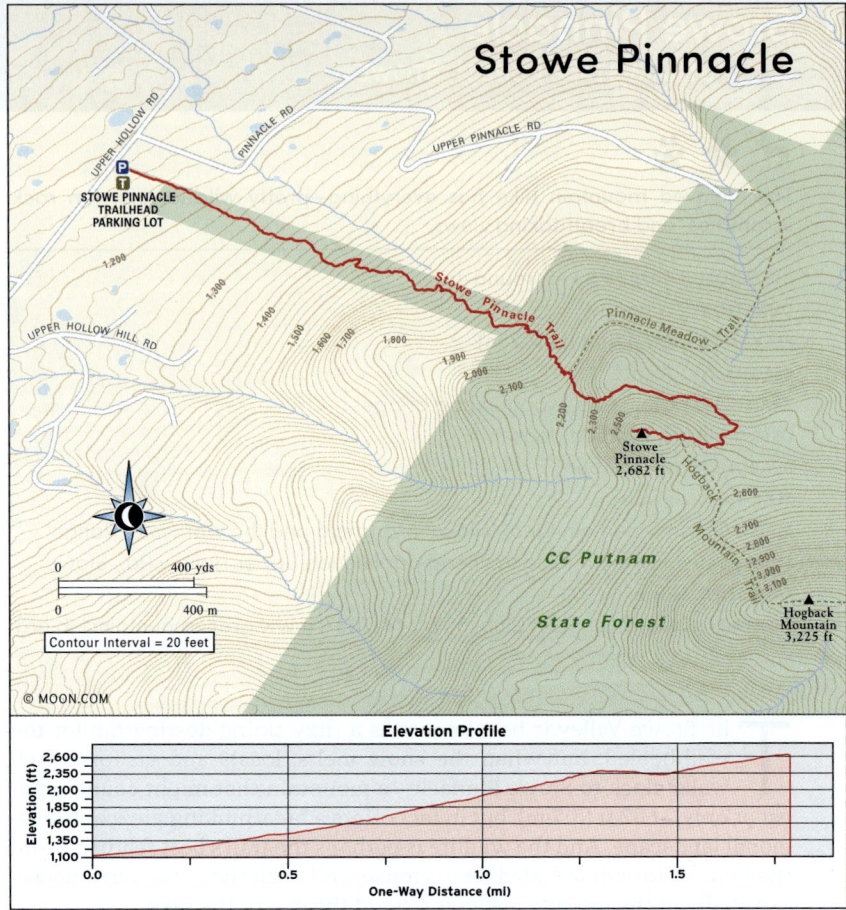

Stowe Pinnacle

STOWE PINNACLE TRAILHEAD PARKING LOT

UPPER HOLLOW RD

PINNACLE RD

UPPER PINNACLE RD

UPPER HOLLOW HILL RD

Stowe Pinnacle Trail

Pinnacle Meadow Trail

Stowe Pinnacle 2,682 ft

Hogback Mountain

CC Putnam State Forest

Hogback Mountain 3,225 ft

0   400 yds
0   400 m

Contour Interval = 20 feet

© MOON.COM

Elevation Profile

Elevation (ft)

One-Way Distance (mi)

▶ **MILE 1.1–1.5: Pinnacle Meadow Trail Junction to Hogback Mountain Trail Junction**

At the junction with Pinnacle Meadow Trail, keep right to stay on Stowe Pinnacle Trail and continue ascending the mountain. Make your way up a steeper series of stone staircases and look for a sign reading Vista nailed to a tree at 1.2 mi (1.9 km). This ledge offers partial views of the Stowe Valley. The forest starts to become airier after this point, hinting at your proximity to the top. The trail starts to curve around the cone of the summit and bypasses a couple of wooden stepladders and a few more (smaller) stone staircases. A junction with the **Hogback Mountain Trail** is at 1.5 mi (2.4 km).

▶ **MILE 1.5–1.7: Hogback Mountain Trail Junction to Stowe Summit**

Turn right at the junction and pass into boreal forest. This final 0.2-mi (0.3-km) stretch becomes a fun scramble up several sloped rock faces. A few stepladders aid your passage. You'll reach the summit of **Stowe Pinnacle** at 1.7 mi (2.7 km).

Once you're ready to return to your car, you can retrace your steps, or you can extend the hike into a loop of 4.7 mi (7.6 km) by backtracking to the junction for **Pinnacle Meadow Trail,** taking a right onto that trail, and descending through the meadows back to the road. It's not as scenic as it sounds—most of the meadow views are obscured by trees—but it's a useful modification for hikers who want more exercise.

DIRECTIONS

From Burlington, drive southeast on I-89 S and take Exit 10 for VT-100 N toward Stowe. Turn left onto VT-100 N and head north for 8 mi (12.9 km). Take a right turn onto Gold Brook Road, cross the bridge over Gold Brook, and then make an immediate left to stay on Gold Brook Road. Drive east to the end of the road, turn right onto Upper Hollow Road, and then make a left turn into the Stowe Pinnacle trailhead parking lot. If the lot is full, you can park alongside the road near the lot.

GPS COORDINATES: 44°26'19.5"N 72°40'03.9"W

> ## BEST NEARBY BITES
>
> There are few better ways to appreciate Vermont's agricultural scene than by munching on a Mediterranean salad or a veggie-loaded, lemon-infused hummus wrap at Stowe's **Green Goddess Café** (618 S Main St., Stowe; 802/253-5255; www.greengoddessvt.com; 7:30am-3pm daily). If it's a post-hike libation you're after, you can't go wrong with a glass of malbec and some charcuterie or tapas at **Cork Natural Wine Shop & Restaurant** (35 School St., Stowe; 802/760-6143; www.corkvt.com; 4pm-9pm Thurs.-Mon.).

5

Little River History Hike

LITTLE RIVER STATE PARK, WATERBURY

This hauntingly beautiful forest hike visits the abandoned houses, orchards, and cemeteries built by some of the first European homesteaders who settled in northern Vermont.

BEST: New England oddities
DISTANCE: 4 mi (6.4 km) round-trip
DURATION: 2 hr
ELEVATION GAIN: 733 ft (223 m)
EFFORT: Easy
TRAIL: Dirt path, rocks, wooden bridges
USERS: Hikers, mountain bikers, leashed dogs
SEASON: June–October
FEES/PASSES: Day-use fee $5/adult
MAPS: Little River State Park website
TRAILHEAD: Information kiosk, Little River Rd., Waterbury
FACILITIES: Restrooms
CONTACT: Little River State Park; 802/244-7103; www.vtstateparks.com/littleriver.html

START THE HIKE

▶ **MILE 0-1.0: Information Kiosk to Log Bridge Ruins**

The hike begins by the trail information kiosk across the road from the day-use parking lot. Pick up the **Dalley Loop Trail,** a gravel road that climbs north and passes through a red access gate. (This trail is shared by hikers and mountain bikers, so keep your ears open at all times.) Keep left at a Y junction; the trail leaves the road and ascends steadily through a deciduous hemlock forest. Down a steep hillside to your left, the monotone rush of water from Stevenson Brook lends the woods a pleasant ambience. Cross a few tiny streams on foot. At 0.5 mi (0.8 km), keep right at the Stevenson Brook Cutoff junction to continue north on the Dalley Loop Trail at a gentler grade, passing some small cascades. After 1 mi (1.6 km), you'll reach the ruins of an old log **bridge** that's still visible in the woods alongside the trail.

▶ **MILE 1.0-1.6: Log Bridge Ruins to Sawmill Trail Junction**

From the log bridge, the trail emerges into a clearing and arrives at a beautiful **farmhouse** built by Almeron Goodell with local timber. A nearby sign tells the history of the Goodell family and their homesteading tribulations here. Beyond the farmhouse, the trail crosses a wooden bridge over a creek, passing through a lush hollow of ferns and then by an **apple orchard,** part of the Patsy Herbert Farm. Continue to reach a junction with the Sawmill Trail at 1.6 mi (2.6 km).

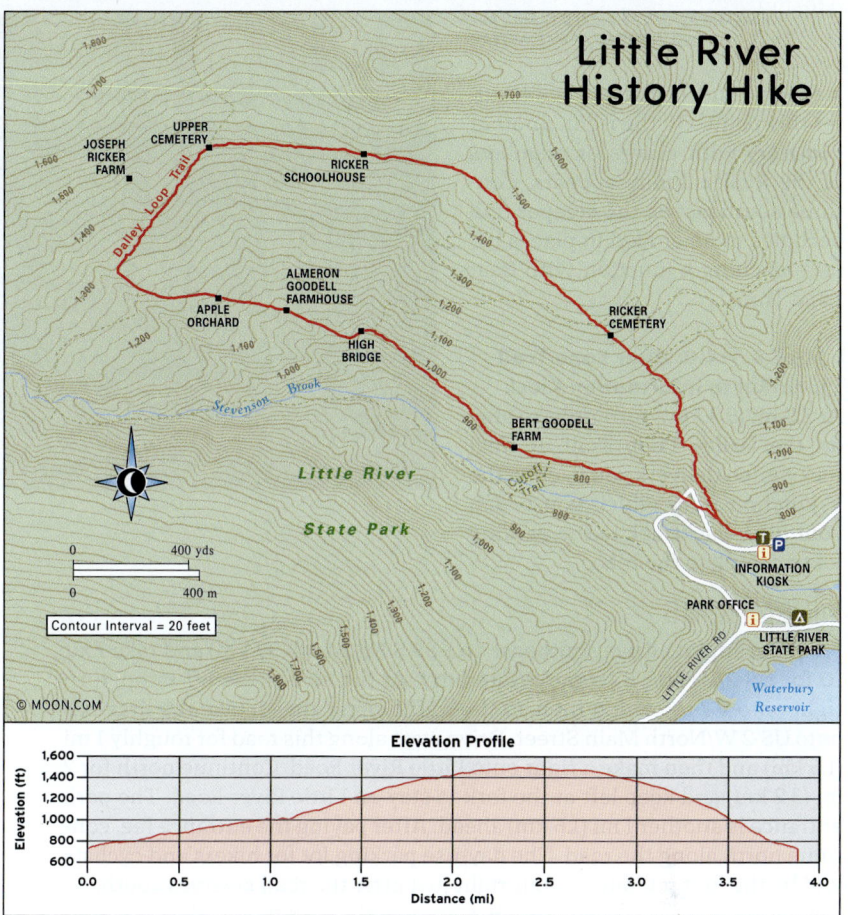

Little River History Hike

JOSEPH RICKER FARM

UPPER CEMETERY

RICKER SCHOOLHOUSE

Dalley Loop Trail

ALMERON GOODELL FARMHOUSE

APPLE ORCHARD

HIGH BRIDGE

RICKER CEMETERY

BERT GOODELL FARM

Stevenson Brook

Little River

State Park

Cutoff Trail

INFORMATION KIOSK

PARK OFFICE

LITTLE RIVER STATE PARK

LITTLE RIVER RD.

Waterbury Reservoir

0   400 yds
0   400 m
Contour Interval = 20 feet

© MOON.COM

Elevation Profile

Elevation (ft)

Distance (mi)

▶ **MILE 1.6–2.1: Sawmill Trail Junction to Patterson Trail Junction**
Turn right to stay on the Dalley Loop Trail, now marked by blue blazes, and amble along crumbling stone walls at a level grade. At 1.7 mi (2.7 km), make another right at the junction and enter the realm of the **Joseph Ricker Farm.** (Ricker was one of the first homesteaders to arrive here—a nearby mountain is named after him.)

As the forest thickens, keep an eye out on your left for the most haunting site yet—the **Upper Cemetery,** where members of the Ricker family are buried. The tombstones are covered with moss and brush. Take in the beauty of this wooded resting place before continuing along the Dalley Loop Trail to reach the Patterson Trail junction at 2.1 mi (3.4 km).

▶ **MILE 2.1–3.3: Patterson Trail Junction to Bear Lane Trail Junction**
Make a right to stay on the Dalley Loop Trail; keep right to stay on this trail at the nearby junction with the cutoff for Kelty Corners. A steady descent begins as the trail heads south alongside a bubbling stream and passes through a few sunlit meadows. You'll reach the Ricker Farm Trail junction in 1 mi (1.6 km). Stay to the right to continue on Patterson Trail, which

steepens and becomes rockier after this point. On the right, another **cemetery** with graves of members of the Ricker family appears. Continue southeast as the steeper trail becomes more eroded in places before reaching a junction with Bear Lane Trail.

▶ **MILE 3.3–4.0: Bear Lane Trail Junction to Information Kiosk**
At 3.3 mi (5.3 km), turn right to stay on the Dalley Loop Trail. A final rocky pitch delivers you back to the Y junction from which you began your hike. Backtrack to the parking lot to complete the hike.

DIRECTIONS

From Burlington, drive southeast on I-89 S for 24 mi (39 km) and take Exit 10 for US-2/VT-100 S toward Waterbury. At the end of the off-ramp, turn right onto VT-100 S and then, at the traffic circle ahead, take the first exit onto US-2 W/North Main Street. Drive west along this road for roughly 1 mi (1.6 km) and then make a right onto Little River Road. Continue north for 2 mi (3.2 km) and keep left at the fork to stay on Little River Road. The park entrance is another 1 mi (1.6 km) ahead. After paying the entrance fee, continue north along the road. The day-use parking lot for hikers and cyclists will be the first pullout on your right just after the road swerves south.

GPS COORDINATES: 44°23'35.9"N 72°45'59.1"W

BEST NEARBY BITES

Little River might be one of Vermont's quieter state parks, but it's a short drive from two of the state's best restaurants. For award-winning, locally sourced New American fare such as monkfish with basil salsa verde and preserved tomato, book a table at **Hen of the Wood** (14 S. Main St., Waterbury; 802/244-7300; www.henofthewood.com; 5pm–10pm Wed.–Mon.).

6

Waterbury Trail to Mount Hunger

C. C. PUTNAM STATE FOREST, WATERBURY

A short but incredibly steep climb, Mount Hunger is a favorite for its sky-high views of the Waterbury-Stowe area and beyond.

DISTANCE: 4.2 mi (6.8 km) round-trip

DURATION: 3 hr

ELEVATION GAIN: 2,158 ft (658 m)

EFFORT: Strenuous

TRAIL: Dirt/rock singletrack

USERS: Hikers, leashed dogs

SEASON: May-October

FEES/PASSES: None

MAPS: Green Mountain Club, "Mount Mansfield and the Worcester Range"

TRAILHEAD: Mount Hunger trailhead parking lot, Sweet Farm Rd., Waterbury Center

FACILITIES: None

CONTACT: Vermont Department of Forests, Parks, and Recreation; 802/793-3432; https://fpr.vermont.gov

START THE HIKE

▶ **MILE 0-1.0: Mount Hunger Trailhead Parking Lot to Waterfall**

Hike east from the parking lot on a wide gravel path that soon turns into dirt singletrack Waterbury Trail. Follow the blue blazes through a forest punctuated by resting boulders and a thick cover of birch trees. The trail steepens in 0.2 mi (0.3 km); hikers ascend with the help of several stone staircases, but in-between sections may be washed out with exposed roots. At 1 mi (1.6 km), arrive at a small **waterfall**.

▶ **MILE 1.0-1.9: Waterfall to White Rocks/Mount Hunger Intersection**

The trail bends right (south) over the creek at the top of the falls and then continues to climb. This is a heavily trafficked trail, so it may be muddy during wet weather. At about 0.7 mi (1.1 km) from the falls, as the vegetation becomes more coniferous, minor rocky scrambles turn into larger rock walls, and hikers will need to use their hands to

◀ SUMMIT OF MOUNT HUNGER

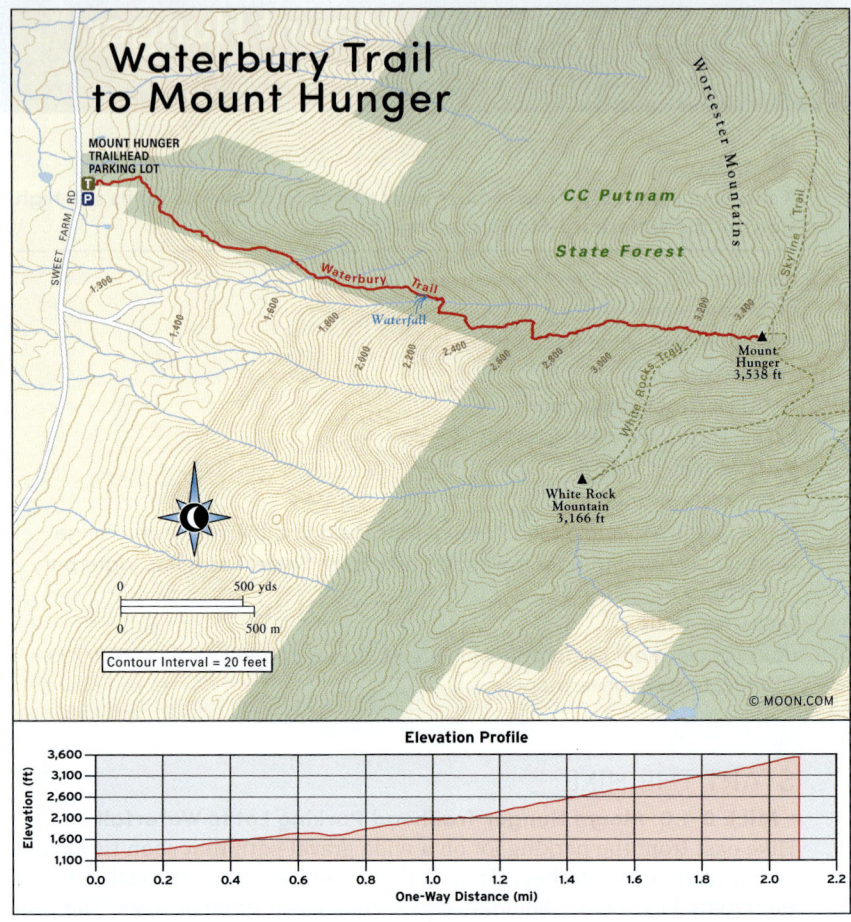

Waterbury Trail to Mount Hunger

MOUNT HUNGER TRAILHEAD PARKING LOT

SWEET FARM RD

Waterbury Trail

Waterfall

1,300
1,400
1,600
1,800
2,000
2,200
2,400
2,600
2,800
3,000
3,200
3,400

CC Putnam State Forest

Worcester Mountains

Skyline Trail

White Rocks Trail

Mount Hunger 3,538 ft

White Rock Mountain 3,166 ft

0   500 yds
0   500 m

Contour Interval = 20 feet

© MOON.COM

Elevation Profile

Elevation (ft)

3,600
3,100
2,600
2,100
1,600
1,100

0.0   0.2   0.4   0.6   0.8   1.0   1.2   1.4   1.6   1.8   2.0   2.2

One-Way Distance (mi)

climb. At the signed intersection for **White Rocks/Mount Hunger** at 1.9 mi (3.1 km), keep straight (east) toward the Mount Hunger summit.

▸ MILE 1.9–2.1: White Rocks/Mount Hunger Intersection to Mount Hunger Summit

After another 0.2 mi (0.3 km) of climbing, the trees part to reveal awesome views of the Worcester Range, Mount Mansfield, and the Waterbury-Stowe valley from a spacious bald granite **summit.** There is plenty of room for hikers to wander the summit, spread out for a picnic, and enjoy the views, but use care to walk only on rocks and not trample delicate alpine vegetation. Keep in mind that this 3,538-ft (1,078-m) peak is quite exposed, so wind and cold can be particularly intense above the tree line, and the bald rocks can be slippery in wet weather. Backtrack to the parking area on the Waterbury Trail.

▲ THE SUMMIT OF MOUNT HUNGER

DIRECTIONS

From VT-100/Waterbury Center, turn onto Howard Avenue. At the end of the road, turn left onto Maple Street. Just after the fire department, turn right onto Loomis Hill Road and go 2 mi (3.2 km), then continue straight onto Sweet Road for another 1.5 mi (2.4 km). The large parking area is marked with a sign for C. C. Putnam State Forest.

GPS COORDINATES: 44°24'08.4"N 72°40'32.3"W

BEST NEARBY BITES AND BREWS

Get your post-hike fuel at **Prohibition Pig** (23 S. Main St., Waterbury; 802/244-4120; www.prohibitionpig.com; 4pm-9pm Mon. and Wed.-Fri., noon-9pm Sat.-Sun., bar open until 10pm Wed.-Sun.), a restaurant/brewery with barbecue sandwiches, mac and cheese, poutine, and other comforting classics.

Champlain Valley and Stowe

VERMONT

Mount Philo

This mountain hike offers an unbeatable view across Lake Champlain into upstate New York and the Adirondacks, as well as a close-up look at some memorable rock formations.

DISTANCE: 2.2 mi (3.5 km) round-trip
DURATION: 1.5 hr
ELEVATION GAIN: 631 ft (192 m)
EFFORT: Moderate
TRAIL: Dirt path, rocks, wooden bridges
USERS: Hikers, leashed dogs
SEASON: June-October
FEES/PASSES: Day-use fee $5/adult
MAPS: Mount Philo State Park website
TRAILHEAD: Mount Philo parking lot, Humphreys Rd., Charlotte
FACILITIES: Restrooms
CONTACT: Mount Philo State Park; 802/425-2390; www.vtstateparks.com/philo.html

You can drive to the gorgeous, grassy summit of Mount Philo, but the wooden Adirondack chairs waiting at the top are even more rewarding when you choose to hike.

START THE HIKE

▶ **MILE 0-0.4: Mount Philo Parking Lot to State Park Road**
Begin the hike at the south end of the Mount Philo parking lot by the park entrance. Find the sign for the **House Rock Trail,** marked by blue blazes. Hike the dirt path northeast through the forest, climbing some wooden stairs and passing several glacial boulders. As the footing gets rootier, the trail arrives at the trail's namesake: **House Rock,** a massive glacial erratic that could easily crush a bungalow if loosened (Indiana Jones-style). Pass under the boulder's overhang, cross a few bog bridges, and ascend some more stairs to reach State Park Road at 0.4 mi (0.6 km).

▶ **MILE 0.4-0.7: State Park Road to Mount Philo Summit**
Take a right onto State Park Road and cross over to the sign for the House Rock Trail, reentering the woods. At a junction with Devil's Chair Trail, keep left to stay on House Rock Trail. The trail steepens considerably with more log stairs before reaching another junction at 0.5 mi (0.8 km); keep left again. Climb a series of rocky switchbacks as the trees start to thin and offer fleeting glimpses of the Charlotte Hills and the Connecticut River. The rock is well worn and slippery in places, even in dry weather, so be careful of your footing. The trail climbs higher before leveling out at 0.6 mi

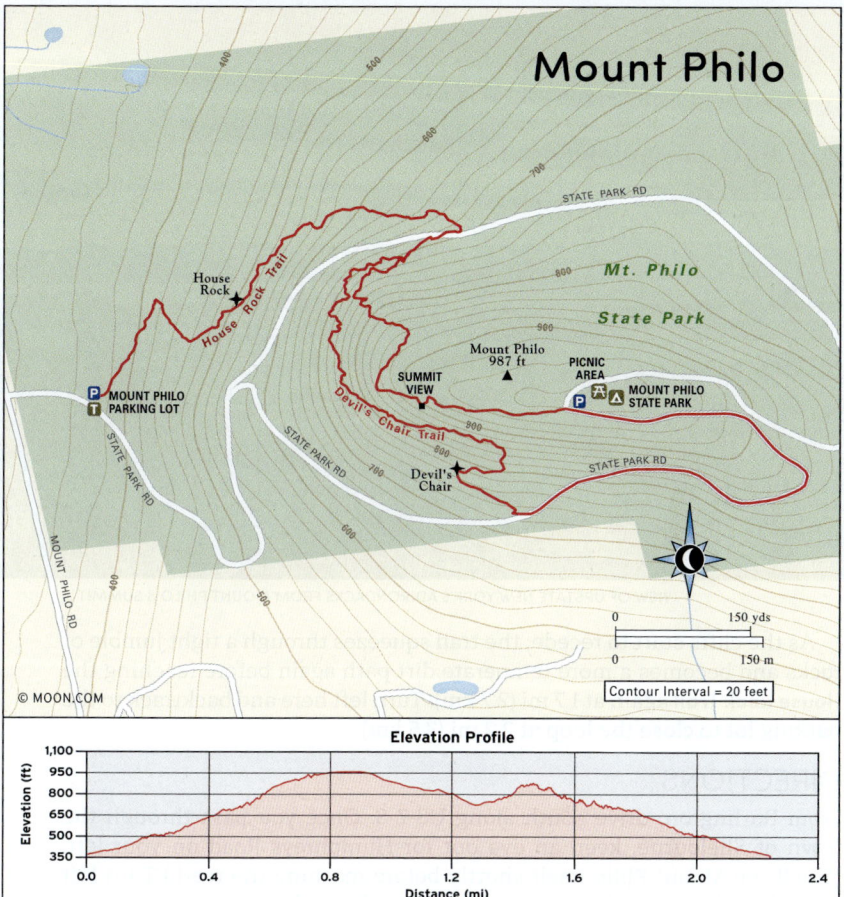

Mount Philo

Elevation Profile

(1 km). Pass a small scenic outlook for a **summit view** before reaching the summit proper at 0.7 mi (1.1 km). Here, hikers have their choice between scrambling up to a rocky height of land with an iron safety rail or taking a seat in one of several Adirondack chairs on a grassy lawn—both of which overlook the epic expanse of Vermont, New York, and the Adirondacks. Take a moment to prepare for the return journey, which has some unique thrills of its own.

▶ **MILE 0.7-2.2: Mount Philo Summit to Mount Philo Parking Lot**
Begin the second half of the hike by walking east past the grassy lawn and across the parking lot for 0.2 mi (0.3 km) until you reach State Park Road. Walk down the auto road for just over 0.4 mi (0.6 km) until you reach the sign for the **Devil's Chair Trail** at 1.4 mi (2.3 km). Turn right here and reenter the forest before arriving at the **Devil's Chair**—a throne-like rock formation that sits on a steep hillside overlooking the woods. The trail zigzags up through the chair and ambles along a series of sheer rock cliffs on somewhat eroded ground. The footing is quite narrow in places and can feel more like a ledge, so go slowly when in doubt.

VIEW OF UPSTATE NEW YORK'S ADIRONDACKS FROM MOUNT PHILO'S SUMMIT ▲

As the cliffs start to recede, the trail squeezes through a tight jumble of rocks and becomes a more temperate dirt path again before reaching the **House Rock Trail** again at 1.7 mi (2.7 km). Turn left here and backtrack to the parking lot to close the loop at 2.2 mi (3.5 km).

DIRECTIONS

From Burlington, drive south along US-7 S. Once you pass through the town of Shelburne, keep an eye out for Humphreys Road on your left. (You'll see Mount Philo itself shortly before reaching the road.) Turn left onto Humphreys Road and continue east to the park entrance.

GPS COORDINATES: 44°16'41.4"N 73°13'20.8"W

BEST NEARBY BITES AND BREWS

Vermont is a strong state for wood-fired pizza, and some of the crispiest and most savory parmesan-crusted pies in the north country can be devoured at **Folino's** (6305 Shelburne Rd., Shelburne; 802/881-8822; www.folinopizza.com; noon-8pm Sun.-Thurs., noon-9pm Fri.-Sat.). Better yet, the pizza parlor is literally connected to the great **Fiddlehead Brewing Company** (6305 Shelburne Rd., Shelburne; 802/399-2994; www.fiddleheadbrewing.com; 4pm-8pm Mon.-Tues., noon-8pm Wed.-Thurs. and Sun., noon-9pm Fri.-Sat.).

8 Camel's Hump

CAMEL'S HUMP STATE PARK, HUNTINGTON

This classic mountain trail takes hikers on a gorgeous and dramatic climb to the top of Vermont's most peculiarly shaped peak.

DISTANCE: 6.8 mi (10.9 km) round-trip

DURATION: 5 hr

ELEVATION GAIN: 2,583 ft (787 m)

EFFORT: Strenuous

TRAIL: Dirt path, rocks, wooden bog bridges

USERS: Hikers, leashed dogs

SEASON: June–October

FEES/PASSES: None

MAPS: Camel's Hump State Park website

TRAILHEAD: Forest City trailhead, Camel's Hump Rd., Huntington

FACILITIES: None

CONTACT: Department of Forests, Parks and Recreation Essex Office; 802/879-6565; www.vtstateparks.com/camelshump.html

Camel's Hump is the tallest undeveloped mountain in the Green Mountain State and one of the most popular day hikes in the Champlain Valley region. There are several ways to ascend Camel's Hump, but the most exciting and beautiful option is to take the Forest City Trail up to the Long Trail, which climbs the exposed south face of the "Hump" in a spectacular rocky fashion. From the top, the Burrows Trail offers a gentler descent route that leads back to the Forest City trailhead to make for a highly photogenic loop hike.

START THE HIKE

▶ **MILE 0-0.3: Forest City Trailhead to Camel's Hump Ascent**

Begin the hike at the east end of the parking area by the trailhead sign for the **Forest City Trail,** marked by blue blazes. Follow a gravel path through birch and beech woods, cross a wooden bridge, and hike east as the trail follows the stream deeper into the woods. Hike 0.3 mi (0.5 km) before reaching the gentle portion of the ascent.

▶ **MILE 0.3-2.1: Camel's Hump Ascent to Long Trail**

As the path transitions to rocks and dirt around 0.4 mi (0.6 km), the sound of rushing water begins to fade away and the grade steepens. Continue hiking 1.7 mi (2.7 km) at a moderate grade through the deciduous woods, which are rich with ferns and vegetation. Stone-and-log stairs become a frequent feature as the forest transitions to boreal trees. Keep climbing east until you reach the junction for the Long Trail at a grassy clearing at 2.1 mi (3.4 km).

Champlain Valley and Stowe

VERMONT

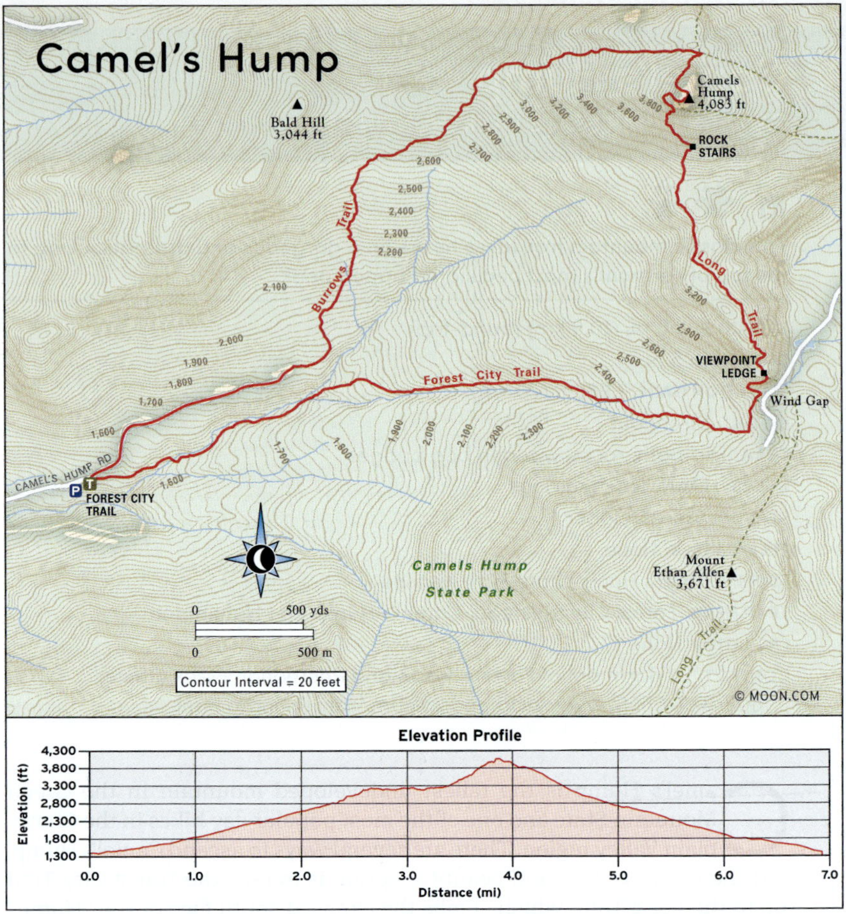

Camel's Hump

Bald Hill
3,044 ft

Camels Hump
4,083 ft

ROCK STAIRS

Long Trail

VIEWPOINT LEDGE

Wind Gap

Burrows Trail

Forest City Trail

CAMEL'S HUMP RD

FOREST CITY TRAIL

Camels Hump State Park

Mount Ethan Allen
3,671 ft

Long Trail

0   500 yds
0   500 m

Contour Interval = 20 feet

© MOON.COM

Elevation Profile

Elevation (ft): 4,300 / 3,800 / 3,300 / 2,800 / 2,300 / 1,800 / 1,300

Distance (mi): 0.0 1.0 2.0 3.0 4.0 5.0 6.0 7.0

▶ **MILE 2.1–3.6: Long Trail to Alpine Trail**

Having ascended the lower haunches of Camel's Hump, the real climb is about to begin. Turn left onto the **Long Trail,** marked by white blazes, and begin climbing a very steep and exposed series of rock faces that are rough enough to offer good natural traction. Continue to the four-way junction with the Dean and Allis Trails at 2.3 mi (3.7 km). Keep left here, and get your camera ready. A **ledge** at 2.4 mi (3.9 km) offers a killer view of Mount Ethan Allen to the south. The trail climbs some more exposed rock slabs for 0.2 mi (0.3 km) before entering a

VIEW OF CAMEL'S HUMP ▶

muddy boreal forest. For another 0.5 mi (0.8 km), the trail weaves along the southern flank of Camel's Hump. Once the trail swings around to the southeastern face of the "Hump" itself at 3.3 mi (5.3 km), you'll climb a very steep and winding series of **rock stairs** before reaching the junction with the Alpine Trail at 3.6 mi (5.8 km).

▶ **MILE 3.6-3.7: Alpine Trail to Camel's Hump Summit**
Take a left onto the **Alpine Trail;** it's only 0.1 mi (0.16 km) more to the tippy-top. The trail ascends a few more stairs before popping out onto the barren and sheer side of the summit. Watch your footing as the trail bypasses some narrow ledges that require a bit of scrambling. Schlep your way up some sloped rock slabs and follow cairns as the trail curves northeast and arrives at the compact and gusty summit of Camel's Hump. Enjoy the panoramic view of the Champlain Valley wilderness, thousands of feet below.

▶ **MILE 3.7-6.0: Camel's Hump Summit to Burrows Trail Parking Lot**
To return to the valley, pick up the **Burrows Trail** by following blue blazes northwest from the summit. You'll descend a moderately graded stone path that quickly reenters the woods. Hike your way through the boreal trees for 0.2 mi (0.3 km) before reaching a clearing; bear left at this junction with the Monroe Trail to continue on Burrows. Hike southwest for another 2 mi (3.2 km). This portion of the trail is a gradual, meandering descent through the forest—surprisingly mellow for a peak as tall and dramatic as Camel's Hump. You'll cross the creek on stones a couple of times.

▶ **MILE 6.0-6.8: Burrows Trail Parking Lot to Forest City Trailhead**
Arrive at the Burrows Trail parking lot at 6 mi (9.7 km). The final 0.8 mi (1.3 km) is a walk back down **Camel's Hump Road,** which passes a few fields and houses. It will give your legs a break before returning to the Forest City trailhead.

DIRECTIONS

From Burlington, drive east on I-89 S and then take Exit 11 for US-2 toward Richmond/Bolton/VT-117. Turn right onto US-2 at the bottom of the off-ramp. After roughly 1 mi (1.6 km), turn right onto Bridge Street and then take another right onto Huntington Road. Continue south on Huntington Road for 4 mi (6.4 km) before making a slight right onto Main Road and heading south for another 2 mi (3.2 km). As you arrive in Huntington Center, turn left onto Camel's Hump Road and take it east as it transitions to dirt. The parking area for the Forest City Trail will be on your right after about 2 mi (3.2 km).

GPS COORDINATES: 44°17'56.4"N 72°55'06.6"W

BEST NEARBY BITES AND BREWS

After the hike, put Camel's Hump in the rearview mirror, an ice-cold German schwarzbier or hoppy West Coast pilsner in your glass, and a plateful of sesame shrimp tacos in your belly at **Stone Corral Brewery** (83 Huntington Rd., Richmond; 802/434-5787; www.stonecorral.com; 4pm-9pm Mon., noon-9pm Tues.-Fri., 11:30am-9pm Sat.-Sun.).

NEARBY CAMPGROUNDS

NAME	LOCATION	FACILITIES	SEASON	FEE
Malletts Bay Campground	88 Malletts Bay Campground, Colchester, 44°32'42.1"N 73°13'04.1"W	Tent sites, RV sites, toilets, showers, potable water, laundry, swimming pool, camp store, Wi-Fi	May-mid-October	$35-65
802/863-6980; www.mallettsbaycamppground.com				
North Beach Campground	60 Institute Rd., Burlington, 44°29'40.7"N 73°14'10.4"W	Tent sites, lean-tos, RV sites, toilets, showers, potable water, snack bar, Wi-Fi	mid-May-mid-October	$37-55
802/862-0942; www.enjoyburlington.com/place/north-beach-campground				
Brewster River Campground	289 Campground Dr., Jeffersonville, 44°36'50.5"N 72°48'43.8"W	Tent sites, lean-to, RV sites, cabin, loft apartment, toilets, showers, potable water	May-mid-November	$49-289
802/324-9631; www.brewsterrivercampground.com				
Underhill State Park	352 Mountain Rd., Underhill, 44°31'44.8"N 72°50'35.9"W	Tent sites, toilets, potable water	late May-mid-October	$28-50
802/636-7220; www.vtstateparks.com/underhill.html				
Gold Brook Campground	1900 Waterbury Rd., Stowe, 44°26'33.3"N 72°42'21.1"W	Tent sites, RV sites, toilets, showers, potable water, laundry, Wi-Fi	July-mid-October	$42-55
802/253-7683; www.facebook.com/goldbrookcampgroundllc				

NEARBY CAMPGROUNDS (continued)

NAME	LOCATION	FACILITIES	SEASON	FEE
Little River State Park	3444 Little River Rd., Waterbury, 44°23'23.2"N 72°46'03.0"W	Tent sites, lean-tos, RV sites, cabins, toilets, showers, potable water	mid-May-late October	$28-50
802/244-7103; www.vtstateparks.com/littleriver.html				
Shelburne Camping Area	4385 Shelburne Rd., Shelburne, 44°23'35.7"N 73°13'03.8"W	Tent sites, lean-tos, RV sites, RV rentals, cabins, toilets, showers, potable water, laundry, swimming pool, camp store, restaurant, Wi-Fi	April-November	$38-140
802/985-2540; www.shelburnecamping.com				
Mount Philo State Park	5425 Mt Philo Rd., Charlotte, 44°16'41.1"N 73°13'20.9"W	Tent sites, lean-tos, toilets, showers, potable water	late May-mid-October	$28-38
802/425-2390; www.vtstateparks.com/philo.html				
Maple Hill Campsites	3825 Quaker St., Lincoln, 44°09'35.1"N 73°00'36.0"W	Tent sites, RV sites, toilets, showers, potable water	mid-May-mid-October	$35-40
802/453-3687; www.maplehillcamp.com				

NORTHEAST KINGDOM

Known for its vibrant displays of fall foliage, and often the first region in New England to "turn" to warm autumnal hues, the Northeast Kingdom of Vermont is a vast and rural landscape that feels untouched by the hands of time. Willoughby State Forest, with its jagged peaks surrounding a lake of the same name, is the hub of adventure in this region, but there are wonderful hidden gems in the wildlife-brimming bogs, sky-high fire towers, and mystical ravines that make up this diverse and wide-ranging patch of New England paradise.

▲ LAKE WILLOUGHBY, SEEN FROM MOUNT PISGAH ▲ LONG TRAIL

1 Long Trail: Jay Pass to Jay Peak
DISTANCE: 3.4 mi (5.5 km) round-trip
DURATION: 3 hr
EFFORT: Moderate/strenuous
PAGE: 408

2 Devil's Gulch via the Long Trail and Babcock Trail
DISTANCE: 4.8 mi (7.7 km) round-trip
DURATION: 3 hr
EFFORT: Moderate/strenuous
PAGE: 410

3 Bald Mountain via the Long Pond Trail
DISTANCE: 4.2 mi (6.8 km) round-trip
DURATION: 2.5 hr
EFFORT: Moderate/strenuous
PAGE: 413

4 Mount Pisgah via the North Trail
DISTANCE: 4.2 mi (6.8 km) round-trip
DURATION: 2.5 hr
EFFORT: Strenuous
PAGE: 416

5 Owls Head Trail
DISTANCE: 4.8 mi (7.7 km) round-trip
DURATION: 3 hr
EFFORT: Moderate
PAGE: 419

6 Little Loop and Peacham Bog Trail
DISTANCE: 5.8 mi (9.3 km) round-trip
DURATION: 3.5 hr
EFFORT: Moderate
PAGE: 422

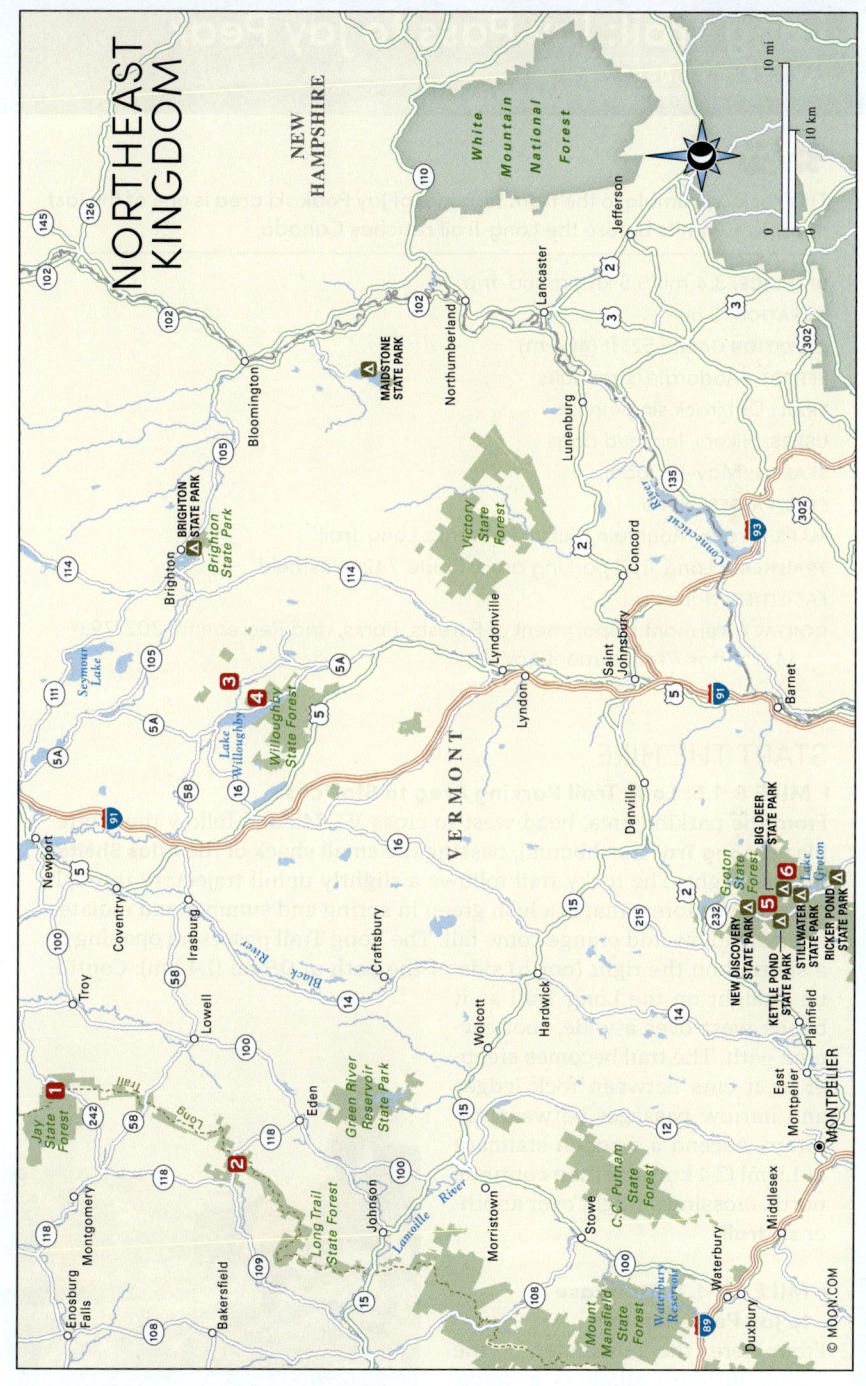

NORTHEAST KINGDOM

NEW HAMPSHIRE

White Mountain National Forest

Jefferson

Lancaster

Northumberland

Lunenburg

Concord

Saint Johnsbury

MAIDSTONE STATE PARK

Bloomington

BRIGHTON STATE PARK

Brighton

Brighton State Park

Victory State Forest

Lyndonville

Lyndon

Danville

Seymour Lake

Lake Willoughby

Willoughby State Forest

Newport

Coventry

Irasburg

Craftsbury

Hardwick

BIG DEER STATE PARK

Groton State Forest

NEW DISCOVERY STATE PARK

KETTLE POND STATE PARK

STILLWATER STATE PARK

RICKER POND STATE PARK

Lake Groton

Troy

Lowell

Eden

Wolcott

Plainfield

East Montpelier

Montgomery

Johnson

Morristown

Stowe

C.C. Putnam State Forest

Middlesex

MONTPELIER

Jay State Forest

Long Trail State Forest

Green River Reservoir State Park

Mount Mansfield State Forest

Waterbury Reservoir

Waterbury

Duxbury

Enosburg Falls

Bakersfield

Connecticut River

Black River

Lamoille River

Long Trail

VERMONT

© MOON.COM

10 mi

10 km

VERMONT

407

❀ 🐾 🚶‍♂️

This rocky scramble to the tram terminal of Jay Peak ski area is one of the last notable summits before the Long Trail reaches Canada.

DISTANCE: 3.4 mi (5.5 km) round-trip

DURATION: 3 hr

ELEVATION GAIN: 1,521 ft (464 m)

EFFORT: Moderate/strenuous

TRAIL: Dirt/rock singletrack

USERS: Hikers, leashed dogs

SEASON: May–October

FEES/PASSES: None

MAPS: Green Mountain Club, "Vermont's Long Trail"

TRAILHEAD: Long Trail parking area, Route 242, Westfield

FACILITIES: None

CONTACT: Vermont Department of Forests, Parks, and Recreation; 802/793-3432; https://fpr.vermont.gov

START THE HIKE

▸ **MILE 0–1.5: Long Trail Parking Area to Staircase**

From the parking area, head west to cross VT-242 and follow the white-blazed **Long Trail** northbound, passing the small shack of the **Atlas Shelter** on your right. The rocky trail follows a slightly uphill trajectory through a deciduous forest that is a lush green in spring and summer and radiates hues of yellow and orange come fall. The Long Trail passes an opening to a ski trail on the right (north) side of the path at 0.9 mi (1.4 km). Continue straight on the Long Trail as it bends west over a wide, root-covered path. The trail becomes steeper as it cuts between rock ledges and narrow passages between conifers. Ascend a wooden staircase at 1.5 mi (2.4 km) and then continue north, crossing straight over another **ski trail.**

▸ **MILE 1.5–1.7: Staircase to Jay Peak Summit**

From here, the remainder of the 0.2-mi (0.3-km) climb is a steep, rocky scramble to the northwest, where the Long Trail meets the top

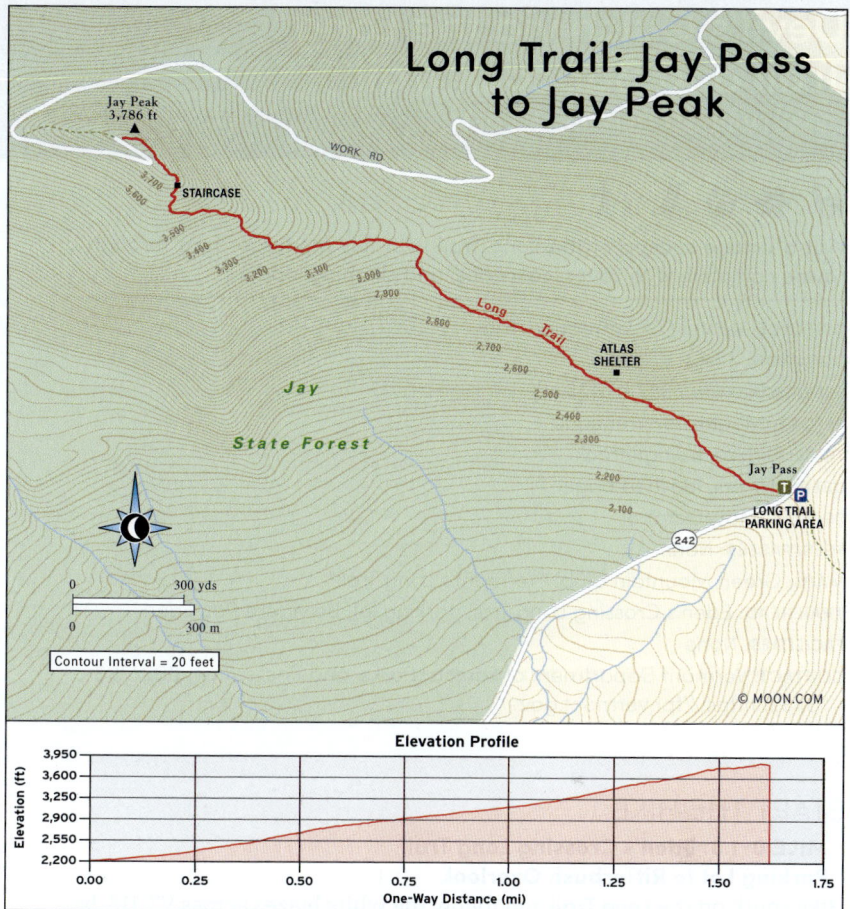

Long Trail: Jay Pass to Jay Peak

Jay Peak
3,786 ft

WORK RD

STAIRCASE

Long Trail

ATLAS SHELTER

Jay

State Forest

Jay Pass

LONG TRAIL
PARKING AREA

242

0   300 yds

0   300 m

Contour Interval = 20 feet

© MOON.COM

Elevation Profile

Elevation (ft)

3,950
3,600
3,250
2,900
2,550
2,200

0.00   0.25   0.50   0.75   1.00   1.25   1.50   1.75

One-Way Distance (mi)

of the summit **tram** line. Great views extend across Vermont and Canada on a clear day, but locals say the peak is frequently shrouded in "the Jay Cloud," a somewhat mystical and precipitous weather system caused by the mountain's unique orientation, elevation, and location; some claim it is responsible for the peak's epic ski conditions. To return to the parking area, backtrack down the Long Trail.

DIRECTIONS

From VT-100, drive to the center of Troy and turn right onto VT-101 N. In 3 mi (4.8 km), turn left onto VT-242 W and drive through the ski area for about 6.5 mi (10.5 km). The trailhead is a large parking turnoff on the left, and the route begins across the street.

GPS COORDINATES: 44°54'46.1"N 72°30'13.6"W

2

Devil's Gulch via the Long Trail and Babcock Trail

LONG TRAIL STATE FOREST, EDEN

Visit a unique section of the Long Trail with this moderate hike through a ravine complete with caves, cascades, and climbing ladders.

DISTANCE: 4.8 mi (7.7 km) round-trip

DURATION: 3 hr

ELEVATION GAIN: 1,387 ft (423 m)

EFFORT: Moderate/strenuous

TRAIL: Dirt/rock singletrack

USERS: Hikers, leashed dogs

SEASON: May–October

FEES/PASSES: None

MAPS: Green Mountain Club, "Vermont's Long Trail"

TRAILHEAD: Eden's Crossing Long Trail parking lot, Belvidere Rd., Eden

FACILITIES: None

CONTACT: Vermont Department of Forests, Parks, and Recreation; 802/793-3432; https://fpr.vermont.gov

START THE HIKE

▶ **MILE 0-1.3: Eden's Crossing Long Trail Parking Lot to Ritterbush Overlook**

Hike south on the **Long Trail** and follow the white blazes across VT-118, being mindful of traffic. The trail traverses a hillside, then winds away from the road and over a series of rolling hills and valleys in an increasingly wild forest. At 1.3 mi (2.1 km), the trail arrives at the **Ritterbush Overlook,** where hikers can take in views of a scenic mountain pond.

▶ **MILE 1.3-1.7: Ritterbush Overlook to Babcock Trail Intersection**

From here, the trail drops in elevation, switchbacking west down the hill and descending a steep stone staircase. Cross over a small stream, using rocks for stepping-stones, and reach the intersection with the **Babcock Trail** at 1.7 mi (2.7 km).

▶ **MILE 1.7-2.3: Babcock Trail Intersection to Devil's Perch Outlook**

Continue straight (west) on the **Long Trail,** following signs for Devil's Gulch. Reach a **cascade** at 2 mi (3.2 km), where the trail turns right (west) and climbs a 6-ft (2-m) wooden ladder. Shortly after, a sign marks the beginning of **Devil's Gulch,** and the path winds through a vibrant ravine with caves, bridges, and rocky scrambles for about 0.2 mi (0.3 km). Continue on the Long Trail until you reach the signed intersection for **Spruce Ledge Camp.** Turn left (east) across the brook and follow the blue blazes 0.1 mi

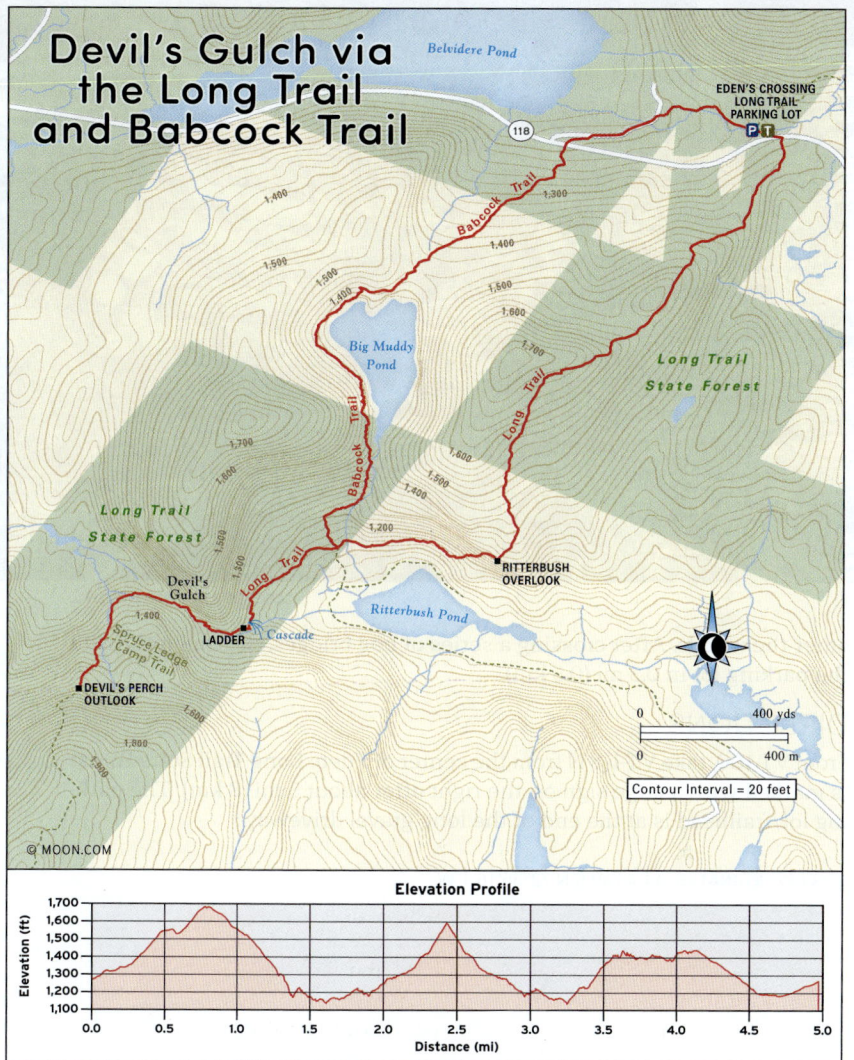

Devil's Gulch via the Long Trail and Babcock Trail

Elevation Profile

(0.2 km) up the stone staircase to Spruce Ledge Camp and the **Devil's Perch Outlook** for great views of the pond, Belvidere Mountain, and its abandoned asbestos mine.

▶ MILE 2.3–4.8: Devil's Perch Outlook to Eden's Crossing Long Trail Parking Lot

When ready, backtrack 0.6 mi (1 km) through the gulch to the intersection with the **Babcock Trail.** Turn left (north) onto the Babcock Trail and follow the blue blazes up the hillside. The trail arrives on the banks of **Big Muddy Pond** at 3.3 mi (5.3 km), then rolls gently downhill. Arrive at VT-118 in 1 mi (1.6 km) and cross the road straight (north) onto the **Babcock Extension Trail.** Turn right (east) onto the gravel road at the end of the path at 4.5 mi (7.2 km), then turn right (east) again at the sign where the blue blazes

CASCADE AT DEVIL'S GULCH ▲

enter the woods. After crossing a series of bog bridges, the trail returns to the parking lot in 0.3 mi (0.5 km).

DIRECTIONS

From VT-100, take VT-118 N from the center of Eden. Long Trail State Forest is marked with a large sign on the right after about 5 mi (8 km). The parking lot/trailhead is at the end of the long gravel driveway.

GPS COORDINATES: 44°45'49.5"N 72°35'16.1"W

BEST NEARBY BREWS

Kingdom Brewing (353 Coburn Hill Rd., Newport; 802/334-7096; https://kingdombrewingvt.com; 4pm-9pm Fri.-Sat.) is a popular name in Vermont beer, and its taproom in Newport, 18 mi (29 km) from the trailhead, is beloved for its ski lodge atmosphere, great live music, and snack bar.

3

Bald Mountain via the Long Pond Trail

WILLOUGHBY STATE FOREST, WESTMORE

A challenging ascent to the pinnacle of Willoughby State Forest features a fire tower with some of the best views in Vermont.

BEST: Fall hikes, vistas

DISTANCE: 4.2 mi (6.8 km) round-trip

DURATION: 2.5 hr

ELEVATION GAIN: 1,233 ft (376 m)

EFFORT: Moderate/strenuous

TRAIL: Gravel fire road, dirt/rock singletrack

USERS: Hikers, leashed dogs

SEASON: May-October

FEES/PASSES: None

MAPS: Vermont Department of Forests, Parks, and Recreation, "Willoughby State Forest Guide"

TRAILHEAD: Long Pond Trail parking lot, Long Pond Rd., Westmore

FACILITIES: None

CONTACT: Vermont Department of Forests, Parks, and Recreation; 802/793-3432; https://fpr.vermont.gov

START THE HIKE

▶ **MILE 0-0.6: Long Pond Trail Parking Lot to Bald Mountain/Long Pond Trail**

Hike north from the parking area, passing through the gate and onto the

gravel logging road. Where the **road forks** at 0.2 mi (0.3 km), bear right (east). The wide road climbs gradually, reaching a **meadow** at 0.6 mi (1 km). Although the meadow is technically a log landing used for forestry, it is a great spot to catch glimpses of wildlife on a quiet day, as well as wildflowers in season and some nice views of rolling hills to the south. Walk straight (east) through the field until you reach a **sign** marked Trail, and then turn right (south) onto a singletrack

◀ LONG POND TRAIL TO BALD MOUNTAIN

Northeast Kingdom

VERMONT

413

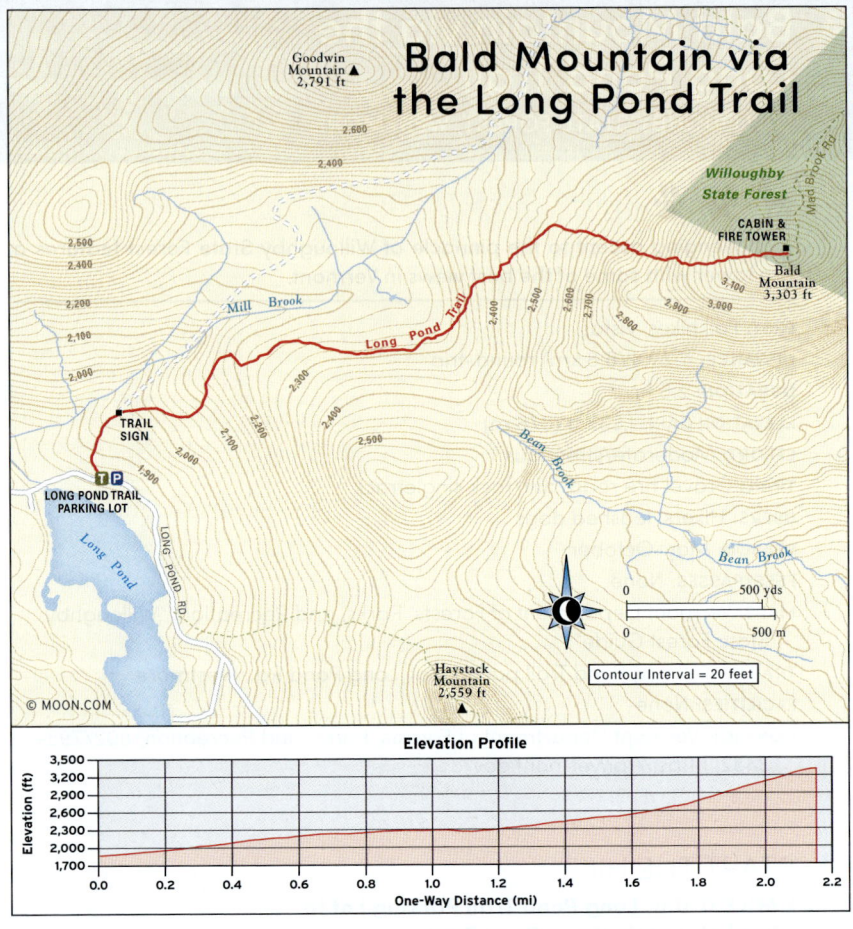

Bald Mountain via the Long Pond Trail

Goodwin Mountain ▲ 2,791 ft

Willoughby State Forest

CABIN & FIRE TOWER

Bald Mountain 3,303 ft

Mill Brook

Long Pond Trail

TRAIL SIGN

LONG POND TRAIL PARKING LOT

Long Pond

LONG POND RD.

Bean Brook

Bean Brook

Mad Brook Rd

0   500 yds
0   500 m

Contour Interval = 20 feet

Haystack Mountain 2,559 ft ▲

© MOON.COM

Elevation Profile

Elevation (ft): 3,500 / 3,200 / 2,900 / 2,600 / 2,300 / 2,000 / 1,700

One-Way Distance (mi): 0.0 0.2 0.4 0.6 0.8 1.0 1.2 1.4 1.6 1.8 2.0 2.2

path. Shortly after, turn left (east) at the trail sign for **Bald Mountain/Long Pond Trail.**

▶ MILE 0.6–1.3: Bald Mountain/Long Pond Trail to Caves

From this point, the trail is marked with blue blazes. Follow the blue blazes along a series of creeks. There are some steep, rooty sections and a few sets of timber steps to help hikers over hills. The trail climbs 0.7 mi (1.1 km) to an area of cool, mossy caves and rock formations that can be observed from the trail.

▶ MILE 1.3–2.1: Caves to Bald Mountain Summit

Continue climbing straight east through this rocky subalpine spruce-fir forest, being mindful of slick terrain. This section of trail is quite strenuous as it leads straight up to the peak of Bald Mountain. The trail emerges on the summit in 0.8 mi (1.3 km). There is a small **cabin** on the summit, which is a newly restored relic of the 1920s effort to create a fire lookout system across the state of Vermont. It holds a woodstove and a few bunks where hikers can spend the night in the company of northern Vermont

wildlife such as snowshoe hares. The lookout's companion **fire tower** is still standing strong, and hikers can climb the steps to the top for 360-degree views stretching across the Northeast Kingdom to New Hampshire's White Mountains. The hike to this 3,314-ft (1,010-m) summit may be tough, but locals agree these are some of the most spectacular views in Vermont. When finished drinking in the sights, backtrack on the Long Pond Trail back to the parking lot.

DIRECTIONS

From St. Johnsbury/I-91, take Exit 23 for US-5 N. In about 8 mi (12.9 km), turn right onto VT-5A N. At the Willoughby Lake Store, turn right onto Long Pond Road. The parking area for the trailhead is about 2.2 mi (3.5 km) up the road on the left, just past the fishing access area. A small sign marks the start of the Long Pond Trail at the end of a gated logging road.

GPS COORDINATES: 44°45'23.6"N 72°01'04.7"W

Northeast Kingdom

VERMONT

4

Mount Pisgah via the North Trail

WILLOUGHBY STATE FOREST, WESTMORE

Climb to incredible vistas on this scenic cliff rising from the banks of shimmering Lake Willoughby.

BEST: Summer hikes

DISTANCE: 4.2 mi (6.8 km) round-trip

DURATION: 2.5 hr

ELEVATION GAIN: 1,326 ft (404 m)

EFFORT: Strenuous

TRAIL: Dirt/rock singletrack

USERS: Hikers, leashed dogs

SEASON: May–October

FEES/PASSES: None

MAPS: Vermont Department of Forests, Parks, and Recreation, "Willoughby State Forest Guide"

TRAILHEAD: Mount Pisgah north trailhead, Route 5A, Westmore

FACILITIES: None

CONTACT: Vermont Department of Forests, Parks, and Recreation; 802/793-3432; https://fpr.vermont.gov

START THE HIKE

▶ **MILE 0-1.8: Mount Pisgah North Trailhead to North Overlook**

Starting at the small sign, hike east from the road and follow the blue blazes up a narrow trail that quickly ascends a series of steep stone steps through the slopes of a thick forest. Traverse a flat hemlock grove and rock-hop across a small stream at 0.2 mi (0.3 km). From the other side of the stream, the trail climbs steadily up several switchbacks to reach a signed intersection with the East Trail at 1.4 mi (2.3 km). Go straight (south) to stay on the **North Trail.** There is a difficult climb up a steep but lovely stone staircase before the trail reaches a sign for North Overlook at 1.7 mi (2.7 km). Turn right (north) onto the spur trail toward **North Overlook.** The narrow spur path leads slightly downhill for 0.1 mi (0.16 km) before emerging at the North Overlook.

FALL FOLIAGE ON THE NORTH TRAIL ▶

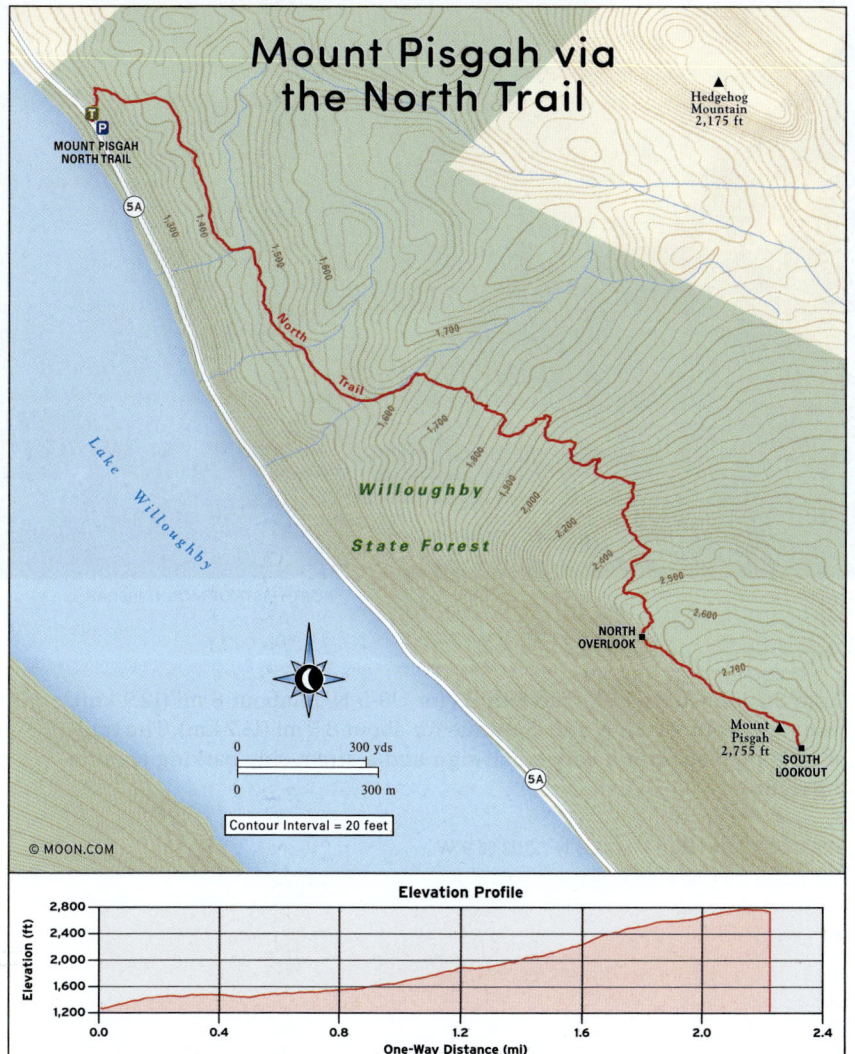

Mount Pisgah via the North Trail

Hedgehog Mountain 2,175 ft

MOUNT PISGAH NORTH TRAIL

North Trail

Lake Willoughby

Willoughby State Forest

NORTH OVERLOOK

Mount Pisgah 2,755 ft

SOUTH LOOKOUT

0   300 yds
0   300 m

Contour Interval = 20 feet

© MOON.COM

Elevation Profile

Elevation (ft)

2,800
2,400
2,000
1,600
1,200

0.0   0.4   0.8   1.2   1.6   2.0   2.4

One-Way Distance (mi)

▶ **MILE 1.8–2.1: North Overlook to South Overlook**

This impressive vista looks directly west over **Lake Willoughby** and **Mount Hor** on the opposite side of the lake. It's a lovely secluded view from a bald granite perch where hikers can see birds soar from the cliffs and canoes and kayaks paddle across the lake below. Use caution; the drop-off is steep and the rocks may be slippery when wet. After enjoying the vista, backtrack 0.1 mi (0.16 km) up the spur trail to the intersection. For more views, hikers can turn right (south) and continue a moderate climb for another 0.3 mi (0.5 km) to the **summit/South Overlook.** Though this is the highest point on **Mount Pisgah,** the thick tree cover obstructs most views, and none are as dramatic as the vista from North Overlook.

When ready, hikers can turn around and backtrack 0.3 mi (0.5 km) to the intersection and then 1.7 mi (2.7 km) north to the road via the North Trail.

Northeast Kingdom

VERMONT

417

NORTH VISTA OF MOUNT PISGAH ▲

DIRECTIONS

From St. Johnsbury/I-91, take Exit 23 for US-5 N. In about 8 mi (12.9 km), turn right onto VT-5A N and continue for about 8.5 mi (13.7 km). The trailhead is marked with a very small sign and a street-side parking area on the right.

GPS COORDINATES: 44°44'42.8"N 72°02'55.9"W

BEST NEARBY BREWS

The Burke Publick House (482 VT-114, East Burke; 802/626-1188; www.burkepub.com; 4pm–9pm Tues.–Thurs., 4pm–10pm Fri.–Sat.), 13 mi (21 km) from the trailhead in East Burke, serves up creative comfort food alongside a great beer and cocktail menu.

5 Owls Head Trail

GROTON STATE FOREST, GROTON

This scenic height of land in Groton State Forest delivers big views of Lake Groton, Kettle Pond, and the Green Mountains after passing through a colorful forest.

DISTANCE: 4.8 mi (7.7 km) round-trip
DURATION: 3 hr
ELEVATION GAIN: 440 ft (134 m)
EFFORT: Moderate
TRAIL: Dirt, rock path
USERS: Hikers, leashed dogs
SEASON: April–October
FEES/PASSES: None
MAPS: Vermont Department of Forests, Parks, and Recreation "Groton State Forest Summer Trails Guide"
TRAILHEAD: Northern parking area, State Forest Rd., Groton
FACILITIES: None
CONTACT: Vermont Department of Forests, Parks, and Recreation; 802/793-3432; https://fpr.vermont.gov

While it's possible to hike to the summit of Owls Head from the end of the Owls Head Scenic Road, the pond-speckled vistas are best paired with a hike through the Osmore Pond Scenic Area. The terrain varies between swampy lowlands, thickly forested hillsides, and sweat-inducing stone staircases before this grab bag of a hike culminates in impressive panoramas.

START THE HIKE

▸ MILE 0-0.8: Northern Parking Area to Owls Head Trail

Head southwest on the doubletrack trail that departs the northern parking area. After 0.2 mi (0.3 km) of slight downhill, arrive at the intersection with the **Telephone Line Trail.** Turn left (east) and cross State Forest Road. This narrow gravel singletrack winds through forest for 0.6 mi (1 km) before reaching the intersection with the **Owls Head Trail.**

▸ MILE 0.8-2.1: Owls Head Trail to Owls Head Parking Area

Turn right (south) onto the blue-blazed Owls Head Trail, following signs toward Owls Head Summit. The trail continues slightly uphill with some logged clearings providing distant views in 0.2 mi (0.3 km). The rolling terrain carries you over a series of roots and rocks, then dips down to a bog bridge through a wet area. In 1.1 mi (1.8 km), emerge near the **Owls Head parking area.**

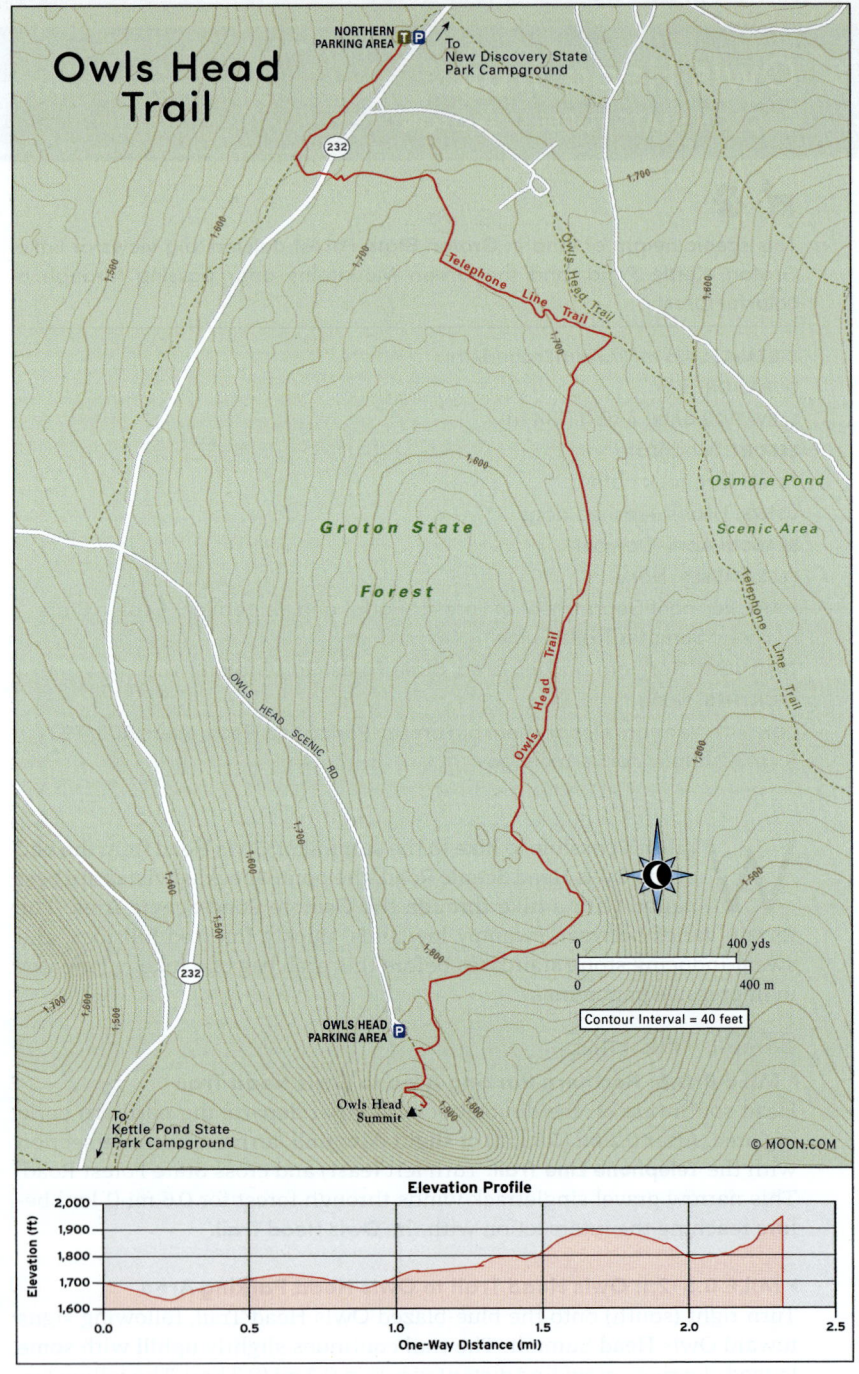

Owls Head Trail

Elevation Profile

▲ VIEW FROM OWLS HEAD

▶ **MILE 2.1-2.4: Owls Head Parking Area to Owls Head Summit**
Turn slightly left (south), following signs for the Owls Head Summit. Wrap around the parking lot to the south for 0.1 mi (0.16 km), then turn left (south) at the next sign for Owls Head Summit. A steep stone staircase carries you 0.2 mi (0.3 km) on your final incline to the summit. At the stone gazebo marking the peak, views stretch out toward Kettle Pond and Camel's Hump to the east and to Lake Groton to the south. Return to the northern parking area the way you came.

DIRECTIONS

From VT-302/Groton, take VT-232 N for about 9 mi (14.5 km). Just past the Owls Head Scenic Road, there will be a sign for the northern parking area on the right side of the road.

GPS COORDINATES: 44°19'07.1"N 72°17'40.0"W

The boardwalk trail through Peacham Bog includes rarities such as carnivorous pitcher plants and boasts great odds for wildlife spotting.

BEST: New England oddities
DISTANCE: 5.8 mi (9.3 km) round-trip
DURATION: 3.5 hr
ELEVATION GAIN: 662 ft (202 m)
EFFORT: Moderate
TRAIL: Dirt/rock singletrack, boardwalk, gravel road
USERS: Hikers, leashed dogs
SEASON: May–October
FEES/PASSES: None
MAPS: Vermont Department of Forests, Parks, and Recreation, "Groton State Forest Summer Trails Guide"
TRAILHEAD: Little Loop trailhead, Boulder Beach Rd., Groton
FACILITIES: Trail map, restrooms, and water at the nature center
CONTACT: Vermont Department of Forests, Parks, and Recreation; 802/793-3432; https://fpr.vermont.gov

START THE HIKE

▸ **MILE 0-0.6: Little Loop Trailhead to Peacham Bog Trail**
Follow the **Little Loop Trail** east out of the parking lot and bear right (south) just after the bridge. The blue-blazed trail winds through a forest decorated with large boulders, then climbs to a ridge above the stream. Pass a **bench** looking out over the marsh at 0.4 mi (0.6 km) and follow the trail as it bends left (west). Reach a signed intersection with the **Peacham Bog Trail** at 0.6 mi (1 km) and turn right (north) onto the Peacham Bog Trail.

▸ **MILE 0.6-2.4: Peacham Bog Trail to Viewing Platform**
Cross straight over Coldwater Brook Road at 0.9 mi (1.4 km) and continue on the blue-and-yellow-blazed trail. The mossy path winds east over rolling hills and small creeks, entering the **Peacham Bog Natural Area** at 1.8 mi (2.9 km). In another 0.6 mi (1 km), the trail emerges from a pine-scented thicket onto a

PEACHAM BOG BOARDWALK ▸

VERMONT
Northeast Kingdom

Little Loop and Peacham Bog Trail

Elevation Profile

boardwalk that carries hikers into the heart of the bog. Bear left at the fork and hike approximately 25 ft (8 m) to the scenic **viewing platform.**

▶ MILE 2.4–4.3: Viewing Platform to Coldwater Road
After enjoying the view at the platform, backtrack to the fork and turn left (east) through the remainder of the bog. Reach an **intersection** at 2.6 mi (4.2 km) and turn right (south), following signs for the **Peacham Bog Trail.** A wide, leafy corridor leads downhill and reaches another sign for Peacham Bog at 3.3 mi (5.3 km). Bear left (south) downhill to reach **Coldwater Road** at 4.3 mi (6.9 km).

▶ MILE 4.3–5.8: Coldwater Road to Little Loop Trailhead
Turn right (north) onto the gravel road and go through a clearing with great views to the west. At the intersection with the Little Loop Trail at 5 mi (8 km), turn left (west) onto the **Little Loop Trail.** Cross the **bridge** and carry on straight (south) for 0.5 mi (0.8 km). Pass straight (south) through the signed intersection of the **Little Loop Trail/Peacham Bog Trail** to return to the parking area in 0.3 mi (0.5 km).

BLACKBERRIES ON THE PEACHAM BOG TRAIL ▲

DIRECTIONS

From VT-302/Groton, take VT-232 N for about 5 mi (8 km), then turn right onto Boulder Beach Road. Park at the Groton Nature Center, which is marked with a sign about 1.5 mi (2.4 km) down the road on the left.

GPS COORDINATES: 44°17'08.3"N 72°15'55.2"W

BEST NEARBY BITES

You won't find many food choices near the trailhead, but **The Meltdown Grilled Cheese and Taproom** (83 Washington St., Barre; 802/622-8277; 11:30am-8pm Sun., 4pm-8pm Mon. and Thurs., 11:30am-9pm Fri.-Sat.) is worth the 25-mi (40-km) drive. Oozing cheese sandwiches with your choice of meat and dips, hand cut fries, and frosty pints will fill up hungry hikers.

NEARBY CAMPGROUNDS

NAME	LOCATION	FACILITIES	SEASON	FEE
Brighton State Park	102 State Park Rd., Island Pond, 44°47'46.7"N 71°51'23.4"W	54 RV/tent sites, 23 lean-to sites, 5 cabins; restrooms	late May-mid-October	$20-68
802/723-4360, www.vtstateparks.com/brighton.html				
Maidstone State Park	5956 Maidstone Lake Rd., Guildhall, 44°38'18.3"N 71°38'35.6"W	34 RV/tent sites, 25 lean-to sites; restrooms	late May-early September	$20-38
802/676-3930; www.vtstateparks.com/maidstone.html				
New Discovery State Park	VT Route 232, Marshfield, 44°19'21.3"N 72°17'22.1"W	38 RV/tent sites, 15 lean-to sites, 8 horse camping sites, 4 remote lean-to sites, 3 remote tent sites; restrooms	late May-mid-October	$20-38
802/426-3042; www.vtstateparks.com/newdiscovery.html				
Kettle Pond State Park	6993 State Forest Rd., Groton, 44°17'38.6"N 72°18'17.1"W	26 group lean-tos, 7 remote lean-tos, 1 remote tent site; composting toilets	mid-May-mid-October	$20-38
802/426-3042; www.vtstateparks.com/kettlepond.html				

NEARBY CAMPGROUNDS (continued)

NAME	LOCATION	FACILITIES	SEASON	FEE
Big Deer State Park	1467 Boulder Beach Rd., Groton, 44°17'10.9"N 72°16'03.2"W	22 tent sites, 5 lean-to sites; restrooms	late May–early September	$20–38

802/584-3822; www.vtstateparks.com/bigdeer.html

NAME	LOCATION	FACILITIES	SEASON	FEE
Stillwater State Park	44 Stillwater Rd., Groton, 44°16'48.9"N 72°16'30.0"W	56 RV/tent sites, 19 lean-to sites; restrooms	mid-May–early September	$20–38

802/584-3822; www.vtstateparks.com/Stillwater.html

NAME	LOCATION	FACILITIES	SEASON	FEE
Ricker Pond State Park	18 Ricker Pond Campground, Groton, 44°14'44.0"N 72°15'13.9"W	26 RV/tent sites, 23 lean-to sites, 5 cabins, 2 cottages; restrooms	late May–mid-October	$50–110

802/584-3821; www.vtstateparks.com/ricker.html

COBBLESTONE BEACH AT MENEMSHA HILLS

MASSACHUSETTS

GREATER BOSTON, NORTH AND SOUTH SHORE

Boston may look like natureless concrete sprawl, but abundant spectacular hikes lie within roughly an hour's drive from the city, including some of the best coastal scenery New England has to offer. The Boston metropolitan area includes the coast to the north of the city, known as the North Shore, and its southern equivalent, the South Shore. Along these coasts, sandy dunes and salt marshes cling to the skirts of the sea while fishing boats bob in the distance. In a crescent around the city, several hills rise up from the coastal plain as sentinels, where one can survey the city skyline against the sparkle of the Atlantic Ocean. The trails in this region prove that even in New England's largest city, a great hike is never far away.

▲ PLANTERS HILL OVERLOOK AT WORLD'S END

▲ CRANE BEACH

◄ BOG AT HEYWOOD'S MEADOW, WALDEN POND

1 **Rock Circuit Trail**
DISTANCE: 4.2 mi (6.8 km) round-trip
DURATION: 4 hr
EFFORT: Moderate/strenuous
PAGE: 434

2 **Carriage Paths**
DISTANCE: 4 mi (6.4 km) round-trip
DURATION: 2 hr
EFFORT: Easy
PAGE: 437

3 **Great Blue Hill via the Skyline Trail**
DISTANCE: 5.7 mi (9.2 km) round-trip
DURATION: 3 hr
EFFORT: Moderate/strenuous
PAGE: 440

4 **Walden Pond via the Alternate Pond Loop**
DISTANCE: 2.2 mi (3.5 km) round-trip
DURATION: 1.5 hr
EFFORT: Easy
PAGE: 443

5 **Mount Wachusett via the Midstate Trail**
DISTANCE: 3.9 mi (6.3 km) round-trip
DURATION: 2 hr
EFFORT: Moderate
PAGE: 446

6 **Mount Watatic via the Wapack Trail**
DISTANCE: 3 mi (4.8 km) round-trip
DURATION: 2 hr
EFFORT: Moderate
PAGE: 449

7 **Castle Neck Trails**
DISTANCE: 5.6 mi (9 km) round-trip
DURATION: 3.5 hr
EFFORT: Moderate
PAGE: 452

GREATER BOSTON, NORTH AND SOUTH SHORE

© MOON.COM

Rock Circuit Trail

MIDDLESEX FELLS RESERVATION, MEDFORD

The roller coaster-like Rock Circuit Trail carries hikers to the highest points in Middlesex Fells Reservation for expansive views of Boston and beyond.

DISTANCE: 4.2 mi (6.8 km) round-trip
DURATION: 4 hr
ELEVATION GAIN: 509 ft (155 m)
EFFORT: Moderate/strenuous
TRAIL: Dirt, rock path
USERS: Hikers, leashed dogs
SEASON: April–November
FEES/PASSES: None
MAPS: Mass DCR, "Middlesex Fells Reservation"
TRAILHEAD: Woodland Path trailhead
FACILITIES: Trail map, picnic tables
CONTACT: Massachusetts Department of Conservation and Recreation; 617/727-1199; www.mass.gov/locations/middlesex-fells-reservation

Middlesex Fells Reservation boasts over 100 mi (160 km) of multi-use trails across 2,575 acres (1,040 hectares) of forests, reservoirs, and hills. The name "Fells" is borrowed from the Saxon word for rocky hills, which is exactly what hikers will traverse on the park's signature Rock Circuit Trail. Highlights of this 4.2-mi (6.8-km) loop include sweeping city views from Melrose Rock, Black Rock, Pinnacle Rock, and Boojum Rock, as well as a seasonal cascade and the former MIT Geodetic Observatory.

START THE HIKE

▶ **MILE 0-0.6: Woodland Path Trailhead to Middlesex Fells Reservoir**
Begin on the Woodland Path. After a slight uphill, pass the end of the Rock Circuit Trail on the right and continue straight. At 0.2 mi (0.3 km) from the trailhead, turn left (north) onto the start of the white-blazed Rock Circuit Trail. Pass **Shiner Pool,** a small bog on the right, then skirt around the edge of the water to arrive at the Hemlock Pool Road, 0.4 mi (0.6 km) from the trailhead. Turn right (east) onto the Hemlock Pool Road. Turn left (north) to continue on the Rock Circuit Trail in 210 ft (64 m). In another 0.1 mi (0.16 km), arrive at the **Reservoir Access Road,** where you'll catch a glimpse of the reservoir shining through the trees.

▶ **MILE 0.6-1.6: Middlesex Fells Reservoir to Melrose Rock**
Keep right, then in 210 ft (64 m) turn left onto Pipe Line Road. In 0.1 mi (0.16 km), the Rock Circuit Trail turns right (east) onto a stretch of woodsy singletrack. Continue along the Rock Circuit Trail for 0.7 mi (1.1 km) until

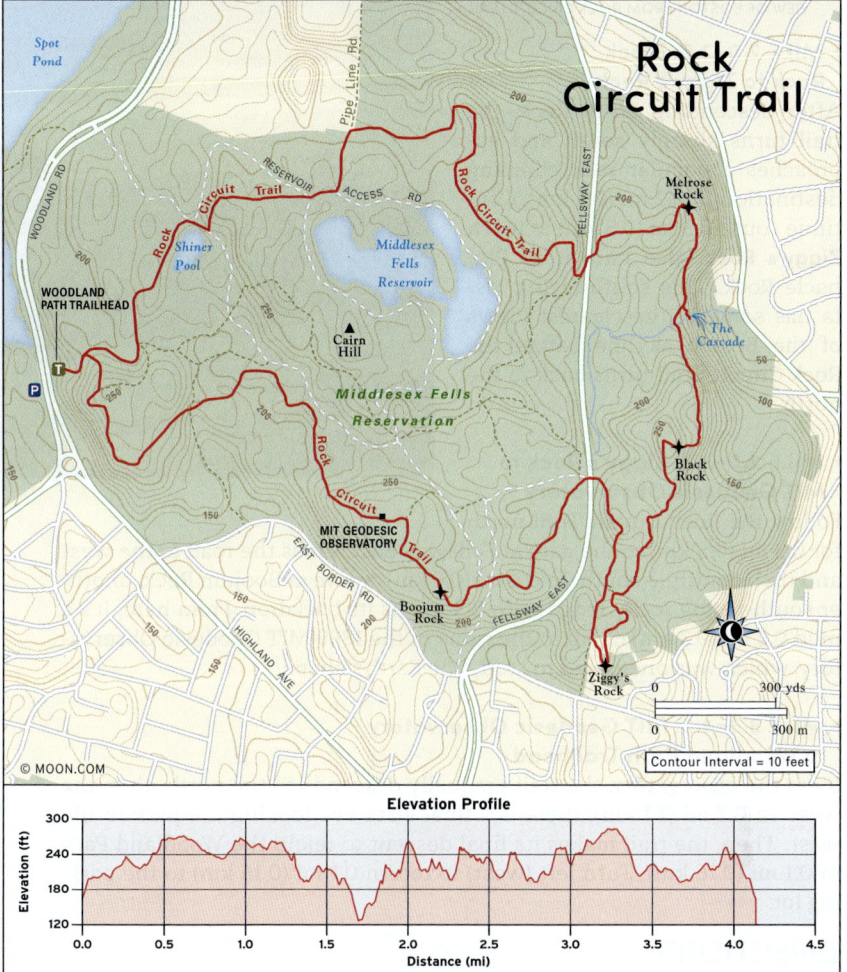

Rock Circuit Trail

Elevation Profile

reaching the intersection with the paved **Fellsway East road.** Cross the road with caution and bear left (north) to rejoin the Rock Circuit Trail. The trail ascends over rocky terrain to reach the high point of Melrose Rock in 0.2 mi (0.3 km), where you can view the center of Melrose to the north and the skyline of Boston to the south.

▶ **MILE 1.6–2.0: Melrose Rock to Black Rock**

In 0.2 mi (0.3 km) after descending Melrose Rock, you'll cross a small footbridge to reach an intersection. Here, you can turn left for a 0.1 mi (0.16 km) round-trip detour to **The Cascade,** a seasonal falls through a section of steep cliff. Otherwise, continue south along the Rock Circuit Trail. A series of ridgeline views unfold as you reach the summit of **Black Rock** in 0.2 mi (0.3 km).

VIEW OF BOSTON FROM ROCK CIRCUIT TRAIL ▶

▶ MILE 2.0-2.5: Black Rock to Ziggy's Rock

After descending Black Rock, the trail turns sharply south and approaches a popular rock climbing destination in 0.2 mi (0.3 km). Continue south 0.3 mi (0.5 km) to reach **Ziggy's Rock,** also known as Pinnacle Rock. This south-facing vista has some of the clearest views of the Boston skyline before the Rock Circuit Trail turns back to the north.

▶ MILE 2.5-3.3: Ziggy's Rock to MIT Geodesic Observatory

Follow the Rock Circuit Trail north for 0.3 mi (0.5 km) to the gate at Fellsway East. Cross the road to the west and then continue south. In 0.4 mi (0.6 km), arrive at Boojum Rock, another south-facing rocky ledge with Boston as its backdrop. From here, it's a mild 0.2 mi (0.3 km) climb to the ruins of the 1899 MIT Geodesic Observatory, which was once used to study the Earth's shape.

▶ MILE 3.3-4.2: MIT Geodesic Observatory to Woodland Path Trailhead

From the observatory, the trail gradually descends to the north, then the west. In 0.7 mi (1.1 km), there is a final vista overlooking the park to the west. Then, the trail makes its final descent to rejoin the Woodland Path in 0.1 mi (0.16 km). Turn left (west) to return 0.1 mi (0.16 km) to the parking lot.

DIRECTIONS

From I-93, take the exit for MA-28 N/Fellsway West. Turn right onto Elm Street, then use the rotary to merge onto Woodland Road. Parking is at the Flynn Rink on the west side of Woodland Road in Medford. The trailhead is east from the parking area, across Woodland Road.

The MBTA line 99 bus stops near the trailhead.

GPS COORDINATES: 42°26'39.8"N 71°05'40.9"W

BEST NEARBY BREWS

Lord Hobo Brewing Company's Woburn taproom (5 Draper St., Woburn; 781/281-0809; www.lordhobo.com/woburn; 4pm-10pm Mon.-Thurs., 11am-midnight Fri.-Sat., 11am-10pm Sun.) is known for its New England-inspired hoppy ales alongside a kitchen that serves pizza, sandwiches, and other bar snacks. It's 7 mi (11.3 km) from the trailhead.

2 Carriage Paths

WORLD'S END, HINGHAM

World's End, a Frederick Law Olmsted-designed park, boasts remarkable trees, scenic coastline, and fantastic views of the Boston skyline from its rolling carriage paths.

BEST: Winter hikes

DISTANCE: 4 mi (6.4 km) round-trip

DURATION: 2 hr

ELEVATION GAIN: 538 ft (164 m)

EFFORT: Easy

TRAIL: Dirt path

USERS: Hikers, leashed dogs

SEASON: Year-round

FEES/PASSES: $10 nonmember vehicles, $6 walk-in on weekdays ($8 on weekends and holidays) or free with a Trustees membership

MAPS: The Trustees of Reservations, "World's End"

TRAILHEAD: Entrance kiosk, Martins Ln., Hingham

FACILITIES: Restroom, trail map

CONTACT: The Trustees of Reservations; 781/740-7233; https://thetrustees. org/places-to-visit/south-shore/worlds-end.html

START THE HIKE

▸ **MILE 0-0.7: Entrance Kiosk to Planters Hill Summit**

Turn right (northwest) from the entrance kiosk over the bridge and follow the **Planters Hill carriage path** straight (north) for 0.4 mi (0.6 km). At the fork with **Barnes Road,** bear right to continue straight (north) up the Planters Hill carriage path. As you ascend the hill, you'll catch intermittent views of the **Boston skyline** to your left (west) and boats bobbing in **Hull Harbor** to your right (east). From the east-facing bench of the Hull Harbor vista, the path curls west, offering great views from the summit of **Planters Hill** (also known as Brewers Grove) at 0.7 mi (1.1 km).

▸ **MILE 0.7-0.9: Planters Hill Summit to Brewer Road Carriage Path**

This is a great spot to lounge in the grass under the shade of massive oaks and drink in the view. Continue on the Planters Hill path as it turns south; at 0.9 mi (1.4 km), turn sharply right (north) onto the **Brewer Road carriage path.**

▸ **MILE 0.9-2.9: Brewer Road Carriage Path to Rocky Neck**

In 0.3 mi (0.5 km), the path cuts through **"The Bar,"** a low and narrow spit between the bays of Hingham Harbor and the Weir River where hikers

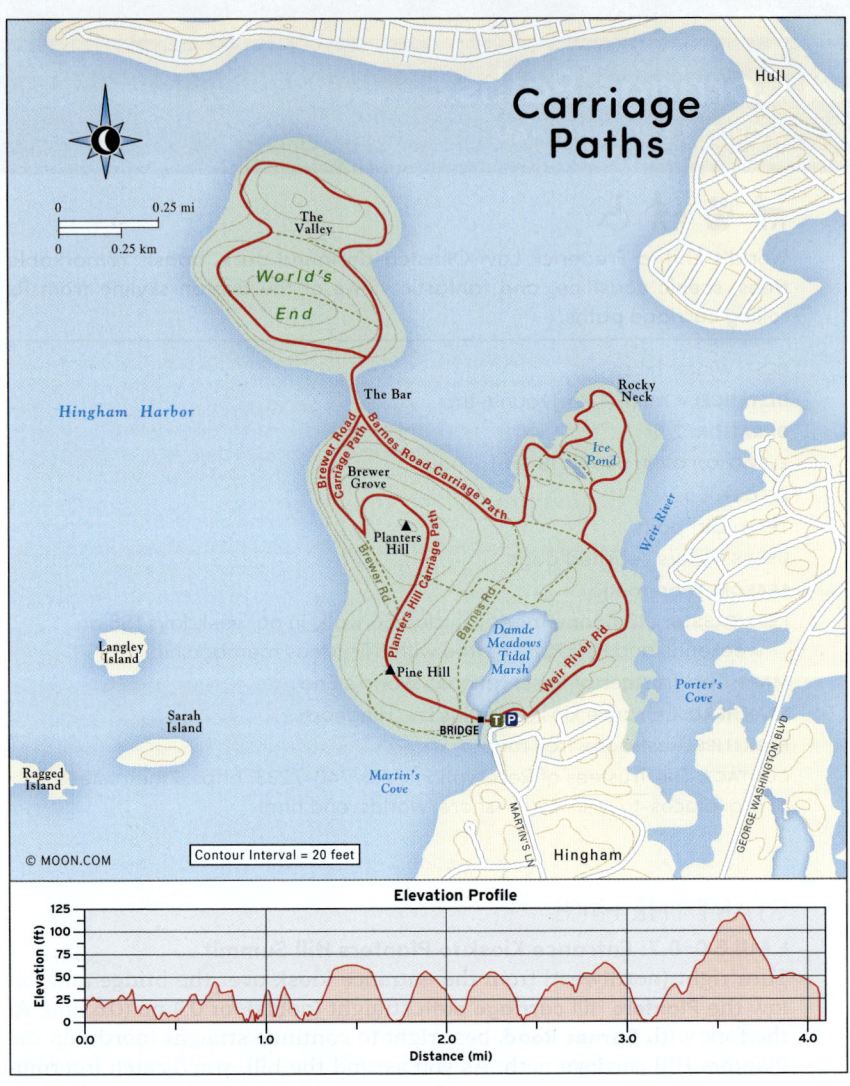

Carriage
Paths

Hull

Rocky
Neck

Ice
Pond

Weir River

The Bar

Hingham Harbor

Brewer Road Carriage Path

Barnes Road Carriage Path

Brewer
Grove

Planters
Hill

Brewer Rd

Planters Hill Carriage Path

Barnes Rd

Damde
Meadows
Tidal
Marsh

Weir River Rd

Porter's
Cove

Langley
Island

Pine Hill

Sarah
Island

BRIDGE

Ragged
Island

Martin's
Cove

MARTIN'S LN

GEORGE WASHINGTON BLVD

Hingham

0   0.25 mi
0   0.25 km

The
Valley

World's
End

© MOON.COM

Contour Interval = 20 feet

Elevation Profile

Elevation (ft)

125
100
75
50
25
0

0.0   1.0   2.0   3.0   4.0

Distance (mi)

may spot waterfowl floating on the water. From The Bar, the path continues north. Turn left (west) where the trail branches off in 0.1 mi (0.16 km).
Stay west on the tree-lined path, which cuts inland to a forested **valley** in
0.5 mi (0.8 km). It's common to catch deer grazing on acorns and other vegetation in these shady lowlands. At the valley, turn left (west) on a slight
uphill trail through thick, green vegetation. The path rounds the northern
tip of World's End, emerging at water views and the sound of waves before
curving south back into the valley in 0.5 mi (0.8 km). Keep left in the valley to follow the eastern path 0.1 mi (0.16 km) back to The Bar. Pass back
through The Bar, turn left onto the **Barnes Road carriage path,** and follow
it for 0.5 mi (0.8 km).

▲ THE BAR

▶ **MILE 2.9-4.0: Rocky Neck to Entrance Kiosk**

Here, hikers can turn left (north) onto the narrow trail around **Rocky Neck.** This slightly more rugged section of trail traverses the coastline jutting into the **Weir River** and is a lovely spot to sit by the water in solitude even when the park is busy. The Rocky Neck trail loops back to the **Weir River Road carriage path** in 0.6 mi (1 km). Turn left (southeast) onto Weir River Road, which wraps around **Damde Meadows tidal marsh.** An observation deck here offers a chance to glimpse coastal birds and other tidal flora and fauna. The trail continues south back to the east side of the parking lot in 0.5 mi (0.8 km).

DIRECTIONS

From MA-3, take Exit 14 onto MA-228 N and travel 6.5 mi (10.5 km). Turn left onto MA-3A and go 0.7 mi (1.1 km). Turn right onto Summer Street; at the Rockland Street intersection, continue straight across onto Martin's Lane. The parking area, marked with a Trustees of Reservations sign, is 0.7 mi (1.1 km) ahead at the end of the road. Walk west from the parking lot, past the restrooms and toward the entrance kiosk, where you will see the trailhead.

GPS COORDINATES: 42°15'30.4"N 70°52'25.1"W

BEST NEARBY BITES AND BREWS

Toast your adventure with a flight of microbrews at **Stars on Hingham Harbor** (2 Otis St., Hingham; 781/749-3200; www.starshingham.com; 7am-10pm Sun.-Thurs., 7am-11pm Fri.-Sat.), which also serves apps and entrées and hosts live music. It's 1.5 mi (2.4 km) from the trailhead.

3

Great Blue Hill via the Skyline Trail

BLUE HILLS RESERVATION, MILTON

🦌 ❀ 🐾

The views of the Boston skyline are unbeatable on this surprisingly wild path just outside the city.

BEST: Vistas
DISTANCE: 5.7 mi (9.2 km) round-trip
DURATION: 3 hr
ELEVATION GAIN: 1,260 ft (384 m)
EFFORT: Moderate/strenuous
TRAIL: Dirt, rock path
USERS: Hikers, leashed dogs, mountain bikers
SEASON: April–November
FEES/PASSES: None
MAPS: Mass DCR, "Blue Hills Reservation"
TRAILHEAD: Skyline Trail trailhead, MA-28/Randolph Ave., Milton
FACILITIES: Water, restrooms, and trail map available at Houghton's Pond Visitors Center south of the trailhead that's on Hillside St.
CONTACT: Massachusetts Department of Conservation and Recreation; 617/698-1802; www.mass.gov/locations/blue-hills-reservationmass

Some 125 mi (200 km) of trails run throughout Blue Hills Reservation, which spans six towns just south of Boston, but the views are most striking from along the challenging Skyline Trail, which covers 9 mi (14.5 km) across the reservation's ridgeline. Our route features a select 5.7-mi (9.2-km) loop with stunning lookouts from Buck Hill and Great Blue Hill, but hikers can shorten the route by parking in the main Hillside Street lot in Milton or complete the entire length of the Skyline Trail starting from Willard Street in Quincy.

START THE HIKE

▶ MILE 0-0.3: Skyline Trailhead to Buck Hill Summit

Hike west from the trailhead off Randolph Avenue, following the blue blazes uphill away from the highway. The trail climbs to a ridge scattered with blueberries, big pine trees, and oaks. At 0.2 mi (0.3 km) from the trailhead, climb the stone staircase 0.1 mi (0.16 km) to the summit of **Buck Hill.** You'll instantly be rewarded with sweeping views of the Boston skyline and harbor to the north.

▶ MILE 0.3-1.0: Buck Hill Summit to Great Blue Hill Vista

The twittering of birds mixes with the sights and sounds of low-flying jets en route to Logan Airport as you descend the Skyline Trail 0.2 mi (0.3 km) west into a cool wood. For 0.5 mi (0.8 km), the trail climbs over North Boyce Hill, then Tucker Hill, the latter of which has a small **vista** looking

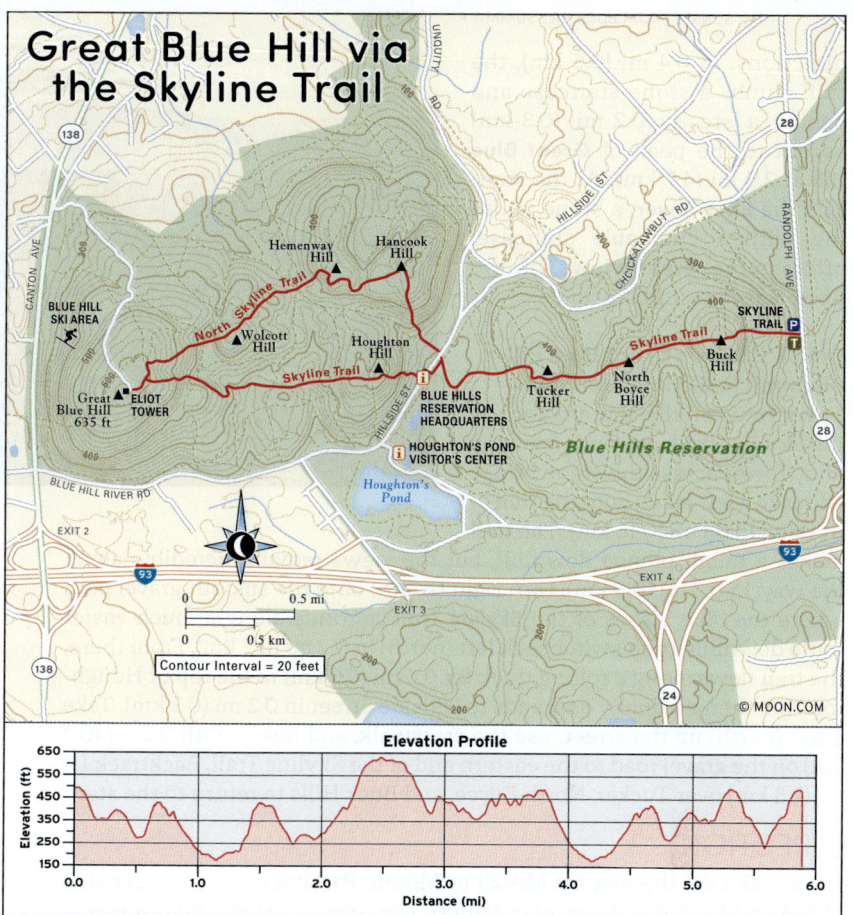

Great Blue Hill via the Skyline Trail

Elevation Profile

west toward **Great Blue Hill.** This view of forested hillside in the distance gives hikers a sneak peek of where they are headed.

▶ MILE 1.0–1.8: Great Blue Hill Vista to Hancock Hill

From the vista, continue straight (west) for 0.3 mi (0.5 km) and then turn right (north) onto the gravel road, which reaches the **Blue Hills Reservation Headquarters** at 1.4 mi (2.3 km). Cross Hillside Street into the headquarters parking lot and find the sign for the continuation of the **North Skyline Trail** to the left of the information center. Turn right (north) up the stone steps, following the blue blazes and signs for the Skyline Trail and Great Blue Hill. This rooty path takes on a challenging ascent of rock slabs leading to **Hancock Hill** at 1.8 mi (2.9 km), then descends.

▶ MILE 1.8–2.9: Hancock Hill to Great Blue Hill Summit

A 0.5 mi (0.8 km) from the peak of Hancock Hill, continue straight (west) across the intersection on the rock-strewn but mellow trail over Hemenway and Wolcott Hills. In spite of dense vegetation and some low-hanging trees, views peek out from these exposed summits in all

directions. In 0.4 mi (0.6 km), the trail climbs a stone staircase and begins a steady 0.2-mi (0.3-km) ascent to the peak of **Great Blue Hill** at 2.9 mi (4.7 km). At the summit, the **Eliot Tower,** a stone building with a climbable staircase, offers more great views of the **Boston skyline** and beyond.

▶ **MILE 2.9–5.7: Great Blue Hill Summit to Skyline Trailhead**

To continue on the south branch of the Skyline Trail, go south from the Eliot Tower across the stone bridge and take a left (east) onto the trail at the sign in 0.1 mi (0.16 km). The trail makes a tough plunge downhill, but the views remain incredible along the way. In 0.3 mi (0.5 km), turn right (south) onto the smooth gravel path where the blue blazes of the **Skyline Trail** continue along a much easier route downhill, then switchback left (north) in 0.2 mi (0.3 km). From there, the trail flows along a rolling track for 0.4 mi (0.6 km) to the top of Houghton Hill, then gradually descends to Hillside Street in 0.2 mi (0.3 km). Take a left (north) up the street, use the crosswalk, and head south 0.2 mi (0.3 km) on the gravel road to the eastern end of the Skyline Trail. Backtrack 1.4 mi (2.3 km) over Tucker, North Boyce, and Buck Hills to return to the start.

DIRECTIONS

From I-93, take the exit for MA-28 to Milton. Parking is on the west side of MA-28 (Randolph Avenue) in Milton. The turnout off this busy street is small and marked only with a trailhead map.

GPS COORDINATES: 42°12'51.2"N 71°04'11.6"W

BEST NEARBY BREWS

Trillium Brewing Company (100 Royall St., Canton; 781/562-0073; https://trilliumbrewing.com; 11am–11pm Mon.–Sat., 11am–10pm Sun.), 8 mi (12.9 km) from the trailhead, serves up what many consider to be the best beer around, and its kitchen includes wood-fired pizza and barbecue options.

4

Walden Pond via the Alternate Pond Loop

WALDEN POND STATE RESERVATION, CONCORD

Historic Walden is well loved for its crystalline swimming water and trails near the former house site of Henry David Thoreau.

DISTANCE: 2.2 mi (3.5 km) round-trip

DURATION: 1.5 hr

ELEVATION GAIN: 251 ft (77 m)

EFFORT: Easy

TRAIL: Dirt and sand path

USERS: Hikers only

SEASON: Year-round

FEES/PASSES: Parking fee $8 MA residents, $30 nonresidents

MAPS: Mass DCR, "Walden Pond State Reservation;" Appalachian Mountain Club, "Bay Circuit Trail Map & Guide"

TRAILHEAD: Walden Pond Visitors Center, Walden St., Concord

FACILITIES: Water, restrooms, trail map at visitor center

CONTACT: Massachusetts Department of Conservation and Recreation; 978/369-3254; www.mass.gov/locations/walden-pond-state-reservation

Hikes don't get much more historic than Walden Pond, where the transcendentalist writer Henry David Thoreau conducted his famous experiment in living simply and deliberately upon the land from 1845 to 1847. The trails in this current-day state park (which is part of the Bay Circuit Trail system) remain inspiring, if a little overcrowded. This route takes hikers to sites on some of the less-traveled park paths, including the Alternate Pond Loop's water views, the scenic bog of Heywood's Meadow, and the peaceful vista of Emerson's Cliff.

START THE HIKE

▶ MILE 0-0.5: Visitor Center to Thoreau's Cove

From the main parking lot near the visitor center, walk southwest across Walden Street and follow the paved ramp toward the beach. In 435 ft (133 m), take a sharp right onto the **Sherwood Trail,** following signs for the **Alternate Pond Loop.** In 0.2 mi (0.3 km), continue straight west on the **Ridge Path,** which treks above the pond for great views to the south. The Alternate Pond Loop continues straight west on the Wyman Path in 0.1 mi (0.16 km), curving northwest over Wyman Meadow. Turn left (south) where the path branches off in 0.2 mi (0.3 km). The trail bends right (west) into **Thoreau's Cove,** where there is a monument to the author's original **cabin site.** The original cabin no longer exists, but you can walk through a replica of Thoreau's "tiny house" back at the visitor center.

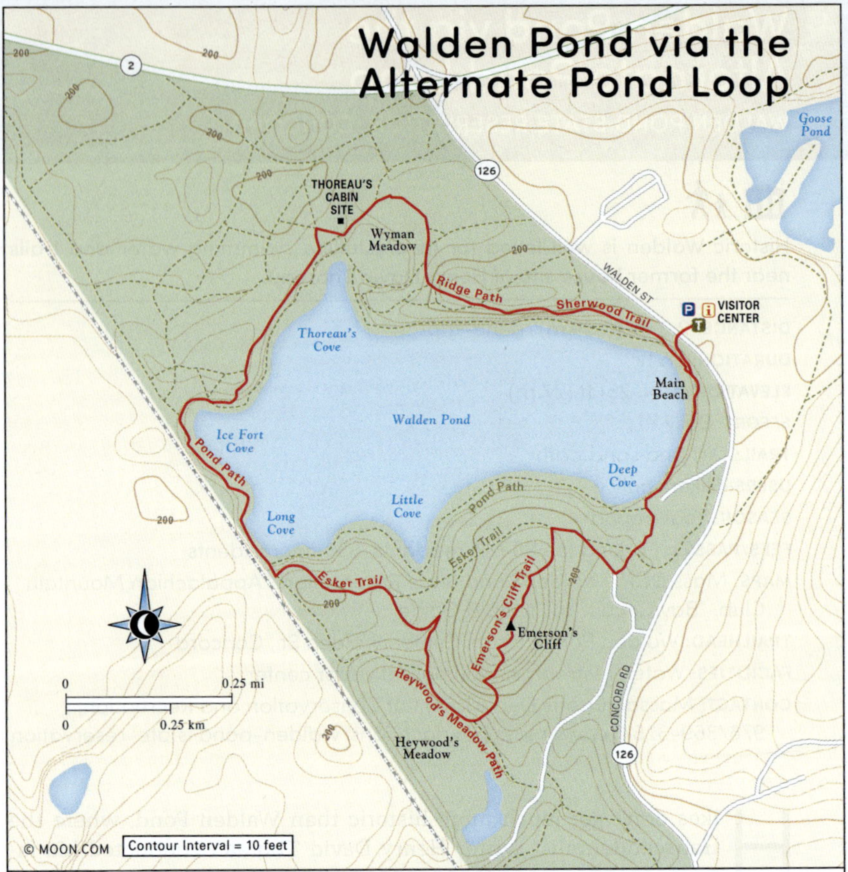

Walden Pond via the Alternate Pond Loop

Elevation Profile

Contour Interval = 10 feet

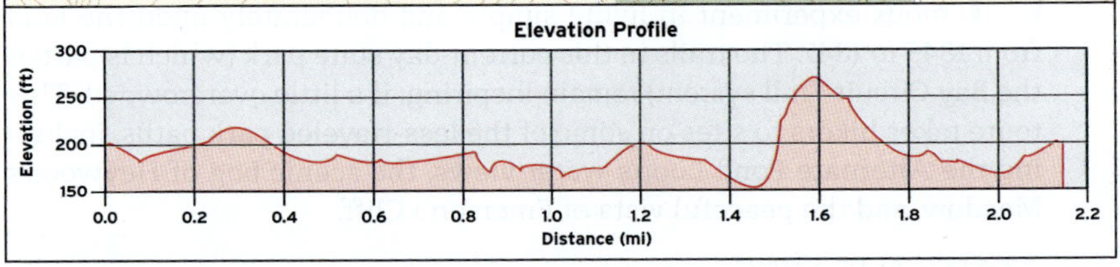

▶ **MILE 0.5-1.3: Thoreau's Cove to Esker Trail**

Continue south from the cabin site on the Alternate Pond Loop, which merges with the main pond loop (Bay Circuit Trail) at Ice Fort Cove in 0.3 mi (0.5 km). The trail passes between the beach on the left (east) and the MBTA Commuter Rail tracks on the right (west). At 1.1 mi (1.8 km), go south up the steps and turn left (east) onto the **Esker Trail.** Bear right (southeast) onto the unmarked Esker Trail loop at 1.3 mi (2.1 km).

▶ **MILE 1.3-1.6: Esker Trail to Emerson's Cliff Vista**

When you reach the next intersection at 1.4 mi (2.3 km), take a sharp right (south) downhill onto the **Heywood's Meadow Path.** This quiet area of the park is less traveled and features a colorful bog scattered with lily pads. Walk southeast, around the bog's banks, for 0.2 mi (0.3 km), then turn left

▲ WALDEN POND

(north) onto the **Emerson's Cliff Trail** at the sign. This short, steep path climbs around some large boulders to a small south-facing vista. Thoreau named this ridge for fellow transcendentalist writer Ralph Waldo Emerson, who once considered building his own rural cabin at this site.

▶ **MILE 1.6-2.2: Emerson's Cliff Vista to Visitor Center**
Continue north across the ridge, then descend back to the **Esker Trail** in 0.3 mi (0.5 km). Turn right (east) onto the Esker Trail and follow it for 0.1 mi (0.16 km) before bearing left (northeast) in the direction of the pond. From the boat launch, use the beach to walk north the remaining 0.2 mi (0.3 km) to the starting point.

DIRECTIONS

From MA-2, take MA-126 (Walden Street) south. The large parking area is well marked on the left side of the street. There is a parking fee, and parking is not permitted anywhere along the street.

GPS COORDINATES: 42°26'26.0"N 71°20'05.9"W

BEST NEARBY BITES

Nashoba Brook Bakery (152 Commonwealth Ave., West Concord; 978/318-1999; http://slowrise.com; 8am-4pm daily) makes sandwiches that are anything but basic, served on their signature slow-rise bread. Nosh with a view at a picnic table along the eponymous brook.

Greater Boston, North and South Shore

MASSACHUSETTS

5 Mount Wachusett via the Midstate Trail

WACHUSETT MOUNTAIN STATE RESERVATION, PRINCETON

Explore the only known old-growth forest east of the Connecticut River on this scenic tour of Mount Wachusett's western slopes.

DISTANCE: 3.9 mi (6.3 km) round-trip

DURATION: 2 hr

ELEVATION GAIN: 1,122 ft (342 m)

EFFORT: Moderate

TRAIL: Dirt and rock path

USERS: Hikers, leashed dogs

SEASON: April–November

FEES/PASSES: No fee at Echo Lake lot. Parking fee ($5 MA residents, $20 nonresidents) charged in main lot.

MAPS: Mass DCR, "Wachusett Mountain State Reservation," *Massachusetts Midstate Trail Guidebook*

TRAILHEAD: Echo Lake Road trailhead, Mountain Rd., Princeton

FACILITIES: None

CONTACT: Massachusetts Department of Conservation and Recreation; 978/464-2987; www.mass.gov/locations/wachusett-mountain-state-reservation

Mount Wachusett is best known as a ski area, but this route around the west side of the state reservation will take hikers through the undeveloped splendor of granite slopes, blossoming meadows, a sprawling old-growth forest, and vistas galore. The hike begins on the quiet, less-traveled trails near Echo Lake and winds its way to the 2,006-ft (611-m) summit using a prized section of the Midstate Trail. From there, views of mountains and lakes stretch from Boston to the Berkshires, and north into New Hampshire and Vermont.

START THE HIKE

▶ MILE 0-0.6: Echo Lake Road Trailhead to Jack Frost Trail

Enter the gate straight ahead of the parking area and hike straight (west) on the flat, dirt-surface **Echo Lake Road** for 0.3 mi (0.5 km). At the **Echo Lake picnic area,** turn right (northeast) onto the **High Meadow Trail.** This sometimes-muddy section may require some rock-hopping, but the path is more reliably dry as it ascends the hill. In 0.2 mi (0.3 km), the trail winds through the apple tree-dotted **High Meadow,** where a bench looks out over grasslands to an east-facing vista of a flat valley stretching toward Boston.

Mount
Wachusett
via the
Midstate Trail

Wachusett Mountain
State Reservation

WACHUSETT
MOUNTAIN
SKI AREA

Mount
Wachusett
2,006'

LOOKOUT
TOWER

ECHO LAKE
PICNIC AREA

Echo
Lake

ECHO LAKE
ROAD TRAILHEAD

Contour Interval = 20 feet

© MOON.COM

Elevation Profile

Continue straight (north) past the bench on the rocky High Meadow Trail for 0.1 mi (0.16 km) and reach the intersection with the **Jack Frost Trail**.

▶ **MILE 0.6-2.0: Jack Frost Trail to West Side (Midstate) Trail**
Take a left (west) onto Jack Frost Trail, where you will descend again on a path through pines and granite boulders. In 0.3 mi (0.5 km), turn right (north) on the **Lower Link Trail,** which intersects with the **Harrington (Midstate) Trail** in 0.3 mi (0.5 km). Turn right (east) onto the red-blazed Harrington Trail and climb it for 0.2 mi (0.3 km). Then, turn left (north) onto the **Semuhenna (Midstate) Trail.** The blue-blazed Semuhenna Trail is mostly flat granite. Follow it north for 0.6 mi (1 km) to reach the **West Side (Midstate) Trail** at 2 mi (3.2 km).

▶ **MILE 2.0–2.6: West Side (Midstate) Trail to Mount Wachusett Summit**

Turn right (east) onto the West Side Trail, which connects with the **Old Indian Trail** in 0.2 mi (0.3 km). Follow signs for the Midstate Trail right (south) and climb the ledges of the Old Indian Trail up through this spectacular section of old-growth forest where sunlight dapples tall, gnarled hardwoods. Reach the summit in 0.4 mi (0.6 km) and enjoy 360-degree views from the **lookout tower.**

▶ **MILE 2.6–3.9: Mount Wachusett Summit to Echo Lake Road Trailhead**

Descend to the south via the Mountain House (Midstate) Trail. In 0.3 mi (0.5 km), bear right for the Jack Frost Trail and follow it through a hemlock forest for 0.3 mi (0.5 km) back to the intersection with the High Meadow Trail. Descend via the High Meadow Trail and Echo Lake Road for a round-trip of 3.9 mi (6.3 km).

DIRECTIONS

From MA-2, take the exit for MA-140 and follow it south to Park Road. Turn right onto Park Road, then bear left onto Mountain Road and follow it for 2 mi (3.2 km) to Echo Lake Road, on the right. The small lot is marked only with a trailhead map.

GPS COORDINATES: 42°28'29.8"N 71°53'00.7"W

BEST NEARBY BREWS

Visit **Wachusett Brewing Company** (175 State Rd. E., Westminster; 978/874-9965; www.wachusettbrewingcompany.com; noon–7pm Sun., noon–9pm Mon.–Thurs., noon–10pm Fri.–Sat.) and the "Brew Yard" for beer served from an Airstream trailer, outdoor seating, live music, and apps and sandwiches. It's 7 mi (11.3 km) from the trailhead.

MASSACHUSETTS

Greater Boston, North and South Shore

Mount Watatic via the Wapack Trail

MOUNT WATATIC STATE RESERVATION, ASHBURNHAM

The starting point of the Wapack Trail, and the only section in Massachusetts, 1,830-ft (558-m) Mount Watatic is known for its spectacular views and blueberry picking.

DISTANCE: 3 mi (4.8 km) round-trip
DURATION: 2 hr
ELEVATION GAIN: 650 ft (198 m)
EFFORT: Moderate
TRAIL: Dirt and rock path
USERS: Hikers, leashed dogs
SEASON: April–November
FEES/PASSES: None
MAPS: Friends of the Wapack, "The Wapack Trail"
TRAILHEAD: Mount Watatic trailhead, Rindge State Rd., Ashburnham
FACILITIES: None
CONTACT: Friends of the Wapack; www.wapack.org

Mount Watatic is off the beaten path, but locals cherish this gem for its scenic views of Ashburnham's many lakes and its abundance of blueberries. It also offers great views of nearby Mount Monadnock and, on a clear day, the Boston skyline. This moderate loop takes hikers over Nutting Hill to the summit of Watatic on the first section of the Wapack Trail, which is also the final section of the Midstate Trail. For more great hiking, continue on the Wapack over the New Hampshire state line.

START THE HIKE

▶ **MILE 0-0.9: Mount Watatic Trailhead to Nutting Hill**

Hike north from the parking lot, following the yellow **Wapack Trail** markers through the gate and over a series of bridges along the bog. In 0.2 mi (0.3 km), you will see signs for the Wapack Trail and **Watatic Summit** pointing right (these indicate the "shortcut" to the summit). Pass the signs and continue straight north on the wide dirt path. This trail follows a gradual rocky incline to another intersection with the Wapack Trail in 0.5 mi (0.8 km). Turn right (southeast) onto the Wapack Trail at this intersection and follow the yellow markers 0.2 mi (0.3 km) to the grass-and-granite slopes of **Nutting Hill,** a lovely bald top with views and bountiful blueberries that looks upon the summit of Watatic to the south.

▶ **MILE 0.9-1.7: Nutting Hill to Mount Watatic Summit**

Follow the cairns south 0.1 mi (0.16 km) as you descend Nutting Hill back into the woods. The path levels out along a stone wall, then bends slightly

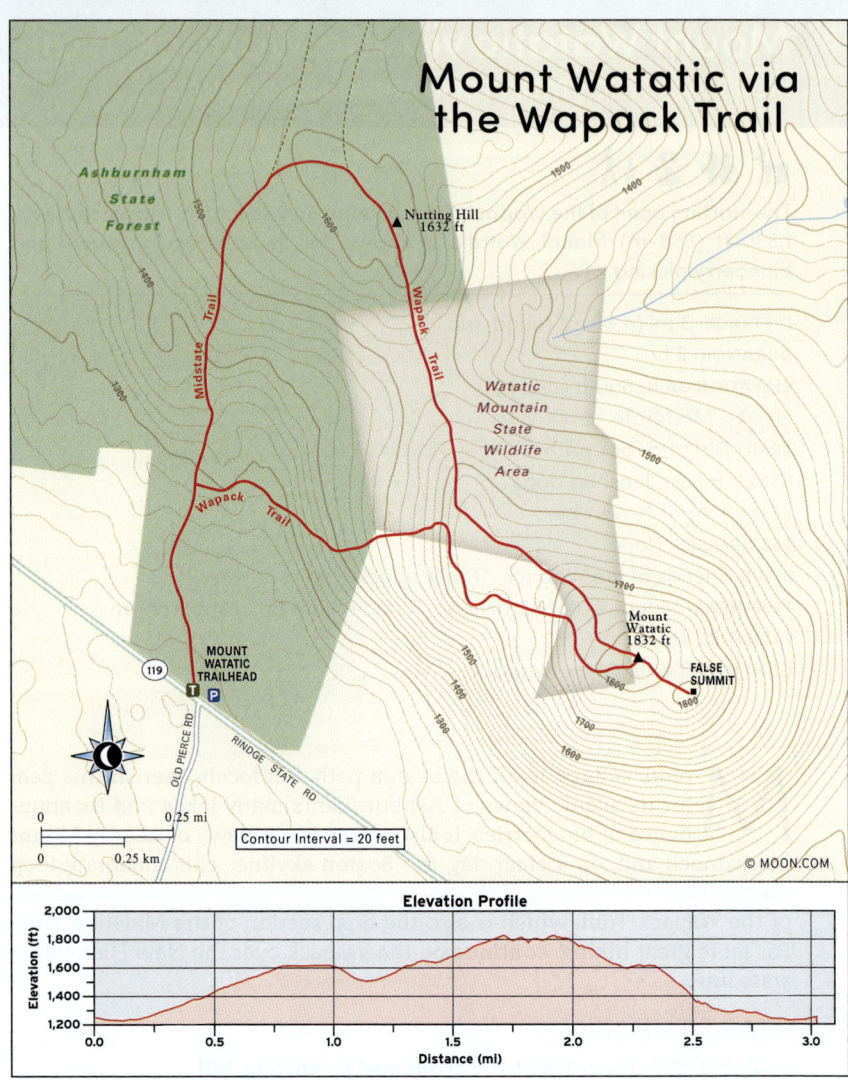

Mount Watatic via the Wapack Trail

Elevation Profile

east through a fern-covered forest floor. In 0.5 mi (0.8 km), the trail begins its gradual ascent to the **Watatic summit.** Cross the gravel access road straight east in 0.1 mi (0.16 km) and climb the final section to the blueberry-speckled summit. The views are even more dramatic from Watatic's false south summit, 0.1 mi (0.16 km) down a rocky corridor, where hikers can view Mount Wachusett, Mount Monadnock, and even the Boston skyline on a clear day.

▶ **MILE 1.7–3.0: Mount Watatic Summit to Mount Watatic Trailhead**
Backtrack 0.1 mi (0.16 km) to the main summit and find the south Wapack Trail to the west. This steep trail descends through granite tumbles and hemlocks, offering another nice west-facing vista in 0.4 mi (0.6 km). From there, the path descends 0.5 mi (0.8 km), winding between two large

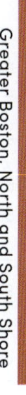

▲ VIEW FROM MOUNT WATATIC'S SOUTH PEAK

boulders and crossing a small stream before leveling to meet the main path in 0.1 mi (0.16 km). Turn left (south) to return 0.2 mi (0.3 km) to the parking lot.

DIRECTIONS

Off MA-119 in Ashburnham, the Mount Watatic parking area is marked with a sign across from Old Pierce Road. Please note: Parking along the side of MA-119 is not permissible.

GPS COORDINATES: 42°41'46.0"N 71°54'14.8"W

BEST NEARBY BITES

While there aren't many commercial businesses in this rural area, a quick trip over the state line to Jaffrey, New Hampshire, takes you to **Kimball Farm** (158 Turnpike Rd., Jaffrey, NH; 603/532-5765; https://kimballfarm.com; 11am-9pm daily in season) a roadside favorite for fried fare—think fish and chips—and super-sized ice cream cones.

Tucked between the Essex River and the Atlantic Ocean, the dunes, forests, and vernal pools of Crane Beach make up one of the most diverse—and beautiful—coastal habitats in southern New England.

BEST: Winter hikes

DISTANCE: 5.6 mi (9 km) round-trip

DURATION: 3.5 hr

ELEVATION GAIN: 100 ft (30 m)

EFFORT: Moderate

TRAIL: Sand path

USERS: Hikers only (leashed dogs permitted with a small fee between October and March)

SEASON: Year-round

FEES/PASSES: Summer: Parking $40 weekdays/$45 weekends, $15 weekdays after 4pm/$25 weekends after 4pm. Shoulder seasons: Parking $15 weekdays/$25 weekends. Off-season: Parking $10. Discounts available with Trustees membership and parking sticker or for hikers and bikers.

MAPS: Trustees of Reservations, "Crane Estate"

TRAILHEAD: Castle Neck Trails trailhead, Argilla Rd., Ipswich

FACILITIES: Water, restrooms, showers, food available at the Snack Shack in season

CONTACT: The Trustees of Reservations; 978/356-4354; https://thetrustees.org/place/crane-beach-on-the-crane-estate

Trekking through the soft sand of the Castle Neck trails on Crane Beach can be tiring, but the chance to get up close and personal with these scenic dune trails is not to be missed. Hikers will wind through pine forests and salt marshes, over sweeping hills and along gentle coastline, to reach stunning vistas of the Essex and Ipswich Bays. Crane Beach is considered a top birding habitat, especially for threatened shorebirds such as the piping plover, and the beach here is widely regarded as one of the prettiest in the Northeast. Take advantage of all Crane has to offer and top off your hike with a refreshing plunge into the Atlantic!

START THE HIKE

▶ **MILE 0-1.3: Castle Neck Trails Trailhead to Wigwam Hill**

Find the trailhead at the far east end of the beach parking lot and head southeast on the sand-and-boardwalk trail through overhanging scrub oak. In 0.1 mi (0.16 km), turn right (south) onto the **Green Trail.** Make sure to hike within the fencing to protect delicate wildlife and vegetation along the trail. The sand path wraps south, then east, along the border of a pine swamp for 0.7 mi (1.1 km) before it intersects with the **Red Trail.** Bear right

Castle Neck Trails

Elevation Profile

(east) on the Red Trail, which climbs 0.5 mi (0.8 km) over the crest of **Wigwam Hill,** a massive dune with sweeping views of the Essex Bay and Choate Island; the 1996 movie *The Crucible* was filmed here.

▶ MILE 1.3–3.4: Wigwam Hill to Essex Bay Beach
From Wigwam Hill, the trail descends steeply into marshland and reaches an intersection in 0.4 mi (0.6 km). Turn left (east) to stay on the **Red Trail.** Reach the **Blue Trail** in 0.3 mi (0.5 km) and turn right (northeast) onto it. The path ascends to a dune-top ridge with great views of Ipswich Bay. Follow the path southeast for 0.3 mi (0.5 km) to where it meets the **Yellow Trail.** Continue southeast on the Yellow Trail for 0.8 mi (1.3 km), then turn left (east) onto the **Black Trail.** This path will deliver you to the beach on the Essex Bay side of the property—a great spot for a picnic or swimming break—in 0.3 mi (0.5 km).

▶ **MILE 3.4-4.3: Essex Bay Beach to Red Trail**

Turn right (northwest) onto the beach and follow the shoreline along the **Castle Neck River.** In 0.6 mi (1 km), cut right (northeast) inland on a white-marked trail through high dune grass, which will return you to the Red Trail. Follow the **Red Trail** for 0.3 mi (0.5 km) back to the Blue Trail intersection, but this time, turn left (north) to stay on the Red Trail.

▶ **MILE 4.3-5.6: Red Trail to Castle Neck Trails Trailhead**

Follow the Red Trail west along the dunes for 0.7 mi (1.1 km), then keep straight west on the **Orange Trail.** This dune-side path skirts a series of vernal pools and cranberry bogs, then wraps back into the pines to meet the Green Trail in 0.3 mi (0.5 km). Take a right (north) onto the Green Trail, which carries on over a boardwalk and back into the dunes. In 0.2 mi (0.3 km), turn right (east) to follow the Green Trail spur 0.1 mi (0.16 km) back to the parking area.

DIRECTIONS

From MA-128 N, take Exit 20A to MA-1A N and continue 8 mi (12.9 km) to Ipswich. Turn right onto MA-133 E; follow it for 1.5 mi (2.4 km) and then turn left onto Northgate Road. In 0.5 mi (0.8 km), turn right onto Argilla Road. The well-marked Crane Beach Trustees of Reservations Parking Lot is in 2.5 mi (4 km) at the end of road, through the gatehouse.

The Cape Ann Transit Authority 12 Ipswich/Essex Explorer bus runs between the Ipswich Commuter Rail station and Crane Beach during the summer months.

GPS COORDINATES: 42°40'58.1"N 70°46'14.8"W

BEST NEARBY BITES

Using only the simplest ingredients, **Riverview Restaurant** (20 Estes St., Ipswich; 978/356-0500; 4pm-10pm Tues.-Sun.) serves up the perfect post-hike personal pizza, with classic toppings as well as local favorites such as kielbasa, in a hometown diner-like atmosphere with a bar. It's 5 mi (8 km) from the trailhead.

NEARBY CAMPGROUNDS

NAME	LOCATION	FACILITIES	SEASON	FEE
Boston Harbor Islands	Peddocks Island, Boston Harbor, 42°17'58.5"N 70°55'38.5"W	33 tent sites, 6 yurts; composting toilets; no water	June–September	$8–140
617/223-8666; www.bostonharborislands.org/campground-reservations				
Wompatuck State Park	204 Union St., Hingham, 42°12'8"N 70°50'52"W	260 RV/ tent sites; restrooms	mid-May–mid-October	$17–54
781/749-7160; www.mass.gov/locations/wompatuck-state-park				
Myles Standish State Forest	194 Cranberry Rd., Carver, 41°50'20.6"N 70°41'30.3W"	400 RV/ tent sites; restrooms	mid-May–mid-October	$17–140
508/866-2526; www.mass.gov/locations/myles-standish-state-forest				
Blue Hills Reservation, Ponkapoag	695 Hillside St., Milton, 42°11'10.6"N 71°05'31.2"W	20 cabins, 2 tent sites; outhouses; no water	year-round	$50–400
781/961-7007; www.ponkapoagcamp.org				
Harold Parker State Forest	305 Middleton Rd., North Andover, 42°36'20"N 71°06'1"W	91 RV/ tent sites; restrooms	early May–mid-October	$17–54
978/686-3391; www.mass.gov/locations/harold-parker-state-forest				
Willard Brook State Forest	10 Townsend Rd., Ashby, 42°39'38"N 71°47'27"W	19 RV/ tent sites, 1 group yurt; restrooms	mid-May–early September	$14–230
978/597-8802; www.mass.gov/locations/willard-brook-state-forest				
Lake Dennison Recreation Area	747 Alger St., Winchendon, 42°38'51.5"N 72°04'51.7"W	151 RV/ tent sites; restrooms	mid-May–early September	$17–54
978/297-1609; www.mass.gov/locations/lake-dennison-recreation-area				

CAPE COD AND THE ISLANDS

Quaint, colorful Cape Cod is a land of flowing dunes and windswept grasses, where plovers tuck away their fragile nests and summer tourists flock to the expansive, pastel-hued beaches. It's also the launching point for the offshore islands of Martha's Vineyard and Nantucket, revered for their beauty by both A-list celebrities and lifelong fishermen. Though many of the shores here are occupied by grandiose mansions and humble beach cottages, a remarkable amount of conservation land has been set aside as the Cape Cod National Seashore, in town preserves, and in land-bank systems on both of the islands. As a result, miles of coastal trails wind through the goldenrod and beach plum, offering seaside vistas that are sure to inspire even the saltiest hearts.

▲ CAPE COD NATIONAL SEASHORE

▲ MENEMSHA HILLS RESERVATION

◄ SUNSET AT SANDY NECK BEACH PARK

1 Great Island Trail
DISTANCE: 5.9 mi (9.5 km) (with longer options at low tide)
DURATION: 3 hr
EFFORT: Moderate
PAGE: 460

2 Marsh Trail
DISTANCE: 7.9 mi (12.7 km) round-trip
DURATION: 4 hr
EFFORT: Moderate
PAGE: 463

3 Menemsha Hills: Prospect Hill and the Great Sand Bank
DISTANCE: 3.1 mi (5 km) round-trip
DURATION: 2 hr
EFFORT: Easy/moderate
PAGE: 466

4 Ocean Walk
DISTANCE: 5.7 mi (9.2 km) round-trip
DURATION: 2.5 hr
EFFORT: Easy
PAGE: 469

CAPE COD
AND THE ISLANDS

To Boston

Cohasset

Hanover

Marshfield

3A

3

Duxbury

Kingston

Plymouth

44

Carver

Myles
Standish
State Forest

3A

3

495

DUNES'
EDGE

Cape

Provincetown

6

Cod

Truro

National

Wellfleet

1

Seashore

Cape Cod
Bay

Eastham

6

SCUSSET BEACH
STATE RESERVATION

Sandwich

SANDY NECK
BEACH PARK

Brewster

Orleans

NICKERSON
STATE PARK

Wareham

6

Bourne

SHAWME-CROWELL
STATE FOREST

2

6A

Barnstable

Dennis

Yarmouth

6A

6

28

195

6

Marion

28

6

Harwich

Chatham

Mattapoisett

28

Mashpee

Hyannis

28

Mashpee
Neck

Monomoy
N.W.R.

28

Falmouth

Woods Hole

Vineyard
Haven

Oak Bluffs

Martha's
Vineyard

Edgartown

3

Chilmark

Polpis

Nantucket

4

Nantucket

0   10 mi
0   10 km

© MOON.COM

Great Island Trail

CAPE COD NATIONAL SEASHORE, WELLFLEET

Traverse pitch pine forests, dunes, and undeveloped beaches with this long hike through the bay side of Cape Cod National Seashore.

BEST: Summer hikes
DISTANCE: 5.9 mi (9.5 km) (with longer options at low tide)
DURATION: 3 hr
ELEVATION GAIN: 153 ft (47 m)
EFFORT: Moderate
TRAIL: Sand, dirt path
USERS: Hikers, leashed dogs
SEASON: Year-round
FEES/PASSES: None
MAPS: National Park Service, "Cape Cod National Seashore"
TRAILHEAD: Great Island Trail parking lot, Chequessett Neck Rd., Wellfleet
FACILITIES: None
CONTACT: National Park Service; 508/771-2144; www.nps.gov/caco

The Great Island Trail, over 8 mi (13 km) long, begins along a coastal salt marsh then alternates between sandy dune paths and pitch pine-lined hills before arriving on the shores of a beautiful beach. At low tide (the best time to hike this trail), hikers can put in extra mileage on the way to Jeremy's Point, a vast expanse of sand that emerges above the waterline to jut into Cape Cod Bay. This pristine shoreline, with its abundant wildlife and magical sunsets, captures the heart and soul of the Cape Cod National Seashore.

START THE HIKE

▶ **MILE 0-1.2: Great Island Trail Parking Lot to Marsh**

Follow the gravel trail southeast from the parking lot and down a series of steps to reach the marsh at 0.2 mi (0.3 km). Turn right (west) onto the **Great Island Trail,** which wraps around the west side of the marsh. At high tide, the marsh section of the trail may be submerged. Follow the grassy west perimeter of the marsh for approximately 1 mi (1.6 km).

MARSH ALONG WELLFLEET'S GREAT ISLAND TRAIL ▶

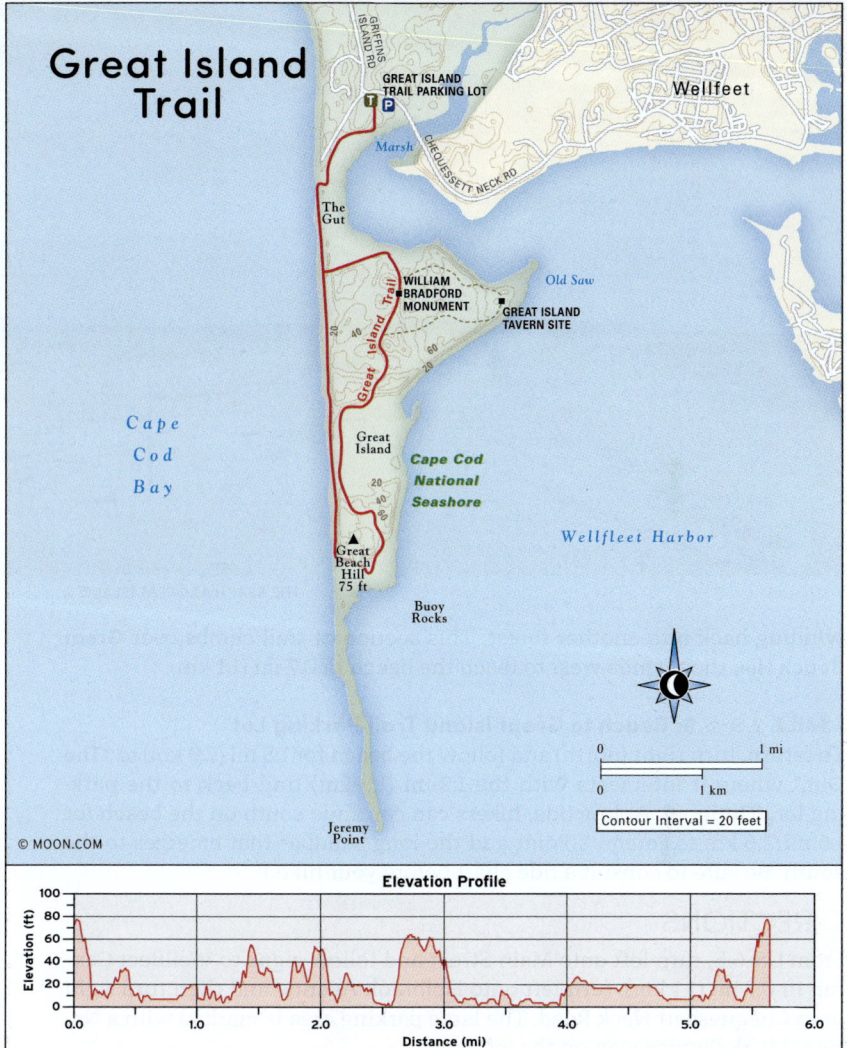

Great Island Trail

GRIFFINS ISLAND RD.

GREAT ISLAND TRAIL PARKING LOT

Wellfleet

Marsh

CHEQUESSETT NECK RD.

The Gut

WILLIAM BRADFORD MONUMENT

Old Saw

GREAT ISLAND TAVERN SITE

20

40

60

20

Cape Cod Bay

Great Island

Cape Cod National Seashore

20

40

Wellfleet Harbor

Great Beach Hill 75 ft

Buoy Rocks

Jeremy Point

© MOON.COM

0   1 mi

0   1 km

Contour Interval = 20 feet

Elevation Profile

Elevation (ft) / Distance (mi)

100, 80, 60, 40, 20, 0

0.0 1.0 2.0 3.0 4.0 5.0 6.0

▶ MILE 1.2-1.7: Marsh to William Bradford Monument and Vista

Here, the trail cuts right (south) into a forest of scrub oak and pitch pine on a springy pine needle path. In 0.3 mi (0.5 km), an optional spur to the left leads to the former site of the **Great Island Tavern.** Continue straight (south) on the main trail, passing a **monument** to William Bradford, a Pilgrim on the Mayflower and the first governor of the Massachusetts Bay Colony. Descend the hill for 0.2 mi (0.3 km), where the path widens into a vista of the marsh and the dunes beyond.

▶ MILE 1.7-2.9: William Bradford Monument and Vista to Beach

At the opening, the trail continues to the right (west) back along the edge of the marsh. Again, depending on the tide, the trail may be wet here. The trail returns to sand in 0.5 mi (0.8 km), climbing over a high dune before winding back into another forest. This section of trail climbs over **Great Beach Hill,** then bends west to reach the beach in 0.7 mi (1.1 km).

▶ **MILE 2.9-5.9: Beach to Great Island Trail Parking Lot**

To return, turn right (north) and follow the beach for 1.8 mi (2.9 km) to **"The Gut,"** where it intersects with the 1.2-mi (1.9-km) trail back to the parking lot. (Optional: At low tide, hikers can continue south on the beach for 1.6 mi/2.6 km to Jeremy's Point and the long sandbar that emerges to the south. Be sure to consult a tide chart before your hike.)

DIRECTIONS

From US-6 E, turn left onto Main Street and follow signs to Wellfleet Center. In 0.7 mi (1.1 km), turn left onto Holbrook Avenue and then turn right onto Chequessett Neck Road. The large parking area is marked with a National Park Service sign on the left.

GPS COORDINATES: 41°55'58.2"N 70°04'08.2"W

BEST NEARBY BREWS

Catch a bite and a live performance at **The Beachcomber** (1120 Cahoon Hollow Rd., Wellfleet; 508/349-6055; www.thebeachcomber.com; 11:30am-1am daily, hours vary seasonally—call ahead), a lively beachfront bar with great summertime vibes. It's 6 mi (9.7 km) from the trailhead.

The expansive marshes and high dunes of this long spit of barrier beach are home to a variety of rare wildlife species.

DISTANCE: 7.9 mi (12.7 km) round-trip

DURATION: 4 hr

ELEVATION GAIN: 214 ft (65 m)

EFFORT: Moderate

TRAIL: Sand

USERS: Hikers, leashed dogs, horseback riders, fat-tire bikes

SEASON: Year-round

FEES/PASSES: Day pass $20

MAPS: Town of Barnstable, "Sandy Neck"

TRAILHEAD: Marsh Trail trailhead, Sandy Neck Rd., West Barnstable

FACILITIES: None

CONTACT: Town of Barnstable; 508/362-8300; https://town.barnstable. ma.us/sandyneckpark

The 6-mi-long (9.7-km) barrier beach of Sandy Neck reaches out between the Barnstable Great Marsh and Cape Cod Bay. The trail through this town park offers excellent opportunities to spot rare wildlife, from diamondback terrapins to river otters. Break up your hike with a one-of-a-kind camping experience at the hike-in tent sites among the dunes.

START THE HIKE

▶ **MILE 0-3.8: Marsh Trail Trailhead to Trail 4**

The **Marsh Trail** begins across from the visitor kiosk and travels east through the gate on a crushed-rock path. Hikers will be rewarded immediately with views of the **Great Marsh** to their right (south) and views of large dunes, gnarled cedar, and scrub oak to their left (north). The path turns to deep sand and walking becomes more strenuous after 0.2 mi (0.3 km). At the signed intersection with Trail 1, 0.5 mi (0.8 km) from the start, keep right on the Marsh Trail. Keep an eye out for unique birds among the many birdhouses and osprey nesting poles in the marsh. Pass the marked left turn for Trail 2 in 1.3 mi (2.1 km)—Trail 3 is no longer open. Reach the sign for **Trail 4** at 3.8 mi (6.1 km).

▶ **MILE 3.8-4.5: Trail 4 to Beach**

Turn left (north) on Trail 4, climbing through the dunes and following signs for the campsite. Bear left at the fork at 4 mi (6.4 km) and hike through the campsite. Trail 4 continues north through a pitch pine forest and over the dunes to reach the beach at 4.5 mi (7.2 km).

Cape Cod and the Islands

MASSACHUSETTS

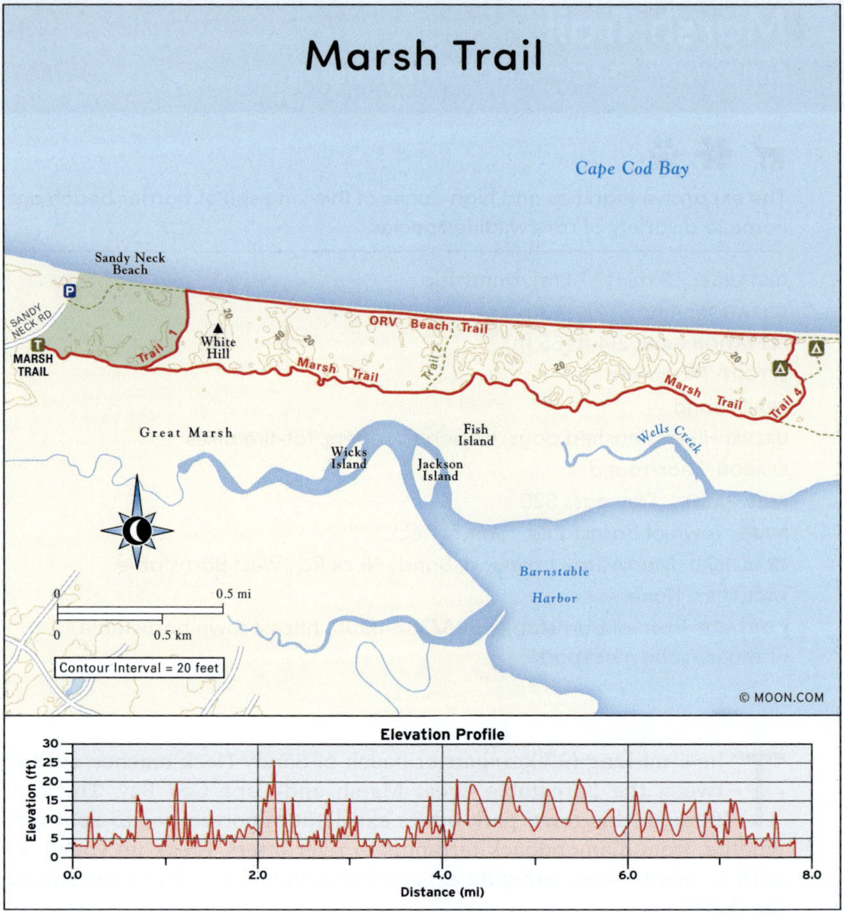

Marsh Trail

Cape Cod Bay

Sandy Neck Beach

SANDY NECK RD

MARSH TRAIL

White Hill

ORV Beach Trail

Trail 1

Trail 2

Marsh Trail

Marsh Trail

Trail 4

Great Marsh

Wicks Island

Jackson Island

Fish Island

Wells Creek

Barnstable Harbor

0   0.5 mi

0   0.5 km

Contour Interval = 20 feet

© MOON.COM

Elevation Profile

Elevation (ft)

Distance (mi)

▶ **MILE 4.5–7.9: Beach to White Hill Vista and Marsh Trail Trailhead**

Turn left (west) onto the beach and follow the shore on the **ORV Beach Trail** for 2.5 mi (4 km) until the intersection with Trail 1, then turn left (south) onto **Trail 1**. Climb south over the dunes of White Hill for a lovely seaside vista, then reach the Marsh Trail again at 7.4 mi (11.9 km). Turn right (west) on the Marsh Trail to return 0.5 mi (0.8 km) to the trailhead.

BEACH ROSES AT SANDY NECK ▶

▲ THE MARSH TRAIL

DIRECTIONS

From US-6 East, take Exit 4 to Chase Road. Follow Chase Road to where it turns into Old County Road and then take a left onto Jones Lane. In 0.5 mi (0.8 km), turn right onto Old King's Highway (MA-6A), and then turn left onto Sandy Neck Road. The gatehouse is about 0.5 mi (0.8 km) down the road. Consult an attendant for fees and parking directions.

GPS COORDINATES: 41°44'06.6"N 70°23'05.7"W

BEST NEARBY BITES

In downtown Hyannis, **emBargo** (453 Main St., Hyannis; 508/771-9700; www.embargorestaurant.com; 4:30pm–1am daily) is a choice spot for cocktails and tapas, with dancing and live entertainment most nights. It's 9 mi (14.5 km) from the trailhead.

3 Menemsha Hills: Prospect Hill and the Great Sand Bank

MENEMSHA HILLS RESERVATION, CHILMARK (MARTHA'S VINEYARD)

Admire views of Vineyard Sound and the Elizabeth Islands from the hills and beaches of Martha's Vineyard's north shore.

DISTANCE: 3.1 mi (5 km) round-trip

DURATION: 2 hr

ELEVATION GAIN: 468 ft (143 m)

EFFORT: Easy/moderate

TRAIL: Dirt path, cobblestone beach

USERS: Hikers, leashed dogs

SEASON: Year-round

FEES/PASSES: None

MAPS: The Trustees of Reservations, "Menemsha Hills"

TRAILHEAD: Harris Loop trailhead, Trustees Ln., Chilmark

FACILITIES: Portable toilet, trail map

CONTACT: The Trustees of Reservations; 508/693-3678; https://thetrustees.org

The Menemsha Hills span 211 acres (85 hectares) of hills, woods, dunes, and coastline along the northwest end of Martha's Vineyard, overlooking Menemsha Bight, Vineyard Sound, the Elizabeth Islands, and the lighthouse-adorned tip of Aquinnah/Gay Head. This lesser-known jewel of public land is one of the finest opportunities for visitors to explore the natural beauty of Martha's Vineyard free of charge.

START THE HIKE

▶ **MILE 0-0.7: Harris Loop Trail to Nashawakemuck Loop**

Hike northeast through the trailhead gate on a gravel trail, which bends west and then reaches an intersection in 150 ft (46 m). Stay left (west) on the **Harris Loop** through a thicket of green woods and vernal pools. The trail curves northwest and gains elevation 0.2 mi (0.3 km) from the trailhead, ascending a series of wood and earthen steps. Continue straight (north) at the intersection at 0.5 mi (0.8 km), following signs for Prospect Hill. (The optional offshoot to the top of **Prospect Hill** will be immediately on your left. The moderate climb up the hill is about 250 ft/76 m, and it ends in spectacular views of the island's west end.) If you climb Prospect Hill, backtrack to the sign at the base of the hill, then continue west on a sandy downhill for 0.1 mi (0.16 km). Cross straight (north) over the dirt road to reach an intersection at 0.7 mi (1.1 km). Turn left (west) onto the

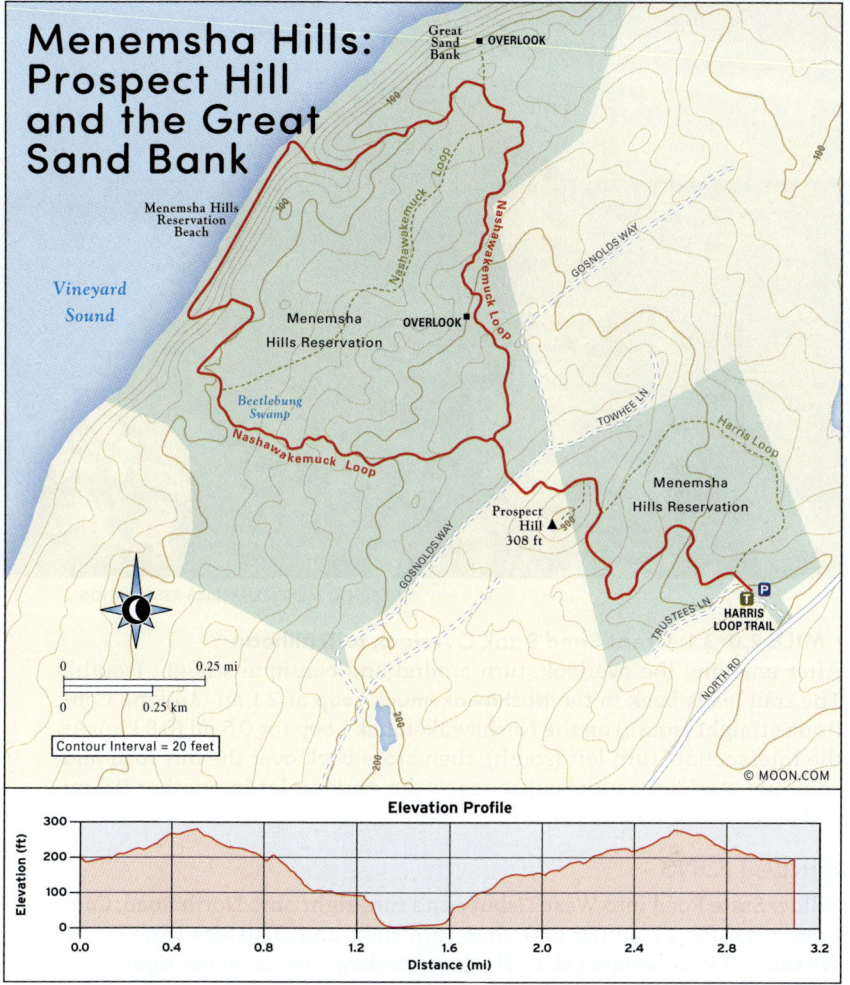

Menemsha Hills: Prospect Hill and the Great Sand Bank

Great Sand Bank ■ OVERLOOK

Menemsha Hills Reservation Beach

Vineyard Sound

Menemsha Hills Reservation

OVERLOOK ■

Nashawakemuck Loop

GOSNOLDS WAY

TOWHEE LN

Beetlebung Swamp

Nashawakemuck Loop

Harris Loop

Menemsha Hills Reservation

Prospect Hill 308 ft ▲

GOSNOLDS WAY

TRUSTEES LN

HARRIS LOOP TRAIL

NORTH RD

0   0.25 mi

0   0.25 km

Contour Interval = 20 feet

© MOON.COM

Elevation Profile

Elevation (ft) — 0, 100, 200, 300

Distance (mi) — 0.0, 0.4, 0.8, 1.2, 1.6, 2.0, 2.4, 2.8, 3.2

narrow dirt path. Before long, the trail opens onto a wide vista of Menemsha Bight, with the Gay Head light twirling above.

▶ **MILE 0.7–2.0: Nashawakemuck Loop to Great Sand Bank Overlook**
Where the Nashawakemuck Loop curves right (east) in 0.4 mi (0.6 km), bear left (north) to follow the trail toward the beach. This path rolls over a high bluff with occasional views of the Vineyard Sound, then descends a staircase to reach the beach at 1.4 mi (2.3 km). Turn right (northeast) onto the beach, stepping with care across the cobblestone shoreline. At a collection of wave-beaten boulders at 1.7 mi (2.7 km), another staircase heads right (southeast) into the dunes. Ascend the staircase and continue on the somewhat steep path as it climbs to the top of the Great Sand Bank. At the intersection on the hilltop at 2 mi (3.2 km), there is a 150-ft (46-m) spur to the left (northwest) that leads to the **Great Sand Bank Overlook**.

▶ **MILE 2.0-3.1: Great Sand Bank Overlook to Trailhead**

After enjoying the overlook, turn around and continue straight (south). The trail leads back to the **Nashawakemuck Loop** at 2.1 mi (3.4 km). Continue straight (south) on the Nashawakemuck Loop for 0.5 mi (0.8 km). At the intersection, turn left (south), then cross back over the dirt road and continue straight (southeast) to reach the parking lot in another 0.5 mi (0.8 km).

DIRECTIONS

Follow State Road into West Tisbury and turn right onto North Road. Continue west for 4.7 mi (7.6 km), then turn right onto Trustees Lane at the Trustees of Reservations sign. The large parking area is on the right.

The Martha's Vineyard Transit Authority number 4 bus stops at the trailhead upon request.

GPS COORDINATES: 41°21'53.7"N 70°44'33.2"W

BEST NEARBY BITES AND BREWS

Grab a local Offshore Ale and BYOB to Menemsha Beach, where you can watch the sun set with some food or ice cream from **The Galley** (515 North Rd.; 508/645-9819; www.menemshagalley.com; 11am-8pm daily, hours vary seasonally—call ahead), 2 mi (3.2 km) from the trailhead.

4 Ocean Walk

SANFORD FARM, RAM PASTURE, AND THE WOODS, NANTUCKET

🦌 ❀ 🐾 🏃 ♿ 🚍

Wind your way to the ocean on this quaint path through historic farmland, exploring sand plains, heaths, and ponds.

BEST: Brew hikes

DISTANCE: 5.7 mi (9.2 km) round-trip

DURATION: 2.5 hr

ELEVATION GAIN: 74 ft (23 m)

EFFORT: Easy

TRAIL: Grass/sand path

USERS: Hikers, leashed dogs, bicyclists

SEASON: Year-round

FEES/PASSES: None

MAPS: Nantucket Conservation Foundation, "A Trail Guide to Sanford Farm, Ram Pasture, and The Woods"

TRAILHEAD: Sanford Farm parking area, Madaket Rd., Nantucket

FACILITIES: None

CONTACT: Nantucket Conservation Foundation; 508/228-2884; www.nantucketconservation.org

This easy but lengthy stroll across Nantucket is a tour of all the island's natural delights: grassy pastures, kettle ponds, unspoiled sandy shoreline. The 5.7-mi (9.2-km) Ocean Walk takes hikers through three key sections of conservation land, starting with Sanford Farm and then traveling through The Woods and Ram Pasture to reach a wide-open sand plain abutting the ocean. Aside from fantastic water views, be on the lookout for deer, osprey, and unique plant life.

START THE HIKE

▶ **MILE 0-1.6: Sanford Farm Parking Area to Historic Barn**
From the **Sanford Farm** parking area, find the trail through the turnstile to the south. The wide sand-and-crushed stone path carries hikers over rolling hills, with grasslands to the right and pond views to the left. The scenic corridor emerges at a historic **barn** atop a hill in about 1.6 mi (2.6 km), with great views stretching across North Head and Hummock Pond to the Atlantic Ocean. This part of the trail is accessible to all-terrain wheelchairs, but you will need to contact the Nantucket Conservation Foundation (508/228-2884) to unlock the entry gate for access.

▶ **MILE 1.6-2.9: Historic Barn to Ram Pasture**
Continue straight (south) down the hill through **The Woods,** where hawthorn, shadbush, and black cherry form a dense thicket around the path. Reach a fork at 2 mi (3.2 km). Bear left (south), skirting the edge of **Ram**

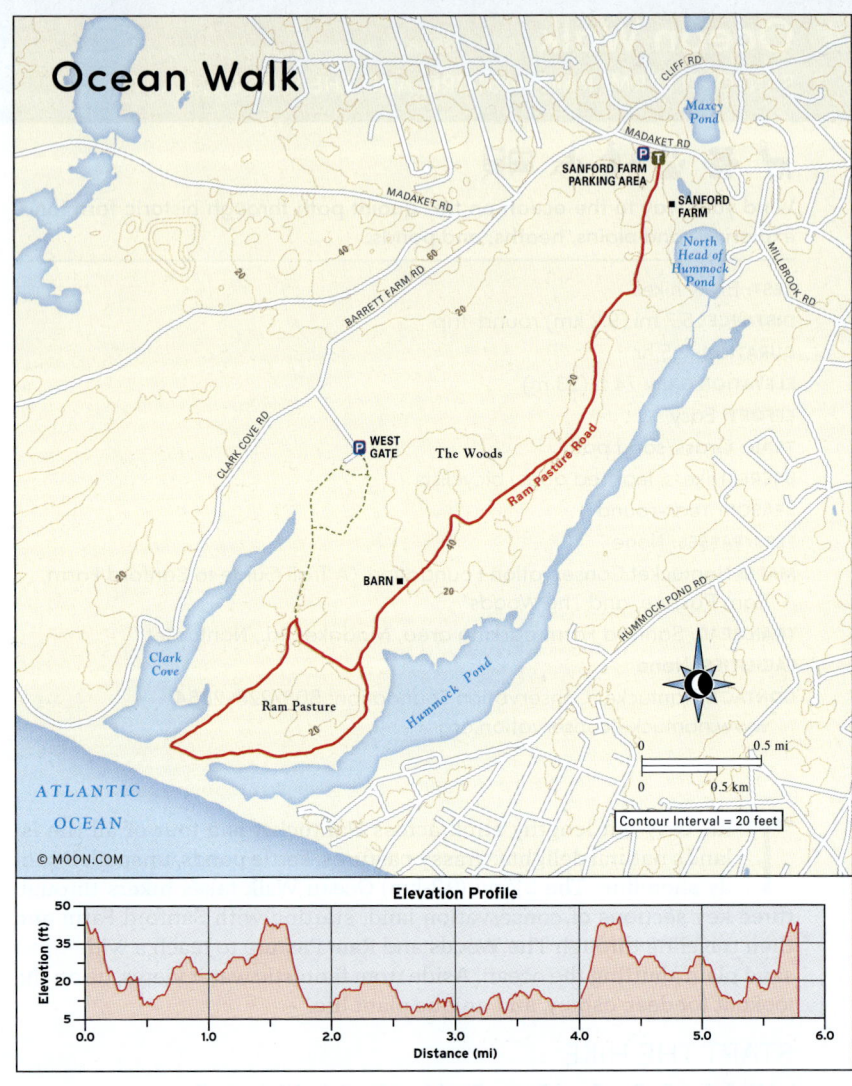

Ocean Walk

SANFORD FARM PARKING AREA

SANFORD FARM

North Head of Hummock Pond

Maxcy Pond

MADAKET RD.

CLIFF RD.

MILLBROOK RD.

BARRETT FARM RD.

CLARK COVE RD.

WEST GATE

The Woods

Ram Pasture Road

BARN

HUMMOCK POND RD.

Clark Cove

Ram Pasture

Hummock Pond

ATLANTIC OCEAN

© MOON.COM

0   0.5 mi
0   0.5 km

Contour Interval = 20 feet

Elevation Profile

Elevation (ft)

Distance (mi)

Pasture, a vast sand plain where birds and insects flitter among colorful grasses. You may even catch a glimpse of an osprey perched atop the nesting pole here. The sound of the ocean draws nearer as the trail wraps west along the coast. An optional side path to the left (south) at 2.9 mi (4.7 km) leads to the **beach.**

▶ MILE 2.9–5.7: Ram Pasture to Sanford Farm Parking Area

The main path turns northeast here, tracing the north edge of Ram Pasture for 0.6 mi (1 km). When you reach the next intersection, turn right (south) to follow the trail east for 0.3 mi (0.5 km) to the main path. Take a left (north) to backtrack 1.9 mi (3.1 km) through The Woods to the Sanford Farm lot.

▲ PATH THROUGH SANFORD FARM

DIRECTIONS

From the center of town, follow Madaket Road west for approximately 1.5 mi (2.4 km). The large parking lot and marked trailhead are on the left, across from 121 Madaket Road.

The Nantucket Regional Transit Authority Madaket bus stops at the trailhead upon request.

GPS COORDINATES: 41°17'01.5"N 70°08'12.6"W

BEST NEARBY BREWS

Stop by **Cisco Brewers** (5 Bartlett Farm Rd.; 508/325-5929; www. ciscobrewers.com; 11am-7pm Mon.-Sat., noon-6pm Sun.) for a fresh local pint and a happening scene that includes food trucks, live music, art, and shopping. It's 4 mi (6.4 km) from the trailhead.

PAINTED TURTLE AT SANFORD FARM ▲

NEARBY CAMPGROUNDS

NAME	LOCATION	FACILITIES	SEASON	FEE
Dunes' Edge Campground	386 US-6, Provincetown, 42°03'38.2"N 70°11'11.3"W	85 tent sites, 15 RV sites; restrooms	mid-May-September	$55-149
508/487-9815; https://thetrustees.org				
Nickerson State Park	3488 Main St., Brewster, 41°46'28"N 70°1'55"W	372 RV/tent sites, 6 yurts; restrooms	May-October	$22-140
508/896-3491; www.mass.gov/locations/nickerson-state-park				
Sandy Neck Beach Park	425 Sandy Neck Rd., West Barnstable, 41°44'07.0"N 70°23'07.1"W	self-contained RVs, 5 primitive tent sites, 1 lean-to site; no restrooms	Memorial Day-Labor Day	$20
508/362-8300; www.town.barnstable.ma.us/SandyNeckPark				
Shawme-Crowell State Forest	42 Main St., Sandwich, 41°45'47"N 70°31'25"W	285 RV/tent sites, 6 yurts; restrooms	May-October	$17-140
508/888-0351; www.mass.gov/locations/shawme-crowell-state-forest				
Scusset Beach State Reservation	20 Scusset Beach Rd., Sagamore Beach, 41°46'45"N 70°30'13"W	98 RV sites, 5 tent sites; restrooms	mid-April-late October; off-season RV camping available	$35
508/888-0859; www.mass.gov/locations/scusset-beach-state-reservation				

THE BERKSHIRES

The Berkshires are perhaps the most popular hiking destination in Massachusetts, and for good reason. Not only do they boast the highest peaks in the state—most notably, Mount Greylock—they emanate a quintessential New England feel, with small artsy towns, rolling farmland, and lush green forests where secluded waterfalls patter out their perpetual rhythms in solitude. Though the region is commonly referred to as the Berkshire Hills, the highlands of western Massachusetts are actually the amalgamation of several mountain ranges, including the southern Green Mountains and the eastern Taconic Mountains. These peaks are your best bet for elevation in southern New England, with sweeping views that reach across state lines to Vermont, Connecticut, New York, and beyond.

▲ APPROACHING THE SUMMIT OF PEESKAWSO PEAK

▲ COTTONWOOD TREE ON THE SPERO TRAIL, BARTHOLOMEW'S COBBLE

◄ THE HALEY FARM TRAIL, MOUNT GREYLOCK

MASSACHUSETTS
The Berkshires

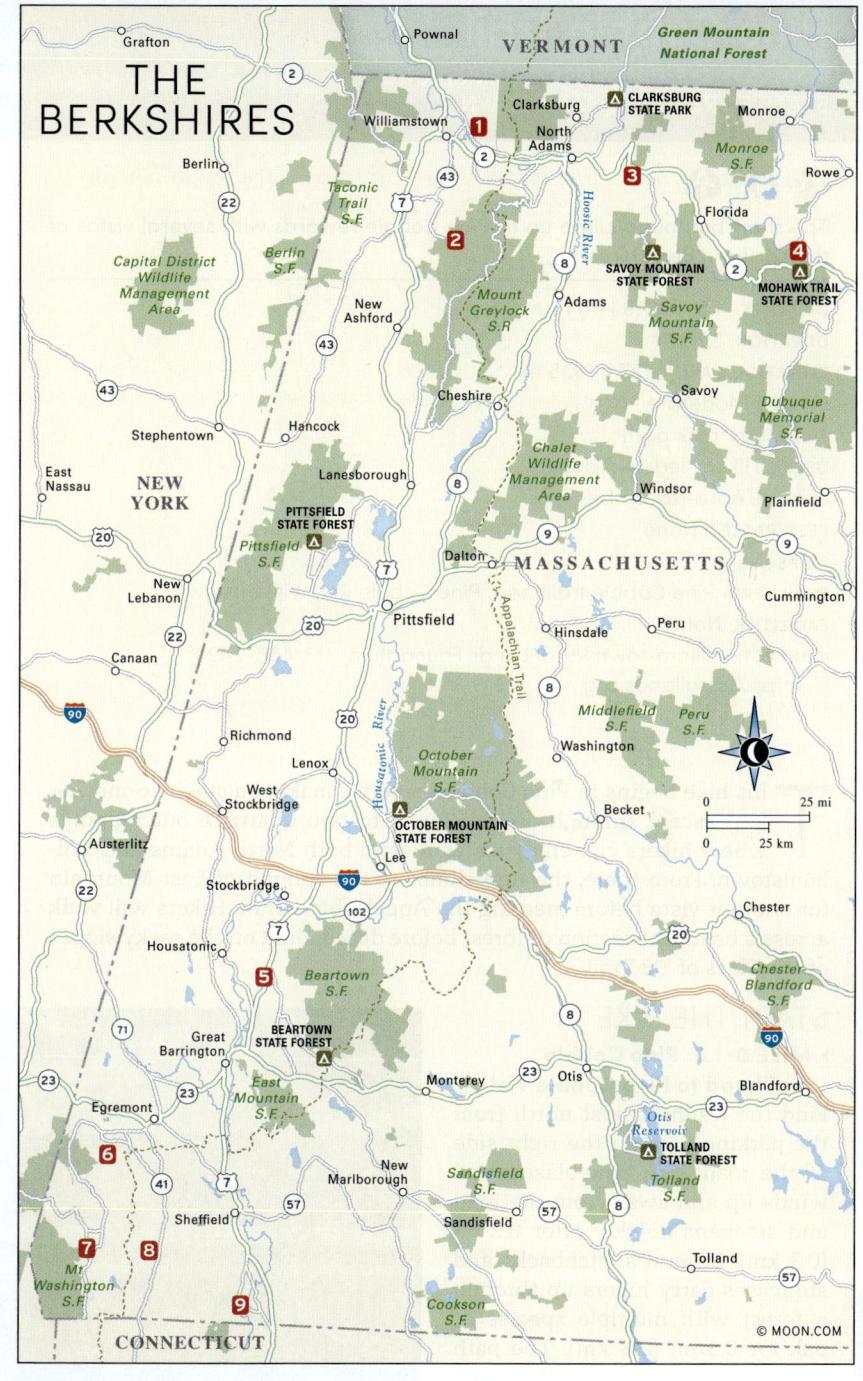

THE BERKSHIRES

VERMONT

Grafton

Pownal

Green Mountain
National Forest

Williamstown

Clarksburg

**CLARKSBURG
STATE PARK**

Monroe

North
Adams

*Monroe
S.F.*

Rowe

Berlin

Taconic
Trail
S.F.

*Berlin
S.F.*

Florida

*Monroe
S.F.*

Capital District
Wildlife
Management
Area

New
Ashford

Mount
Greylock
S.R

Adams

**SAVOY MOUNTAIN
STATE FOREST**

*Savoy
Mountain
S.F.*

**MOHAWK TRAIL
STATE FOREST**

Hoosic River

Stephentown

Hancock

Cheshire

Savoy

*Dubuque
Memorial
S.F.*

East
Nassau

**NEW
YORK**

Lanesborough

*Chalet
Wildlife
Management
Area*

Windsor

Plainfield

New
Lebanon

**PITTSFIELD
STATE FOREST**

*Pittsfield
S.F.*

Dalton

MASSACHUSETTS

Cummington

Canaan

Pittsfield

Hinsdale

Peru

Richmond

Lenox

*Middlefield
S.F.*

*Peru
S.F.*

West
Stockbridge

*October
Mountain
S.F.*

Washington

Becket

0   25 mi

0   25 km

Austerlitz

**OCTOBER MOUNTAIN
STATE FOREST**

Lee

Stockbridge

Chester

Housatonic

*Beartown
S.F.*

*Chester-
Blandford
S.F.*

**BEARTOWN
STATE FOREST**

Great
Barrington

*East
Mountain
S.F.*

Monterey

Otis

Blandford

Egremont

*Otis
Reservoir*

**TOLLAND
STATE FOREST**

New
Marlborough

*Sandisfield
S.F.*

*Tolland
S.F.*

Sheffield

Sandisfield

Tolland

*Mt.
Washington
S.F.*

*Cookson
S.F.*

CONNECTICUT

© MOON.COM

MASSACHUSETTS

477

1 Pine Cobble Trail

PINE COBBLE PRESERVE/CLARKSBURG STATE FOREST, WILLIAMSTOWN

The short but tough climb up to Pine Cobble rewards with several vistas of the northern Berkshires.

DISTANCE: 4.9 mi (7.9 km) round–trip
DURATION: 2.75 hr
ELEVATION GAIN: 1,427 ft (435 m)
EFFORT: Moderate
TRAIL: Dirt/rock path
USERS: Hikers, leashed dogs
SEASON: April–November
FEES/PASSES: None
MAPS: None
TRAILHEAD: Pine Cobble trailhead, Pine Cobble Rd., Williamstown
FACILITIES: None
CONTACT: Williamstown Rural Lands Foundation; 413/458-2494; https://rurallands.org

This hike begins in Pine Cobble Preserve, making a steep 1.6-mi (2.6-km) ascent through an oak forest to two quartzite outcroppings where hikers can enjoy vistas toward both North Adams and Williamstown. From there, the trail climbs to the summit of East Mountain for another vista before meeting the Appalachian Trail. Hikers will walk across a beautiful section of forest before descending on the rocky slopes of the Class of '98 Trail.

START THE HIKE

▸ **MILE 0-1.6: Pine Cobble Trailhead to Pine Cobble Vista**
Find the trailhead just north from the parking area on the right side of the road. The blue-blazed trail winds up and away from the road and steepens quickly after 0.2 mi (0.3 km). Several switchbacks and staircases carry hikers up through a forest with multiple species of oak for 0.5 mi (0.8 km). The path flattens for 0.2 mi (0.3 km) and passes the intersection with the Class of '98 Trail. Continue straight

PINE COBBLE WEST VISTA VIEW ▸

MASSACHUSETTS

The Berkshires

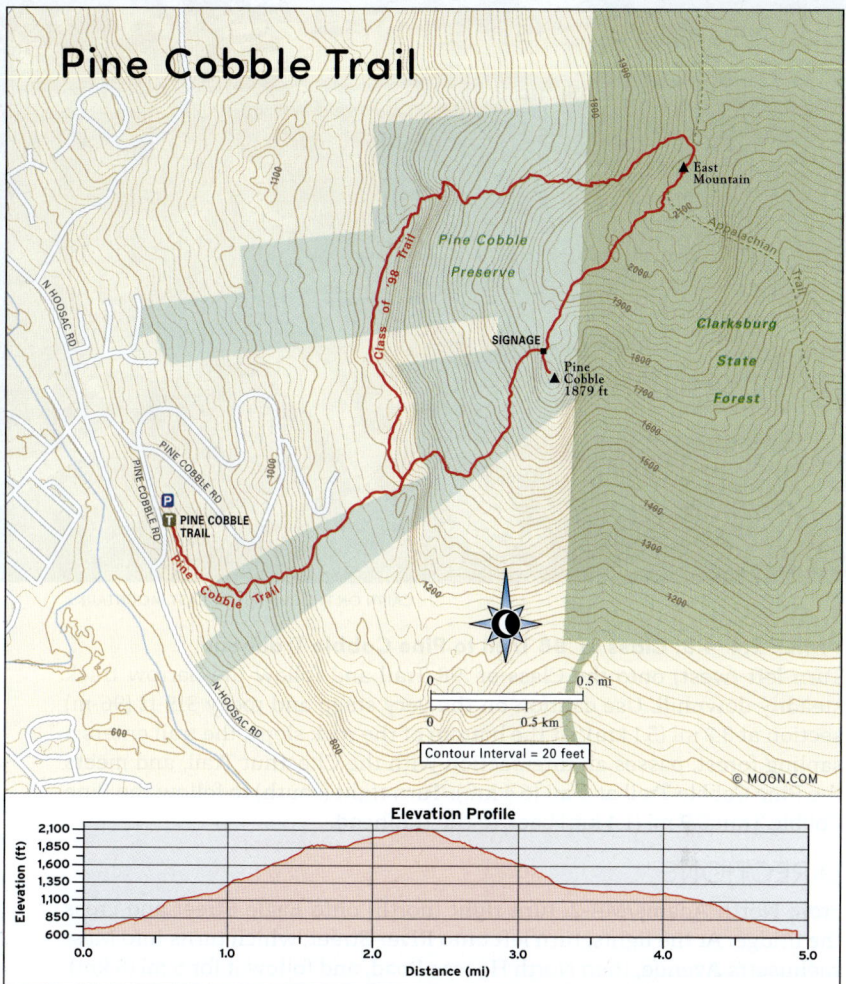

Pine Cobble Trail

East Mountain

Pine Cobble
Preserve

Class of '98 Trail

SIGNAGE

Pine
Cobble
1879 ft

Appalachian Trail

Clarksburg
State
Forest

PINE COBBLE RD

PINE COBBLE RD

N. HOOSAC RD

P

T PINE COBBLE
TRAIL

Pine Cobble Trail

N. HOOSAC RD

0   0.5 mi
0   0.5 km

Contour Interval = 20 feet

© MOON.COM

Elevation Profile

northeast. The path becomes quite rocky as it makes its final 0.6-mi (1-km) climb to a sign for Pine Cobble at 1.5 mi (2.4 km). Take the spur to Pine Cobble Vista.

▶ MILE 1.6–2.2: Pine Cobble Vista to East Mountain Summit

After enjoying the views, backtrack to the sign for Pine Cobble and continue straight north. The narrow path continues uphill through forest for 0.5 mi (0.8 km) before merging with the Appalachian Trail (AT) just south of the East Mountain summit. A 0.1-mi (0.16-km) climb over quartz tumbles will deliver you to the summit of **East Mountain,** marked with cairns.

▶ MILE 2.2–2.4: East Mountain Summit to Class of '98 Trail

Continue north on the white-blazed AT and follow it for 0.2 mi (0.3 km). Look out for the sign for the **Class of '98 Trail** on the left side of the path at 2.4 mi (3.9 km)—it may be slightly overgrown.

CAIRN ON THE SUMMIT OF EAST MOUNTAIN ▲

▶ **MILE 2.4–4.9: Class of '98 Trail to Pine Cobble Trailhead**

Turn left (west) onto the Class of '98 Trail and follow the narrow track steadily downhill. Use caution on the very steep and rocky 315-ft (96-m) section at 3.2 mi (5.1 km). At the bottom of the rock slope, the trail enters a sapling forest, passes an intersection with the Chestnut Trail, and meets the Pine Cobble Trail at 4 mi (6.4 km). Turn right (south) to follow the Pine Cobble Trail 0.9 mi (1.4 km) back to the trailhead.

DIRECTIONS

From North Adams/MA-2, turn right (north) onto Eagle Street and cross the bridge. At the lights, turn left onto River Street, which turns into Massachusetts Avenue, then North Hoosac Road, and follow it for 5 mi (8 km). Then, turn right onto Pine Cobble Road. The parking area is marked with a sign 0.1 mi (0.16 km) north on the left. The trailhead is across the street.

GPS COORDINATES: 42°42'58.9"N 73°11'06.5"W

2 Mount Greylock via the Money Brook and Appalachian Trails

MOUNT GREYLOCK STATE RESERVATION, WILLIAMSTOWN

As the tallest mountain in Massachusetts, Mount Greylock calls for a long exploratory loop with waterfalls and breathtaking views.

BEST: Fall hikes, vistas

DISTANCE: 11.8 mi (19 km) round-trip (with optional additions)

DURATION: 6 hr

ELEVATION GAIN: 2,647 ft (807 m)

EFFORT: Strenuous

TRAIL: Dirt/rock path, gravel road

USERS: Hikers, leashed dogs

SEASON: April–November

FEES/PASSES: None

MAPS: Massachusetts DCR, "Mount Greylock State Reservation and Greylock Glen"

TRAILHEAD: Hopper Trailhead, Hopper Rd., Williamstown

FACILITIES: Portable toilet, trail map

CONTACT: Massachusetts Department of Conservation and Recreation, Mount Greylock State Reservation Visitor Center, 30 Rockwell Rd., Lanesborough, MA; 413/499-4262; www.mass.gov/locations/mount-greylock-state-reservation

There are so many great trails on Mount Greylock that it's hard to pick a favorite way up. This long loop covers some of the reservation's best trails, starting on the east side of the mountain. The Money Brook Trail meanders along its namesake waterway to a stunning falls, then climbs to the Appalachian Trail, where it traverses the scenic Greylock Range ridgeline to the 3,488-ft (1063-m) summit. Descend via the Hopper Trail, Sperry Road, and the Haley Farm Trail, hitting March Cataract Falls and the pristine vista of Stony Ledge along the way.

START THE HIKE

▸ **MILE 0-2.8: Hopper Trailhead to Money Brook Falls**

Hike east from the parking lot on the Hopper Trail and pass through the gate into the Hopper Natural Area. Reach an intersection in 0.3 mi (0.5 km) and continue straight on the **Money Brook Trail.** Follow the light blue blazes for 2.5 mi (4 km) through the forest, along a bubbling brook, over several bridges, and then up a steep ascent over the valley. At 2.8 mi (4.5 km), reach a sign that reads Money Brook Falls 100 Yards Ahead at the top of

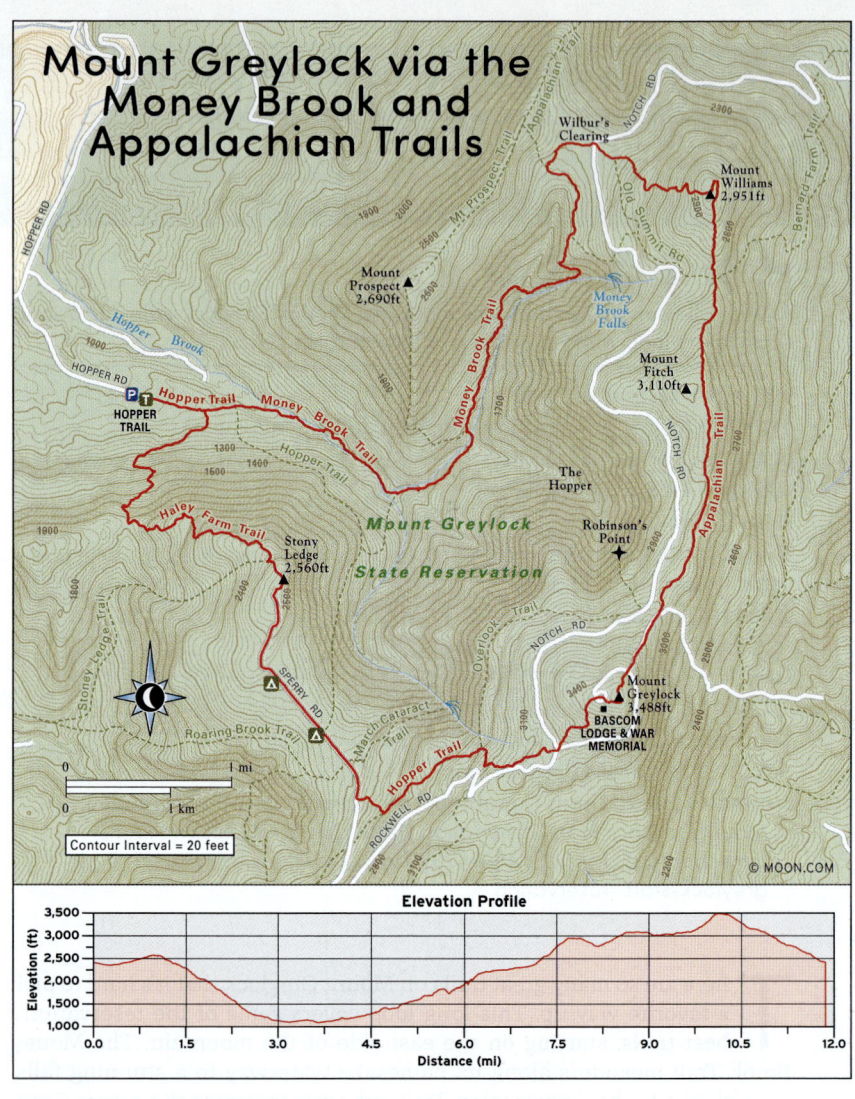

Mount Greylock via the Money Brook and Appalachian Trails

Contour Interval = 20 feet

© MOON.COM

Elevation Profile

the ascent. **Money Brook Falls,** just to the east of the sign, is a remarkable 80-ft (24-m) cascade.

▶ **MILE 2.8–3.5: Money Brook Falls to Appalachian Trail**
When you're finished admiring the falls, head back to the sign, then hike west for 0.3 mi (0.5 km) on a steep uphill toward Notch Road. Reach another posted intersection and turn left (north) toward **Wilbur's Clearing.** This flat section of trail passes the Wilbur's Clearing camping area and meets the **Appalachian Trail (AT)** at a junction of bog bridges at 3.5 mi (5.6 km).

▶ **MILE 3.5–4.6: Appalachian Trail to Mount Williams Summit**
Turn right (north) on the AT southbound, following the white blazes toward **Notch Road.** The AT crosses the paved road at 3.8 mi (6.1 km) and

▲ MARCH CATARACT FALLS

then begins a steep, rocky ascent to the summit of **Mount Williams.** Reach the north-facing vista at 4.6 mi (7.4 km), then continue east on the south-bound AT.

▶ **MILE 4.6–7.0: Mount Williams Summit to Greylock Summit**
From here, the trail traverses the ridgeline of Mount Fitch, dropping into the only boreal forest in Massachusetts. Follow the trail for 1.9 mi (3.1 km) to the intersection with the **Bellows Pipe Trail.** Turn right (south) to continue on the AT, which climbs a steep, rocky path for 0.4 mi (0.6 km) to meet Notch Road again. Cross straight (south) over Notch Road and continue on the asphalt path for 0.1 mi (0.16 km) to the **Veterans War Memorial** tower at **Greylock's summit.** This 93-ft (28-m) stone tower, topped with a light globe, honors Massachusetts casualties of World War I. The best views from the summit are facing east toward the town of Adams.

▶ **MILE 7.0–8.7: Greylock Summit to Sperry Road**
To descend from the summit, head west and rejoin the southbound AT, passing the **Bascom Lodge** and following signs for the **Hopper Trail.** Where the rocky downhill trail meets the road at 7.5 mi (12.1 km), cross the road and turn right (west) onto the Hopper Trail. Pass a pond and reach another intersection at 7.6 mi (12.2 km). Bear right (north) to remain on the Hopper Trail. At the signed intersection with the Overlook Trail at 7.9 mi (12.7 km), bear left (west). The wide rock-and-gravel path reaches a sign pointing toward Sperry Road at 8.5 mi (13.7 km). Turn right (west) and reach the gravel track of Sperry Road at 8.7 mi (14 km). Turn right (north) on **Sperry Road.** Optional: Turn right (east) at the sign in 0.1 mi (0.16 km) for a 1.6-mi (2.6-km) out-and-back detour to **March Cataract Falls.**

▶ **MILE 8.7–9.7: Sperry Road to Stony Ledge Vista**
Follow Sperry Road north through the campground to its terminus at the **Stony Ledge vista** at 9.7 mi (15.6 km). Many consider this peak to be the best view in Greylock, looking out over the Hopper and the ridgeline you've just crossed.

▶ **MILE 9.7–11.8: Stony Ledge Vista to Hopper Trailhead**
Descend to the left (north) on the Haley Farm Trail, which drops 1.9 mi (3.1 km) through a gorgeous hardwood forest to the Hopper Trail. Turn left (west) onto the Hopper Trail and continue 0.2 mi (0.3 km) to return to the trailhead.

DIRECTIONS

Follow US-7 to its intersection with MA-43 and take MA-43 N (Green River Road) for 2.3 mi (3.7 km). Turn right onto Hopper Road and follow it until the end. The trailhead is marked with a sign in a dirt parking lot on the right side of the road.

GPS COORDINATES: 42°39'19.1"N 73°12'15.4"W

3

Hoosac Range Trail to Spruce Hill

HOOSAC RANGE RESERVE AND SAVOY MOUNTAIN STATE FOREST, NORTH ADAMS

Reach stunning views at the summit of Spruce Hill with very little climbing on this pleasant ridgeline hike.

DISTANCE: 5.4 mi (8.7 km) round-trip

DURATION: 2.75 hr

ELEVATION GAIN: 823 ft (251 m)

EFFORT: Moderate

TRAIL: Dirt/rock trail

USERS: Hikers, leashed dogs

SEASON: April–November

FEES/PASSES: None

MAPS: Berkshire Natural Resources Council, "Hoosac Range Reserve"

TRAILHEAD: Hoosac Range Trailhead, MA-2, North Adams

FACILITIES: Trail map at trailhead

CONTACT: Berkshire Natural Resources Council; 413/499-0596; www.bnrc.org

Just before MA-2 W plummets down a hairpin turn into North Adams, hikers have the opportunity to hop on the Hoosac Range Trail across the Western Summit. This 5.4-mi (8.7-km) out-and-back carries hikers across a scenic ridgeline from the west-facing Sunset Rock to the expansive panorama of Savoy Mountain State Forest's Spruce Hill. Visitors don't have to work too hard for the reward—the valley floor simply drops down from the trailhead, leaving nothing but views.

START THE HIKE

▶ **MILE 0-0.7: Trailhead to Sunset Rock Vista**

Go south through the fence at the trailhead. The trail heads through maple, beech, and hobblebush, following the red and white blazes. Gain elevation climbing several switchbacks and reach a posted intersection at 0.4 mi (0.6 km). Turn left (north) to visit **Sunset Rock.** The narrow path through grass and ferns reaches the vista at 0.7 mi (1.1 km), with great views of **North Adams** tucked between the **Greylock Range** and the Hoosic River. As the name suggests, it's a wonderful place to watch the sun lower itself behind Mount Greylock.

▶ **MILE 0.7-2.1: Sunset Rock Vista to Schist Rock Ledge**

Continue south from Sunset Rock and reach another posted intersection. Turn left (east) toward Spruce Hill. This fun, winding path snakes between boulders and birch forest for 1.3 mi (2.1 km), with hints of a view in both directions, before reaching a sign pointing to another vista at 2 mi (3.2 km). Follow the sign left (east) for a side trip (0.1 mi/0.16 km round-trip)

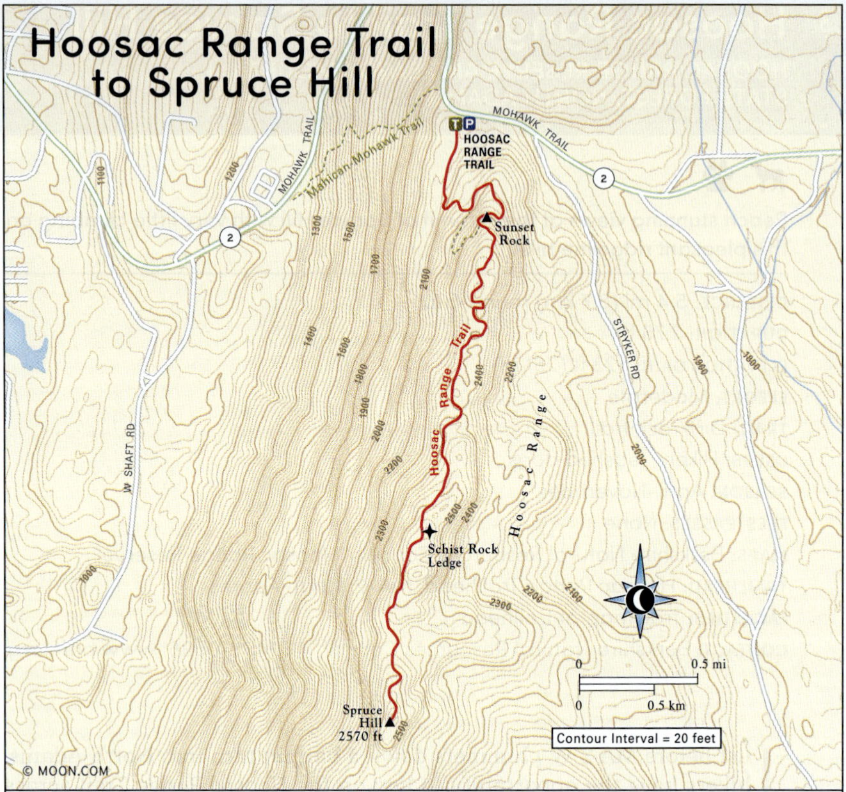
Hoosac Range Trail to Spruce Hill
MOHAWK TRAIL
Mahican-Mohawk Trail
HOOSAC RANGE TRAIL
MOHAWK TRAIL
2
2
Sunset Rock
Hoosac Range Trail
STRYKER RD
W SHAFT RD
Hoosac Range
Schist Rock Ledge
Spruce Hill 2570 ft
0
0.5 mi
0
0.5 km
Contour Interval = 20 feet
© MOON.COM

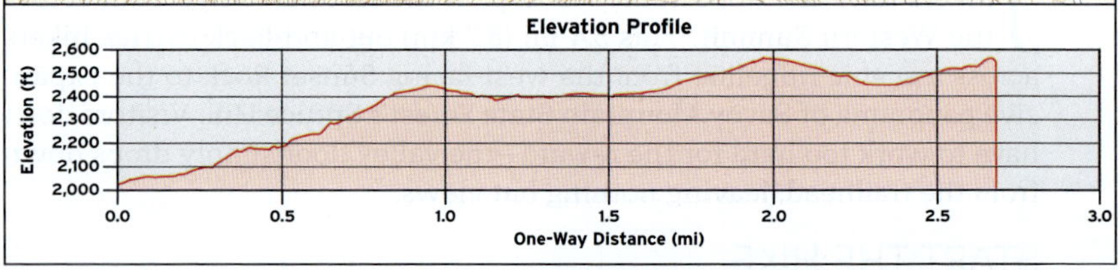
Elevation Profile
Elevation (ft)
2,600
2,500
2,400
2,300
2,200
2,100
2,000
0.0
0.5
1.0
1.5
2.0
2.5
3.0
One-Way Distance (mi)

to a **schist rock ledge** offering great views of Flat Rock Hill and the Cold River.

▸ MILE 2.1-2.7: Schist Rock Ledge to Spruce Hill

Backtrack from the ledge to the main path and continue straight south for 0.3 mi (0.5 km), skirting the edge of a hill, passing grass-covered rock formations and vernal pools, and traveling under a set of power lines. At 2.6 mi (4.2 km), when the blazes turn to light blue, follow the side trail right

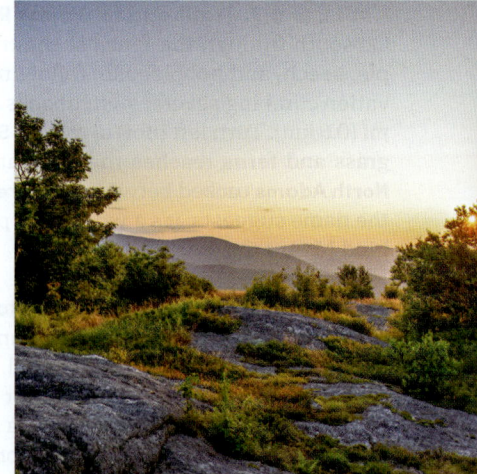

VISTA ALONG THE HOOSAC RANGE TRAIL ▸

(west) over the rock slabs and up the steps. Reach the summit of **Spruce Hill** at 2.7 mi (4.3 km), with panoramic views looking across the **Hoosic River Valley** to **Mount Greylock.** It's a great place to take in the beauty of the **Berkshires** and look for migrating raptors before returning to the parking lot along the same route.

DIRECTIONS

Follow MA-2 W through the town of Florida and continue for 4 mi (6.4 km). The parking lot is on the left just after Stryker Road and before the hairpin turn where the road descends into North Adams.

GPS COORDINATES: 42°41'48.1"N 73°03'54.1"W

4

Todd Mountain via the Mahican–Mohawk Trail

MOHAWK STATE FOREST, CHARLEMONT

Follow in the footsteps of the Berkshires' Indigenous peoples on this section of the Mahican–Mohawk trail along the Deerfield River and up Todd Mountain.

DISTANCE: 5 mi (8 km) round-trip
DURATION: 2.5 hr
ELEVATION GAIN: 1,158 ft (353 m)
EFFORT: Strenuous
TRAIL: Dirt doubletrack, dirt/rock path
USERS: Hikers, leashed dogs
SEASON: April–November
FEES/PASSES: $5 MA resident, $20 nonresident
MAPS: Massachusetts DCR, "Mohawk Trail State Forest"
TRAILHEAD: Mahican–Mohawk parking area, Cold River Rd., Charlemont
FACILITIES: Restrooms, water, trail map
CONTACT: Mohawk Trail State Forest; 413/339-5504; www.mass.gov

T he 40-mi-long (64-km) Mahican-Mohawk Trail, which traverses railroad beds, riverways, and footpaths across the Deerfield River Valley, is a nod to the ancient routes first traveled by the Mohawk and neighboring tribes. The oldest documented section of this trail is this path over the summit of Todd Mountain. This steep hike includes grassy fields and views along the banks of the Deerfield and Cold Rivers.

START THE HIKE

▶ **MILE 0-0.5: Mahican– Mohawk Parking Area to Mahican–Mohawk Trail**

Walk southeast 0.2 mi (0.3 km) from the parking area, back toward the bridge at the entrance of the park. Pass through the gate onto a gravel doubletrack, marked with a sign for the **Mahican–Mohawk Trail.** Continue southeast along the **Cold River** for 0.3 mi (0.5 km), where you reach another sign for the Mahican–Mohawk trail on the left. Turn left (northeast) into the

COLD RIVER IN MOHAWK TRAIL STATE FOREST ▶

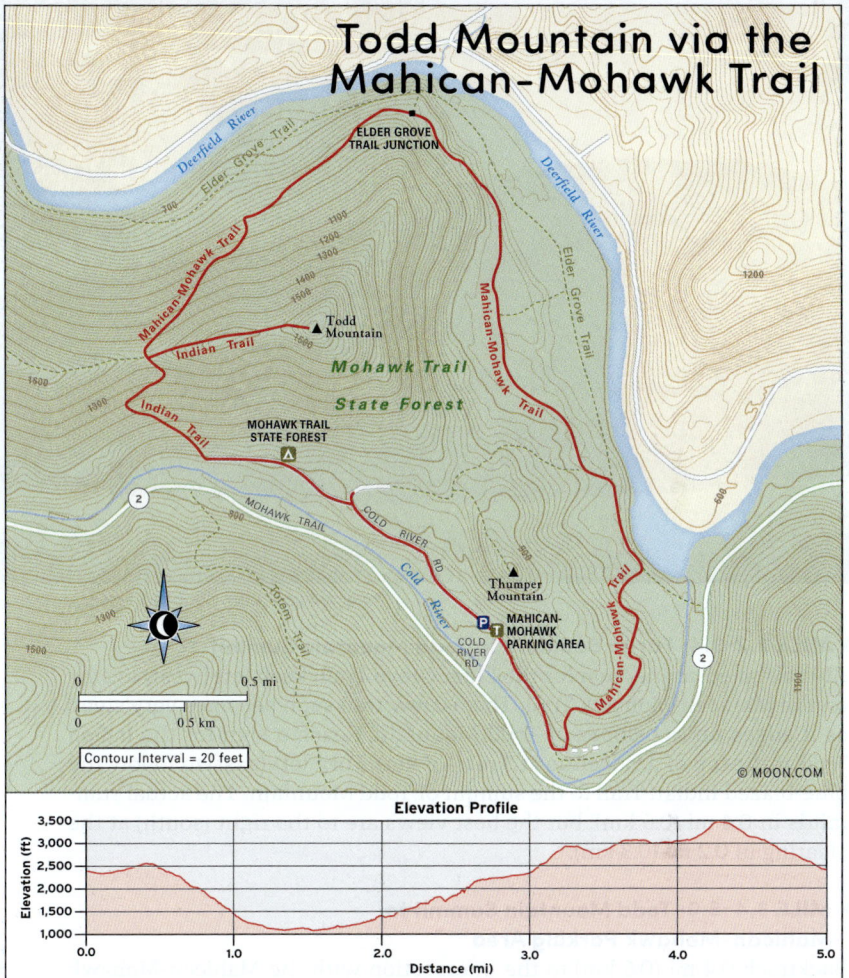

Todd Mountain via the Mahican-Mohawk Trail

Elevation Profile

woods on the Mahican-Mohawk Trail and follow the white blazes through a shady pine forest.

▶ MILE 0.5-2.2: Mahican-Mohawk Trail to Large Boulders

Keep straight (north) past the Thumper Mountain spur, following signs toward the **Todd Lookout.** The trail reaches an intersection at the bank high above the Deerfield River at 1.1 mi (1.8 km). Follow signs for the Mahican-Mohawk Trail, going left (west) on another wide doubletrack path. At the fork at 1.3 mi (2.1 km), bear left (northwest). Follow signs at 1.4 mi (2.3 km), where the trail turns right (north) back onto a narrow forested track. Pass through an opening in the stone walls of a 1700s **sheep range** into a grassy clearing with Todd Mountain rising above it. Continue straight (west) on the trail for 0.3 mi (0.5 km) as it plunges back into a pine grove. Follow the path another 0.5 mi (0.8 km) past large boulders as it skirts the hillside.

TRAIL APPROACHING TODD MOUNTAIN ▲

▶ **MILE 2.2–3.4: Large Boulders to Todd Mountain Summit**

At the signed connection for the Elder Grove Trail, keep left (west) to stay on the Mahican-Mohawk Trail. The narrow trail soon becomes very steep as it edges up the slopes of Todd Mountain. Reach a sign for the **Indian Trail** at the top of a ridgeline at 3 mi (4.8 km). Turn left (east) to follow the blue-blazed Indian Trail to the summit of Todd Mountain. The actual summit is in 0.4 mi (0.6 km), but the best views are to the right (south) at the clearing in 0.2 mi (0.3 km).

▶ **MILE 3.4–5.0: Todd Mountain Summit to Mahican-Mohawk Parking Area**

Backtrack 0.4 mi (0.6 km) to the intersection with the Mahican-Mohawk Trail and turn left (south) down the hill on the Indian Trail, following signs for the campground. The trail descends on a steep slope through laurel. Reach the bottom of the hill in 0.4 mi (0.6 km) and turn left (east) through the gate to the paved road. Follow the road southeast through the campground for 0.8 mi (1.3 km) to return to the parking area.

DIRECTIONS

Follow MA-2 west through the town of Charlemont and continue for 4.2 mi (6.8 km). Just after a dirt turnoff on the highway, turn right onto Cold River Road, which is marked with a large Mohawk Trail State Forest sign. Cross the bridge and turn left toward the check-in station. After checking in at the gate, day-hiker parking is located to the left.

GPS COORDINATES: 42°38'14.3"N 72°56'06.2"W

5

Monument Mountain via the Mohican Monument Trail

MONUMENT MOUNTAIN RESERVATION, GREAT BARRINGTON

The pale quartz vistas of Monument Mountain offer inspiring views of the Berkshires, Taconics, and Catskills in exchange for a short climb.

DISTANCE: 2.4 mi (3.9 km) round-trip

DURATION: 1.25 hr

ELEVATION GAIN: 601 ft (183 m)

EFFORT: Moderate

TRAIL: Dirt/rock path

USERS: Hikers, leashed dogs

SEASON: April–November

FEES/PASSES: $6 per vehicle parking fee for nonmembers (pay at kiosk)

MAPS: The Trustees of Reservations, "Monument Mountain"

TRAILHEAD: Mohican Monument trailhead, US-7, Great Barrington

FACILITIES: Trail map

CONTACT: The Trustees of Reservations; 413/298-3239; https://thetrustees.org

Monument Mountain is an extremely popular hike for its ease of access, but don't be fooled—this quick climb boasts some of the most spectacular views around and some surprisingly steep rock scrambles. Begin on the Mohican Monument Trail, climb up to the scenic Devil's Pulpit and Peeskawso Peak overlooks via the Peeskawso Peak Trail, and return via the Hickey Trail.

START THE HIKE

▸ **MILE 0-0.9: Mohican Monument Trailhead to Peeskawso Peak Trail**
Hike south on the **Mohican Monument Trail,** following the blue blazes from the left (south) side of the parking lot. The rocky path winds through boulders and hemlock forest, skirting the road for about 0.2 mi (0.3 km). Traffic noise dissipates as the trail bends north away from the road. Here, the wide path gains elevation at a gentle grade. At 0.6 mi (1 km), turn sharply right (east) onto the red-blazed **Peeskawso Peak Trail.** The trail heads uphill through tangles of roots followed by a jagged quartz ridge. At 0.9 mi (1.4 km), it bends west to reach a series of south-facing viewpoints over the Housatonic River valley.

▸ **MILE 0.9-1.0: Peeskawso Peak Trail to Devil's Pulpit**
At 1 mi (1.6 km), continue straight through the intersection and climb the stone steps toward **Devil's Pulpit**—a rocky perch with views of hoodoo-like quartzite cliffs across a steep drop-off. Enjoy the views, then backtrack on the Peeskawso Peak Trail to the intersection.

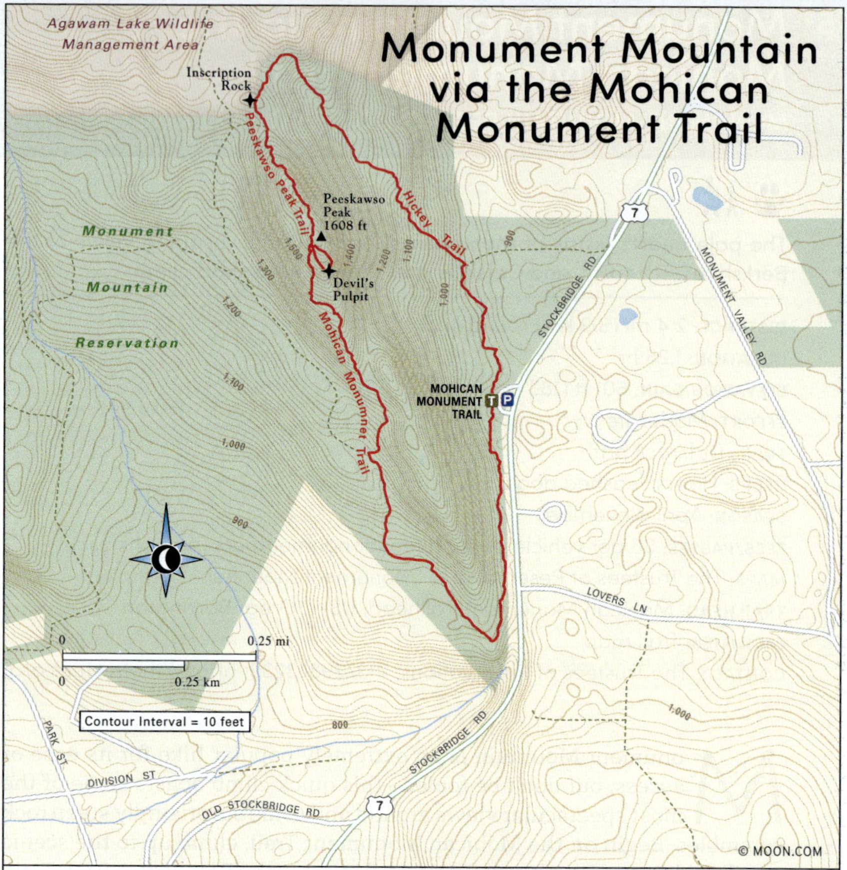

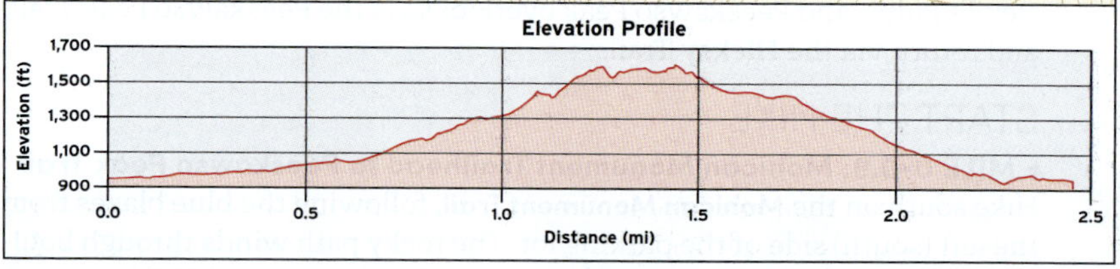

Monument Mountain via the Mohican Monument Trail

Agawam Lake Wildlife Management Area

Inscription Rock

Peeskawso Peak Trail

Peeskawso Peak 1608 ft

Hickey Trail

Devil's Pulpit

Monument Mountain Reservation

Mohican Monument Trail

MOHICAN MONUMENT TRAIL

STOCKBRIDGE RD

MONUMENT VALLEY RD

LOVERS LN

0   0.25 mi
0   0.25 km

Contour Interval = 10 feet

PARK ST

DIVISION ST

OLD STOCKBRIDGE RD

STOCKBRIDGE RD

7

© MOON.COM

Elevation Profile

Elevation (ft) vs Distance (mi)

▶ **MILE 1.0-1.2: Devil's Pulpit to Peeskawso Peak Summit**

Turn right (north) at the intersection and follow the Peeskawso Peak Trail for 0.2 mi (0.3 km) toward the summit of **Peeskawso Peak.** The massive quartz formations of the summit provide views in all directions, most notably of Mount Greylock to the north, the Catskill Range to the west, and the Housatonic River just below. Use caution

▲ PEESKAWSO PEAK

following the trail along the summit, especially in wet weather; the trail surface can be slippery.

▶ **MILE 1.2–2.4: Peeskawso Peak Summit to Mohican Monument Trailhead**

After 0.2 mi (0.3 km) across the summit, the trail begins to descend. Reach the **"Inscription Rock,"** dedicating the reservation to the people of the Berkshires, at 1.5 mi (2.4 km). Then, turn right (north) onto the yellow-blazed **Hickey Trail.** At 1.7 mi (2.7 km), the trail switchbacks south and steadily declines through boulder fields and hemlock forest to return to the parking lot in 2.4 mi (3.9 km).

DIRECTIONS

From Great Barrington center, follow US-7 north for 4 mi (6.4 km). From other points, use MA-102 E to connect to US-7 S, then follow the latter for 3 mi (4.8 km). The large parking area is marked with a Trustees of Reservations sign. Pay at the kiosk.

GPS COORDINATES: 42°14'35.1"N 73°20'07.2"W

❀ 🐾 🚶

The high, open meadows of Jug End State Reservation offer some of the most distinctive and secluded hiking in the Berkshires.

DISTANCE: 4.4 mi (7.1 km) round-trip

DURATION: 2 hr

ELEVATION GAIN: 508 ft (155 m)

EFFORT: Easy/moderate

TRAIL: Dirt/grass path

USERS: Hikers, leashed dogs

SEASON: Year-round

FEES/PASSES: None

MAPS: Massachusetts DCR, "Mt. Washington State Forest"

TRAILHEAD: Loop Trail trailhead, Jug End State Reservation and Wildlife Management Area parking, Jug End Rd., Egremont

FACILITIES: None

CONTACT: Massachusetts Department of Conservation and Recreation, Mount Washington State Forest; 413/528-0330; www.mass.gov/orgs/department-of-conservation-recreation

Jug End is a beloved vista of the famously beautiful Riga Plateau section of the Appalachian Trail, but the other features of this gorgeous ridgeline are front and center at Jug End State Reservation. The park's Loop Trail winds along Fenton Brook and climbs through an enchanting forest to an old stone chimney. From there, the east end of the loop winds through a series of wide, open meadows brimming with butterflies and wildflowers. Though it's widely regarded as one of the Berkshires' most kid-friendly hikes, Jug End is a treat for all ages.

START THE HIKE

▶ **MILE 0-0.3: Loop Trail Trailhead to Fenton Brook**

Head west on the **Loop Trail,** cross the bridge, and turn left (south) into the woods. The grassy path, shaded by large trees, follows bubbling **Fenton Brook** for 0.2 mi (0.3 km) with views of the ridgeline ahead. Where the path branches, stay left (south) along Fenton Brook.

STONE CHIMNEY AT JUG END ▶

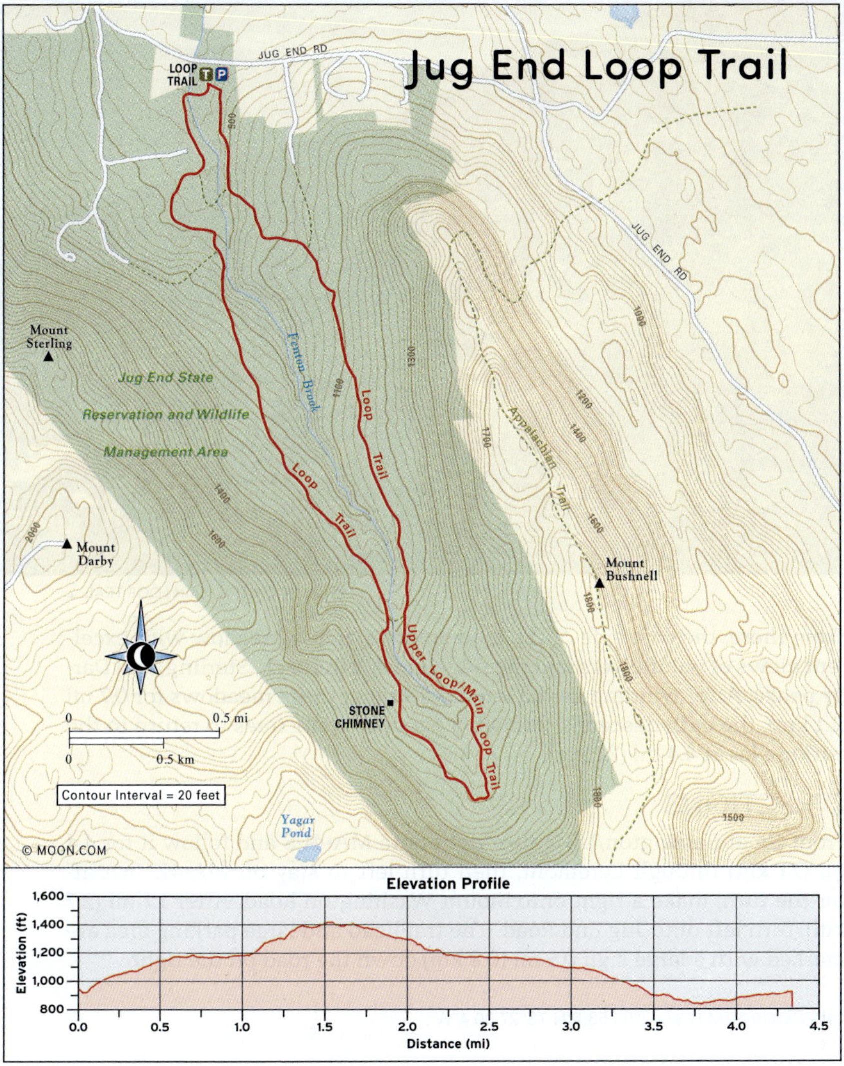

Jug End Loop Trail

LOOP TRAIL

JUG END RD

Mount Sterling

Jug End State Reservation and Wildlife Management Area

Fenton Brook

Loop Trail

Mount Darby

Loop Trail

Upper Loop/Main Loop Trail

STONE CHIMNEY

Mount Bushnell

Appalachian Trail

JUG END RD

0   0.5 mi

0   0.5 km

Contour Interval = 20 feet

© MOON.COM

Yagar Pond

Elevation Profile

▶ **MILE 0.3–1.7: Fenton Brook to Upper Loop/Main Loop**

The trail winds in and out of an open field for 0.5 mi (0.8 km) until reaching another fork. Turn right (south) and begin a gradual ascent through a shady mixed hardwood forest, following the blue blazes. The wide track gains elevation for 0.9 mi (1.4 km) above the Fenton Brook valley before narrowing into a flat path. Shortly after the path narrows and becomes noticeably flat, you'll reach the **Upper Loop/Main Loop** intersection where an abandoned **stone chimney** remains from Jug End's days as a ski resort.

▶ **MILE 1.7–4.4: Upper Loop/Main Loop to Loop Trail Trailhead**

Continue straight south onto the **Upper Loop,** a narrow track that carries uphill through fern and jewelweed to a hemlock forest. The path curls east in 0.6 mi (1 km), then back north for 0.6 mi (1 km) to the **Main Loop.**

From there, the east side of the loop enters a grassy meadow with excellent views of wildflowers and the ridgeline of Whitbeck, Sterling, and Darby peaks. After winding in and out of several of these meadows for 0.7 mi (1.1 km), the path descends through a patch of apple trees to return to the parking lot at 4.4 mi (7.1 km).

DIRECTIONS

From Great Barrington/US-7, turn right onto MA-41 S and follow it for 4.4 mi (7.1 km) through Egremont, then turn left to stay on MA-41. Just after the turn, make a right onto Mount Washington Road. After 1.7 mi (2.7 km), turn left onto Jug End Road. The trailhead and large parking area are marked with a large sign 0.5 mi (0.8 km) down the road on the right.

GPS COORDINATES: 42°08'53.5"N 73°27'00.4"W

🦌 ✿ 🐾

This hike is a favorite for its trail along a bubbling brook and long tristate views from the Alander Mountain summit.

BEST: Vistas
DISTANCE: 6 mi (9.7 km) round-trip
DURATION: 3.5 hr
ELEVATION GAIN: 1,012 ft (308 m)
EFFORT: Moderate
TRAIL: Dirt/rock path
USERS: Hikers, leashed dogs, horseback riders
SEASON: April–November
FEES/PASSES: None
MAPS: Massachusetts DCR, "Mount Washington State Forest"
TRAILHEAD: Alander Mountain trailhead, East St., Mount Washington
FACILITIES: Trail map at trailhead
CONTACT: Massachusetts Department of Conservation and Recreation, Mt. Washington State Forest; 413/528-0330; www.mass.gov

ocated in the very southwest corner of Massachusetts, the spacious summit of Alander Mountain offers some of the best views in the state—stretching far into New York and Connecticut. This out-and-back hike to the viewpoint is just as pleasant, climbing through a serene forest along Ashley Hill Brook. There is a primitive campground along the way for those who want to extend their trip into an overnight. (Note: A second Massachusetts access point to Alander Mountain, via a connec- tor trail to the South Taconic Trail at Bash Bish Falls State Park, is now closed. The South Taconic Trail can be accessed at Taconic State Park in New York.)

START THE HIKE

▶ **MILE 0-1.6: Alander Mountain Trailhead to Camping Area**
Go west from the trailhead sign and hike through a grassy field, follow- ing signs for the **Alander Mountain Trail.** When the trail enters a pine forest, the wide, flat path is marked with blue blazes. Reach a sign at 0.3 mi (0.5 km) and bear left (west) on

◀ CANADA LILY

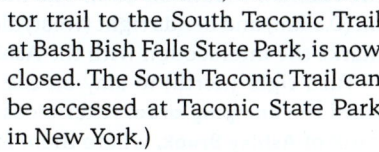

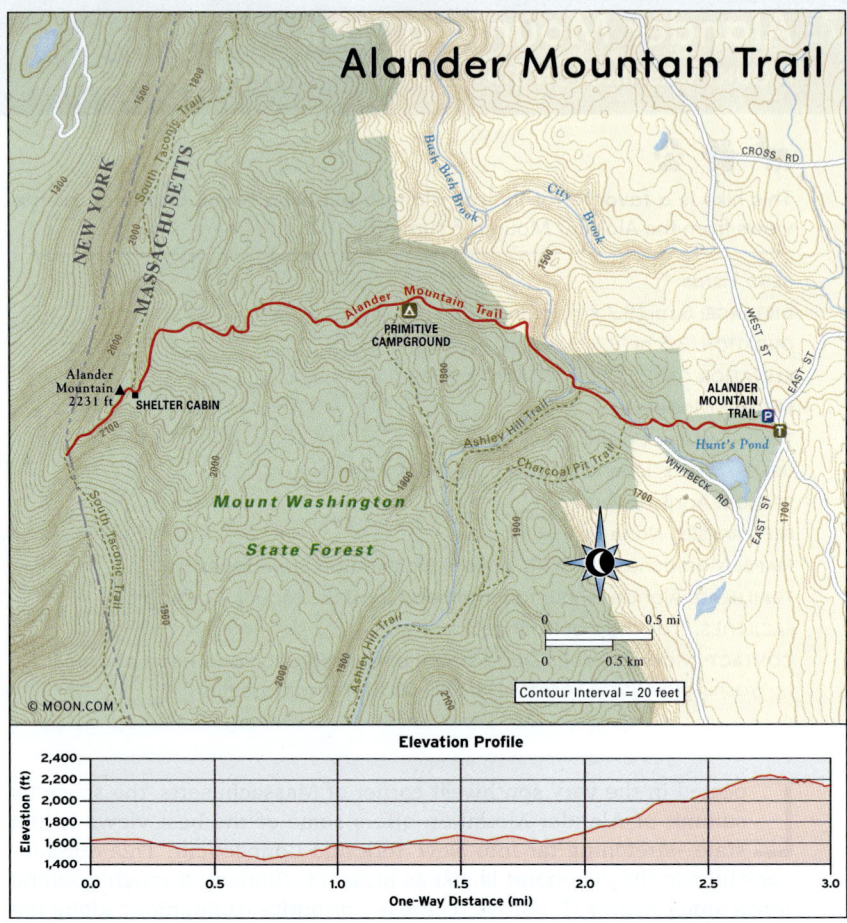

Alander Mountain Trail

Elevation Profile

the Alander Mountain Trail. The dirt trail crosses a wooden bridge at 0.5 mi (0.8 km) and bends right (west) along the brook. A sign at 0.7 mi (1.1 km) marks the intersection with the **Ashley Hill Trail.**

Turn right (north) to stay on the Alander Mountain Trail, heading toward the **camping area.** After crossing another bridge, the trail hugs the bank of **Ashley Brook,** where there is a small (approximately 3-ft/1-m) cascade. Reach a sign pointing to the camping area at 1.6 mi (2.6 km) and continue straight (west), following signs for **Alander Summit.**

▶ MILE 1.6–2.8: Camping Area to Shelter Cabin

The trail narrows into a loose rock and gravel path through a corridor of laurel, passing a mossy tributary of the brook. Arrive at a fork in front of a rugged shelter **cabin** 1.2 mi (1.9 km) from the campground trail.

▶ MILE 2.8–3.0: Shelter Cabin to Alander Summit

Follow signs to the right (west) toward the Alander summit, ascending a steep rock face. At the cairn atop the rock face, go left (south), following the narrow path through blueberry bushes. The trail reaches the summit

▲ THE SUMMIT OF ALANDER MOUNTAIN

at 3 mi (4.8 km). For a variety of vantage points, hikers can wander along the long summit ridge on the South Taconic Trail. After enjoying the broad tristate views, backtrack to the Alander Mountain Trailhead.

DIRECTIONS

From Great Barrington/US-7 S, turn right onto MA-41 S; follow it for 4.4 mi (7.1 km) through Egremont and then turn left to stay on US-41. Make an immediate right onto Mount Washington Road and follow it for 4.4 mi (7.1 km). Turn left onto East Street; in 1 mi (1.6 km), turn left to stay on East Street. In 3.6 mi (5.8 km), Mount Washington State Forest Headquarters is marked with a sign on the right. Turn right, pass the headquarters building, and find the parking area/trailhead to the left.

GPS COORDINATES: 42°05'10.7"N 73°27'43.6"W

MASSACHUSETTS
The Berkshires

8 Race Brook Falls and Mount Race via the Appalachian Trail

MOUNT WASHINGTON STATE FOREST, SHEFFIELD

Visit a plunging cascade and traverse a favorite ridgeline of the Appalachian Trail on this strenuous out-and-back.

BEST: Waterfalls

DISTANCE: 5.8 mi (9.3 km) round-trip

DURATION: 4 hr

ELEVATION GAIN: 1,455 ft (443 m)

EFFORT: Strenuous

TRAIL: Dirt/rock path

USERS: Hikers, leashed dogs

SEASON: April–November

FEES/PASSES: None

MAPS: Massachusetts DCR "Mount Washington State Forest"

TRAILHEAD: Race Brook Falls trailhead, S. Undermountain Rd., Sheffield

FACILITIES: Trail map at trailhead

CONTACT: Massachusetts Department of Conservation and Recreation, Mt. Washington State Forest; 413/528-0330; www.mass.gov

The 100-ft-high (30-m) Race Brook Falls, which carves through a gash of mossy rock on the west side of the Riga Plateau, is a must-see destination in the Berkshires in spite of a tough 900-ft (274-m) elevation gain in the first 1 mi (1.6 km) of this trail. From the falls, hikers can continue along the scenic length of Race Brook, past a primitive campground, to meet the Appalachian Trail (AT). The best views are on the southbound stretch of the AT, looking out from the summit of Mount Race.

START THE HIKE

▶ **MILE 0-0.9: Race Brook Falls Trail to Upper Race Brook Falls**

Hike south on the Race Brook Falls Trail, following the blue blazes over a dry creek bed and through a meadow. At the signed fork at 0.3 mi (0.5 km), turn left (southwest)

CROSSING RACE BROOK ▶

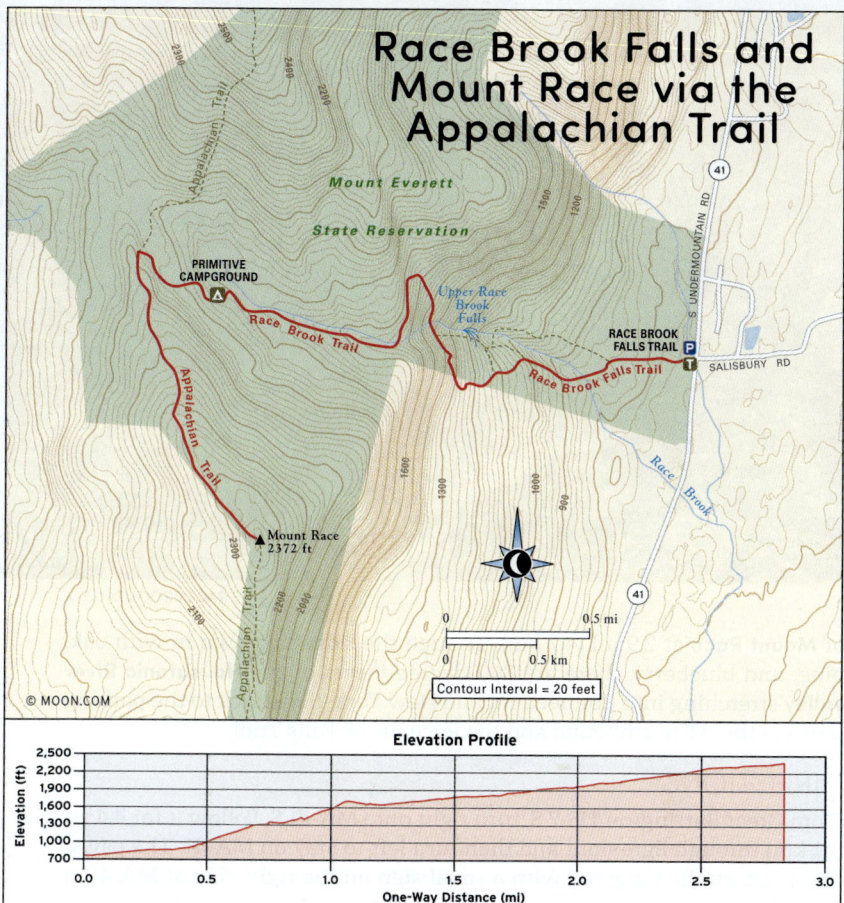

Race Brook Falls and Mount Race via the Appalachian Trail

Elevation Profile

toward Upper Falls/Campsite/AT. The trail goes along the brook, then hops along rocks to cross the water to the left (south) at 0.4 mi (0.6 km). From here, the path begins climbing above the gorge, becoming very rocky and steep. Reach the base of **Upper Race Brook Falls** at 0.9 mi (1.4 km).

▶ MILE 0.9-2.0: Upper Race Brook Falls to Appalachian Trail
From the falls, the trail continues north across the brook, and the narrow, rocky path works its way up to a ridgeline at 1.2 mi (1.9 km), where there is a small vista to the east. Shortly after, reach the brook again and turn right (west) upstream. This more level section of trail wanders along the lush plain of the brook, reaching the **primitive campground** at 1.6 mi (2.6 km). Follow the blue blazes through the campground, continuing west toward the Appalachian Trail (AT). Reach the intersection with the AT at 2 mi (3.2 km) and turn left (south) onto the AT southbound toward Laurel Ridge.

▶ MILE 2.0-2.9: Appalachian Trail to Mount Race Summit
The trail heads over a slight incline to a rocky ridgeline. You may need to use your hands at times to navigate over steep rocks. Arrive at the summit

of **Mount Race** at 2.9 mi (4.7 km). Though the ridge is grown in with oak, pine, and blueberry, there are 360-degree views of the **Housatonic River valley** stretching into Connecticut and New York. Backtrack to the parking area via the AT northbound and the Race Brook Falls Trail.

DIRECTIONS

From Great Barrington/US-7 S, turn right onto MA-41 S. Follow it for 4.4 mi (7.1 km) through Egremont and then turn left to stay on MA-41. The paved parking turnoff is marked with a small sign on the right side of MA-41 in 5 mi (8 km).

GPS COORDINATES: 42°05'23.3"N 73°24'40.2"W

Hurlburt's Hill and Bartholomew's Cobble

BARTHOLOMEW'S COBBLE RESERVATION, SHEFFIELD

This amazingly diverse property includes rock formations, sections along the Housatonic River, and views of the Berkshire–Taconic Range from Hurlburt's Hill.

BEST: Fall hikes, New England oddities
DISTANCE: 3.2 mi (5.1 km) round-trip
DURATION: 1.75 hr
ELEVATION GAIN: 400 ft (122 m)
EFFORT: Easy/moderate
TRAIL: Dirt path, grass/dirt doubletrack
USERS: Hikers only
SEASON: Year-round
FEES/PASSES: $5 for nonmembers, $1 child (6-12)
MAPS: The Trustees of Reservations, "Bartholomew's Cobble"
TRAILHEAD: Bartholomew's Cobble Reservation Visitor Center, Weatogue Rd., Sheffield
FACILITIES: Picnic table, restrooms, water available at visitor center in season
CONTACT: The Trustees of Reservations; 413/229-8600; https://thetrustees.org

Bartholomew's Cobble is a popular hike for families with kids due to its fairly easy terrain, explorable rock features, and frolic-friendly fields. However, this National Natural Landmark is also a favorite among naturalists for its fascinating ecology. As hikers visit riverbanks, forests, and meadows, they can appreciate a number of plant species, including one of the largest cottonwood trees in the state and one of the greatest diversities of ferns in North America. To top it off, the captivating view from Hurlburt's Hill is a picture-perfect Berkshires scene.

START THE HIKE

▸ **MILE 0-0.4: Visitor Center to Bailey Trail**
Follow the trail east behind the visitor center for 200 ft (61 m) and then turn left (northeast) onto the **Ledges Trail.** This flat, pine needle-covered path cuts through ledges and boulders, winding along a section of the **Housatonic River.** At 0.4 mi (0.6 km), the trail reaches a grassy clearing with a sign for the **Bailey Trail.**

▸ **MILE 0.4-1.6: Bailey Trail to Spero Trail**
Turn left (south) onto the Bailey Trail, which crosses over several bridges, following the length of the river for 0.3 mi (0.5 km). At the intersection, turn left (east) on the Spero Trail. Follow the yellow blazes through a forest of huge pines for approximately 0.1 mi (0.16 km), then turn left (north) onto

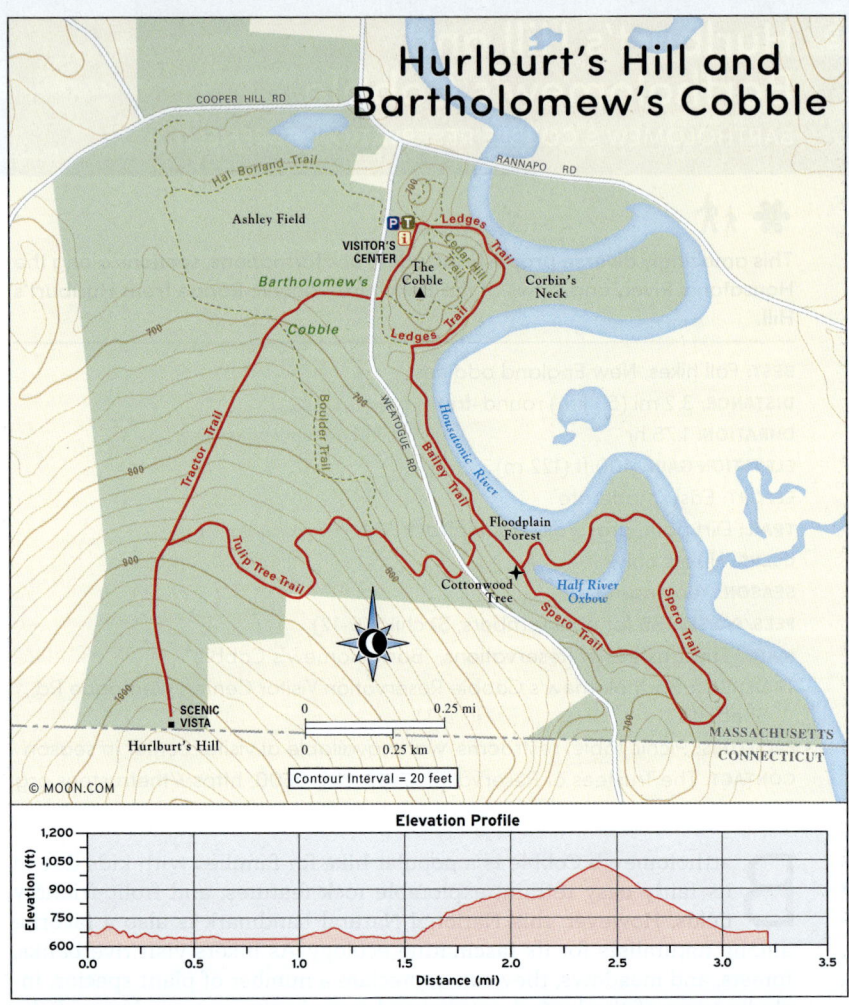

Hurlburt's Hill and Bartholomew's Cobble

Elevation Profile

the **Spero Trail.** This grassy path winds from the **Half River Oxbow** through a silver maple floodplain forest that offers great views of the Housatonic. After passing through a field, the trail doubles back through a hemlock grove, returning to the end of the loop at 1.6 mi (2.6 km). Note the huge **cottonwood** to the left (west) here—it's one of the largest in the state.

▶ **MILE 1.6-1.7: Spero Trail to Tulip Tree Trail**
Continue straight west toward the Tulip Tree Trail for 0.1 mi (0.16 km) and then turn left (west) up the hill on the white-blazed **Tulip Tree Trail.** At the top of the hill, the trail crosses straight (west) over a dirt road, after which it meanders through a forest of rare and varied ferns.

▶ **MILE 1.7-2.5: Tulip Tree Trail to Hurlburt's Hill Summit**
At the signed intersection with the Boulder Trail at 1.9 mi (3.1 km), turn left (west) to stay on the Tulip Tree Trail. After a wildflower meadow and a series of bridges and stepping-stones, the path meets the **Tractor Path**

▲ HURLBURT'S HILL

at 2.3 mi (3.7 km). Turn left (south) onto the Tractor Path, following signs for the **Hurlburt's Hill summit.** The grassy path heads uphill through a bird-house-lined meadow for 0.2 mi (0.3 km), where it ends at a series of benches overlooking an incredible **scenic vista** of the Housatonic River valley, the Riga Plateau, and the many farms and peaks beyond.

▶ MILE 2.5-3.2: Hurlburt's Hill Summit to Visitor Center

Descend north for 0.7 mi (1.1 km) on the wide tractor path through forests and meadows until it ends at the dirt road. Cross the road straight (east) through the fence, then turn immediately left (north) onto the short leg of the Ledges Trail that returns to the visitor center.

DIRECTIONS

From Great Barrington/US-7, follow US-7 south 8 mi (12.9 km) through Sheffield, then keep right onto MA-7A. In 0.5 mi (0.8 km), turn right onto Rannapo Road. In 1.5 mi (2.4 km), turn right again onto Weatogue Road. The visitor center and parking area are marked with a Trustees of Reservations sign on the left in 0.1 mi (0.16 km).

GPS COORDINATES: 42°03'27.4"N 73°21'03.6"W

BEST NEARBY BITES AND BREWS

Part of the Berkshires' charm is its rural nature, with miles of farm stretching out between rolling mountain ranges. However, that means you may have to travel a few miles to reach any semblance of civilization—and even then, some of the small villages only include bare-bones amenities. Luckily, most of our routes are centered on two of the Berkshires' most beloved cultural hubs: Great Barrington in the south and North Adams in the north. These towns' artsy downtown areas are your best bets for scoring top-notch food and drink after your hike.

GREAT BARRINGTON

- **Baba Louie's** (42/44 Railroad St.; 413/528-8100; www.babalouiespizza. com; noon-3pm and 5pm-8pm Sun., 5pm-8pm Mon. and Thurs., noon-3pm and 5pm-9pm Fri.-Sat.) creates flavorful, offbeat, and classic sourdough pizza in cozy digs with a good bar menu.
- **The Well** (312 Main St.; 413/528-3651; https://wellgb.com; 3pm-9pm Wed.-Sat.) has unique burgers and other classic American staples, plus a nice bar specializing in top-shelf whiskeys.
- **Prairie Whale** (178 Main St.; 413/528-5050; 5pm-10pm Thurs.-Mon.) is an upscale option for those feeling fancy, offering creative New American dishes and amazing cocktails.

NORTH ADAMS

- **Public eat+drink** (34 Holden St.; 413/664-4444; http://publiceatanddrink. com; 4pm-close Tues.-Sat.) boasts an extensive local beer list, tasty burgers, and other New American options in a relaxed brick bar and dining room.
- **Ramunto's** (67 Main St.; 413/398-5152; https://ramuntos.com; 11am-10pm Mon.-Thurs., 11am-11pm Fri.-Sat., 11am-9pm Sun.) is the place to carboload with soft garlic knots and chewy brick-oven pizza. This casual wood-paneled restaurant has beer on draft and a trivia night.
- At **Korean Garden** (139 Ashland St., Williamstown; 413/346-4097; 11am-9pm Tues.-Thurs., 11am-9:30pm Fri.-Sun.), sushi lovers will rejoice at the fresh and varied options at this hot spot with a full bar.

NORTH ADAMS ⌄

NEARBY CAMPGROUNDS

NAME	LOCATION	FACILITIES	SEASON	FEE
Clarksburg State Park	1199 Middle Rd., Clarksburg, 42°44'01.8"N 73°04'34.1"W	45 RV/ tent sites; restrooms	late May- early September	$17-54
413/664-8345; www.mass.gov/locations/clarksburg-state-park				
Mohawk Trail State Forest	Cold River Rd., Charlemont, 42°38'11.1"N 72°56'08.3"W	53 RV/tent sites, 6 cabins; restrooms	early May- mid-October	$17-170
413/339-5504; www.mass.gov/locations/mohawk-trail-state-forest				
Savoy Mountain State Forest	260 Central Shaft Rd., Florida, 42°38'55.5"N 73°02'49.0"W	45 RV/tent sites, 4 cabins; restrooms	mid-May- mid-October	$17-150
413/663-8469; www.mass.gov/locations/savoy-mountain-state-forest				
Pittsfield State Forest	1041 Cascade St., Pittsfield, 42°29'9"N 73°18'8"W	40 RV/ tent sites; restrooms	mid-May- mid-October	$17-54
413/442-8992; www.mass.gov/locations/pittsfield-state-forest				
October Mountain State Forest	317 Woodland Rd., Lee, 42°20'14"N 73°13'57"W	44 RV/tent sites, 3 yurts; restrooms	early May- mid-October	$17-140
413/243-1778; www.mass.gov/locations/october-mountain-state-forest				
Beartown State Forest	69 Blue Hill Rd., Monterey, 42°12'21"N 73°17'31"W	12 RV/ tent sites; composting toilets	early May- mid-October; off-season camping available	$14-40
413/528-0904; www.mass.gov/locations/beartown-state-forest				
Tolland State Forest	410 Tolland Rd., East Otis, 42°8'50"N 73°2'39"W	93 RV/ tent sites; restrooms	mid-May- mid-October	$17-54
413/269-6002; www.mass.gov/locations/tolland-state-forest				

THE PIONEER VALLEY AND NORTH QUABBIN

The Pioneer Valley occupies the fertile rift where the Connecticut River flows through Massachusetts, separating the eastern hills from the Berkshire Range to the west. This central section of the state is known as a patchwork of farmlands and college towns, but it's also one of the most geologically significant areas of New England. The Metacomet Ridge stretches up the river from Connecticut, forming a roller coaster of teardrop-shaped mountains over which runs the Metacomet-Monadnock section of the New England National Scenic Trail. To the east of the valley, the 38.6-sq-mi (100-sq-km) Quabbin Reservoir—created as the water supply for Boston—is surrounded by beautiful forestland where waterfalls plunge toward the Tully and Millers Rivers. Hikers in this region can take in dramatic views from high cliff faces or explore waterways in the valleys below.

▲ TRILLIUM IN BLOOM AT HIGH LEDGES

▲ MOUNT TOBY'S ROARING BROOK FALLS

◀ TRAPROCK CLIFFS NEAR MOUNT TOM SUMMIT

1 **Doane's Falls via the Tully Trail**
DISTANCE: 6 mi (9.7 km) round-trip (with optional additions)
DURATION: 4 hr
EFFORT: Easy/moderate
PAGE: 512

2 **High Ledges via the Sanctuary Road Loop**
DISTANCE: 3.3 mi (5.3 km) round-trip (with optional additions)
DURATION: 2 hr
EFFORT: Easy
PAGE: 515

3 **Hermit's Castle via the Metacomet-Monadnock Trail**
DISTANCE: 5.7 mi (9.2 km) round-trip
DURATION: 4 hr
EFFORT: Moderate
PAGE: 518

4 **Mount Toby via the Robert Frost Trail**
DISTANCE: 4.3 mi (6.9 km) round-trip (with optional additions)
DURATION: 3 hr
EFFORT: Moderate
PAGE: 521

5 **Norwottuck Horse Caves and Rattlesnake Knob via the Metacomet-Monadnock Trail**
DISTANCE: 3.9 mi (6.3 km) round-trip
DURATION: 3 hr
EFFORT: Moderate
PAGE: 524

6 **Mount Tom via the Metacomet-Monadnock Trail**
DISTANCE: 6.6 mi (10.6 km) round-trip
DURATION: 3 hr
EFFORT: Moderate
PAGE: 528

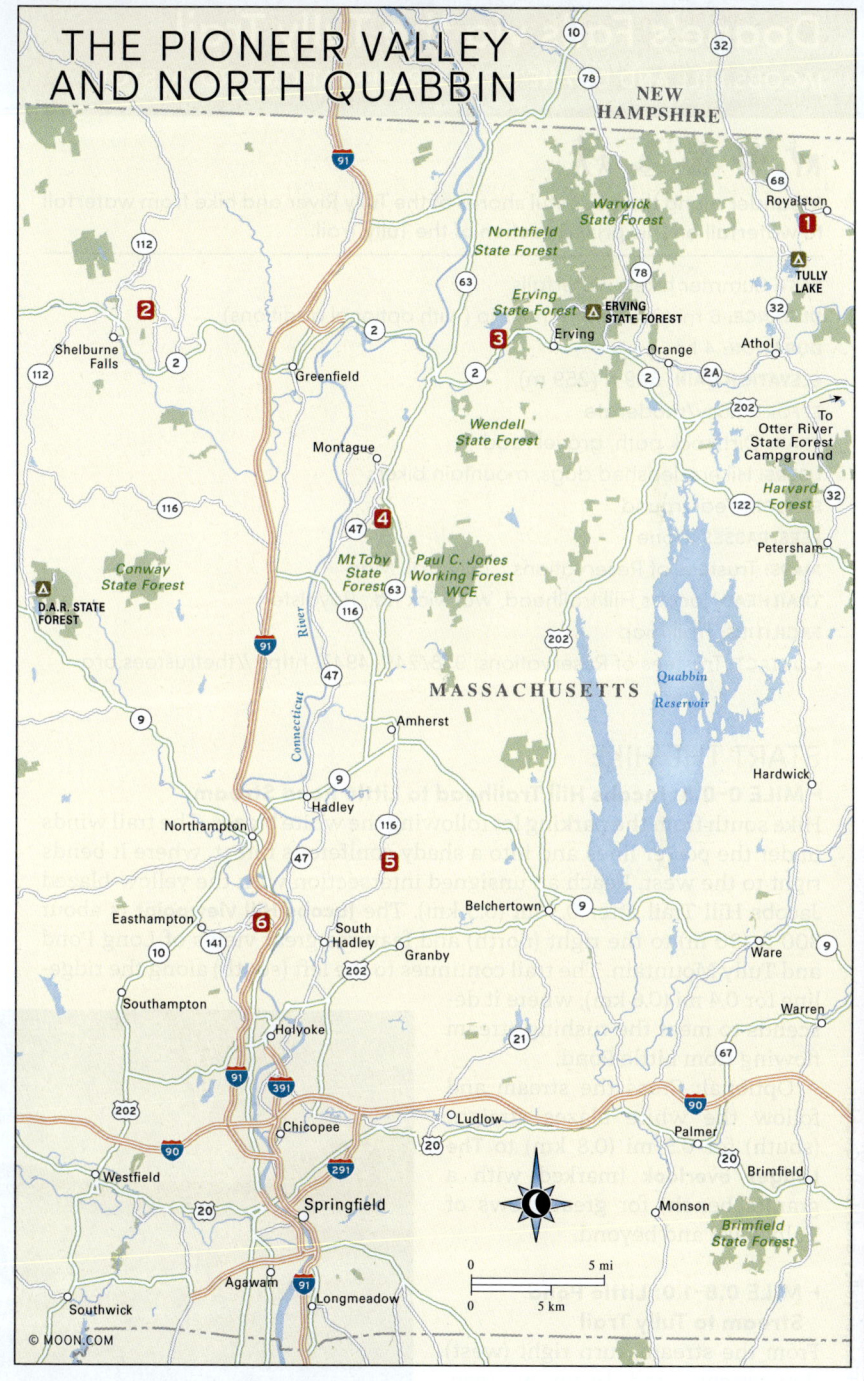

THE PIONEER VALLEY AND NORTH QUABBIN

NEW HAMPSHIRE

Warwick State Forest

Royalston

1

TULLY LAKE

Northfield State Forest

Erving State Forest

ERVING STATE FOREST

Erving

Orange

Athol

3

Shelburne Falls

Greenfield

To Otter River State Forest Campground

Wendell State Forest

Harvard Forest

2

Montague

Petersham

Conway State Forest

Mt Toby State Forest

Paul C. Jones Working Forest WCE

D.A.R. STATE FOREST

4

Quabbin Reservoir

MASSACHUSETTS

Amherst

Hardwick

Northampton

Hadley

Belchertown

Ware

Easthampton

South Hadley

Granby

5

6

Warren

Southampton

Holyoke

Chicopee

Ludlow

Palmer

Brimfield

Westfield

Springfield

Monson

Brimfield State Forest

Southwick

Agawam

Longmeadow

0   5 mi

0   5 km

© MOON.COM

Connecticut River

MASSACHUSETTS

Doane's Falls via the Tully Trail

JACOBS HILL AND DOANE'S FALLS RESERVATIONS, ROYALSTON

Meander along the peaceful shores of the Tully River and hike from waterfall to waterfall on this prized section of the Tully Trail.

BEST: Summer hikes, waterfalls
DISTANCE: 6 mi (9.7 km) round-trip (with optional additions)
DURATION: 4 hr
ELEVATION GAIN: 849 ft (259 m)
EFFORT: Easy/moderate
TRAIL: Dirt/rock path, gravel road
USERS: Hikers, leashed dogs, mountain bikers
SEASON: Year-round
FEES/PASSES: None
MAPS: Trustees of Reservations, "Tully Trail Map"
TRAILHEAD: Jacobs Hill trailhead, Warwick Rd., Royalston
FACILITIES: Trail map
CONTACT: Trustees of Reservations; 978/249-4947; https://thetrustees.org

START THE HIKE

▶ **MILE 0-0.8: Jacobs Hill Trailhead to Little Pond Stream**

Hike south from the parking lot following the white blazes. The trail winds under the power lines and into a shady coniferous forest, where it bends right to the west. Reach an unsigned intersection with the yellow-blazed Jacobs Hill Trail after 0.3 mi (0.5 km). The **Jacobs Hill viewpoint** is about 300 ft (90 m) to the right (north) and features great views of Long Pond and Tully Mountain. The trail continues to the left (south) along the ridge-line for 0.4 mi (0.6 km), where it de-

scends to meet the rushing stream flowing from Little Pond.

Optional: Cross the stream and follow the white blazes straight (south) for 0.5 mi (0.8 km) to **The Ledges overlook** (marked with a granite bench) for great views of Tully Lake and beyond.

▶ **MILE 0.8-1.0: Little Pond Stream to Tully Trail**

From the stream, turn right (west) downstream and begin a steep, rocky descent to **Spirit Falls,** fol-lowing the yellow blazes. Continue

LONG POND ▶

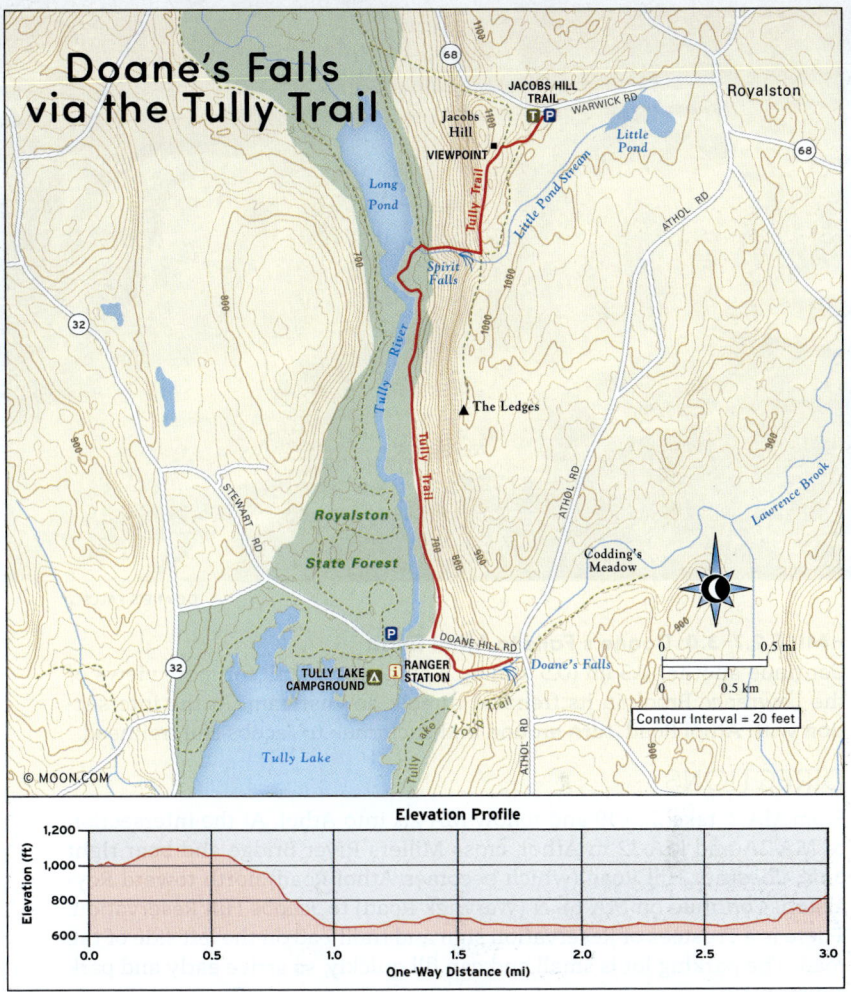

Doane's Falls via the Tully Trail

Elevation Profile

0.2 mi (0.3 km) west toward the **Tully River,** passing a dramatic section of the falls. Cross the bridge over the stream and turn left (south) on the red-blazed Tully Trail.

▶ MILE 1.0–2.7: Tully Trail to Doane's Falls

This section is flat and peaceful, with lovely views from the blueberry-lined banks of **Long Pond** and the Tully River, plus plenty of opportunities for swimming. The trail passes the ranger station after 1.2 mi (1.9 km) and joins the wide doubletrack **Mountain Bike Trail** for 0.3 mi (0.5 km) to the intersection with Doane Hill Road. Cross the road and turn left (east) to find the **Doane's Falls** trailhead. This accessible gravel trail heads southeast for 0.2 mi (0.3 km) before reaching the first section of the falls.

DOANE'S FALLS ▲

▶ **MILE 2.7–3.0: Doane's Falls to Athol Road**

Continue another 0.3 mi (0.5 km) up a singletrack trail for more views of the Lawrence Brook in its frenzied tumble downstream. At the intersection with Athol Road, turn around and backtrack to Jacobs Hill trailhead.

DIRECTIONS

From MA-2, take Exit 19 and follow MA-2A into Athol. At the intersection of MA-2A and MA-32 in Athol, cross Millers River Bridge and bear right onto Chestnut Hill Road (which becomes Athol Road) north toward Royalston. Continue on MA-68 N (Warwick Road) to Jacobs Hill Reservation. There is a Trustees of Reservation sign and trailhead on the left side of the road. The parking lot is small and can fill quickly, so arrive early and park courteously.

GPS COORDINATES: 42°40'34.9"N 72°11'58.4"W

BEST NEARBY BITES

Los Agaves (491 Main St., Athol; 978/830-0001; 11am-9pm Sun.-Thurs., 11am-10pm Fri.-Sat.) does tacos, street corn, and margaritas to the max in a laid-back bar room with fair-weather outside seating.

2

High Ledges via the Sanctuary Road Loop

HIGH LEDGES WILDLIFE SANCTUARY, SHELBURNE FALLS

✿ 🚶

Botany lovers will delight in High Ledges' vibrant Orchid Swamp, but this property also features a seasonal waterfall, a west-facing vista, and the option to visit a fire tower for 360-degree views.

BEST: Spring hikes
DISTANCE: 3.3 mi (5.3 km) round-trip (with optional additions)
DURATION: 2 hr
ELEVATION GAIN: 637 ft (194 m)
EFFORT: Easy
TRAIL: Dirt/gravel path
USERS: Hikers
SEASON: Year-round
FEES/PASSES: Donations appreciated
MAPS: Mass Audubon, "High Ledges Wildlife Sanctuary"
TRAILHEAD: Mass Audubon High Ledges Wildlife Sanctuary parking lot, Patten Rd., Shelburne Falls
FACILITIES: Trail map at trailhead
CONTACT: Mass Audubon; 978/464-2712; www.massaudubon.org

This short hike may be rated as easy, but it delivers big views of the Deerfield River and Mount Greylock from its namesake ledges. Most hikers visit strictly for the view, but as you venture further into the forest, a surprise is around every corner—whether it's a tumbling falls or a rare orchid hidden at the fringe of a swamp. For added mileage and views, hike 1.6 mi (2.6 km) out and back to the stone fire tower atop Massaemett Mountain (Bald Mountain).

START THE HIKE

▸ **MILE 0-0.5: Parking Lot to Sanctuary Road**

Head southwest down **Sanctuary Road** for 0.1 mi (0.16 km) and continue straight through the gate. The path curls slightly uphill on a gravel doubletrack surface. Reach an intersection in 0.2 mi (0.3 km). Stay straight (west)—do not follow the orange arrows—and arrive at a clearing at 0.5 mi (0.8 km). Continue straight (west) to remain on Sanctuary Road.

Optional: Turn left (south) and follow the Shelburne Trails signs for 0.8 mi (1.3 km) to the stone **Shelburne Fire Tower** on Massaemett Mountain (Bald Mountain) for great 360-degree views of the valley.

▸ **MILE 0.5-0.8: Sanctuary Road to High Ledges Lookout**

Sanctuary Road continues straight (west) through another gate and down a smooth gravel path, passing a vernal pond. At 0.8 mi (1.3 km), turn left

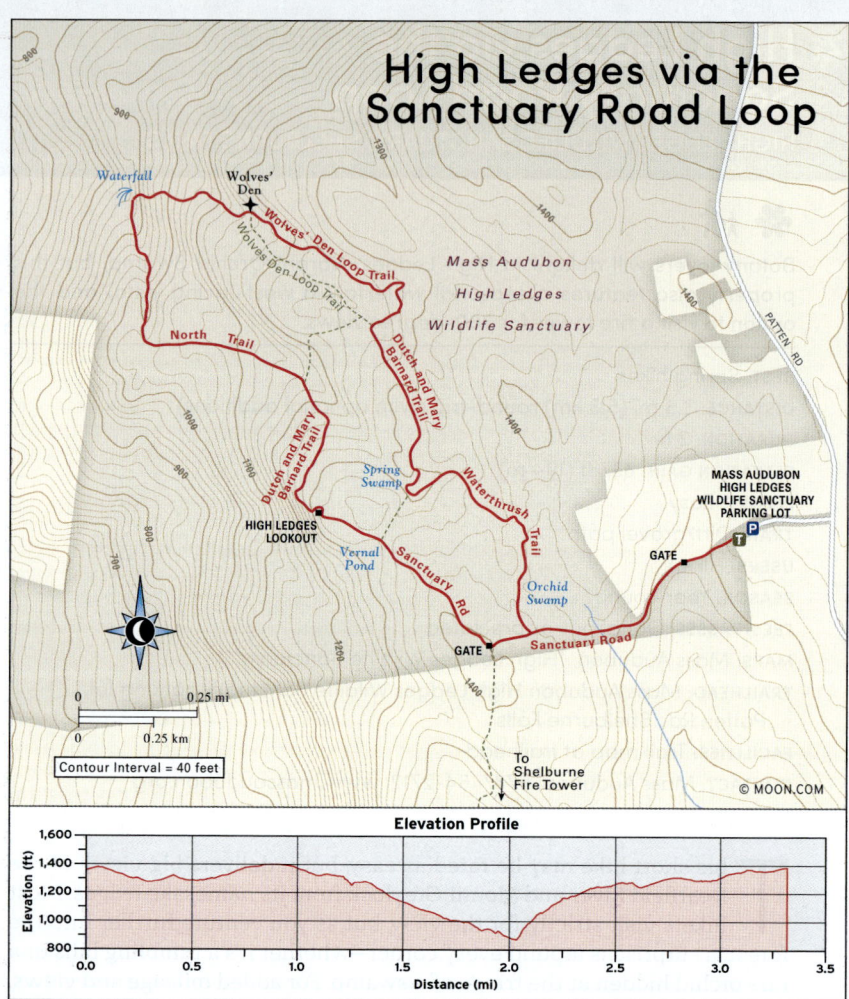

High Ledges via the Sanctuary Road Loop

Waterfall
Wolves' Den
Wolves' Den Loop Trail
Wolves Den Loop Trail
North Trail
Dutch and Mary Barnard Trail
Dutch and Mary Barnard Trail
Mass Audubon High Ledges Wildlife Sanctuary
Spring Swamp
Waterthrush Trail
HIGH LEDGES LOOKOUT
Vernal Pond
Sanctuary Rd
Orchid Swamp
GATE
Sanctuary Road
GATE
PATTEN RD
MASS AUDUBON HIGH LEDGES WILDLIFE SANCTUARY PARKING LOT

0   0.25 mi
0   0.25 km
Contour Interval = 40 feet

To Shelburne Fire Tower

© MOON.COM

Elevation Profile

(west) to find the **High Ledges lookout,** an incredible vista with views of the Deerfield River stretching toward Mount Greylock in the distance.

▶ **MILE 0.8-2.0: High Ledges Lookout to Wolves' Den Loop Trail**
From the lookout, the blue-blazed **Dutch and Mary Barnard Trail** begins to the right (north) of the High Ledges. Follow this thin, rocky path as it drops into a valley to meet a stream in 0.2 mi (0.3 km). Take a left (west) on the **North Trail,** which follows the brook downstream and then parallels a stone wall. The path crosses over a spring and descends to meet a minor **waterfall** at 1.5 mi (2.4 km). The trail crosses the water and heads downstream for 0.1 mi (0.16 km). Here, turn right (east) up over the ledges. This section is steep, but short, and the blazes change from blue to yellow. Reach the intersection with the **Wolves' Den Loop Trail** at 2 mi (3.2 km), and stay left. The Wolves' Den loop stretches under a series of ledges with some small caves and pockets to explore.

▲ SUNSET AT HIGH LEDGES

▶ **MILE 2.0–3.3: Wolves' Den Loop Trail to Parking Lot**
Continue on the Wolves' Den loop for 0.3 mi (0.5 km) to an intersection with the **Dutch and Mary Barnard Trail.** Turn left (south) to follow the yellow blazes of the Barnard Trail. The trail bends through a maze of laurel for 0.3 mi (0.5 km) until it reaches **Spring Swamp.** Follow the trail west around the swamp, cross the bridge, and turn left (east) onto the **Waterthrush Trail.** Be on the lookout for wildflowers where the trail borders **Orchid Swamp,** an ideal habitat for these delicate blossoms. The Waterthrush Trail returns to Sanctuary Road in 0.5 mi (0.8 km). Take a left (east) to return 0.2 mi (0.3 km) to the parking area.

DIRECTIONS

From MA-2, take Frank Williams Road to Little Mohawk Road, then take a left onto Patten Road. The parking lot is about 1 mi (1.6 km) down Patten Road on the left, and it's marked with a Mass Audubon sign.

GPS COORDINATES: 42°37'12.2"N 72°42'20.2"W

BEST NEARBY BITES AND BREWS

Grab a beer flight and some New American fare at **The Blue Rock Restaurant and Bar** (1 Ashfield St.; 413/625-8133; https://thebluerockrestaurant.com; 5pm-9pm Thurs.–Mon.) in Shelburne Falls, 7 mi (11.3 km) from the trailhead.

3

Hermit's Castle via the Metacomet-Monadnock Trail

FARLEY LEDGES, ERVING

This playground of boulders and precipitous ledges is a favorite of New England rock climbers, but hikers can enjoy exploring waterfalls, caves, and vistas of the Millers River.

BEST: New England oddities
DISTANCE: 5.7 mi (9.2 km) round-trip
DURATION: 4 hr
ELEVATION GAIN: 1,158 ft (353 m)
EFFORT: Moderate
TRAIL: Dirt/rock path
USERS: Hikers, leashed dogs, rock climbers
SEASON: April–November
FEES/PASSES: None
MAPS: Appalachian Mountain Club, "Massachusetts Trail Map #4 and #5"
TRAILHEAD: Metacomet-Monadnock trailhead, Wells St., Erving
FACILITIES: None
CONTACT: Western Massachusetts Climbers' Coalition; https://climbgneiss.org

Combined with the tough Red Trail circling Rattlesnake Mountain and the Farley Ledges, this route follows the Metacomet-Monadnock Trail past a scenic overlook of the Millers River and arrives at the Hermit's Castle rock formation, where Scottish recluse John Smith lived from 1867 to 1899. Other highlights include the tumbling waters of Briggs Brook Falls and the chance to watch climbers spidering up the gneiss.

START THE HIKE

▶ **MILE 0-0.7: Metacomet-Monadnock Trailhead to Farley Ledges**
Follow the red and white blazes for the **Metacomet-Monadnock Trail** heading straight (north). The narrow path winds along Briggs Brook and arrives at **Briggs Brook Falls** at 0.2 mi (0.3 km). At the falls, turn left (south) and follow the red blazes toward **Farley Ledges.** The trail becomes increasingly rocky as it travels south into an enormous boulder field at the base of the cliffs, where huge slabs of granite rest in the shade of oak and grapevine. Pass a series of wooden signs that designate popular rock-climbing routes.

▶ **MILE 0.7-1.3: Farley Ledges to Rattlesnake Mountain Summit**
The trail gets steep straight west of the ledges at 0.8 mi (1.3 km). A series of rope holds tied to trees are available to assist hikers with this strenuous section. At the top of the ropes, the trail bears left, wrapping northwest

Hermit's Castle via the Metacomet-Monadnock Trail

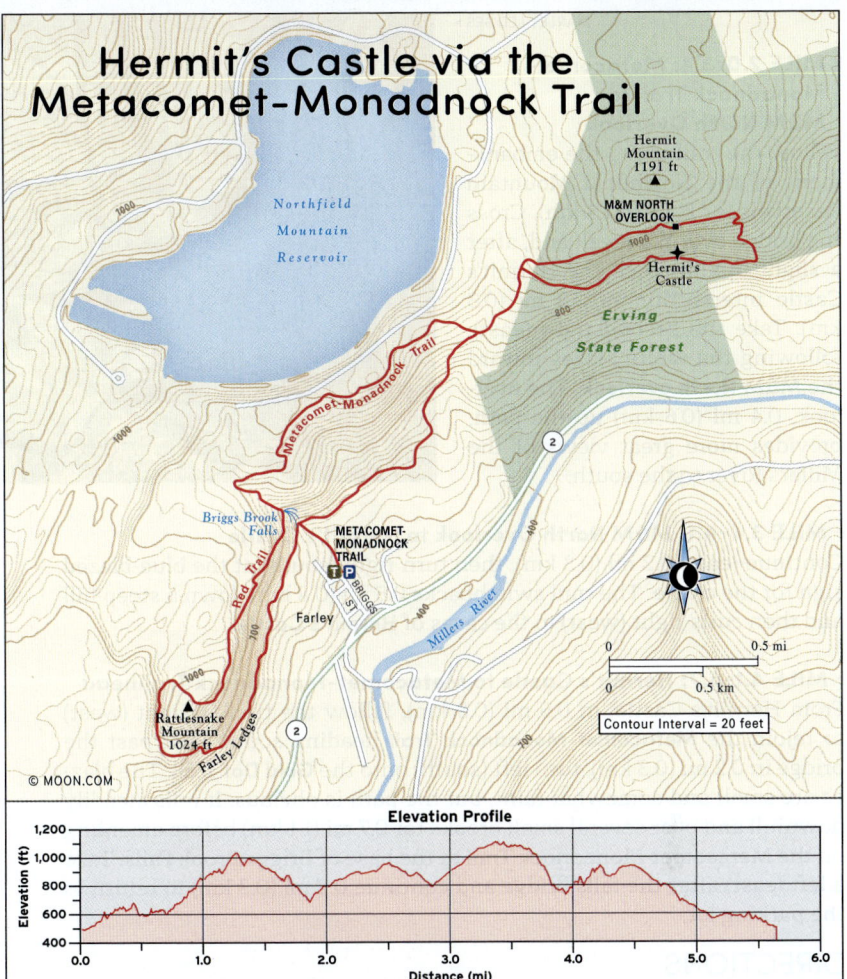

Elevation Profile

around the ledges into a tangle of mountain laurel and hemlock. Reach the summit of **Rattlesnake Mountain** at 1.3 mi (2.1 km), where a south-facing vista looks out over the Millers River.

▶ **MILE 1.3-1.8: Rattlesnake Mountain Summit to Briggs Brook**
From the lookout, continue straight north to stay on the Red Trail, which traverses the Rattlesnake ridgeline. This descent involves lowering yourself over rocks. The trail crosses Briggs Brook at the top of the falls in 0.5 mi (0.8 km).

▶ **MILE 1.8-2.0: Briggs Brook to Metacomet-Monadnock Trail**
Just after the crossing, turn left to follow the white blazes of the **Metacomet-Monadnock Trail.** The path leads 0.2 mi (0.3 km) upstream, crisscrossing the brook. At the third crossing, follow the white blazes right (east) at the sign for Hermit's Castle.

▶ MILE 2.0-3.4: Metacomet–Monadnock Trail to M&M North Overlook

Follow the trail along the embankment of the Northfield Mountain Reservoir for 0.8 mi (1.3 km). Cross the bridge over the creek and, after a slight uphill, reach the Hermit's Castle intersection in 0.2 mi (0.3 km). Take the second right (east), following the white blazes toward the **M&M North overlook.** The overlook, 0.4 mi (0.6 km) up the path, provides more great views of the Millers River to the south.

▶ MILE 3.4-4.1: M&M North Overlook to Hermit's Castle

Continue (east) 0.2 mi (0.3 km), then turn right (south) at the blue-blazed sign for the castle. The trail switchbacks 0.5 mi (0.8 km) down a steep hill and then curls right (west) to the caves of **Hermit's Castle.**

▶ MILE 4.1-5.7: Hermit's Castle to Metacomet-Monadnock Trailhead

From Hermit's Castle, in 0.5 mi (0.8 km), follow the trail straight (west) to rejoin the **Metacomet-Monadnock Trail** heading south. Just past the bridge in 0.2 mi (0.3 km), turn left (south) onto the **Gold Dot Trail.** The blazes are small and somewhat faint, but the path is obvious. It rolls steadily downhill and over several small brooks for 0.7 mi (1.1 km) before emerging on the Metacomet-Monadnock Trail at the base of Briggs Brook Falls. Take a left (east) after the falls bridge and continue 0.2 mi (0.3 km) to return to the parking lot.

DIRECTIONS

From MA-2, turn onto Holmes Avenue and follow Briggs Street north to Cross Street. Parking for this route is located off Cross Street. The trailhead is to the east of the parking area, at the end of Briggs Street. The parking lot is small and fills quickly, so arrive early and park courteously.

GPS COORDINATES: 42°36'04.8"N 72°26'24.4"W

BEST NEARBY BREWS

Element Brewing Company (16 Bridge St., Millers Falls; 413/835-6340; www.elementbeer.com; 1pm-6pm Wed., 1pm-8pm Thurs., noon-9pm Fri.-Sat., noon-6pm Sun.), 4 mi (6.4 km) from the trailhead, has a great selection of craft brews, a game room, and a small menu including burgers, wings, and nachos.

4

Mount Toby via the Robert Frost Trail

MOUNT TOBY RESERVATION, SUNDERLAND

With a summit fire tower, caves, and waterfalls, the Robert Frost Trail through Mount Toby offers endless exploration opportunities.

DISTANCE: 4.3 mi (6.9 km) round-trip (with optional additions)

DURATION: 3 hr

ELEVATION GAIN: 1,017 ft (310 m)

EFFORT: Moderate

TRAIL: Dirt/rock path, gravel road

USERS: Hikers, leashed dogs, horseback riders, mountain bikers

SEASON: April–November

FEES/PASSES: None

MAPS: University of Massachusetts, "The Trails of Mount Toby," www.umass.edu

TRAILHEAD: Robert Frost trailhead, Reservation Rd., Sunderland

FACILITIES: Trail map

CONTACT: University of Massachusetts Amherst Department of Environmental Conservation; www.umass.edu

S ituated just north of Amherst, Mount Toby Reservation is the demonstration forest for University of Massachusetts ecology students. Its extensive trail network is worthy of a full day of hiking, replete with waterfalls, secret caves, and relics of the maple sugar industry. Not to mention, the views from the summit fire tower are second to none. (Note: Be careful to follow only trail blazes here—many trees are marked for teaching purposes.)

START THE HIKE

▶ **MILE 0-0.5: Robert Frost Trailhead to Cave Trail Intersection**
Hike west on the red-orange blazed **Robert Frost Trail (RFT),** a short walk west from parking lot, as it winds uphill over a rock path and through a hemlock grove before reaching an intersection at 0.5 mi (0.8 km).

Optional: At the signed intersection 0.5 mi (0.8 km) from the trailhead, bear right to visit the caves via the blue-blazed Sugar Farms Trail and the green-blazed Cave Trail. This 1.1-mi (1.8-km) round-trip detour affords the rare opportunity to climb through a large cave where surreal ice columns form in winter—if you are feeling fit and are equipped with a flashlight. The cave entrance is located on the west side of the cliff, downhill from the trail's end. Return to the RFT via the yellow-blazed Bridle Path.

The Pioneer Valley and North Quabbin

MASSACHUSETTS

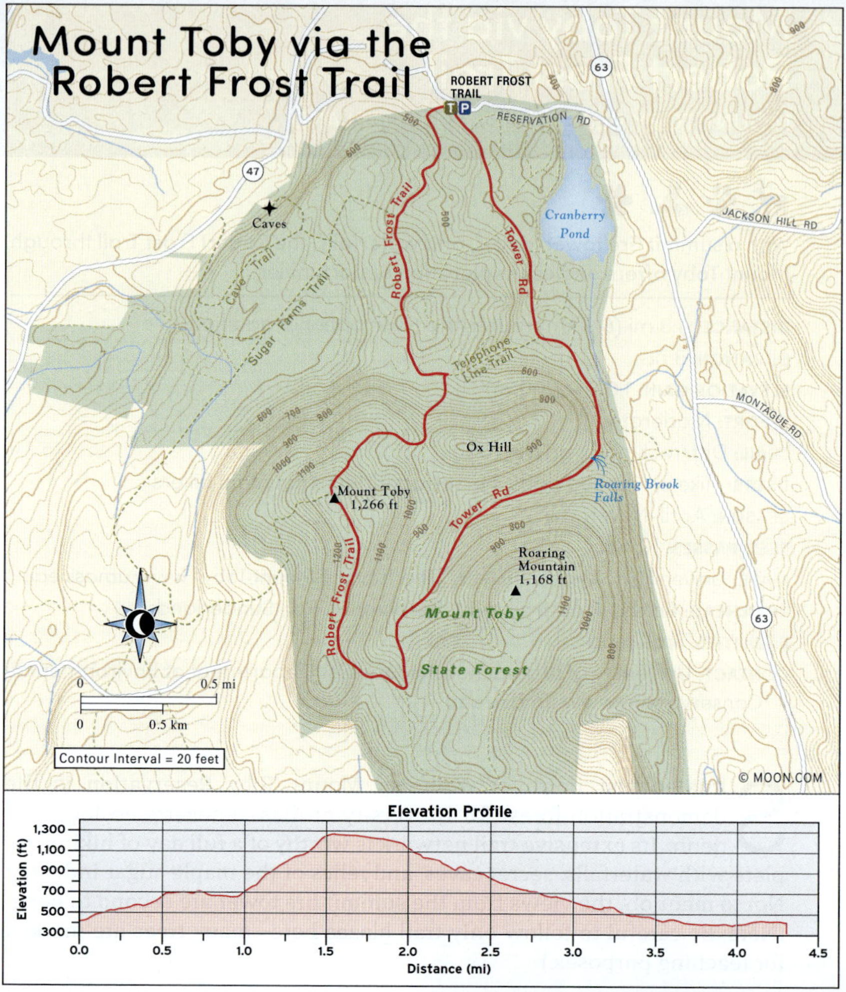

Mount Toby via the Robert Frost Trail

ROBERT FROST TRAIL

RESERVATION RD

Caves

Robert Frost Trail

Cave Trail

Sugar Farms Trail

Telephone Line Trail

Tower Rd

Cranberry Pond

JACKSON HILL RD

MONTAGUE RD

Ox Hill

Roaring Brook Falls

▲ Mount Toby 1,266 ft

Tower Rd

Robert Frost Trail

▲ Roaring Mountain 1,168 ft

Mount Toby

State Forest

63

47

63

0 0.5 mi

0 0.5 km

Contour Interval = 20 feet

© MOON.COM

Elevation Profile

Elevation (ft) — Distance (mi)

1,300 / 1,100 / 900 / 700 / 500 / 300

0.0 0.5 1.0 1.5 2.0 2.5 3.0 3.5 4.0 4.5

▶ **MILE 0.5-2.2: Cave Trail Intersection to Mount Toby Summit**

Continue south on the RFT and begin your ascent of Mount Toby, following the red-orange blazes. In 1 mi (1.6 km) from the intersection, turn right (south) to stay on the RFT.

Here, the trail steepens and joins the corridor of the phone lines. In 0.2 mi (0.3 km), reach the intersection with the Upper Link Trail and turn right (west) to continue uphill on the RFT. Reach the summit after a tough 0.5-mi (0.8-km) climb. For

ENTRANCE TO THE CAVES AT MOUNT TOBY ▶

▲ ROBERT FROST TRAIL IN WINTER

the best views, climb to the top of the fire tower. This 360-degree panorama includes stunning views of the Connecticut River and surrounding peaks.

▶ **MILE 2.2-4.3: Mount Toby Summit to Robert Frost Trailhead**
When you're ready, descend to the east via the **RFT/Tower Road,** a long gravel doubletrack that sweeps down the eastern slope of the mountain following Roaring Brook. Where the RFT diverges east at 1 mi (1.6 km), continue straight north on Tower Road. The parking lot is 1.1 mi (1.8 km) north on Tower Road from the falls intersection.

Optional: Take a right (east) 0.6 mi (1 km) from where the RFT diverges and follow the blue blazes 440 ft (134 m) downhill to reach **Roaring Brook Falls.**

DIRECTIONS

From the intersection of MA-116 and MA-47 in Sunderland, follow MA-47 north to the Montague town line. Just after the town sign, turn right onto Reservation Road. The parking area and trailhead are about 0.5 mi (0.8 km) down on the right. When you park, take care not to block the access road or the school bus turnaround. Parking is free.

GPS COORDINATES: 42°30'13.5"N 72°31'48.2"W

> ## BEST NEARBY BITES
> Peruse the shelves of the **Montague Book Mill** (440 Greenfield Rd., Montague; 413/367-9206; www.montaguebookmill.com; 10am–6pm daily), which serves beer, coffee, and more from its **Lady Killigrew Café** (https://theladykilligrew.com; 8am–9pm daily).

5

Norwottuck Horse Caves and Rattlesnake Knob via the Metacomet-Monadnock Trail

MOUNT HOLYOKE RANGE STATE PARK, AMHERST

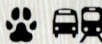

The overhanging rock ledges of the Norwottuck Horse Caves and the secluded bald vistas overlooking the Connecticut River valley are iconic features of the Metacomet-Monadnock Trail as it winds through Mount Holyoke Range State Park.

DISTANCE: 3.9 mi (6.3 km) round-trip

DURATION: 3 hr

ELEVATION GAIN: 875 ft (267 m)

EFFORT: Moderate

TRAIL: Dirt/rock path

USERS: Hikers, leashed dogs

SEASON: April–November

FEES/PASSES: None

MAPS: Massachusetts DCR, "Joseph Allen Skinner and Mt. Holyoke Range State Parks"; Appalachian Mountain Club, "Massachusetts Trail Map #4 and #5"

TRAILHEAD: Notch Visitor Center parking lot, West St., Amherst

FACILITIES: Water, restrooms available inside visitor center when open

CONTACT: Massachusetts Department of Conservation and Recreation; 413/253-2883; www.mass.gov

START THE HIKE

▶ **MILE 0-0.5: Notch Visitor Center to Metacomet-Monadnock Trail**

Starting from the **Notch Visitor Center** parking lot, find the trailhead behind the building to the southeast. Follow the red, white, and blue blazes, which designate the **Robert Frost Trail** (red), **Metacomet-Monadnock Trail** (white), and **Ken Cuddebank Trail** (blue). The trail reaches a set of power lines where it turns right (east) and then descends to an intersection. Continue straight (east) on the gravel double-track past the quarry, following the

NORWOTTUCK HORSE CAVES ▶

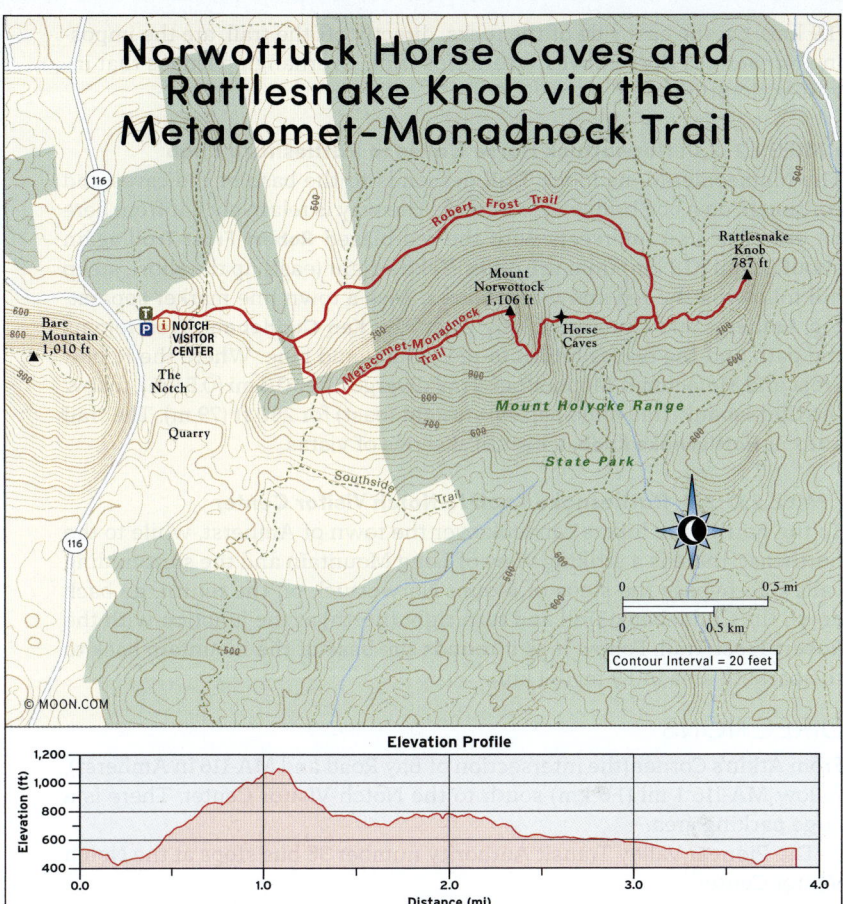

Norwottuck Horse Caves and Rattlesnake Knob via the Metacomet-Monadnock Trail

Elevation Profile

red and white blazes. (Note: You may hear gunfire from a nearby private shooting range, but the trail eventually moves out of earshot.) Turn right (south) onto the **Metacomet-Monadnock Trail** at 0.5 mi (0.8 km), following the white blazes.

▸ MILE 0.5-1.0: Metacomet-Monadnock Trail to Mount Norwottuck Summit

This moderate section of trail climbs steeply and steadily through a mixed oak and hickory forest, gaining over 500 ft (150 m) of altitude. The white blazes are sparse along this section of the ridge, but the path is clear as it levels out, dips, and then ascends a brief section of steep scree. Reach the summit of **Mount Norwottuck** at 1 mi (1.6 km) and enjoy nearly 360-degree views of the valley below from atop a grassy knob.

▸ MILE 1.0-1.2: Mount Norwottuck Summit to Norwottuck Horse Caves

Descend via the Metacomet-Monadnock Trail to the north. Be mindful of loose rock as you step down the cliffside. The trail winds through a large boulder field and cuts through a narrow crack between two rocks at 1.2 mi

(1.9 km). On the east side of the rocks, directly off the trail, are the imposing **Norwottuck Horse Caves**, a series of wide, overhanging ledges that invite exploration.

▶ **MILE 1.2–2.0: Norwottuck Horse Caves to Rattlesnake Knob**
The Metacomet-Monadnock Trail descends to the base of the caves and continues on a bog bridge over a creek. The way is relatively flat from here on out. The trail intersects with the red-blazed **Robert Frost Trail** again about 0.5 mi (0.8 km) from the caves. Take a right (east) up the short, steep hill following the red and white blazes. Pass a town line marker separating Amherst and Granby. Shortly after, the **Ken Cuddebank Trail** rejoins the path and the blazes return to red, white, and blue. Where the Robert Frost and Metacomet-Monadnock Trail diverge after 0.3 mi (0.5 km), follow the Cuddebank Trail (blue blazes) straight (east) for 260 ft (79 m). The trail ends at **Rattlesnake Knob,** a beautiful series of vistas.

▶ **MILE 2.0–3.9: Rattlesnake Knob to Notch Visitor Center**
To the northwest, hikers can look over the town of Amherst, while to the northeast, there is a striking view of Long Mountain and the surrounding valley. To bypass the steps of Mount Norwottuck on the return, go back down the Cuddebank Trail and turn right (north) at the junction with the Robert Frost Trail. Follow it as it rounds the base of the mountain back to the parking area in 1.9 mi (3.1 km).

DIRECTIONS

From Atkin's Corner (the intersection of Bay Road and MA-116 in Amherst), follow MA-116 1 mi (1.6 km) south to the Notch Visitor Center. There is a large parking area.

The Pioneer Valley Transit Authority number 38 bus stops at the Notch Visitor Center.

GPS COORDINATES: 42°18'18.2"N 72°31'42.3"W

BEST NEARBY BITES AND BREWS
Visit the brew aficionados at **The Moan & Dove** (460 West St., Amherst; 413/256-1710; 3pm-1am Mon.-Fri., 1pm-1am Sat.-Sun.), 3 mi (4.8 km) from trailhead in Amherst, for a recommendation from their extensive beer list. Takeout is available next door at **Mission Cantina** (485 West St.; 413/230-3580; www.themissioncantinaamherst.com; 4pm-10pm Wed.-Sat., 4pm-9pm Sun.) or **Sibie's Pizza** (481 West St.; 413/256-6100; www.sibiespizza.com; 3pm-8:30pm Mon., 11am-8:30pm Tues.-Wed., 11am-9pm Thurs.-Sat.).

▲ LONG MOUNTAIN FROM RATTLESNAKE KNOB

Mount Tom via the Metacomet-Monadnock Trail

MOUNT TOM STATE RESERVATION, HOLYOKE

This trail traverses a series of sheer cliffs that are some of the best bird-watching perches in the state, especially for raptor species such as broad-winged hawks.

BEST: Brew hikes
DISTANCE: 6.6 mi (10.6 km) round-trip
DURATION: 3 hr
ELEVATION GAIN: 1,246 ft (380 m)
EFFORT: Moderate
TRAIL: Dirt/rock path
USERS: Hikers, leashed dogs, cross-country skiers
SEASON: April-November
FEES/PASSES: $5 MA residents, $20 nonresidents (in-season)
MAPS: Massachusetts DCR, "Mount Tom State Reservation"; Appalachian Mountain Club, "Massachusetts Trail Map #4 and #5"
TRAILHEAD: Universal Access trailhead, Reservation Rd., Holyoke
FACILITIES: Trail map, picnic tables; restrooms available in visitor center when open
CONTACT: Massachusetts Department of Conservation and Recreation; 413/534-1186; www.mass.gov

This hike ascends the eastern side of the Mount Tom Range and then follows a section of the Metacomet-Monadnock Trail along a vast stretch of cliffs with spectacular views to the west. Hikers have a good chance of spotting hawks soaring from the high traprock faces. The hike culminates at the teardrop-shaped summit of Mount Tom, purportedly the inspiration for Mount Crumpit in Dr. Seuss's *How the Grinch Stole Christmas*.

START THE HIKE

▸ **MILE 0-0.2: Universal Access Trail to Kay Bee Trail**
Begin on the **Universal Access Trail,** a wide gravel path that wraps west around **Lake Bray.** Turn right (north) onto the blue-blazed **Kay Bee Trail** at the intersection at 0.2 mi (0.3 km).

▸ **MILE 0.2-2.0: Kay Bee Trail to Metacomet-Monadnock Trail**
The trail immediately ascends several switchbacks, rolling over a traprock bed and through a hemlock forest. After 0.5 mi (0.8 km), arrive at a four-way intersection. Continue straight (west) to stay on the Kay Bee Trail. Commence climbing 0.4 mi (0.6 km) to reach another intersection. Continue straight (west) onto the **Keystone Extension Trail,** following the orange blazes. The Keystone Extension winds around a series of small hills until it descends into a valley with a creek flowing through it. Cross the

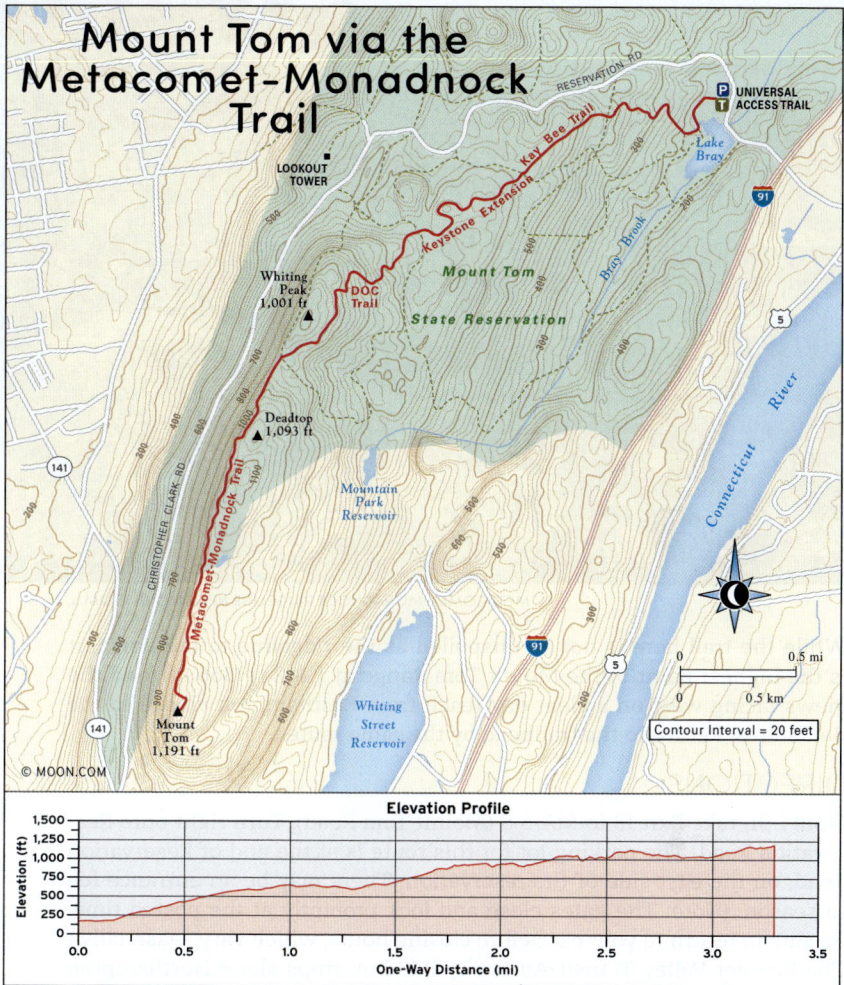

Mount Tom via the Metacomet-Monadnock Trail

Elevation Profile

footbridge and continue straight (west) onto the **D.O.C. Trail** (red blazes). The D.O.C. gains moderate elevation, offering great views to the south in winter and spring when there are no leaves on the trees. The trail arrives at the top of the ridgeline and meets the white-blazed **Metacomet-Monadnock Trail** at 2 mi (3.2 km).

▶ **MILE 2.0–3.3: Metacomet-Monadnock Trail to Mount Tom Summit**
Turn left (south) on the **Metacomet-Monadnock Trail** toward Mount Tom. The views from here on out are spectacular as the trail skirts Deadtop, the rugged traprock ridge between Whiting Peak and Mount Tom. Keep an eye out for raptor species riding currents from the steep cliffs, but use caution in wet weather—the bare rock can be slick. The trail extends straight (south) with a series of vistas and some rocky scrambles. You may need to use your hands to climb up and down. After 1.3 mi (2.1 km) on the Metacomet-Monadnock Trail, reach the summit of Mount Tom, punctuated by various communication towers, graffiti, and remnants of a former ski area.

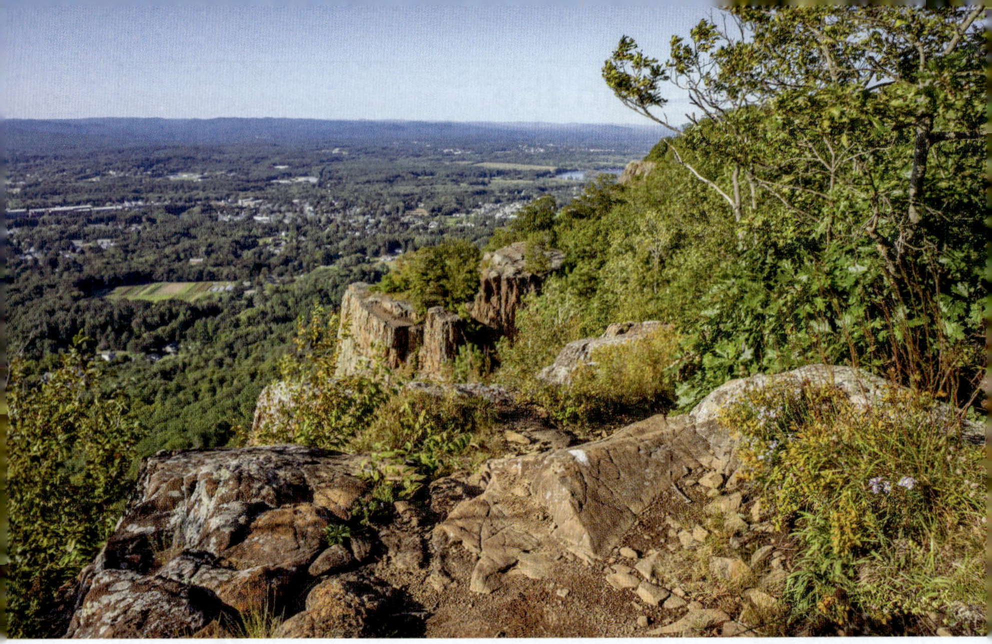

METACOMET-MONADNOCK RIDGELINE NEAR MOUNT TOM ▲

While the trail here is not as unspoiled as the ridgeline to the north, it is the highest point of the Mount Tom Range at 1,202 ft (366 m), and the views facing west on a clear day reach from Easthampton village to the Berkshires. Return to the trailhead by the same route.

DIRECTIONS

From I-91, take Exit 18 to MA-5 S (Mount Tom Road). Turn right onto Reservation Road. The parking lot for this route is at the end of Reservation Road, on the east side of the reservation. There may be an entrance fee in season. (Note: The gates close and lock promptly at the posted time. Be sure to return to your car before closing hours, which vary seasonally.) The Pioneer Valley Transit Authority B48 bus stops along Northampton Street.

GPS COORDINATES: 42°16'07.9"N 72°36'59.8"W

BEST NEARBY BREWS

Enjoy views of Mount Tom and live music at the taproom of **Fort Hill Brewery** (30 Fort Hill Rd., Easthampton; 413/203-5754; www.forthillbrewery.com; 4pm-7pm Thurs., 4pm-8pm Fri., 2pm-8pm Sat., 2pm-6pm Sun.), 4 mi (6.4 km) from the trailhead. Food trucks frequent Fort Hill, but you are also welcome to bring your own grub.

NEARBY CAMPGROUNDS

NAME	LOCATION	FACILITIES	SEASON	FEE
Tully Lake Campground	25 Doane Hill Rd., Royalston, 42°39'02.1"N 72°12'34.6"W	33 tent sites; restrooms	May–October	$37–49
978/249-4957; https://thetrustees.org				
Erving State Forest	1 Laurel Lake Rd., Erving, 42°37'10"N 72°22'12"W	27 RV/ tent sites; restrooms	mid–May– early September	$17–54
978/544-7745; www.mass.gov				
D.A.R. State Forest	78 Cape St., Goshen, 42°27'41"N 72°47'36"W	51 RV/ tent sites; restrooms	mid–May– mid–October	$17–54
413/268-7098; www.mass.gov				
Otter River State Forest	86 Winchendon Rd., Baldwinville, 42°37'39"N 72°4'46"W	73 RV/tent sites, 4 yurts; restrooms	early May– mid–October	$17–140
978/939-8962; www.mass.gov				

▲ LITTLE POND LOOP BOARDWALK TRAIL

CONNECTICUT

LITCHFIELD HILLS

Geologically speaking, the Litchfield Hills are the southern continuation of the Berkshires, and they offer many of same spectacular interstate views, high rocky peaks, and abundant farmland fed by the flow of the Housatonic River. This rolling, rural landscape is a respite from the suburban feel that dominates much of Connecticut, and therefore a popular destination for vacationers and second-home owners. Those seeking outdoor adventure flock to the northernmost hills to ascend the highest peaks in the state, while the wide watershed of the Housatonic provides plenty of waterfront scenery at lower elevations. From the trusty corridor of the Appalachian Trail to the isolated lowland forests, there is a trail in northwestern Connecticut to suit every inclination.

▲ TUNNEL AT STEEP ROCK PRESERVE

▲ A FLIGHT OF LOCAL BEERS

CONNECTICUT
Litchfield Hills

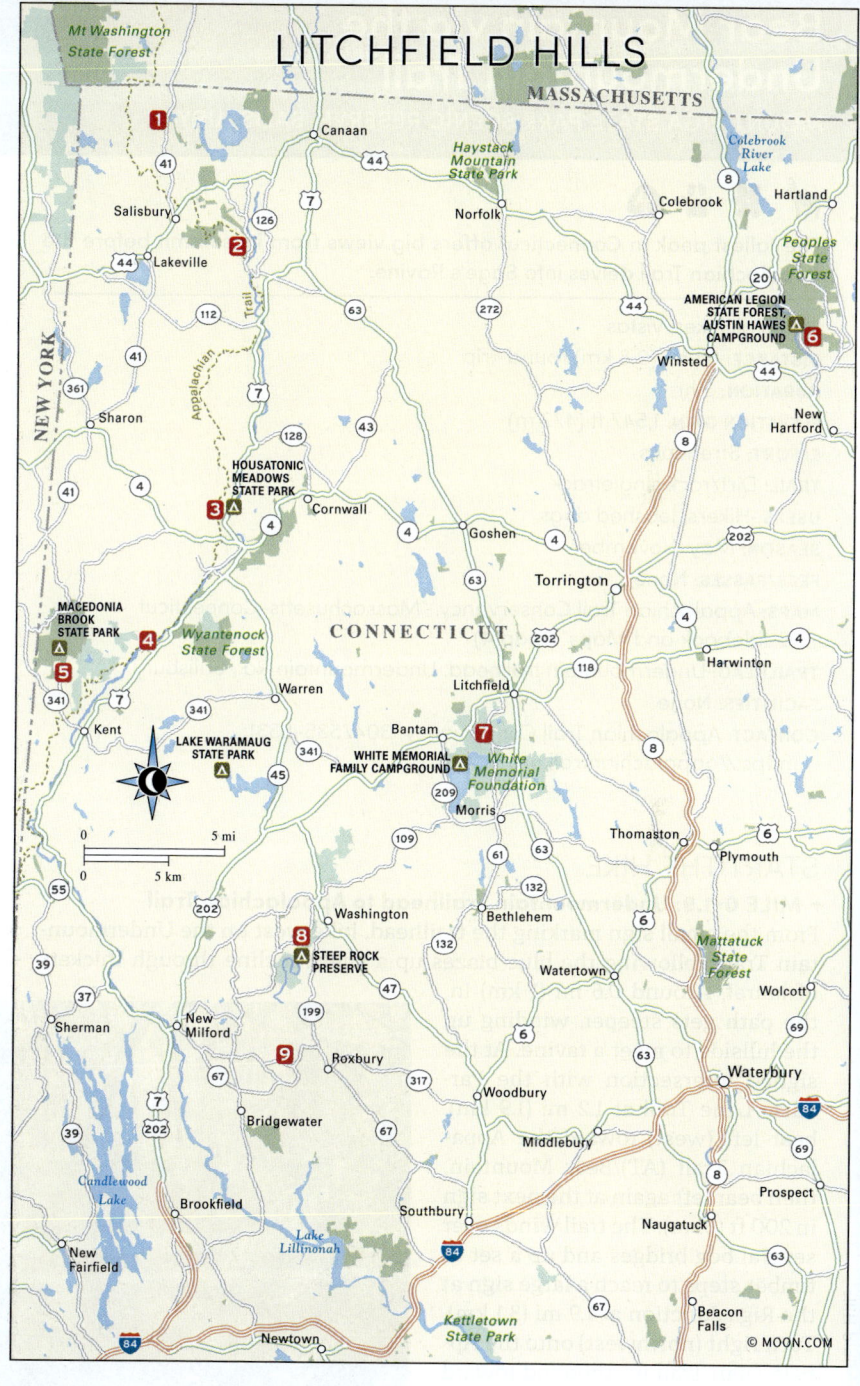

LITCHFIELD HILLS

MASSACHUSETTS

Mt Washington State Forest

Canaan

1

41

44

Haystack Mountain State Park

Colebrook River Lake

8

Salisbury

126

7

Norfolk

Colebrook

Hartland

Peoples State Forest

44

Lakeville

2

112

63

272

44

20

AMERICAN LEGION STATE FOREST, AUSTIN HAWES CAMPGROUND **6**

41

361

7

Winsted

44

Sharon

128

43

8

New Hartford

41

HOUSATONIC MEADOWS STATE PARK

3

Cornwall

4

4

Goshen

4

202

CONNECTICUT

MACEDONIA BROOK STATE PARK

4

Wyantenock State Forest

63

Torrington

202

4

Harwinton

5

Warren

Litchfield

118

4

341

7

341

Bantam

8

Kent

341

LAKE WARAMAUG STATE PARK

45

7

WHITE MEMORIAL FAMILY CAMPGROUND

White Memorial Foundation

209

0   5 mi

0   5 km

109

Morris

6

Thomaston

Plymouth

61

63

55

202

132

Washington

Bethlehem

Mattatuck State Forest

Wolcott

8

STEEP ROCK PRESERVE

132

6

Watertown

39

37

199

47

63

69

Sherman

New Milford

9

Roxbury

317

Woodbury

Waterbury

84

67

Bridgewater

67

Middlebury

69

39

202

Candlewood Lake

Brookfield

Lake Lillinonah

Southbury

8

Prospect

New Fairfield

84

Naugatuck

63

67

Beacon Falls

Newtown

Kettletown State Park

© MOON.COM

NEW YORK

The tallest peak in Connecticut offers big views from its summit before the Appalachian Trail delves into Sage's Ravine.

BEST: Fall hikes, vistas
DISTANCE: 6.1 mi (9.8 km) round-trip
DURATION: 3 hr
ELEVATION GAIN: 1,547 ft (472 m)
EFFORT: Strenuous
TRAIL: Dirt/rock singletrack
USERS: Hikers, leashed dogs
SEASON: May–November
FEES/PASSES: None
MAPS: Appalachian Trail Conservancy, "Massachusetts-Connecticut Guidebook and Maps" (map 4)
TRAILHEAD: Undermountain trailhead, Undermountain Rd., Salisbury
FACILITIES: None
CONTACT: Appalachian Trail Conservancy; 304/535-6331; https://appalachiantrail.org

START THE HIKE

▶ **MILE 0-1.9: Undermountain Trailhead to Appalachian Trail**

From the small sign marking the trailhead, hike west on the Undermountain Trail, following the blue blazes up a slight incline through thickets of laurel. Around 0.6 mi (1 km) in, the path gets steeper, winding up the hillside to meet a ravine. At the signed intersection with the Paradise Lane Trail at 1.2 mi (1.9 km), bear left (west) toward the Appalachian Trail (AT)/Bear Mountain, then bear left again at the next sign in 200 ft (61 m). The trail winds over several bog bridges and up a set of timber steps to reach a large sign at the Riga Junction at 1.9 mi (3.1 km). Turn right (northwest) onto the Appalachian Trail northbound toward Bear Mountain.

MOUNTAIN LAUREL ON THE PARADISE LANE TRAIL ▶

CONNECTICUT | Litchfield Hills

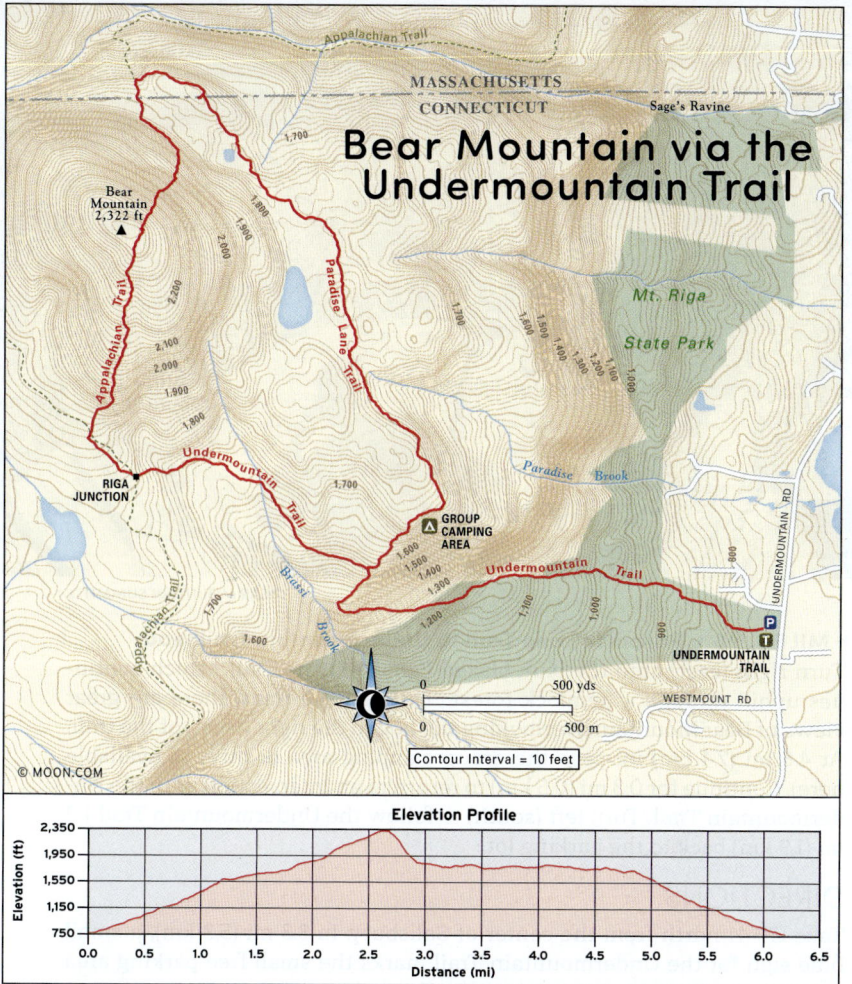

Bear Mountain via the Undermountain Trail

MASSACHUSETTS
CONNECTICUT

Sage's Ravine

Bear Mountain 2,322 ft

Mt. Riga State Park

RIGA JUNCTION

Paradise Lane Trail

Appalachian Trail

Undermountain Trail

GROUP CAMPING AREA

Paradise Brook

Brassie Brook

Appalachian Trail

UNDERMOUNTAIN RD

UNDERMOUNTAIN TRAIL

WESTMOUNT RD

© MOON.COM

0   500 yds
0   500 m

Contour Interval = 10 feet

Elevation Profile

Elevation (ft)

2,350
1,950
1,550
1,150
750

0.0 0.5 1.0 1.5 2.0 2.5 3.0 3.5 4.0 4.5 5.0 5.5 6.0 6.5
Distance (mi)

▶ **MILE 1.9–2.6: Appalachian Trail to Bear Mountain Summit**

Follow the white-blazed trail to a fork at 2 mi (3.2 km), and bear right (northeast). From here, a set of stone steps begins an ascent to the bare, rocky peak. Vistas improve the higher hikers climb, but the crown jewel is the rock tower atop the summit at 2.6 mi (4.2 km). The best views stretch northwest toward Mount Everett and Mount Race in Massachusetts and northeast toward the "twin lakes" of Salisbury.

▶ **MILE 2.6–3.1: Bear Mountain Summit to Paradise Lane Trail**

Continue north on the AT, descending a steep, rocky slope. Use caution through this section, especially during wet weather. The trail flattens in 0.5 mi (0.8 km) and briefly enters Massachusetts, where hikers will reach a large sign for Sage's Ravine at 3.1 mi (5 km).

Optional: Continue straight on the AT for 0.7 mi (1.1 km) to Sage's Ravine Falls.

▶ **MILE 3.1-6.1: Paradise Lane Trail to Undermountain Trailhead**

Turn right (east) onto the blue-blazed Paradise Lane Trail, which continues uphill through a hemlock forest. Through the trees, there are great views of Bear Mountain overlooking the bog to the right (west) of the trail. At 4.6 mi (7.4 km) in, pass the group camping area (a privy is available here). Continue for 0.3 mi (0.5 km) to return to an intersection with the Undermountain Trail. Turn left (south) to follow the Undermountain Trail 1.2 mi (1.9 km) back to the parking lot.

DIRECTIONS

Take CT-41 north from the center of Salisbury. In 3.3 mi (5.3 km), a small blue sign for the Undermountain Trail marks the small free parking area on the left side.

GPS COORDINATES: 42°01'43.6"N 73°25'43.4"W

Appalachian Trail: Prospect Mountain and Rand's View

APPALACHIAN NATIONAL SCENIC TRAIL, FALLS VILLAGE

Wander over the summit of Mount Prospect to the sprawling fields of Rand's View, tucked underneath the peaks of the Berkshire hills.

BEST: Spring hikes, vistas

DISTANCE: 5.2 mi (8.4 km) round-trip

DURATION: 2.5 hr

ELEVATION GAIN: 979 ft (298 m)

EFFORT: Moderate

TRAIL: Dirt/rock singletrack

USERS: Hikers, leashed dogs

SEASON: May–November

FEES/PASSES: None

MAPS: Appalachian Trail Conservancy, "Massachusetts-Connecticut Guidebook and Maps" (map 3)

TRAILHEAD: Great Falls Reservoir parking lot, Housatonic River Rd., Salisbury

FACILITIES: None

CONTACT: Appalachian Trail Conservancy; 304/535-6331; https://appalachiantrail.org

START THE HIKE

▶ **MILE 0-1.6: Great Falls Reservoir Parking Lot to Prospect Mountain Summit**

From the gated parking area at the falls, cross Housatonic River Road and hike west, following the white blazes uphill for 0.2 mi (0.3 km). The trail winds past a large boulder and enters a meadow, a great spot to glimpse deer and other wildlife feeding in the morning and evening.

Travel through an airy beech and maple forest for another 0.2 mi (0.3 km), then dip alongside a stream on the right (east) side of the trail. Cross the stream on foot heading straight (north) and follow the path over several rolling hills for 0.5 mi (0.8 km) until the trail bends sharply left (northwest). Begin the 0.7-mi

◀ MUSHROOMS ON THE APPALACHIAN TRAIL

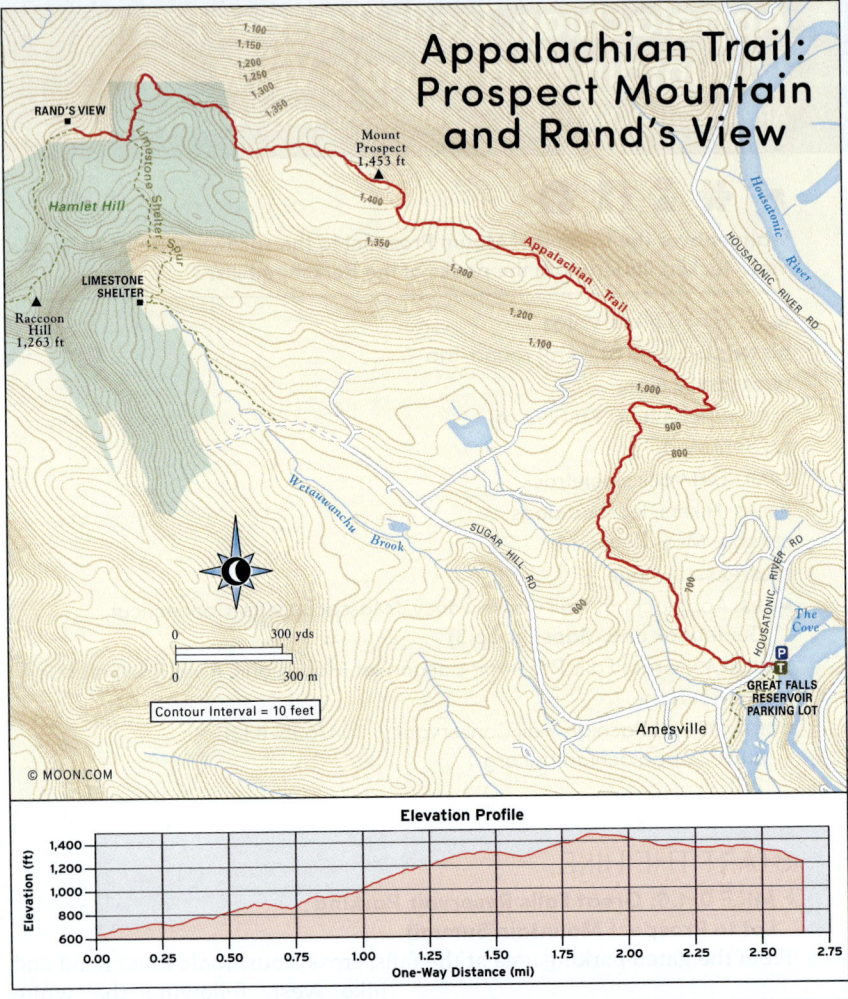

Appalachian Trail: Prospect Mountain and Rand's View

Elevation Profile

(1.1-km) ascent to the rocky ridgeline of **Prospect Mountain.** The trail eases into a soft dirt track leading to the summit of Prospect at 1.6 mi (2.6 km). A narrow but pretty vista looks west toward the Housatonic River and a series of marshes bordered by green hills.

▶ **MILE 1.6–2.6: Prospect Mountain Summit to Rand's View**
The trail continues straight (west) along the summit. Cross a stone wall and then descend a hill to the signed intersection with the **Limestone Shelter** spur at 2.5 mi (4 km). Turn right (west) to stay on the **Appalachian Trail.** In 0.1 mi (0.16 km), the trail arrives at **Rand's View,** a grassy, wide-open clearing with wildflowers and fantastic views of the Berkshire Range. After enjoying the view, turn around and backtrack the same route across Prospect Mountain and down the ridgeline to the parking lot on Housatonic River Road.

▲ RAND'S VIEW

DIRECTIONS

Take US-7 to the intersection with CT-126 in Falls Village and go west on CT-126. Pass through the center of town, turn left onto Water Street, and pass under a railroad bridge. Shortly after, cross an iron bridge and take the first right onto Housatonic River Road. There is a large gated gravel parking area at the falls in 0.4 mi (0.6 km).

GPS COORDINATES: 41°57'47.8"N 73°22'22.9"W

A quick hike along rolling cascades up to the Pine Knob lookouts results in lovely views of the Litchfield Hills.

BEST: Waterfalls

DISTANCE: 2.5 mi (4 km) round-trip

DURATION: 2 hr

ELEVATION GAIN: 765 ft (233 m)

EFFORT: Moderate

TRAIL: Dirt/rock singletrack

USERS: Hikers, leashed dogs

SEASON: May–November

FEES/PASSES: None

MAPS: Connecticut Forest and Park Association, "Blue Blazed Hiking Trail System/Connecticut Walk Book"

TRAILHEAD: Pine Knob Loop trailhead, Route 7, Sharon

FACILITIES: None; restrooms and water available at Housatonic Meadows Campground

CONTACT: Connecticut Forest and Park Association; 860/346-8733; https://ctwoodlands.org

START THE HIKE

▶ **MILE 0-1.0: Pine Knob Loop Trailhead to First Vista**

For this counterclockwise route, turn right (north) along the stone wall. The flat trail winds over several creeks, passing the spur to the **Housatonic Meadows State Park Campground** in 0.4 mi (0.6 km).

From the spur, the path climbs switchbacks to meet a small **waterfall** at 0.6 mi (1 km). Continue past the waterfall and climb a rocky ridgeline with some scrambling to reach the **first vista** at 1 mi (1.6 km). This east-facing lookout peers over nearby conifers for fantastic views of the Litchfield Hills and the Housatonic River valley on a clear day. Fog coming off the river below can add an enchanted quality to the forested vista on a cool morning.

FOGGY VIEW FROM PINE KNOB VISTA ▶

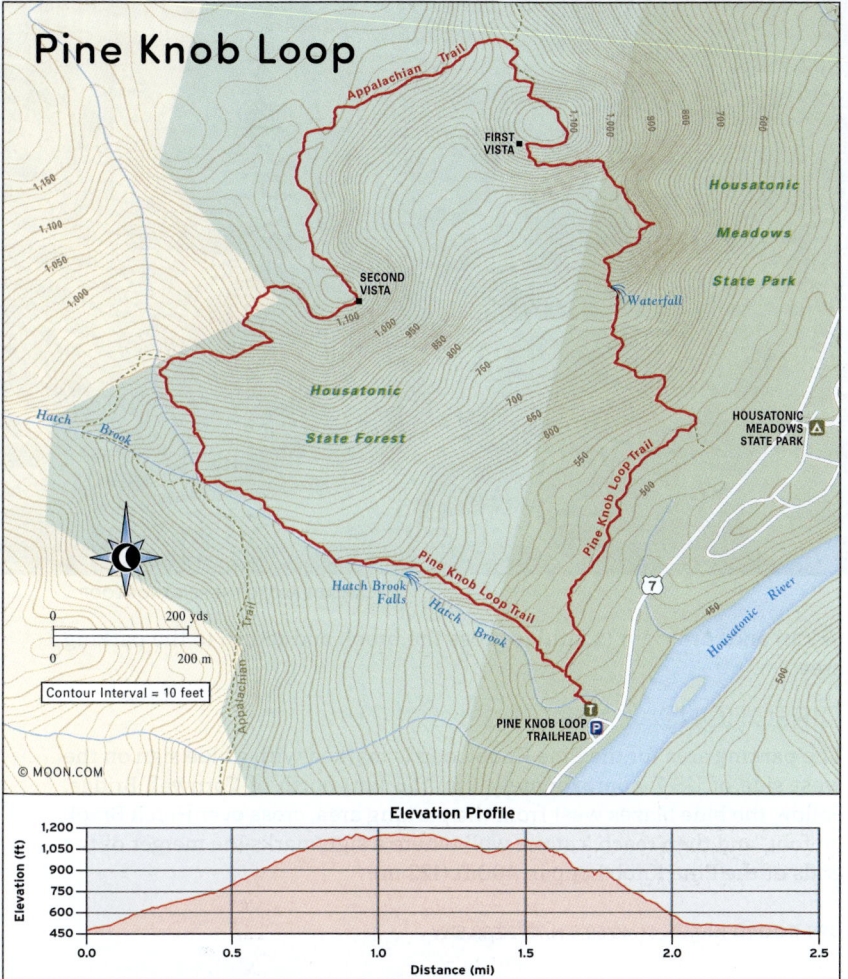

Pine Knob Loop

Elevation Profile

▶ MILE 1.0–1.6: First Vista to Second Vista

Cross over the hilltop northwest of the vista, descend, and reach a sign marking the intersection with the Appalachian Trail (AT) at 1.1 mi (1.8 km). Turn left (west) onto the AT southbound to continue the Pine Knob Loop. The blazes become white and blue when the Pine Knob Trail and the AT merge. The trail traverses the flat saddle between Pine Knob's two peaks. Reach the narrow, **east-facing vista** atop the second peak at about 1.6 mi (2.6 km).

▶ MILE 1.6–2.5: Second Vista to Pine Knob Loop Trailhead

After taking in the vista, continue another 1.9 mi (3.1 km), where the Pine Knob Loop departs the Appalachian Trail at a marked intersection and the white-and-blue blazes end. Turn left (southeastfv) following only the blue blazes, which continue downstream along Hatch Brook. Hikers will pass large boulders and a series of cascades culminating in the impressive Hatch Brook Falls at 2.3 mi (3.7 km). Return to close the loop at 2.5 mi

(4 km) and turn right (south) to cross the brook and return to the parking area.

DIRECTIONS

The parking area for the Pine Knob Loop is marked with a blue sign on the west side of US-7, approximately 1 mi (1.6 km) north of Cornwall Bridge. Follow the blue blazes west from the parking area, cross over Hatch Brook on foot, and then reach a stone wall where a sign marks the merger of the ends of the Pine Knob Loop in 400 ft (122 m).

GPS COORDINATES: 41°49'59.6"N 73°22'59.8"W

4 Appalachian Trail: Housatonic River Walk

APPALACHIAN NATIONAL SCENIC TRAIL, KENT

This easygoing meander along the Housatonic River comprises a favorite flat section of the Appalachian Trail.

BEST: Winter hikes, brew hikes

DISTANCE: 7.6 mi (12.2 km) round-trip

DURATION: 3.5 hr

ELEVATION GAIN: 122 ft (37 m)

EFFORT: Easy

TRAIL: Dirt singletrack

USERS: Hikers, leashed dogs

SEASON: Year-round

FEES/PASSES: None

MAPS: Appalachian Trail Conservancy, "Massachusetts–Connecticut Guidebook and Maps"

TRAILHEAD: Canoe Access trailhead, River Rd., Kent

FACILITIES: None

CONTACT: Appalachian Trail Conservancy; 304/535-6331; https://appalachiantrail.org

START THE HIKE

▶ **MILE 0-1.3: Canoe Access Trailhead to Stewart Hollow Brook Bridge**

Hike north from the parking area, following the white blazes upstream on a wide, flat gravel path. The partially shaded trail follows a stone wall lined with a number of large maples, then crosses over North Kent Brook, a fairly wide stream. There is no bridge, so hikers may have to leap to make it over without getting wet. At 0.5 mi (0.8 km) from the trailhead, the trail narrows and enters a stand of tall, skinny beech trees, which are particularly beautiful in fall when draped in yellow leaves. At 0.9 mi (1.4 km) the trail returns to hug the

◀ BRIDGE OVER THE STEWART HOLLOW BROOK

CONNECTICUT

Litchfield Hills

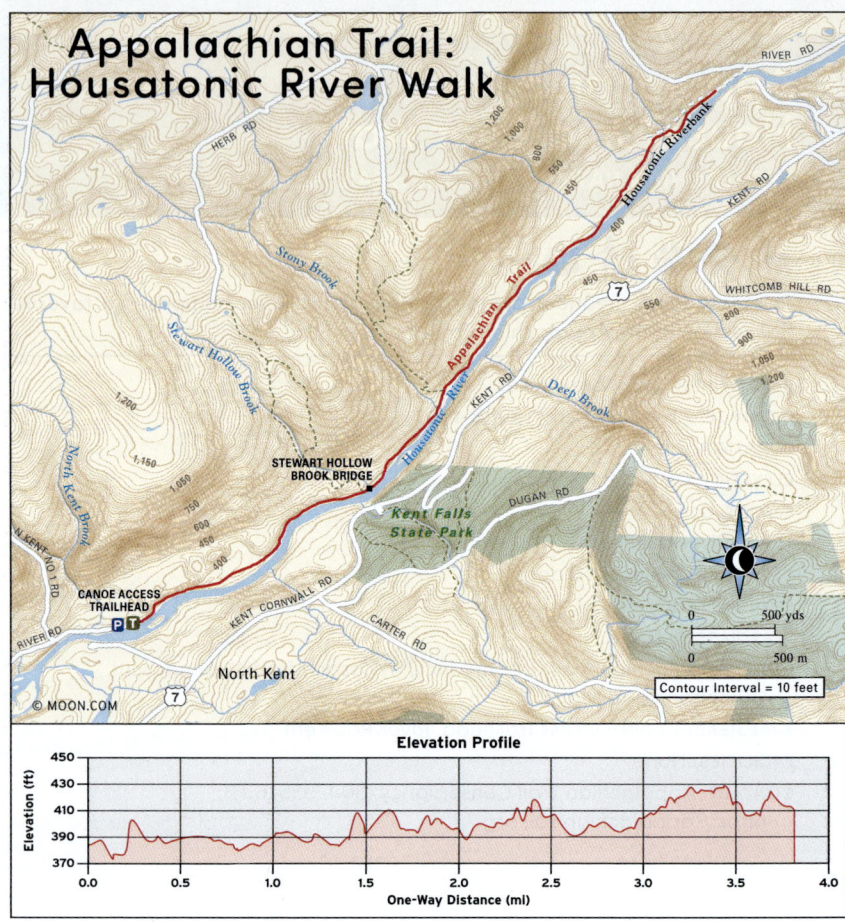

Appalachian Trail: Housatonic River Walk

Elevation Profile

west bank of the Housatonic River. Cross over the Stewart Hollow Brook on a **wooden bridge** at 1.3 mi (2.1 km), and pass the turnoffs to the **Stewart Hollow** campsite and group area.

▶ **MILE 1.3–3.4: Stewart Hollow Brook Bridge to Housatonic Riverbank**
The area includes a privy and a lean-to shelter that is a nice spot for a break. Continue to where the path diverts west away from the river and through a grassy open **field** with great views of the tree-covered Kent hillside rising up to the west, 2.9 mi (4.7 km) in. At 3.4 mi (5.5 km), the path winds through bramble back to the water's edge. This unique ecosystem is a popular place to spot rare bird species.

▶ **MILE 3.4–3.8: Housatonic Riverbank to Canoe Access Trailhead**
When the trail reaches an intersection with a gravel road at 3.8 mi (6.1 km), turn around and backtrack to the trailhead to complete the 7.6-mi (12.2-km) hike.

▲ THE HOUSATONIC RIVER

DIRECTIONS

From downtown Kent, take CT-341 west for about 0.2 mi (0.3 km), then turn right onto Skiff Mountain Road. At the fork in 1 mi (1.6 km), bear right onto River Road. The parking area and trailhead is at the end of the road in about 2.5 mi (4 km).

GPS COORDINATES: 41°46'06.5"N 73°26'06.8"W

Macedonia Ridge Trail

MACEDONIA BROOK STATE PARK, KENT

A woodsy loop around a hillside includes views from Cobble Mountain and scenic stretches along the Macedonia Brook.

DISTANCE: 6.4 mi (10.3 km) round-trip

DURATION: 3.5 hr

ELEVATION GAIN: 1,429 ft (436 m)

EFFORT: Moderate/strenuous

TRAIL: Dirt/rock singletrack, gravel road

USERS: Hikers, leashed dogs

SEASON: May–November

FEES/PASSES: Camping only

MAPS: Connecticut DEEP, "Macedonia Brook State Park"

TRAILHEAD: Macedonia Ridge trailhead, Macedonia Brook Rd., Kent

FACILITIES: Vault toilet; water available at campground office

CONTACT: Connecticut Department of Energy and Environmental Protection; 860/526-2336; https://portal.ct.gov/deep

START THE HIKE

▸ **MILE 0-1.5: Macedonia Ridge Trailhead to Cobble Mountain Summit**
To complete the loop clockwise, hike toward the red outhouse and then turn left (south), crossing a stream via a **bridge** and following the blue blazes. Ascend a hill and cross the stream again in 0.3 mi (0.5 km). The trail climbs up to a **ridgeline** with increasingly good east-facing views of the Housatonic River valley. Blueberry bushes line the way as the path dips into a pocket of laurel, then ascends a grassy slope to the summit of **Cobble Mountain** 1.5 mi (2.4 km) in.

▸ **MILE 1.5-2.7: Cobble Mountain Summit to**
  Macedonia Brook State Park
Follow the blue-and-white blazes north across the summit. There are great vistas facing east over the Macedonia Brook valley and west into New York and the Taconic Range. From Cobble Mountain, the trail descends through ledges for 0.8 mi (1.3 km); hikers may need to use their hands to lower themselves. At the end of the descent, the trail meets a wide gravel road. Turn left (north) and follow the gravel road straight across the paved street and through the gate on the other side. The route travels along a rock wall and meets another gate at the wooden **Macedonia Brook State Park** sign at 2.7 mi (4.3 km).

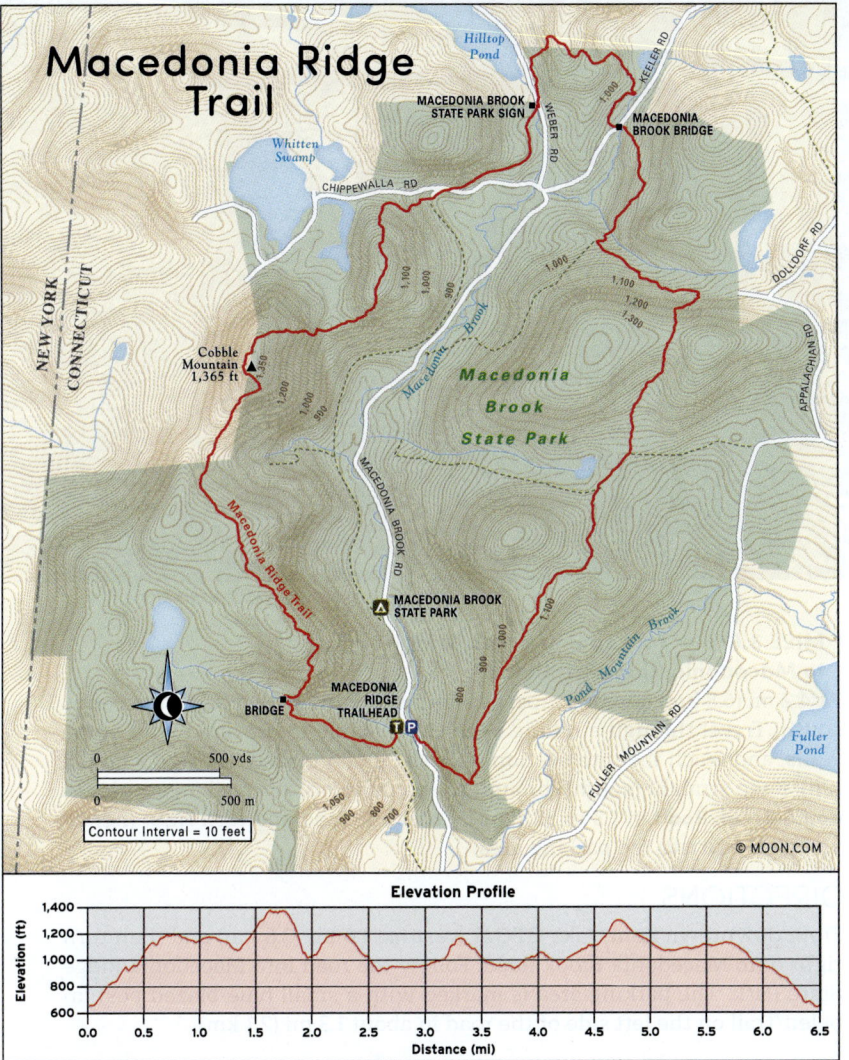

Macedonia Ridge Trail

Elevation Profile

▶ MILE 2.7–3.6: Macedonia Brook State Park to Macedonia Brook Bridge

Cross the street, and walk left (north) for about 100 ft (30 m) to a trail sign. At the trail sign, turn right (east) into the woods. There are glimpses of **Hilltop Pond** to the left (east) as the trail winds up a hillside of hemlock for 0.3 mi (0.5 km). Cross through an opening in a stone wall and past a meadow and bog for another 0.3 mi (0.5 km). The trail bends alongside Macedonia Brook for 0.2 mi (0.3 km), then crosses over the brook and Keeler Road on a bridge at 3.6 mi (5.8 km).

▶ **MILE 3.6–6.4: Macedonia Brook Bridge
to Macedonia Ridge Trailhead**

At 4.2 mi (6.8 km), the trail crosses another narrow stream and then bends south. Travel through a rolling beech and maple forest lined with stone walls, and reach the intersection with the green-blazed trail at 4.9 mi (7.9 km). Keep straight (south) through the woods until the trail meets **Macedonia Brook Road** in 1.3 mi (2.1 km). Cross the road and turn right (northwest) to return to the parking area.

DIRECTIONS

From downtown Kent, take CT-341 west for 1.6 mi (2.6 km) and then turn right onto Macedonia Brook Road. Follow the road into Macedonia Ridge State Park. The parking area is marked with a small blue-blazed post labeled Trail on the left side of the road in about 1.3 mi (2.1 km).

GPS COORDINATES: 41°45'39.4"N 73°29'37.8"W

6

Robert Ross and Agnes Bowen Trails

PEOPLE'S STATE FOREST, BARKHAMSTED

This beautiful hike through pristine forest and over bubbling brooks delivers big views from its overlooks with very little effort.

BEST: Brew hikes

DISTANCE: 6.4 mi (10.3 km) round-trip

DURATION: 3.5 hr

ELEVATION GAIN: 1,019 ft (311 m)

EFFORT: Moderate

TRAIL: Dirt/rock singletrack

USERS: Hikers, leashed dogs

SEASON: May–November

FEES/PASSES: $15 for nonresidents on weekends and holidays, $10 weekdays. No charge for CT residents.

MAPS: Friends of American Legion and People's State Forest, "American Legion and People's State Forest Trail Map"

TRAILHEAD: Matthies Grove parking lot, East River Rd., Barkhamsted

FACILITIES: Restrooms, picnic tables, trail map

CONTACT: Connecticut Department of Energy and Environmental Protection; 860/526-2336; https://portal.ct.gov/DEEP

START THE HIKE

▶ **MILE 0-0.3: Parking Lot to Robert Ross Trail**

Start from the trailhead at the Matthies Grove parking lot. Follow signs toward the **Nature Museum,** an educational facility built by the Civilian Conservation Corps in 1935. Reach the museum at 0.2 mi (0.3 km) and turn left (north) toward the Agnes Bowen and Robert Ross Trail signs, following the blue and orange-blue blazes. At 0.3 mi (0.5 km), bear left on the blue-blazed **Robert Ross Trail.**

▶ **MILE 0.3-2.2: Robert Ross Trail to Jessie Gerard Trail**

The route chugs steadily uphill through an eclectic mix of trees and shrubs. At 1 mi (1.6 km) from the trailhead, the trail widens and arrives at the **King Road** intersection. Turn left (northwest) to stay on the Robert Ross Trail. The path rolls downhill until intersecting the

GREAT CHAUGHAM LOOKOUT ▶

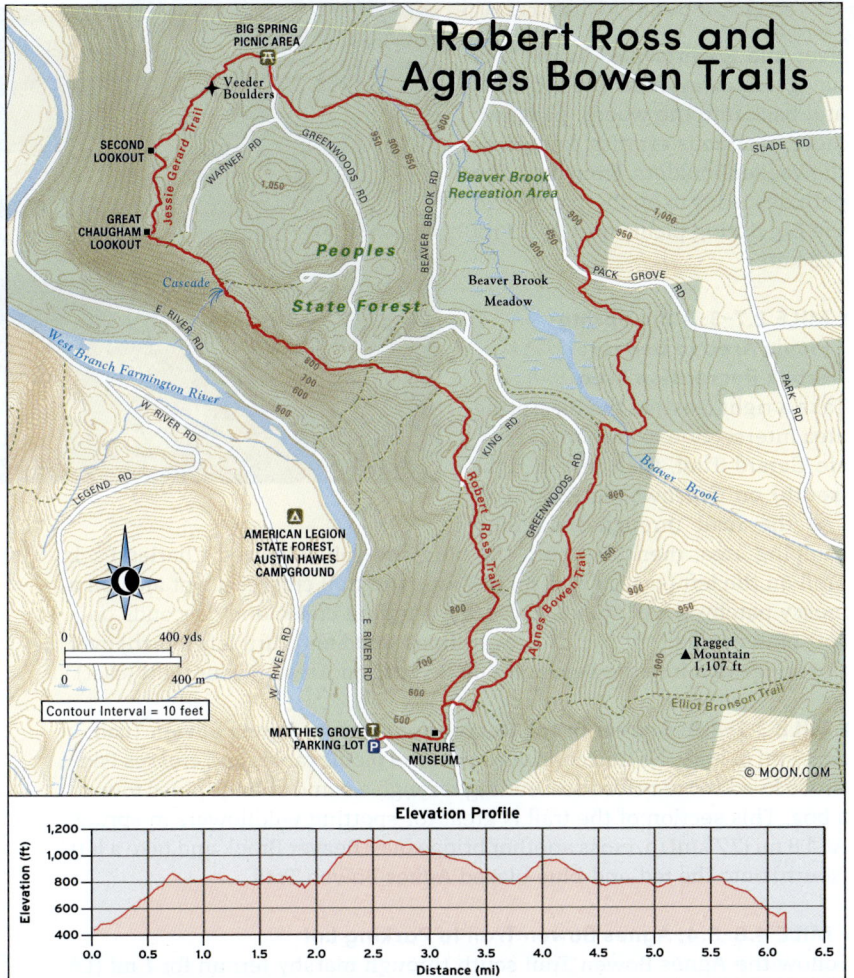

Robert Ross and Agnes Bowen Trails

Elevation Profile

Agnes Bowen Trail again at 1.5 mi (2.4 km). Turn right (north) and then bear left (west) to continue on the **Robert Ross Trail,** which winds through a clearing and over a creek where a glacial erratic boulder keeps sentinel. There are some views to the west as the trail climbs uphill and wraps around a series of ledges. At 1.9 mi (3.1 km), reach the intersection with the Jessie Gerard Trail. Stay right on Robert Ross to reach the bridge and the intersection with Falls Cutoff at 2 mi (3.2 km). Check out the falls to the left (west) before following the Robert Ross Trail straight through the intersection on a rocky uphill path. At 2.2 mi (3.5 km), reach Warner Road and take the blue-and-yellow-blazed Jessie Gerard Trail straight north.

▶ MILE 2.2–2.7: Jessie Gerard Trail to Big Spring Picnic Area

At this steepest point in the hike, hundreds of stone steps lead uphill to the **Great Chaugham Lookout.** The vista offers excellent views of the Farmington River disappearing into a horizon of hills. At 2.4 mi (3.9 km) from the trailhead, reach the second lookout, which faces northwest toward the

river and Robertsville. As the trail navigates away from the lookouts and back into the woods, pass two more enormous erratics, known as the Veeder Boulders. From here, the path descends to an intersection at the Big Spring picnic area at 2.7 mi (4.3 km).

▶ **MILE 2.7–3.7: Big Spring Picnic Area to Beaver Brook Recreation Area**

Take a right (east) at the Big Spring area intersection to stay on the Jessie Gerard Trail, then take a right (south) on Greenwoods Road. Follow the road through the group camping area, then turn onto the blue-and-yellow-blazed Charles Pack Trail on the left (east). At 2.8 mi (4.5 km), the trail crosses a wet area on a mossy patchwork of stones, crosses a gurgling creek, and descends on a soft pine needle trail. Reach Beaver Brook Road and turn left (north) over the bridge and into the Beaver Brook Recreation Area on your right (east).

▶ **MILE 3.7–4.8: Beaver Brook Recreation Area to Agnes Bowen Trail**

At 3.7 mi (6 km), the trail continues past the picnic tables and crosses Pack Grove Road twice before descending through a stand of huge pines toward a bog. This section of the trail is great for spotting wildflowers in spring. At 4.8 mi (7.7 km) in, cross another bridge over Beaver Brook and take a left (south) onto the red-and-blue-blazed Agnes Bowen Trail.

▶ **MILE 4.8–6.4: Agnes Bowen Trail to Parking Lot**

Follow the Agnes Bowen Trail south through marshy terrain for 1 mi (1.6 km). At 5.8 mi (9.3 km), pass a camping area, continue downhill with the stream on your right (west), and then cross a road before meeting the Robert Ross Trail again. Take a left (south) to arrive back at the Nature Museum. Turn right (west) to return to the parking lot, completing the 6.4-mi (10.3-km) hike.

DIRECTIONS

From US-44, turn onto CT-318 in Barkhamsted. Cross the bridge and immediately turn left onto East River Road. The park entrance is on the left after 1 mi (1.6 km).

GPS COORDINATES: 41°55'32.0"N 72°59'57.8"W

This novel hike includes more than a mile of boardwalk over the scenic marshland of Little Pond and the Bantam River.

DISTANCE: 3.2 mi (5.1 km) round-trip

DURATION: 1.75 hr

ELEVATION GAIN: 139 ft (42 m)

EFFORT: Easy

TRAIL: Gravel road, dirt singletrack, wooden boardwalk

USERS: Hikers, leashed dogs

SEASON: Year-round

FEES/PASSES: None

MAPS: White Memorial Conservation Center, "WMF Property Map"

TRAILHEAD: White Memorial Conservation Center Nature Museum, Whitehall Rd., Litchfield

FACILITIES: Restrooms, trail map

CONTACT: White Memorial Conservation Center; 860/567-0857; https://whitememorialcc.org

START THE HIKE

▶ **MILE 0-0.5: Nature Museum to Bissell Road**

With the museum to your right, follow the gravel road east for about 0.2 mi (0.3 km). At the stone-pillared gate, turn left (north) onto the blue-blazed Mattatuck Trail, which runs through a boggy area along a section of the Bantam River. Reach the intersection with Bissell Road, 0.5 mi (0.8 km) from the trailhead, and cross straight (north) through the gate and into a forest of tall pines.

▶ **MILE 0.5-1.0: Bissell Road to Boardwalk Trail**

In approximately 400 ft (122 m), turn right (east) onto the black-and-white-blazed Little Pond Loop Trail. After crossing Whites Woods Road, the trail continues east down a grassy path. At the intersection at 1 mi (1.6 km), turn right (south) to start the boardwalk circuit counterclockwise. **Sutton's Bridge,** a high wooden arch bridge at the beginning of the boardwalk, is a particularly scenic perch to look out over the river and the high cattails and colorful grasses that envelop the trail. Hikers with keen eyes may spot waterfowl, beavers, and a variety of wildflowers in the spring and early summer.

SUTTON'S BRIDGE OVER THE BANTAM RIVER ▲

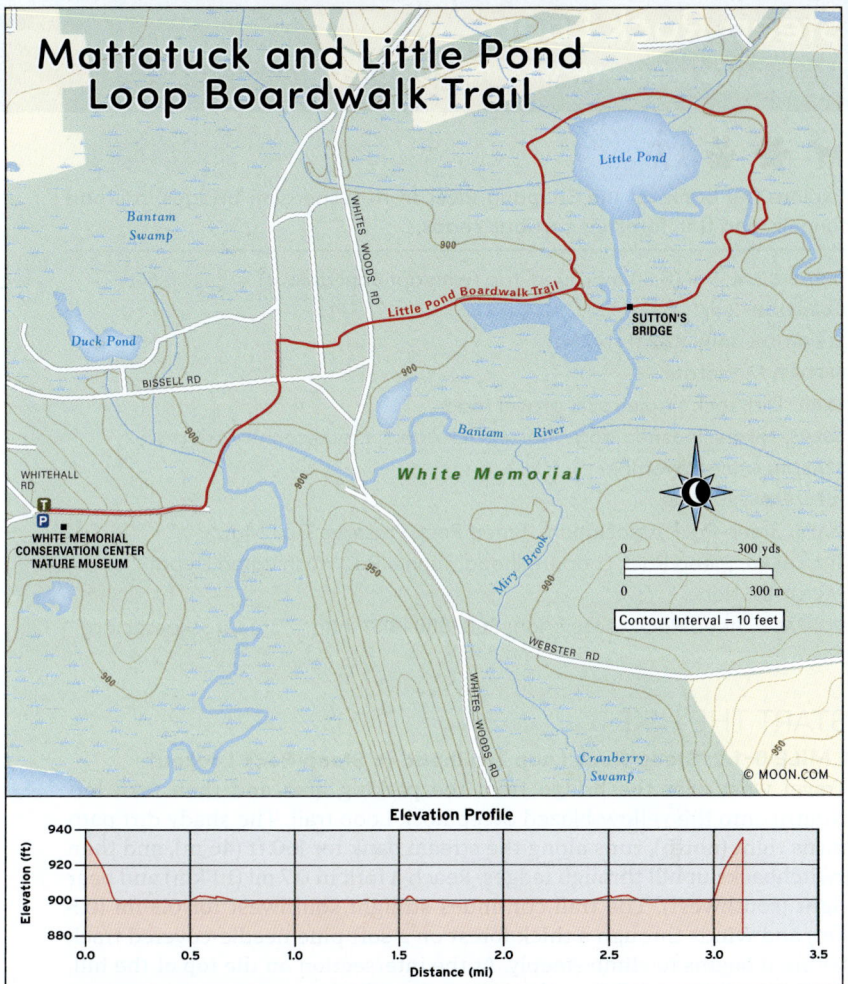

Mattatuck and Little Pond Loop Boardwalk Trail

Elevation Profile

▶ MILE 1.0–3.2: Boardwalk Trail to Nature Museum

The 1.2-mi-long (1.9-km) boardwalk winds over the Bantam River and around the surrounding marsh. There's a split in 0.8 mi (1.3 km) as you continue counterclockwise; keep left to stay on the Little Pond Loop Trail, which ends back at the intersection in 0.4 mi (0.6 km). Turn right (west) at the intersection to backtrack 1 mi (1.6 km) to the museum and parking area.

DIRECTIONS

From Litchfield Center, take US-202 west for 2 mi (3.2 km), then turn left onto Bissell Road. In 100 ft (30 m), turn right onto Whitehall Road. There is a large parking area and a trail sign at the White Memorial Conservation Center.

GPS COORDINATES: 41°43'27.3"N 73°12'46.5"W

8

Steep Rock Loop
STEEP ROCK PRESERVE, WASHINGTON DEPOT

Explore the banks of the Shepaug River from suspension bridges, railroad tunnels, and flat, forested carriage roads.

DISTANCE: 4.1 mi (6.6 km) round-trip (with optional detour)
DURATION: 2 hr
ELEVATION GAIN: 482 ft (147 m)
EFFORT: Moderate
TRAIL: Dirt/rock singletrack, gravel road
USERS: Hikers, leashed dogs, horseback riders, cross-country skiers
SEASON: May–November
FEES/PASSES: None
MAPS: Steep Rock Association, "Steep Rock Preserve Trail Map"
TRAILHEAD: Steep Rock Loop trailhead, Tunnel Rd., Washington Depot
FACILITIES: None
CONTACT: Steep Rock Association; 860/868-9131; https://steeprockassoc.org

START THE HIKE

▶ **MILE 0-1.2: Steep Rock Loop Trailhead to Steep Rock Lookout**
Travel west over the bridge from the parking area and then turn left (south) onto the yellow-blazed Steep Rock Loop trail. The shady dirt path turns right (north), runs along the stream bank for 150 ft (46 m), and then switchbacks uphill through ledges. Reach a fork in 0.7 mi (1.1 km) and bear right (southwest). The trail continues straight southwest for 0.3 mi (0.5 km) and winds through a thick forest on a soft pine needle-covered track before it begins to climb steeply. At the intersection on the top of the hill, turn right (west) to follow the yellow blazes to the Steep Rock lookout at 1.2 mi (1.9 km), with great views of the Shepaug River.

▶ **MILE 1.2-2.2: Steep Rock Lookout to Suspension Bridge**
After enjoying the view, backtrack 0.2 mi (0.3 km) east to the intersection and continue straight (south). The trail descends a hill and then bends right (west), following both yellow and green blazes for 0.8 mi (1.3 km) along a wide carriage road overlooking the river. Drop into a

STEEP ROCK LOOKOUT ▶

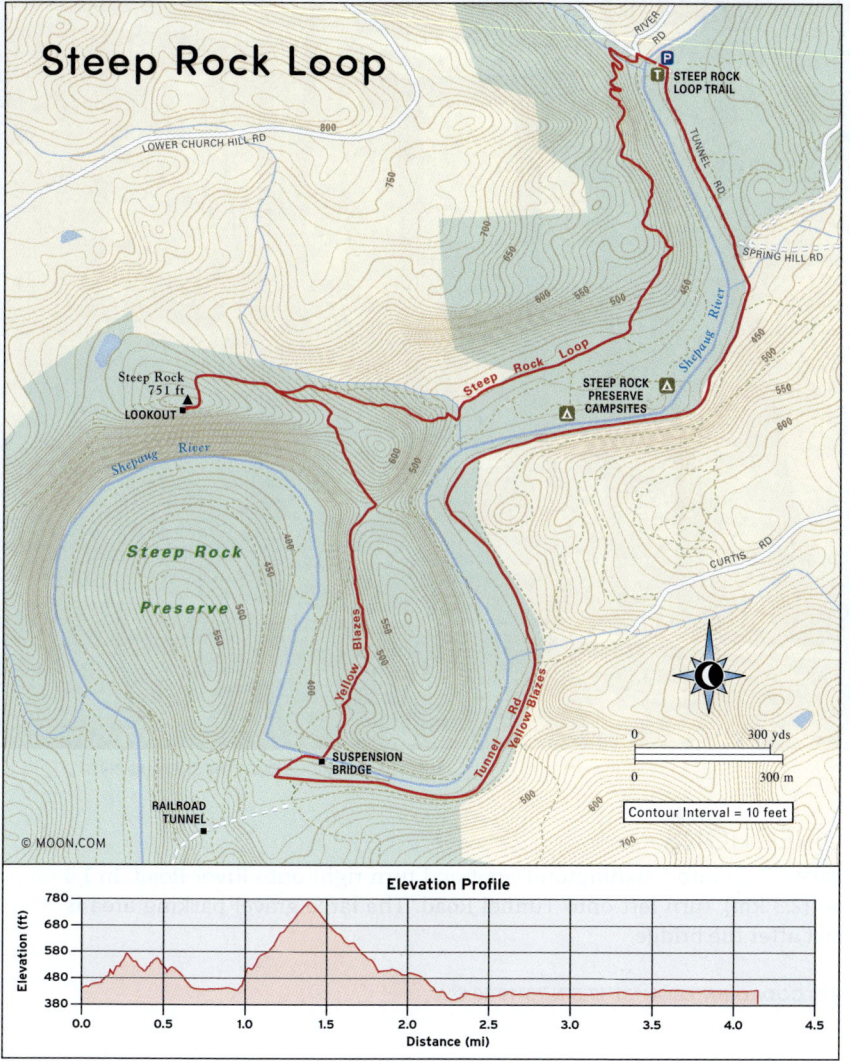

Steep Rock Loop

Elevation Profile

forest of massive pines and arrive at a suspension bridge over the river at 2.2 mi (3.5 km).

▶ **MILE 2.2–4.1: Suspension Bridge to Steep Rock Loop Trailhead**
Cross the bridge and then turn right (west) to follow the yellow blazes 0.1 mi (0.16 km) to a gravel road. Continue east on the wide gravel Tunnel Road, following the yellow blazes upstream directly alongside the river. The road arrives back at the parking area in 1.8 mi (2.9 km).

Optional: After the suspension bridge, follow the blue trail west for 0.3 mi (0.5 km) one-way to hike through the 235-ft-long (72-m) rock railroad tunnel, a photogenic underpass originally constructed as part of the Shepaug Valley Railroad.

SUSPENSION BRIDGE OVER THE SHEPAUG RIVER ▲

DIRECTIONS

Take CT-47 into Washington Depot and turn right onto River Road. In 1.4 mi (2.3 km), turn left onto Tunnel Road. The large gravel parking area is just after the bridge.

GPS COORDINATES: 41°37'17.5"N 73°19'30.6"W

9

Donkey Trail and Hodge Road Loop

MINE HILL PRESERVE, ROXBURY

Delve into Connecticut's mining history on these trails surrounding the ruins of an 1860s ironworks.

BEST: New England oddities
DISTANCE: 3.5 mi (5.6 km) round-trip
DURATION: 2.75 hr
ELEVATION GAIN: 675 ft (114 m)
EFFORT: Moderate
TRAIL: Dirt/rock singletrack, gravel road
USERS: Hikers, leashed dogs, horseback riders, cross-country skiers
SEASON: May–November
FEES/PASSES: None
MAPS: Roxbury Land Trust, "Mine Hill Preserve/Carter Preserve Trail Map"
TRAILHEAD: Mine Hill trailhead, Mine Hill Rd., Roxbury
FACILITIES: None
CONTACT: Roxbury Land Trust; 860/350-4148; https://roxburylandtrust.org

START THE HIKE

▶ **MILE 0-0.6: Mine Hill Trailhead to Tunnel Entrance**

Follow the blue blazes east from the trailhead to an intersection in 390 ft (119 m), then turn left (north) onto the **Donkey Trail.** This blue-blazed path carries hikers for 0.2 mi (0.3 km) above the former Roasting Ovens, double stone cylinders used by the ironworks to heat raw ore. From the furnace ruins, the route continues straight north on a raised rock path. Pass the bog and Nature Trail on the right (east) side of the trail, then arrive at a grated tunnel entrance (you can't walk through it) on the left (west) at 0.6 mi (1 km).

▶ **MILE 0.6-1.7: Tunnel Entrance to Hodge Road Trail**

Follow the trail left (west) uphill past the tunnel for 0.1 mi (0.16 km) to the grated "bat cages," which protect the entrances to several bat hibernacula. At 1 mi (1.6 km), reach a signed intersection where the Donkey Trail bends right (north) to wander through laurel and ledges.

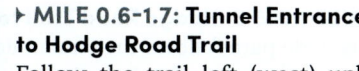

◀ MINE HILL TRAIL

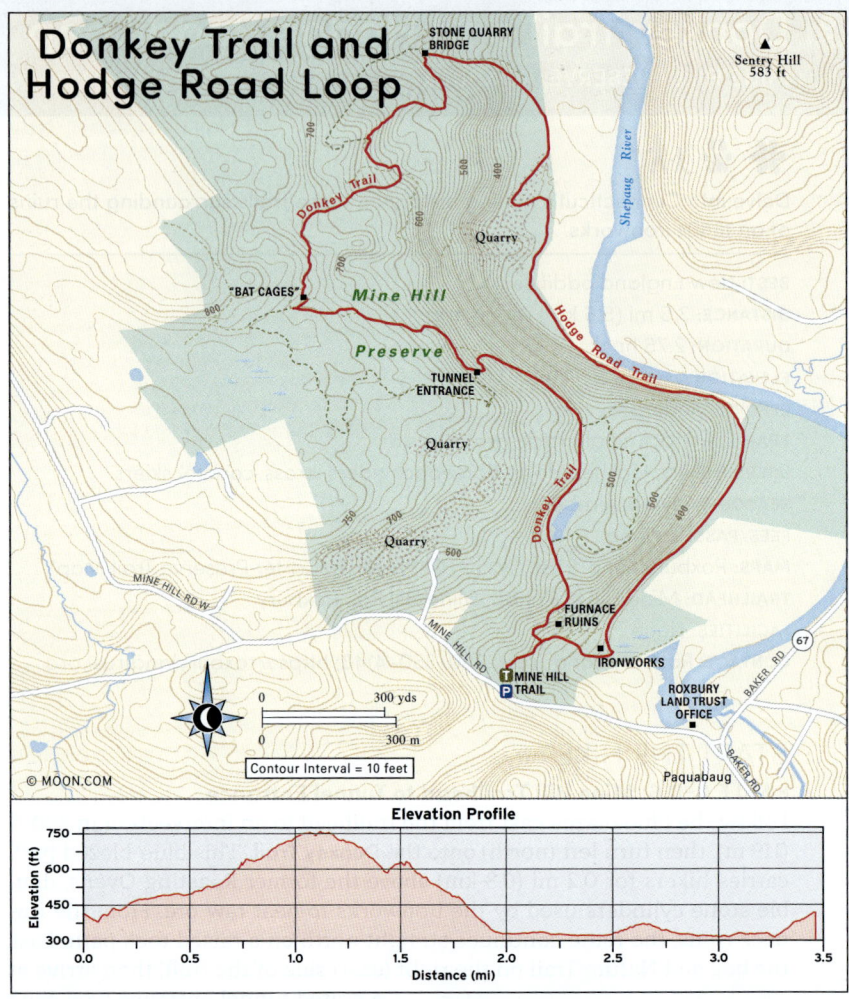

Donkey Trail and Hodge Road Loop

STONE QUARRY BRIDGE

▲ Sentry Hill 583 ft

Shepaug River

Donkey Trail

Quarry

"BAT CAGES"

Mine Hill

Hodge Road Trail

Preserve

TUNNEL ENTRANCE

Quarry

Donkey Trail

Quarry

Quarry

MINE HILL RD W.

MINE HILL RD.

FURNACE RUINS

IRONWORKS

67

BAKER RD.

MINE HILL TRAIL

ROXBURY LAND TRUST OFFICE

0   300 yds

0   300 m

Contour Interval = 10 feet

BAKER RD.

Paquabaug

© MOON.COM

Elevation Profile

At the cliff and the small granite quarry bridge at 1.7 mi (2.7 km), turn right (east) onto the Hodge Road Trail.

▶ **MILE 1.7–3.5: Hodge Road Trail to Mine Hill Trailhead**

This wide path follows the stream downhill for 0.5 mi (0.8 km) and delves into a spacious forest where the terrain flattens into a field. Reach a sign at the edge of the field and follow Hodge Road to the right (south). This gravel road parallels the Shepaug River for about 1 mi (1.6 km) before reaching the enormous stone cold-blast furnace, brick chimney, and other remnants of the 19th-century ironworks. This is a good spot to stop, explore, and read the interpretive signs before heading southwest on the trail 0.3 mi (0.5 km) back to the parking area.

▲ REMNANTS OF THE COLD-BLAST FURNACE AT MINE HILL

DIRECTIONS

Take CT-67 west from Roxbury for 2.3 mi (3.7 km), then turn right onto Mine Hill Road. The parking area is marked with a large sign on the right-hand side.

GPS COORDINATES: 41°33'35.1"N 73°20'17.9"W

BEST NEARBY BITES AND BREWS

When traveling in the Litchfield Hills, most hikers flock to the touristic centers of Kent and Litchfield for refreshment and entertainment. These idyllic New England towns, situated just 20 mi (32 km) apart, offer myriad options for breweries and tasty eats. These are some of our top recommendations.

- **Kent Falls Brewing Company** (33 Camps Rd., Kent; 860/398-9645; https://kentfallsbrewing.com; 2pm-7pm Thurs.-Fri., 1pm-6pm Sat.-Sun.), a "working farm" brewery, offers tours of the farm in addition to pints, flights, and growlers to go in an inviting taproom.

- Breakfast, lunch, and brunch get the farm-to-table treatment at **Mountainside Café** (251 Route 7 S, Falls Village; 860/824-7876; https://mountainside.com/cafe; 7am-3pm Wed.-Sun.), where delectable sandwiches, omelets, and baked goods are sourced from local ingredients.

- **Meraki Kitchen** (239 West St., Litchfield; 860/361-9777; www.merakifood.com; 7am-4pm Tues.-Sat.) offers tasty to-go and eat-in foods ranging from soups and sandwiches to a "salad case" curated from local ingredients. Also look for their food truck at local breweries.

- A classic pub, the **White Horse** (258 New Milford Turnpike/Route 202, New Preston; 860/868-1496; www.whitehorsecountrypub.com; 11:30am-close Mon.-Sat., 11am-close Sun.) offers great values on heaping plates of comfort pub food with gorgeous indoor and outdoor seating by the river.

- The New Hartford microbrewery **Brewery Legitimus** (283 Main St., New Hartford; 860/238-7870; www.brewerylegitimus.com; 3pm-9pm Tues., 3pm-10pm Wed.-Thurs., noon-10pm Fri.-Sat., noon-9pm Sun.) has a focus on Belgian and American ales and hosts live music, food trucks, and other events year-round in its indoor/outdoor space.

NEARBY CAMPGROUNDS

The Housatonic River Walk, Rand's View, and Bear Mountain hikes have primitive campsites on or near the routes.

NAME	LOCATION	FACILITIES	SEASON	FEE
American Legion State Forest, Austin Hawes Campground	198 W. River Rd., Barkhamsted, 41°55'48"N 73°0'0"W	30 RV/tent sites, 6 cabins; restrooms	mid-April– early October	$17-60
860/379-0922; https://portal.ct.gov				
Housatonic Meadows State Park	90 Route 7, Sharon, 41°52'48"N 73°21'36"W	59 RV/tent sites, 4 cabins; restrooms	late May– early September	$17-60
860/672-6772; https://portal.ct.gov				
Macedonia Brook State Park	159 Macedonia Brook Rd., Kent, 41°45'36"N 73°29'24"W	51 RV/tent sites; toilets	mid-April– early September	$14-24
860/927-4100; https://portal.ct.gov				
Lake Waramaug State Park	30 Lake Waramaug Rd., New Preston, 41°42'36"N 73°22'48"W	76 RV/tent sites, 6 cabins; restrooms	late May– early September	$17-60
860/868-0220; https://portal.ct.gov				
White Memorial Family Campground	N. Shore Rd., Bantam, 41°42'46.4"N 73°13'37.5"W	65 RV/tent sites; toilets	early May–early September	$10 wooded sites, $16 waterfront, $19.50 RV
860/567-0857; www.whitememorialcc.org/family-camping				
Steep Rock Preserve	2 Tunnel Rd., Washington Depot, 41°37'17.4"N, 73°19'30.9"	3 tent sites; toilets	mid-April– mid-November	$35
860/868-9131; www.steeprockassoc.org/explore/camping				

Litchfield Hills

CONNECTICUT

METACOMET RIDGE

The Metacomet Range is the fault block ridge that winds its way up from Long Island Sound, through central Connecticut, and well into western Massachusetts alongside the Connecticut River. The steep and narrow ridge is home to miles of hiking trails that creep along traprock cliff faces then descend through bubbling stream corridors and vividly hued swamps. As the only high ground within miles of farmland and the sprawling metropolitan area of Hartford, the ridge is a popular destination for outdoor recreation. Its trails include the southern section of the 114-mi (183-km) Metacomet-Monadnock Trail, as well as several local and state parks that are the pride and joy of Connecticut.

▲ DOG ON THE BLUE TRAIL

▲ PATH NEAR CHAPMAN FALLS

◄ CLIFFSIDE VIEWS AT CHAUNCEY PEAK

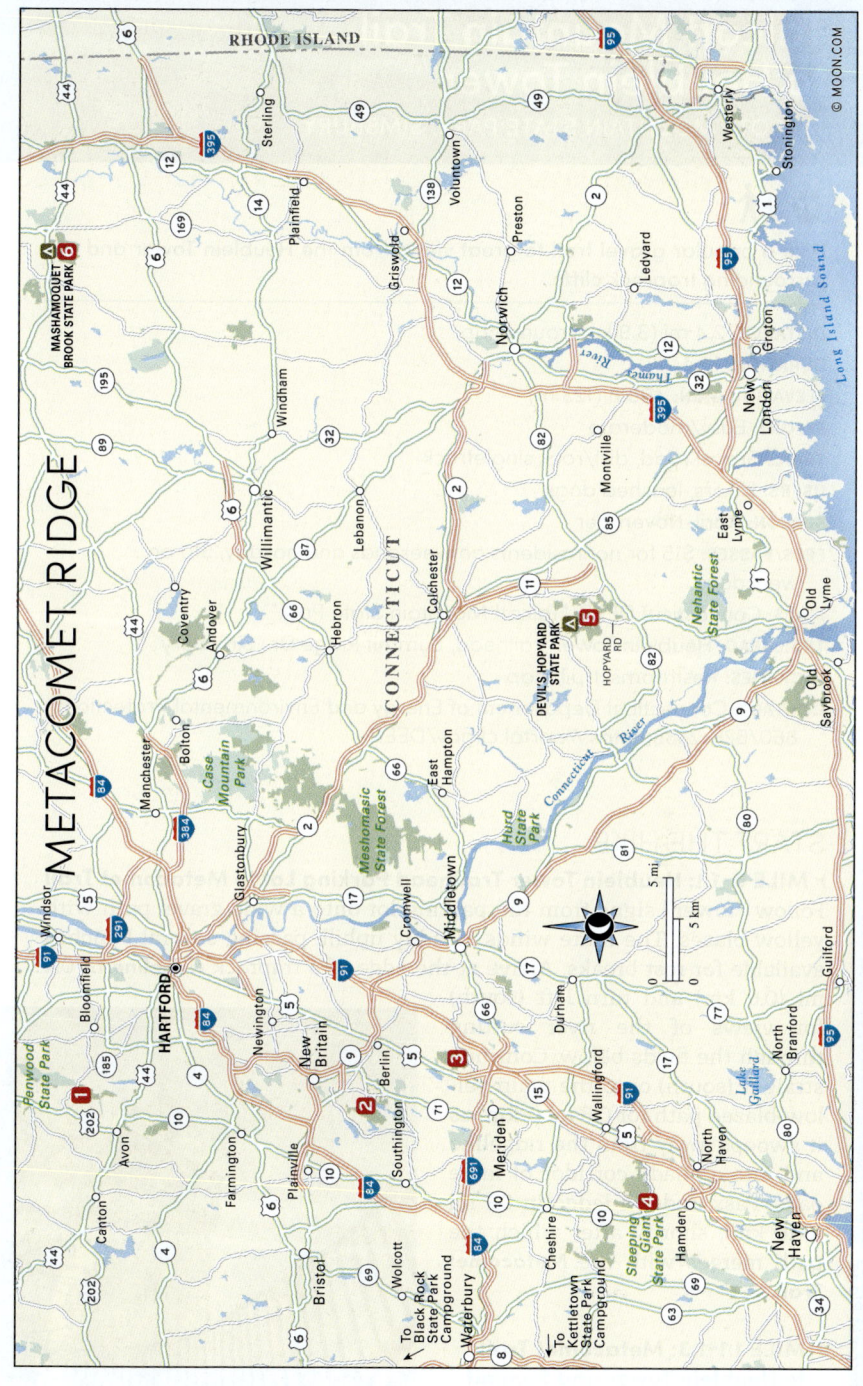

MASHAMOQUET BROOK STATE PARK

RHODE ISLAND

METACOMET RIDGE

CONNECTICUT

Sterling
Plainfield
Griswold
Voluntown
Preston
Ledyard
Norwich
Montville
Windham
Willimantic
Lebanon
Hebron
Colchester
Coventry
Andover
Bolton
Manchester
Glastonbury
HARTFORD
Windsor
Bloomfield
Newington
New Britain
Berlin
Southington
Plainville
Farmington
Canton
Avon
Bristol
Wolcott
Waterbury
Cheshire
Meriden
Wallingford
Hamden
North Haven
New Haven
North Branford
Guilford
Durham
Middletown
Cromwell
East Hampton
East Haddam
Groton
New London
East Lyme
Old Lyme
Old Saybrook
Westerly
Stonington

Case Mountain Park
Meshomasic State Forest
Hurd State Park
Penwood State Park
Nehantic State Forest
Sleeping Giant State Park

DEVIL'S HOPYARD STATE PARK

Connecticut River
Thames River

Long Island Sound

To Black Rock State Park Campground
To Kettletown State Park Campground

5 mi
5 km

© MOON.COM

CONNECTICUT

571

1 Talcott Mountain Trail to Heublein Tower

TALCOTT MOUNTAIN STATE PARK, SIMSBURY

Hike a popular gravel trail to great views from the Heublein Tower and the surrounding traprock cliffs.

DISTANCE: 2.4 mi (3.9 km) round-trip
DURATION: 1 hr
ELEVATION GAIN: 403 ft (123 m)
EFFORT: Easy/moderate
TRAIL: Gravel road, dirt/rock singletrack
USERS: Hikers, leashed dogs
SEASON: April–November
FEES/PASSES: $15 for nonresidents on weekends and holiday, $10 on weekdays
MAPS: Connecticut DEEP, "Talcott Mountain State Park"
TRAILHEAD: Heublein Tower trailhead, Summit Ridge Dr., Simsbury
FACILITIES: Restrooms, trail map
CONTACT: Connecticut Department of Energy and Environmental Protection; 860/526-2336; https://portal.ct.gov/DEEP

START THE HIKE

▶ **MILE 0-1.1: Heublein Tower Trailhead Parking Lot to Metacomet Trail**
Follow "tower" signs from the parking lot onto a wide gravel path with yellow blazes. The route winds steadily uphill, passing several benches available for rest breaks. Arrive at the edge of a traprock **ridgeline** in 0.4 mi (0.6 km) and turn left (south) for views of the river cutting through the fields below. Continue straight (south) onto the main yellow-blazed path for 0.6 mi (1 km) as it swoops away from the ridgeline and into a shady corridor of large oaks. Pass under a ledge in 0.1 mi (0.16 km), shortly after which the path merges with the **Metacomet Trail.**

▶ **MILE 1.1-1.3: Metacomet Trail to Heublein Tower and Summit**
Turn right (south) to follow the blue and yellow blazes. At the sign for

HEUBLEIN TOWER ▶

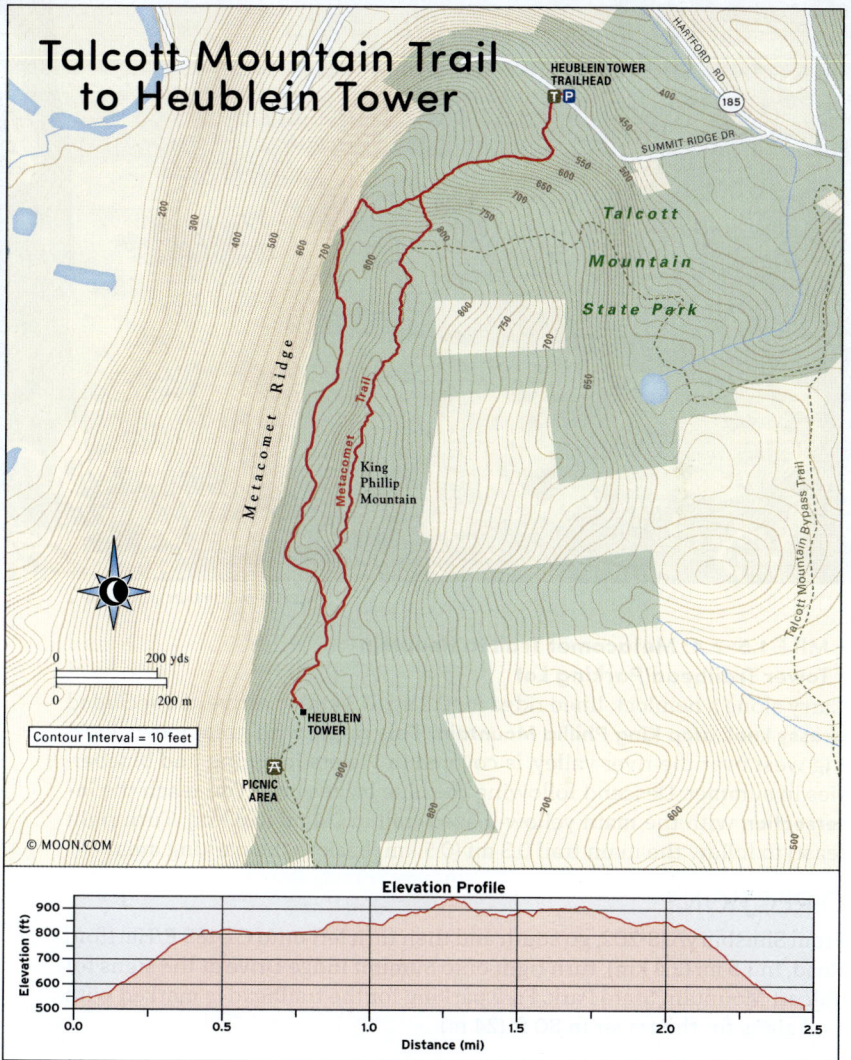

Talcott Mountain Trail to Heublein Tower

Elevation Profile

the tower in 0.1 mi (0.16 km), turn right (south) up the hill on the blue-and-yellow-blazed path. Follow a set of stone steps between the gate and the ledges, and reach the **Heublein Tower** and **picnic area** in 0.1 mi (0.16 km). This Bavarian-inspired former summer home of a food and drink magnate provides panoramic views of the Hartford skyline and the Farmington River. Due to the easy access and stunning scenery, the summit can be quite crowded during peak hours. Those in search of solitude can return via the Metacomet Trail.

▶ **MILE 1.3-1.5: Heublein Tower and Summit to Metacomet Trail**
Backtrack north for 0.2 mi (0.3 km) following the blue and yellow blazes to the intersection where the yellow trail and the Metacomet Trail split. Bear right (northeast) onto the Metacomet Trail.

▶ **MILE 1.5–2.4: Metacomet Trail to Heublein
Tower Trailhead Parking Lot**

Carry along a hemlock-lined ridge for 0.2 mi (0.3 km) to arrive at a secluded **grassy knoll atop King Phillip Mountain.** This ridge, with great views looking west over the river valley, is covered in violets in spring and blueberries in summer. Descend following the blue blazes until you reach the **intersection** with the main yellow-blazed trail in 0.4 mi (0.6 km). Turn right (east) to follow the main trail 0.3 mi (0.5 km) back to the parking area.

DIRECTIONS

From Simsbury/US-202, go south and then turn left onto CT-185 E/Hartford Road. In 1.5 mi (2.4 km), turn right onto Summit Ridge Drive at the signs for Talcott Mountain State Park. Free parking for the trailhead is marked with trail signs for the tower in 80 ft (24 m).

GPS COORDINATES: 41°50'17.8"N 72°47'26.4"W

BEST NEARBY BITES AND BREWS

Burgers, beer, and bourbon? What more could a famished and parched hiker ask for? Three miles (4.8 km) from the trailhead, stop in to the warm, brick-laced dining room of **Plan B Burger Bar** (4 Railroad St., Simsbury; 860/658-4477; https://burgersbeerbourbon.com; 11:30am–11pm daily) for a good sampling of craft drinks and unique burgers.

2 Ragged Mountain via the Preserve and Metacomet Trails

RAGGED MOUNTAIN PRESERVE, SOUTHINGTON

Although the climb to the summit of Ragged Mountain is relatively gentle, the views from its sheer traprock precipices overlooking the reservoirs and hills of central Connecticut are rewarding.

BEST: Vistas
DISTANCE: 5.3 mi (8.5 km) round-trip
DURATION: 2 hr
ELEVATION GAIN: 637 ft (194 m)
EFFORT: Easy
TRAIL: Dirt/gravel path
USERS: Hikers
SEASON: April-November
FEES/PASSES: Donations appreciated
MAPS: Connecticut Forest and Park Association, "Ragged Mountain Preserve"
TRAILHEAD: Preserve trailhead, West Ln., Berlin
FACILITIES: None
CONTACT: Ragged Mountain Foundation; http://raggedmtn.org

START THE HIKE

▶ **MILE 0-0.8: Preserve Trailhead to Blue and White Trail Junction**
Follow the blue and red blazes of the **Preserve Trail** west from the trailhead to a three-way intersection at 215 ft (66 m). Turn right (north) at the intersection, then turn left (west) in 0.2 mi (0.3 km) to stay on the Preserve Trail.

◀ RED-TAILED HAWK

The path is a wide, rolling double-track for 0.1 mi (0.16 km) until it jumps a creek on stepping-stones and ascends a steep, very rocky section for 0.1 mi (0.16 km). Just after this rocky section, the path skirts a grassy slope, gradually gaining elevation to the north. At 0.8 mi (1.3 km), the Preserve Trail reaches an intersection with the **Blue and White Trail.**

▶ **MILE 0.8-1.4: Blue and White Trail to Metacomet Trail**
Go straight (north) on the Blue and White Trail for the best views. At

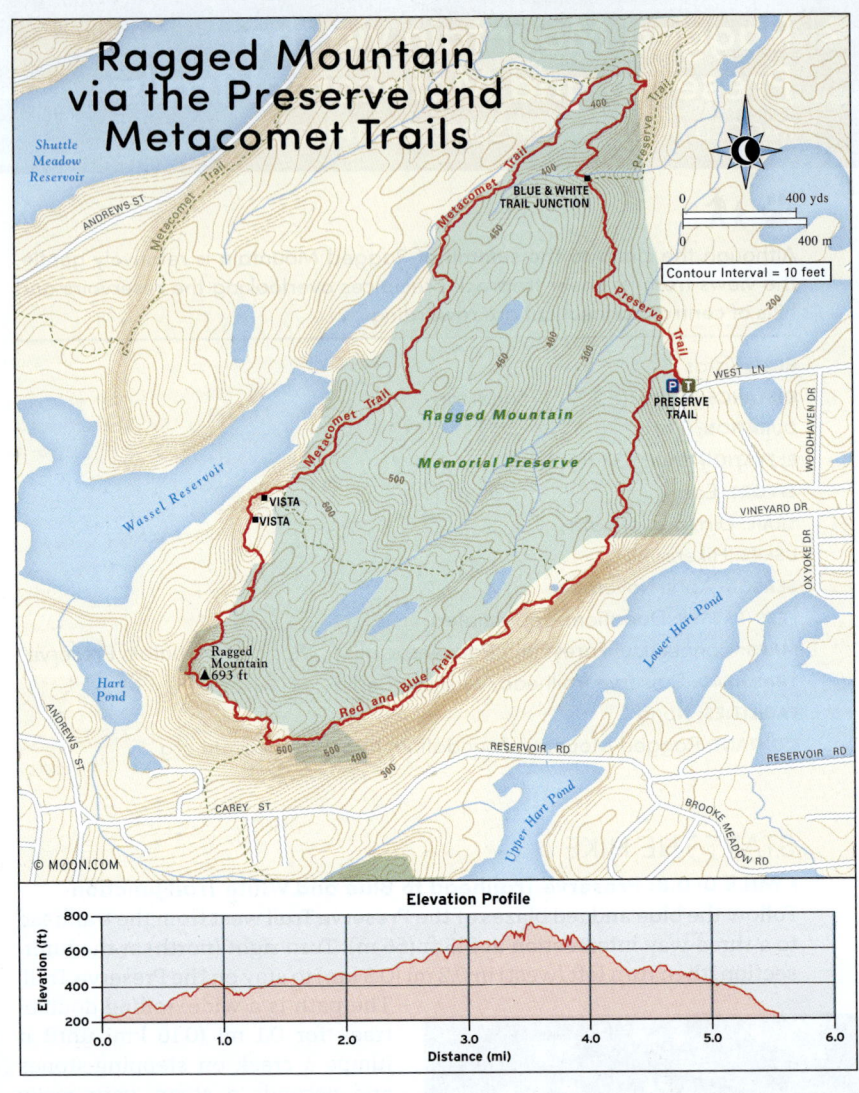

Ragged Mountain via the Preserve and Metacomet Trails

Shuttle Meadow Reservoir

ANDREWS ST

Metacomet Trail

BLUE & WHITE TRAIL JUNCTION

Preserve Trail

WEST LN

P T PRESERVE TRAIL

WOODHAVEN DR

Contour Interval = 10 feet

VINEYARD DR

OX YOKE DR

Ragged Mountain Memorial Preserve

Wassel Reservoir

VISTA
VISTA

Metacomet Trail

Lower Hart Pond

Hart Pond

Ragged Mountain 693 ft

Red and Blue Trail

RESERVOIR RD

RESERVOIR RD

ANDREWS ST

CAREY ST

Upper Hart Pond

BROOKE MEADOW RD

© MOON.COM

Elevation Profile

Elevation (ft) / Distance (mi)

1.2 mi (1.9 km), there is a nice **vista** to the right (east). Enjoy the views looking out on the wooded hillside from this grassy knoll, but be mindful of poison ivy. From the overlook, the trail drops quickly in and out of a deep rocky ravine for 0.1 mi (0.16 km) before it levels out and reaches a signed intersection at 1.4 mi (2.3 km). Take a left (south) onto the blue-blazed **Metacomet Trail**.

▶ **MILE 1.4–3.4: Metacomet Trail to Hartford Skyline Vista**

From here, the hike is mostly over a flat ridge top brimming with vernal pools. The trail passes some minor intersections, but keep following the blue blazes to stay on the Metacomet Trail. At 2.9 mi (4.7 km), reach a **west-facing vista** with nice views of the reservoirs below. At 3.4 mi (5.5 km),

arrive at another, even wider **vista** where you can spot the Hartford skyline to the north.

▶ **MILE 3.4-3.8: Hartford Skyline Vista to Ragged Mountain Summit**
From here, the trail snakes back into the woods, descends a ledge, and rolls over some rooty ups and downs. Arrive at the **summit** at 3.8 mi (6.1 km), with views facing primarily south toward Short Mountain.

▶ **MILE 3.8-5.3: Ragged Mountain Summit to Preserve Trailhead**
Descend via the **Red and Blue Trail,** which serves up views of the Hart Ponds to the east from various lookouts along the way. The traprock trail is rugged as it passes this vista, but it smooths out about 1 mi (1.6 km) from the summit. From here, the trail widens and continues north 0.5 mi (0.8 km) to the trailhead.

DIRECTIONS

From New Britain, turn left (south) onto Kensington Avenue, which becomes High Road. In 1.8 mi (2.9 km), turn right onto West Lane. The roadside parking area is marked with a sign on the right in about 0.8 mi (1.3 km).

GPS COORDINATES: 41°37'41.8"N 72°48'13.6"W

BEST NEARBY BITES

A sushi lover's dream, **Sweet Mango** (692 West St., Southington; 860/276-5888; www.sweet-mango.com; 11am-10pm Mon.-Thurs., 11am-11pm Fri.-Sat., noon-10pm Sun.) also serves Japanese and Thai entrées and hibachi in a festive setting with a full bar. It's 8 mi (12.9 km) from the trailhead.

Lamentation Mountain and Chauncey Peak via the Mattabesett Trail

GIUFFRIDA PARK, MERIDEN

This little gem of a park right outside the city of Meriden includes a quick climb to the ledges of Lamentation Mountain and Chauncey Peak, with placid views over Crescent Lake.

DISTANCE: 3.8 mi (6.1 km) round-trip
DURATION: 2 hr
ELEVATION GAIN: 598 ft (182 m)
EFFORT: Moderate
TRAIL: Dirt/rock singletrack, gravel road
USERS: Hikers, leashed dogs
SEASON: April–November
FEES/PASSES: None
MAPS: Meriden Land Trust, "Giuffrida Park"
TRAILHEAD: Mattabesett trailhead, Westfield Rd., Meriden
FACILITIES: Picnic tables, trail map
CONTACT: Meriden Land Trust; 203/630-4259; https://meridenlandtrust.org

START THE HIKE

▶ **MILE 0-1.2: Mattabesett Trailhead to Lamentation Mountain Summit**
Hike north from the parking lot, following the blue-blazed Mattabesett Trail with the wide, pine needle-lined shores of Crescent Lake to your right (east). In 0.3 mi (0.5 km), the Mattabesett Trail turns left (northwest) away from the water, crosses a paved street, and then turns right (northeast) onto a gravel access road in 160 ft (49 m). Follow the gravel road north along the power lines for about 100 ft (30 m), then continue right (north) on the Mattabesett Trail where it retreats into the woods. There is a quick, taxing uphill hike for 0.1 mi (0.16 km) to a lower ridge with intermittent views of Chauncey Peak through the trees. In 0.1 mi (0.16 km), reach an intersection and continue straight (north) following the blue blazes. Reach another intersection

LAMENTATION MOUNTAIN ▶

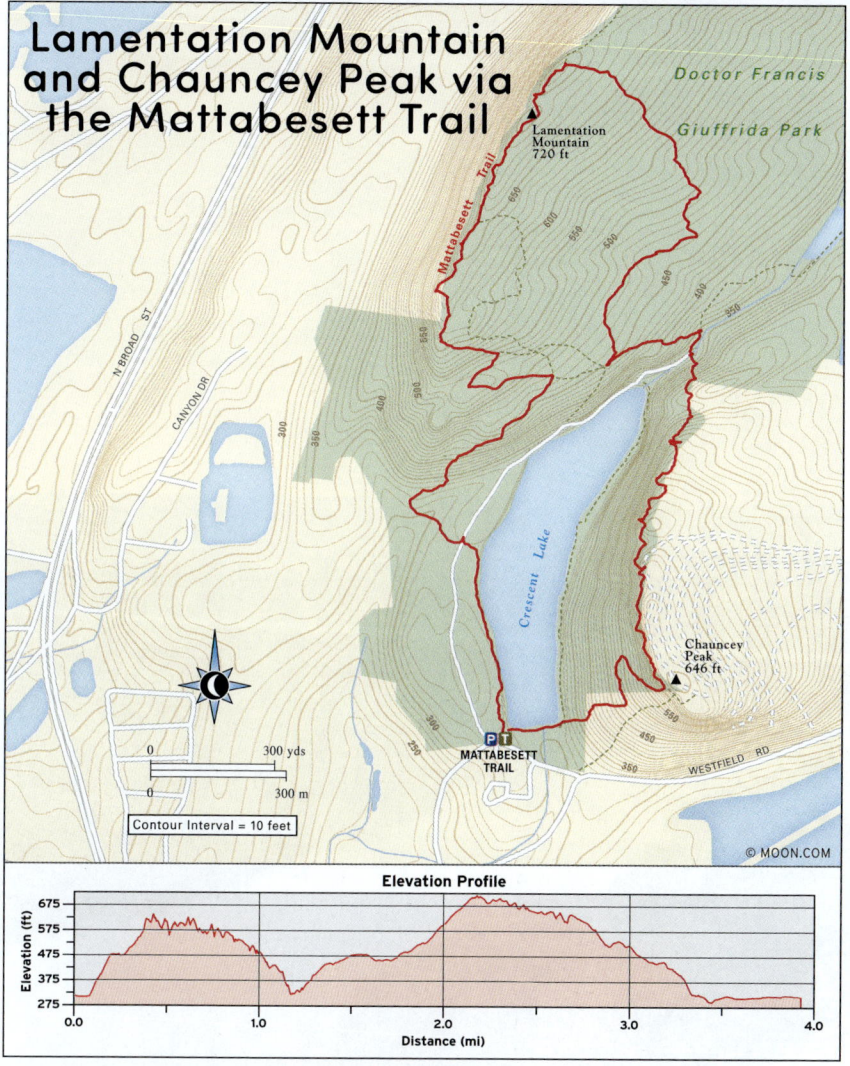

Lamentation Mountain and Chauncey Peak via the Mattabesett Trail

Doctor Francis

Giuffrida Park

Lamentation Mountain 720 ft

Mattabesett Trail

Crescent Lake

Chauncey Peak 646 ft

WESTFIELD RD

N BROAD ST

CANYON DR

P T MATTABESETT TRAIL

0 — 300 yds
0 — 300 m

Contour Interval = 10 feet

© MOON.COM

Elevation Profile

Elevation (ft)

Distance (mi)

in 0.4 mi (0.6 km) and turn left (west), following the blue blazes again. In 0.3 mi (0.5 km), the trail climbs to the summit of Lamentation Mountain.

▶ MILE 1.2–2.9: Lamentation Mountain Summit to Chauncey Peak

There are several west-facing vistas along this narrow, grassy, cliff-top path, from which you can spot the Hartford skyline as well as soaring turkey vultures. At the intersection with the yellow-blazed trail at 1.8 mi (2.9 km), turn right (east) to follow the yellow-blazed trail, which descends from the summit on a rocky path. At the intersection at 2.5 mi (4 km), turn left (northeast) onto the red-blazed trail, which descends east toward Crescent Lake. In 0.2 mi (0.3 km), it rejoins with the blue-blazed Mattabesett Trail. Turn right (south) to follow the blue blazes on the wide crushedstone path along the deep water-filled ravine to your left (east). Cross left

VIEW FROM CHAUNCEY PEAK ▲

(east) over the ravine on the small wooden bridge in 210 ft (64 m). The blue-blazed trail then ascends the north side of Chauncey Peak with some steep but short climbs. At 2.9 mi (4.7 km), reach the first of many vistas along the summit of Chauncey Peak.

▶ **MILE 2.9–3.8: Chauncey Peak to Mattabesett Trailhead**
These sheer traprock cliffs offer great views of Crescent Lake and Lamentation Mountain, and their west-facing orientation makes them great for watching a sunset. Continue straight (south) along the ridge. At the signed intersection at 3.4 mi (5.5 km), turn right (west) to descend the south side of the peak on the Mattabesett Trail. This 0.4-mi (0.6-km) return to the parking lot is a combination of steep staircases and loose traprock where copperhead snakes can linger, so descend with care!

DIRECTIONS

From Meriden, take I-691 E and then take Exit 8 for US-5. Turn right onto US-5 N, then turn right onto Westfield Road in 0.5 mi (0.8 km). At the intersection in 1 mi (1.6 km), turn left to stay on Westfield Road. A large sign on the left marks the entrance to the park in 0.4 mi (0.6 km).

GPS COORDINATES: 41°33'22.8"N 72°45'50.5"W

BEST NEARBY BITES

The Little Rendezvous (256 Pratt St., Meriden; 203/235-0110; https://thelittlevous.com; 1pm–8pm Wed.–Thurs., 11am–9pm Fri.–Sat., 1pm–8pm Sun.), a cash-only pizza joint, attracts big crowds on weekends for its straightforward but delectable coal-fired brick-oven pies. It's 2 mi (3.2 km) from the trailhead.

Climb across a long ridgeline resembling a giant in repose and enjoy stunning views from its summit tower and traprock cliffs.

BEST: Fall hikes

DISTANCE: 4.6 mi (7.4 km) round-trip

DURATION: 3 hr

ELEVATION GAIN: 1,215 ft (370 m)

EFFORT: Strenuous

TRAIL: Dirt/rock singletrack

USERS: Hikers, leashed dogs

SEASON: April-November

FEES/PASSES: $15 for nonresidents ($6 after 4 pm) on weekends and holidays, $10 on weekdays

MAPS: Connecticut DEEP, "Sleeping Giant State Park"

TRAILHEAD: Blue trailhead, Mount Carmel Ave., Hamden

FACILITIES: Picnic tables

CONTACT: Connecticut Department of Energy and Environmental Protection; 860/526-2336; https://portal.ct.gov/DEEP

START THE HIKE

▶ **MILE 0-0.1: Blue Trailhead to Mill River Intersection and Bridge**
Follow the paved road northwest from the parking area to the north end of the **picnic area** loop. From the top of the picnic area loop, follow the blue blazes downhill west for 0.1 mi (0.16 km) to the intersection at the Mill River.

▶ **MILE 0.1-0.6: Mill River Intersection and Bridge to Quinnipiac and New Haven Vista**
Turn right (north) over the small wooden bridge and continue straight (north) on the **Blue Trail.** Ascend the hill and reach the first of many vistas in 0.2 mi (0.3 km). Descend, merging with the Red Trail for about 100 ft (30 m), then turn right (east) up the hill, continuing to follow the blue blazes. The way becomes incredibly steep—almost sheer at times—and hikers may need to use their hands to scramble up for 0.3 mi (0.5 km). At the top of the scramble, there are great vistas looking back to the south and west, taking in Quinnipiac and New Haven.

▶ **MILE 0.6-1.3: Quinnipiac and New Haven Vista to Summit Castle**
The path descends for 0.2 mi (0.3 km), first crossing straight east over the Red Trail, then crossing straight southeast over the Tower Trail. Continue

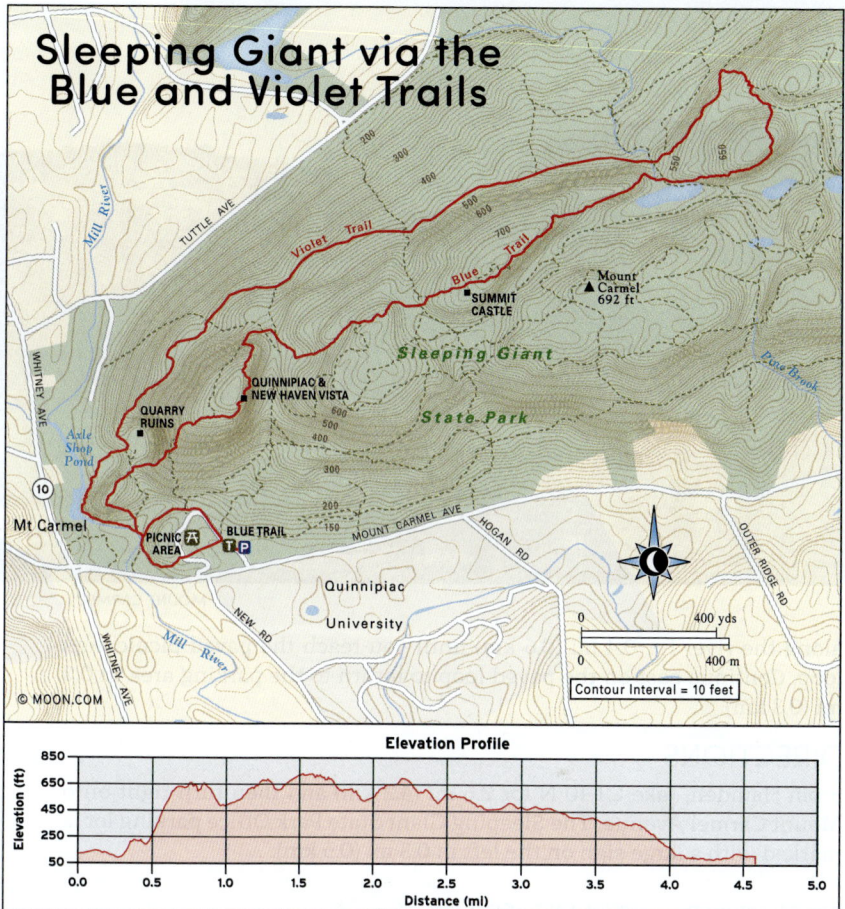

Sleeping Giant via the Blue and Violet Trails

Elevation Profile

straight (east) uphill on the Blue Trail, cross the Red Trail and the Tower Trail again in 0.3 mi (0.5 km), then hike 0.2 mi (0.3 km) more to reach the **stone summit castle,** which boosts hikers to incredible views of the valley below. Hikers can see miles of farmland rolling out in all directions below the mountain, as well as Long Island Sound meeting the horizon to the south. There are also restrooms at the summit tower.

▶ **MILE 1.3-2.2: Summit Castle to Violet Trail**
From the summit, continue northeast on the **Blue Trail** for 0.4 mi (0.6 km), then cross straight (east) over the Red Trail. At the next intersection in 0.4 mi (0.6 km), turn left (northwest) onto the **Blue/Violet Connector** trail. At the intersection in 0.1 mi (0.16 km), turn left (south) onto the violet-blazed **Violet Trail.**

▶ **MILE 2.2-4.6: Violet Trail to Blue Trailhead**
The Violet Trail bends around the north flank of the Giant, crossing over the Red Trail four times and passing an old **quarry** before it meets the edge of the **Mill River** in 1.8 mi (2.9 km). Follow the violet blazes southeast

MOUNT CARMEL ▲

along the river for 0.4 mi (0.6 km) until you reach the paved picnic area loop. Continue east on the paved loop to return to the parking area in 0.2 mi (0.3 km).

DIRECTIONS

From Hamden, take CT-10 N for 2.6 mi (4.2 km) and then turn right onto Mount Carmel Avenue. The Sleeping Giant State Park Office parking lot is marked with a large sign on the left in 0.3 mi (0.5 km).

GPS COORDINATES: 41°25'21.4"N 72°54'02.4"W

BEST NEARBY BREWS

Come for the varied small plates and excellent selection of craft beers, stay for the cozy-yet-classy atmosphere at **Mikro Depot** (0 Depot Ave., Hamden; 203/553-7676; www.mikrodepot.com; 4pm–9pm Tues.–Thurs., noon–10pm Fri.–Sat., 11:30am–8pm Sun.), a unique gastropub that also serves brunch. It's just 1 mi (1.6 km) from the trailhead.

CONNECTICUT

Metacomet Ridge

DEVIL'S HOPYARD STATE PARK, EAST HADDAM

✽ 🐾 🏞 🚶

Start your hike with an enormous cascade and wander along the banks of the Eight Mile River to an impressive vista.

BEST: Spring hikes, waterfalls

DISTANCE: 2.4 mi (3.9 km) round–trip

DURATION: 1.5 hr

ELEVATION GAIN: 506 ft (154 m)

EFFORT: Easy

TRAIL: Dirt path

USERS: Hikers, leashed dogs

SEASON: Year–round

FEES/PASSES: None

MAPS: Connecticut DEEP, "Devil's Hopyard State Park"

TRAILHEAD: Vista trailhead, Chapman Falls parking lot, Foxtown Rd., East Haddam

FACILITIES: Picnic tables; restrooms available near covered bridge

CONTACT: Connecticut Department of Energy and Environmental Protection; 860/526–2336; https://portal.ct.gov/DEEP

START THE HIKE

▶ **MILE 0–0.2: Vista Trailhead to Picnic Area and Covered Bridge**
From the parking area, cross Foxtown Road and head straight south toward **Chapman Falls.** The best viewing area for the majestic falls is about 425 ft (130 m) down the unblazed trail on the left (east). Use caution along the river at the end of the trail, as the rocks can be slick. Backtrack from

the viewing area to the main trail, which continues 0.2 mi (0.3 km) south into the picnic area, where you'll find a covered bridge over the river.

▶ **MILE 0.2–0.6: Picnic Area and Covered Bridge to Devil's Oven**
Cross left (east) over the **covered bridge** and continue straight east on the wide, flat dirt path through low-hanging vegetation. In 0.2 mi (0.3 km), the trail enters a clearing where the sights and sounds of the **Eight Mile River** pour through huge pine trees. The orange-blazed Vista

◀ CHAPMAN FALLS

Metacomet Ridge

CONNECTICUT

585

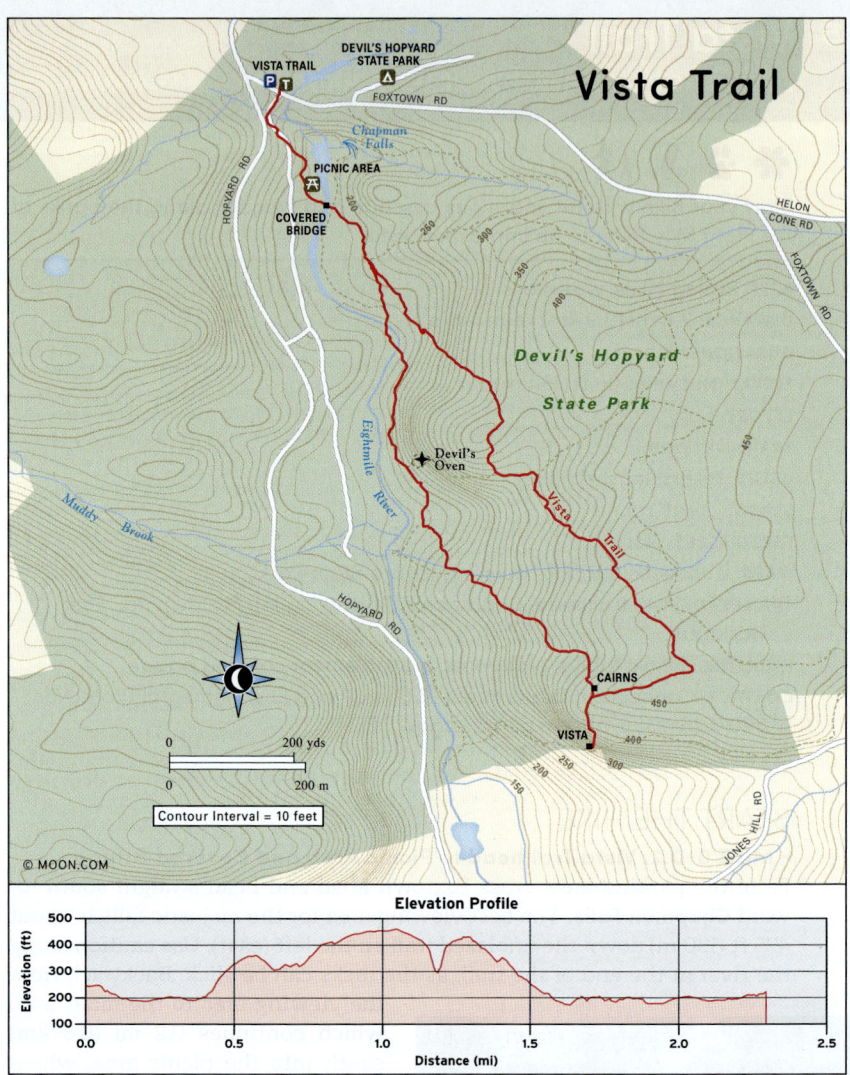

Vista Trail

Elevation Profile

Trail branches out to both the southeast and southwest. Bear right (southwest) to stay on the west side of the Vista Trail, keeping the river to your right (west). At 0.6 mi (1 km), reach an intersection with the side trail for **Devil's Oven.**

Optional: Turn left (east) for a taxing 400-ft (122-m) climb up to some interesting rock formations, including the Devil's Oven, a stove-shaped hole in the cliff. Backtrack to the intersection on the same path.

▶ **MILE 0.6–1.0: Devil's Oven to Vista Lookout Point**

From the Devil's Oven intersection, the orange-blazed Vista Trail continues straight (south) and then bends left (east) away from the river. After a couple of wildflower-dotted stream crossings on log bridges, the path begins to gain elevation. At 0.9 mi (1.4 km), arrive at a hilltop clearing where

hikers have built a vast collection of **cairns.** Continue straight (south) for 0.1 mi (0.16 km) to the vista, which looks south into the river valley and takes in the surrounding hills.

▶ **MILE 1.0–1.6: Vista Lookout Point to Vista Trail Intersection**
After enjoying the view, backtrack 0.1 mi (0.16 km) to the cairns. Here, turn right (east) onto the east side of the Vista Trail to continue the loop. Follow the orange blazes east, then north, on the fern-lined trail as it crosses back over the bubbling streams flowing toward the river. There are some nice ridge views looking over the river along the way. At the intersection at 1.6 mi (2.6 km), turn left (west) to stay on the east side of the Vista Trail.

▶ **MILE 1.6–2.4: Vista Trail Intersection to Chapman Falls and Vista Trailhead**
The path descends another 0.4 mi (0.6 km) before it reaches the intersection where the east and west sides of the Vista Trail meet. Continue straight north to backtrack the final 0.4 mi (0.6 km) to Chapman Falls and the parking area.

DIRECTIONS

From CT-82, turn onto CT-434 and continue north for 3.5 mi (5.6 km). Then, turn right onto Foxtown Road. A large Chapman Falls Park parking/picnic area marked with a sign for Chapman Falls is on the left in 135 ft (41 m).

GPS COORDINATES: 41°29'03.6"N 72°20'31.3"W

BEST NEARBY BITES

Stop in for coffee, breakfast, lunch, or ice cream at **Two Wrasslin' Cats** (374 Town St.; 860/891-8466; 7am-5pm daily), 7 mi (11.3 km) from the trailhead in East Haddam. The staff at this quirky cat-themed café will treat you like family.

Wolf Den and Indian Chair via the Blue Trail

MASHAMOQUET BROOK STATE PARK, POMFRET

Amble around a bubbling brook to several interesting rock formations, including a legendary wolf's den and a natural granite "chair."

BEST: New England oddities
DISTANCE: 4.4 mi (7.1 km) round-trip
DURATION: 2.5 hr
ELEVATION GAIN: 650 ft (198 m)
EFFORT: Easy/moderate
TRAIL: Dirt/rock singletrack
USERS: Hikers, leashed dogs, horseback riders
SEASON: April–November
FEES/PASSES: None
MAPS: Connecticut DEEP, "Mashamoquet State Park"
TRAILHEAD: Yellow trailhead, Mashamoquet Rd., Pomfret Center
FACILITIES: Restrooms, water, picnic tables
CONTACT: Connecticut Department of Energy and Environmental Protection; 860/526-2336; https://portal.ct.gov/DEEP

START THE HIKE

▶ **MILE 0-0.7: Yellow Trailhead to Meadow**

Cross the Mashamoquet Brook on the wooden **bridge** just to the west of the parking area and bear left (southwest) following signs for Hiking Trails. Follow the yellow blazes upslope and meet the **Blue Trail** in 0.2 mi (0.3 km). Turn right (south) onto the Blue Trail, which crosses a bridge over another brook in 0.1 mi (0.16 km). Wind through a green forest of deciduous trees and lush ferns for 0.4 mi (0.6 km) and arrive on the left (west) side of a **meadow** dotted with wildflowers—a great spot for bird-watching.

▶ **MILE 0.7-1.7: Meadow to Wolf Den**

From here, the trail cuts through a stand of mountain laurel. Arrive at a dirt road in 0.7 mi (1.1 km). Continue across and to the right (west)

WOLF DEN ▶

CONNECTICUT

Metacomet Ridge

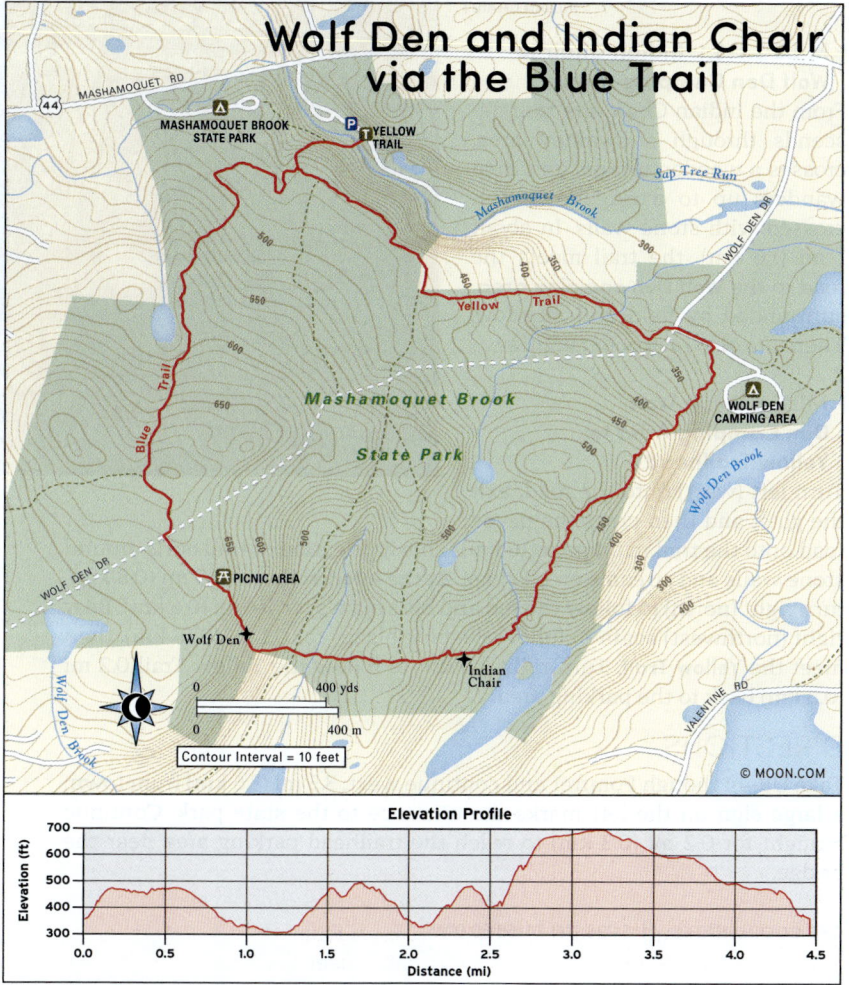

Wolf Den and Indian Chair via the Blue Trail

Elevation Profile

toward the Wolf Den Entrance sign. Follow the dirt road north through the parking and picnic area for 0.2 mi (0.3 km), after which the singletrack trail resumes. Bear right (south) toward signs for Wolf Den/Indian Chair and follow the red and blue blazes. The trail continues downhill on a series of stone steps and arrives at the Wolf Den—a narrow cave where Connecticut's last wolf lived and was killed—in 0.1 mi (0.16 km).

▶ MILE 1.7-2.1: Wolf Den to Indian Chair

From here, the trail descends in and out of ledges and then crosses a footbridge over a stream. At the intersection in 0.4 mi (0.6 km), continue straight (east) on the Blue Trail. Shortly after, the trail arrives at the **Indian Chair,** a bench-like granite structure overlooking the forest floor from atop a ledge. The boulder's perfect positioning is a coincidence caused by glacial movements, but it is a great spot to stop for a snack and enjoy the views.

▶ **MILE 2.1–3.1: Indian Chair to Wolf Den Camping Area**

From the Indian Chair, the trail descends through a swampy area, crosses a wooden **bridge,** and then wanders up to a ridgeline crisscrossed with stone walls. In about 1 mi (1.6 km), the trail meets the road to the **Wolf Den camping area,** surrounded by field and meadow. There are also restroom facilities.

▶ **MILE 3.1–4.4: Wolf Den Camping Area to Yellow Trailhead**

Turn left (west) onto the road, exit the gate, and then cross the paved road onto the trail in 0.1 mi (0.16 km). This flat section of trail curls around stone walls and streams on all sides. At the **intersection** in 0.5 mi (0.8 km), turn right (north) to follow the red and blue blazes for 0.4 mi (0.6 km). Bear right (northwest) again to follow the blue blazes for 0.1 mi (0.16 km), then meet the **Yellow Trail.** Turn right (north) to follow the Yellow Trail 0.2 mi (0.3 km) back to the parking area.

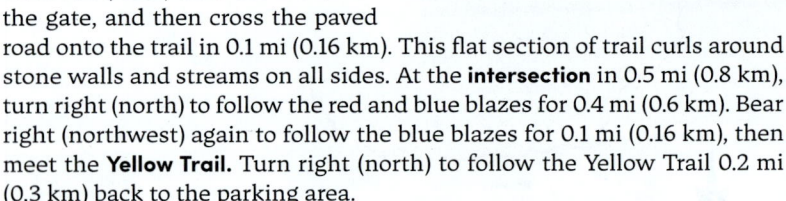

DIRECTIONS

Take US-44 though Pomfret and continue west; 3.5 mi (5.6 km) from town, a large sign on the left marks the entrance to the state park. Continue straight for 0.2 mi (0.3 km) to reach the trailhead parking area near the bridge.

GPS COORDINATES: 41°51'28.7"N 71°58'50.0"W

BEST NEARBY BITES

In addition to fresh comfort food made with local ingredients, the **Vanilla Bean Café** (450 Deerfield Rd., Pomfret; 860/928-1562; https://thevanillabeancafe.com; 8am-8pm Thurs.–Sun., 8am-3pm Mon.–Tues.) hosts live music events throughout the year. It's 4 mi (6.4 km) from the trailhead.

NEARBY CAMPGROUNDS

NAME	LOCATION	FACILITIES	SEASON	FEE
Devil's Hopyard State Park	366 Hopyard Rd., East Haddam, 41°29'24"N 72°20'24"W	21 RV/tent sites; restrooms, no water	early April–early October	$14–24
860/526-2336; https://portal.ct.gov				
Black Rock State Park	2065 Thomaston Rd., Watertown, 41°39'0"N 73°5'24"W	78 RV/tent sites, 4 cabins; restrooms	early May–early October	$17–60
860/283-8088; https://portal.ct.gov				
Kettletown State Park	1400 Georges Hill Rd., Southbury, 41°25'12"N 73°11'59"W	61 RV/tent sites, 6 cabins; restrooms	late May–early October	$17–60
203/264-5678; https://portal.ct.gov				
Mashamoquet Brook State Park	320 Mashamoquet Rd., Pomfret Center, 41°52'12"N 71°58'48"W	53 RV/tent sites; restrooms	early April–early October	$14–24
860/928-6121; https://portal.ct.gov				

RHODE ISLAND

RHODE ISLAND

From offshore Block Island to the Narragansett Bay, Rhode Island's vast sandy beaches, imposing clay cliffs, and swaying grasses are a dream for boaters, birders, and hikers. Inland, the state's kettle ponds, erratic rocks, and vibrant plant life are just as alluring. The hikes here are not particularly steep or challenging, but the scenery along these trails is key to understanding the diversity of New England's southeastern landscape, which can fluctuate from gentle and subdued to jagged and dramatic with the turn of a corner. Nowhere is this more true than tiny, watery Rhode Island, which is guaranteed to enchant in spite of its size.

▲ SIGNS AT NORMAN BIRD SANCTUARY

▲ POND ON THE GRASSY POINT TRAIL

◄ PINK LADY'S SLIPPERS AT PULASKI WILDLIFE MARSH

RHODE ISLAND

Douglas State Forest
Buck Hill Management Area
George Washington Management Area

Woonsocket

Burrillville

1 GEORGE WASHINGTON STATE CAMPGROUND

Glocester

Smithfield

Foster

Johnston

PROVIDENCE

East Providence

Rehoboth

Attleboro

Pawtucket

Scituate

Scituate Reservoir

Cranston

Warwick

Barrington

Warren

Bristol

Fall River

Sterling

Coventry

West Warwick

2

3

West Greenwich

4

Big River Management Area

East Greenwich

Narragansett Bay

Prudence Island

Portsmouth

Voluntown

Exeter

North Kingstown

Middletown

Aquidneck Island

Richmond

5

6

Great Swamp Management Area

South Kingstown

Narragansett

Jamestown

Conanicut Island

Newport

9 SECOND BEACH FAMILY CAMPGROUND

10

Hopkinton

Westerly

BURLINGAME STATE CAMPGROUND

7

CHARLESTOWN BREACHWAY

EAST BEACH

Charlestown

FISHERMEN'S MEMORIAL STATE CAMPGROUND

Point Judith

Rhode Island Sound

Block Island Sound

8 Block Island

New Shoraham

0   5 mi
0   5 km

© MOON.COM

MASSACHUSETTS
RHODE ISLAND
CONNECTICUT

Walkabout Trail

GEORGE WASHINGTON MANAGEMENT AREA, CHEPACHET

Built by a group of Australian sailors in 1965, the Walkabout Trail is a secluded loop through woods and around sparkling lakes.

BEST: New England oddities

DISTANCE: 7.8 mi (12.6 km) round-trip

DURATION: 3.75 hr

ELEVATION GAIN: 375 ft (114 m)

EFFORT: Easy/moderate

TRAIL: Dirt/rock path

USERS: Hikers, leashed dogs, horseback riders

SEASON: Year-round

FEES/PASSES: $2 per vehicle daily visitors pass

MAPS: Rhode Island Division of Parks and Recreation, "George Washington/ Pulaski Wildlife Management Area"

TRAILHEAD: Bowdish Reservoir Beach, George Washington State Park Trail, Chepachet

FACILITIES: Restrooms, water

CONTACT: Rhode Island Division of Parks and Recreation; 401/568-2085; https://riparks.ri.gov

START THE HIKE

▶ **MILE 0-3.3: Bowdish Reservoir Beach to Pulaski Management Area**
Start at the Bowdish Reservoir beach and hike north, following the trail with orange, red, and blue blazes into the woods. The muddy path traces the edge of the lake, highlighting unspoiled waterfront and enormous granite boulders. The trail bends east toward **Wilbur Pond** in 0.4 mi (0.6 km). Cross the road and continue straight east in 0.3 mi (0.5 km). The blue trail branches off to the east at 0.8 mi (1.3 km). Turn left (north) to follow the orange and red blazes around Wilbur Pond. At the next intersection at 2 mi (3.2 km), turn left (west) to follow only the orange blazes. The trail crosses straight across several dirt roads and through a hemlock grove. At the intersection at 3.3 mi (5.3 km), follow the orange blazes straight

PULASKI WILDLIFE MARSH ▶

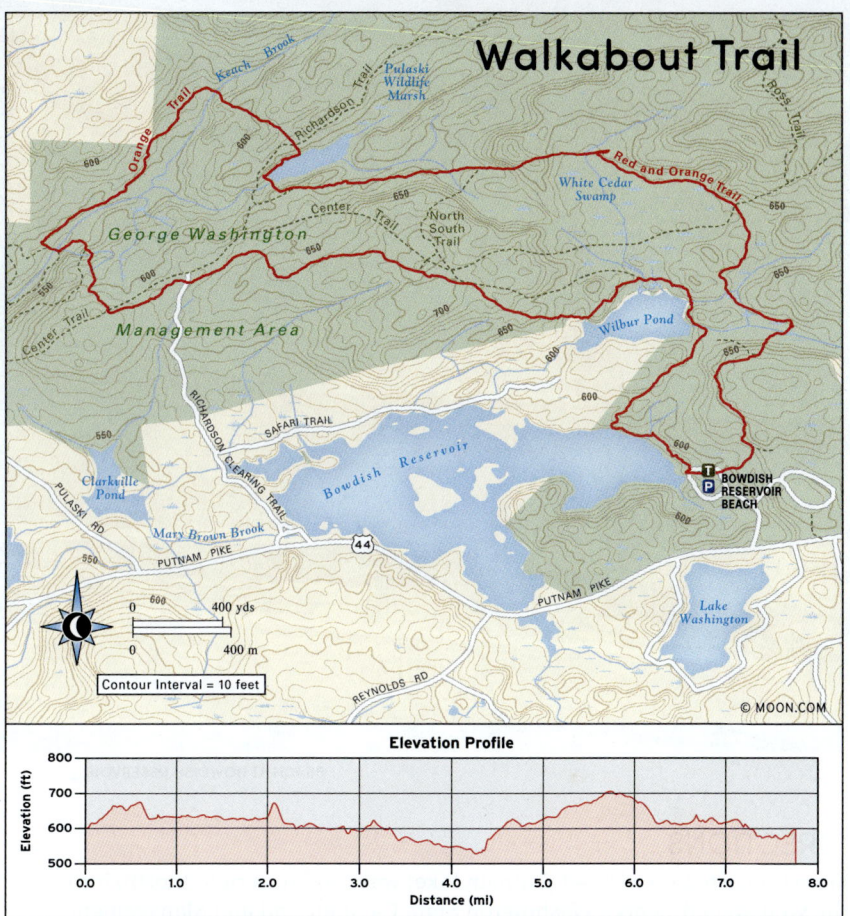

Walkabout Trail

Elevation Profile

(north) downhill. Cross a long wooden footbridge and enter **Pulaski Management Area.**

▶ **MILE 3.3-4.5: Pulaski Management Area to Pulaski Wildlife Marsh**
Just after the sign, turn right (northeast) and continue to follow the orange blazes through a wetland area along a stream. At 4.5 mi (7.2 km), the trail crosses another dirt road and arrives at the **Pulaski Wildlife Marsh.**

▶ **MILE 4.5-7.8: Pulaski Wildlife Marsh to Bowdish Reservoir Beach**
Continue south along the edge of the marsh. At the southwest edge of the marsh, turn left (east) and follow signs for the **North South Trail** across the levee bridges and into the woods. Turn left again to stay on the orange-blazed North South Trail heading north. The trail winds through a swamp, merging with the red trail at 5.1 mi (8.2 km). Follow the orange and red blazes east through a muddy cedar swamp with plenty of interesting log bridges to help your footing. The path joins the blue trail in 1.5 mi (2.4 km). Keep straight, following the red, orange, and blue blazes south for 1.2 mi (1.9 km) back to the beach.

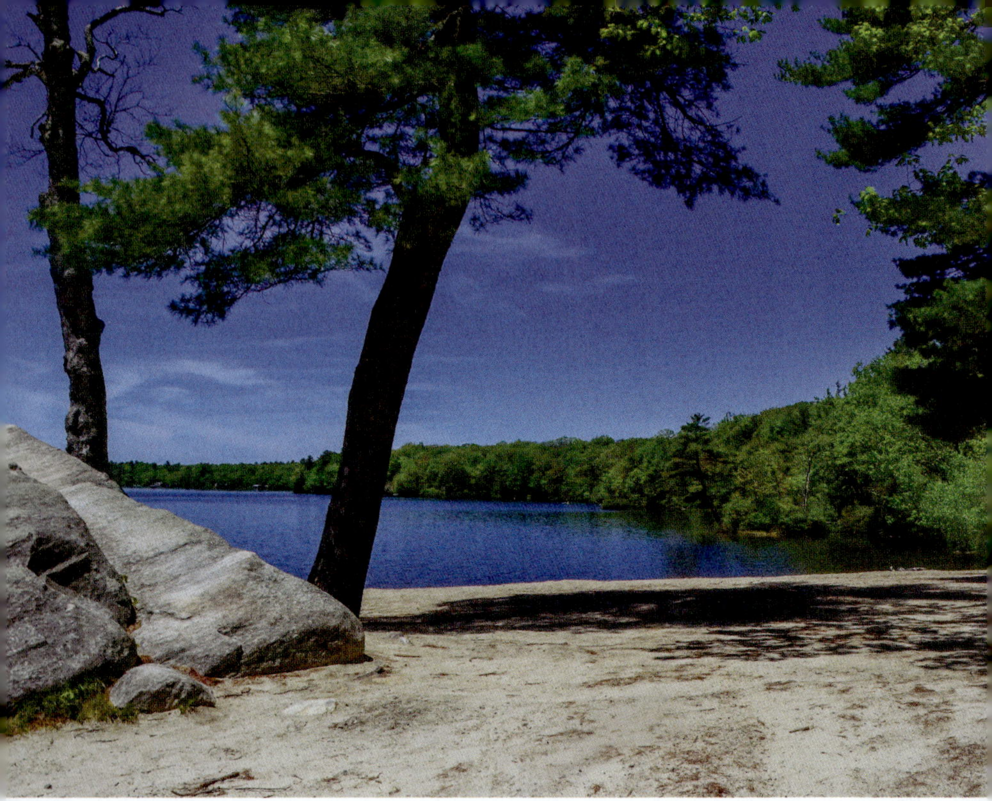

BEACH AT BOWDISH RESERVOIR ▲

DIRECTIONS

From Glocester, take US-44 (Putnam Pike) west and turn right (north) into the well-signed George Washington State Campground and Management Area. After checking in at the gate, continue north to the parking area/restrooms near the Bowdish Reservoir beach.

GPS COORDINATES: 41°55'11.4"N 71°45'17.9"W

With stone walls, historical sites, and enormous glacial erratic rocks, this hike in and around a bubbling brook is a pleasant setting for birding and wildlife viewing.

DISTANCE: 6 mi (9.7 km) round–trip

DURATION: 4 hr

ELEVATION GAIN: 611 ft (186 m)

EFFORT: Easy

TRAIL: Dirt path, boardwalk

USERS: Hikers only

SEASON: Year–round

FEES/PASSES: None

MAPS: Audubon Society of Rhode Island, "George B. Parker Woodland Wildlife Refuge"

TRAILHEAD: Parker Woodland Wildlife Refuge parking lot 1, Maple Valley Rd., Coventry

FACILITIES: Trail map in parking lot

CONTACT: Audubon Society of Rhode Island; 401/295–8283; https://asri.org

Hikers can enjoy the warbles and twitters of birds in the greenery while traversing long boardwalks through wetlands, exploring gigantic boulders along a brook, or seeking out deer on the edge of a pastoral meadow.

START THE HIKE

▶ **MILE 0-0.5: Parker Woodland Wildlife Refuge Parking Lot to Coventry Loop**

The trail heads north out of the parking lot. Take a left (west) toward the meadow at the sign and follow the path through a grassy field, a great spot for wildlife viewing when quiet. Continue along the orange-blazed trail as it enters the woods and reaches an intersection at 0.2 mi (0.3 km). Stay straight (north) on the orange trail, which bounds over a series of long boardwalks and bog bridges. Reach the intersection with the blue-blazed Coventry Loop in 0.3 mi (0.5 km).

▶ **MILE 0.5-0.8: Coventry Loop to Foster Loop**

Turn left (west) onto the Coventry Loop to complete the circuit clockwise. The path winds along stone walls, through a beech and oak forest, and passes the historic **Vaughn Farm site.** After descending past several overhanging ledges, the rolling trail arrives at a massive boulder at 0.8 mi (1.3 km), where a sign marks the yellow-blazed connector trail leading toward the **Foster Loop.**

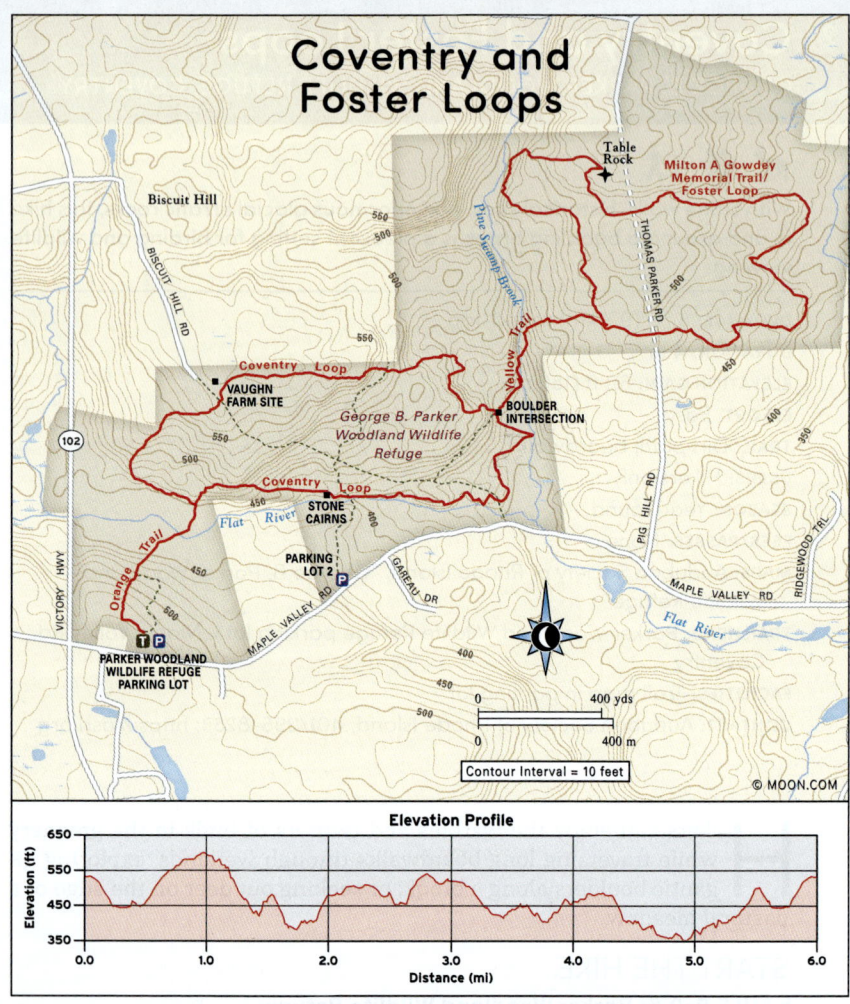

Coventry and Foster Loops

Biscuit Hill

Table Rock

Milton A Gowdey Memorial Trail/ Foster Loop

THOMAS PARKER RD

Pine Swamp Brook

Yellow Trail

Coventry Loop

VAUGHN FARM SITE

George B. Parker Woodland Wildlife Refuge

BOULDER INTERSECTION

Coventry Loop

STONE CAIRNS

Flat River

PARKING LOT 2

PIG HILL RD

RIDGEWOOD TRL

MAPLE VALLEY RD

Flat River

Orange Trail

VICTORY HWY

MAPLE VALLEY RD

GAREAU DR

PARKER WOODLAND WILDLIFE REFUGE PARKING LOT

0   400 yds
0   400 m

Contour Interval = 10 feet

© MOON.COM

Elevation Profile

Elevation (ft) / Distance (mi)

▶ **MILE 0.8–1.6: Foster Loop to Milton A. Gowdey Memorial Trail**

Turn left (northeast) and follow the yellow blazes, which trek through a boulder field and along the stream. The yellow connector trail reaches the **Milton A. Gowdey Memorial Trail/Foster Loop** (marked with blue blazes) at 1.6 mi (2.6 km).

▶ **MILE 1.6–4.2: Milton A. Gowdey Memorial Trail to Coventry Loop**

Turn left (north) onto this blue-blazed loop, which rolls through an enormous field of blueberries, descends in and out of a brook valley, and passes the flat granite slab known as **Table Rock**. The trail crosses a dirt road and goes through a gate in 2 mi (3.2 km); it returns to the junction with the connector trail 0.2 mi (0.3 km) later. Take a left (west) and follow the yellow-blazed trail 0.4 mi (0.6 km) back to the intersection with the large boulder.

▲ A BOG BRIDGE ON THE TRAIL

▶ **MILE 4.2–6.0: Coventry Loop to Parker
  Woodland Wildlife Refuge Parking Lot**

Turn left (south) around the boulder to join with the other end of the blue-blazed Coventry Loop. This section of trail travels along the brook banks for about 1 mi (1.6 km) before reaching an intersection with the path toward parking lot 2. Stay straight on the blue-blazed trail toward parking lot 1, which passes a collection of more than 100 historic **stone cairns.** Reach the intersection with the orange trail in another 0.3 mi (0.5 km), and turn left (south) onto the orange trail back toward the lot.

DIRECTIONS

From West Greenwich, head north on RI-102 (Victory Highway) for 6.5 mi (10.5 km), then turn right onto Maple Valley Road. The well-marked gated parking area is 0.1 mi (0.16 km) down the road on the left.

GPS COORDINATES: 41°43'00.1"N 71°41'53.0"W

3

Pond, Coney Brook, and Flintlock Loops

TILLINGHAST POND MANAGEMENT AREA, WEST GREENWICH

Enjoy views of a pristine pond surrounded by field and forest on the trails of the Nature Conservancy's largest preserve.

BEST: Winter hikes
DISTANCE: 5.4 mi (8.7 km) round-trip
DURATION: 2.75 hr
ELEVATION GAIN: 204 ft (62 m)
EFFORT: Easy
TRAIL: Dirt path
USERS: Hikers, paddlers
SEASON: Year-round
FEES/PASSES: None
MAPS: The Nature Conservancy, "Tillinghast Pond Management Area"
TRAILHEAD: Pond Loop trailhead, Plain Rd., West Greenwich
FACILITIES: Trail map, vault toilet
CONTACT: The Nature Conservancy; 401/331-7110; www.nature.org

START THE HIKE

▶ **MILE 0-1.9: Pond Loop Trailhead to Cascades**

Walk to the **Pond Loop** trailhead at the north corner of the parking lot and hike north, following the white blazes. Turn left (west) onto the orange-blazed **Coney Brook Loop** at 0.1 mi (0.16 km). The trail crosses straight west over **Plain Road,** then becomes narrow as it winds through a stand of pines.

Bear left (west) to stay on the orange-blazed Coney Brook Loop at 0.1 mi (0.16 km). The trail opens into a field of blueberries with views of the hills to the west, then turns into the woods after 0.3 mi (0.5 km). Hike along the slopes of a fern-covered mixed forest, then arrive at a frog-filled bog in 0.4 mi (0.6 km). Turn right (north) to stay on the Coney Brook Loop, which reaches Coney Brook at 1.7 mi (2.7 km). Follow the brook and hike east upstream along the gorge, descend the wooden staircase, and cross the bridge to

BENCH ON THE CONEY BROOK LOOP ▶

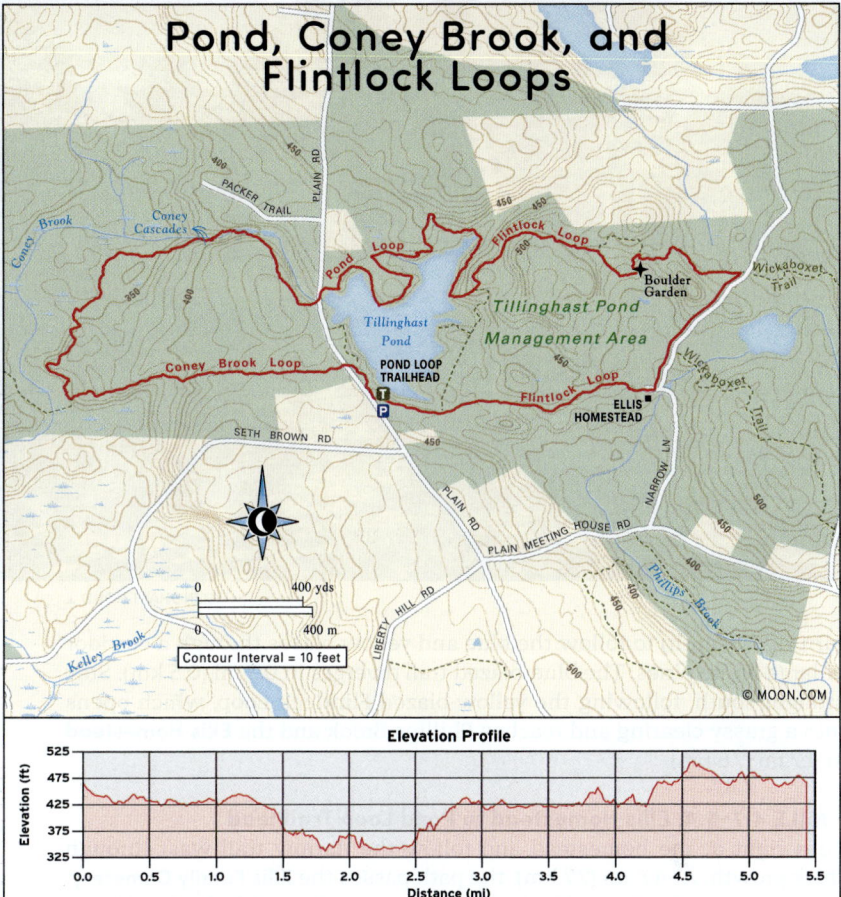

Pond, Coney Brook, and Flintlock Loops

Elevation Profile

reach a small series of **cascades.** At the dam, the trail turns right (south) around a pond. The trail may be slightly flooded here. Arrive at an open field of daisies and black-eyed Susans in 0.2 mi (0.3 km).

▶ **MILE 1.9–3.4: Cascades to Flintlock Loop**
Continue south along the edge of the field and reach the road in 0.2 mi (0.3 km). Turn left (north) onto the road and find the white-blazed **Pond Loop** where it enters the forest to the right (east). The Pond Loop trail alternates between fields of hay and the pine-forested shoreline as it traces Tillinghast's northern shore. Turn left (north) onto the yellow-blazed **Flintlock Loop** in 1.2 mi (1.9 km).

▶ **MILE 3.4–4.7: Flintlock Loop to Ellis Homestead**
The narrow path climbs slightly uphill to a fork in 0.4 mi (0.6 km). Turn right at the fork to follow the south spur to the **Boulder Garden,** where large rocks seem to sprout from tufts of grass. At 0.2 mi (0.3 km) east of the Boulder Garden, turn right (east) to return to the main Flintlock Loop. At the unsigned intersection with the Wickaboxet Trail at 4.3 mi (6.9 km),

TILLINGHAST POND ▲

turn right (south) to follow the blue and yellow blazes through a corridor of large white pines. The blue-blazed trail diverges in 0.3 mi (0.5 km). Stay straight south, following the yellow-blazed Flintlock Loop, which opens into a grassy clearing and reaches Phillips Brook and the **Ellis Homestead** at 4.7 mi (7.6 km).

▶ MILE 4.7-5.4: Ellis Homestead to Pond Loop Trailhead
Turn right at the homestead and follow the narrow trail west through thick growth. At 4.8 mi (7.7 km), the path passes the **Ellis Family Cemetery.** Continue west for 0.4 mi (0.6 km) to the intersection with the **Pond Loop.** Hike straight west, following the white blazes between the pond and a stone wall for 0.2 mi (0.3 km) back to the parking area.

DIRECTIONS
From West Greenwich on RI-102, turn left onto Plain Meetinghouse Road. At the four-way intersection, turn right onto Plain Road and continue for 0.5 mi (0.8 km). The large Tillinghast Pond Management Area parking lot on the right is marked with a Nature Conservancy sign and trailhead kiosk.

GPS COORDINATES: 41°38'47.2"N 71°45'28.7"W

4

North South Trail to Stepstone Falls

ARCADIA MANAGEMENT AREA, EXETER

This hidden gem in the Arcadia Management Area features a waterfall and a pleasant walk along the banks of the Falls River, where a variety of rare wildflowers grow.

BEST: Spring hikes, waterfalls, brew hikes
DISTANCE: 5.2 mi (8.4 km) round-trip
DURATION: 3.75 hr
ELEVATION GAIN: 312 ft (95 m)
EFFORT: Easy
TRAIL: Dirt path
USERS: Hikers, leashed dogs (horseback riders, mountain bikers permitted on some sections)
SEASON: Year-round
FEES/PASSES: None
MAPS: None
TRAILHEAD: North South trailhead, Barber Rd., Exeter
FACILITIES: None
CONTACT: Rhode Island Division of Parks and Recreation; 401/539-2356

Rhode Island's North South Trail stretches 78 mi (126 km) across the state, and this segment through the Arcadia Management Area is one of the most scenic and unspoiled sections, traveling on secluded footpaths through the heart of the park. It's a gentle trail, but rare plant life, a rushing river, and a series of uniquely shaped falls make this hike feel truly wild.

START THE HIKE

▶ **MILE 0-1.2: North South Trailhead to Plain Road**

Heading northwest from the trailhead, follow the blue-blazed North South Trail from where it splits from Barber Road. From the marshy meadow off Barber Road, the narrow trail bends into a secluded pine grove on a flat, winding track. Boardwalks assist hikers through muddy portions, and blueberries are prevalent along the trailside. Pass the Escoheag Trail, keeping right to stay on the well-marked North South Trail. Arrive at **Plain Road** at 1.2 mi (1.9 km).

▶ **MILE 1.2-2.4: Plain Road to Wooden Bridge**

Cross the road, then take a left (north) just before the bridge. Here, the North South Trail merges with the yellow-blazed **Ben Utter Trail** and heads north upstream along the river. (The following length of trail, approximately 1 mi/1.6 km, is truly spectacular, with crafted footbridges, rushing

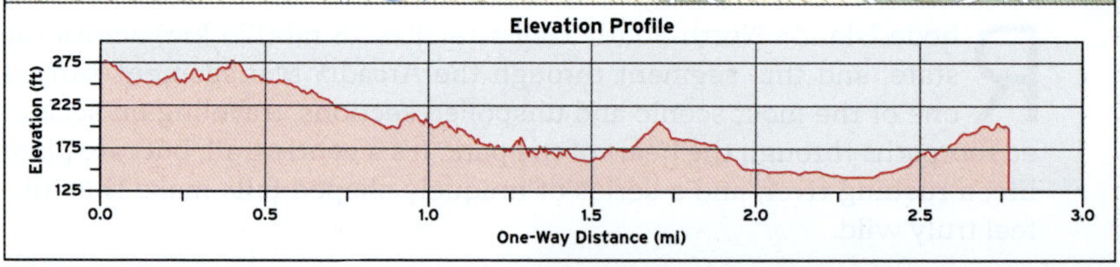

North South Trail to Stepstone Falls

Elevation Profile

(Map showing North South Trail to Stepstone Falls through Arcadia Management Area, with features including Wooden Bridge, Stepstone Falls, Ben Utter Trail, Wood River, Kelley Brook, North South Trail, Mount Tom 429 ft, and various roads. Contour Interval = 10 feet. Scale: 500 yds / 500 m. © MOON.COM)

water, and blossoms of rare wild-flowers, such as pink lady's slippers and azaleas along the riverbanks.)

At 0.5 mi (0.8 km) from the start of the Ben Utter Trail, reach a dirt road and turn right (east) to stay on the blue-blazed trail. At the fork in 0.6 mi (1 km), bear right (east) again to stay on the **North South Trail.** The trail becomes rocky as the river widens through swampland. Arrive at a wooden bridge across the river at 2.4 mi (3.9 km).

WILD PINK AZALEA ▶

▲ BRIDGE ALONG THE FALLS RIVER

▶ **MILE 2.4–2.6: Wooden Bridge to Stepstone Falls**

Turn right (east) onto the bridge, then turn immediately left (north) to follow the river upstream. In 0.2 mi (0.3 km), reach **Stepstone Falls,** a cascade over a series of square-shaped boulders. Backtrack from the falls for a 5.2-mi (8.4-km) round-trip.

DIRECTIONS

From RI-3 or I-95, take RI-165 W (Ten Rod Road). Turn right into the Midway parking area and continue north on the dirt road, following the blue blazes of the North South Trail. In 0.5 mi (0.8 km), turn left over the bridge onto Barber Road and follow it for 0.9 mi (1.4 km). Park at the turnoff where the North South Trail splits into the woods on the right.

GPS COORDINATES: 41°35'07.9"N 71°44'02.5"W

5

Long and Ell Pond Trail

ROCKVILLE MANAGEMENT AREA, HOPKINTON

The trail to Long Pond is like a natural playground—there are boulders to scramble over, stairs to climb, bridges to cross, and some of the most spectacular inland views in Rhode Island.

BEST: Vistas
DISTANCE: 4.4 mi (7.1 km) round-trip
DURATION: 2.5 hr
ELEVATION GAIN: 405 ft (123 m)
EFFORT: Easy/moderate
TRAIL: Dirt/rock path
USERS: Hikers, leashed dogs
SEASON: April–November
FEES/PASSES: None
MAPS: Audubon Society of Rhode Island, "Long Pond Woods"
TRAILHEAD: Long and Ell Pond trailhead, Stubtown Rd., Hope Valley
FACILITIES: None
CONTACT: Audubon Society of Rhode Island; 401/949-5454; https://asri.org

Movie buffs might recognize sections of the Narragansett Trail to Long Pond from the 2012 Wes Anderson film *Moonrise Kingdom*. It's no wonder Anderson chose this scenic trail as his set—its large granite boulders make for fun scrambles and picture-perfect vistas. This route begins on the south side of the Rockville Management Area before wrapping around Asheville Pond and climbing steadily to the overlook above Long Pond.

START THE HIKE

▶ **MILE 0-1.5: Long and Ell Pond Trailhead to Green Valley**

Hike north from the trailhead toward **Asheville Pond.** The dirt trail winds along the west edge of the pond and continues north for 0.5 mi (0.8 km). Here the trail bends sharply right (east), then wraps to the west, and then switchbacks east again through a tunnel of giant laurel bushes.

Pass the **Canonchet Road parking area** at 1.2 mi (1.9 km) and turn left (west). The trail gains elevation

WOODEN BRIDGE OVER WETLANDS ▶

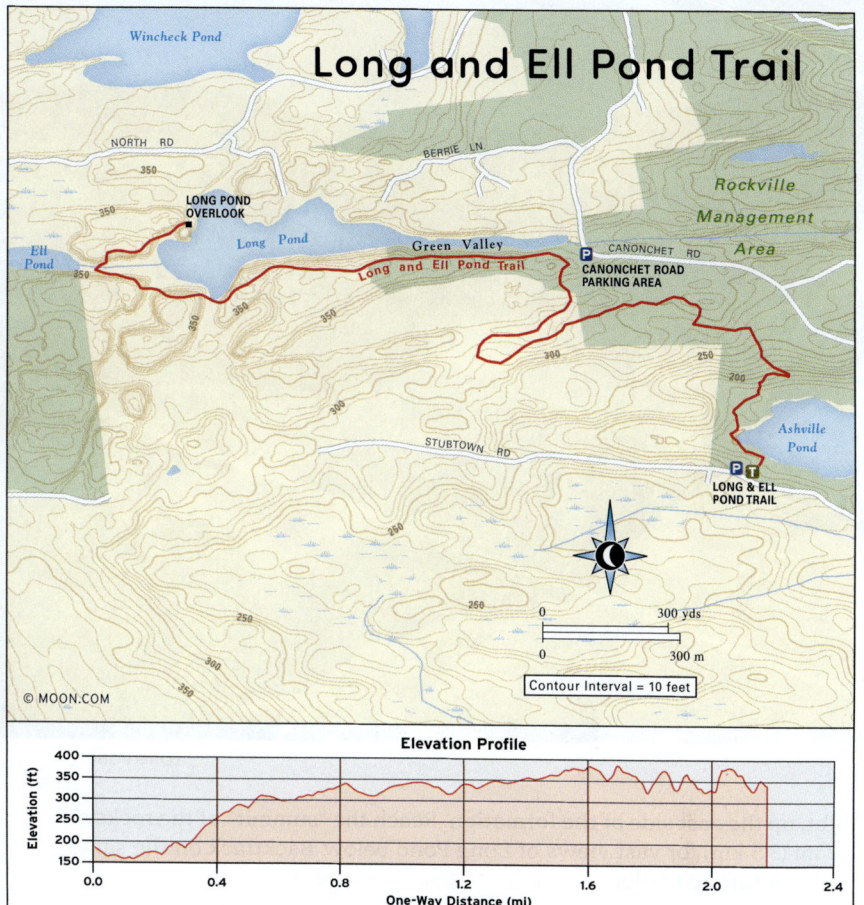

Long and Ell Pond Trail

Contour Interval = 10 feet

Elevation Profile

along a rock ridge, passes a pair of huge boulders, and follows a stone wall west for about 0.3 mi (0.5 km). As the trail reaches the top of a hill, the waters of Long Pond peek out from beyond the trees. The trail then leads hikers down through a pile of boulders and into a green valley.

▶ MILE 1.5–1.9: Green Valley to Long Pond Overlook

Past the valley, make a steep ascent to the top of a ridge. The trail continues to ascend and descend for 0.3 mi (0.5 km) before skirting the east edge of a root-bound hill. At the bottom of the hill, go down the stairs and cross the long wooden bridge through a cedar bog. At the other end of the bridge, climb through a final steep corridor of rock to arrive at an intersection at 1.9 mi (3.1 km). Go straight (north) through the intersection for the trail leading to **Long Pond overlook.**

▶ MILE 1.9–2.2: Long Pond Overlook to Summit

The path passes several rock outcroppings and then descends a hill. It reaches a towering rock formation at 2.1 mi (3.4 km). Follow the trail around to the north side of the rocks. At the End of Trail sign, ascend to the

LONG POND ▲

right, up the east side of the formation. Reach the "summit" of the rocks at 2.2 mi (3.5 km) for vast views of Long Pond below. Backtrack on the same trail to return to the lot.

DIRECTIONS

From RI-3, turn north onto Canonchet Road. Then turn left onto Stubtown Road. The Asheville Pond parking area is marked with a Rockville Management Area sign.

GPS COORDINATES: 41°29'59.4"N 71°45'37.4"W

6

Grassland, Moraine, and Old Pasture Loops

FRANCIS C. CARTER MEMORIAL PRESERVE, CHARLESTOWN

This peaceful woodland trail is punctuated by vernal pools, historic stonework, and open grasslands that attract diverse bird species.

DISTANCE: 4.4 mi (7.1 km) round-trip
DURATION: 2 hr
ELEVATION GAIN: 227 ft (84 m)
EFFORT: Easy
TRAIL: Dirt/grass path
USERS: Hikers, horseback riders
SEASON: Year-round
FEES/PASSES: None
MAPS: The Nature Conservancy, "Carter Preserve Trail System"
TRAILHEAD: Grassland Loop trailhead, Old Mill Rd., Charlestown
FACILITIES: Vault toilet, trail map
CONTACT: The Nature Conservancy; 401/331-7110; www.nature.org

START THE HIKE

▸ **MILE 0-0.3: Grassland Loop Trailhead to Old Pasture Loop**
Head straight west from the trailhead on a wide grass path; turn right (north) onto the yellow-blazed **Grassland Loop** in 135 ft (41 m). The narrow, flat trail is lined with heavy vegetation, and it's a great place to pick blueberries along the way in season. At the intersection at 0.3 mi (0.5 km), turn right (north) onto the blue-blazed **Old Pasture Loop** trail.

▸ **MILE 0.3-0.9: Old Pasture Loop to Moraine Loop**
Cross the stone wall and then follow alongside it in a black oak forest dotted with fern and pitch pine. Reach a fork in another 0.3 mi (0.5 km) and keep right (east) on the blue-blazed trail. When you reach the large boulder and intersection with the **Moraine Loop** at 0.9 mi (1.4 km), turn right (south) to follow the orange blazes.

◂ BENCH ON THE GRASSLAND LOOP

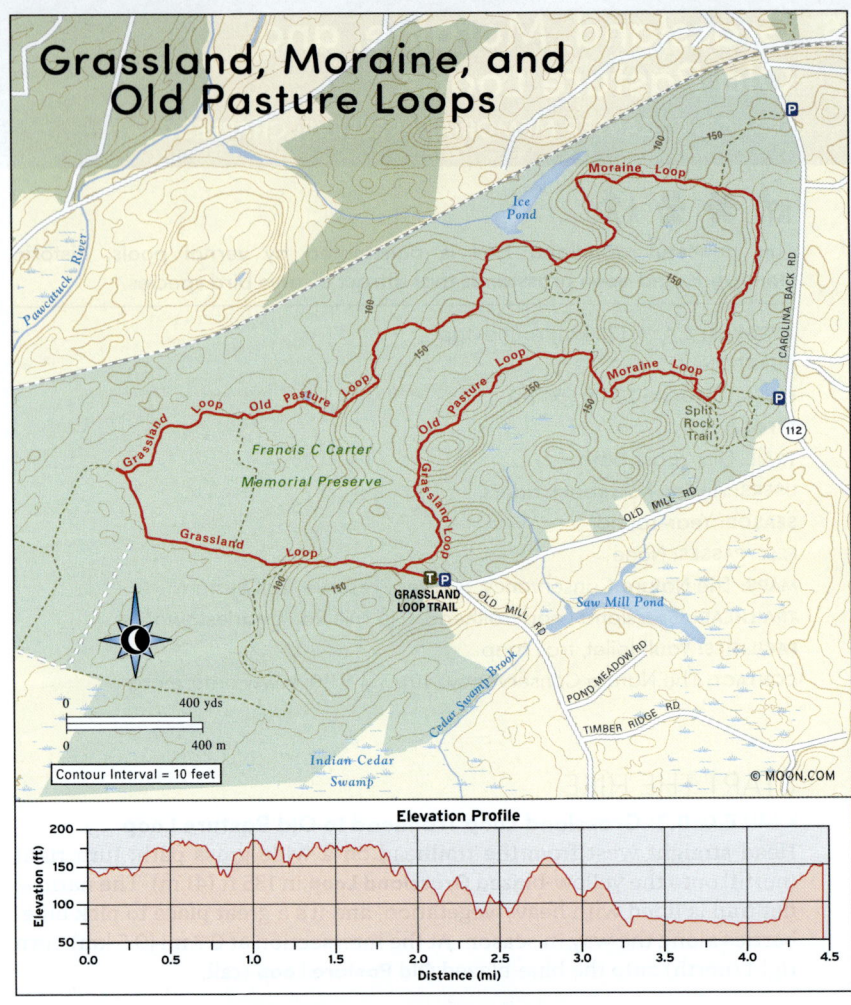

Grassland, Moraine, and Old Pasture Loops

Contour Interval = 10 feet

© MOON.COM

Elevation Profile

▶ **MILE 0.9–3.0: Moraine Loop to Grassland Loop**

The trail climbs slightly uphill to the south before bending back northwest. At the intersection with the Split Rock Loop at 1.2 mi (1.9 km), stay left (east) on the orange-blazed trail. Pass the other end of the Split Rock Trail at 1.6 mi (2.6 km), then another spur trail at 2.2 mi (3.5 km), keeping left (north) at both intersections. Continue on the Moraine Loop and pass several giant boulders and a stone wall, then cross over the historic dam at 2.7 mi (4.3 km). Reach the intersection with the **Old Pasture Loop** and bear right (north) to follow the blue blazes. The trail winds along a bog and through a patch of tall ferns before it reaches the intersection with the **Grassland Loop** at 3 mi (4.8 km).

▶ **MILE 3.0–4.4: Grassland Loop to Grassland Loop Trailhead**

Turn right (north) onto the yellow-blazed trail, which passes the bog and winds left uphill to a bench. The trail here can sometimes be brushy and overgrown, but it shortly emerges in an open field at 3.2 mi (5.1 km). At the

▲ STONE WALL ON THE PASTURE LOOP

field, turn right (west) onto the grass path and follow it along the northern border of the meadow. When you reach the intersection with the Narragansett Loop at 3.7 mi (6 km), keep left on the Grassland Loop, which eventually enters a pitch pine forest and leads straight southeast back to the parking area in 0.7 mi (1.1 km).

DIRECTIONS

From I-95, take Exit 3 to RI-138 E and follow it to the intersection with RI-112. Follow RI-112 past a sign for Carter Preserve and take the next right onto Old Mill Road. At the next Carter Preserve sign, bear right onto the dirt road and follow it to the large parking area at the end of the drive.

GPS COORDINATES: 41°25'33.2"N 71°39'46.8"W

7

Foster Cove, Cross Refuge, and Grassy Point Trails

NINIGRET NATIONAL WILDLIFE REFUGE, CHARLESTOWN

Hike on this gentle grass and gravel track to a scenic barrier beach where shorebirds and wildflowers flourish.

BEST: New England oddities, brew hikes
DISTANCE: 4.5 mi (7.2 km) round-trip
DURATION: 2 hr
ELEVATION GAIN: 22 ft (7 m)
EFFORT: Easy
TRAIL: Grass/gravel path
USERS: Hikers, bikers
SEASON: Year-round
FEES/PASSES: None
MAPS: U.S. Fish and Wildlife Service, "Ninigret National Wildlife Refuge Salt Pond Unit"
TRAILHEAD: Foster Cove Loop trailhead, Post Rd., Charlestown
FACILITIES: Vault toilet available at main parking area
CONTACT: U.S. Fish and Wildlife Service Ninigret Refuge Headquarters; 401/364-9124; www.fws.gov/refuge/Ninigret

START THE HIKE

▶ **MILE 0-0.5: Foster Cove Loop Trailhead to Cross Refuge Trail**
From the trailhead sign, go right (west) onto the **Foster Cove Loop,** a wide grass and gravel track surrounded by thick vegetation and perfumed with honeysuckle. The flat and easy trail arrives at water views of Foster Cove in 0.2 mi (0.3 km). Reach an intersection 0.3 mi (0.5 km) farther on the trail.

▶ **MILE 0.5-1.6: Cross Refuge Trail to Auxiliary Air Station Runway**
Stay straight (south) for the **Cross Refuge Trail,** which crosses over a strip of pavement and returns to a gravel surface. The trail slips between two lily pad-laden bogs. At the gated intersection at 1.3 mi (2.1 km), bear left (east). The vegetation opens into a spacious, grassy

BRIDGE AT NINIGRET NATIONAL WILDLIFE REFUGE ▶

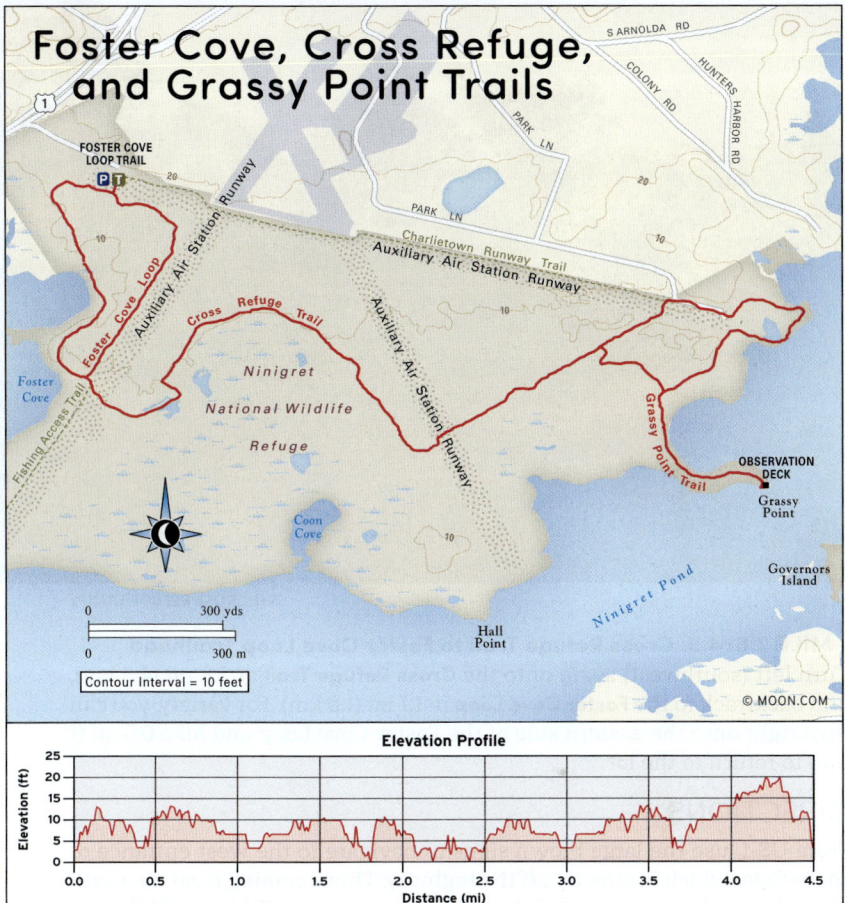

Foster Cove, Cross Refuge, and Grassy Point Trails

Elevation Profile

habitat where wildflowers and birds abound. Reach the parking area at 1.6 mi (2.6 km), and walk right (east) through the lot to the site of an old **runway** from Ninigret's days as Naval Auxiliary Air Station Charlestown.

▶ **MILE 1.6–1.8: Auxiliary Air Station Runway to Grassy Point Trail**
The trail continues on the far east side of the runway. Turn left (northeast) onto the **Grassy Point Trail,** which passes into the woods and then hugs the edge of Ninigret Pond, with great water views. After 0.2 mi (0.3 km), cross the bridge and then turn left (south) to follow the grassy trail to the end of the point.

▶ **MILE 1.8–2.6: Grassy Point Trail to Cross Refuge Trail**
At the trail's terminus in 0.5 mi (0.8 km), you can enjoy more water views and wildlife from the **observation deck.** Backtrack 0.3 mi (0.5 km) to an intersection and turn left (west), following signs for the **Cross Refuge Trail.**

▶ **MILE 2.6–4.5: Cross Refuge Trail to Foster Cove Loop Trailhead**
Turn left (southwest) again onto the **Cross Refuge Trail** at 2.8 mi (4.5 km), and backtrack to the **Foster Cove Loop** in 1.1 mi (1.8 km). For variety, you can turn right onto the eastern side of the Foster Cove Loop and hike 0.6 mi (1 km) to return to the lot.

DIRECTIONS

From US-1, use the large brown signs to navigate to the west entrance of the refuge, which is directly off the highway. Those coming from the north should pass the entrance and then double back onto US-1 N at Wildflower Road. There is a large parking lot at the trailhead.

GPS COORDINATES: 41°22'05.9"N 71°40'19.6"W

8 Clay Head Nature Trail and the Maze

CLAY HEAD PRESERVE, NEW SHOREHAM, BLOCK ISLAND

Explore Block Island's sentinel cliffs from this ambling seaside path with beach access and a labyrinth of unmarked trails.

BEST: Summer hikes
DISTANCE: 2.9 mi (4.7 km) round-trip
DURATION: 2 hr
ELEVATION GAIN: 114 ft (35 m)
EFFORT: Easy
TRAIL: Dirt/grass path
USERS: Hikers, leashed dogs, swimmers
SEASON: Year-round
FEES/PASSES: None
MAPS: None
TRAILHEAD: Clay Head trailhead, Clay Head Trail Rd., New Shoreham
FACILITIES: None
CONTACT: The Nature Conservancy; 401/331-7110; www.nature.org

START THE HIKE

▶ **MILE 0-0.5: Clay Head Trail to Beach**
The trail sets out from the left (north) side of the parking lot at the end of Clay Head Trail Road. Follow the narrow dirt track straight (east) past the trailhead sign and through a tangle of thick bramble. The vegetation parts to expose great views of the pond and the ocean sprawling below in 0.1 mi (0.16 km). Descend a hill, hike across a boardwalk, and at 0.5 mi (0.8 km) reach a side path opening to a gorgeous sandy beach on the right (east) side.

▶ **MILE 0.5-1.0: Beach to Pond**
Turn left (northeast) to stay on the sandy trail as it winds uphill. From here, the trail is marked with waist-high posts with blue arrows. You will pass several side paths to the left that lead into "The Maze," an unmarked network of intertwining trails lined with thick vegetation. Follow the blue arrows straight

◀ VIEWS FROM THE CLAY HEAD BLUFF

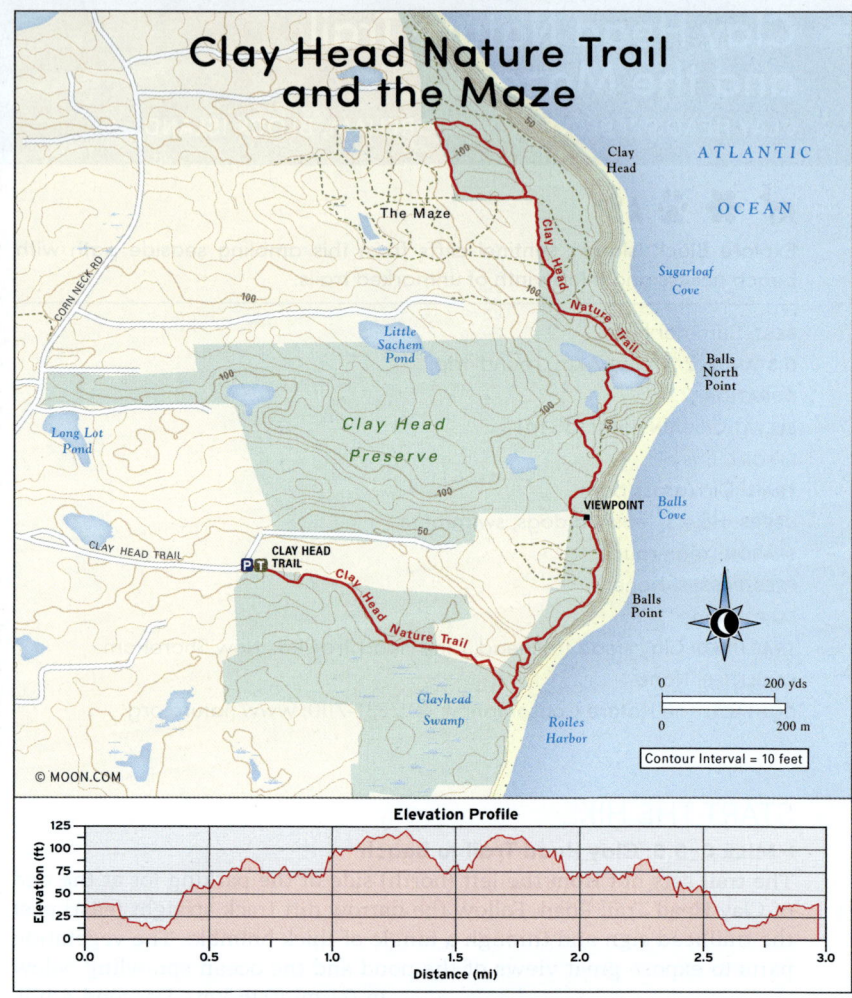

Clay Head Nature Trail and the Maze

Elevation Profile

north to stay on the main Clay Head Trail, which emerges on a bluff at 0.7 mi (1.1 km) to reveal ocean vistas from the top of the 800-ft (244-m) clay cliffs. As the trail winds along, it passes lovely stone walls and meadows. Arrive at a secluded pond at 1 mi (1.6 km), which offers great chances to glimpse rare wildlife such as the yellow-crowned night heron.

▶ MILE 1.0-2.9: Pond to Clay Head Trail

Continue straight north from the pond and reach a fork at 1.2 mi (1.9 km). Bear left (northwest) to follow the red arrows for a brief tour of The Maze. This counterclockwise loop (keep turning left) will return you to the fork in about 0.6 mi (1 km). From here, backtrack straight south on the blue-arrow trail to return to the parking lot.

▲ CLAY HEAD TRAIL

DIRECTIONS

Take the ferry to New Shoreham, Block Island. Take Water Street north around the bend where it becomes Dodge Street. At the four-way intersection, turn right on Corn Neck Road and continue for 2.6 mi (4.2 km). Turn right onto Clay Head Trail Road and follow it until the end. The road ends in a large dirt parking lot with a Clay Head Nature Trail sign.

GPS COORDINATES: 41°12'30.7"N 71°33'43.8"W

Bird lovers will delight at the diverse collection of fields, woods, ponds, and ledges at Norman Bird Sanctuary, which attracts a variety of species.

BEST: Vistas

DISTANCE: 2.8 mi (4.5 km) round-trip

DURATION: 1.5 hr

ELEVATION GAIN: 188 ft (57 m)

EFFORT: Easy/moderate

TRAIL: Dirt/rock path, boardwalk

USERS: Hikers

SEASON: Year-round

FEES/PASSES: $7 adult, $6 senior/military, $3 student/child

MAPS: Norman Bird Sanctuary, "Norman Bird Sanctuary Trail Map"

TRAILHEAD: Norman Bird Sanctuary Welcome Center, Third Beach Rd., Middletown

FACILITIES: Restrooms available at Welcome Center

CONTACT: Norman Bird Sanctuary; 401/846-2577; http://normanbirdsanctuary.org

The many trails of Norman Bird Sanctuary offer myriad habitats, but hikers are often most attracted to the park's "ridge trails"—long pudding stone fingers that reach out toward the Atlantic Ocean. To access the ridges, our route follows the main Universal Trail through field, shrub, and forest, and then forms a loop on the Red Fox, Nelson Pond, and Gray Craig Trails.

START THE HIKE

▶ MILE 0-0.4: Welcome Center to Red Maple Pond

Check in at the Welcome Center and then walk north on the **Universal Trail** through fields and around the garden. Reach an intersection at 0.2 mi (0.3 km) and keep right (west) on the gravel path. The trail ventures into shady woods and along a stone wall to reach another intersection at 0.4 mi (0.6 km). Turn left (south) and hike along the long boardwalk, which ends at the observation deck on **Red Maple Pond.**

▶ MILE 0.4-0.7: Red Maple Pond to Red Fox Trail

Head around the pond and over the bridge. Follow the stone steps for 0.1 mi (0.16 km) and then turn left (south). Almost immediately, turn right (west) onto another boardwalk, following signs toward Nelson Pond. Continue to bear right following signs for the **Red Fox Trail.** Then, at 0.7 mi (1.1 km), bear left (south) onto the Red Fox Trail.

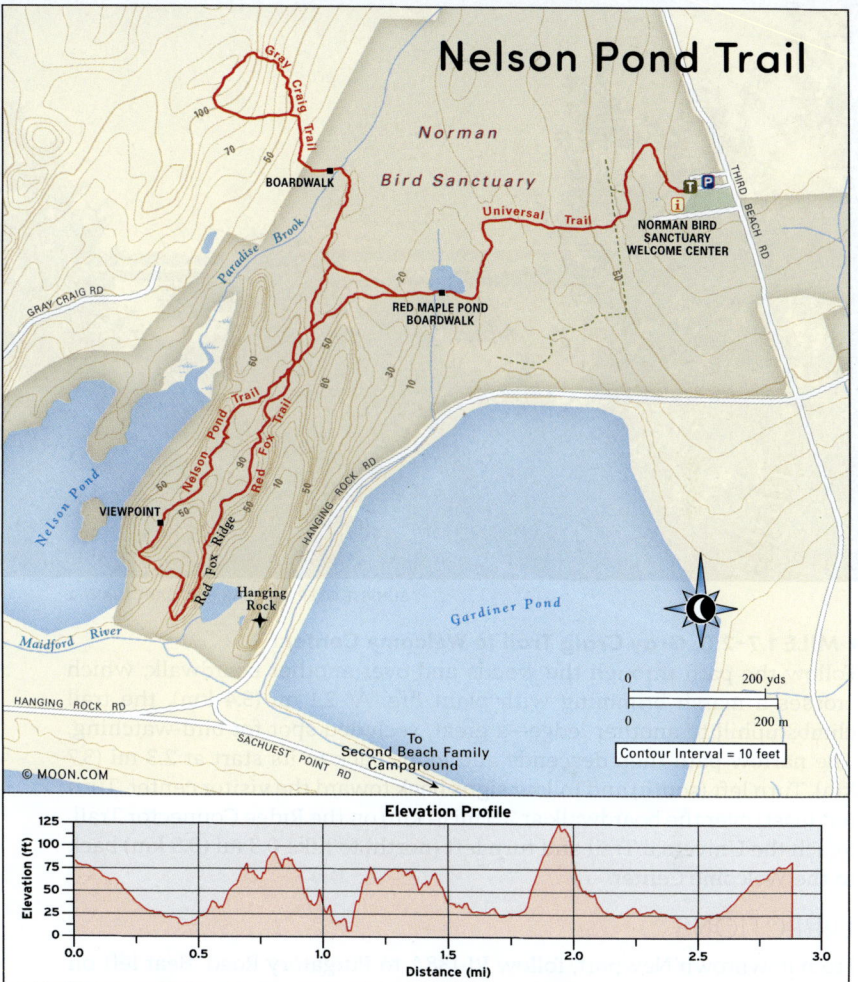

Nelson Pond Trail

Elevation Profile

▶ **MILE 0.7–1.1: Red Fox Trail to Red Fox Ridge**

The path enters a cool forest protected by massive beech trees and climbs slightly uphill over a series of ledges, with deep green valleys on either side. Reach the end of the Red Fox ridge at 1.1 mi (1.8 km), with great views looking east toward **Hanging Rock** and south to the ocean.

▶ **MILE 1.1–1.7: Red Fox Ridge to Gray Craig Trail**

Descend straight to the south and follow the low, grassy trail for 0.1 mi (0.16 km). Turn left (west) onto the boardwalk, then follow the trail left (west) as it climbs the ledges to more great views. The trail continues north on easy terrain, reaching a rocky viewpoint of **Nelson Pond** at 1.5 mi (2.4 km). Follow the viewpoint trail to the left (west); it descends to the main path at 1.5 mi (2.4 km). At the signed intersection at 1.7 mi (2.7 km), bear left (north) onto the **Gray Craig Trail.**

▶ **MILE 1.7-2.8: Gray Craig Trail to Welcome Center**

Follow the path through the woods and over another boardwalk, which crosses a marsh brimming with plant life. At 2.1 mi (3.4 km), the trail climbs uphill to another ledge—a great, secluded spot for bird-watching. The narrow path then descends and loops back to its start at 2.3 mi (3.7 km). Turn left (south) and follow signs back toward the visitor center. Turn left (east) over the boardwalk at 2.5 mi (4 km) on the Ridge Connector Trail. Reach the Universal Trail and turn left (north) to hike 0.3 mi (0.5 km) back to the Welcome Center.

DIRECTIONS

From downtown Newport, follow RI-138A to Purgatory Road. Bear left on Hanging Rock Road and then turn left on Third Beach Road. The well-marked and signed parking lot is on the left. Be sure to check in at the Welcome Center before hiking the trails.

GPS COORDINATES: 41°29'59.3"N 71°15'00.9"W

10 Flint Point and Ocean View Loops

SACHUEST POINT NATIONAL WILDLIFE REFUGE, MIDDLETOWN

Enjoy miles of waterfront views on this easy trail that winds between golden fields and a rocky peninsula jutting into the Atlantic Ocean.

BEST: Summer hikes, brew hikes
DISTANCE: 2.3 mi (3.7 km) round-trip
DURATION: 1.25 hr
ELEVATION GAIN: 46 ft (14 m)
EFFORT: Easy
TRAIL: Gravel path
USERS: Hikers
SEASON: Year-round
FEES/PASSES: None
MAPS: U.S. Fish and Wildlife Service, "Sachuest Point National Wildlife Refuge"
TRAILHEAD: Flint Point Loop trailhead, Sachuest Point Rd., Middletown
FACILITIES: Restrooms, water available at visitor center
CONTACT: U.S. Fish and Wildlife Service; 401/619-2680; www.fws.gov

Situated on a peninsula just east of Newport, the 242-acre (98-hectare) Sachuest Point refuge is both a destination for migratory shorebirds and a prized fishing area. Our route follows the park's two main trails—Flint Point and Ocean View—which follow the coastline on an easy gravel track featuring observation platforms, grassy bird habitat, and a hypnotizing jagged shoreline.

START THE HIKE

▶ **MILE 0-0.6: Flint Point Loop Trailhead to Flint Point Observation Deck**

Find the trailhead in the northeast corner of the parking area and head straight east toward the Flint Point Loop on the wide gravel path. In 600 ft (183 m), bear left (north) on the **Flint Point Loop,** which winds through rolling grassland before arriving at ocean views. Reach the **Flint Point observation deck** at 0.6 mi (1 km), where you can view boats bobbing in the Sakonnet River to the north and east.

▶ **MILE 0.6-1.1: Flint Point Observation Deck to Ocean View Loop**

From here, the path bends east then south along the coast through wild beach rose and honeysuckle. Shoreline views of sunbathing cormorants and sailboats persist to the east. Reach another **observation deck** at 1 mi (1.6 km). In another 0.1 mi (0.16 km), keep left to continue south onto the **Ocean View Loop.**

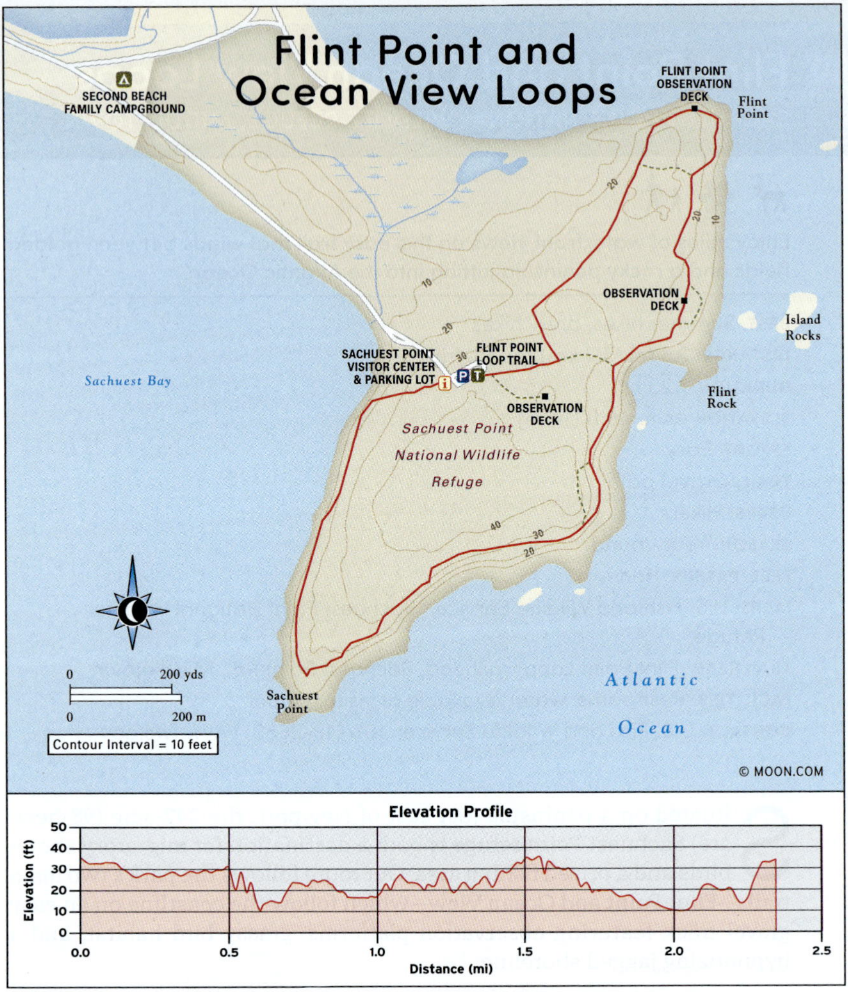

Flint Point and Ocean View Loops

Map labels:

SECOND BEACH FAMILY CAMPGROUND

FLINT POINT OBSERVATION DECK

Flint Point

OBSERVATION DECK

Island Rocks

SACHUEST POINT VISITOR CENTER & PARKING LOT

FLINT POINT LOOP TRAIL

Flint Rock

Sachuest Bay

OBSERVATION DECK

Sachuest Point National Wildlife Refuge

Sachuest Point

Atlantic Ocean

0   200 yds
0   200 m

Contour Interval = 10 feet

© MOON.COM

Elevation Profile

Elevation (ft) / Distance (mi)

▶ MILE 1.1–2.3: Ocean View Loop to Flint Point Loop Trailhead

As you hike south on the Ocean View Loop, vast fields unfold to one side while the rocky coastline becomes increasingly dramatic on the other. Reach the tip of **Sachuest Point** at 1.8 mi (2.9 km). Here, you may want to take some time to explore the rocks before continuing the 0.5 mi (0.8 km) on the path north back to the visitor center and parking area.

SUNSET OVER SACHUEST POINT ▶

▲ OCEAN VIEW LOOP AT SACHUEST POINT

DIRECTIONS

From US-1, take RI-138 E over the Newport Bridge. Take the Newport exit and pass through downtown Newport on RI-138A. After First Beach, take a right onto Purgatory Road. Then turn right onto Sachuest Point Drive and follow it to **Sachuest Point Visitor Center** at the very end of the road, where you'll find a parking lot.

GPS COORDINATES: 41°28'47.4"N 71°14'38.0"W

BEST NEARBY BITES AND BREWS

Despite its small size, Rhode Island boasts a great list of cool spots for post-hike brews and bites.

- Build-your-own tacos, burritos, and quesadillas are the center of the menu at **The Taco Shop** (459 Chapel St., Burrillville; 401/568/8226; www.thetacoshopri.com; noon-8pm Tues.-Sat.) in the northern part of the state.

- Visit **Tavern on the Hill** (809 Nooseneck Hill Rd., West Greenwich; 401/385-3835; https://tavernonthehillri.com; noon-1am Fri.-Mon., 3pm-1am Tues.-Thurs.) for drinks, barbecue specials, and fun live music including Bluegrass Sundays.

- Grab a drink at the **Charlestown Rathskeller** (489A Old Coach Rd., Charlestown; 401/792-1000; www.thecharlestownrathskeller.com; noon-10pm Wed.-Sun.), a restored 1930s speakeasy. It has a classic American pub and seafood menu and famous fries.

- Rhode Island's first farm brewery, **Tilted Barn Brewery,** (1 Hemsley Place, Exeter; http://tiltedbarnbrewery.com; 4pm-8pm Wed., noon-8pm Thurs.-Sat.., noon-5pm Sun.) is the ideal spot to enjoy a pint. Savor fresh brews with offerings from a rotating list of food trucks.

- Tucked in the state's southwest corner, **Grey Sail** (63 Canal St., Westerly; 401/212-7592; https://greysailbrewing.com; 3pm-8pm Wed.-Fri., noon-8pm Sat., noon-6pm Sun.) is one of Rhode Island's favorite breweries, with an airy beer garden and pizza options from Vetranos Wood Fired Pizza.

- Stop by **Poor People's Pub** (33 Ocean Ave., Block Island; 401/466-8533; www.pppbi.com; 11:30am-1am daily) on your way back to the New Shoreham ferry terminal for a cold cocktail or beer on the porch, plus skillet mac and cheese, burgers, pizzas, sandwiches, and more.

- Treat yourself to a pint and house-made pretzel at **Taproot Brewing Company** (909 E. Main Rd., Middletown; 401/848-5161; http://newportvineyards.com/taproot-brewing; hours vary seasonally). Reservations are not required for bar service, but you'll want to book your spot for the full dining experience.

- The extensive cocktail menu and tasty entrées at the **Brick Alley Pub and Restaurant** (140 Thames St., Newport; 401/849-6334; www.brickalley.com; 11:30am-9:30pm Sun.-Thurs, 11:30am-10 pm Fri.-Sat.) make it a local icon for dinner and a drink.

- Enjoy a seasonal brew at **Whalers Brewing Company** (1174 Kingstown Rd., South Kingstown; 401/552-0002; http://whalers.com; 4pm-10pm Tues.-Thurs., 1pm-10pm Fri., 11:30am-10pm Sat., 11:30am-7pm Sun.) after hiking the Foster Cove, Cross Refuge, and Grassy Point Trails.

NEARBY CAMPGROUNDS

NAME	LOCATION	FACILITIES	SEASON	FEE
George Washington State Campground	2141 Putnam Pike, Chepachet, 41°55'11.7"N 71°45'17.9"W	76 RV and tent sites, 4 cabins; restrooms	mid–April–October	$18–75
401/568-6700; https://riparks.ri.gov				
Burlingame State Campground	1 Burlingame State Park Rd., Charlestown, 41°55'11.7"N 71°45'17.7"W	700 standard sites, 20 cabins; restrooms	mid–April–mid-October	$18–74
401/322-8910; https://riparks.ri.gov				
East Beach Campground	East Beach Rd., Charlestown, 41°20'40.7"N 71°41'13.9"W	20 sites for "camping unit" vehicles; no utilities; beach permit required	late May–early September	$28–55
401/322-8910; https://riparks.ri.gov				
Charlestown Breachway	Charlestown Beach Rd., Charlestown, 41°21'26.5"N 71°38'12.5"W	75 RV sites	mid–April–October	$18–36
401/322-8910; https://riparks.ri.gov				
Fishermen's Memorial State Campground	1011 Point Judith Rd., Narragansett, 41°22'48.3"N 71°29'17.8"W	182 RV and tent sites; restrooms	mid–April–October	$18–55
401/789-8374; https://riparks.ri.gov				
Second Beach Family Campground	474 Sachuest Point Rd., Middletown, 41°29'13.9"N 71°15'09.7"W	44 RV sites; hookups; restrooms with showers	early May–mid-October	$79–90
401/846-6273; www.middletownri.com				

HIKING TIPS

SAFETY

Safety is paramount to making sure your day on the New England trails is an enjoyable experience for all. The best way to ensure safety is to plan for your hike ahead of time. Consider preparedness your first defense in the prevention of accidents and mishaps. If something does go wrong, have an emergency plan in place that will allow you to seek help while keeping all members of your group safe. A Wilderness First Aid class is a great resource for anyone who spends time outdoors. Check out the SOLO Wilderness Medicine School for classes across New England.

BEFORE YOU GO

Before you set out on your hike, review a map and research your desired route. Keep in mind that a 2-mi (3.2-km) hike straight up a mountain peak may require more time, effort, and resources than a gentle 2-mi (3.2-km) hike along a beach. Consider your route's unique terrain and weather as well as the size and ability of your group when planning and packing for your hike. In addition to "The 10 Essentials" listed, make sure you have any equipment required for enjoyment and comfort on your hike. It's also a good idea to double-check the fit and quality of essential gear ahead of time. Does your footwear give you uncomfortable blisters? Does that tear in your rain jacket let in excess moisture? If you foresee trouble with any of your supplies, repair or replace those items before the need to use them arises.

Always be sure to let someone know where you are traveling and when you plan to return, no matter how easy, close to home, or familiar a hike seems. If an accident happens on the trail, this valuable information could be the key to making sure you return home safely. Cell phones and communication devices are prone to battery failures and lapses in service, and should not be relied on as your sole method for obtaining help.

The 10 Essentials

No matter where you travel, experts agree that these "10 Essentials" should make their way into your backpack.

Hydration: Water bottle or hydration pack, plenty of water, and filtration/purification system

Nutrition: Plenty of food, plus extra snacks in case you are out longer than anticipated

Navigation: A detailed map and compass, a GPS device, and knowledge of how to use them

First Aid Kit: Be sure your kit includes enough supplies for the length of your trip and the size of your group

Illumination: A headlamp (even if you don't expect to be out after dark)

Sun Protection: Sunblock, a hat, and breathable layers to cover your skin

Insulation: Warm layers, preferably made of wool or synthetics that insulate even when wet

Fire: A lighter or waterproof matches in case you need to start a fire for warmth

Pocketknife/Repair Tools: A blade or multi-tool can come in handy throughout a trip, especially if your equipment needs repair or adjusting

Emergency Survival Gear: If stranded, an emergency blanket, tent, and sleeping bag can help protect you from the elements; a whistle and flares allow you to signal for help

Hiking Prep

Hiking is remarkable in that almost everyone can do it, regardless of age or body type. That said, it's important to know both your strengths and your limitations when choosing a trail in New England. Some of the trails listed in this book require a high baseline of existing physical fitness and endurance. Hikers should be trained and confident in their physical abilities before attempting trails marked "strenuous." We absolutely recommend that hikers challenge themselves mentally and physically when exploring New England, but it's a good idea to start small and work your way up to more challenging trails as your body is ready.

ON THE TRAIL

A good understanding of navigation is one of the best tools a hiker can have. In addition to map and compass skills, familiarize yourself with the various forms of trail markers. Most hiking trails use "blazes," colored markers painted or nailed along the route to mark the way (usually found on trees or rocks). Most trails are marked with a single color or symbol that differentiates that trail from other trails in a park. Some hikes, especially those above the tree line, utilize cairns—pyramid-like towers of rock that mark a pathway. While the majority of the hikes in this book are well marked, hikers should pay especially close attention at intersections to ensure they remain on the right track. If you're unsure which way to go, don't be afraid to reach out! Most hikers are friendly and more than willing to help.

Practice common courtesy on the trail. Respect other visitors by yielding and creating space where necessary, controlling your pets, and keeping voices at a polite volume.

WEATHER

There is a saying in New England that "if you don't like the weather, wait five minutes and it will change." In a nutshell, New England weather is unpredictable and often extreme. Summers (late May-September) bring pleasantly warm daytime temperatures and cooler evenings. Still, summer weather can be chilly, especially in the north and at high elevations, and thunderstorms are frequent in warmer weather. Spring and fall consist of cooler daytime temperatures and often cold nights. Spring also brings on the notorious New England "mud season" caused by excessive rain and snow runoff. Winters are long and cold, and snowfall is likely, especially in the mountainous northern states. Snow and frigid temperatures may begin as early as October and linger into April.

Hikers should take extra precautions against weather-related incidents of hypothermia and frostbite, especially on New England's high peaks. Use additional caution in the event of thunder and lightning storms. Avoid high peaks, open spaces, and water during lightning events.

New England water can be quite cold, even in summertime, and coastal surf can be dangerous. Always heed local warnings regarding swimming and never swim alone.

WILDLIFE

While hikers are unlikely to encounter hostile wildlife on New England trails, it is important to take precautions to ensure your safety and the safety of any animals you encounter. Observe wild animals from a safe distance and do not attempt to approach or follow them. Be especially cautious around injured, mating, nesting, and young animals, and report any odd or aggressive behavior to local authorities. Always heed local signs regarding wildlife and avoid any restricted areas designated to protect them.

Avoid feeding wildlife intentionally or accidentally by storing and transporting your food and trash properly. A taste of human food can change the feeding behaviors of wild animals in ways that are dangerous for both humans and wildlife. This applies not only to large creatures, but also smaller animals like rodents and birds.

Moose

Moose are gentle and elusive creatures, and most hikers are lucky to spot them in their natural habitat. However, moose are responsible for hundreds of car accidents each year. Use caution driving to and from the trailhead, especially in areas marked with Moose Crossing signs.

Bears

Black bears are common across Maine, New Hampshire, Vermont, and the western parts of Massachusetts and Connecticut, although they may be spotted elsewhere. In general, these creatures are harmless, but they may cause problems when they have been exposed to human food, or if they feel threatened. When camping, secure food and other scented items in a bear hang or a bear-proof box. If you encounter a bear on the trail, speak in calm tones and slowly wave your arms. This will help the bear identify you as human and it will usually flee. Move away slowly sideways. If the bear charges or makes aggressive movements towards you, stand your ground. Never run or climb a tree, and never place yourself between a mother bear and its cubs. As long as hikers behave respectfully, most bear encounters are exciting experiences that do not result in injury.

Snakes

Most species of snakes found in New England are harmless. However, although they are endangered and rarely encountered, timber rattlesnakes and northern copperheads are present throughout New England. These venomous pit vipers are marked by a triangular head. Timber rattlesnakes have black tails with a distinctive rattle at the end, and are most commonly found in rocky areas of western Massachusetts. Reddish-hued copperheads are most common from Massachusetts southward. Both species are wary of humans and are unlikely to strike unless provoked. When climbing, always look before placing your hand, and never attempt to pick up a snake. In the unlikely event you are bitten by a venomous snake, wrap the wound distally to proximally in an Ace bandage and seek immediate medical treatment.

Insects

Biting insects such as mosquitoes, blackflies, no-see-ums, and greenheads are a fact of life in New England. While cases of eastern equine encephalitis (EEE) and other mosquito-borne illnesses have occurred in the region, most insect bites are little more than an itchy nuisance. Biting insects usually reach their peak in midsummer, and they can be especially vicious in the evening, in shady areas, and near water. Protect yourself with long-sleeved clothing and insect repellent. Various species of bees can also be found in New England. Bee stings can be painful and uncomfortable, but they may also cause serious allergic reactions in some individuals. If someone in your party has a history of allergic reactions to bee stings, carry an epinephrine injector and an antihistamine such as Benadryl in your first aid kit.

Ticks

Though some are only as big as a pinhead, ticks are one of the most ubiquitous hazards of hiking in New England. These ectoparasites feed on the blood of humans and other species and may transmit potentially serious illnesses including Lyme disease, babesiosis, and anaplasmosis. While deer ticks (also known as black-legged ticks) are implicated in the spread of most tick-borne diseases in New England, dog ticks and lone star ticks can also spread pathogens. To prevent tick-borne illness, use insect repellent and wear long clothing. Perform a "tick check" after spending time outdoors by scanning your body for crawling or embedded ticks, which prefer warm crevices in the skin. An embedded tick is no cause for alarm, but it should be removed as soon as possible to decrease the likelihood of disease transmission. Simply grasp the tick with a pair of tweezers as close to the skin as possible and pull the entire body straight out, firmly but gently. A little bit of irritation is normal, but if you notice a rash, fever, or flu-like symptoms following a tick bite, consult your physician immediately. Most tick-borne illnesses are mild when caught early and can be easily treated with antibiotics.

HAZARDOUS PLANTS

Rash-causing plants like poison ivy and poison sumac can put a serious damper on your experience of the great outdoors. These prevalent New England plants contain a compound called urushiol, which causes an extremely itchy, blistery contact dermatitis in most humans. The best defense against both plants is knowing how to identify and avoid them.

Poison ivy is the more common of the two plants. Most New Englanders stand by the rule "Leaves of three, let it be." The plant is notorious for its three almond-shaped leaves (sometimes notched) with a reddish dot where the leaves meet. Leaves are green in summer, reddish or yellow in fall, and may appear to have a shiny coat. Poison ivy is most often encountered on a hairy vine but can also grow as a shrub or as individual sprouts. In late summer and fall, it produces clusters of whitish, waxy berries.

Poison sumac is also widespread in New England, though it is most commonly found in and surrounding wetlands. This woody shrub has long ovoid leaves that sometimes take on a reddish hue, and white clustered berries. While less common on the trail, poison sumac is even more toxic than poison ivy, and it should be identified and avoided accordingly.

If you suspect you've come into contact with either of these plants, it's important to wash your skin and clothing as soon as possible to reduce the risk of rash. Specialty products like Tecnu can help break down urushiol, but most regular soaps will help remove the rash-causing oil. A typical laundry cycle will remove urushiol from clothing. If a rash breaks out, keep the area clean and ventilated, and avoid scratching. Topical over-the-counter anti-itch treatments can bring some relief, but if the rash is persistent, widespread, or on sensitive areas of the body, a prescription steroid may be necessary.

PROTECT THE ENVIRONMENT

Help preserve the beauty and tranquility of the natural spaces you visit by following the seven "Leave No Trace" principles as outlined by the Leave No Trace Center for Outdoor Ethics.

Plan Ahead and Prepare: Unprepared hikers are more likely to impact the environment if they become ill, injured, or lost. View the "Safety" section to ensure you and your group have the right equipment, skills, and plan for an enjoyable and environmentally friendly trip.

Travel and Camp on Durable Surfaces: Trails do not only exist to mark the way and make hiking easier. Restricting foot traffic to designated areas helps reduce human impact, especially in frequently visited areas. Trail crews work hard to maintain safe, weather- and traffic-resistant trails—use them! Staying on-trail helps protect sensitive areas, such as alpine zones, from overuse.

Dispose of Waste Properly: Carry in, carry out! Most backcountry trails are not equipped with trash cans, so hikers should plan to pack out any waste with them. Make sure to scan your area for "microtrash"—items like bottle caps and wrapper corners that are easily left behind. While many trailheads are equipped with outhouses or restroom facilities, hikers should familiarize themselves with protocol for when nature calls on the trail. Bury solid human waste in a "cathole" 6 in (15 cm) deep and at least 200 ft (61 m) away from trails, water, or camping areas. Pack out toilet paper and hygiene products along with other trash.

Leave What You Find: Finding a beautiful flower, a shed antler, or a historical artifact is one of the many joys of hiking in New England. Let others enjoy the same experience by leaving what you find where you find it. This not only preserves history and natural spaces, but helps eliminate the introduction and transport of non-native species.

Minimize Fire Impacts: While there are other ways of cooking, staying warm, and finding entertainment outdoors, fires can be a great experience when enjoyed safely and sustainably. Where fires are allowed, keep them small, contain them to designated or low-impact areas, and extinguish them properly. Avoid transporting firewood from nonlocal areas to prevent the spread of pests and diseases.

Respect Wildlife: Treat wildlife and their habitats with caution and dignity. Observe wildlife from a distance and never feed wild animals. See also the "Wildlife" section.

Be Considerate of Other Visitors: Allow other hikers to enjoy a peaceful and pleasant trail experience by sharing spaces, controlling volume, and practicing common courtesy and respect.

PASSES, PERMITS, AND FEES

Veterans of the U.S. military can access most New England parks free of charge.

America the Beautiful Pass: Covers entrance fees to all U.S. national parks and national wildlife refuges, plus day-use fees to all national forests, grasslands, and lands managed by the Bureau of Land Management, Bureau of Reclamation, and U.S. Army Corps of Engineers for the driver and up to four adults per vehicle. Valid for one year from date of purchase: $80. Purchase at https://store.usgs.gov/pass; 888/275-8747; or at most park entrances.

Maine State Parks Annual Passes: Vehicle season pass admits pass holder and occupants of vehicle to day-use facilities at most Maine state parks and historic sites (some exclusions apply): $105. Individual season pass admits only pass holder: $55. Senior discounts available. Valid for one calendar year. Purchase at www.maine.gov/dacf/parks; 207/624-9950; or at most park entrances.

New Hampshire State Parks Annual Passes: Individual season pass admits pass holder to most day-use New Hampshire state parks (some exclusions apply): $60. Family season passes admit two adults and up to four dependents: $105 residents/$120 nonresidents. Youth discounts available. Valid for one calendar year. Purchase at www.nhstateparks.org; 603/271-3556; or at most park entrances.

Vermont State Parks Annual Passes: Season vehicle passes admit pass holder and up to eight passengers to all Vermont state parks. $90. Individual season pass admits only pass holder. $30. Valid for one calendar year. Purchase at www.vtstateparks.com; 888/409-7579; or at most park entrances.

Massachusetts State Parks Annual Passes: The Department of Conservation and Recreation Annual Parking Pass covers parking fees at most Massachusetts state parks: $60 Massachusetts residents only. Valid for one calendar year. Senior lifetime pass: $10. Purchase at https://yodelportal.com/massdcr or 617/626-1420.

Connecticut State Parks Annual Pass: Nonresidents may purchase a season pass to cover parking fees at most Connecticut state parks (park

HIKING WITH CHILDREN

It's never too early for kids to hit the trail and start learning about the natural beauty that surrounds them. But remember, your young companions are depending on you to prepare for the day with supplies and information. Here are some tips to help turn first-timers into lifelong hikers.

- **Gear Up:** While they may not be carrying as heavy a pack, kids should still have all the essential gear to keep them comfortable for a day on the trail. This includes appropriate footwear and plenty of layers to stay warm and dry in all conditions. For younger kids, consider a carrying pack for when they need a break.

- **Know Your Limits:** Visit shorter, less-steep trails when traveling with little legs, and factor in extra time for rest breaks, play, and exploration. You may also want to pick a hike with a special destination or activity (like swimming) so kids have something to look forward to.

- **Double Down on Snacks:** Proper hydration and nutrition is crucial to keeping us all energized on the trail, but children may be especially sensitive to missed snack times. Having plenty of tasty treats on hand can help improve energy and mood and provide necessary encouragement on tough trails.

- **Make It a Learning Experience:** Foster curiosity about the natural world by asking and answering questions about where you are, what you're doing, and why. Use events on the trail as "teaching moments." Even a tough day on the trail can help inspire tenacity and perseverance in young minds.

BEST HIKES WITH KIDS

- Maine: Wells Reserve (page 127)
- New Hampshire: The Flume (page 208)
- Vermont: Devil's Gulch via the Long Trail and Babcock Trail (page 410)
- Massachusetts: Hurlburt's Hill and Bartholomew's Cobble (page 503)
- Connecticut: Lamentation Mountain and Chauncey Peak via the Mattabesett Trail (page 578)
- Rhode Island: Nelson Pond Trail (page 622)

admission is free): $112. No on-site charge for CT residents. Valid for one calendar year. Purchase at www.ctdeepstore.com; 860/424-3105; or at most park entrances.

Rhode Island Beaches Season Pass: Covers admission and parking at all Rhode Island state beaches for the pass holder's vehicle and all passengers: $30 residents/$60 nonresidents. Senior discounts available. Valid for one calendar year. Purchase online at https://riparks.ri.gov.

Trustees of Reservations Membership: Provides free or discounted membership to all Trustees of Reservations properties in Massachusetts. Memberships start at $55 individual/$80 family. Additional parking permit

HIKING APPS

Smartphones can be useful both on the trail and while planning your trip. Not only can they help with navigation, but they can be a fun way to learn more about the natural environment, whether it's identifying flora and fauna or predicting the weather. Though cell service is not always reliable in some hiking areas, many apps have offline components.

- **Gaia GPS:** This navigation app shows detailed topographic maps, hiking trails, and landmarks, but it also tracks your hike as you go along, providing information on distance, time, elevation, and more. Free. A $59.90 premium membership unlocks additional useful features. Available for Android and iOS.
- **First Aid American Red Cross:** Keep your cool in any medical emergency with this preloaded guide to treating common illnesses and injuries. English and Spanish translations. Free. Available for Android and iOS.
- **Weather Live:** One of the most accurate weather apps out there, Weather Live provides real-time forecast information complete with easy-to-read radar, maps, and helpful warnings regarding sudden weather changes. Free. Available for Android and iOS.
- **PeakVisor:** Get the most out of each mountain vista with PeakVisor, which helps users identify each summit in their line of sight using their phone's camera and GPS. Free. Available for Android and iOS.
- **Merlin Bird ID:** From the Cornell Lab of Ornithology, this acclaimed birding app allows users to identify avian species by uploading a picture or using the "Bird ID Wizard." Free. Available for Android and iOS.

Be sure to ask park staff if there is an app for the hiking area you're visiting. Many organizations have apps with additional maps and interpretive information.

needed for Crane Beach. Valid for one year from date of purchase. Purchase at https://thetrustees.org/membership.

White Mountain National Forest Season Pass: Covers parking and admission for one vehicle at developed White Mountain National Forest sites that require a recreation fee (most WMNF areas are free): $30 individual/$40 household. Holders of the America the Beautiful Pass do not need to purchase an additional WMNF pass. Valid for one year from date of purchase. Purchase at www.myscenicdrives.com or WMNF offices and information centers.

Baxter State Park Season Pass: Admits vehicles to Baxter State Park for summer season: $42. Additional fees apply for camping. Purchase at park entrance. Info at www.baxterstatepark.org or 207/723-5140.

CLUBS AND MEMBERSHIPS

Appalachian Mountain Club
A great resource for Appalachian Trail maps, lodging, and trail information, especially in the White Mountains. Annual membership saves pass holders 20 percent on AMC lodging, programs, and maps, plus gear discounts, a magazine subscription, and more. Valid for one year from date of purchase. Starting at $50. Purchase at www.outdoors.org/get-involved; 800/372-1758; or at most AMC locations.

Appalachian Trail Conservancy
Provides helpful information and maps for the Appalachian Trail, especially for thru-hikers. Help protect the Appalachian Trail with an annual ATC membership. Benefits include a map, magazine subscription, retail/lodging discounts, and more. NextGen members under 30 "pay your age." Other memberships start at $50. Purchase at https://appalachiantrail.org.

Green Mountain Club
The best contact for maps and information about the Long Trail in Vermont. Annual membership gives the pass holder a discount on GMC gear, workshops, and publications, plus deals at participating retailers, inns, and B&Bs. Valid for one year from date of purchase. Starting at $45. Purchase at www.greenmountainclub.org; 802/241-8325; or at the GMC Visitor Center.

Mass Audubon
Independent of the National Audubon Society, this Massachusetts group is dedicated to protecting the nature of the commonwealth through conservation lands, programming, and more. Members receive free admission to properties and discounts on programs and gear. Starting at $35. Discounts for members under 30 years old. Purchase at www.massaudubon.org.

National Audubon Society
Aims to protect birds and manages conservation areas throughout the United States. Members receive a magazine subscription, membership in a local chapter, admission to special events, and more. Starting at $20. Purchase at www.audubon.org.

Nature Conservancy
A membership with this conservation organization helps support many of the properties in this book. Members receive news, magazines, and more. Starting at $50. Purchase at www.nature.org.

Randolph Mountain Club

This beloved local group helps maintain trails and shelters in the White Mountains. A great resource for trail information. Members receive discounts on lodging, and fees directly benefit trails: $45 individual/$85 family. Purchase at https://randolphmountainclub.org.

Trustees of Reservations

A great resource for trail information and special events at select properties in Massachusetts. See "Passes, Permits, and Fees."

WEATHER AND SAFETY

In case of emergency, dial 911.

HikeSafe

Great information on hiker preparedness and education (https://hikesafe.com).

Mount Washington Observatory

Best resource for weather information in the White Mountains (2779 White Mountain Hwy., P.O. Box 2310, North Conway, NH 03860; 603/356-2137; www.mountwashington.org).

National Oceanographic and Atmospheric Administration

Best resource for tidal and weather information nationwide (1401 Constitution Ave. NW, Room 5128, Washington, DC 20230; www.noaa.gov).

NH Hike Safe Card

Purchase of this voluntary card helps support New Hampshire Fish and Game search and rescue efforts, and pass holders are not required to repay costs in the event they need rescue (not applicable in instances of negligence): $25 individual/$35 family. Purchase at www.nhfishandgame.com or at the Fish and Game office in Concord.

SOLO Wilderness Medicine School

Provides classes for Wilderness First Aid, Wilderness First Responder, and Wilderness EMT certifications (623 Tasker Hill Rd., Conway, NH 03818; 603/447-6711; https://soloschools.com).

NATIONAL PARKS, FORESTS, AND SEASHORES

Acadia National Park

P.O. Box 177, Bar Harbor, ME 04609; Hulls Cove Visitor Center, Route 3, Bar Harbor, ME 04609; 207/288-3338; www.nps.gov/acad

Cape Cod National Seashore

99 Marconi Site Rd., Wellfleet, MA 02667; 508/771-2144; www.nps.gov/caco

Green Mountain National Forest

231 N. Main St., Rutland, VT 05701; 802/747-6700; www.fs.usda.gov/main/gmfl

White Mountain National Forest
71 White Mountain Dr., Campton, NH 03223; 603/536-6100; www.fs.usda.gov/main/whitemountain

FEDERAL WILDLIFE AGENCIES
United States Fish and Wildlife Service
1849 C St. NW, Washington, DC 20240; 800/344-9453; www.fws.gov

STATE WILDLIFE AGENCIES
Connecticut Department of Energy and Environmental Protection (DEEP), Bureau of Natural Resources
79 Elm St., Hartford, CT 06106; 860/424-3000; https://portal.ct.gov/deep

Maine Department of Inland Fisheries and Wildlife (Maine Warden Service)
284 State St., Augusta, ME 04333; 207/287-8000; www.maine.gov/ifw/warden-service

Massachusetts Division of Fish and Wildlife (MassWildlife)
1 Rabbit Hill Rd., Westborough, MA 01581; 508/389-6300; www.mass.gov/orgs/division-of-fisheries-and-wildlife

New Hampshire Fish and Game Department
11 Hazen Dr., Concord, NH 03301; 603/271-3421; www.wildlife.nh.gov

Rhode Island Division of Fish and Wildlife
235 Promenade St., Providence, RI 02908; 401/222-4700; https://dem.ri.gov/natural-resources-bureau/fish-wildlife

Vermont Fish and Wildlife Department
1 National Life Dr., Dewey Building, Montpelier, VT 05620; 802/828-1000; http://vtfishandwildlife.com

STATE PARK AGENCIES
Connecticut Department of Energy and Environmental Protection (DEEP), Bureau of Outdoor Recreation
79 Elm St., Hartford, CT 06106; 860/424-3200; https://portal.ct.gov/deep

Maine Bureau of Parks and Lands
22 State House Station, 18 Elkins Ln., Augusta, ME 04333; 207/287-3821; http://maine.gov/dacf/parks

Massachusetts Department of Conservation and Recreation (DCR)
251 Causeway St., 9th Floor, Boston, MA 02114; 617/626-1250; www.mass.gov/orgs/department-of-conservation-recreation

New Hampshire Division of Parks and Recreation
172 Pembroke Rd., Concord, NH 03301; 603/271-3556; www.nhstateparks.org

Rhode Island Division of Parks and Recreation
1100 Tower Hill Rd., North Kingstown, RI 02852; 401/667-6200; https://riparks.ri.gov

Vermont Department of Forests, Parks, and Recreation
1 National Life Dr., Davis 2, Montpelier, VT 05620; 888/409-7579; www.vtstateparks.com

MAPS
Appalachian Mountain Club
10 City Square, Boston, MA 02129; 800/262-4455; https://amcstore.outdoors.org

Appalachian Trail Conservancy
Kellogg Conservation Center, P.O. Box 264, South Egremont, MA 01258; 304/535-6331; www.atctrailstore.org

Green Mountain Club
4711 Waterbury-Stowe Rd., Waterbury Center, VT 05677; 802/244-7037; https://store.greenmountainclub.org

United States Forest Service
www.fs.usda.gov/visit/maps

United States Geological Survey
888/275-8747; www.usgs.gov/products/maps

NEW ENGLAND'S LONG TRAILS
Appalachian National Scenic Trail
2,180 mi (3,510 km) from Georgia to Maine. Managed in New England by the Appalachian Trail Conservancy and the Appalachian Mountain Club (P.O. Box 50, Harpers Ferry, WV 25425; 304/535-6278; www.nps.gov/appa).

Bay Circuit Trail
230 mi (370 km) circling the Boston area. Managed by the Appalachian Mountain Club and the Bay Circuit Alliance (www.baycircuit.org).

Cohos Trail
175 mi (282 km) from the White Mountains to the Canadian border. Managed by the Cohos Trail Association (P.O. Box 82, Lancaster, NH 03584; www.cohostrail.org).

The Long Trail
273 mi (439 km) through Vermont to the Canadian border. Managed by the Green Mountain Club (Waterbury-Stowe Rd., Waterbury Center, VT 05677; 802/244-7037; www.greenmountainclub.org).

Midstate Trail

92 mi (148 km) through central Massachusetts from the Rhode Island border to the New Hampshire border. Managed by the Midstate Trail Committee (2 Westinghouse Pkwy., Worcester, MA 01606; www.midstatetrail.org).

Monadnock-Sunapee Greenway

48 mi (77 km) through central New Hampshire. Managed by the Monadnock-Sunapee Greenway Trail Club (P.O. Box 164, Marlow, NH 03456; www.msgtc.org).

New England National Scenic Trail

215 mi (346 km) from the Connecticut coast through Massachusetts to the New Hampshire border. Managed by the National Park Service, the Appalachian Mountain Club, and the Connecticut Forest and Park Association (https://newenglandtrail.org).

North South Trail

77 mi (124 km) from the Rhode Island coast to the Massachusetts border. Managed by the North South Trail Council and the Appalachian Mountain Club (www.outdoors.org/Narragansett).

The Wapack Trail

21 mi (34 km) from north-central Massachusetts into southern New Hampshire. Managed by Friends of the Wapack Trail (P.O. Box 115, West Peterborough, NH 03468; http://wapack.org).

INDEX

PHOTO CREDITS

Title page © Kelsey Perrett; page 4 © Miles Howard; page 6 © Kelsey Perrett; page 7 © (top) Kelsey Perrett; (middle) Kelsey Perrett; (bottom) Kelsey Perrett; page 8 © (top) NPS; (bottom) Steve Callahan | Dreamstime.com; page 9 © (top) Kelsey Perrett; (bottom) Mass Bay Brewing Co.; page 10 © (top) Kelsey Perrett; (bottom) Mikael Males | Dreamstime.com; page 11 © Miles Howard; page 12 © Miles Howard; page 14 © Miles Howard; page 16 © Justinhoffmanoutdoors | Dreamstime.com; page 18 © Miles Howard; page 19 © Miles Howard; page 21 © Kelsey Perrett; page 22 © Miles Howard; page 23 © Kelsey Perrett; page 25 © Mass Bay Brewing Co. /John Lundquist

Maine; New Hampshire all photos © Miles Howard except: page 26 © Alexey Stiop | Dreamstime.com; page 28 © Claudia M. | Dreamstime.com; page 29 © (left) Kumpyashka | Dreamstime.com; page 35 © Joseph Bilek | Dreamstime.com; page 38 © Jason Busa | Dreamstime.com; page 46 © Liz Grogan | Dreamstime.com; page 53 © hawkeye978 | shutterstock.com; page 60 © Ajjphotos | Dreamstime.com; page 61 © Quietside Campground; page 65 © (left) Bncc369| Dreamstime.com; page 73 © Lynnemariehale | Dreamstime.com; page 93 © Lauraganz | Dreamstime.com; page 110 © Monika Salvan | Shutterstock.com; page 137 © (left) Daniel Wiley| Dreamstime.com; (right) Klinc207 | Dreamstime.com; page 172 © Joseph Jacobs | | Dreamstime.com; page 173 © (left) Drew Groves | Dreamstime.com; page 182 © Wangkun Jia | Dreamstime.com; page 206 © Richard Howard; page 227 © (left) Billgreen162 | Dreamstime.com; (right) © William Jacovina | Dreamstime.com; page 247 © Salajean | Dreamstime.com; page 251 © Sue Feldberg | Dreamstime.com; page 265 © Joseph Jacobs | Dreamstime.com; page 277 © Jeffrey Holcombe | Dreamstime.com; page 281 © Jamie Erickson | Dreamstime.com; page 286 © Matthew Benoit | Dreamstime.com; page 290 © Jon Bilous | Dreamstime.com; page 293 © Melissa A Lombard/USGS; page 300 © Deborah Hewitt | Dreamstime.com

Vermont; Massachusetts; Connecticut; Rhode Island; Hiking Tips all photos © Kelsey Perrett except: page 314 © Sam Moore; page 326 © Sam Moore; page 333 © Jim Lawrence | Dreamstime.com; page 371 © Amanda Nicastro; page 374 © Ann Moore | Dreamstime.com; page 375 © (left) Miles Howard; (right) Miles Howard; page 380 © Miles Howard; page 383 © Miles Howard; page 384 © Miles Howard; page 389 © Miles Howard; page 392 © Miles Howard; page 398 © Miles Howard; page 400 © Ann Moore | Dreamstime.com; page 413 © Sam Moore; page 415 © Sam Moore; page 422 © Sam Moore; page 424 © Sam Moore; page 425 © Sam Moore; page 431 © (left) Sam Moore; page 451 © Matthew Smith | Dreamstime.com; page 457 © (left) Sam Moore; page 460 © Sam Moore; page 462 © Sam Moore; page 475 © Sam Moore; page 476 © (right) Sam Moore; page 478 © Sam Moore; page 499 © Sam Moore; page 506 © Joe Sohm | Dreamstime.com; page 535 © (right) Darya Petrenko | Dreamstime.com; page 584 © Chengusf | Dreamstime.com; page 619 © Amanda Nicastro; page 621 © Amanda Nicastro

Get inspired for your next adventure

Follow **@moonguides** on Instagram or
subscribe to our newsletter at **moon.com**

#TravelWithMoon

National Parks Travel Guides from Moon

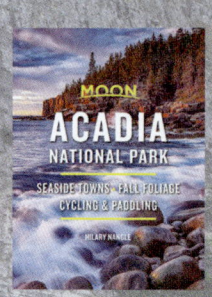

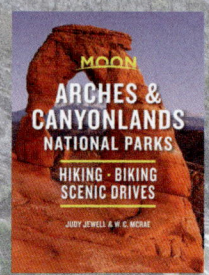

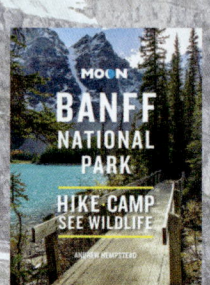

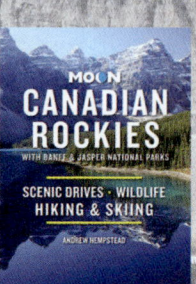

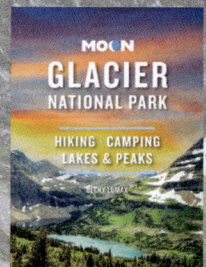

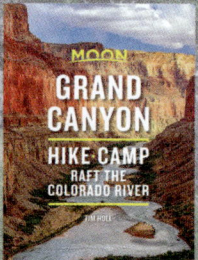

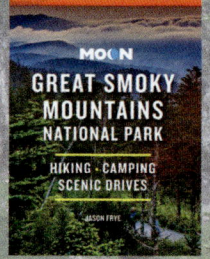

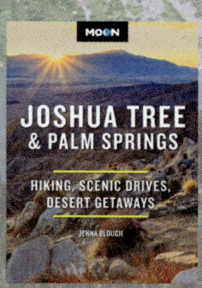

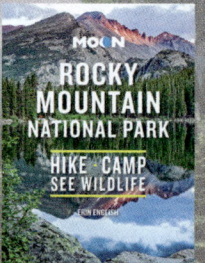

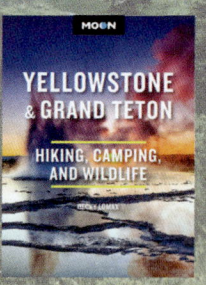

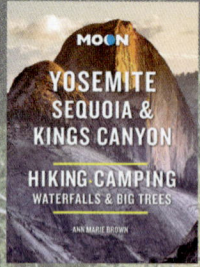

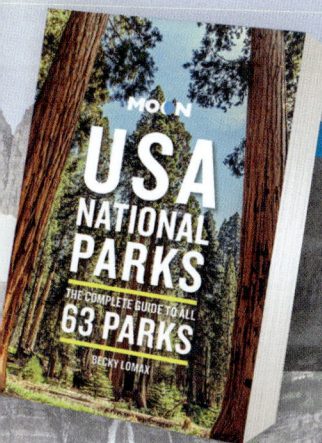

Get the bestselling all-parks guide, or check out Moon's new Best Of Parks series to make the most of a 1-3 day visit to top parks.

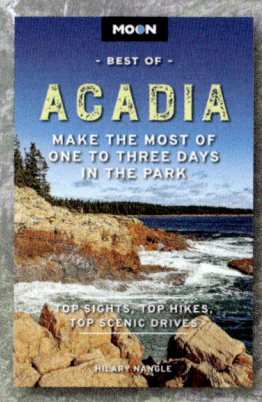

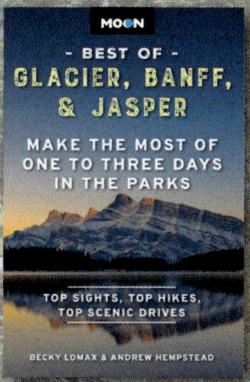

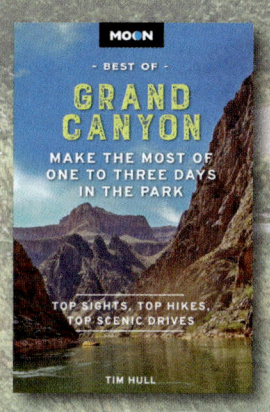

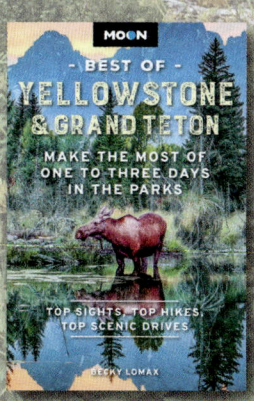

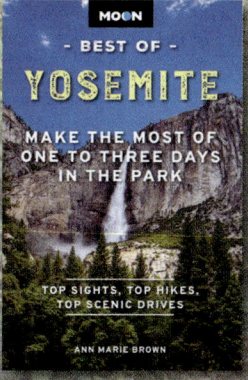

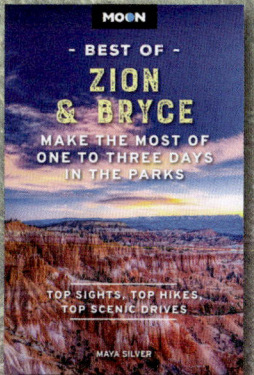

TRAILS AT A GLANCE

PAGE	HIKE NAME	DISTANCE	DIFFICULTY	
Maine: Acadia				
32	Cadillac Mountain via the Gorge Path	4.6 mi rt	Strenuous	
36	The Beehive	1.6 mi rt	Moderate	
40	Ocean Path	3.6 mi rt	Easy	
43	South Bubble and Jordan Pond	3.6 mi rt	Moderate	
47	Penobscot Mountain via the Jordan Cliffs Trail	3.3 mi rt	Strenuous	
51	Hadlock Falls	2 mi rt	Easy	
54	Perpendicular and Razorback Trails	2.6 mi rt	Moderate	
58	Ship Harbor	1.4 mi rt	Easy	
Maine: Baxter, the Highlands, and the Carrabassett Valley				
68	South Turner Mountain	3.6 mi rt	Moderate/strenuous	
71	Mount Katahdin	9.4 mi rt	Strenuous	
75	Little and Big Niagara Falls	2.4 mi rt	Easy	
78	Blueberry Ledges	3.6 mi rt	Easy	
81	Debsconeag Ice Caves	2 mi rt	Easy	
84	Mount Kineo	3.5 mi rt	Moderate	
87	Gulf Hagas	8.2 mi rt	Strenuous	
91	Mount Bigelow	10 mi rt	Strenuous	
95	Poplar Stream Falls	4.4 mi rt	Easy	
98	Orono Bog	1.5 mi rt	Easy	
Maine: Midcoast, Casco Bay, and the Maine Beaches				
108	Mount Megunticook	2.8 mi rt	Moderate	
111	Ragged Mountain	4.8 mi rt	Moderate/strenuous	
114	Lane's Island Preserve	1 mi rt	Easy	
117	Oven's Mouth Preserve	3.1 mi rt	Easy	

TRAILS AT A GLANCE

SEASONAL ACCESS	DOG-FRIENDLY	WATER FEATURES	WILDLIFE
June-Oct		X	X
June-Oct			X
Apr-Nov	X		X
June-Oct			X
June-Oct			X
May-Oct		X	
June-Oct	X		X
May-Oct			X
May-Oct			X
June-Sept		X	X
June-Oct		X	X
May-Sept		X	X
May-Sept			X
May-Oct			X
June-Sept	X	X	X
June-Sept	X		X
June-Oct		X	X
May-Nov			X
June-Oct	X	X	X
May-Nov	X		X
May-Nov	X		X
May-Oct	X		X

TRAILS AT A GLANCE (CONTINUED)

PAGE	HIKE NAME	DISTANCE	DIFFICULTY
Maine: Midcoast, Casco Bay, and the Maine Beaches, continued			
121	Harpswell Cliff Trail	2.2 mi rt	Easy
124	Fore River and Jewell Falls	3.3 mi rt	Easy
127	Wells Reserve	2.8 mi rt	Easy
130	Mount Agamenticus	2.5 mi rt	Easy/moderate
Maine: The Mahoosucs, Evans Notch, and Rangeley Lakes			
140	Angel Falls	1.4 mi rt	Easy
143	Tumbledown Mountain	5.8 mi rt	Strenuous
147	Dunn Falls	2.6 mi rt	Moderate
151	Old Speck	7.6 mi rt	Strenuous
155	Caribou Mountain	6.7 mi rt	Strenuous
158	Bickford Slides	2.3 mi rt	Easy/moderate
161	Lord Hill	4.3 mi rt	Easy
164	Androscoggin Riverlands	7.2 mi rt	Moderate
New Hampshire: White Mountain National Forest			
176	Giant Falls	3 mi rt	Easy
180	Mount Adams	8.6 mi rt	Strenuous
184	Mount Washington via Tuckerman Ravine	8.2 mi rt	Strenuous
188	Basin Rim	4.4 mi rt	Moderate
191	Zealand Valley and Thoreau Falls	9.4 mi rt	Moderate
195	Mount Willard	3 mi rt	Easy
198	Arethusa Falls via Bemis Brook	2.8 mi rt	Easy/moderate
201	Bridal Veil Falls	4.4 mi rt	Easy/moderate
204	Mount Lafayette and Franconia Ridge	8.4 mi rt	Strenuous
208	The Flume	2 mi rt	Easy

SEASONAL ACCESS	DOG-FRIENDLY	WATER FEATURES	WILDLIFE
May–Nov	X	X	X
May–Nov	X	X	X
May–Oct			X
Apr–Oct	X		X
May–Oct	X	X	X
June–Oct			X
June–early Oct	X	X	X
June–Oct		X	
June–Oct	X	X	X
June–Oct	X	X	X
May–Oct	X		X
June–Oct	X		X
May–Oct	X	X	X
June–Sept		X	X
June–Sept		X	X
June–Oct	X	X	X
June–Oct	X	X	X
June–Oct	X	X	X
May–Oct	X	X	X
May–Oct	X	X	X
June–Oct		X	X
June–Oct		X	X

PAGE	HIKE NAME	DISTANCE	DIFFICULTY	
New Hampshire: White Mountain National Forest, continued				
211	Mount Carrigain	10.4 mi rt	Strenuous	
214	Mount Moosilauke	7.6 mi rt	Strenuous	
217	Greeley Ponds	4.2 mi rt	Easy/moderate	
220	Mount Chocorua	7.4 mi rt	Moderate/strenuous	
New Hampshire: Great North Woods and Dixville Notch				
230	Fourth Connecticut Lake	2.1 mi rt	Moderate	
233	Little Hellgate Falls	1.5 mi rt	Easy	
237	Table Rock	1.6 mi rt	Moderate/strenuous	
241	South and North Percy Peaks	4.6 mi rt	Strenuous	
245	The Devil's Hopyard	2 mi rt	Easy	
New Hampshire: Winnipesaukee and the Lakes District				
254	Welch and Dickey Mountains	4.2 mi rt	Moderate/strenuous	
257	West and East Rattlesnake Mountains	3.8 mi rt	Easy/moderate	
260	Markus Wildlife Sanctuary	2 mi rt	Easy	
263	Mount Cardigan	3.4 mi rt	Moderate/strenuous	
266	Welton Falls	2.6 mi rt	Easy	
269	Belknap Mountain	2.5 mi rt	Moderate	
272	Devil's Den Mountain	5.4 mi rt	Easy/moderate	
275	Lake Solitude	4.2 mi rt	Easy/moderate	
New Hampshire: Monadnock, Merrimack Valley, and the Seacoast				
284	Sweet Trail	5.6 mi rt	Easy	
287	Odiorne Point State Park	3.3 mi rt	Easy	
291	Skatutakee Mountain and Thumb Mountain	5 mi rt	Moderate	
294	Madame Sherri Forest	4 mi rt	Easy/moderate	

SEASONAL ACCESS	DOG-FRIENDLY	WATER FEATURES	WILDLIFE
June-Oct	X	X	X
June-Oct	X		X
June-Oct	X		X
June-Oct	X	X	X
June-Oct			X
June-Sept	X	X	X
May-Oct	X		X
June-Sept			X
June-Oct			X
June-Oct	X		X
June-Oct	X		X
May-Oct			X
June-Oct	X		X
May-Oct	X	X	X
May-Oct	X		X
May-Oct			X
June-Oct	X		X
Apr-Oct	X		X
Year-round			X
May-Oct	X		X
May-Oct	X		X

TRAILS AT A GLANCE (CONTINUED)

PAGE	HIKE NAME	DISTANCE	DIFFICULTY	
New Hampshire: Monadnock, Merrimack Valley, and the Seacoast, continued				
297	Monte Rosa and Mount Monadnock	4.6 mi rt	Strenuous	
301	Purgatory Falls	5 mi rt	Easy/moderate	
Vermont: Northern Green Mountains				
312	Long Trail: Lincoln Gap to Mount Abraham	4.8 mi rt	Strenuous	
315	Abbey Pond Trail	4.4 mi rt	Easy/moderate	
318	Skylight Pond Trail and Long Trail to Breadloaf Mountain	6.9 mi rt	Moderate	
321	Falls of Lana and Rattlesnake Cliffs	4.9 mi rt	Moderate	
324	Long Trail: Brandon Gap to Mount Horrid Great Cliff and Cape Lookout	3.6 mi rt	Moderate/strenuous	
327	Killington Peak via the Bucklin Trail	7.4 mi rt	Strenuous	
330	Mount Tom via Mountain Road	3.6 mi rt	Moderate	
Vermont: Southern Green Mountains				
340	Haystack Mountain	3.2 mi rt	Moderate	
343	White Rocks Cliffs	3.6 mi rt	Moderate/strenuous	
346	Mount Ascutney via the Weathersfield Trail	5.2 mi rt	Strenuous	
349	Baker Peak and Griffith Lake	8.4 mi rt	Strenuous	
352	Antone Mountain via Old Town Road	5.2 mi rt	Moderate	
355	Gettysburg Quarry and Gilbert Lookout	3.4 mi rt	Moderate/strenuous	
357	Mount Equinox and Lookout Rock	5.4 mi rt	Strenuous	
360	Lye Brook Falls Trail	4.4 mi rt	Moderate	

SEASONAL ACCESS	DOG-FRIENDLY	WATER FEATURES	WILDLIFE
May-Oct			X
Apr-Oct	X	X	X
May-Oct	X		X
May-Oct	X	X	X
May-Oct	X		X
June-Oct	X	X	
May-Oct	X		
May-Oct	X		X
May-Oct	X		
May-Oct	X		
May-Oct	X		X
Apr-Nov	X	X	
May-Oct	X	X	X
Year-round	X		
Apr-Oct	X		X
May-Oct	X		X
Year-round	X	X	X

PAGE	HIKE NAME	DISTANCE	DIFFICULTY	
Vermont: Southern Green Mountains, continued				
363	Stratton Pond Trail	7.4 mi rt	Easy/moderate	
366	Hamilton Falls via the West River Trail	4.3 mi rt	Easy/moderate	
369	Everett Cave	2.7 mi rt	Easy	
Vermont: Champlain Valley and Stowe				
378	Calm Cove at Niquette Bay	3.7 mi rt	Easy/moderate	
381	Sterling Pond	2.6 mi rt	Moderate	
384	Mount Mansfield via the Sunset Ridge Trail	5.2 mi rt	Strenuous	
387	Stowe Pinnacle	3.4 mi rt	Moderate	
390	Little River History Hike	4 mi rt	Easy	
393	Waterbury Trail to Mount Hunger	4.2 mi rt	Strenuous	
396	Mount Philo	2.2 mi rt	Moderate	
399	Camel's Hump	6.8 mi rt	Strenuous	
Vermont: Northeast Kingdom				
408	Long Trail: Jay Pass to Jay Peak	3.4 mi rt	Moderate/strenuous	
410	Devil's Gulch via the Long Trail and Babcock Trail	4.8 mi rt	Moderate/strenuous	
413	Bald Mountain via the Long Pond Trail	4.2 mi rt	Moderate/strenuous	
416	Mount Pisgah via the North Trail	4.2 mi rt	Strenuous	
419	Owls Head Trail	4.8 mi rt	Moderate	
422	Little Loop and Peacham Bog Trail	5.8 mi rt	Moderate	
Massachusetts: Greater Boston, North and South Shore				
434	Rock Circuit Trail	4.2 mi rt	Moderate/strenuous	
437	Carriage Paths	4 mi rt	Easy	

SEASONAL ACCESS	DOG-FRIENDLY	WATER FEATURES	WILDLIFE
Apr–Oct	X		X
May–Oct	X	X	
Apr–Nov	X		
May–Oct	X		X
May–Oct	X		X
May–Oct	X		X
May–Oct	X		X
June–Oct	X	X	X
May–Oct	X	X	
June–Oct	X		X
June–Oct	X		X
May–Oct	X		
May–Oct	X	X	X
May–Oct	X		X
May–Oct	X		
Apr–Oct	X		X
May–Oct	X		X
Apr–Nov	X	X	
Year-round	X		X

PAGE	HIKE NAME	DISTANCE	DIFFICULTY	
Massachusetts: Greater Boston, North and South Shore, continued				
440	Great Blue Hill via the Skyline Trail	5.7 mi rt	Moderate/strenuous	
443	Walden Pond via the Alternate Pond Loop	2.2 mi rt	Easy	
446	Mount Wachusett via the Midstate Trail	3.9 mi rt	Moderate	
449	Mount Watatic via the Wapack Trail	3 mi rt	Moderate	
452	Castle Neck Trails	5.6 mi rt	Moderate	
Massachusetts: Cape Cod and the Islands				
460	Great Island Trail	5.9 mi rt	Moderate	
463	Marsh Trail	7.9 mi rt	Moderate	
466	Menemsha Hills: Prospect Hill and the Great Sand Bank	3.1 mi rt	Easy/moderate	
469	Ocean Walk	5.7 mi rt	Easy	
Massachusetts: The Berkshires				
478	Pine Cobble Trail	4.9 mi rt	Moderate	
481	Mount Greylock via the Money Brook and Appalachian Trails	11.8 mi rt	Strenuous	
485	Hoosac Range Trail to Spruce Hill	5.4 mi rt	Moderate	
488	Todd Mountain via the Mahican-Mohawk Trail	5 mi rt	Strenuous	
491	Monument Mountain via the Mohican Monument Trail	2.4 mi rt	Moderate	
494	Jug End Loop Trail	4.4 mi rt	Easy/moderate	
497	Alander Mountain Trail	6 mi rt	Moderate	

SEASONAL ACCESS	DOG-FRIENDLY	WATER FEATURES	WILDLIFE
Apr–Nov	X		X
Year-round			
Apr–Nov	X		X
Apr–Nov	X		
Year-round			X
Year-round	X		X
Year-round	X		X
Year-round	X		X
Year-round	X		X
Apr–Nov	X		
Apr–Nov	X	X	X
Apr–Nov	X		X
Apr–Nov	X		X
Apr–Nov	X		
Year-round	X		
Apr–Nov	X		X

PAGE	HIKE NAME	DISTANCE	DIFFICULTY
Massachusetts: The Berkshires, continued			
500	Race Brook Falls and Mount Race via the Appalachian Trail	5.8 mi rt	Strenuous
503	Hurlburt's Hill and Bartholomew's Cobble	3.2 mi rt	Easy/moderate
Massachusetts: The Pioneer Valley and North Quabbin			
512	Doane's Falls via the Tully Trail	6 mi rt	Easy/moderate
515	High Ledges via the Sanctuary Road Loop	3.3 mi rt	Easy
518	Hermit's Castle via the Metacomet-Monadnock Trail	5.7 mi rt	Moderate
521	Mount Toby via the Robert Frost Trail	4.3 mi rt	Moderate
524	Norwottuck Horse Caves and Rattlesnake Knob via the Metacomet-Monadnock Trail	3.9 mi rt	Moderate
528	Mount Tom via the Metacomet-Monadnock Trail	6.6 mi rt	Moderate
Connecticut: Litchfield Hills			
538	Bear Mountain via the Undermountain Trail	6.1 mi rt	Strenuous
541	Appalachian Trail: Prospect Mountain and Rand's View	5.2 mi rt	Moderate
544	Pine Knob Loop	2.5 mi rt	Moderate
547	Appalachian Trail: Housatonic River Walk	7.6 mi rt	Easy
550	Macedonia Ridge Trail	6.4 mi rt	Moderate/strenuous
554	Robert Ross and Agnes Bowen Trails	6.4 mi rt	Moderate

SEASONAL ACCESS	DOG-FRIENDLY	WATER FEATURES	WILDLIFE
Apr–Nov	X	X	X
Year-round			
Year-round	X	X	X
Year-round			
Apr–Nov	X	X	
Apr–Nov	X	X	X
Apr–Nov	X		
Apr–Nov	X		
May–Nov	X		X
May–Nov	X		
May–Nov		X	X
Year-round	X		X
May–Nov	X		X
May–Nov	X	X	X

PAGE	HIKE NAME	DISTANCE	DIFFICULTY	
Connecticut: Litchfield Hills, continued				
557	Mattatuck and Little Pond Loop Boardwalk Trail	3.2 mi rt	Easy	
560	Steep Rock Loop	4.1 mi rt	Moderate	
563	Donkey Trail and Hodge Road Loop	3.5 mi rt	Moderate	
Connecticut: Metacomet Ridge				
572	Talcott Mountain Trail to Heublein Tower	2.4 mi rt	Easy/moderate	
575	Ragged Mountain via the Preserve and Metacomet Trails	5.3 mi rt	Easy	
578	Lamentation Mountain and Chauncey Peak via the Mattabesett Trail	3.8 mi rt	Moderate	
582	Sleeping Giant via the Blue and Violet Trails	4.6 mi rt	Strenuous	
585	Vista Trail	2.4 mi rt	Easy	
588	Wolf Den and Indian Chair via the Blue Trail	4.4 mi rt	Easy/moderate	
Rhode Island				
598	Walkabout Trail	7.8 mi rt	Easy/moderate	
601	Coventry and Foster Loops	6 mi rt	Easy	
604	Pond, Coney Brook, and Flintlock Loops	5.4 mi rt	Easy	
607	North South Trail to Stepstone Falls	5.2 mi rt	Easy	
610	Long and Ell Pond Trail	4.4 mi rt	Easy/moderate	
613	Grassland, Moraine, and Old Pasture Loops	4.4 mi rt	Easy	

SEASONAL ACCESS	DOG-FRIENDLY	WATER FEATURES	WILDLIFE
Year-round	X		X
May-Nov	X		X
May-Nov	X		
Apr-Nov	X		
Apr-Nov	X		
Apr-Nov	X		
Apr-Nov	X		
Year-round	X	X	
Apr-Nov	X		X
Year-round	X		X
Year-round			X
Year-round	X	X	
Year-round	X	X	
Apr-Nov	X		
Year-round	X		X

PAGE	HIKE NAME	DISTANCE	DIFFICULTY	
Rhode Island, continued				
616	Foster Cove, Cross Refuge, and Grassy Point Trails	4.5 mi rt	Easy	
619	Clay Head Nature Trail and the Maze	2.9 mi rt	Easy	
622	Nelson Pond Trail	2.8 mi rt	Easy/moderate	
625	Flint Point and Ocean View Loops	2.3 mi rt	Easy	

SEASONAL ACCESS	DOG-FRIENDLY	WATER FEATURES	WILDLIFE
Year-round			X
Year-round	X		X
Year-round			X
Year-round			X

MOON NEW ENGLAND HIKING

Avalon Travel
Hachette Book Group, Inc.
555 12th Street, 18th Floor
Oakland, CA 94607, USA
www.moon.com

Editor: Devon Lee
Managing Editor: Hannah Brezack
Copy Editor: Deana Shields
Graphics and Production
    Coordinator: Ravina Schneider
Cover Design: Toni Tajima
Interior Design: Avalon Travel
Map Editor: John Culp
Cartographers: John Culp, Abby
    Whelan, Brian Shotwell, and Lohnes + Wright
Proofreader: Callie Stoker-Graham
Indexer: Greg Jewett

ISBN-13: 979-8-88647-078-9

Printing History
1st Edition — 2020
2nd Edition — March 2025
5 4 3 2 1

Front cover photo: Cadillac Mountain,
Acadia National Park. © Jon Bilous
| Dreamstime.com

Back cover photo: Spruce Hill, Berkshires. © Kelsey Perrett

Printed in China by RR Donnelley

ICON AND MAP SYMBOLS KEY

- 🚶 Kid-friendly
- 🏛 Historic landmarks
- 🐾 Wildlife
- ✿ Wildflowers
- 🐾 Dog-friendly
- 🥾 Water features
- ⛰ Appalachian Trail
- 🚉 Public transit
- ♿ Wheelchair accessible

Expressway	Feature Trail	♠ Park	🏕 Picnic Table/Area	
Primary Road	Other Trail	✚ Natural Feature	▪ Point of Interest	
Other Road	1,200 Index Contour Line	▲ Mountain Peak	ⓘ Information	
Unpaved Road	Contour Line	🥾 Waterfall	🎿 Ski Area	
Paved Path	🅣 Trailhead	✦ Water Feature	○ City	
Stairs	🅟 Parking Area	🅰 Camping Area	○ Town/Village	
			✈ Airport	

 QUICK-REFERENCE CHART: TRAILS AT A GLANCE